**WITHDRAWN
NDSU**

THE STEAM NAVY

...OF THE...

UNITED STATES.

A HISTORY OF THE GROWTH OF THE STEAM VESSEL OF WAR
IN THE U. S. NAVY, AND OF THE NAVAL
ENGINEER CORPS

WITH NUMEROUS ILLUSTRATIONS.

BY

FRANK M. BENNETT,

PASSED ASSISTANT ENGINEER, UNITED STATES NAVY.

GREENWOOD PRESS, PUBLISHERS
WESTPORT, CONNECTICUT

Library of Congress Cataloging in Publication Data

Bennett, Frank Marion, 1857-1924.
   The steam navy of the United States.

   1. U. S. Navy--History. 2. U. S.--History, Naval
--To 1900. 3. Warships. 4. Marine engineers.
I. Title.
VA55.B48 1972   359'.00973   70-98814
ISBN 0-8371-2949-4

Copyrighted 1896 by Frank M. Bennett

Originally published in 1896 by W. T. Nicholson Press,
Pittsburgh, Pennsylvania

Reprinted by Greenwood Press,
a division of Williamhouse-Regency Inc.

First Greenwood Reprinting 1972
Second Greenwood Reprinting 1974

Library of Congress Catalog Card Number 70-98814

ISBN 0-8371-2949-4

Printed in the United States of America

CONTENTS.

CHAPTER I.
Introductory 1

CHAPTER II.
The DEMOLOGOS, or FULTON, the First Steam War Vessel ever Built—Robert Fulton—The SEA GULL—The FULTON, 2D—Mr. Chas. H. Haswell, the First Engineer in the United States Navy—Captain M. C. Perry's Recomendations Regarding Engineers' Force—Regulations Governing Appointment of Engineers—Performance of the FULTON Under Steam—Her Subsequent Career—Captain Perry's Interest in Engineers............ 8

CHAPTER III.
The ENGINEER—The MISSISSIPPI and MISSOURI—Establishment of the Engineer Corps by Act of Congress—Destruction of the MISSOURI—Career of the MISSISSIPPI—Steamers Transferred to the Navy from the War Department—The MICHIGAN... 32

CHAPTER IV.
Experiments with the "Hunter Wheel"—The UNION—The WATER WITCH—The ALLEGHANY—The Stevens Battery.. 48

CHAPTER V.
Introduction of the Screw Propeller—John Ericsson—The PRINCETON, and Her Remarkable Engine—Great-Gun Accident on the PRINCETON and Consequent Breach of Friendship Between Ericsson and Captain Stockton—Subsequent Career of the PRINCETON.. 61

CHAPTER VI.
Reorganization of the Engineer Corps—Case of Chief Engineer C. B. Moss—All Assistant Engineers Examined and Rearranged According to Proficiency—Laws and Regulations Affecting the Engineer Corps from 1845 to 1850—Resignation of Chief Engineer John Faron, Jr................... 75

CHAPTER VII.
The War With Mexico—Naval Operatians in California—Important Service of Surgeon William Maxwell Wood—Blockade of the Gulf Coast—Commodore Perry and the MISSISSIPPI—Valuable Professional Service of Engineer-in-Chief Haswell—Bombardment of Vera Cruz—"Alvarado Hunter"—Steamers Bought for Temporary Service—Naval Engineers Engaged in the Mexican War—Results of the War................................. 88

CHAPTER VIII.
New Steamers Authorized for the Navy in 1847—The SUSQUEHANNA, POWHATAN, SARANAC, and SAN JACINTO—Mr. Haswell Succeeded as Engineer-in-Chief by Charles B. Stuart—Circumstances Connected with Mr. Haswell's Leaving the Navy—His Great Services to the Naval Engineer Corps—His Subsequent Career... 102

CHAPTER IX.
The Expedition to Japan and Treaty with that Country—Services of Engineers in the Expedition—Value of Steamers in Impressing the Japanese—Other Naval Affairs in the Far East.. 126

CONTENTS.

CHAPTER X.
PAGE.

End of the Experimental Period and Beginning of the Creationary Period of the American Steam Navy—The FRANKLIN—The MERRIMAC Class of Steam Frigates—The NIAGARA—Services of Chief Engineer Everett in Connection with the Atlantic Cable Laid by the NIAGARA—The HARTFORD Class of Large Screw Sloops—Mr. Archbold Succeeds Mr. Martin as Engineer-in-Chief—The MOHICAN Class—The PAWNEE—The Paraguay Expedition—Small Steamers Purchased for the Navy—Project to Convert Old Line-of-Battle-Ships into Steam Frigates.................................... 137

CHAPTER XI.

The Engineer Corps from 1850 to the Beginning of the Civil War—Congress Petitioned to Increase the Corps—Pay Increased by United Effort of all Officers—Rank of Engineers Defined—New Regulations Governing Appointment and Promotion Issued—Opinions of Chief Engineer Gay in Relation of Sails and Steam... 177

CHAPTER XII.

The Civil War... 193

CHAPTER XIII.

1861—The Civil War, Continued—Engineers and Steam Vessels in the Navy at the Outbreak of Hostilities—Resignation and Dismissal of Officers—Chief Engineer B. F. Isherwood Appointed Engineer-in-Chief of the Navy—Increase of the Engineer Corps—Qualifications of the Volunteer Engineers—Remarkable Career of Don Carlos Hasseltino—Vessels Added to the Fleet During the Year.—The KEARSEARGE and CANANDAIGUA Classes of Steam Sloops—The Ninety-Day Gunboats—The First Double-Enders 201

CHAPTER XIV.

1861—The Civil War, Continued—The Norfolk Navy Yard—Attempt to Save the Frigate MERRIMAC—Endeavors of Engineer-in-Chief Isherwood—Destruction of the Yard—Attack on Hatteras Inlet—Destruction of the Privateer JUDAH at Pensacola... 230

CHAPTER XV.

1861—The Civil War, Continued—Expedition of Flag Officer DuPont to Port Royal—Loss of the GOVERNOR—Naval Battle at Port Royal—Killing of Assistant Engineer Whittemore on the MOHICAN—Affair of the TRENT... 245

CHAPTER XVI.

1861—The Civil War, Continued—The First American Iron Clads—The Stevens Battery Condemned by a Board of Naval Officers—Authority to Build Armored Vessels Conferred by Act of Congress—Report of Board on Iron Clad Vessels—The GALENA, NEW IRONSIDES, and MONITOR—Armored Vessels on the Mississippi River.. 262

CHAPTER XVII.

1862—The Civil War, Continued—Capture of Roanoke Island and Elizabeth City—The MERRIMAC and Her Raid—Destruction of the CONGRESS and CUMBERLAND—The MONITOR Completed and Commisioned—Her Chief Engineer, Isaac Newton—Voyage of the MONITOR from New York and Her Arrival in Hampton Roads... 286

CHAPTER XVIII.

1862—The Civil War, Continued—First Fight of Iron Clads—Effects of the Battle—Extraordinary Services Rendered by Chief Engineer Stimers—Attack on Drury's Bluff—The GALENA Badly Injured—Gallantry of Assistant Engineer J. W. Thomson.. 301

CONTENTS.

CHAPTER XIX.

1862—The Civil War, Continued—Naval Operations in the Mississippi River—Battles Below New Orleans—Catastrophe to the MOUND CITY—Attack on Vicksburg—Warfare on the Atlantic Coast—Wreck of the ADIRONDACK—Loss of the MONITOR—Peril of the PASSAIC—Heroism of Assistant Engineer H. W. Robie...... 318

CHAPTER XX.

1862—The Civil War, Continued—Increase of the Navy—Steamers Purchased Mississippi Flotilla Transferred to the Navy Department—Steam Vessels of War Placed Under Construction—The PASSAIC Class of Monitors—The DICTATOR and PURITAN—The MIANTONOMOH Class—Other Monitors—The KEOKUK—The DUNDERBERG—Legislation Regarding the Navy—Retired List Established—Creation of the Bureau of Steam Engineering—Pensions...... 337

CHAPTER XXI.

1863—The Civil War, Continued—Disasters at Galveston—Loss of the *Columbia*—Raid of Rebel Rams off Charleston—Loss of the *Isaac Smith*—The *Florida*, and Her Pursuit by the *Sonoma*—Investment of Washington, North Carolina—Assembling of Ironclads off Charleston — Remarkable Breakdown and Repairs to the Machinery of the *Weehawken*—Attack on Fort McAllister — First Attack on Fort Sumter — Destruction of the *Keokuk*—The *Atlanta-Weehawken* Duel—Protracted Investment of the Charleston Forts by the Monitors—Sinking of the *Weehawken*...... 362

CHAPTER XXII.

1863—The Civil War, Continued—The War on the Western Waters—Passage of Port Hudson—Destruction of the Frigate MISSISSIPPI—Minor Operations in the West — New Vessels Placed Under Construction — The Light-Draft Monitors—Iron Double-Enders—Large Wooden Frigates and Sloops-of-War—The First Swift Cruisers—The KALAMAZOO Class of Monitors—Assimilated Rank of Staff Officers Raised—New Regulations Governing Promotion in the Engineer Corps Issued...... 384

CHAPTER XXIII.

1863—The Civil War, Continued—Controversy as to the Efficiency of Iron-Clads—Rear Admiral DuPont Reports Adversely to Them—Chief Engineer Stimers Reports in Their Favor—Rear Admiral DuPont Prefers Charges Against Chief Engineer Stimers—The Case Investigated by a Court of Inquiry—Vindication of Mr. Stimers...... 403

CHAPTER XXIV.

1864—The Civil War, Continued—Confederate Successes in the Use of Torpedoes—Blowing Up of the Sloop of War HOUSATONIC—Minor Naval Operations—Boiler Explosion on the CHENANGO—The KEARSARGE-ALABAMA Fight—The Great Battle in Mobile Bay—Loss of the TECUMSEH—Capture of the Privateer FLORIDA by the WACHUSETT—The Gunboat OTSEGO Sunk by a Torpedo—First Attack on Fort Fisher...... 423

CHAPTER XXV.

1864—The Civil War, Continued—Naval Operations in the North Carolina Sounds—The Ram ALBEMARLE—Sinking of the SOUTHFIELD and defeat of the MIAMI—The Naval Battle of May Fifth—Disaster to the SASSACUS and Heroism of Her Chief Engineer—Daring Attempt of Enlisted Men to Destroy the Ram—Her Destruction by Lieutenant Wm. B. Cushing—Battle and Capture of Plymouth—Prize Money Distributed on Account of the ALBEMARLE...... 447

CONTENTS.

CHAPTER XXVI.

1864—The Civil War, Continued—New Ships and Machinery Begun—The SERAPIS Class—The RESACA Class—Competitive Machinery of the QUINNEBAUG and SWATARA—The STROMBOLI, or SPUYTEN DUYVIL—The Light-Draft Monitors—Petition of the Engineer Corps Addressed to Congress and its Results.. 474

CHAPTER XXVII.

1865—The Civil War, Concluded—Loss of the SAN JACINTO—Second Attack on Fort Fisher—The PATAPSCO Destroyed by a Torpedo—Charleston Abandoned by the Confederates—The Monitors MILWAUKEE and OSAGE Sunk—Loss of the SCIOTA and ADA—Restoration of Peace—Some Naval Lessons of the War—Armed Merchant Vessels Unsuited for Operations of War—Casualities of the Engineer Corps During the Rebellion........... 495

CHAPTER XXVIII.

Competitive Trials of Steam Machinery—The NIPSIC and KANSAS—Failure of the SACO—The Famous ALGONQUIN-WINOOSKI Controversy—Performance of the IDAHO—Her Success as a Sailing Ship—Trial Trip of the CHATTANOOGA—Trial of the MADAWASKA—Comparative Table of Results of Trials of the IDAHO, CHATTANOOGA, MADAWASKA and WAMPANOAG—Subsequent Career of the MADAWASKA, or TENNESSEE................................ 514

CHAPTER XXIX.

The Trial Trip of the WAMPANOAG—Remarkable Speed Developed—Official Reports of Commanding Officer and Board of Chief Engineers—Attempt of the Press to Discredit Her Performance—Her Success Verified by the Trial of the AMMONOOSUC—The Real Reasons for Building Swift Cruisers During the Civil War—The WAMPANOAG Condemed by a Board of Naval Officers—Her Subsequent Career................................ 353

CHAPTER XXX.

Some Naval Events After the Civil War—The Voyage of the MONADNOCK to California—The MIANTONOMOH Visits Europe—The MOHONGO in a Pampero—Loss of the NARCISSUS—Yellow Fever on the KEARSARGE and MUSCOOTA—Wreck of the SACRAMENTO—Earthquakes and Tidal Waves—Wreck of the SUWANEE—The Affair of the FORWARD—Loss of the ONEIDA—Wreck of the SAGINAW... 584

CHAPTER XXXI.

Condition of the Engineer Corps after the War—Resignations—The Question of Brevet Rank—First and Second Assistant Engineers Become Commissioned Officers—Chief Engineer J. W. King Appointed Engineer-in-Chief—Sweeping Reduction in Rank of Staff Officers—Use of Steam Discontinued on Ships of War—The Pay Act of 1870—The Act of 1871......................... 603

CHAPTER XXXII.

Shipbuilding Progress in the Navy, 1865–1880—The ALASKA and Class—Captured Blockade-Runners—Sale of Monitors—Rebuilding of the MIANTONOMOH Class—The PURITAN—The New SWATARA and Class—Compound Engines—Chief Engineer Wood Appointed Engineer-in-Chief—Costly Experiments with Two-Bladed Propellers—The ALERT Class of Iron Gunboats—The ENTERPRISE Class—The TRENTON—The NIPSIC—The DESPATCH—The ALARM and INTREPID.. 622

CHAPTER XXXIII.

The Training of Naval Engineers at the Naval Academy............................ 652

CONTENTS.

CHAPTER XXXIV.

Steam Vessels of the United States Navy in the Arctic Ocean—The POLARIS Expedition—Cruise of the JUNIATA and TIGRESS—The JEANNETTE Expedition—Retreat on the Ice—Heroism and Fortitude of Chief Engineer Melville—Voyage and Loss of the RODGERS—Naval and Congressional Investigations Into the Loss of the JEANNETTE—The Greely Relief Expedition—Tardy Promotion of Chief Engineer Melville for Heroism Displayed in the JEANNETTE Expedition 679

XXXV.

Uniforms and Corps Devices of the Engineer Corps 713

CHAPTER XXXVI.

The Connection of the Naval Engineer Corps with Technical Education in the United States—Engineers Detailed to Colleges by Authority of Congress—Success of the Experiment—Its Discontinuance 732

CHAPTER XXXVII.

Brief Mention of Events of Engineering Interest Since 1872—Peril of the MANHATTAN—Titles of Assistant Engineers Changed—Chief Engineer Wm. H. Shock Appointed Engineer-in-Chief—Loss of the HURON—Cruise of the MARION to Heard Island—Reduction of Engineer Corps in 1882—Case of the Discharged Cadet Engineers—Wreck of the ASHUELOT—Longevity Pay for Passed Assisant Engineers—Chief Engineer C. H. Loring Succeeds Mr. Shock as Engineer-in-Chief—Naval Disaster at Samoa—Naval Engineers at the Columbian Exposition and Midwinter—Fair Loss of the KEARSARGE—Casualty on the MONTEREY 744

CHAPTER XXXVIII.

The New Navy—Naval Advisory Boards—First Acts of Congress Providing for the Rebuilding of the Navy—The ATLANTA, BOSTON, CHICAGO, and DOLPHIN—The NEWARK, YORKTOWN, and PETREL—The CHARLESTON—The TEXAS, MAINE, and BALTIMORE—The Dynamite-Gun Cruiser—The MONTEREY—The PHILADELPHIA and SAN FRANCISCO—Chief Engineer George W. Melville Appointed Engineer-in-Chief of the Navy 771

CHAPTER XXXIX.

The New Navy, Continued—The NEW YORK and OLYMPIA—The DETROIT Class—The CINCINNATI and RALEIGH—The BANCROFT, CASTINE and MACHIAS—The Ammen Ram—Coast-Line Battle-Ships—The ERICSSON—The COLUMBIA—Her Remarkable Voyage Across the Atlantic Ocean—The MINNEAPOLIS—The BROOKLYN and IOWA—New Torpedo Boats and Gunboats—The New KEARSARGE 809

CHAPTER XL.

Conclusion 845

APPENDIX A.

An Alphabetical List of the Names of All Members of the Regular Corps of the Navy from the Introduction of Steam to the Present Day 853

APPENDIX B.

List of Steam Vessels of War of the United States, with Principal Data Regarding them and a Brief Synopsis of Service; Arranged in Chronological Order 893

APPENDIX C.

"Uncle Samuel's Whistle and What it Costs;" An Illustrated Satire of the Old Navy 919

PREFACE.

HAVING completed this work, the author desires to express his thanks to many friends and acquaintances whose assistance, given in the form of books, letters, manuscripts, etc., has made the collection of much of the contained information possible. Especial thanks are due to Mr. Chas. H. Haswell of New York, a veteran engineer, and one of the few survivors of the earliest steam period of our navy; his clear mind has supplied a fund of information regarding the birth of our steam navy that could not have been obtained elsewhere, and which has made possible the rescue from oblivion of much of the subject-matter included in the first chapters. Chief Engineer B. F. Isherwood, U. S. Navy, has also kindly supplied much information and many references to documents from which valuable knowledge has been derived.

Chief Engineers James W. King, William H. Shock, Charles H. Loring, George W. Melville, David P. Jones, James Entwistle, F. G. McKean, Harrie Webster, and James H. Perry; Passed Assistant Engineers Robert S. Griffin, F. C. Bieg, Walter M. McFarland, H P. Norton, F. C. Bowers, G. Kaemmerling, and Chief Naval Constructor Philip Hichborn, have all afforded so much aid in the way of papers, manuscripts, photographs, etc., that it is a pleasure to thank them by name. Mr. T. C. Brecht, formerly of the naval engineer corps, and Mr. A. O. Blaisdell of New York, have contributed valuable drawings of machinery of older ships, which might not have been found elsewhere, which are greatly appreciated. Mr. E. H. Hart, the well-known photographer of Brooklyn, has placed the author under many obligations by allowing the use of photographs upon which he holds copyrights. Besides those already named, nearly three hundred others—officers and ex-officers of the navy, ship and engine builders, and civilians interested in naval progress—have by letter or verbally given much assistance; all whom are now formally thanked.

In all matters of historical importance the aim has been to adhere strictly to official accounts written at the time by persons most directly concerned. With this idea in view, the annual reports of the Secretary of the Navy for more than fifty years, covering the period since steam was introduced into the navy, have been carefully studied, as have also the reports of commanding officers of fleets, squadrons, and ships, especially those relating to the operations of the Civil War. The records of the naval Bureaus of Steam Engineering and Construction and Repair have been found mines of useful knowledge. Many reports made by committees of Congress on naval matters have also been used and much information gained from them, they being official and impartial to the same extent as departmental reports, and therefore equally suitable. From these official sources and from individuals of undoubted reliability the material for this book has been obtained.

In addition to official documents, many books have been used for reference. Some of these are mentioned in the text; among others, those found most useful have been, "The Atlantic and Gulf Coast," by Rear Admiral Daniel Ammen; C. B. Boynton, "History of the Navy During the Cival War;" Charles B. Stuart, "Naval and Merchant Steamers of the United States;" J. R. Soley, "The Blockade and the Cruisers;" Geo. F. Emmons, "Navy of the United States, 1775-1853;" Rear Admiral Preble, "History of Steam Navigation;" Dr. R. H. Thurston, "Growth of the Steam Engine;" Captain A. T. Mahan, "Gulf and Inland Waters;" T. H. S. Hamersly, "General Register of the U. S. Navy;" J. T. Scharf, "History of the Confederate States Navy;" Bennet Woodcroft, "Origin of Steam Navigation;" Wm. C. Church, "Life of John Ericsson;" H. O. Ladd, "The War With Mexico;" Chief Engineer B. F. Isherwood, "Engineering Precedents," and "Experimental Researches;" Chief Engineer George W. Melville, "In the Lena Delta;" Mrs. Emma De Long, "The Voyage of the Jeannette;" Chief Engineer James W. King, "European Ships of War," and Wm. Fairbairn, "History of Iron Ship-Building." The Journal of the American Society of Naval Engineers has furnished complete data regarding naval and commercial steamers of the United States and foreign countries for the past seven years, or ever since that journal was established.

Appendix A is known to be imperfect in not containing the names of that great body of patriotic Americans who served their country so well as volunteer engineers in the navy during the long war for the preservation of the Union: they numbered upwards of twenty-five hundred and their names and records when displayed in tabular form were found to fill so many pages as to exceed the limits proposed for this volume, which obliged the author reluctantly to abandon his original intention of including them in the list of officers of the regular service.

Appendix B is also incomplete for lack of space. To properly present in tables all the important data relating to our naval steamers, their engines, boilers, builders, synopsis of service, etc., would require pages of folio, or at least quarto, size, the tables given being consequently limited by the size of these pages to a few columns of the most important items. Lack of space has also caused the omission from these tables of the names of a large number of steamers purchased or captured during the Civil War and used temporarily as war vessels. An excellent list of naval vessels, giving all useful information, was published in book form in 1853 by Lieutenant (afterwards rear admiral) George F. Emmons, but nothing of the kind has appeared recently. Some officer with a liking for statistics could not be better employed at present than in the preparation of similar tables brought up to date, using the Emmons book as a model, for it cannot be improved upon in form and arrangement. Unless this is done soon, much useful and interesting information will be lost, as the author, with all the records of the Navy Department to refer to, found great difficulty in collecting data pertaining to ships not more than thirty years old.

Appendix C, "Uncle Samuel's Whistle and What It Costs," is amusing rather than instructive. It is reprinted to gratify requests made by a number of present and former members of the engineer corps. It is hoped it will please the older officers of the navy to see it again in print, while it certainly will amuse the younger men of the service who have never seen it.

The author submits no apology for making this book. It is a custom in armies and navies for the histories of distinct corps, departments, regiments, and even ships, to be written, and, although the supply of books in the world is far too great, there is room for one more to tell the story of steam in the American Navy. The only regret felt by the writer in giving this volume to his friends and the public is because of its imperfections: the subject deserves better treatment, and with more time and better opportunities to bestow upon it could be made more valuable as a history and more attractive in literary form. As it is, it has cost much research and hard work in the intervals of busy employment afloat and ashore, and it is now open to criticism. F. M. B.

New York, August, 1896.

THE
STEAM NAVY
OF THE
UNITED STATES

THE STEAM NAVY OF THE UNITED STATES.

CHAPTER I.

"For we are to bethink us that the Epic verily is not *Arms and the Man*, but *Tools and the Man*—an infinitely wider kind of Epic."—THOMAS CARLYLE: *Past and Present, Book IV., Chapter 1.*

INTRODUCTORY.

A glorious epic of the olden world, with the first lines of which most modern men are familiar, sings in stately rythm of "The arms and the man who first from the shores of the Trojan into Italy came," and this association of man and his weapons has remained through all the ages as the symbol and corner stone of all human government, power, and progress. The events of the century now drawing to its end have to a considerable extent shaken this ideal, for other things than arms have come to be recognized in the story of man's development a change in sentiment expressed to perfection by that prince of modern philosophers in the words that appear at the head of this chapter. In undertaking the subject of this volume the author does not propose to sing, or try to sing, of tools and men alone, nor will he attempt to elevate either tools or arms to the disadvantage of the other; but rather, believing that the adoption of steam machinery for purposes of war furnishes the most perfect illustration in existence of the mutual dependence and co-operation of these two great factors in civilization, he will endeavor to treat them as equals, for the arm is a tool and the tool is an arm, and their uses and purposes are identical within the limits of the subject of this book.

The story of the application of steam power to navigation, especially to the navigation and operation of ships of war, is a long one, and one which must be imperfectly told in the following chapters for the reason that the slow acceptance and growth of the new element will be considered with reference to one country and one navy only. Men who have made a study of the history of war, or who have given even a reasonable amount of reading to the subject are familiar with the reluctance with which the older weapons were laid aside for those which came in with the use of gunpowder. "Villainous saltpetre" was for a long era an object of dislike and distrust and those who used it were regarded with disfavor if not with contempt; they did not meet the enemy in hand-to-hand conflict with sword and spear; they begrimed their hands and clothing with burnt powder; they could not join in the rush and blood-stirring excitement of the charge, but stood off from friend and foe encumbered with their heavy weapons, creating an ill-smelling smoke and discordant noises, and their labors were very grudgingly admitted to be of any real advantage. So strong was the aversion to the new implement that in 1544, two hundred years after cannon are known to have been used by civilized nations in battle,[1] an historian dealing with the subject wrote that a monk was the inventor of cannon; adding that "the villian who brought into the world so mischievous a thing is not worthy that his name should remain in the memory of men."

As they did not take part in hand-to-hand conflict, gunners were looked upon as non-combatants, quite inferior to the warriors of the broad-sword and battle-axe variety, and as their weapon was very slow in its development they remained in an inferior military position for many centuries. It is an historical fact that it was not until just before the beginning of the American Revolution that the artillery branch of the British army, after a protracted but triumphant struggle with prejudice, "had vindicated its right to be, and was considered an important combatant arm."[2] So complete has been the change of sentiment with respect to cannon within about one hundred years that men belonging to military establishments now, especially navies, who make a point of priding themselves upon being essentially combatants, base their claim wholly upon the circumstance that their business is to handle cannon and gunpowder. The effect

---

[1] At Crècy in 1346. Traditions more or less authentic carry the use of "fire pipes" or other obscurely described weapons back almost to the beginning of the Christian era.

[2] Lieutenant W. E. Birkhimer: "Historical Sketch of the Artillery, U. S. Army."

of the prejudice of centuries against firearms is still visible in the lingering regiments of lancers, armed with the spear, occasionally met with in the great armies of the most progressive powers.

The introduction of steam into naval operations has revolutionized the fighting tactics of navies to fully as great an extent as gunpowder changed the methods of fighting on land, and in precisely the same manner has the development of steam been hindered by a prejudice born of older things and intolerant of change. Gunpowder has long since won its struggle, and steam on shore has been equally successful, but steam at sea is still in the very thickest of the fight for recognition upon its merit, and this in spite of the fact that the vehicle for its use—the marine engine—has advanced further toward perfection within the hundred years of its life than did the cannon during all the centuries from Crècy to Sedan, and is now in a stage of development fully abreast, if not actually ahead of the most perfected pieces of ordnance. That steam will win an equal place and equal honor with gunpowder and the propelling and auxiliary engines of a ship of war will come to be recognized as arms fully as important in making up the ship's combative qualities, as the turret and machine guns is a matter of simple logic; it only remains to be seen how long it will be before preconceived notions will admit the value of a new weapon.

It is proposed to begin with the first steam war-vessel ever built, which happened to be in our own navy, and to trace from that clumsy beginning the slow development of the naval steamer, with such illustrations as have been obtainable, in such manner that the chapters of this book will be an orderly and progressive account of the growth of the war-steamer and the marine engine in the United States. Into this narrative, as a most essential part, will be woven the history of the engineer corps of the navy, whose members have, in the face of much that was discouraging, kept the standard of our steamers fully up to that of other nations and have made the new navy, with its swift steel ships and perfected machinery, an established fact. Naval histories, of which there are many, deal almost entirely with the deeds of those who fight in ships that they have received completed from the hands of the builders, and in a majority of cases have little or nothing to say of the ships themselves or of their makers, or of that other class of officials who not only design and build the vitals of all modern war-ships but fight in the ships themselves as part of their naval duties. In making this work statistical to a considerable extent with regard to our naval steamers it is therefore proper that the lives and deeds of those who have been so intimately connected with them be also told, descriptively as well as statistically, and in so doing the author believes he will supply a lack that many beside himself have noticed in the older and more pretentious histories of our navy.

It has been written that it is difficult to become sentimental about the engineer. This idea is born of the belief that he deals only with material things and takes no part in the glorious possibilities of war or in the victories that are won from storms. This theory is absolutely false; his post of duty is as dangerous, as responsible, and as romantic, if you will, as any in a ship if people did but know it, and it is only because of a cultivated fondness for things that have been long celebrated in song and story that they do not know it. The life of the old-time sailor was in reality commonplace enough to satisfy even a ploughman, but an admiration for the sea and those who face its dangers on the part of those who never go to sea has made of the sailor's existence a picturesque ideal that has become an article of faith with all landsmen. And this faith excludes the new type of seaman—the man of the engine and boiler rooms—from any share in the romance of the sea because he faces dangers of another kind and performs his duty in another atmosphere, though equally exposed to the dangers that are peculiar to a life afloat. When some poet with a clearer vision and a willingness to enter an untrodden field shall appear and sing the song of steam it will be a revelation to the multitude; for there is music and romance and poetry as well as the embodiment of power about the mechanisms that drive the great ships of to-day.

From a habit of thought, then, rather than from any real state of affairs, the engine-room men of modern fleets are denied participation and honor in much of the life in which they take a leading part. With but little change, Napier's famous comparison of the conditions surrounding the British and French soldiers in the Peninsular War applies most aptly to the relation between the artificer and sailor classes in modern navies. The British soldier, though patiently fighting to conquer, could look forward to no honors to reward his daring; no despatch gave his name to the plaudits of his countrymen; his life of danger and hardship was uncheered by hope, his death unnoticed. At the same time, "Napoleon's troops fought in bright fields, where every helmet caught some beams of glory." In just the same way the naval engineer and his men toil in darkness in the depths of the ship, knowing full well that much they do will be unknown and unnoticed, however important it may be; and they often meet emergencies so bravely that their ships are saved from destruction or disablement both in peace and war, as will be shown hereafter by a few notable instances of duty, well done, that have come to light out of the many that have been performed.

Few naval engineeers of any length of service have not *once* at least, been suddenly brought face to face with death in its most fearful form by being called upon to act in an emergency resulting from a damaged boiler or steam pipe, and the instances are few where they have failed to prevent a calamity by sticking to their posts and encouraging their men to do the needful work, often so quietly that knowledge of the danger averted does not extend beyond the fireroom. If equal danger were faced from shot and shell in the smoke of battle, popular applause and military rewards would follow, but the engineer, encountering his peril in clouds of scalding steam and in the choke and wither of fierce fires suddenly hauled, does not appeal to the popular idea of heroism, though his acts are heroic and his performance of duty in navies is a military act just as much as nailing a flag to a mast, stopping a shot hole, or fishing a mast under fire, are military duties. Nor has he even the consoling thought when confronted with an emergency of meeting a death accounted heroic, for if he dies it must be like a rat in a hole, for which there is no glory, popular fancy regarding no death for one's country glorious, unless it is met not only beneath the flag but in full sight of it.

Popular ideas of naval administration are based upon a partial knowledge of an order of things that is no more, and not upon familiarity with conditions that really exist. Whatever notions the public may entertain, the fact remains that a much firmer and finer degree of courage is required in the officer who controls a division of men, either in peace or war, imprisoned beneath the battle-hatches of a war-steamer than in him whose men are in the open air and in sight of their danger. If the habit of command is ever needed in an officer it is in the trying emergencies and conditions that beset the naval engineer, and he who posesses it to the degree that enables him in a critical moment to keep his men at their posts and free from panic, thereby making of them and the machinery they handle a fighting factor that can be relied upon, is aiding his commanding officer in carrying out a plan of battle to fully as great an extent as can any other officer who directs the handling of two or four guns; and the officer who does this is most thoroughly and essentially a combatant, performing duties directly contributory to the fighting capabilities of the ship. This proposition needs no proof to those familiar with modern naval conditions, but as one of the purposes of this book is to set the position of American naval engineers in a true light before the public a number of instances of gallantry and professional efficiency on their part will be recited to prove that they actually and by right, by virtue of the duties they perform, belong to the combatant class of naval officers, *of* the navy as well as *in* the navy.

As the Civil War furnishes the example of the most prolonged and arduous service that our navy has ever been called upon to perform, and is, moreover, the first and only instance of great naval operations being carried on by means of steam vessels, it will be taken as the proper field for illustrating the nature and importance of the duties that engineers have rendered this country in its naval service. Though nearly one-half of this volume will be devoted to the work of the navy during the Civil War, no idea has been entertained of giving even an outline of our naval history during that period. A sufficient number of naval engagements and undertakings will be narrated in chronological order to give an ordinarily good idea of the general services performed by the navy, and an effort will be made to trace with some care the changes in type of naval steam-ships and marine engines resulting from the experiences of the war. In all of this no undue or undeserved prominence will be given to the naval engineer corps or to any of its members, but where engineers have rendered conspicuous service, either in battle or in preparing ships and machinery for use in war, full credit will be accorded them. This being a history of engines and engineers, it is natural that engineers should be frequently mentioned, but that does not leave the inference that they were the only officers engaged in carrying on the war on the part of the navy; on the contrary, the aim is simply to show that they did contribute much to the success of the Union arms and were much more than civilian adjuncts to the officers charged with the execution of general operations, whom they helped so well. The latter cannot at this late day regret that the story of the devotion of their engineer colleagues is to be told, especially as the story of their own deeds has been told often and well and has become a glorious part of our naval history.

CHAPTER II.

"Soon shall thy arm, unconquer'd Steam! afar
Drag the slow barge, or drive the rapid car;
Or on wide-waving wings expanded bear
The flying chariot through the fields of air."
ERASMUS DARWIN.

The DEMOLOGOS,[1] or FULTON, the First Steam War-Vessel ever Built—Robert Fulton—The SEA GULL—The FULTON, 2D—Mr. Charles H. Haswell, the First Engineer in the United States Navy—Captain M. C. Perry's Recommendations Regarding Engineers' Force—Regulations Governing Appointment of Engineers—Performance of the FULTON Under Steam—Her Subsequent Career—Captain Perry's Interest in Engineers.

THE first steam vessel for war purposes in the United States navy, or in any navy for that matter, was the *Demologos*, or *Fulton*, designed by Mr. Robert Fulton and built under his supervision in New York in 1814, while the war with Great Britain was going on. Owing to difficulties in obtaining material and skilled labor, this vessel, or floating battery, was not completed in time to be used against the British fleet, then constantly hovering about the port of New York, an unfortunate circumstance that is to be regretted for more reasons than one. The subsequent performance of this peculiar craft under steam makes it

WAR STEAMER FULTON THE FIRST, OR, DEMOLOGOS.

---

[1] "Voice of the People."

certain that with her powerful battery and independence of wind and tide she would have been entirely successful over the sailing-frigates she was built to assail, her advantage over them being not unlike that possessed by a savage, tireless wolf attacking a flock of sheep. Her earlier advent would have saved us the loss of the *President* frigate, and thus deprived the enemy of one of the very few causes for rejoicing over naval victories that the events of that war afforded.

Of much more importance would have been the incalculable impulse given to steam as a factor in naval warfare that would have followed the success of the *Demologos* in battle, and which would have set forward the development of the times in this regard almost half a century. The duel between the rudely-fashioned ironclads *Monitor* and *Merrimac* completely changed the naval architecture of the world, but who can tell of the absolute revolution, not only in naval architecture but in the methods of naval warfare, that would have resulted from the trial of Fulton's invention in actual war? Instead of being afterward obliged to fight its way inch by inch and foot by foot, compelled to struggle against every obstacle and every objection which jealousy, conservatism, and ignorance could bar against its progress, slowly and painfully forcing an unwilling and qualified recognition from the very element that should have championed its cause, steam-power would have appeared in the arena fully armed and equipped from the brain of its master, and would have been hailed not only as an auxiliary, but as an all-important arm in naval warfare.

The dimensions of the *Demologos* were: length, one hundred and fifty-six feet; breadth, fifty-six feet; depth, twenty feet; tonnage, two thousand four hundred and seventy-five; water-wheel, sixteen feet in diameter, fourteen feet wide, four feet dip; engine, cylinder forty-eight inches diameter, and five feet stroke; boiler, length, twenty-two feet; breadth, twelve feet; depth, eight feet.

The total cost of the vessel was $320,000, or about the cost of a first-class frigate, the *Constitution*, built in 1797, having cost originally $302,719.

A comparision of these dimensions with the views of this pioneer war-steamer given in this chapter shows that the drawings are somewhat out of proportion to the scale marked on them; they are, nevertheless, of great interest and value as being exact copies of the

"DEMOLOGOS"

Figure 1st Transverse section A her Boiler B the steam Engine C the water wheel E E her wooden walls 5 feet thick, diminishing to below the waterline as at FF, draught of water 9 feet D D her gun deck.

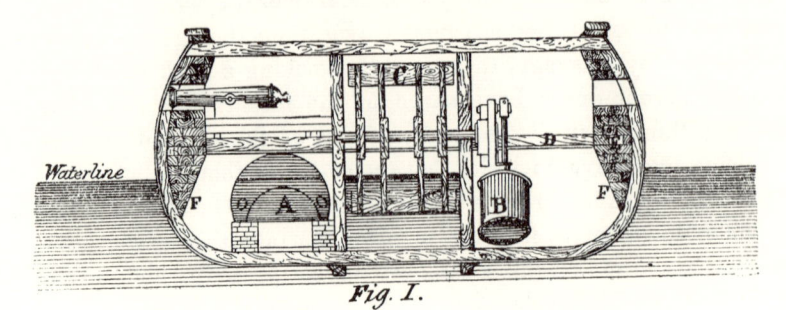

Fig. I.

Fig. II.

Figure II This shews her gun deck 140 feet long 26 feet wide, mounting 20 guns A the Water wheel.

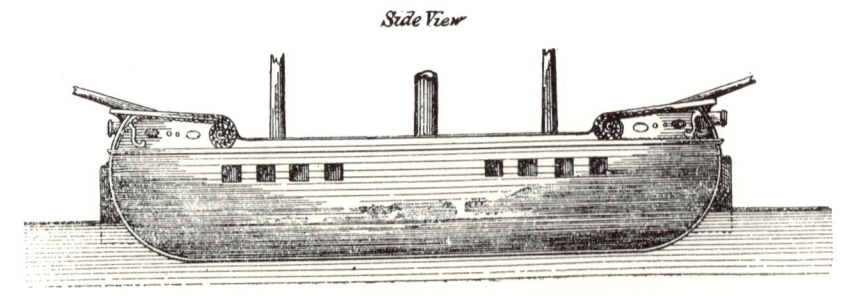

Side View

Fig. III.

ROBERT FULTON
November 1813

FROM STUART'S NAVAL AND MAIL STEAMERS OF THE UNITED STATES.

originals made by Robert Fulton and exhibited by him to the President of the United States when advocating his plan of applying steam to naval warfare. Fulton had his interview with the Executive late in 1813 and his project was zealously accepted, Congress, in March, 1814, authorizing the President to have built and equipped one or more such floating batteries for the defense of the coast.

The Coast and Harbor Defense Association, having charge of the building of war vessels, committed the building of the *Demologos* to a sub-committee of five prominent gentlemen, and Robert Fulton was appointed the engineer in charge of the work. The complete vessel—hull, engines and boilers—was designed by Fulton and the engines and boilers were built by him at his machine works on the North River. The hull was built at the ship-yard of Adam and Noah Brown on the East River and was launched in the presence of a great multitude of spectators, October 29, 1814, a little more than four months after the *keels* were laid. The plural is used intentionally, as the structure, as may be seen from the drawings, consisted of two hulls with the paddle-wheel working in a channel or canal between them; this canal was not continuous from end to end of the vessel, but is described as occupying a space of about sixty feet adjacent to the wheel, with its approaches presumably sloped off to prevent the action of the wheel from being inutile.

In November the hull was moved from the ship-yard to Fulton's engine works and the machinery installed, that labor being completed by the end of May, 1815. Certain changes were made in the vessel about this time on the recommendation of Captain David Porter, who had just returned home from his unfortunate cruise with the *Essex* and had been assigned to the command of the war-steamer. The original plan was to rely upon steam alone for propulsion, but Porter regarded this with misgiving and caused two large masts to be stepped to support latteen sails, and bowsprits for jibs, with all the accompanying top-hamper; he also had the sides, originally stopped flush at the spar deck, carried up to form protecting bulwarks for the sailors who would be on deck attending to the sails and rigging that had been added. The boiler, or "caldron for preparing her steam," as the gentlemen having charge of the work called it in their report, was also changed, probably by Fulton's direction, and two boilers were installed instead of one. Owing to the rigor of the British blockade about New York, guns for the vessel had to be hauled overland from Philadelphia, they having been taken from an armed British ship named *John of Lancaster*, captured by the *President* early in the war. In June, 1815, the *Demologos* steamed about New York Bay to try her machinery and found its performance to exceed every expectation; in the words of an early writer, "she exhibited a novel and sublime spectacle to an admiring people."

On the fourth of July of the same year, she made a passage to the ocean and back, steaming fifty-three miles in all, without any aid from her sails, in eight hours and twenty minutes; the wind and tide were partly in her favor and partly against her, the average rather in her favor. In September she made another trial trip to the sea, and having at this time the weight of her whole armament on board, she went at an average of five and a half miles an hour, with and against the tide. When stemming the tide, which ran at the rate of three miles an hour, she advanced at the rate of two and a half miles an hour. This performance was not more than equal to Robert Fulton's expectations, but it exceeded what he had promised to the government, which was that she should be propelled by steam at the rate of from three to four miles an hour.

The British were not uninformed as to the preparations which were making for them, nor inattentive to their progress. It is certain that the steam battery lost none of her terrors in the reports or imaginations of the enemy, as we find the following information in a treatise on steam vessels published in Scotland at that time, the author stating that he had taken great care to procure full and accurate accounts:

"Length on deck, *three hundred feet;* breadth, *two hundred feet;* thickness of her sides, *thirteen* feet of alternate oak plank and cork wood—carries forty-four guns, four of which are *hundred pounders*; quarter-deck and forecastle guns, forty-four pounders; and further to annoy an enemy attempting to board, can discharge *one hundred gallons of boiling water in a minute*, and by mechanism brandishes *three hundred cutlasses* with the utmost regularity over her gunwales; works also an equal number of heavy iron pikes of great length, darting them from her sides with prodigious force, and withdrawing them every quarter of a minute!"

LAUNCHING OF FULTON THE FIRST, OR DEMOLOGOS.

By one of those inexplicable cruelties of fate, Mr. Fulton, whose heart and soul were absorbed in the progress of his structure, was taken ill and died suddenly in February, 1815, before the vessel was completed, so he never knew of the great success he had achieved. Referring to this sad event, the report of the construction committee says: "Their exertions were further retarded by the premature and unexpected death of the engineer. The world was deprived of his invaluable labors before he had completed his favorite undertaking. They will not inquire, wherefore, in the dispensations of a Divine Providence, he was not permitted to realize his grand conception. *His discoveries, however, survive for the benefit of mankind*, and will extend to unborn generations."

The same committee report, signed by Messrs. Samuel L. Mitchell, Thomas Morris, and Henry Rutgers, contains many opinions and recommendations of great wisdom, indicating that the men of those days were more far-seeing and thoughtful than those of a later generation, and more disposed to appreciate the importance of new discoveries. Although written eighty years ago, the following paragraphs from the report sound not unlike the more progressive naval opinions of to-day, especially in that part relating to the necessity of training men for steam service, a subject that has been recommended and as regularly neglected from time to time ever since 1815:

"The Commissioners congratulate the Government and the nation on the event of this noble project. Honorable alike to its author and its patrons, it constitutes an era in warfare and the arts. The arrival of peace, indeed, has disappointed the expectations of conducting her to battle. That last and conclusive act of showing her superiority in combat, has not been in the power of the Commissioners to make.

"If a continuance of tranquility should be our lot, and this steam vessel of war be not required for the public defense, the nation may rejoice that the fact we have ascertained is of incalculably greater value than the expenditure—and that if the present structure should perish, we have the information never to perish, how, in a future emergency, others may be built. The requisite variations will be dictated by circumstances.

"Owing to the cessation of hostilities, it has been deemed inexpedient to finish and equip her as for immediate and active employ. In a few weeks everything that is incomplete could receive the proper adjustment.

"After so much has been done, and with such encouraging results, it becomes the Commissioners to recommend that the steam frigate be officered and manned for discipline and practice. A discreet commander, with a selected crew, could acquire experience in the mode of navigating this peculiar vessel. The supplies of fuel, the tending of the fires, the replenishing of the expended water, the management of the mechanism, the heating of shot, the exercise of the guns, and various matters, can only become familiar by use. It is highly important that a portion of the seamen and marines should be versed in the order and economy of the steam frigate. They will augment, diffuse, and perpetuate knowledge. When, in process of time, another war shall call for more structures of this kind, men, regularly trained to her tactics, may be dispatched to the several stations where they may be wanted."

There being no active service in the navy against the enemy; the *Demologos*, or *Fulton*, as she was afterward named, was taken to the Brooklyn navy yard and used as a receiving ship for many years, until, on the fourth day or June, 1829, her magazine, containing two and one-half barrels of damaged powder used for firing the morning and evening gun, blew up, entirely destroying the vessel, killing twenty-four persons and wounding nineteen others. Lieutenant S. M. Breckenridge was among the killed, as was also a woman who happened to be on board at the time. The cause of the explosion has never been known, although there was a tale current at the time that it was the deliberate act of a gunner's mate who had been disrated and flogged the morning of the day on which the catastrophe occurred. It is also said to have resulted from gross carelessness, survivors stating that the powder was kept in open kegs and that in the "bag-room" next the magazine, and separated from it only by a light bulkhead in which was a *sliding* door, the marine sergeant had a desk and was allowed to use an open light. Whatever the cause, the destruction was complete, and terminated the history of the *first steam vessel of war ever built.*

No engineers came into the navy because of the existence of the *Demologos*, men from Fulton's works having operated the machinery on the three occasions when she was under way with her own steam, and her engines were not moved after she was laid up in the navy yard. The next steamer to appear in the navy was the galliot *Sea Gull*, of one hundred tons, purchased in New York for $16,000 in 1822 and used as a despatch boat in Porter's "Mosquito fleet," employed in the West Indies for the suppression of piracy in 1823-24. There is no record of the men who had charge of the machinery of this little craft and we can only surmise that they were probably the same who had run her before she was purchased, and that their connection with the service was merely temporary. The *Sea Gull* was laid up in 1825 at Philadelphia, where she remained until 1840 when she was sold for $4,750.

For ten years after the *Sea Gull* was laid up, steamers do not appear in the official literature of the navy, though the same period witnessed a most wonderful development of the application of steam to navigation for commercial purposes, and steamers had visited India, China, the West Indies and other parts of the world, as well as having made the trans-Atlantic voyage no longer a marvellous one when performed under steam. That our navy was not the only one to remain in ignorance and indifference while this great change in marine affairs was going on all about it, is shown by the circumstance that in 1831 a steamer built in Quebec was, while on a peaceful voyage to London, fired on by a British frigate in the Gulf of St. Lawrence and compelled to heave-to until the officers of the frigate were satisfied that there was nothing diabolical in her construction. This same steamer, the *Royal William* by name, was sold after arriving in London to the Spanish government, and, under the name of *Isabella the Second*, became the first steam war-ship of that nation.

In 1835, under date of June 26, Mr. Mahlon Dickerson, then Secretary of the Navy, addressed a letter to the Board of Navy Commissioners, calling attention to an act of Congress dated April 29, 1816, which authorized the construction of a steam vessel, and requesting that the Board take immediate measures for commencing and completing such vessel; further directing that plans of the vessel and machinery be submitted to the Department for the approval of the President.

At that time there were about 700 steam vessels in use on the waters of the United States, the most of them being on the rivers and lakes, although some coastwise steamship lines had been established: with few exceptions these vessels were not larger than a modern steam tug, and their machinery was of the most crude design and workmanship, the chief object being to hammer together a boiler that would not leak too much to prevent the accumulation of some steam within it, and to hew out of heavy iron castings a cylinder with a roughly-fitted piston that could be forced to move back and forth under steam-pressure with reasonable regularity. There were at that time, of course, men of scientific attainments who were giving attention to the theory of the steam engine, and who had made considerable progress toward the solution of those thermo-dynamic problems, the knowledge of which in our own day has made the steam engine a comparatively economical machine.

To these experts, who were usually the managers or superintendents of the larger engine-building establishments then in existence, the Board of Navy Commissioners appealed for advice and help, but it does not appear from the records that any great amount of comfort was derived in this manner. One Wm. Kemble, who was the agent for the West Point Foundry Association, cheerfully supplied the Board with dissertations on the comparative merits of condensing and high-pressure engines and the theory of working steam expansively, giving copious opinions of Watt, Trevithick, Oliver Evans, and other authorities, all of which must have been highly interesting reading for the Board. One of these letters closes as follows: "I have given you our views candidly, but we are ready to execute any plan which the more extensive views and experience of the Board may decide on." Whether this was the irony of an expert who appreciated the humor of the situation, or was simply the homage demanded by the standing of the Board of Navy Commissioners, is open to doubt, but as no catastrophe to Mr. Kemble followed, we may conclude that the Board accepted this insinuation of its engineering wisdom as a proper and customary due.

Construction work on the hull of the vessel went forward rapidly at the New York navy yard, but the Navy Commissioners do not seem to have made corresponding progress in mastering the science of marine engineering, for we find them presently driven to the extremity of addressing the following letter to the Secretary of the Navy:

"NAVY COMMISSIONERS' OFFICE, December 30, 1835.

"SIR: The Commissioners of the Navy have, in conformity with the terms of your letter of the 26th instant, caused an advertisement to be published asking for proposals for furnishing the steam engines for the the steam vessel now building at New York. From their ignorance upon the subject of steam engines they are in doubt whether the advertisement gives the necessary information to enable persons to make proper offers. They are satisfied that they are incompetent themselves, and have no person under their direction who could furnish them with the necessary information to form a contract for steam engines that may secure the United States from imposition, disappointment, and loss, should the lowest offers happen to be made by persons whose general character and responsibility would not offer great security for their completing the engines in the best manner, according to the intentions and wishes of the board, in case the precise terms of the contract should leave them a legal opportunity of evading its spirit.

"The board beg leave, therefore, to request your authority for engaging some person who may be deemed competent to advise them upon this subject, and to superintend and inspect the engines during their progress, and until they shall be satisfactorily tested, and to designate the fund from which his compensation shall be paid.

"Respectfully, etc.,
"JOHN RODGERS."

This request for the professional services of an engineer not meeting with any immediate response from the Secretary, the board renewed its call for help a month later by the following communication:

"SIR: The board would respectfully recall your attention to their letter of the 30th ultimo, in relation to the employment of an engineer; his services will be much wanted in superintending the construction and arrangement of the engines and boilers, and afterwards to work them in the vessel. As it will be desirable to obtain satisfactory testimonials of the qualifications of any person who may be thus employed, which may consume some time, an early decision may prove advantageous.

"Respectfully, etc.,
"JOHN RODGERS."

Mr. Charles H. Haswell of New York became an applicant for the position of engineer which the Board of Navy Commissioners was so anxious to have filled, but his appointment was not made until the Board had taken occasion, while admitting the excellence of his professional knowledge as shown by his testimonials and conversation, to express grave doubts as to his *practical* familiarity with the manipulation of marine machinery, from which circumstance we of this day, who not infrequently encounter the same criticism, may see that the mistrust, inconsequential as it is, is by no means new. The Board qualified its doubt in Mr. Haswell's case with the following ingenuous confession: "How far such practical knowledge may be absolutely necessary, or can be supplied by superior information upon the construction of the engine itself, the Board has no means of determining, except such as are common to other persons." Mr. Haswell's appointment, made two days after the comments of the Board were submitted to the Department, reads as follows:

"NAVY DEPARTMENT, February 19, 1836.

"SIR: In your letter to the Commissioners of the Navy yesterday, you offer to furnish draughts of a high and low-pressure steam engine and boiler, on different elevations, suitable for the steam vessel now constructing by the Government of the United States, for the purposes stated.

"You are therefore appointed, for the term of two months, to make such draughts and report the same to the Board of Navy Commissioners, for which you will receive a compensation of two hundred and fifty dollars.

"MAHLON DICKERSON.
"To Mr. C. H. Haswell, *Washington.*"

In mid-summer following, under date of July 12th, 1836, Mr. Haswell was appointed chief engineer for the *Fulton*, as the steam-vessel then building was named; he thus becoming the first person to hold the position of engineer in the United States navy. Mr. Haswell was then an engineer of ability and established professional reputation, being earnestly engaged in the task, at that time a doubtful one, of proving the reliability of steam as a marine motor, independent of any aid from sails. To him has been granted a privilege that comes to few men in any calling on this earth, for it has been his fortune to witness the emblem of his profession—the steamship—grow from its awkward infancy to its present gigantic and perfected form, a development in which he has had a prominent part during all these decades, and which in the completeness of the changes that have been wrought, far exceeds the magical transformations of a dream or the enchantments of a fairy-tale. In the great harbor where, as a young man, he saw the embryo steamer timidly and alone making its uncertain wake, an object so rare that curious crowds always flocked to watch it, he has been spared until now to see in his old age the crude and clumsy *Fulton* transformed into the *Columbia* or the *New York*, and the pioneer passenger steamers changed, as if by the magician's wand, into the *Umbria*, the *Majestic*, and the *Campania*.

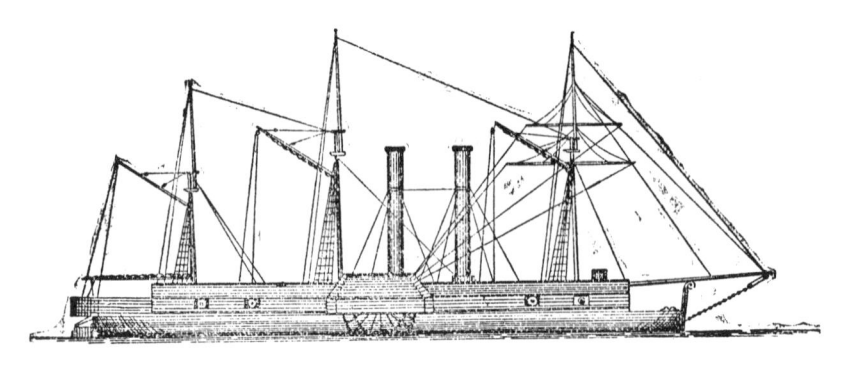

U. S. STEAMER FULTON (THE SECOND), 1837.

The following were the principal dimensions of the *Fulton:*
Length of vessel between perpendiculars.. 180 ft.
Beam on deck (extreme) .... 34 " 8 in.
Depth of hold........................... 12 " 2 "
Mean draft.............................. 10 " 6 "
Immersed midship section at mean draft... 308 square ft.
Weight of hull.......................... 470 tons.
Depth of keel .... 12 inches.
Displacement at mean draft (about).........1,200 tons.

The engines and boilers were built by the West Point Foundry Association of New York, under a contract dated January 23, 1837, the engines in type and location being from the designs prepared for the Board of Navy Commissioners by Mr. Haswell, and the boilers from the designs of Mr. Charles W. Copeland, the engineer of the West Point company. There were two horizontal condensing engines located *on the spar deck*, the cylinders being of nine feet stroke and fifty inches in diameter, each engine turning a side-wheel twenty-two feet nine inches in diameter, and eleven feet six inches wide. The contract provided for a thwartship shaft to connect the two wheel shafts, at an additional cost of $2,000, if required, but the requirement was not made and the vessel was completed without such connection. So undeveloped was the art of iron manufacture at that time that the cranks and shafts were made of cast iron. The contract price for the engines was $40,000, to which was added $198.57 for authorized changes. The wheels cost $9,000. The boilers were built by the contractors at the New York navy yard for eight and one-half cents a pound, the Government furnishing the material, which consisted of copper plates and rivet rods provided in 1816 for another vessel like the *Demologos*, which was never built. The total cost of boilers, including the material and labor, was $93,396.06. Originally there were four wagon-shaped boilers of the return-flue type, each sixteen feet long, ten feet six inches wide, and nine feet three inches high, but these were afterward changed to two boilers twenty-five feet nine inches long, the other dimensions remaining unchanged. These boilers were located in the hold under the engines, and were supplied with separate smoke pipes. The total cost of the vessel when completed—hull, equipments and machinery—was $299,649.81.

The weight of engines was 81 tons; of boilers, including smoke pipes, steam pipes and connections, 119 tons, and water in the boilers, 41 tons. On a trial trip the following winter, Chief Engineer Haswell computed the horse-power developed to be 625, from which we observe that the weight of machinery per horse-power was about three times as much as under present practice.

The steamer was launched May 18, 1837, and the work of installing the machinery immediately undertaken; this work was much hindered by the action of the Board of Navy Commissioners in refusing to allow the hull to be taken to the engine builders' works on the North river, thus compelling the contractors to transport the engines in pieces to the navy yard. The Commissioners, in refusing the application to have the hull moved, said that they did not "feel themselves justified in permitting the vessel to be moved from the navy yard to a place over which they have no control," although why they should have felt this way is not apparent, as they had previously confessed their incompetency to deal with matters relating to the vessel's machinery. This action forced the contractors to file a claim for "increased expense in the putting up of the work, together with an additional delay of not less than three weeks," just as contractors do now when their work is retarded by the interference of naval officers. Truly, there is no new thing under the sun.

About the first of September Captain Matthew C. Perry took general charge of the steamer, and immediately began investigating the subject of *personnel* required for her operation, the result of his researches being communicated to the Navy Commissioners by the following report:

"NEW YORK, September 11, 1837.

"GENTLEMEN:—I have sought to obtain the best information in reference to the number of engineers, firemen, &c., that will be required for the steam frigate *Fulton*, and the following is the result of the combined opinions of the various persons consulted:

"The lowest number for putting the engines in operation—

"2 1st-class assistant engineers, at $800 per annum.

"2 2nd-class assistant engineers, at $500 per annum.

"8 firemen, at from $25 to $30 per month. The firemen to be paid either of those amounts, at the discretion of the captain, as suitable persons can be obtained.

"4 or 6 coal heavers, at $15 per month.

"Add to this when the vessel is in actual operation—

"1 chief engineer, 4 additional firemen and 4 coal heavers.

"The coal holes are at the ends of the boilers, opposite to the furnaces, and the coal must necessarily be transported some distance.

"These are the estimates of Mr. Haswell, Mr. Kimble, and several other competent persons with whom I have conferred on the subject.

"It is apparent that no less than four engineers will answer, as it requires *two* constantly at the levers, by which the engines are stopped and put in motion, which are worked on the *spar deck*, and two at the engines and boilers *below deck*, to watch the machinery and attend the water in the boilers—a most important consideration, as by the least neglect in this particular some accident occurs or the boilers are burnt.

"It is necessary, also, that the firemen should be somewhat acquainted with the operation of the engines, the mode of supplying the boilers, &c., as also the mode of placing the coals to prevent the burning of the furnaces.

"The gentlemen all agree that the above is the least number that prudence and economy would authorize.

"The large North river and Rhode Island boats have three engineers each, and their firemen understand starting and stopping the engines, regulating the steam, &c. Their wages are—for the chief engineer, $1,000 per annum; two assistants, at $360 and $600 per annum. Add to this their board, which, in the navy, would be defrayed by themselves all beyond the ration of 20 cents per day.

"Those denominated first-class assistants for the navy should correspond in qualifications with the chief engineers of private steamers, and their assistants with the second-class proposed for the navy, as it is supposed that the Government can hire persons on lower terms.

"It has been suggested, in which I fully concur, that there should be these several described rates among the engineers and firemen in our national steamers, the better to distribute authority and responsibility, and to produce a proper ambition with the inferior rates to rise to the higher classes.

"I enclose herewith a letter from Captain William Comstock, giving his views on the subject. And it may be remarked here, that all concur in the opinion of the necessity of separating the regular crew from any interference with the engineers.

"I would respectfully invite the attention of the Commissioners to the consideration of the *tenure* by which these assistant engineers are to hold their appointment, and by what authority they are to be granted. It seems to me the process of their discharge, at least, should be summary, and entirely divested of the legal forms of arrest, court-martial, &c. The slightest appearance of intemperance, neglect, carelessness, &c., should be sufficient cause for their certain dismissal from the service. With whom is to rest the authority to judge of these delinquencies, and the necessity of the infliction of the penalty, will, of course, be determined on in time, and made known to the persons on receiving the appointment.

"I have the honor to be, gentlemen, your obedient servant,
"M. C. PERRY.
"To the Commissioners of the Navy, Washington, D. C."

This letter is important in our history as a corps, being the earliest official document containing so much as a hint of the necessity of organizing a permanent corps of naval engineers.

The Board of Naval Commmissioners agreed to Captain Perry's recommendations as to wages for engineers and firemen, although remarking that for the latter the pay appeared high in addition to the ration, and referred the matter to the Department with various recommendations. The Department let the matter rest for more than a month, until, about the end of October, Captain Perry reported the vessel ready for steam, and called attention to the fact that no authority existed for the employment of assistant engineers, adding that their services were much needed. The suggestions made by the Board of Navy Commissioners on September 15 were promulgated as the regulations of the Department governing the appointment of "these descriptions of persons for the steamer." The recommendations of the Board, which became the Department's regulation, is another important document in the history of the engineer corps, and is here given:

"Upon the subject of *appointments* of the engineers, etc., the Board respectfully suggest the expediency of allowing, for the present, the commandant to nominate the assistant engineers, after collecting, as far as practicable, proofs or certificates of their character and qualifications, subject to the confirmation of the commander of the station, when time will allow of an immediate reference; in other cases, to be made by the commander of the vessel.

"That they receive a letter of appointment, revocable at any time by the commander of the station upon complaints of intemperance, incapacity, insubordination, negligence, or other misconduct, by the commander of the vessel, if proved to the satisfaction of such commanding officer of the station.

"The commander of the vessel, of course, to have the power of suspending them from duty, if he deems it necessary.

"The engineers to sign some proper instrument, which will legally render them liable to the laws for the government of the navy, but to be exempt from corporal punishment; which instrument is to be transmitted to the Secretary of the Navy, with the letter accepting their appointment.

"The firemen and coal-heavers to sign the shipping articles and be removable at the pleasure of the commander of the vessel, as authorized for the reduction and punishment of petty officers and seamen."

This order was dated October 31, 1837, and was carried into effect by the appointment of John Faron, Jr., and Nelson Burt as first assistant engineers on November 15, and of J. C. Hines and Hiram Sanford as second assistants on November 21. These appointments were made by Captain Perry himself, as shown by the following extract from a report made December 16 on the steam trial of the *Fulton:*

"The assistant engineers appointed by me promise to be highly industrious and useful men. I have been much pleased with their conduct, and, so far as I am yet capable of judging, consider them well acquainted with their duty; of one thing I am certain, that if the vessel is to be employed at all, sixteen, instead of eight firemen will be indispensably necessary."

On November 1 the engines of the *Fulton* were put in motion for the first time and the result was highly satisfactory; "twelve inches of steam was produced in less than an hour by chips from the yard," to quote from Captain Perry's report. During the ensuing winter the *Fulton* was thoroughly tried in free route and proved herself a success as a steamer, although certain peculiarities in construction precluded her use as a cruiser for general sea purposes: in fact she was not built for such service, the primary idea in her construction being to provide a harbor-defense vessel to take the place of the first *Fulton*, or *Demologos*.

Captain Perry reported in February that her usual speed at a medium pressure of steam and twenty revolutions per minute of the engines had been proved to be about twelve knots, and that her maximum speed, at a forced pressure, might be extended to fifteen knots. He spoke highly of her efficiency as an armed vessel, in comparision with vessels of war not propelled by steam, and gave an opinion resulting from his observations that "there is not the least doubt that *sea steamers* of 1,400 or 1,500 tons can be constructed and equipped to cruise at sea, for limited periods (say twenty days,) as efficient vessels of war, to be as safe from the disasters of the sea as the finest frigate, and at an expense considerably less." Lieutenant Lynch, attached to the vessel, in a written report stated that "For harbor and coast defense, in *light winds and calms*, with a battery of long 64-pounders, the *Fulton*, with slight alterations, would be perfectly efficient, and more useful than any number of armed ships not propelled by steam," and the opinions of the other officers, all whom had to make reports to Captain Perry, generally agreed to this. In Chief Engineer Haswell's report we find the following carefully itemized statement of current expenses of running the engines, which is both curious and interesting at this date:

Engines, 3 quarts of oil, at 18¾c.................	$0.56
Engines and boilers, 5 pounds of tallow, at 10c.........	.50
Engines, 2½ pounds of hemp, at 12c.................	.30
2 pounds of spun yarn, at 12c...............	.24
½ pound of black lead, at 10c................	.10
Paints and brushes........................	.75
Boilers, Indian meal.....................................	.24
Engines and boilers, white lead, 2 pounds at 12c......	.24
Lamps and lanterns.................	.10
Shovels, brooms, and axes........	.23
Tools.............................	.50
For twelve hours............	$3.66
Off one-sixth per diem of ten hours......................	.61
	$3.05

More light on the operation of the machinery is given by the synopsis of the engine-room log, here following in the form of the engineer's weekly report for one of the weeks that the vessel was under steam a considerable part of the time:

THE STEAM NAVY OF THE UNITED STATES. 27

ENGINEER'S WEEKLY REPORT, (ENDING MONDAY, 22D, 1838), UNITED STATES STEAMER FULTON, M. C. PERRY, Esq., COMMANDER.

Time of setting fire.	Time of raising steam.	Boilers used.	Engines used.	Average pressure.	Average vacuum.	Average revolutions.	Engines at rest.	Time of blowing off.	Engines in operation.	Time consuming fuel.	Cords of wood consu'd.	Bu. of coal consumed.		
	H M						H M	H M	H M	H M			Total time firing, 20 hours, 34 minutes. Total wood consumed, 23 cords, 96 feet. Total coal consumed, 78 ch., 12 bushels.	REMARKS.—Slip joints of starboard engine leaked some, but were screwed up after every trip. Lost five water-wheel arms and three buckets. Lengthened larboard piston rod one-fourth of an inch. Set grate bars in after larboard furnaces for burning coal. On 20th let fires in forward boilers go down after under way, and carried six inches steam, and engines made thirteen revolutions with the two remaining boilers.
17th, A. M.	10 30	4	2	10	11	17	0 15 P.M.	3 17	3 22	4 47	10	105		
18th, A. M.	11 40	4	2	7.5	10	14	0 40 P.M.	12 12	1 32	3 07	6	65		
	9 5 10													
20th, A. M.	8 40 9 30	4 2	2 2	11 6	12 18 12 13		0 20 P.M.	2 35	4 45	5 55	2⅝	205		
22d, A. M.	8 45 9 50	4	2	11	12	17.5	1 0 P.M.	3 30	4 40	6 45	5⅛	285		
									14 19	20 34	23¾	660		

CHAS. H. HASWELL, Engineer.

APPROVED: M. C. PERRY, Captain.

New York, January 23, (S. A.), 1838.

When the *Fulton* was put in commission with a regular complement of officers and men on board, the question of what to do with the engineers as to their quarters and messing arrangements came up, and was a difficult one to settle, because there were no precedents to follow and no regulations regarding the new class of officials. Fortunately for Mr. Haswell, and for those who came after him as well, his social status was such that his place among the officers was obviously in the ward room, and to that part of the ship he was assigned irrespective of the fact that he held no commission and no rank in the service. The precedent thus established of assigning the chief engineer to the ward-room operated to the benefit of other chief engineers in the following years, until, in 1842, the quarters for chief engineers on board ship were specified by law to be in the ward-room. The assistant engineers of the *Fulton* were berthed and messed with the warrant officers.

In April, 1838, the *Fulton* visited Norfolk and Washington and was an object of general attention, especially at the national capitol. In September of the same year, in consequence of a discussion that was related to the Secretary of the Navy, she was ordered back to

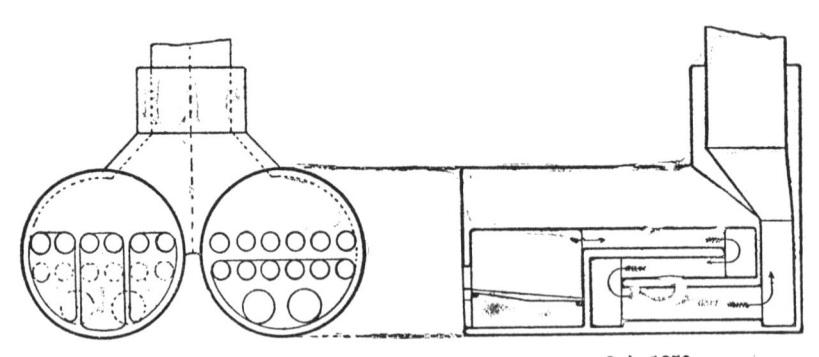

RETURN DROP-FLUE BOILERS, U. S. FULTON(3D), 1850.

Diameter of shells 10 feet, 6 inches. Length, 22 feet.
Length of furnace, 7 feet. Height of furnace 6 feet, 3 inches.
Diameter of flues, two upper rows, 16 inches. Lower row, 25 inches.
Diameter of steam drum, 7 ft, 3 in. Diameter of smoke pipe, 5 ft. 3 in.

New York for the express purpose of testing her speed with that of the British steamer *Great Western*, running between New York and Liverpool. The *Fulton* followed the latter vessel to sea on the occasion of her regular departure, ranged up alongside and passed her rapidly. After being employed in active service along the Atlantic coast of the United States until 1842, the *Fulton* was laid up in ordinary at the New York navy yard, where she remained a neglected and useless hulk until 1851. In the latter year the machinery was entirely replaced by a different type, designed under the direction of Mr. Charles B. Stuart, then engineer-in-chief of the navy. There was a single inclined engine mounted on a wooden frame, the cylinder being fifty inches in diameter and ten feet four inches stroke, provided with a Sickel's cut-off. The old copper boilers were replaced with two wrought iron ones of the double-return, drop-flue variety, ten feet six inches in diameter and twenty-two feet long. Feathering paddle wheels were substituted for the original radial wheels. The shaft of this engine was of wrought iron.

The hull was hauled on the ways and thoroughly repaired, the upper deck and high bulwarks being removed and the interior arrangements were completely changed because of the altered arrangement of the machinery, but the original lines of the ship were not disturbed. The rig was changed to a two-masted fore-topsail schooner. A trial trip was run January 1, 1852, in New York harbor, seventy-one and one-half miles being run under steam between various intervals of stopping, sailing, backing, etc., which interruptions completely destroy the results as a steam trial. The report of this trial gives the average steam pressure as twenty-five pounds; average vacuum, twenty six inches; average revolutions, twenty-one, and average speed, 13.34 *miles* per hour. For a period of twenty-one minutes at the end of the performance, with thirty pounds of steam and twenty-three revolutions, the distance run is given as seven miles, or at the rate of twenty miles per hour. Unfortunately the report does not state the condition of the wind and tide at that period, so we do not know whether the high speed was due entirely to the engines or not. It is a matter of record, however, that the vessel had a reputation in the service as a very fast steamer. She was employed on general cruising duty in the home squadron and West Indies for several years, was one of the vessels of the Paraguay expedition in 1858, and in 1861 was in ordinary at the Pensacola navy yard.

The Pensacola yard was surrendered to the Confederates January 10, 1861, and the *Fulton* thus fell into their hands; she was then in very bad condition, having sometime previously been stranded and nearly wrecked near Pensacola, but her captors hauled her on the building-ways and began repairing her. May 9, 1862, military operations compelled the Confederates to abandon the yard, they burning everything behind them. An account of this destruction is given in Mr. J. T. Scharf's History of the Confederate States Navy, in which account appears the last historical reference to this famous old steamer—"The *Fulton*, that was on the stocks in the navy yard, was burned."

This story of the old *Fulton* would be incomplete without a special reference to the invaluable services rendered by Captain M. C. Perry to the steam navy which her example called into life, his able championship of engines and engineers in connection with her having properly given him a place in our naval history as the father of the American steam navy. Matthew C. Perry was a younger brother of that other Perry who overcame the British on Lake Erie in 1813, which event is so nearly synonymous in the public mind with the name of Perry that the deeds of the younger brother, some of which were of more lasting importance than the mere winning of a battle, have been dimmed by contrast. Captain Perry's services to the naval engineer corps in connection with his command of the *Fulton* were both important and lasting, and can best be told by quoting from his biography, written by a distinguished civilian, Reverend Wm. E. Griffis, another of whose books, "The Mikado's Empire," has been a source of instruction and pleasure to hundreds of our naval officers of the present time who have had the privilege of seeing the shores of beautiful Japan:

"Perry took command of the *Fulton* October 4th, 1837, when the smoke-pipes were up, and the engines ready for an early trial. His work meant more than to hasten forward the completion of the new steam battery. He was practically to organize an entirely new branch of naval economy. There were in the marine war service of the United States absolutely no precedents to guide him.

"Again he had to be 'an educator of the navy.' To show how far the work was left to him, and was his own creation, we may state that no authority had been given and no steps taken to secure firemen, assistant engineers, or coal heavers. The details, duties, qualifications, wages, and status in the navy of the whole engineer corps fell upon Perry to settle. He wrote for authority to appoint first and second-class engineers. He proposed that $25 to $30 a month, and one ration, should be given as pay to firemen, and that they should be good mechanics familiar with machinery, the use of stops, cocks, gauges, and the paraphernalia of iron and brass so novel on a man-of-war.

"Knowing that failure in the initiative of the experimental steam service might prejudice the public, and especially the incredulous and sneering old salts who had no faith in the new fangled ideas, he requested that midshipmen for the *Fulton* should be first trained in seamanship prior to their steamer life. He was also especially particular about the moral and personal character of the 'line' officers who were first to live in contact with a new and strange kind of 'staff.' It is difficult in this age of war-steamers, when a sailing man-of-war or even a paddle-wheel steamer is a curiosity, to realize the jealousy felt by sailors of the old school towards the un-naval men of gauges and stop-cocks. They foresaw only too clearly that steam was to steal away the poetry of the sea, turn the sailor into a coal heaver, and the ship into a machine.

"Perry demanded in his line officers breadth of view sufficient to grasp the new order of things. They must see in the men of screws and levers equality of courage as well as of utility. They must be of the co-operative cast of mind and disposition. From the very first, he foresaw that jealousy amounting almost to animosity would spring up between the line and staff officers, between the deck and the hold, and he determined to reduce it to a minimum. The new middle term between courage and cannon was *caloric*. He would provide precedents to act as anti-friction buffers so as to secure a maximum of harmony.

"That was Matthew Perry—ever magnifying his office and profession. He believed that responsibility helped vastly to make the man. He suggested that engineers take the oath, and from first to last be held to those sanctions and to that discipline, which would create among them the *esprit* so excellent in the line officers."

CHAPTER III.

> "So shalt thou instant reach the realm assigned,
> In wondrous ships, self-moved, instinct with mind;
> . . . .
> Though clouds and darkness veiled the encumbered sky,
> Fearless, through darkness and through clouds they fly."
> ALEXANDER POPE, *translation of the Odyssey.*

The ENGINEER—The MISSISSIPPI and MISSOURI—Establishment of the Engineer Corps by Act of Congress—Destruction of the MISSOURI—Career of the MISSISSIPPI—Steamers Transferred to the Navy from the War Department—The MICHIGAN.

BEFORE the completion of the *Fulton*, a single steam vessel appeared in the navy in the form of a small paddle-wheel tugboat of 142 tons, which was bought in Baltimore in 1836 for $18,997, and was named the *Engineer*. This boat had a single beam engine of about one hundred horse-power, and one iron flue boiler: the vessel was used as a tug and dispatch boat about the Norfolk navy yard for a number of years, and also did some service on the southern coast as a surveying vessel. Although not a war vessel in any sense, this craft is here referred to because she was for a short time the only steamer in the navy, and was a familiar object to the early members of the engineer corps, many of whom were assigned to her for temporary service while getting broken in to the rules of the navy.

In 1839 two boards of officials were convened in Washington to consider the method of carrying out the provisions of an act of Congress authorizing the construction of two or more steam vessels of war. One of these boards was composed of commodores, and was directed to "consider and decide upon the qualities and power which it was desirable to secure in the vessels:" the other was composed of naval constructors and one engineer, Mr. Haswell being the latter, with instructions to scrutinize the report of the commodores, and determine whether the qualities and powers recommended by them could be combined practically, and if so, to prepare the details for carrying them out. The result of this labor set in process of construction two large side-wheel frigates named the *Mississippi* and

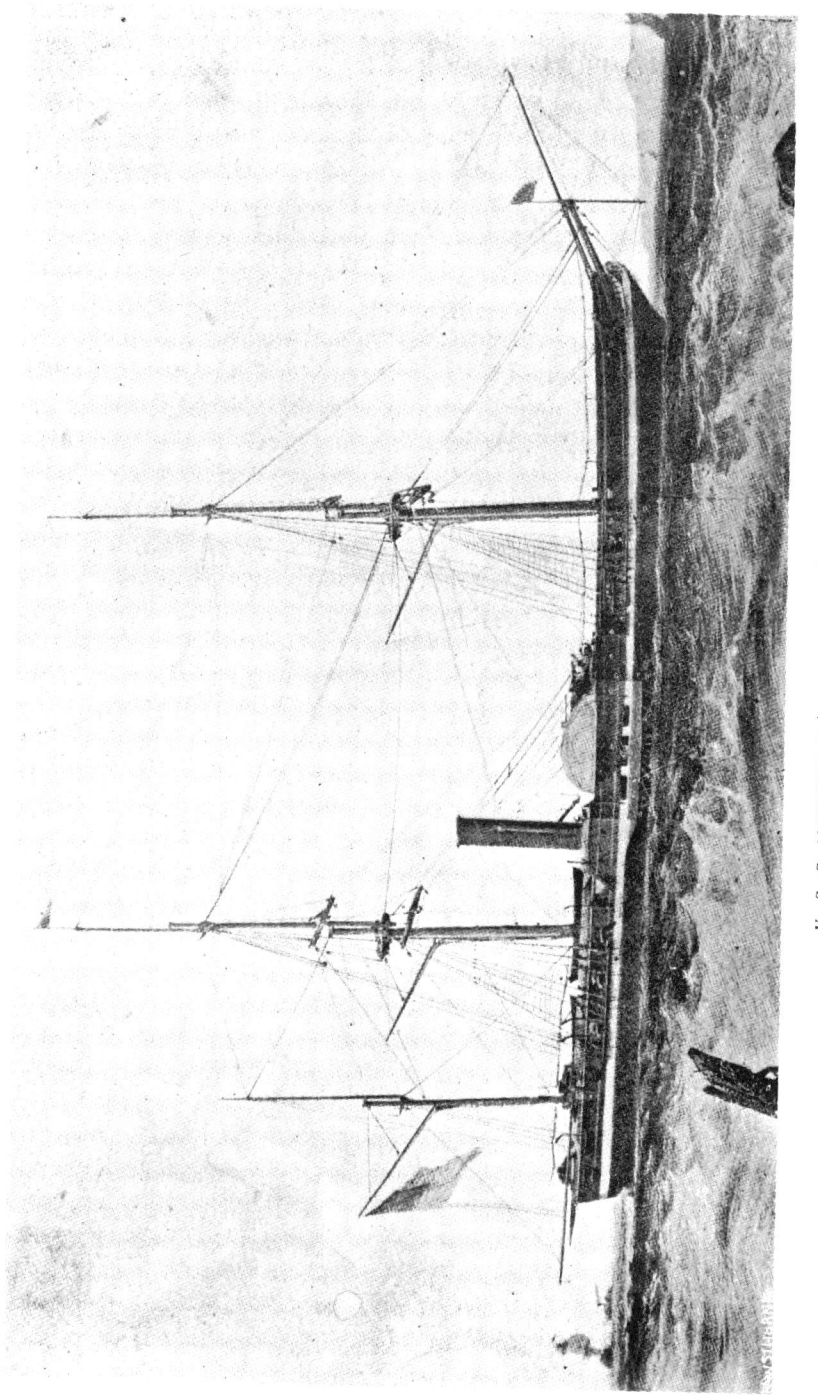

U. S. S. MISSISSIPPI (AND MISSOURI), 1842.

Missouri, precisely alike in all respects, except the type of engines. It is not to be supposed that the inauguration of the policy of building steam vessels for the navy was unattended with skepticism and opposition; like the application of all great scientific discoveries, the introduction of steam power was combatted and misunderstood, abroad as well as in our own country. The logic, if it may be so called, of the opposition is well indicated by the vehement utterance of Lord Napier in the British House of Commons in a speech fiercely antagonistic to the building of steamers of war: "Mr. Speaker, when we enter Her Majesty's naval service and face the chances of war, we go prepared to be hacked in pieces by cutlasses, to be riddled with bullets, or to be blown to bits by shot and shell; but, Mr. Speaker, we do not go prepared to be *boiled alive*."

The principal data common to both the *Mississippi* and *Missouri* were the following:

Length over all	229 feet.
Beam	40 feet.
Mean draft	19 feet.
Displacement at mean draft	3,220 tons.

The vessels were bark-rigged, spreading 19,000 square feet of canvas in plain sails to top-gallant sails inclusive. Each vessel had three copper boilers of the double return ascending flue variety, with three furnaces and eighty square feet of grate surface in each boiler; the heating surface of each boiler was 2,000 square feet, or exactly twenty-five times the grate surface. The paddle-wheels were twenty-eight feet in diameter and eleven feet broad. The battery of each vessel consisted of two X-inch and eight VIII-inch shell guns. The *Mississippi* had two side-lever engines with cylinders seventy-five inches in diameter and seven feet stroke, and the *Missouri* had two inclined direct-acting engines with cylinders sixty-two and one-half inches diameter and ten feet stroke: the cubical contents of the cylinders of the two vessels were practically the same, a difference being made in the length of the stroke to test the relative merits of long and short stroke engines.

The hulls were of wood, that of the *Mississippi* being constructed at the navy yard, Philadelphia, and that of the *Missouri* at the New York navy yard. The *Mississippi's* machinery was built by Merrick and Towne in the city of Philadelphia, and that for the *Missouri* by the West Point Foundry Association at their works at Cold Spring, New York. The machinery for both vessels was designed by Mr. Charles W. Copeland, referred to in a previous chapter as the superintending engineer of the West Point Foundry Association at the time the engines for the *Fulton* were built. He had been employed as a consulting engineer for the Board of Navy Commissioners, and, with the title of Principal Engineer, held that position for several years, during which time he did much excellent work in designing machinery for the new steam navy, although he never was in the naval service in the sense of holding a commission as an officer or being amenable to military law and discipline.

In the fall of 1839, when the work of building these two vessels began, Mr. Haswell was detached from the *Fulton* and assigned to duty with Mr. Copeland in New York to prepare drawings of machinery for both vessels. It was in the course of this work that Mr. Haswell laid down the boilers of both the new vessels in full size, designed and determined the dimensions of each plate, and thus for the first time in the history of boiler manufacture were the plates rolled and trimmed to measure. In January, 1840, Mr. Faron, the senior engineer of the *Fulton*, was promoted to be a chief engineer, detached from the *Fulton* and detailed to superintend the building of the *Mississippi's* engines in Philadelphia, his place on the *Fulton* being filled by Mr. Andrew Hebard, who was appointed chief engineer from civil life. Shortly afterward Mr. Haswell was named as superintendent of the engines building for the *Missouri*.

The two frigates were completed early in 1842, and a number of engineers were appointed in the manner indicated by the Department's regulation on the subject, quoted in a former chapter. A remarkable fact in connection with the building of these two ships is the close parallelism of their cost, although they were built in different cities, and had engines radically different in details of construction: in 1853 the Navy Department, in obedience to a resolution of the House of Representatives, informed Congress that the actual cost of the *Mississippi* to the time of her first sailing, exclusive of ordnance, was $569,670.70, and of the *Missouri*, $568,806. Mr. Faron was the first chief engineer of the *Mississippi*, and Mr. Hebard of the

MR. CHARLES W. COPELAND,

Principal Engineer, U. S. Navy. Designer of the machinery of the *Mississippi, Missouri*, etc.

Missouri, he being temporarily assigned to that vessel while Mr. Haswell was engaged with Mr. Copeland on the designs of a new steamer—the *Michigan*. This latter work was completed in October, 1842, when Mr. Haswell returned to the *Missouri* as her chief engineer.

After the appointments for the two new frigates were made there were twenty engineers in the service, with prospects for the need of many more in the near future, as the policy of building war steamers was so well established that there was no longer any hope for success on the part of the conservative element which had struggled against the new order of things so stubbornly. The engineers were very much dissatisfied with various anomalies and evils incident to their connection with the navy, and began an agitation which speedily resulted in the legal establishment of the engineer corps as a permanent part of the naval organization. Their pay did not compare favorably with the wages of competent engineers in civil employment, and consequently was unsatisfactory to them; the irregular manner in which they were appointed, and their uncertain tenure of office, were also grievances, and early in the year with which we are now dealing an incident occurred which so provoked the engineers that they felt constrained to lay their troubles before Congress. This incident was the appointment as an engineer in the navy of a young man who made no pretense to knowledge of engineering, he being the *protege* of a powerful politician and simply wanted a salaried position under the Government, without bothering himself as to what the duties of that position might be. That the engineers then in the service resented this appointment is good proof that there already existed among them that pride in their calling and the *esprit de corps* that have for so long kept them united and made continuous progress possible in the midst of many discouragements.

Mr. Haswell, as the senior and most prominent of the engineers, took the matter in charge, and appealed to Congress for a redress of grievances. Mr. Gilbert L. Thompson, a prominent politician and man about town in Washington in those days, took up Mr. Haswell's cause and gave him much assistance, although his motives were not entirely philanthropic, as we shall presently see. The result of this effort was an act of Congress regulating the appointment and pay of engineers in the navy, which act was approved August 31, 1842, and read in full as follows:

SECTION 1. *Be it enacted, etc.*, That the Secretary of the Navy shall appoint the requisite number of chief engineers and assistant engineers, not to exceed one chief engineer, two first assistant, two second assistant, and three third assistant engineers for each steamship of war, for the naval service of the United States, who shall be paid, when in actual service, as follows:

To the chief engineer, fifteen hundred dollars per annum and one ration per day; to the first assistant engineer, nine hundred dollars per annum and one ration per day; to the second assistant engineer, seven hundred dollars per annum and one ration per day; to the third assistant engineer, five hundred dollars per annum and one ration per day. The chief engineer shall be entitled to mess in the wardroom of ships of war, and in all cases of prize-money he shall share as a lieutenant; the first assistant engineer shall share as a lieutenant of marines; the second assistant engineer shall share as a midshipman; the third assistant engineer shall share as the forward officers; but neither the chief nor the assistant engineers shall hold any other rank than as engineers.

SEC. 2. *And be it further enacted*, That the Secretary of the Navy shall be authorized to enlist and employ the requisite number of firemen, who shall receive, each, thirty dollars per month and one ration per day; and the requisite number of coal-heavers, who shall receive, each, eighteen dollars per month and one ration per day; and the said firemen and coal-heavers shall in all cases of prize-money share as seamen.

SEC. 3. *And be it further enacted*, That the said chief engineer and the assistant engineers when waiting orders shall be paid as follows: to the chief engineer, twelve hundred dollars per annum; to the first assistant engineer, seven hundred dollars per annum; to the second assistant engineer, five hundred dollars per annum; to the third assistant engineer, three hundred and fifty dollars per annum.

SEC. 4. *And be it further enacted*, That the Secretary of the Navy shall appoint a skillful and scientific engineer-in-chief, who shall receive for his services the sum of three thousand dollars per annum, and shall perform such duties as the Secretary of the Navy shall require of him touching that branch of the service.

SEC. 5. *And be it further enacted*, That the Secretary of the Navy shall be authorized to prescribe a uniform for the said chief engineers and assistant engineers, and to make all necessary rules and regulations for the proper arrangement and government of the corps of engineers and assistant engineers not inconsistent with the Constitution and laws of the United States. The said engineers and assistant engineers shall be in all respects subject to the laws, rules, and regulations of the naval service in like manner with other officers of the service.

SEC. 6. *And be it further enacted*, That the said chief engineers shall be appointed by commission, and the assistant engineers shall be appointed by warrant from the Secretary of the Navy, in such form as he may prescribe.

SEC. 7. *And be it further enacted*, That the Secretary of the Navy be and he is hereby authorized to establish, at such places as he may deem necessary, suitable depots of coal or other fuel for the supply of steam ships of war.

The day following the approval of this act Mr. Gilbert L. Thompson was appointed engineer-in-chief of the navy; this to the great amazement and disgust of Mr. Haswell, who had seen in him only a benevolent and influential gentleman disposed to devote his time to the support of the cause simply because it was right. Benevolent gentlemen with unlimited time and influence to expend in the righting of wrongs abound in the harmless works of fiction distributed by the tract societies, but in real life they are extremely rare. Of Mr. Gilbert L. Thompson one of his contemporaries has written the author: "Mr. Thompson was a lawyer, and knew absolutely nothing of engineering. He was a gentleman, a scholar, a diplomatist, and a son of a previous Secretary of the Navy; but his engineering was purely nominal, and confined to a very prompt and efficient drawing of his salary."

In the spring of 1843 the *Missouri*, after a prolonged cruise in the Gulf of Mexico, was ordered to Washington, where Mr. Thompson caused her smoke-pipe, seven feet in diameter, to be removed and replaced with two pipes, each *three feet six inches* in diameter. The two pipes diverged out towards the sides and connected with the wheel-houses with the idea that the centrifugal action of the wheels would induce a strong draught by forcing air up through the pipes. In this connection it must be known that the boiler room of the *Missouri* was abaft the engines and the wheels consequently were forward of the smoke-pipes, which arrangement would have seriously interfered with the operation of the forced draught scheme in a head wind, even if there had been any merit in it under other conditions. Mr. Haswell, the chief engineer of the *Missouri*, protested against the design and declared it impracticable, but his professional opinion was unheeded. Engineer-in-Chief Thompson was so confident of success that he had the members of the Cabinet invited on board to witness the trial of his discovery, but they attended a funereal feast, for the scheme failed most dismally in operation. A scapegoat being necessary, Mr. Haswell was selected and suspended from duty because he had "not used sufficiently inflammable material in lighting the fires," although it is not apparent at this late date just what the manner of lighting fires would have to do with any subsequent performance with steam raised. Mr. Haswell was later offered to be restored to duty and proceed with the ship to the Mediterranean, where she had been ordered, on condition that he would apologize to the captain for his error (?), but this he declined to do, notwithstanding the requests of his messmates, saying that he would "rather suffer injustice from another than be unjust to himself." Whereupon he was detached from the vessel and Chief Engineer Faron ordered to take his place.

The experiment, above related, definitely established the fact that Mr. Thompson was not an engineer, whatever ability he might have in other directions, and his opinions were no longer sought in the councils of the Navy Department. After leaving the *Missouri*, Mr. Haswell was employed in designing machinery for four Revenue cutters, and in December was completely vindicated for his affair on the *Missouri* by being ordered to the Navy Department and assigned to the duties of engineer-in-chief; October 3 of the following year (1844) Mr. Thompson's name was dropped from the list and Mr. Haswell was regularly appointed engineer-in-chief of the navy.

The smoke-pipe of the *Missouri* was restored to its original form and the vessel proceeded to the Mediterranean, arriving at Gibraltar on the 25th of August after a voyage of nineteen days from the Capes of the Chesapeake. The next day, August 26, 1843, the engineer's yeoman broke a demijohn of spirits of turpentine in the store-room, which ignited and started a fire that spread so rapidly that all hope of saving the vessel had to be abandoned, and the crew barely escaped with their lives. In a few hours this splendid vessel was reduced to a blackened and sinking hulk. Her commander, Captain J. T. Newton, and Chief Engineer John Faron, Jr., were tried by court-martial upon their return home and were sentenced to suspension from duty, the former for a period of two years, and the latter for one year, which sentences were remitted after the captain had served four months and the chief engineer eight months. Congress appropriated sixty thousand dollars later to be expended in removing the sunken wreck from Gibraltar harbor. When chief engineer of the *Missouri* the year before she burned, Mr. Haswell had asked for a leaden tank in which to keep the spirits of turpentine, but the requisition was refused.

The *Mississippi* had a long and famous career, but eventually met a far more tragic fate than did her sister ship. She is said to have been a beautiful vessel, and from having had a succession of able commanders and common-sense officers in full accord with each other, she won the enviable reputation of being a "happy ship," and with this reputation was the most popular and best known of all the steamers of the old navy. She was the flagship of Commodore M. C. Perry in the Mexican War, and also his flagship in the expedition to Japan; she carried the famous Hungarian exile, Kossuth, from Turkey to France, and brought a number of his fellow-exiles to the United States. As the flagship of Flag Officer Josiah Tatnall in 1859 she was present at the engagement in the Pei Ho river,

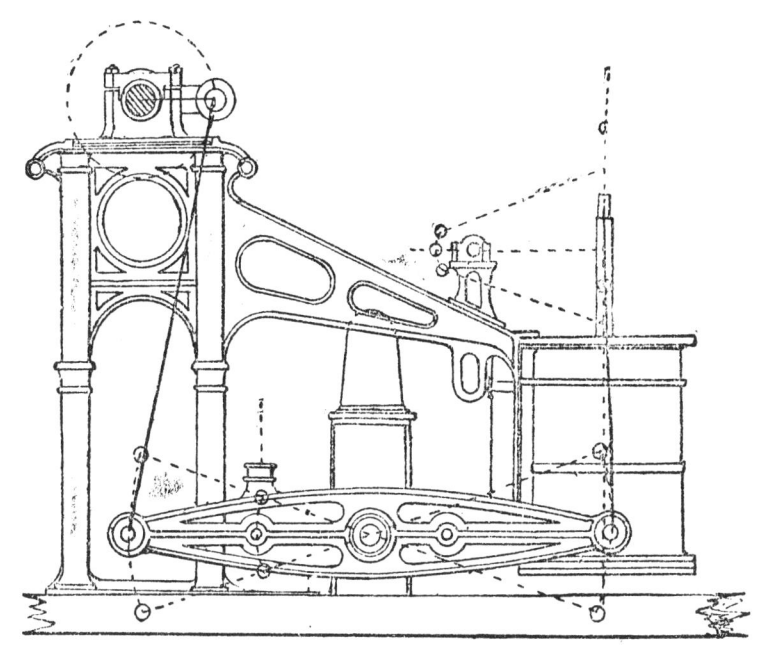

SIDE LEVER ENGINE, U. S. S. MISSISSIPPI.

where the "blood is thicker than water," sentiment is said to have originated, and at the outbreak of the Civil War was one of the first vessels to go to the front. She had twice circumnavigated the globe, and it was said of her, probably truly, that she had cruised more miles under steam than any war vessel of her time. Eventually a combination of circumstances, so strange that their suggestion during her palmy days would have been scouted as the climax of absurdity, brought this noble frigate with hostile intent into the great river whose name she had so long and so worthily carried about the world, and there one dark night in a storm of shot and shell, in fire and smoke, she sank to her long rest, a coffin for many of her crew, on the bosom of her false god-mother.

While the *Mississippi* and *Missouri* were being built, the Government was bringing to an end a long and bloody war with the Seminole Indians of Florida. It had been decided to remove this tribe from its lands and deport it to the wilds beyond the western frontiers, but when efforts were made to carry the decision into effect the savages declined to be moved, they viewing the matter in the same light that we may imagine the present inhabitants of Florida would regard a similar project to eject them from their homes and belongings. Under their great chief, Osceola, the Seminoles took up arms and a long and devastating war followed, costing the United States ten million dollars and nearly fifteen hundred lives. The result was the same as of all other weary struggles on this continent of the original possessors of the soil against the encroachments of the dominant race, and the aborigines went to the wall. The nature of the country in which the struggle took place made the employment of small steamers for the transportation of men and war material absolutely necessary, and the War Department accordingly found itself with a number of such vessels on its hands when the Seminole War was over, three of which were disposed of by transfer to the Navy Department.

The steamers thus added to the navy establishment were the *General Taylor*, of 152 tons; the *Colonel Harney*, of 300 tons, and the *Poinsett*, of 250 tons. They were employed for a few years on the Florida waters to prevent the spoliation of Government live oak preserves, one or two naval engineers being usually attached to each. The *Poinsett* was sold in 1845 for $5,000, and the *Harney* was returned to the War Department in 1846. The *General Taylor*, after being the tender at the Pensacola navy yard for several years, was sold in 1852 for $3,000.

In 1841 and 1842 plans were prepared for the paddle-wheel steamer *Michigan*, the hull being designed by Naval Constructor Samuel Hartt, and the engines and boilers by Mr. C. W. Copeland. There were two inclined direct acting condensing engines, placed side by side, the cylinders being 36 inches in diameter and eight

U. S. S. MICHIGAN.

feet stroke; these engines are now, more than fifty years after the *Michigan* was first commissioned, still in the vessel and in excellent working order. The two original return-flue iron boilers lasted nearly fifty years, they having been replaced as recently as the winter of 1892-93. The engines and boilers were built by Stackhouse & Tomlinson in Pittsburgh, Pa. The hull was built of iron, the plates, frames and other iron material being all prepared in Pittsburgh ready for assembling and then transported overland to Erie, Pa., where the vessel was put together and launched in 1843, making her first cruise on the Great Lakes in 1844. She was the first iron vessel afloat on those waters, and is still in active service, a striking illustration of the difference between fresh and salt water as agents for the deterioration of iron vessels. It should be mentioned, however, that the extraordinary longevity of the *Michigan* is partly due to the fact that she has to lie up in a winter harbor for about six months each year, and thus the chances for her untimely destruction by the usual perils of the sea have been reduced one-half. The first commander of the *Michigan* was William Inman, and her first chief engineer Andrew Hebard.

CHAPTER IV.

"A little learning is a dangerous thing."
ALEXANDER POPE.

Experiments with the "Hunter Wheel"—The UNION—The WATER WITCH—The ALLEGHANY—The Stevens Battery.

THE work of the engineers in designing and building machinery for the new naval steamers, while it excited suspicion and opposition from some who were well satisfied with the navy as it was, attracted a certain amount of admiration from others and it was not long before amateur imitators of their work sprung up in the service. Early in 1842, Lieutenant W. W. Hunter of the navy secured a patent for a submerged wheel, claiming a great improvement over the ordinary side wheels in propelling vessels. Experiments were made on the old canal in Washington with a small boat named the *Germ* fitted with Hunter's wheels, and the results obtained presented to the Navy Department in such a favorable light that it was determined to build a war-steamer to test the invention on a large scale.

The Hunter wheel consisted essentially of a drum with the paddles projecting from its surface like the teeth of a large gear wheel or pinion; the axis of the wheel was placed vertically and the wheel so located in the vessel, below the water line, that as it revolved the paddles, when at right angles to the keel, would project their whole width from the side of the ship through a suitable aperture. To keep the water from flowing into the ship through this opening the drum was cased inside the ship with a box or coffer-dam made to fit as closely as safety permitted, in practice a clearance of about two inches on all sides being allowed. A wheel was fitted on each side of the ship. In operation it will be observed that this wheel would act on the water on precisely the same principle as that governing the ordinary side wheel, but unlike the latter its idle side, instead of revolving through the air, had to do work all the time by sweeping around the water inside the casing. It had an advantage in dispensing with the large wheel-houses which were exposed to shot and offered much resistance to the wind, beside blocking space belonging to broadside guns, but this was practically offset by the disadvantage of having so much space in the hold occupied by the drum cases, while the enormous loss of work involved in constantly churning the water inside the cases, appeared at once to every engineer and mechanic to be a fatal defect in the device.

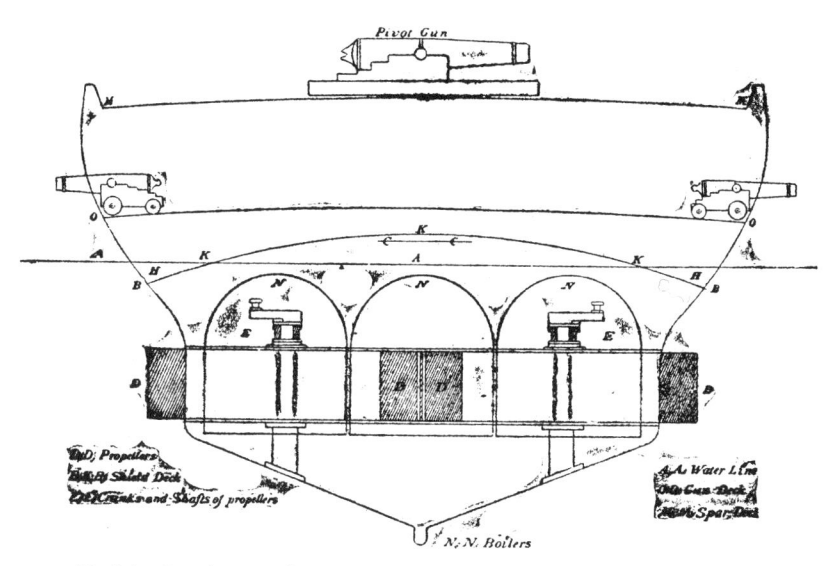

Sketch showing section of vessel and arrangement of Hunter's wheels. This is a reproduction of a drawing submitted by Lieut. Hunter to the Navy Department under date of Nov. 29, 1843, and is particularly interesting from the fact that it shows the principle of the protective or shield deck, believed by many to be a recent invention. None of Hunter's vessels had such a deck as built. This drawing was first published in the annual report of the secretary of the navy, about 1844.

However, the Navy Department ordered the building of a vessel on Mr. Hunter's plans and the work was carried out at the Norfolk navy yard in 1842. The vessel, named the *Union*, was 185 feet long, 33 feet beam, and displaced 900 tons on a draft of eleven feet. The rig was that of a three-masted topsail schooner, and the battery consisted of four 68-pounder guns. The engines were built at the Washington navy yard according to Mr. Hunter's ideas and consisted of a horizontal non-condensing engine for each wheel, the cylinders being twenty-eight inches in diameter and four feet stroke. There were three iron tubular boilers, eighteen feet long and six feet six inches in diameter, they being of the usual commercial pattern for land service. The propelling wheels were fourteen feet in diameter, each fitted with twenty paddles four feet long and ten inches wide.

The *Union* was completed at the end of 1842 and Mr. William P. Williamson, who had assisted Mr. Hunter in his experiments with the *Germ*, was appointed a chief engineer in the navy and ordered to the new vessel. In 1843 she was engaged in experimental cruising about the coast, under command of Lieutenant Hunter, but was unable to develop a better average than five knots per hour, while the slip or lost work of the wheels in pumping water through the drum cases, was from fifty to seventy per cent. The boilers, carrying nearly one hundred pounds of steam for the high-pressure engines, rapidly accumulated scale causing an equally rapid deterioration, they being intended only for land service, were unprovided with means or accessibility for scaling, and in about a year new boilers fit for use at sea were supplied from designs of Chief Engineer Haswell, but the wheels continued to waste their energy by acting as centrifugal pumps instead of propelling the vessel. An average of five knots on a daily expenditure of eighteen tons of coal was the best that could be done with the ship. With a favorable wind she made on some occasions nine and ten knots for short periods, and Lieutenant Hunter reported one performance of about twelve knots sustained for five hours with a moderate breeze. In 1846 it was concluded the engines were not powerful enough, so they were removed and replaced with a pair of condensing engines, four feet stroke and forty inches diameter of cylinders; at the same time the boilers were thoroughly repaired and the wheels so altered that they had ten paddles each instead of twenty, the new paddles being four feet long and two feet wide; all this failed to increase the efficiency of the wheels and the *Union* was finally, in 1848, put to use as a receiving ship at the Philadelphia navy yard. The machinery was removed at this time and sold for $3,840. The total cost of this experiment was:

Hull, to period of first sailing....................$107,065.67
Engines and dependencies, do..... .... 51,062.93
Repairs at various times 68,549.13

      Total......................$226,677.73

While the troubles of the "Hunter wheel" in the *Union* were progressing, similar experience was being gained with a small iron steamer named the *Water Witch*. This vessel was built at the Washington navy yard in 1843 from Lieutenant Hunter's plans and was intended for a steam water tank to supply the vessels at the Norfolk station, but when completed it was discovered that she could not go through the locks of the Dismal Swamp canal, which had to be done in order to get at the water supply, so she was fitted for a harbor vessel and tug. Her length was 100 feet and beam 21 feet; the machinery consisted of two non-condensing engines with cylinders 22 inches in diameter and four feet stroke, driving two Hunter wheels 16 feet in diameter. The maximum speed of this contrivance was six and one-half knots per hour, which was so unsatisfactory considering her small size and great power, that the vessel was condemned and taken to Philadelphia to be rebuilt. The experiment with the Hunter wheel in this vessel stops at this point, but it will be interesting to trace the subsequent career of the *Water Witch* since she has been introduced.

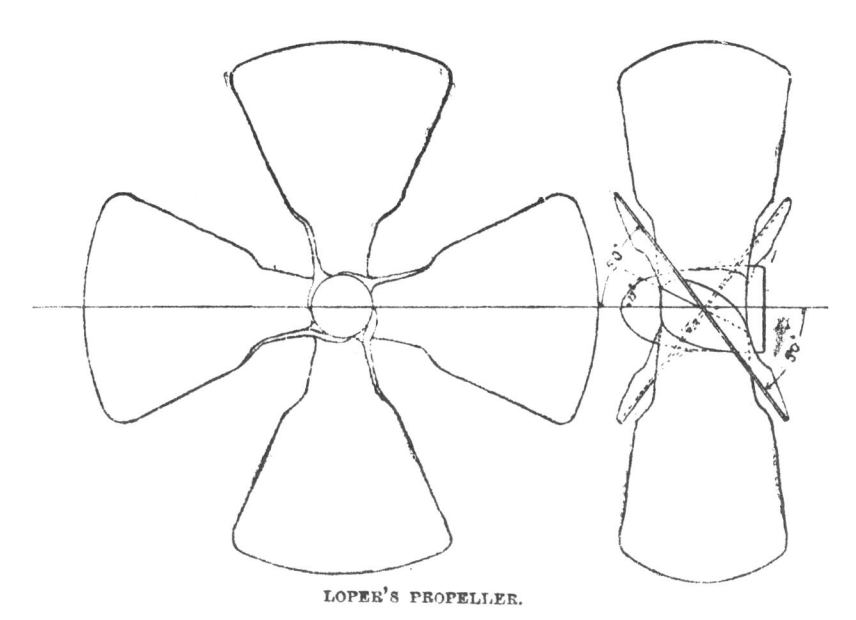

LOPER'S PROPELLER.

A peculiarity claimed by the inventor for this instrument was that it was not a screw because "the propeller blades form an angle with the center line in the same."

At Philadelphia the vessel was lengthened thirty feet and the entire machinery removed, new machinery driving a "Loper" propeller as an experiment being substituted. This also was pronounced unsatisfactory, although when tried by a committee of the Franklin Institute in the Delaware river a speed of nearly nine knots was obtained, and in 1847 an inclined condensing engine driving side wheels, designed by Engineer-in-Chief Haswell, was substituted. With this alteration the *Water Witch* was actively employed in the Gulf during the Mexican War, but she had been the victim of so much patch-work on an originally faulty model that it required much labor to keep her in working order. In 1851 she sailed from Norfolk for a coastwise voyage and hopelessly broke down on the first day out, after which exploit the machinery was removed and the hull put to good practical use as a target for gunnery practice at Washington. The machinery being perfectly good, a new hull of wood, somewhat larger than the old was built at the Washington yard in 1852 and a reasonably efficient little gunboat thus produced, still bearing the original name. This new steamer was employed for a number of years in the Rio de la Plata region of South America, and later saw some very active service during the first three years of the Civil War. June 3, 1864, she was captured in Ossabaw Sound by a large boarding party of the enemy after a most desperate struggle, in which her paymaster, Mr. Luther G. Billings, killed Lieutenant Pelot the Confederate commander in a hand-to-hand fight, and also saved the life of his own commanding officer by killing the man who had cut him down and was about to despatch him. The Union prisoners were taken to Savannah where they came under the control of the Confederate officer commanding that naval station, and who, singularly enough, was the same Hunter whose wheels had propelled the original *Water Witch*, he having resigned as a commander in 1861 and cast his fortunes with the Confederacy. The coincidence does not seem to have appealed to his magnaminity to any great extent, for it is a matter of official record that he treated his prisoners with considerable harshness.

To return to the experience of the Navy Department with the Hunter wheel. The experiments with the *Union* and *Water Witch* not being conclusive to Mr. Hunter and his supporters, the Department was prevailed upon to try the invention on a larger scale than

THE STEAM NAVY OF THE UNITED STATES. 53

before. On the 11th of July, 1843, the Secretary of the Navy, Mr. A. P. Upshur, directed Captain Beverly Kennon, chief of the Bureau of Construction, "to take proper steps for building at Pittsburgh, Pennsylvania, an iron steamer on plans to be submitted by Lieutenant William W. Hunter," and a contract was accordingly made with Joseph Tomlinson for an iron steamer on Hunter's plan, together with engines, propellers, machinery, and all metal appurtenances, and Lieutenant Hunter was ordered by the Navy Department to superintend the construction of the whole. Work on this vessel, named the *Alleghany*, began in 1844 and was completed in April, 1847, when she descended the Ohio and Mississippi rivers to New Orleans, and thence steamed around to Norfolk, Va.

The *Alleghany* was 185 feet long, 33 feet beam, 13 feet 6 inches mean draft, at which her displacement was 1,020 tons. She was bark-rigged and mounted originally four 8-inch Paixham guns, weighing 10,000 pounds each, but this battery was reduced one-half before the vessel sailed for a foreign cruise. There were two horizontal condensing engines with cylinders of four feet stroke and 60 inches diameter, and two iron return-flue boilers containing 2,000 square feet of heating surface and 55 square feet of grate surface each. The boilers were designed by Mr. Haswell, but the engines and hull were Mr. Hunter's, modified by such suggestions as he collected from the engineers and constructors. The horizontal propelling wheels were 14 feet 8 inches outside diameter, fitted with eight paddles each, the paddles being 3 feet 6 inches long and 2 feet 2 inches wide.

On the trip from New Orleans to Norfolk the mean results of her best steaming performances in smooth sea and calms gave a speed of 4.9 knots on an expenditure of 2,000 pounds of coal per hour. At Norfolk it was concluded to cut out every other paddle, leaving only four in each wheel, and thus altered the *Alleghany* sailed for Brazil, on which station and in the Mediterranean she was employed until 1849, when she returned to the United States and went on duty in the Gulf of Mexico until October of that year. After the reduction of the paddles the average performance for eighty-eight hours' steaming at sea in calm weather was 5.9 knots per hour on an hourly consumption of 2,096 pounds of coal. The mean results of eleven hundred and ninety hours under steam and sail in the Atlantic and Mediterranean during her cruise were as follows:

Mean pressure in boilers	11.77 pounds
Throttle	One-half open
Cut-off	28.100 of stroke
Coal consumption per hour	1,940 pounds
Average revolution of wheels	27.2 per minute
Vacuum	25 inches
Speed of vessel per log	5,883 knots

Upon the return of the *Alleghany* from the Gulf of Mexico in October, 1849, a survey was held on her by order of Commodore C. W. Skinner, chief of the Bureau of Construction, etc., the board of survey being composed of Commander J. B. Montgomery, Naval Constructor John Lenthal, Engineer-in-Chief C. H. Haswell, Chief Engineer Wm. P. Williamson, and Mr. Wm. Ellis, the supervising engineer of the Washington navy yard. Their report was a condemnation of the Hunter wheel, and a recommendation to substitute a common side wheel, but as the engines could be adapted to a screw propeller, and not to paddle wheels, a propeller was decided upon, as the cost of new engines would thereby be saved. This report definitely ended the career of Hunter's wheel and put a stop to needless expenditure of public money. The entire history of these experiments in the navy only confirms the correctness of an old adage a "shoemaker should stick to his last."

The actual cost of the *Alleghany* to the period of her departure from Pittsburg was:

Hull and fittings	$118,635.27
Engines, boilers, fittings and connections	113,640.65
Patent right for Hunter's wheels	10,320.00
Total	$242,595.92

In 1851–52 the *Alleghany* was rebuilt at the works of A. Mehaffy & Co., Portsmouth, Va., under the supervision of Chief Engineer Wm. P. Williamson, U. S. Navy. The iron hull, having been constructed by an establishment accustomed to building vessels for river service, had been found too weak for rough cruising in the open sea, a number of frames having buckled inward, and an attempt to remedy this was made by putting in additional frames and braces. The openings in the side for the Hunter wheels were built in, and a new stern post, suitable for the passage of a propeller shaft, was substituted for the old one. The cylinders of the old engines, which worked fore and aft, were used in the new engine to work athwartship from the diagonally opposite corners of a new bed plate, the connecting rods reaching backward from cross-tails, and many of the minor parts of the old engines were likewise adapted in the new structure. The alterations in the engines were regarded by engineers at the time as very ingenious and were devised by Mr. B. F. Isherwood, a young chief engineer who had entered the service a few years previously. His arrangement of the cylinders with a back-acting motion, will be recognized as the fore-runner of the type so universally known some years later as the Isherwood engine.

Three new iron boilers, aggregating 5,500 square feet of heating surface and 200 square feet of grate surface were provided; these were of an English patent type known as "Lamb and Summer" boilers, hitherto unknown in the United States, although used successfully to some extent in England. They were installed in the *Alleghany* at the instance of Mr. Charles B. Stuart, the engineer-in-chief at the time, a royalty of forty-five cents per superficial foot of heating surface being paid to the patentees. Pirsson's patent double-vacuum condenser, to which was attached an evaporator for making up the waste of fresh water, was fitted in this steamer at this time, which was the first appearance in our naval service of that once popular type of condenser.

The cost of all these alterations and additions was about $130,000, which, when added to the original cost of the vessel and about $25,000 spent for repairs when she was in service, brings the total cost up to nearly $400,000.

The screw propeller was made of cast iron, $13\frac{1}{2}$ feet in diameter, with four blades $3\frac{1}{2}$ feet wide, having an expanding pitch from 27 to 33 feet. So curious was this propeller in comparison with the modern pear-shaped development of the same instrument, that a reduced copy of the original drawing is shown on next page, the author feeling confident it will interest all his readers who ever had any connection with the profession of marine engineering.

The *Alleghany* was promised for the Perry expedition to Japan, which fitted out in the summer of 1852, but so many vexatious delays in her rebuilding occured that she was not ready for a steam trial until nearly a year after Commodore Perry sailed for Japan in the *Mississippi*. On trial the *Alleghany* proved to be an absolute and unqualified failure; the hull was too weak to withstand the action of the engines and this resulted in the engine bed plates breaking in several places; the boilers were entirely inadequate for supplying the

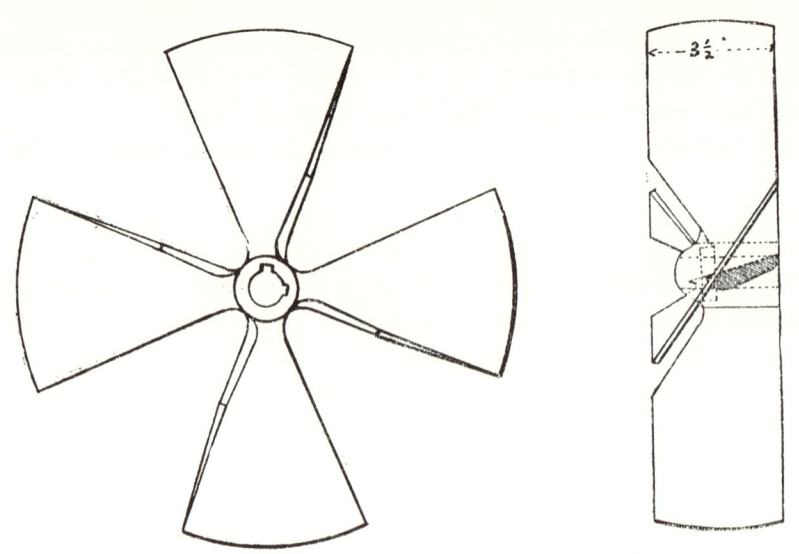

SCREW-PROPELLER, U. S. S. ALLEGHANY, 1852.

engines with steam, and things were at sixes and sevens generally. Misfortunes with other ships will be referred to in due time, which occurred during the same year and with the fiasco of the *Alleghany* caused public attention and much adverse criticism to be directed at the management of the Navy Department. Mr. Secretary Dobbin, in response to the popular clamor, organized a board of engineers with instructions to institute a searching investigation, not only as to the causes of the disasters, but also the officers or individuals who were responsible. This board consisted of Engineer-in-Chief D. B. Martin (Mr. Stuart had resigned in June of that year); Chief Engineer Henry Hunt, U. S. Navy, and Mr. C. W. Copeland. Mr. John Lenthal, the chief constructor of the navy, was ordered to act with the board and advise its members in matters relating to his specialty.

In the case of the *Alleghany*, the report of this board was not especially flattering to any who had been concerned in her building and repair, amounting to a general condemnation of the vessel as being totally unsuited for naval purposes. The hull, originally built for the reception of Hunter's wheels, was of a very peculiar form, the cross section being shaped like an inverted bell; a shape manifestly inconsistent with structural strength to withstand outside pressure, as well as a dangerous model for sailing, and it was found that the additional frames put in were so placed and fastened as not to add to the strength, while considerably increasing the weight. The English boilers, originally adopted as experimental, had been radically altered after another set of the same boilers had failed in another ship—the *Princeton*—and this fact was unfavorably dwelt upon by the board, although there was no reason for believing that this type would have been successful in the *Alleghany* after it had failed in another case. Chief Engineer Isherwood was scored for not providing, in the design and strength of the engine frames, for the weakness of the ship's bottom, and on his side he of course contended that it was his task to provide an engine only; not a hull to support it. With more experience, at a later period of his professional career, when it became his duty to provide power for a great number of war vessels with all sorts of hulls, his engine frames were made proof against any amount of racking they might receive, and then a hue and cry was raised again, not because the engines were too light, but because they were too heavy. Philosophers say that it is much easier to be critical than correct, and the belief that the most successful critics are those who have failed in other callings has long since passed into a proverb.

The great fault in this affair appears, from a careful study of the documents in the case, to have been the original attempt to make a serviceable war vessel out of a structure that in shape and scantling of material was utterly unfit for the reception of adequate power. After her lamentable failure the *Alleghany* was laid up in ordinary at Washington navy yard for a year or two and was then moved to Baltimore, where she remained for many years as a store ship, being eventually sold in 1869 for $5,250.

During this same experimental period a project for constructing an iron-clad steam battery was submitted to the government by Mr. Robert L. Stevens of Hoboken, New Jersey, and was so well received that Congress, by an act approved April 14, 1842, authorized the Secretary of the Navy to enter into contract with Mr. Stevens "for the construction of a war steamer, shot and shell proof, to be built principally of iron, upon the plan of the said Stevens," the act appropriating two hundred and fifty thousand dollars towards carrying the law into effect and providing that the whole cost of the steamer should not exceed the average cost of the *Mississippi* and *Missouri*. Although the steamer thus originated was never completed, and its history reached forward into a period far ahead of that with which we have yet begun to deal, it was such an object of interest to the early engineers that it is entitled to mention in this place, especially as the present chapter has been devoted to the recital of upset theories and blasted hopes.

Mr. Stevens was the son of the famous American inventor, John Stevens, who, as early as 1804, had successfully operated a small experimental steamer with twin screw propellers in place of paddle-wheels; who, in 1812, had prepared a complete set of plans for a circular iron-clad steam battery, and whose name was for many years intimately associated with the beginning of steam navigation and railway operations in this country. Robert L. Stevens inherited his father's inventive genius and his incomplete inventions, among them the idea of the armored steam battery. The original plan for this vesssel was for a large iron steamer (about two hundred and fifty feet long) to be protected with plates of four and one-half inch iron armor plate, Mr. Stevens having proved to the satisfaction of the Coast Defense Board, composed of army and navy officers, that iron plates of this thickness could withstand the fire of any possible gun. Unfortunately for Stevens, another great genius, who will appear prominently in the next chapter, arrived on the scene about this time with a large wrought-iron gun of English manufacture, with which he proceeded to demonstrate by actual experiments that plates of iron four and one-half inches thick could be easily penetrated. This was a great discouragement to Mr. Stevens and occasioned so much official interference with his work that the project languished until 1854, when work on a modified battery was begun in earnest and carried almost to completion before it was brought to a stand still by the death of Mr. Stevens in 1856. The vessel thus constructed was much larger than the original design, being 420 feet long, 53 feet beam, and of about 6,000 tons displacement. The iron armor projected for this formidable craft was to be six and three quarter inches in thickness.

The machinery, which was completed in 1856, was designed for 8,600 horse-power, then an enormous engine power and equal to that of the famous *Great Eastern*. The vessel had twin screws, the shafts being eight feet apart at the engines and diverging towards the stern, at which point they were twenty-two feet apart; they also were designed to point down a little to get a better hold of the water, the screw ends being about a foot lower than the engine ends. The total length of each shaft was 184 feet, with a maximum diameter of seventeen inches. Each shaft was operated by a row of four vertical cylinders placed outboard of the shaft and connected to the cranks by means of overhead walking beams six feet long and the usual interposition of connecting rods, an arrangement that engineers familiar with our modern navy will recognize as remarkably like the beam engines adopted by the Advisory Board for the *Chicago*. The cylinders of these two sets of engines were all of the same dimensions, viz: forty-five inches in diameter and forty-two inches stroke. The four cranks of each shaft were placed ninety degrees apart, and the crank shafts, forged separately, were coupled together in a manner closely similar to modern practice. The engine frames were built up of iron plates. The fore-and-aft fire-room, seventy-six feet long, had five boilers on each side, aggregating 26,000 square feet of heating surface. Unlike the typical boilers of that time, these boilers were fitted with tubes two and a quarter inches in diameter instead of the large flues so generally used.

Up to this time the government had appropriated five hundred thousand dollars for this undertaking and the inventor had expended two hundred thousand dollars of his own money on it besides. At Robert Stevens' death, the unfinished structure became the property of his two brothers, Edwin A. and John C. Stevens, who, being very wealthy from having successfully followed out the railway and shipping enterprises of their father, offered in 1861 to complete the vessel at their own expense if the government would pay for it if it proved to be successful. This liberal offer was rejected by the Navy Department through the medium of a board of naval officers who reported adversely to the project, in spite of the fact that the country was sorely in need of armored vessels and at that very time another naval board was in daily session listening to the claims of every inventor who came along with a scheme of any kind for an iron clad. In an effort to prove the practicability of their plan the Stevens brothers fitted out at their own expense a small steamer named the *Naugatuck*, with their arrangement of protective armor, and loaned her to the Navy Department; this craft was in action at Drury's Bluff on the James river in 1862 and had to fall out of battle owing to the bursting of her Parrott gun, so her armor did not receive the desired test, and she never figured as a national vessel on the official navy list.

In 1868 Mr. Edwin A. Stevens died, and by the terms of his will gave the unfinished battery to the State of New Jersey, bequeathing $1,000,000 to be used in completing it. General George B. McClellan of Army of the Potomac fame, was appointed as the engineer to determine on the plans for completing the vessel, and Mr. Isaac Newton, who as an engineer in the navy during the war had won a high professional reputation, was appointed General McClellan's technical assistant. These officials determined to convert the structure into a ram, with a revolving turret similar to that of Ericsson's monitor type. The bow was strengthened accordingly, an inner skin, on the double bottom principal, and transverse water-tight bulkheads were introduced, and the old machinery was entirely replaced with ten large boilers and two sets of powerful engines of the "Maudsley & Field" vertical overhead-crosshead type, designed to propel the vessel at a speed of fifteen knots per hour.

In 1874 the million dollars left by Mr. Stevens was exhausted and the vessel not yet completed, although far enough along to justify the claim that she would be the most formidable war vessel in the world if completed. New Jersey was not disposed to spend the necessary money for her completion and opened negotiations for her sale to the United States, a bargain to that end being practically completed so far as the Navy Department was concerned, but Congress refused to appropriate the money to make the necessary payments, and the structure fell back upon the hands of the State of New Jersey. Proposals for her sale, either as a whole or in parts, were then advertised, and in 1874 and 1875 the most of the material and machinery was disposed of in that way, even the new engines being sold for old iron.

Although borne on the official navy list as a national vessel for several years, this troublous craft never had any other name than the designation of the "Stevens Battery."

CHAPTER V.

"Ericsson's career proved that the PENCIL, as well as the pen, is mightier than the sword. Napoleon did not effect greater changes in the face of Europe than has Ericsson produced in naval warfare, and these latter are lasting, while the former have long since passed into other forms."
J. VAUGHAN MERRICK IN CHURCH'S *Life of John Ericsson.*

Introduction of the Screw Propeller—John Ericsson.—The PRINCETON, and Her Remarkable Engine.—Great-gun Accident on the PRINCETON and Consequent Breach of Friendship Between Ericsson and Captain Stockton.—Subsequent Career of the PRINCETON.

THIS narrative of the early steam vessels and engineers of our navy has now progressed to the point where there appears on the scene the most remarkable marine engineer whose genius has ever impressed itself upon the engineering practice of the world, his advent into our naval history being due to the adoption of a war-steamer, the product of his brain, which in many particulars radically and successfully departed from the accepted dogmas of engineers of the time regarding the application of steam power to marine propulsion. Experiments with screw propellers of various types had been made in the United States, England, and elsewhere, and the practicability of the instrument had been visibly demonstrated by more than one inventor, notwithstanding which many engineers persisted in maintaining that its theoretical loss by oblique action, and other alleged defects, were fatal to its adoption in practice. Foremost among the experimenters in England was the Swedish engineer, John Ericsson, who, failing to gain recognition from the Admiralty although he had constructed entirely successful screw-propelled vessels, left that country in disgust and came to the United States, if not at the instance, certainly to the gratification of Captain Richard F. Stockton of the U. S. Navy.

Captain Stockton had been in England at the time the experiments with Ericsson's propeller were attracting public attention and he became thoroughly converted to the importance and value of the invention. Becoming well acquainted with the great engineer, he had talked to him at length of his wish to have the United States

Government build a steamer on Ericsson's plan of propulsion, and had made many flattering promises of success to the latter should he ever take up the practice of his profession in America. The Act of Congress of 1839, under which the *Mississippi* and *Missouri* were built, had authorized the construction of three vessels, and at the urgent and repeated solicitations of Captain Stockton the Department, late in 1841, directed the construction of the third vessel from plans suggested by him. As soon as authority to build the ship was granted, Stockton summoned Ericsson to his aid and engaged him to make all the necessary designs for the hull and machinery, as well as to act as general superintendent of the construction of the same.

This vessel, named the *Princeton* after Captain Stockton's home town in New Jersey, was built in Philadelphia during the years 1842 and 1843, the hull at the navy yard and the machinery by the engineering firm of Merrick and Towne. She was 164 feet long, 30½ feet beam, and displaced 954 tons at her mean draft of

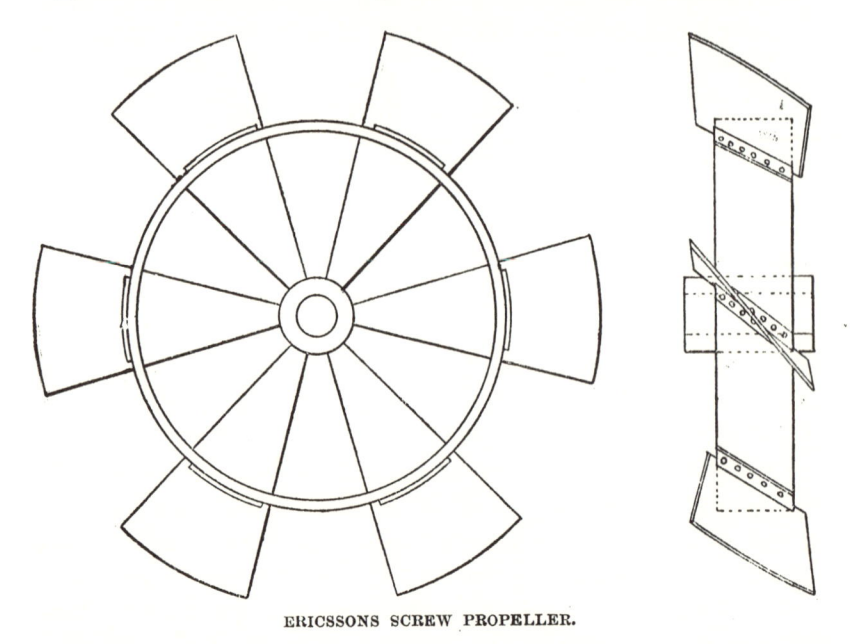

ERICSSONS SCREW PROPELLER.

16½ feet. The peculiarity of model consisted in a very flat floor amidships, with great sharpness forward and excessive leanness aft, the run béing remarkably fine. She was ship-rigged, spreading fourteen thousand four hundred and thirteen square feet of canvas in plain sails. The screw propeller originally used was of the form known as "the Ericsson": it was composed of a cast brass hub with six arms, the latter being surrounded by a copper band or drum, on which six brass blades were riveted, the general appearance of the instrument being shown as in the annexed sketch. Both arms and blades were of true helicoidal twist. In Mr. Robert Macfarlane's History of Steam Navigation, published in 1851, this form of propeller is thus spoken of:—"The advantage of the Ericsson screw is in having a ring within the arms, whereby any number of blades can be fixed, and a large area of surface obtained." The *Princeton's* propeller was of the following dimensions :

Diameter, extreme............................	14	feet.
Diameter of drum.................	8	"
Diameter of hub.............	1	" 8 in.
Pitch of screw..................................	35	"
Length of hub and arms in direction of axis.	2	"
Width of blades.................................	4	" 1 in.
Weight of screw...............................12,000		pounds.

In 1845, about a year after the completion of the vessel, the original propeller was removed and a six-bladed screw without any supporting drum was substituted, the new screw being 14½ feet in diameter, $32\frac{44}{100}$ feet pitch, with blades about 4¼ feet wide. Experiments made on the *Princeton* under similar conditions showed that the common screw was about 11 per cent. more efficient than Ericsson's. The *Princeton* had three iron boilers, designed by Ericsson to burn hard coal, aggregating 2,420 square feet of heating surface and 124 square feet of grate surface.

The *Princeton* was the *first screw steam war-vessel ever built*, although followed closely by H. M. S. *Rattler*, launched soon after she was. The *Rattler* was begun some time before the *Princeton* and was intended originally for side-wheels, but was changed while building owing to a change in sentiment regarding screw propellers. To this circumstance may be attributed the fact that the *Rattler* is frequently claimed to have been the first screw war-steamer. The *Princeton* was also the first vessel of war in which all the machinery was placed entirely below the water line out of reach of shot. She was also the first war-vessel with boilers designed to burn anthracite coal, thus avoiding the volume of black smoke to betray her presence to an enemy : blowers were used for the first time in naval practice, and she was the first steamer provided with a telescopic smoke pipe. Ericsson was the first engineer to couple the engine direct to the screw shaft, other experimenters with screws using intermediate gearing in deference to the theories of the day.

The engine of the *Princeton* may be roughly described as a half-cylinder, in which a rectangular piston vibrated like a barn door on its hinges, and was beyond doubt the most remarkable modification of the steam engine ever carried into successful practice. The principle of a vibrating rectangular piston is an old mechanical device, so old, in fact, that it was embraced in Watt's patent as one of the modes of transmitting the power of steam to machinery, but, until Ericsson's time, engineers had failed to build successful engines on this plan. Ericsson's plan differed radically from previous attempts, from the fact that he introduced, opposite the main semi-cylinder, a much smaller one with its piston a prolongation of of the large one on the opposite side of the shaft, both being acted on by the steam at the same time and the difference in their powers being the effective force transmitted to the crank levers.

In the *Princeton* this combined or double semi-cylinder was eight feet long and placed horizontal with the smaller semi-cylinder uppermost. The smaller, or re-acting, piston was ten inches wide and the lower, or working piston thirty-six inches wide. This difference leaves twenty-six inches of effective width of piston, with its center of pressure located $10+13=23$ inches from the center of the piston shaft. The effective piston area therefore was $26 \times 96 = 2,516$ square inches, moving back and forth through an arc of ninety degrees with an arm or radius of twenty-three inches, the distance of the center of pressure from the center of the piston shaft.

Before laughing at this contrivance as a crude effort of olden times it is well to investigate a little, and we will find that it possessed peculiar merits. The vibration of the working piston will be found to correspond closely to the beat of a pendulum ; and therefore its swing during the first half of each vibration would be materially assisted by the force of gravity. The arrangement with the steam ports underneath, facilitated the outflow of condensed water and prevented any dangerous accumulation in the cylinder. Centrifugal force aided the outward tendency of the packing, and in the case of the lower piston this was further assisted by the force of gravity. The crank levers were attached to the piston shafts in nearly the same plane with the pistons, which relieved the journals of that shaft from irregular strains. The small angular movement (ninety degrees) of the main piston was also an important feature. A greater motion would increase the power of any given sized engine but would also increase the strain on all the principal bear-

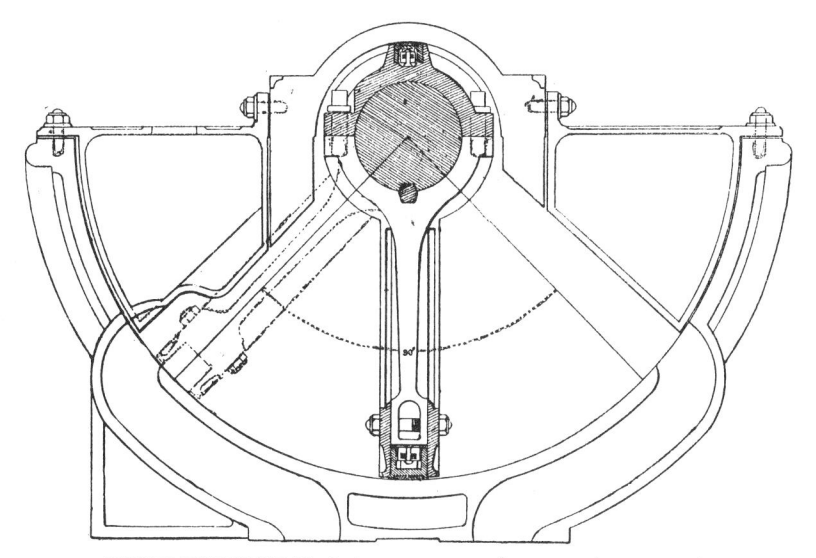

PISTON MOVEMENT U. S. S. PRINCETON (ERICSSON'S PATENT.)

ings, as the force of the piston obviously increases in the inverse ratio of the sines of the angles of the piston shaft cranks, with reference to the position of the connecting rods. A moderate increase of diameter would make up the loss of power due to the short arc through which the piston vibrates. Another advantage resulting from this short vibration was the possibility of fitting deep cylinder covers to resist the upward pressure of the steam. Finally it will be noticed that there are very few working parts, and the moving parts are fewer than in any other type of steam engine, except possibly the oscillating engine with the piston rod connected directly to the crank.

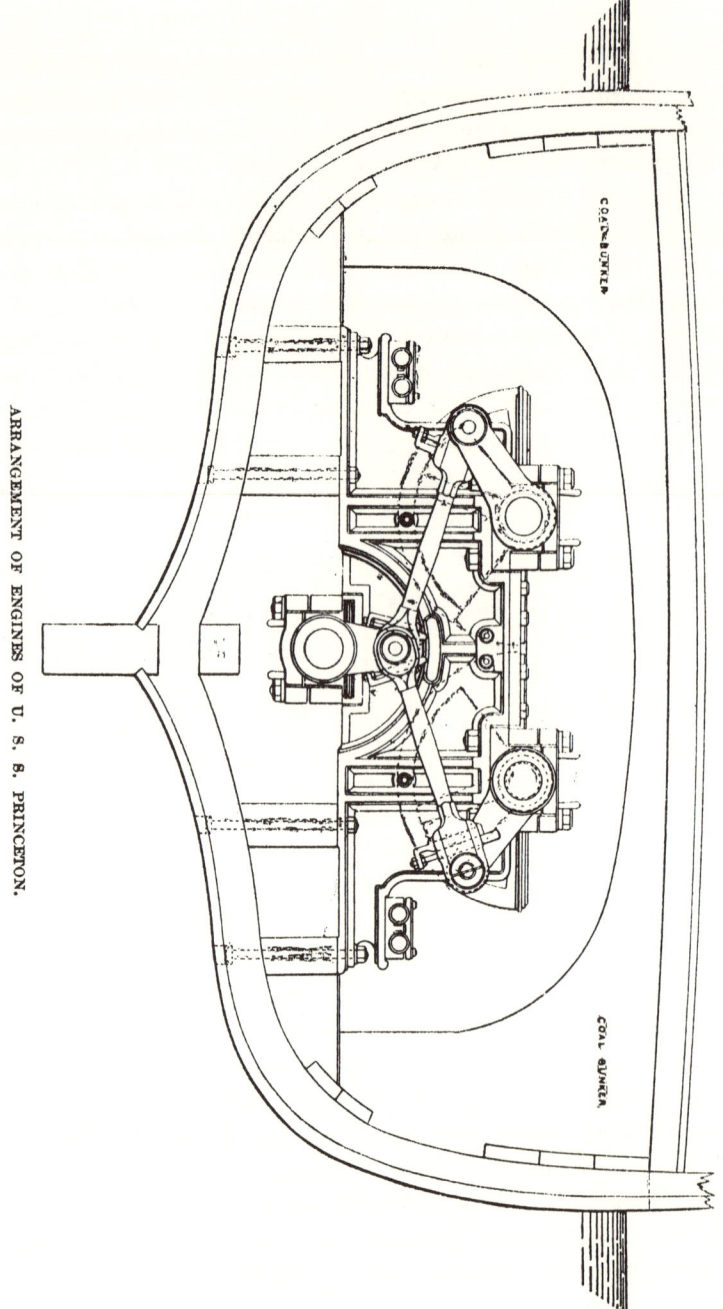

ARRANGEMENT OF ENGINES OF U. S. S. PRINCETON.

Ordinary slide valves of the locomotive type were fitted to this peculiar engine. Two of these engines were fitted in the *Princeton*, parallel to the crank-shaft and imparting motion by the connections shown in the outline sketch.

The ship was completed and ready for sea about the first of January, 1844, and was exhibited as a marine wonder at various places along the coast. Although this was some time after the enactment of the law regulating the appointment of engineers in the naval service, Captain Stockton appointed the first ones for this ship as though the ship belonged to him ; indeed it is not improbable he felt a certain right to ownership, he being a man of wealth had spent much of his own money on the vessel. When the vessel was completed he sent the following report to the Secretary of the Navy, which is very interesting and gives the best description of the *Princeton* in existence :

"U. S. SHIP PRINCETON,
"PHILADELPHIA, Feb. 5th, 1844.
"SIR:

"The United States Ship *Princeton* having received her armament on board, and being nearly ready for sea, I have the honor to transmit to you the following account of her equipment, etc.:

"The *Princeton* is a full rigged ship of great speed and power, able to perform any service that can be expected from a ship of war. Constructed upon the most approved principles of naval architecture, she is believed to be at least equal to any ship of her class with her sail, and she has an auxiliary power of steam and can make greater speed than any sea going steamer or other vessel heretofore built. Her engines lie snug in the bottom of the vessel, out of reach of an enemy's shot, and do not at all interfere with the use of the sails, but can at any time be made auxiliary thereto. She shows no chimney, and makes no smoke, and there is nothing in her external appearance to indicate that she is propelled by steam.

"The advantages of the *Princeton* over both sailing ships and steamers propelled in the usual way are great and obvious. She can go in and out of port at pleasure, without regard to the force or direction of the wind or tide, or the thickness of the ice. She can ride safely with her anchors in the most open roadstead, and may lie-to in the severest gale of wind with safety. She can not only save herself, but will be able to tow a squadron from the dangers of a lee shore. Using ordinarily the power of the wind and reserving her fuel for emergencies, she can remain at sea the same length of time as other sailing ships. Making no noise, smoke, or agitation of the water (and if she chooses, showing no sail), she can surprise an enemy. She can take her own position and her own distance from an enemy. Her engines and water wheel being below the surface of the water, safe from an enemy's shot, she is in no danger of being disabled, even if her masts should be destroyed. She will not be at daily expense for fuel as other steamships are. The engines being seldom used, will probably outlast two such ships. These advantages make the *Princeton*, in my opinion, the cheapest, fastest, and most certain ship of war in the world.

"The equipments of this ship are of the plainest and most substantial kind, the furniture of the cabins being made of white pine boards, painted white, with mahogany chairs, table, and sideboard, and an American manufactured oil cloth on the floor.

"To economize room, and that the ship may be better ventilated, curtains of American manufactured linen are substituted for the usual and more customary and expensive wooden bulkheads, by which arrangement the apartments of the men and officers may in an instant be thrown into one, and a degree of spaciousness and comfort is attained unusual in a vessel of her class.

"The *Princeton* is armed with two long 225-pounder wrought iron guns, and twelve 42-pounder carronades, all of which may be used at once on either side of the ship. She can consequently throw a greater weight of metal at one broadside than most frigates. The big guns of the *Princeton* can be fired with an effect terrific and almost incredible, and with a certainty heretofore unknown. The extraordinary effects of the shot were proved by firing at a target, which was made to represent a section of the two sides and deck of a 74-gun ship, timbered, kneed, planked and bolted in the same manner. This target was 560 yards from the gun. With the smaller charges of powder, the shot passed through these immense masses of timber (being fifty-seven inches thick), tearing it away and splintering it for several feet on each side, and covering the whole surface of the ground for a hundred yards square with fragments of wood and iron. The accuracy with which these guns throw their immense shot (which are *three feet* in circumference), may be judged by this: the six shots fired in succession at the same elevation struck the same horizontal plank more than half a mile distant. By the application of the various arts to the purposes of war on board the *Princeton*, it is believed that the art of gunnery for sea service has for the first time been reduced to something like mathematical certainty. The distances to which these guns can throw their shot at every necessary angle of elevation has been ascertained by a series of careful experiments. The distance from the ship to any object is readily ascertained with an instrument on board, contrived for that purpose by an observation which it requires but an instant to make, and by inspection without calculation. By self-acting locks, the guns can be fired accurately at the necessary elevation, no matter what the motion of the ship may be. It is confidently believed that this small ship will be able to battle with any vessel, however large, if she is not invincible against any foe. The improvements in the art of war adopted on board the *Princeton* may be productive of more important results than anything that has occured since the invention of gunpowder. The numerical force of other navies, so long boasted, may be set at naught. The ocean may again become neutral ground, and the rights of the smallest as well as the greatest nations may once more be respected. All of which, for the honor and defense of every inch of our territory, is most respectfully submitted to the honorable Secretary of the Navy, for the information of the President and Congress of the United States.

" By your obedient and faithful servant,

"R. F. STOCKTON,

"Captain, U. S. Navy.

On February 28, 1844, the *Princeton* sailed from Washington on a pleasure and trial trip down the Potomac river, having on board President Tyler and his Cabinet and a distinguished party of civil and military officials, invited by Captain Stockton to witness the performance of the vessel and her machinery. The trip was a great success professionally and convivially, and Captain Stockton was lionized as the greatest inventor of the times, it being the general impression that the ship and all that was in her had sprung from his vigorous brain. On the return trip one of those irresponsible persons who are always doing something that ought not to be done and whose names are never known afterward, wanted to have the big gun known as "Peacemaker," fired again "just for fun," to which Captain Stockton dissented, as the guns had been thoroughly exercised earlier in the day; he yielded, however, upon the good-natured wish expressed by the Secretary of the Navy to let the guests have all the sport they wished, and the gun was fired. It burst, injuring many people, among them Stockton himself, and killing the Hon. Abel P. Upshur, Secretary of State; Hon. Thomas. W. Gilmer, Secretary of the Navy; Captain Beverly Kennon, U. S. Navy; Hon. Virgil Maxey of Maryland; Mr. David Gardiner, and a colored servant. Mr. Gilmer had been Secretary of the Navy less than two weeks, and Mr. Upshur had been Secretary of the Navy at a period shortly before he received the portfolio of the Department of State. Mr. Gardiner was a descendant of the "lords of the manor" of Gardiner's Island, and his tragic death was the cause of an interesting romance; his body was taken to the White House by direction of the President, and in the resulting distress and sympathy President Tyler developed such an interest in Gardiner's beautiful daughter Julia that he afterward married her.

When Ericsson came to the United States he brought among many other inventions a large wrought iron gun, designed by himself and made in England. On trial this gun developed cracks which Ericsson remedied by an expedient now in general use in gun making, namely, by shrinking bands on it. Thus altered it was fired more than one hundred times with great success, its projectiles piercing a $4\frac{1}{2}$-inch wrought iron target, and it was placed on board the *Princeton*, with the name of "Oregon," as one of the two heavy guns of that vessel; the name "Oregon" was adopted because that word was in everybody's mouth owing to an international controversy then in progress, the British Lion being engaged in an attempt to place his heavy paw upon our extreme north-western territories. The other great gun of the *Princeton*—the "Peacemaker"—was Captain Stockton's gun, and was simply an imitation of Ericsson's, being regarded as an improvement over the latter, as its breach was a foot greater in diameter and the gun was heavier throughout, the quality of its metal being over looked in the effort to provide quantity; it was of the same calibre, viz, twelve inches. Its weight was about ten tons and was claimed to be the largest forging then in the world and a great manufacturing triumph, as only a few years before the forges of the United States could not produce a wrought-iron shaft for the second *Fulton*.

It is a matter of simple history that Captain Stockton allowed the belief to become general that he was the originator of everything connected with the *Princeton* and tacitly, if not directly, withheld from Ericsson the credit which was his due. In the eulogistic account of the *Princeton* before quoted, the name of John Ericsson does not appear, although every detail mentioned with so much enthusiasm as great improvements was his invention. The hull of the *Princeton* was designed by Ericsson; the engines were of his patent, and so was the screw propeller; the telescopic smoke pipe and fire room blowers were his; the banded gun was his invention; the range finder was his; the automatic gun lock was his; the *Princeton* was essentially the child of Ericsson's brain. So long as the career of the *Princeton* amounted to a triumphal procession from one city to another, John Ericsson remained in the shadow of obscurity, but with the bursting of the "Peacemaker" he was remembered and summoned to Washington. "Captain Stockton," as Mr. Church very pointedly remarks, "bethought himself of Ericsson. If he was not disposed to share the credit of success with him he was quite ready to give him his full measure of responsibility for disaster." Ericsson declined to be held responsible for an imitation gun not of his making and his letter in reply to the summons to proceed to Washington is a veritable gem of irony and independence. Stockton never forgave him and greatly injured him afterward by preventing the payment by the Government of Ericsson's bill for his patents and his invaluable professional work for the two years that the ship was under construction. In denying Ericsson's claim for payment for his services Stockton referred to him as a "mechanic of some skill," and made the remarkable statement that he had allowed him, "*as a particular act of favor and kindness*," to superintend the construction of the *Princeton's* machinery. Not many months before, at a dinner in Princeton, celebrating the launching of the ship, Captain Stockton had introduced Ericsson as the man for whom he had searched all over the world, who was capable of inventing and carrying out all that was necessary to make a complete ship of war. Ericsson experienced all the weary circumlocution of bills in Congress, suits in the court of claims, &c., and to the great shame of our country eventually died with the bills for his services on the *Princeton* still unpaid. The whole miserable story is told in Mr. Wm. C. Church's admirable history of the life of John Ericsson, a book that is well worth the study of all engineers.

The *Princeton* was employed in the home squadron during the years 1845, '46 and '47, and was actively engaged in the Mexican War, her performance under sail and steam at all times being highly satisfactory, and her reliability as a steamer remarkable. The mean results, when under steam alone during this period, were as follows:

Mean steam pressure in boilers..............11.75 pounds.
Mean initial pressure in cylinders (throttle
    one-fifth open)...................... 6.3   "
Double vibrations of piston, per minute...22.58   "
Consumption of anthracite coal per hour,
    fan blast...................................1,293   "
Mean effective pressure throughout stroke,   9   "
Horse-power developed by engines.........191.893
Speed of ship in knots, per hour............ 7.29
Slip of the screw......................... 10.38 per cent.
Sea water evaporated per hour per pound
    of coal.. 6.64 pounds.

In 1847 the *Princeton* was supplied with new boilers of the same number and external dimensions as the old, but with about twenty per cent. more heating surface; thus improved she sailed for the Mediterranean station where she remained two years under the command of Commander Frederick Engle. Mr. Henry Hunt was her chief engineer the first part of this cruise, succeeded by Joshua Follansbee. On this cruise the performance under steam was much better than it had been with the original boilers and it was claimed that she was, considered in connection with the amount of fuel consumed, the most efficient steamer in existence. She was an object of interest and admiration to European engineers and her cruise in the Mediterranean did much to break down the prejudice of sailors against steamers, and of engineers against the screw and the practice of coupling engines direct to the shaft. At sea she was readily handled, either with steam or sail, and had no bad quality except the fault of pitching violently owing to her great leanness forward and aft. Under sail, with the propeller uncoupled, she was claimed to be as fast and handy as most sailing vessels, and she is said to have beaten some sloops of war and frigates in clawing off a lee shore in a heavy gale, under sail and dragging her screw.

The old navy captains had strenuously asserted that steam could never be practically applied to naval warfare, and the defects in the first side wheel steamers and failure of Hunter's system of submerged propulsion added weight to their predictions. The appearance and successful performances of the *Princeton*, without any objectionable side-wheels and with the machinery entirely below the water line, left the objectors with no argument except their own sentimental predilections in favor of sails, and for this reason the *Princeton* may truly be credited with the honor of being the germ of our steam navy, for after her first service there was no longer any doubt in the minds of sensible men that the old order of things must yield to the new. Besides inaugurating the era of steam men of war, the *Princeton* may be credited with introducing another new factor into the problem of marine warfare. It has been previously mentioned that Ericsson's wrought-iron gun had been used to perforate an iron target, and, although that particular gun was removed from the ship after the disaster to its copy, this fact set people thinking about how to resist the fire of such guns. As Lieutenant Jacob W. Miller very aptly says in an essay read before the U. S. Naval Institute, "When the U. S. S. *Princeton, propelled by Ericsson's screw* and armed by *Ericsson's wrought-iron gun*, was launched the war between armor and projectiles began."

When the *Princeton* returned from the Mediterranean in 1849 she was condemned by a survey and immediately broken up at the Boston Navy Yard. It is asserted in Commodore Stockton's biography that the hasty condemnation and destruction of this ship was the work of certain naval captains who were jealous of the fame and popularity he had won in championing the cause of steam in the navy, and it is certain that much hard feeling was occasioned by the event, but this quarrel may well be passed over in silence, especially as its principals have long since ceased the contentions of this world. Two years later when Stockton was a member of the United States

Senate he prevailed upon the Navy Department to rebuild his ship, and a new hull was accordingly built at the Boston navy yard, such of the old timbers as were fit being worked into the new structure. The new *Princeton* was a clipper-built ship, 177 feet long, 33 feet 8 inches beam, and of 1370 tons displacement at mean draft, which dimensions it will be noticed correspond very closely with those of our present *Enterprise* class of corvettes. The old Ericsson semi-cylinder engines, being in good order, were not destroyed with the ship, and these were taken to Baltimore and thoroughly overhauled at the Vulcan Iron Works, under the supervision of Chief Engineer Wm. H. Shock, U. S. Navy. The only material change made in them was in the addition of Sickel's adjustable cut-off. Three iron boilers of the " Lamb and Summer " patent, previously referred to in connection with the *Alleghany*, were supplied by the Baltimore firm; also a four-bladed composition propeller, 16 feet in diameter, not unlike in general form the propellers in use fifteen years ago.

A long delay in completing the ship occured on account of a controversy between the engine builders and the Navy Department as to whether the machinery was to be installed in Boston or Baltimore, but the Department, being anxious to get the ship for the Japan expedition, finally sent her to Baltimore and the machinery was put in place during the summer of 1852. Eventually completed, the *Princeton* sailed from Annapolis in November, 1852, in company with the *Mississippi*, but on the voyage down Chesapeake Bay the boilers gave so much trouble that she was detained at Norfolk and the *Mississippi* sailed without her. The Board of Engineers named in Chapter IV. as having been organized to investigate the failures of certain vessels, reported in the case of the *Princeton* that the addition of the Sickel's cut-off was injudicious and that the failure of the ship was attributable to the patent boilers; so far as any individual was to blame for the failure, the report stated that Mr. Stuart, the former engineer-in-chief, who had recommended the use of the Lamb and Summer boilers was the responsible person. Commodore Stockton felt that his pet ship had been terribly bungled in rebuilding, possibly maliciously so, and he denounced the whole affair by a vigorous speech in the Senate, referring to the new *Princeton* as "an abortion in the naval service." After lying idle in Norfolk for a year or two, the *Princeton* was taken to Philadelphia and used as a receiving ship until October 9, 1866, when she was sold.

CHAPTER VI.

"I hold every man a debtor to his profession; from the which as men of course do seek to receive countenance and profit, so ought they of duty to endeavour themselves by way of amends to be a help and ornament thereunto,"
FRANCIS BACON.

Reorganization of the Engineer Corps—Case of Chief Engineer C. B. Moss—All Assistant Engineers Examined and Re-arranged According to Proficiency—Laws and Regulations Affecting the Engineer Corps from 1845 to 1850—Resignation of Chief Engineer John Faron, Jr.

THE act of August 31, 1842, creating the engineer corps of the navy, authorized the Secretary of the Navy to appoint the engineer-in-chief and the chief engineers, as well as the assistant engineers. In the original draft of this bill it was provided that the engineer-in-chief and chief engineers should be commissioned officers, nominated by the President and confirmed by the Senate, which provision met with approval, but disappeared at the last moment when the bill assumed its final form. This omission was said to be due to the exertions of Mr. Gilbert L. Thompson, who had arranged to be appointed to the new office of engineer-in-chief, and, not being an engineer by profession, was fearful that the Senate would not confirm him when nominated; so he used his political influence to further his interests by making the way to the desired office as free from legislative and legal forms and ceremonies as possible.

After Mr. Thompson's short career as engineer-in-chief, his successor, Mr. Haswell, immediately undertook the task of remedying the defect in organization occasioned by the diplomacy of his predecessor, his efforts being so successful that the naval appropriation bill of the following year (approved March 3, 1845) contained the following:—

SEC. 7. *And be it further enacted*, That in lieu of the mode heretofore provided by law, the engineer-in-chief and chief engineers of the navy shall be appointed by the President, by and with the advice and consent of the Senate, and that the President, by and with the like advice and consent, may appoint six engineers, to be employed in the revenue service of the United States, and the Secretary of the Treasury may appoint six assistant engineers, to be employed in the like service, one engineer and one assistant to be assigned to each steamer in the said service, if the same shall be deemed necessary by the Secretary of the Treasury, who shall prescribe the duties to be performed by said officers respectively; each of the said engineers shall be entitled to receive the same pay as now is, or hereafter may be, by law, allowed to first lieutenants in the revenue service; and that each assistant engineer shall be entitled to receive the same pay that now is, or hereafter may be, by law, allowed to third lieutenants in said service.

The enactment of this law made it necessary for the names of the chief engineers to be sent to the Senate for confirmation for commissions, and this furnished the engineer-in-chief with an opportunity to re-arrange them in what, according to his judgment, was their proper order of merit, his recommendation on the subject to the Secretary of the Navy, dated May 9, 1845, being approved and a re-arrangement accordingly made by numbering the commissions. There were then seven chief engineers ranking with each other according to date of appointment in the following order:

John Faron, Jr., appointed January 13, 1840.
Andrew Hebard, appointed February 6, 1840.
James Thompson, appointed April 14, 1842.
Wm. P. Williamson, appointed October 20, 1842.
Charles B. Moss, appointed May 29, 1844.
Wm. Sewell, Jr., appointed February 11, 1845.
W. W. W. Wood, appointed March 15, 1845.

By Mr. Haswell's recommendation, this order of precedence was changed to the following, in order of number of commission:

1. John Faron, Jr.
2. Andrew Hebard.
3. Wm. Sewell, Jr.
4. W. W. W. Wood.
5. James Thompson.
6. Wm. P. Williamson.
7. Charles B. Moss.

This new arrangement was of course not agreeable to those who were reduced in standing, Mr. Williamson especially feeling aggrieved at having Messrs. Sewell and Wood, who had just entered the corps as chief engineers direct from civil life, placed above him, and the case does appear to savor of hardship, but the judgment of the engineer-in-chief was allowed to stand as final, and Mr. Williamson's protests to the Department availed him nothing. Chief Engineer Moss also came to grief at the hands of the Department at the same time. He was a close friend of President Tyler, and had been his private secretary prior to receiving an appointment as a chief engineer in the navy, and after that remained in Washington as a member of the President's household. President Tyler's term of office expired March 4, 1845, and the following day the Navy Department took possession of Mr. Moss by ordering him to Pittsburgh as inspector of machinery, building in that city for the *Alleghany*. Two months later, when Mr. Haswell recommended the rearrangement of the chief engineers, he reported to the Department that "Mr. Moss, without the advantages of personal observation consequent upon the immediate management of the steam engine, has made himself well acquainted with its operation and possesses high attainments in physics and mathematics." *Proteges* of President Tyler were not popular with the new administration, however, and the Navy Department detached Mr. Moss from his duty in Pittsburgh, placed him on furlough, and ordered him to report at a future date to the engineer-in-chief for an examination as to his qualifications for sea duty, the letter of explanation accompanying the order stating:

"In consequence of the Department's want of confidence in your ability to assume the detailed direction and perform the practical duties of a chief engineer attached to a sea-going steamer, and at the same time, entertaining the disposition to concede to you all proper indulgence and facilities, it has decided that for the purpose of giving you an opportunity practically to acquire the knowledge which it conceives you to be in want of, you will be detached from your present duties and put on furlough until the 15th of December next."

About the middle of January following, Mr. Moss was ordered before an examining board composed of the engineer-in-chief and the two senior chief engineers of the navy, which resulted in his receiving the following notification from Secretary Bancroft:

"In consequence of the result of your examination, which has been communicated to you, I am authorized by the President to inform you that your commision as a chief engineer in the navy of the

United States is hereby revoked, and you are no longer a chief engineer.

"A warrant as a second assistant engineer in the navy, in accordance with the report of the Board of Engineers before which you were examined, will be given you upon your signifying your readiness to accept it."

This letter was dated January 30, 1846, and as Mr. Moss did not signify his willingness to accept the proffered warrant, his connection with the service ceased on that date. The affair is narrated as an illustration of the danger of relying upon political influence for official position, and also as serving to show the uncertain tenure of a commission in the navy in olden times, which latter uncertainty was not confined to the young engineer corps, but menaced all commissioned officers alike.

Having disposed of the chief engineers, Mr. Haswell turned his attention to the assistants, and recommended that they all, irrespective of grade or length of service in the navy, be subjected to an examination to establish their fitness for the service and determine their relative merits, which recommendation was approved by Secretary Bancroft, and an examining board convened by his order in the city of Washington on the 9th of July, 1845. This board consisted of Engineer-in-Chief Haswell as president and Chief Engineers John Faron, Jr., and Wm. W. W. Wood as members, and before it all the assistant engineers who were within summoning distance were ordered to appear.

The proceedings of the examining board partook largely of "star chamber" methods, as may be seen from the following letter of instructions issued to the board by the chief of the Bureau of Construction, Equipment and Repairs, who represented the Secretary of the Navy for the time, and to which bureau the engineering branch was attached as a sub-department or bureau:

"MESSRS. C. H. HASWELL,
  JOHN FARON, } Engineers.
  W. W. W. WOOD.

"INSTRUCTIONS FOR A BOARD FOR EXAMINATION OF ASSISTANT ENGINEERS.

"The board will take particular care to ascertain the qualifications of the candidates for all the duties that may be required of them, as assistant engineers, and satisfy themselves of their moral, as well as professional fitness for the public service.

"Having ascertained the merits of the candidates as above, the board will proceed to class them as first, second and third assistants—taking into view professional and moral fitness and other circumstances which may give claim to preference.

"Having classed the candidates as above, the board will arrange them in their several classes according to merit.

"The appointments now held by assistant engineers are to be considered as temporary, and not giving claim to precedence, except in cases when candidates may be thought to be equal in merit, then preference will be given to the senior appointment.

"The board will admit but one candidate for examination at a time, the examination is to be considered private and confidential, and it will impress upon the mind of each candidate, and enjoin it on him, that he is not to disclose to any one the course of examination, the questions asked him, or anything that may occur in the session of the board.

"The decisions at which the board may arrive are to be communicated to no one; but are, when the whole examination is completed, to be submitted to the Secretary of the Navy, for such action as he may deem proper.

"By order of the Secretary of the Navy.

"W. B. SHUBRICK,
"for Com. Morris,
"Bureau of Construction, Equipment and Repairs, July 8, 1845."

At that time the different grades of assistant engineers were composed of the following members, arranged in order of seniority according to length of service:

FIRST ASSISTANTS.	SECOND ASSISTANTS.	THIRD ASSISTANTS.
1. Hiram Sanford,	A. S. Palmer,	Smith Thompson,
2. William Scott,	J. S. Rutherford,	Joshua Follansbee,
3. James Cochrane,	J. K. Mathews,	Wm. F. Mercier,
4. Henry Hunt,	Gilbert Sherwood,	John Gallagher,
5. D. B. Martin,	N. C. Davis,	William Taggart,
6. John Alexander,	Daniel Murphy,	Samuel Archbold,
7. James Atkinson,	J. M. Middleton,	John Serro,
8. Thomas Copeland,	William Luce,	Thomas Dickson.
9. Levi Griffin,	Levi T. Spencer,	Theodore Zeller,
10. B. F. Isherwood,	J. F. Dryburgh.	M. M. Thompson,
11. Alexander Birkbeck.	....	James W. King,
12.	....	Robert Danby,
13.	....	William H. Shock,
14.	....	Charles Coleman.

After examining all the available assistant engineers the result of the examination was reported as follows:

"OFFICE OF ENGINEER CORPS, U. S. N.,
"July 28th, 1845.

"SIR:—

"In behalf of the Board for the examination of Assistant Engineers that was convened on the 9th instant, I have to report:

"That there were twenty-seven Assistants examined, one of whom was rejected.

"The accompanying paper contains a list of the names of those that were passed, arranged in the several grades and numbered in the order in which they are recommended to be placed.

"In consideration of this being the first occasion since the organization of the Engineer Corps that duty of this nature has been performed, and as many changes in the different grades are recommended to be made, I deem it proper to recur to the irregular manner in which the present tenure of appointments of those examined originated.

"Thus from 1837 to 1842 there did not exist the grade of Third Assistant, and not until 1842 was there an examination prior to admission into the corps, and even up to the present time there has not been an appointment under any defined regulations or restrictions.

"With these facts in view it is fair to infer that errors of position could not have been avoided; added to which, observation, ambition, and a difference in capacity, have secured to some (since their appointments in the service) that advantage which is so readily obtained when their attendant results are contrasted with indifference and a less regard to the exactions of advancement.

"The want of a working model of a condensing engine for the purposes of illustration and reference was much felt, and in future examinations of candidates for admission into the corps much inconvenience will be experienced without the use of one. I recommend that one be constructed at the navy yard in Washington—the cost of which should not exceed $300.

"Mr. Alexander Birkbeck, Jr., is recommended as worthy of an examination for promotion to a Chief Engineer whenever the Department may see fit to add to the number of that grade. First Assistant Thomas Copeland from physical infirmity, added to the want of professional experience as a marine engineer, is considered unfit to discharge the duties pertaining to an Assistant Engineer in the Naval Service.

'I am, very respectfully,
"Your obedient servant,
"CHAS. H. HASWELL."

The paper referred to in the above report as giving the names of the assistant engineers, re-arranged in the order of merit recommended by the examining board, shows that the following order, which was officially approved, was recommended:

FIRST ASSISTANTS.	SECOND ASSISTANTS.	THIRD ASSISTANTS.
1. Alexander Birkbeck, Jr	Joshua Follansbee,	John M. Middleton,
2. Henry Hunt,	John Alexander,	Wm. F. Mercier,
3. Daniel B. Martin,	James Atkinson,	William Taggart,
4. Hiram Sanford.	Levi Griffin,	William Luce,
5. James Cochrane,	Levi T. Spencer,	James W. King,
6.	Albert S. Palmer,	James R. Dryburgh,
7.	Jesse S. Rutherford,	Theodore Zeller,
8.	Samuel Archbold,	Robert Danby,
9.	Naylor C. Davis,	William H. Shock,
10.	Daniel Murphy,	John Serro,
11.	....	M. M. Thompson.

Of the eight assistants not examined in July, two, Second Assistant Gilbert Sherwood and Third Assistant Smith Thompson, declined the examination and resigned. The other six, the vessels to which they were attached having returned to the United States, were ordered before the board in December and January following, and examined, Chief Engineer Andrew Hebard being then one of the examiners in place of Mr. Wood, who had been sent to New Orleans to superintend a general overhauling of the machinery of the *General Harney*. Those examined were first assistants Wm. Scott and B. F. Isherwood; second assistant John K. Mathews, and third assistants John Gallagher, Thomas Dickson, and Charles Coleman. The result of the examination was that Messrs. Scott and Isherwood were reduced to second assistants; Mr. Mathews advanced to the head of the second assistants list; Mr. Gallagher promoted to second assistant, and Messrs. Dickson and Coleman placed on the list of third assistants next after Wm. H. Shock and M. M. Thompson respectively.

This whole proceeding was most radical and arbitrary, and occasioned much heart-burning among those unfortunates who lost grade or numbers in the final arrangement; nevertheless, it was demanded by the lack of homogeneity in the corps which had resulted from the irregular manner in which the first engineers had been appointed, and the advantages of establishing professional competency as a requisite for membership in the corps, and of starting fair, even though a trifle late, with the engineering *personnel* graded according to merit, much more than offset any grievances of individuals resulting from the rearrangement. Of high professional ability and broad general education himself, Mr. Haswell felt that the requirement of similar ability from all the members of his corps was the only proper method of elevating its standard, and the imposition of this arbitrary examination upon the junior engineers was the first step in that direction. That the step was of great subsequent benefit to the corps is manifest, and its inception indicates a degree of corps pride and far-sightedness on the part of the engineer-in-chief to be admired and commended more than any other of his numerous acts which operated to the lasting benefit of his corps. Moral courage of a high order was necessary to the carrying out of this reform, for it could be of no possible personal benefit to its pro-

CHAS. H. HASWELL.

The first engineer in the United States Navy: appointed Chief
Engineer July 12, 1836. Engineer-in-chief of the Navy
from October 3, 1844, until December 1, 1850.

jector, and by its character was bound to make enemies for him within his own corps, where friends were most needed; enemies who treasured up their wrongs, real or imaginary, and patiently waited for the time, which eventually came, when they could safely combine to seek their revenge.

Mr. Haswell's scheme for the reformation and reorganization of his corps was further perfected this same year by the promulgation of a set of regulations governing the admission and promotion of members of the engineer corps. This order was dated July 8, 1845, and established limits of age for candidates, made the performance of a certain amount of sea service in each grade a requirement for promotion, and fixed a scale of mental requirements much in advance of what had been previously demanded. The initial examination for admission as a third assistant engineer was elementary compared with modern requirements, but the subsequent advances in grade were guarded by examinations that increased in difficulty in what may be termed geometrical progression, until the candidate for promotion to the list of chief engineers was required to pass a very exacting ordeal, calculated to establish the possession of much scientific and mechanical ability.

Chief engineers of excellent professional and general information were habitually selected for the duty of examiners, and it was an established rule that a failure to pass the required examination meant an end to the naval career of the delinquent. This furnished a strong incentive to the young engineers to fit themselves for advancement, and almost immediately after the reorganization of the corps a much keener incentive to study and self improvement appeared in the development of an intense spirit of corps pride which made the engineers quick to recognize their own short-comings and to strive to overcome them. Opposition from within the service to the new branch was the chief cause for the early inception of this *esprit de corps*, and, although disagreeable to those who had to resist it, should now be regarded as a blessing in disguise to the engineers, for it prompted all but the laggards not only to overcome the deficiencies charged against them, but to outstrip their competitors in the pursuit of knowledge.

The Naval Academy was opened the same year that the systematic reorganization of the engineer corps was effected, and as soon as the two systems were well in operation the young men of the two branches of the service fell into an intellectual rivalry, which was good for both classes, and especially for the engineers. The result of this feeling was frankly confessed by a distinguished naval captain some years ago, who, in a discussion regarding naval education, remarked that under the old system a newly graduated midshipman was much better informed on general subjects than was a newly appointed third assistant engineer, but at the end of the first cruise the young engineer would generally be found to be much the better informed man of the two.

Immediately after being appointed engineer-in-chief, Mr. Haswell prepared a list of instructions for the government of the engineer department of vessels of war, which instructions were issued by the Secretary of the Navy in the form of a general order to commanding officers under date of February 26, 1845. This order defined in general, the duties and responsibilities of engineers afloat, precautions to be observed in the care and preservation of machinery, etc., and were so well considered and prepared that some of the sections still remain in the steam instructions without modification, except in matters of detail demanded by the changes in engineering practice.

August 1, 1847, the Navy Department issued a circular order regarding the enlistment of firemen and coal heavers, which directed that no fireman should be shipped in the future until he had passed a satisfactory examination before a board of engineers and demonstrated his ability to manage fires properly with different kinds of fuel, and to use skillfully smiths' tools in the repair of boilers and machinery. Two classes of firemen were established by the order, and a regular system of promotion from coal heaver to the two grades of firemen was directed. First class firemen were declared eligible for advancement to the warrant rank of third assistant engineer if they could qualify before the examining board.

The next year Congress, by an Act approved August 11, 1848, extended the benefits of existing laws, respecting naval pensions, to the engineer corps and to enlisted men of the engineers' force, the wording of the act being as follows:

"SEC. 2.—That engineers, firemen, and coal heavers in the navy shall be entitled to pensions in the same manner as officers, seamen, and marines, and the widows of engineers, firemen and coal heavers in the same manner as the widows of officers, seamen, and marines: *Provided,* That the pension of a chief engineer shall be the same as that of a lieutenant in the navy, and the pension of the widow of a chief engineer shall be the same as that of the widow of a lieutenant in the navy; the pension of a first assistant engineer shall be the same as that of a lieutenant of marines, and the pension of the widow of a first assistant engineer shall be the same as that of the widow of a lieutenant of marines; the pension of a second or a third assistant engineer the same as that of a forward officer, and the pension of the widow of a second or third assistant engineer the same as that of the widow of a forward officer."

A new schedule of pay for engineer officers, by which an increase for all grades was effected, was created by the following section from the naval appropriation bill approved March 3, 1849:

SEC. 6. *And be it further enacted,* That the engineers in the navy shall hereafter receive the following pay, viz:

Chief engineers on duty first five years	$1,500
Chief engineers on duty after five years	2,000
Chief engineers on leave first five years	1.200
Chief engineers on leave after five years	1,400
First assistant engineers on duty	1,000
First assistant engineers on leave	850
Second assistant engineers on duty	800
Second assistant engineers on leave	600
Third assistant engineers on duty	600
Third assistant engineers on leave	400

The engineer corps experienced a decided loss at this period by the resignation of the senior chief engineer in the service, Mr. John Faron, Jr., who tendered his resignation in April, 1848, in order to accept the position of Superintending Engineer of the newly established Collins line of transatlantic mail steamers. Mr. Faron, it will be remembered, was the first assistant engineer appointed to the *Fulton* in 1837, and became a chief engineer in January, 1840. He was a thoroughly capable and efficient marine engineer, and was prominently identified with the designing, building and management of the early naval steamers, as well as being a prominent factor as a member of the examining board, in the work of reorganizing the engineer corps. His name was continued on the navy list by the admission into the corps of a third assistant engineer named John Faron, a few months after his resignation.

CHAPTER VII.

"I believe that if the question had been put to Congress before the march of the armies and their actual conflict, not ten votes could have been obtained in either house for the war with Mexico under the existing state of things."— WEBSTER.

The War With Mexico—Naval Operations in California—Important Service of Surgeon Wm. Maxwell Wood—Blockade of the Gulf Coast—Commodore Perry and the MISSISSIPPI—Valuable Professional Service of Engineer-in-Chief Haswell—Bombardment of Vera Cruz—"Alvarado Hunter"—Steamers Bought for Temporary Service—Naval Engineers Engaged in the Mexican War—Results of the War.

THIS volume being devoted to the deeds of naval men, it is hardly within its province to deal with the causes, or pretexts, which brought about the war with Mexico. Without referring to the political and sectional interests involved, it will be sufficient to say in regard to the direct cause of the war that the Mexican State of Texas, after having achieved its independence after a short but exceptionally cruel war, and after having enjoyed the dignity of a sovereign republic for ten years, asked for admission into the North American Union, and was admitted late in 1845, bringing with her a bitter quarrel with her parent country as to the exact boundary line between them, and a vast assortment of fierce and bloody border feuds handed down from the days of the Alamo, Goliad and San Jacinto. The new administration, that of President Polk, resolved to defend by force if necessary the position taken by the Texans in regard to their boundary dispute, and within a few months collisions of troops in the disputed territory gave the American Congress the opportunity of declaring, May 11, 1846, that "By the acts of the Republic of Mexico, a state of war exists between the United States and that Republic."

Mexico, being miserably poor, distracted, misgoverned, and revolutionary, had no national navy, and the navy of the United States therefore was restricted to a rather limited share in the operations of the war, being forced to unromantic blockading and transport duties along the coasts, and denied the glory of battles at sea for lack of an enemy to meet on that element. Nevertheless, some of the acts of the naval force were productive of most important and lasting results in the prosecution of the war, while the maintenance of a blockade, imperfect as it was from being held by a fleet mainly composed of sailing ships on coasts famous for sudden storms, contributed greatly to hasten the end of hostilities: otherwise the war might have been prolonged by the sending of war material and supplies into Mexico by other nations had her ports been left unguarded.

One of the very first events of the war was of the greatest importance, and in all human probability its result was to give to the United States instead of Great Britain possession for all time of the vast region then composing the Mexican territory, or province, of California. The Mexican national debt was largely held by British capitalists, and fearing they would never realize on their investments because of the constant political turmoil of the feeble young republic, had appealed to their own government for assistance, which was readily attempted, as the foreign policy of England very properly includes the protection of the pockets of her subjects as well as their personal safety. Through the regular diplomatic channels propositions were made to Mexico to mortgage California and allow its occupation by England until the bonds were paid: a most astute scheme, and one that would have resulted in due time in the British government assuming the payment of the debt to its subjects and becoming the owner in fee simple of the territory held as security. While negotiations to this end were pending, the prospect of war between the United States and Mexico became threatening, and a subject of great interest to the British admiral in the Pacific, who is believed to have had instructions to seize upon California at the first news of hostilities, and thus insure his countrymen against financial loss.

In the spring of 1846 the American Pacific squadron, composed of sailing vessels, was lying at Mazatlan on the west coast of Mexico, Commodore John D. Sloat in the frigate *Savannah* being in command. The British admiral, Seymour, in the *Collingwood*, was also there, both watching each other and waiting eagerly for news, which came slowly in those days, without railways and telegraphs. It often happens that important events in the history of nations result from the acts of individuals not prominently connected with them, or from obscure circumstances of which the public is not cognizant, and one these events was now to come about. Surgeon Wm. Maxwell Wood, of the *Savannah*, having been relieved by another surgeon, left Mazatlan April 30 on his way home, his plan being to cross Mexico and take a steamer for the United States before war began, if a war was really to result. He was commissioned by Commodore Sloat to convey important information verbally to the Secretary of the Navy, the condition of the country being such that it was not deemed safe to trust his despatches or letters to be carried across the country. Dr. Wood spoke Spanish fluently, and when well started on his journey, at Guadalajara, overheard a conversation not intended for his ears from which he learned that hostilities had actually occurred on the Rio Grande. He was a most phlegmatic man, and consequently was able to absorb the startling intelligence without any outward show of interest; furthermore, his manner and personal appearance were those of a prosperous Englishman, in which character he was traveling, so he was comparatively free from suspicion.

At the earliest possible moment Surgeon Wood wrote out a detailed account of what he had heard, and despatched it by messenger to Commodore Sloat at Mazatlan, this act involving great personal risk, for had the despatch been intercepted its author would certainly have been hunted down and treated as a spy. By good luck more than anything else the letter reached Commodore Sloat safely, and that officer was not slow to appreciate the importance of the news and the exigency of the occasion. He at once sent two of his vessels—the *Cyane* and *Levant*, names that had before been historically associated—to the northward, and followed soon after in the *Savannah*. Within a few days the British admiral learned of the beginning of the war, and, surmising the mission of the American squadron, sailed at once on the same errand; but he was too late. On the 7th of July the American vessels took possession of Monterey, the chief city of Upper California, and of San Francisco, the best harbor, and that territory has ever since remained a part of the American Republic, thanks in the first instance to Surgeon Wood for his quick perception of his duty in the emergency in which he was accidentally placed, and in the second to Commodore Sloat for assuming the responsibility of seizing upon a vast territory without orders and without any assurance that his action would be upheld, or that a force sufficient to hold it would be supplied.

That Commodore Sloat acted wholly on his own judgment is proved by the fact that orders from Washington directing him to take possession of San Francisco Bay in the event of war were received by him long after the act had actually been performed. The importance of Surgeon Wood's part in the affair is testified to by Commodore Sloat, who, writing him some years later in relation to the event, said: "The information you furnished me at Mazatlan from Guadalajara (at the risk of your life) was the only reliable information I received of that event, and which induced me to proceed immediately to California, and upon my own responsibility to take posession of that country, which I did on the 7th of July, 1846." Had California become a British instead of American possession, the subsequent influence upon the progress of the United States, especially in the ultimate settlement of differences between the free and the slave states, is a subject quite beyond the bounds of any possible historical speculation.

Commodore Sloat was succeeded in command of the Pacific squadron by Commodore Stockton (of *Princeton* fame,) who, in cooperation with a small army under General Kearney, quelled an insurrection in the captured province and held it in hand until by the terms of the treaty of peace it became definitely a possession of the United States. His vessels also maintained as good a blockade of the ports on the western coast of Mexico as the nature of their motive power permitted. The action of Commodore Sloat in seizing upon the California coast was by all odds the most far-reaching move of the war, and the credit for it rests entirely with the navy.

An account of naval operations on the gulf coast of Mexico is largely a history of Captain M. C. Perry and his favorite war-vessel —the steamer *Mississippi*. Within a few weeks after the beginning of hostilities on the Rio Grande a reasonably efficient blockade of the Mexican ports was established, although the stormy character of that coast made blockading a rather difficult matter with the force at hand. This squadron, under the command of Commodore Connor, consisted of the steamers *Mississippi* and *Princeton*, the frigates *Raritan* and *Potomac*, several sloops-of-war, among which were the ill-fated *Albany* and *Cumberland*, and a number of schooners, bomb-ketches and small steamers, the latter being mentioned more particularly hereafter. The principal military operation undertaken by Commodore Connor was an expedition against Alvarado in October, but owing to the grounding of a schooner on the bar and signs of an approaching "norther," signal was made to return to the station off Vera Cruz, the abandonment of the attack greatly displeasing the subordinate officers and eventually proving something of a reflection upon Commodore Connor.

In August, Captain Perry was ordered to take two small steamers to Mexico and upon his arrival to relieve Captain Fitzhugh in command of the *Mississippi*. The steamers were the *Vixen* and *Spitfire*, small side-wheel vessels of about 240 tons burden, fitted with horizontal half-beam engines. They were twin vessels and had been built by Brown & Bell of New York for the Mexican government, but being unfinished at the time the war began they were bought by the United States from the builders for about $50,000 each. The *Spitfire* was sold at the close of the war and was lost on her first voyage as a commercial vessel; the *Vixen* was continued in the navy until 1855, when she was sold. Captain Perry arrived on the station with these steamers in September, after which there was a practical division of the squadron, Commodore Connor, who does not seem to have had much faith in steamers as war vessels, allowing Perry to control the steamers while he directed the operations of the sailing vessels, although he of course, as the senior, officially commanded the whole squadron.

At the time of Commodore Connor's demonstration against Alvarado, Perry with the *Mississippi*, *Vixen*, and some gun-schooners, reinforced by two hundred marines from the sailing ships, went to attack Tobasco up the river of the same name. Frontera, at the mouth of the river, was taken without resistance on October 23, a river steamer named *Petrita* which was afterward of great use being taken at this time. On the 26th Tobasco was captured after a smart fight, but the enemy, after having surrendered, attacked the naval force unexpectedly and this act obliged Perry to bombard the town, doing it a great deal of damage and completely subduing the war spirit of the Mexicans, the *Vixen* taking a prominent part in the cannonading. Not having a force with which to occupy the town,

Perry took away the small vessels he had captured and returned to rejoin the fleet. One of the vessels taken at Tobasco was a steamer named the *Champion*, formerly employed on the James River in Virginia, which as a despatch boat became afterward most useful to the American squadron. Although the captured city was not occupied, the expedition against it was not without value, for it infused new life into the men who were growing discontented under the monotony of looking at the enemy's shores from a distance.

About the middle of November both Connor and Perry went to attack Tampico, about two hundred miles north of Vera Cruz, and gained possession of that place without firing a shot, the appearance of the squadron off the bar being the signal for surrender. It being desirable for military reasons to retain this place, Perry with his ever-ready *Mississippi* was sent to Matamoras near the mouth of the Rio Grande to communicate with the army authorities and ask that troops be sent. After doing this he went on his own responsibility to New Orleans, where he obtained from the governor of Louisiana a battery of field guns and a quantity of shovels, picks, wheelbarrows, etc., much needed for entrenching purposes. Returning, he arrived at Tampico after just one week's absence, his quick trip amazing the old seamen in the fleet who were almost persuaded into the belief that a steamer might after all be good for something.

By the end of the year constant service under steam began to tell on the *Mississippi*, repairs being so urgently needed that early in January, 1847, Perry proceeded in her to Norfolk, where he turned her over to the navy yard authorities, going himself to Washington to consult with the Navy Department officials relative to the conduct of the war. A board of survey reported that it would require six weeks to fit the *Mississippi* for service, which was very discouraging news to Perry who felt that important events were impending in Mexico and who had his own reasons for wishing to be present during their occurrence. In this emergency he fell back on his old friend Haswell, the engineer-in-chief, knowing that if anyone could help him out Haswell was the man. The engineer-in-chief went to Norfolk and, after a critical examination of the ship, declared that she could be made ready in two weeks by working night and day, and this feat was actually accomplished under his personal direction. " We may safely add that, by his energy, and ability in getting the *Mississippi* ready at this time, Mr. Haswell saved the government many thousands of dollars and contributed largely to the triumphs of a quick war which brought early peace."[1]

Commodore Perry's familiarity with steam vessels was utilized during his enforced stay in the United States at this time by putting him in charge of the fitting out of a flotilla of lightdraft vessels for service in Mexico. These were the steamers *Scourge* and *Scorpion*, and a number of bomb-ketches with imported volcanic names— *Vesuvius*, *Stromboli*, and the like—intended to be towed by the steamers. The *Scourge* was a small vessel of 230 tons burden, purchased in New York for $44,825; she was fitted with two of the Loper flat-bladed propellers, and was sold at New Orleans at the close of the war. The *Scorpion* was a paddle-wheel steamer of 340 tons burden, bought in New York for $80,505, and sold in 1848 for $14,500. Although not a part of this flotilla, two other steamers added to the naval establishment for Mexican War service may properly be mentioned here. These were the *Iris*, a paddle-wheel vessel of 388 tons burden, fitted with a steeple engine, bought in New York in 1847 for $35,991 and sold in Norfolk in 1849 for about one-fourth that amount, and the *Polk*, a revenue cutter very similar to the *Scorpion*; the *Polk* was transferred to the Navy Department is 1846, but was found unseaworthy and defective in machinery, having broken down on an attempted voyage to the Gulf, in consequence of which she was returned to the Treasury Department.

Perry returned to Vera Cruz with the *Mississippi* early in March, carrying with him orders to relieve Commodore Connor and take command of the American fleet, which he did March 21, 1847, and immediately thereafter a vigorous and aggressive policy was inaugurated. General Winfield Scott's army had already landed and begun the siege of Vera Cruz, but found itself without ordnance heavy enough to make much impression upon the city walls. To General Scott's request for the loan of heavy guns from the fleet, Perry refused, unless his own men might go with their guns, a condition that Scott first declined, but when he fully realized that his

---

[1] William E. Griffis; "Biography of Matthew Calbraith Perry;" p. 211.

own batteries could not breach the walls he accepted it, and a heavy battery of six guns with ship's mounts and picked crews was at once landed and laboriously dragged through the sand in the night-time some three miles to the spot where it was to be located for most effective use. The earthwork defenses for this battery were laid out by an engineer of General Scott's staff—Captain Robert E. Lee. It may be interesting to mention that in the army before Vera Cruz at this time, gaining experience for a far greater war, were the following named young officers: First Lieutenants James Longstreet, P. G. T. Beauregard, John Sedgwick, and Earl Van Dorn, and Second Lieutenants U. S. Grant, George B. McClellan, Fitz John Porter, W. S. Hancock, and Thomas J. (Stonewall) Jackson.

After the installation of the naval battery the cannonading became more deadly and furious, resulting in the surrender four days later of the beleagured city. The details of this exploit are not especially pleasant for the American historian to dwell upon. The Mexican general, Morales, had declined General Scott's summons to surrender and had not availed himself of the privilege offered to remove the inhabitants of the city before the bombardment began. The fire of the heavy naval guns was directed successfully to the breaching of the wall, but the army guns and mortars kept up an incessant storm of shot, shell and bombs, rained over the walls into the city. Ages ago Cicero established the maxim that "Laws are silent in war," and the truth of this was well illustrated by the tragedy of Vera Cruz. Whole families were destroyed in the ruins of their shattered homes; women and children praying in an agony of fear before the altars of their churches were torn and mangled by bombs and shells crushing through the roofs; even the sepulchres of the dead were torn to pieces and the corpses scattered about the streets. The damage done to combatants was small compared with the horrors inflicted upon the wretched populace.

An exhibition of bravado in the fleet was the only touch of comedy connected with the bombardment of Vera Cruz. The famous stone castle of San Juan d'Ulloa, built by the Spaniards in the 16th century at a cost of forty million dollars, stands in the harbor about a mile in front of the city, and its fire soon proved a serious annoyance to some of the investing batteries, the exact range of which had been ascertained by repeated firing. To divert this fire, Perry ordered Commander Tatnall in the steamer *Spitfire* to approach and open fire on the castle. Tatnall, always disputatious, asked for specific directions as to what point he should attack, to which "Ursa Major," as Perry was known behind his back, replied not too gently, "Where you can do the most execution, sir!" With this flea in his ear Tatnall proceeded with the *Spitfire*, in company with the *Vixen*, Commander Joshua R. Sands, to within a stone's throw of the castle and opened furiously against its massive walls. This close proximity probably saved the two little steamers, for they were untouched, although the men on board were thoroughly drenched with the water splashed over them by the storm of cannon balls. The spectacle was exciting to the crews of the on-looking ships, and ludicrous as well on account of its futility. Perry, both amused and provoked at the exhibition of temper on the part of his subordinate, made signal for the steamers to withdraw, but Tatnall failed to see any signals, assuring the officer who reported them that he was mistaken and was looking the wrong way. It finally became necessary to endanger a boat's crew by sending it to call him back. Mr. Wm. H. Shock, who was the engineer in charge of the machinery of the *Spitfire* on this occasion, has stated in a magazine article that when the vessels went out of action he heard Tatnall say in tones of regret, "Not a man wounded or killed."

After the fall of Vera Cruz, a combined army and naval expedition was planned against Alvarado, the place that had previously been proceeded against without results by Commodore Connor. The chief object in gaining this town was to supply Scott's army with animals for transportation in his projected invasion of Mexico, horses being abundant in the Alvarado neighborhood. General Quitman with a considerable force of artillery, cavalry and infantry, started overland, while Perry organized an expedition with small steamers manned by picked men from the fleet to proceed against the place by water. Lieutenant Charles G. Hunter in the *Scourge* was directed to blockade the threatened town and report the movements of the enemy to Captain Breese of the sloop-of-war *Albany*. This young officer, observing signs of the enemy abandoning the town, landed some men and took possession of it, a very presumptuous act when a general and a commodore had designs upon the position and the honor of capturing it. Hunter was promptly arrested by order of Commodore Perry, tried by court-martial for disobedience of orders, and sent home in disgrace. In the United States he was given many dinners and receptions, and as "Alvarado Hunter" was the hero of the hour, while Perry was made the target for a multitude of newspaper attacks. All of which was natural enough on the part of the public, which saw nothing in the affair except the capture of a town without regard for the rank of the captor. As a matter of fact, by exceeding his authority Hunter completely defeated the real object of the expedition; his act forewarned the Mexicans and gave them ample time to remove with their horses and portable property before the army forces had hemmed them in.

The next naval operation of consequence in this war was Perry's capture in June of the city of Tobasco, after severe fighting. This is an important event in our naval history, as it is the first occasion on which a large force of blue-jackets was regularly organized into a naval brigade for prolonged military operations on shore, which was done under the personal direction and command of Commodore Perry. The necessity for this proceeding was brought about by the circumstance that the marines of the fleet had been formed into a regiment and sent with Scott's army on the march to the city of Mexico. The year before, Commodore Stockton had used his sailors to some extent for guard and garrison duty in California, but the credit for the first real naval brigade is given to Perry by the historians of our navy. The small steamers of the fleet were invaluable in the capture of Tobasco; in fact, without them the expedition would hardly have been practicable. Commodore Perry so fully appreciated the value of this type of vessel that he repeatedly asked for more light-draft steamers from home, and eventually so provoked the conservative old officers about the Navy Department that he got a stiff reprimand from the Secretary of the Navy for his persistence in this regard.

To First Assistant Engineer George Sewall is due credit for having repaired in a most ingenious manner without any convenient appliances the two steamers *Vixen* and *Spitfire*, which had become unseaworthy and unfit for use owing to leaky Kingston valve connections, thus giving to the Government two steamers for war operations.

Yellow fever broke out in July on the *Mississippi*, and that invaluable ship eventually had to be sent off the station, going to Pensacola with about two hundred invalids on board. A short time before the appearance of this pestilence a fire from spontaneous combustion had gained such headway in the *Mississippi's* coal bunkers that it was only extinguished by flooding the bunkers, and it was believed that the moisture remaining in the nooks and corners of the ship after this accident gave a foothold for the disease. Two of the *Mississippi's* engineers—First Assistant Charles A. Mapes, and Third Assistant Emerson G. Covel—died on board their ship of this epidemic and were buried in the soil of Mexico.

General Scott entered the city of Mexico on the 17th of September, 1847, and that practically ended the war, although the naval force continued the blockade of the coast until the treaty of peace was signed the following February. Then the vessels were gradually withdrawn, the larger ones to other stations and the small purchased steamers were sold for what they would bring. The most beneficial lesson to the navy derived from this war was that steamers were vastly superior to sailing vessels for war purposes, and the prejudice against the new motor were so broken down that naval opposition to the policy of building war steamers was materially diminished thereafter, although not wholly extinguished. The demonstrated value of the small steamers for river and harbor operations had quite as much to do with bringing about this change of sentiment as had the general utility exhibited by the *Princeton* and *Mississippi*.

With the return of peace, the steam navy was augmented by the transfer from the War Department of two steamers which had been used for troop-ships. The larger of these was the *Massachusetts*, a full-rigged ship of 750 tons burden with auxiliary steam power, which had been bought in 1847 for $80,000. This ship had been the pioneer in a line of auxiliary steam packets employed in the New York and Liverpool trade, and was fitted with two small engines of Ericsson's design, driving an Ericsson screw only $9\frac{1}{2}$ feet in diameter, the screw being attached to the shaft by a coupling that could be disengaged and the screw hoisted on deck in a few minutes. The propeller shaft passed out of the stern at the side of the stern post, to which was bolted the stern bearing of the shaft, the latter projecting far enough to allow the screw to operate abaft the rudder. The rudder had a slot, or "shark's mouth" cut in it to prevent its striking the projecting shaft when put hard over. Both the stern bearing attached to the post and the cut in the rudder were features patented by John Ericsson. The *Massachusetts* was some years afterward converted into a bark-rigged sailing vessel, and under the name of *Farrallones* remained in the naval service until after the Civil War, when she was sold.

The other transferred transport was the auxiliary steam bark *Edith*, of 400 tons burden, which had Ericsson machinery of the same type as that described in the case of the *Massachusetts*. She had been in the East India trade and was on record as having made the quickest voyage then known between Calcutta and Canton. After being fitted for war purposes the *Edith* was sent on a cruise to the Pacific station, where, in 1850, she was run ashore and wrecked, but without loss of life.

The following list of engineers of the navy who served on vessels actively employed in the Mexican War is made up from a list given in General C. M. Wilcox's *History of the Mexican War:*

Chief Engineer John Faron, Jr.
" " D. B. Martin.
" " William Sewell.
First Assistant Engineer Saml. Archbold.
" " " L. S. Bartholomew.
" " " E. G. Covel.
" " " T. H. Faron.
" " " Jesse Gay.
" " " J. K. Matthews.
" " " Hiram Sanford.
" " " George Sewell.
Second Assistant Engineer James Atkinson.
" " " N. C. Davis.
" " " Joshua Follansbee.
" " " John Gallagher.
" " " A. P. How.
" " " B. F. Isherwood.
" " " R. M. Johnson.

Second Assistant Engineer, J. M. Middleton.
"   "   "   A. S. Palmer.
"   "   "   Theodore Zeller.
Third Assistant Engineer J. M. Adams.
"   "   "   Lafayette Caldwell.
"   "   "   John Carroll.
"   "   "   Charles Coleman.
"   "   "   Wm. E. Everett.
"   "   "   Edward Faron.
"   "   "   B. F. Garvin.
"   "   "   J. R. Hatcher.
"   "   "   J. W. King.
"   "   "   William Luce.
"   "   "   Charles A. Mapes.
"   "   "   J. W. Parks.
"   "   "   W. H. Shock.
"   "   "   William Taggart.
"   "   "   J. C. Tennent.
"   "   "   M. M. Thompson.
"   "   "   J. A. Van Zandt.
"   "   "   Wm. C. Wheeler.
"   "   "   Edward Whipple.

The material benefits to the United States resulting from the Mexican War were enormous, and entirely out of proportion to the outlay of life and treasure involved, notwithstanding it is difficult at this distance in time for one to grow enthusiastic over the events of that unequal struggle. Desperate battles were fought; many noteworthy deeds of valor were performed, and both army and navy achieved that peculiar distinction called *glory*, but to the American student of his country's history the fact that the military power of our great republic was ruthlessly used to overwhelm with woe and desolation a small sister republic struggling to maintain self-government on the democratic principles professed by the nation which inflicted upon her the horrors of war, must ever remain prominent. The cause of freedom had then enough to contend with, without the greatest nation governed by its own people tearing to pieces a feeble follower of its institutions.

The territory of the United States was increased one-third by the terms of the treaty which concluded the war, and a vast extent of sea coast on the Pacific Ocean was gained. The benefits to our country and to the world in general, resulting from this transfer of territory cannot be over-estimated, and this, as a manifestation of Providence forwarding the destiny of the Anglo-Saxon race, must be our chief apology for the manner in which that vast region changed hands. California under Mexican rule gave little promise for the future, but in the hands of the energetic and investigating American became almost in a day both famous and wealthy. It had long been known to the Mexicans of California that their rivers ran over golden sands, but the indolent and ease-loving people preferred the shade of their haciendas to the labor of exploring the mountains; *manana* or "the day after," would be ample time in which to investigate, and thus the great discovery bade fair to be neglected for an indefinite time.

The prying American lost no time in exploring his new posessions and within a year had proclaimed such wonderful discoveries that ships freighted with tools and men were converging upon the Golden Gate from every quarter of the globe; steamship lines before impossible, were established, and the transcontinental railways, which have hastened the development of the North American continent and the civilization of the Far East at least a century, were projected. It is a favorite statement of historians that the amount of gold produced by California since 1848 exceeds in value the enormous national debt incurred by the United States in the war for the preservation of the Union. Granting this to be true, and admitting that the mineral wealth of the territory acquired from Mexico is yet beyond computation, the greater truth remains that all this is actually secondary in value to the wonderful agricultural resources of the same region. But for the aggressive and perhaps undemocratic policy which led the United States to despoil a neighbor whose form of government should have been her defense, California, with sources of wealth far greater than those possessed by more than one empire which has ruled the world, might yet be the hunting ground of hungry savages, her fields untilled, her orchards unplanted, and the treasure of her streams and mountain ledges still undisturbed save by the hoof of the antelope and the paw of the bear.

CHAPTER VIII.

"The wheel of fortune turns incessantly round, and who can say within himself, 'I shall to-day be uppermost.'"—CONFUCIUS.

New steamers authorized for the navy in 1847—The SUSQUEHANNA, POWHATAN, SARANAC, and SAN JACINTO—Mr. Haswell Succeeded as Engineer-in-Chief by Charles B. Stuart—Circumstances Connected with Mr. Haswell Leaving the Navy—His Great Services to the Naval Engineer Corps—His Subsequent Career.

STEAM, as we have seen, did not play an important part in the naval operations of the Mexican war, but the numerous opportunities and advantages lost or not used simply for lack of motive power more reliable than the winds, served as excellent object lessons to direct naval and public attention to the necessity of having a fleet of steam war vessels if the navy were to be thereafter a useful military arm. In the report of the Secretary of the Navy for the year 1846 a policy of building war-steamers was urged, and in December of that year Mr. Fairfield, Chairman of the Senate Committee on Naval Affairs, asked the Department by letter for a statement as to the size, type, cost, &c., of the vessels desired. The rep'y was to the effect that at least four steamers, at an average cost of $500,000 each should be immediately undertaken, and the authority asked for was conferred by the naval appropriation bill then under consideration, which was approved March 3, 1847. The same act directed the Secretary of the Navy to enter into contract with E. K. Collins and his associates for the transportation of the United States mails between New York and Liverpool; with A. G. Sloo for the transportation of the mails between New York and New Orleans, touching at Havana, and with some other agent, not named, for the transportation of the mails from Panama to Oregon Territory. In the first two cases, the steamers of the contractors were to be built under the supervision of a naval constructor and were to be adapted to use as war vessels, the contractors being also required by the terms of the act to receive on board each of their steamers four passed midshipmen of the navy to act as watch officers.

Mr. John Y. Mason, Secretary of the Navy, on March 22, 1847, ordered a board, consisting of Commodores Morris, Warrington and Smith, Engineer-in-Chief Haswell, Naval Constructors Grice, Lenthall and Hartt, and Mr. Charles W. Copeland, the eminent civilian engineer employed by the Navy Department, to assemble in Washington and determine upon the various features of the proposed vessels, the order stating in general terms some of the requirements to be observed, and directing that one of the vessels " should be propelled by some of the various screw propellers." Later, Commodore Skinner and Chief Engineer John Faron, Jr. were added to the board, which met at frequent dates from March 23 until July 3, 1847, on which latter date its final report and recommendations were submitted to the Department. So many interesting points arose later about the ships recommended by this board, and such a bitter controversy grew out of alleged defects in the design of at least one of them that the matter eventually became the subject of congressional inquiry, and its history in detail thus got into print in the form of a public document—Executive Document 65; House of Representatives, Thirty-third Congress; First Session: this document the author has been fortunate enough to discover in that vast mine of information almost inaccessibly buried in the crypt of the Capitol, and from it the principal facts presented in this chapter are derived.

The proceedings of the board indicate that the *Mississippi* was regarded as a model from which to copy as much as possible. Without going into all the differences of opinion, lengthy debates, and yea and nay votes indulged in by the commodores, constructors and engineers of the board, it is sufficient to say the resultant recommendations were the building of two large side-wheel steamers, similar to the *Mississippi*, but sufficiently large to carry coal, provisions, &c., for long voyages to foreign stations, and two smaller steamers, of about 2,100 tons displacement, one of the latter, to be fitted with a screw propeller. Wood was designated as the material from which these vessels were to be built, the vote of the Board showing that Mr. Haswell was the only member who favored iron as building material for even one of them. The board also decided that Naval Constructors Grice and Lenthall should each design the hull of one of the larger steamers and that Mr. Hartt should design both of the smaller ones, Messrs. Haswell and Copeland each to design machinery for one large and one small vessel. All these recommendations were approved by the Navy Department, and on the 13th of July, 1847, the Secretary promulgated the President's order that the two large ships be built at Philadelphia and Norfolk respectively, and the smaller ones at Kittery and New York.

The large steamer designed by Mr. Lenthall was named *Susquehanna*, and was built in the navy yard at Philadelphia, where she was launched in April, 1850, and was entirely completed with machinery ready for service at the end of that year. She was bark-rigged, 250 feet long, 45 feet beam and displaced 3,824 tons at her load draft of 19½ feet. The engines, designed by Charles W. Copeland, were built by Murray & Hazelhurst of Baltimore, under the supervision of Chief Engineer Wm. P. Williamson, U. S. Navy, and consisted of two inclined direct-acting condensing engines, with cylinders 70 inches in diameter and 10 feet stroke, fitted with inclined air pumps. The paddle wheels were of the ordinary radial type, 31 feet in diameter. There were four copper boilers of the double return, ascending flue type, containing 342 square feet of grate surface and 8,652 square feet of heating surface.

In June, 1851, the *Susquehanna* sailed for the Asiatic station, then known as the East India Station, her first commander being Captain J. H. Aulick and her chief engineer Mr. Samuel Archbold. On the passage to Rio de Janeiro some defects or injuries to her engines and spars were discovered, resulting in a delay of some two months at the Brazilian capital, during which time repairs to the extent of about $3,500 were made at the marine arsenal, mostly to the air pumps and paddle-wheels. Her performance thereafter was excellent, and most creditable to her engineers, as may be seen from the following report of the commanding officer, which report is of special interest in these days when we rather pride ourselves on our ability to cross wide seas under steam without an extravagant use of fuel, showing that the men of a previous generation were not wholly ignorant of the same desirable experience:

U. S. STEAM FRIGATE SUSQUEHANNA,
TABLE BAY, CAPE OF GOOD HOPE, October 17, 1851.

SIR: I have the honor to report our arrival here on the 15th nstant, eighteen days from Rio de Janeiro.

This passage has thoroughly and severely tested the strength of our masts and engines. The weather for the greater part of the time was very stormy, and the sea higher than I have ever known it before, causing the ship to roll and plunge to such a degree that frequently one wheel was eight or ten feet entirely clear of the sea, when the other was full half its diameter buried in it; but nothing of any importance gave way, and the engines were never stopped from the time we weighed our anchor in "Rio;" until it was let go in this bay. I, however, did not neglect to use our sails and economize fuel; when the wind was fair, and the weather permitted, we used only two boilers, and with a daily expenditure of less than fourteen tons of coal, keeping up only sufficient steam to turn our wheels, we averaged for a number of days more than two hundred miles in the twenty-four hours. I adopted this course in preference to taking off the floats, for the reason that it is very difficult, if not impossible, to un-ship and re-ship them in a heavy seaway. We expended on the passage only about half the coal with which we left "Rio." I am, &c.,

J. H. AULICK,
Commanding Squadron, East Indies and China.
Hon. WILLIAM A. GRAHAM, Secretary of the Navy,
Washington, D. C.

The *Susquehanna* continued an efficient cruising steamer for many years, and was a prominent ship during the war of the rebellion; a few years after its close her machinery was entirely removed and the work of converting her into a screw steamer undertaken, but never completed, and she never went to sea again.

Constructor Grice's steamer was the *Powhatan*, launched at the Norfolk navy yard February 14, 1850. The principal dimensions of the hull were practically the same as those of the *Susquehanna*, but as her load draft when completed was about a foot less than that of the latter vessel, her displacement was also somewhat less; she was bark-rigged. The engines were designed by Engineer-in-Chief Haswell and were built by Mehaffy & Co., of Gosport, Va., under the inspection of Chief Engineer William Sewell, U. S. Navy. There were two inclined direct-acting condensing engines with the same cylinder dimensions as those of the *Susqeuhanna*, differing from that vessel in design, having vertical air pumps and a novelty in engine framing, the frames being of wrought iron, built up on the box-girder principle. There were four copper boilers of the same general dimensions as those of the sister ship, but differing from them considerably in details of arrangement, fittings, etc. The lower flues were made elliptical to increase the heating surface.

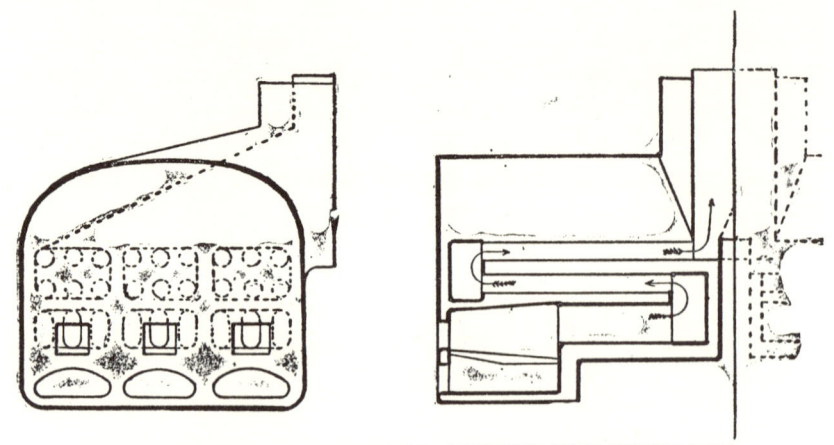

COPPER BOILER, U. S. S. POWHATAN; ASCENDING-FLUE RETURN TYPE.
Length, 16 feet; breadth, 15 feet 3 inches; height, 13 feet; grate surface, 88½ square feet; heating surface, 1,971 square feet.

A new feature in marine engineering practice appeared in this vessel in the introduction of a small one-furnace auxiliary boiler, intended primarily for supplying a hoisting engine to aid in coaling ship. The *Powhatan* also was fitted with two Worthington steam pumps, which is believed to be the first appearance in our navy of that now familiar auxiliary.

Owing to a lack of professional and clerical aid, Engineer-in-Chief Haswell personally designed every detail of the *Powhatan's* machinery and made the working drawings with his own hands in the intervals between attention to the necessary duties of his office. So pressed was he for time that he was unable to lay out a general design of the engines to work up to, but had to develop the various parts progressively. This feat is probably unprecedented in designing work of such magnitude, and, considered together with the remarkable success of the *Powhatan's* engines, furnishes a most valuable index to the rare professional accomplishments of Mr. Haswell.

U. S. S. POWHATAN (AND SUSQUEHANNA), 1850.

(When first put in service the smoke pipes of these ships had flaring or bell mouthed tops).

The *Powhatan* was employed in service, almost continously for a longer period than any steamer ever in the navy, with the sole exception of the *Michigan*, which latter vessel owes her longevity, as has been pointed out before, to the fact that her career has been confined to summer cruising on the fresh-water lakes of the Northwest. The copper boilers of the *Powhatan* of course had to be replaced in time, but her original engines remained thoroughly efficient and trustworthy to the end, a monument to the ability of their designer and the skill of the men who built them. When the *Powhatan* was attached to the Japan expedition squadron, her chief engineer, George Sewell, wrote home that in a trip of three thousand miles under steam a hammer had not been touched to her engines, which ran with such rhythmic regularity that they seemed set to music.

Even in her old age the *Powhatan* was a faster steamer than almost any other on the navy list and was decidedly the most comfortable and popular with both officers and men. With ten pounds of steam and her great wheels making ten revolutions per minute she was proverbially capable of making ten knots an hour, and that without much reference to the state of the weather. In 1878, after she had outlived almost every steamer of her date, she fought for her life off Hatteras, under the command of that splendid old seaman, Captain T. S. Fillebrown, through one of the most awful cyclones that any ship ever survived, and though terribly battered and strained, remained able to breast the sea for several years thereafter. In that storm it is reported by the indisputable evidence of many observers that her fore yard-arm dipped into the sea. In 1887, to the genuine regret of all in the navy, the *Powhatan* was condemned by a board of survey, being actually worn out in the service, and an unsentimental administration sold her poor old bones to the ghouls of the ocean—the ship-breakers.

One of the two smaller vessels was built at the navy yard at Kittery, Maine, and named *Saranac*. She was the first of the four steamers to be completed, being launched in November, 1848, and sailed for a cruise in the West Indies in April, 1850. She was 216 feet long, 38 feet beam, and of 2,200 tons displacement at the mean draft of 17 feet. The machinery, designed by Engineer Copeland, was built by Coney & Co. of Boston, under the inspection of Chief Engineers Wm. W. W. Wood and D. B. Martin, and consisted of a pair of inclined direct-acting condensing engines with cylinders 60 inches in diameter and 9 feet stroke, driving radial paddle-wheels 27 feet in diameter. The engines were fitted with Stevens' patent cut-offs. There were three copper double-return drop-flue boilers, designed to carry twelve pounds of steam pressure, aggregating 188 square feet of grate surface and 5,127 square feet of heating surface. At an ordinary engine speed of about twelve revolutions per minute about eight knots an hour could easily be maintained. The rig was that of a bark, and her lines were so graceful and the external finish so perfect that she was regarded as an ornament to the service. After a long career for a war vessel the *Saranac* came to a violent end in June, 1875, by running ashore and becoming a total wreck in Seymour Narrows, while on her way to Alaska.

The fourth one of these steamers—the *San Jacinto*—was, like the wrath of Achilles, "the direful spring of woes unnumbered," to almost everyone ever prominently connected with her, her campaign of destruction beginning with blasting the naval career of Engineer-in-Chief Haswell. Designed by the same constructor, Mr. Hartt, who designed the *Saranac*, the hull was an exact counterpart of that vessel, and the rig was the same. She was built at the navy yard, New York, where she was launched in April, 1850. The engines were designed by Mr. Haswell and were built by Merrick and Towne of Philadelphia, under the inspection at different times of Chief Engineers Faron, Wood and Hunt, and finally Mr. Haswell himself. They consisted of two "square" engines, as they were termed, operating the shaft of a screw propeller; the cylinders were $62\frac{1}{2}$ inches in diameter and 50 inches stroke, and were placed athwartship, inclined upward and outboard with the inner, or lower heads, in contact over the crank shaft. Long cross-heads carried two connecting rods for each engine, reaching backward and downward on each side of the cylinders to take hold of the cranks. There were three copper boilers of the same external dimensions as those of the *Saranac*, but somewhat better designed, as they displayed more grate and heating surface.

There were some strange things about this ship, one of which was the location of the propeller shaft twenty inches to one side of

U. S. S. SAN JACINTO, 1850.

the center line of the keel, which was done at the instance of the three naval constructors, members of the board that settled upon the plans for the vessel. These gentlemen were eminent in the business of ship designing and building, but screw-propelled ships were new to them and they could not bring themselves to agree to any application of steam power that involved cutting a big hole for a shaft through the stern post. It transpired that Ericsson, who had patents on a multitude of marine appliances, useful and otherwise, had a patent on a precisely similar arrangement. This location entailed the projection of the propeller shaft far enough beyond the stern to allow the screw to work abaft the rudder, which plan Mr. Haswell had opposed in the Board, but made his designs in accordance when it was finally decided upon. The board also fixed the location of the engines so far aft and in such a cramped space that the engineer who had to design them was so handicapped that it was practically impossible for him to arrive at an arrangement of details that would allow proper room for examination, repairing and adjustment of the machinery when assembled in place. The screw itself as designed was a ponderous six bladed affair, five feet wide axially and weighing some seven tons, which weight, overhanging the stern five feet at least, was manifestly a menace to the safety of the ship. Mr. Haswell claimed, and with propriety as the records of the Board show, that he was forced to such a design by the board's exaction that no patents be infringed, and the lighter types of screws then in use, having thin supported blades, were covered by Ericsson's patents.

As the engines of the *San Jacinto* approached completion it began to be gossiped abroad among engineers that the engineer-in-chief had made a fearful botch of his designs, and the various naval engineers and machinery contractors who fancied they had been wronged by him in the fearless performance of his official duties, according to his conscientious judgment, gathered their forces for his overthrow, the movement being simply a manifestation of the natural tendency of mankind to assail and humble the eminent. In a primitive state of society, man kills his rival with a club and eats him, partly in revenge, partly to remove an obstacle to his ambition, and partly to provide subsistence for himself. As we become enlightened, the older and more natural code of ethics is abandoned in deferenc to certain artificial prejudices which are adjuncts of civilization, and while less rude are equally effective methods of personal warfare. This seems to be a necessity, for the natural predilection of man is a love of hostility to his species, as exhibited in personal rivalries and jealousies when a state of war does not afford an outlet for his passions under the guise of patriotism.

Such a condition of society may be sad to contemplate in these closing years of the nineteenth century, and there are doubtless many who are thoughtlessly ready to controvert the proposition. A little reflection, however, will be convincing to the majority; for as we look about the world it appears that in spite of all the doctrines of peace and good-will to man, promulgated by the apostles of christianity and other great religions, there does not and never has existed, the nation large enough to permit of the harmonious existence within its borders at the same time, two great statesmen, soldiers, or others of the same calling; nor is there a village so small that two carpenters, shoemakers or blacksmiths within its limits fail to become rivals, each claiming his fellow craftsman to be incompetent and an imposter. Even the clergy, the anointed apostles of the doctrine of peace, take delight in bitter quarrels of creed, or, failing in opportunities for that, turn upon each other in the same denomition and institute heresy trials, and critical inquisitions regarding their profession of faith.

Unpalatable as it may be, it is nevertheless a plain, unvarnished truth that fondness for war and strife is an instinct inherent in the human breast. Without this instinct success in any undertaking is well-nigh impossible, as society is at present constituted. Nothing proves this more clearly than the history of nations, which, when analyzed, are simply tales of the contention of individuals striving for supremacy. He who becomes foremost in any walk in life must succeed at the expense of his fellows who are struggling for the same eminence, and it is literally "to him that overcometh," who, according to Revelation, " shall be given power over the nations."

Returning to the subject, after this digression, it must be admitted that there were some radically bad features connected with the design of the *San Jacinto's* machinery, but the assertions freely made at the time that the engines were an " object of ridicule to all

Mr. Charles B. Stuart,
Engineer-in-Chief of the Navy, December 1, 1850, to June 30, 1853.

engineers who have seen them," and a "standing monument of Mr. Haswell's incompetency and folly," were more ridiculous in view of Haswell's reputation and achievements as an engineer than any defect in these engines could possibly have been. Some of the faults of the *San Jacinto's* engines were forced upon the designer by conditions imposed by superior authority and were as well known to him as they could have been to any of his critics, while many of the other alleged defects existed chiefly in the minds of those who had decided the time had come to thrust him from the pedestal he occupied above all other scientific engineers of his time.

The hue and cry had its effect, and late in November, 1850, the President appointed Mr. Charles B. Stuart of New York to the office of engineer-in-chief of the Navy from December 1st, Mr. Haswell resuming his place at the head of the list of chief engineers. Mr. Stuart was a civil engineer of prominence, being the superintendent of the Erie Canal at the time of his appointment, and made no pretense to knowledge of marine engineering, though he acquired considerable knowledge by experience while engineer-in-chief. His was purely a political appointment as a reward for party service, and he never was an enrolled member of the naval engineer corps. Some serious engineering mistakes, which have been or will be noted in these pages, occurred in the navy during his administration, the result of which was that when he resigned, after an occupancy of his office for two years and a half, the custom was adopted of selecting the engineer-in-chief from the chief engineers of the navy, who were familiar with the service and the peculiarities of its steam vessels. While engineer-in-chief, Mr. Stuart performed good service for the engineering world by collecting the necessary data and publishing two remarkably valuable and reliable books on naval material—"The Naval Dry Docks of the United States," and "The Naval and Mail Steamers of the United States."

The day after Mr. Stuart's induction into office, Mr. Haswell was ordered to assume the duty of superintendent of the installation of the *San Jacinto's* machinery, and Chief Engineer B. F. Isherwood, who before entering the naval service had been associated with Mr. Stuart in the civil engineering work of the Erie canal, was detached from duty under the Light House Board and ordered as technical assistant to the engineer-in-chief. Shortly thereafter, letters expressing grave doubts about the *San Jacinto* were sent by the engineer-in-chief to the chief of the bureau of construction, and requests made that a survey be held before the work of completing the ship was allowed to go further. As a result, a board consisting of Chief engineers Wm. P. Williamson, Wm. Sewell and Henry Hunt, provided with a categorical list of fifteen questions, the answers to which, it was supposed would damn the machinery of the *San Jacinto*, was assembled at New York to examine the vessel and report discoveries, a report being made February 10, 1851. It

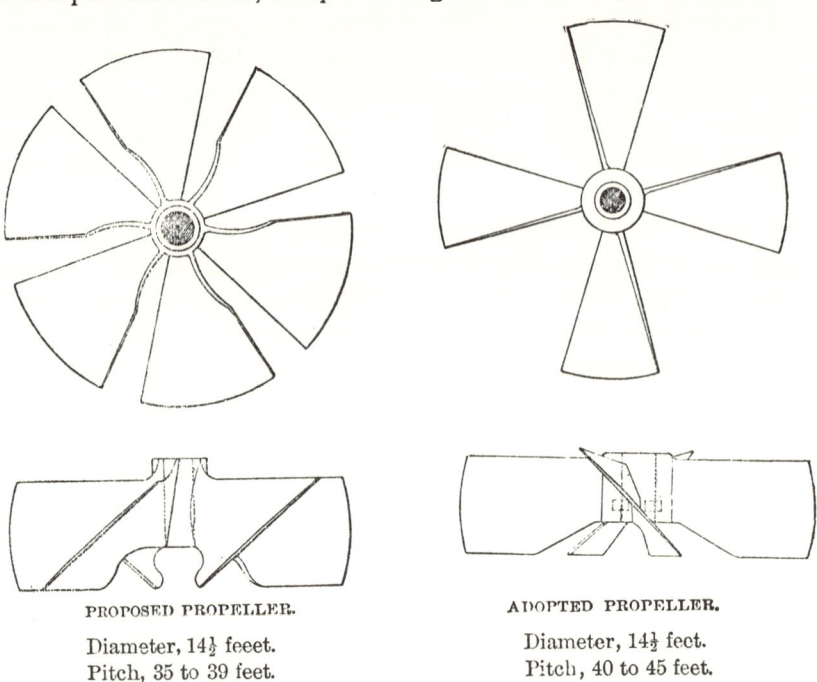

PROPOSED PROPELLER.
Diameter, 14½ feeet.
Pitch, 35 to 39 feet.

ADOPTED PROPELLER.
Diameter, 14½ feet.
Pitch, 40 to 45 feet.

was decidedly unfavorable to the engines in general, and especially severe in regard to the heavy projecting propeller and the side location of the shaft, both of which objectionable features were recommended for alteration. The propeller was altered accordingly, it so happening that the one originally designed had not yet been cast, although its mold was completed; the modified screw, as recommended by the Board and designed by Mr. Isherwood, together with the one originally designed being represented by the outline sketches here inserted.

The shaft passage through the stern having been cut, the recommendation of the board of engineers regarding its modification was not carried out. It has been previously noted that Captain Ericsson had a patent on such an arrangement and he, through an attorney promptly made claim for infringement; the claim was referred to Engineer-in-Chief Stuart for an opinion, and that official made a most lengthy report, acknowledging in rather indirect terms that the shaft arrangement was practically the same as that described in the specification of Ericsson's patent and was therefore an infringement for which the patentee was entitled to damages. Besides this question, which was the only real point raised by Ericsson's claim, the engineer-in-chief dilated upon other features of the *San Jacinto's* machinery involved very indirectly, if at all, in the claim, and of course proved they were not infringements, the object of this digression being apparently to make an occasion to reflect upon the machinery designs of the ex-engineer-in-chief, which reflection was introduced into the report somewhat neatly by the following sentence: "I cannot discover that the construction of the 'engines' of the *San Jacinto* involves the infringement of Captain Ericsson's patent in any particular, nor do I think he would upon inspection of them, make any claim for the 'novelties' introduced in their construction."

The chief of the bureau of Construction was unable to extract any conclusions from the mass of verbiage with which the engineer-in-chief's opinions were clothed, and returned the report to him as being "too indefinite to authorize a settlement of the question." In replying to this, Mr. Stuart did himself no great credit by saying that if the report was indefinite it was "owing to the extreme illness under which I was suffering at the time of writing the report." This excuse, taken into consideration with the uncalled-for comments injected into the original report, has been conclusive proof to the author in his patient investigation of this case, that professional zeal was not the only motive that inspired the engineer-in-chief, and that in his effort to disparage his predecessor he rather stultified himself.

Chief Engineer Haswell, not giving satisfaction as an inspector of machinery to the new administration of the steam department, was eventually relieved from that duty and placed on waiting orders, the *San Jacinto* being completed and fitted for sea under the supervision of Chief Engineer Henry Hunt. When the ship was ready for sea, Mr. Haswell was ordered to her, his orders being brought about by the following recommendation, which explains itself fully as to animus and motives:

OFFICE OF THE ENGINEER-IN-CHIEF, U. S. N.,
August 25, 1851.

SIR: I respectfully recommend that chief engineer Henry Hunt be detached from the United States steamer *San Jacinto*, and ordered to the United States steamer *Fulton*; and that chief engineer Charles H. Haswell, now waiting orders at New York, be ordered to the United States steamer *San Jacinto*.

The propriety of the above recommendations will be obvious from the following considerations:

The machinery of the *San Jacinto* was designed by Mr. Haswell, and has been executed (with the exception of the propeller) in conformity with those designs. Upon my acceptance of the office of engineer-in-chief, the machinery of the *San Jacinto* was one of the first things that came under my notice, and struck me so entirely unfavorably, that I reported my opinion to the bureau, with the recommendation that a board of chief engineers be ordered to examine it, and report their opinion. The bureau acted on this recommendation, and the resulting report of the board completely sustained my own views; their condemnation of the engines and propeller was full and unlimited, while, with a view to save the vessel from utter failure, the board proposed a new propeller of such proportions as the mal-design of the machinery had rendered necessary. This report was approved by the bureau, the new propeller was made in conformity with it, and is at present fitted to the vessel now about completed.

As the professional reputation of Mr. Haswell is involved in the performance of the machinery of this vessel, the propriety of sending him to sea in charge of it, instead of in charge of chief engineer Hunt, who was one of the board that condemned it, is too apparent for argument.

Furthermore, the *Fulton* has machinery designed by me, and

executed in conformity with my instructions; and as it is necessary, owing to the limited number of chief engineers in the service, that Mr. Haswell be ordered either to the *San Jacinto* or *Fulton*, as he is the only chief engineer unemployed, the impropriety of putting him in charge of machinery designed by one who was compelled by his position and sense of duty to the disagreeable task of pointing out the defects of, and condemning Mr. Haswell's machinery, cannot fail to be properly appreciated.

Independently of the above considerations, the health of Mr. Hunt is such as to utterly incapacitate him for a long cruise, while he is sufficiently able to perform the short runs which will probably constitute the chief duty of the *Fulton*.

I have, therefore, in justice and delicacy to all parties, to conclude with the suggestion that the detachment of Mr. Hunt from the *San Jacinto* and ordering to the *Fulton*, and the ordering of Mr. Haswell to the *San Jacinto*, be made, to take effect on the 15th September next, which will give sufficient time for the performance of the trial trip of the *San Jacinto*, and the putting her in the hands of Mr. Haswell with her machinery in complete order.

I have the honor to be, sir, very respectfully your obedient servant.

CHAS. B. STUART,
Engineer-in-Chief.
Per B. F. ISHERWOOD,
Chief Engineer.

Com. CHAS. WM. SKINNER,
Chief of Bureau of Construction, &c.

At that time Mr. Haswell was a confirmed invalid from a torpid liver and chronic dyspepsia, which caused his subjection to a medical survey, two of the three members of the medical board reporting him unfit for sea service. When this report reached the Department the Secretary was absent and the Secretary of War was acting in his stead; that official, although he had said in private conversation that Mr. Haswell was unfit for service, inadvertantly signed a dissent from the decision of the medical board, which the chief clerk, had laid before him with all the letters of the day. As soon as the *San Jacinto* was put in commission, the surgeon reported

Mr. Haswell as being unfit for sea duty, and not long afterward the surgeon and his assistant joined in a report to the same effect. No notice of these reports being taken, Mr. Haswell wrote to Commodore Morris, with whom he had been associated for several years, saying that he would be forced to resign on account of his health, but he was dissuaded from that by the commodore obtaining from the Secretary of the Navy a promise that in case the chief engineer's health did not improve by the time the vessel arrived at Gibraltar he would be invalided home, upon which assurance Mr. Haswell agreed to remain in the ship.

When the ship was about to sail, the surgeon and commanding officer both reported that Mr. Haswell was unable to proceed, and he, fearing that his friend, Commodore Morris, would think he had been instrumental in obtaining these reports, and thus had broken faith both with him and the agreement with the Secretary as to his remaining in the ship, telegraphed to Commodore Morris that the reports were not made at his instance. The commodore went to the Secretary, who was in the act of signing the order relieving Haswell from duty, and by exhibiting the telegram convinced him that the detachment was unnecessary. In this manner it happened that from an over sensitiveness regarding the estimate of his integrity he remained in the ship, and the misunderstanding of the telegram lost him his detachment, and in the end his commission as well. Three days after the vessel sailed he was put on the sick list and relieved from duty. Upon the arrival of the vessel at Cadiz he proceeded to Gibraltar to get the necessary orders for detachment from the commander-in-chief of the station, in accordance with the promise of the Secretary of the Navy, but that officer declined to take any action in the matter.

Sick, relieved from duty, denied the immunity of four reports of surgeons as to his physical unfitness, the promise of the Secretary of the Navy ignored, disgusted with his treatment, and mentally depressed, Chief Engineer Haswell left his ship on his own responsibility and returned to his own country, for which act, regardless of his past invaluable services for the steam navy, he was dropped from the rolls of the navy, the date of this action of the Department being May 14, 1852. Some years later (in 1859) the President at the close of a session of Congress sent his name to the

Senate for confirmation as a chief engineer in his former position, but Congress adjourned before the nomination was reached, and Mr. Haswell made no effort to have the matter revived, as he was very profitably employed at the time.

The engineer corps owes much to Mr. Haswell as its organizer and steady champion, and we of this day cannot but wonder at the great progress he made considering his limited official power and the intense prejudice he had to struggle against. Not only were many of the most influential of the old naval officers bitterly opposed to the invasion of steam into the domain they regarded as their own, but at least one Secretary of the Navy shared the same conservative sentiment. Mr. Secretary Paulding, who ruled the Navy Department when the steam navy was very young, set naval progress back a number of years by blocking the attempts to introduce the new power. In his diary he complained of being *steamed* to death, and wrote that he "never would consent to see our grand old ships supplanted by these new and ugly sea-monsters," the sea-monsters referred to especially being the beautiful steamers *Mississippi* and *Missouri*.

Mr. Haswell was master of the engineering science of his time and fully appreciated the magnitude of the change in naval methods meant by the introduction of steam, never missing an opportunity to teach and preach his belief. Without having any faith in Lieutenant Hunter's scheme of submerged propulsion, he nevertheless gave that officer much aid in his projects and furnished him with designs for machinery simply because Hunter needed steam, and his vessels, although fore-doomed to failure, were still additions to the steam navy. Captain Stockton, also, found in him a staunch supporter, always ready to supply professional facts and arguments in refutation of the many objections raised by the old conservatives against Stockton's scheme for a war-steamer.

Especially fortunate was Mr. Haswell in being associated with Captain M. C. Perry at the beginning of his naval career, for in him he found a friend of his profession and a supporter broadminded enough to realize that a new era in naval construction had dawned, and that the interests of the naval service demanded its recognition to the subordination of all the prejudices of the past. To quote from Captain Perry's biographer, he, "first, last, and always honored the engineer and believed in his equal possession, with the line officers, of all the soldierly virtues, notwithstanding that the man at the lever, out of sight of the enemy, must needs lack the thrilling excitement of the officers on deck. He felt that courage in the engine-room had even a finer moral strain than the more physically exciting passions of the deck.''

As this is probably the last appearance in this history of the eminent engineer who was the first leader and pioneer of the naval engineer corps, except by occasional reference to his works, it is fitting that this chapter should close with a brief review of his career and achievements.

Charles H. Haswell was born in the city of New York in the year 1809, and from earliest youth exhibited a decided talent for mechanical investigations and pursuits, having at the age of fifteen constructed a small fire-engine and later a steam engine of such excellence that both were readily disposed of to pecuniary advantage. After receiving a classical education, he entered upon the calling to which his natural bent directed by entering the employ of the engineering establishment of James P. Allaire of New York, where he developed into a thorough competent theoretical and practical mechanical engineer. In 1836, when twenty-seven years of age, and with the reputation of being one of the best scientific engineers in New York, he was appointed by the Navy Department as superintending engineer and later chief engineer of the steamer *Fulton*, his naval career in connection with that vessel and others having already been told. While connected with the *Fulton* at the New York navy yard Mr. Haswell (in 1837) lengthened the gig of the sloop-of-war *Ontario* and fitted in it a small engine and boiler with which the boat was run about the harbor; this was undoubtedly the first successful essay of a steam launch, notwithstanding the many claims that have been put forth regarding the origin of that useful application of steam.

In 1846, while engineer-in-chief of the navy, Mr. Haswell conceived the idea of placing zinc slabs in marine boilers to divert oxidation from their plates and had zinc placed in the boilers of the *Princeton* that year for the same purpose. He also had zinc placed in the hold of an iron steamer, the *Legare* of the Revenue Marine fleet, with the same object in view. This use of zinc was nearly thirty years before it was tried in England as a new invention.

Since leaving the naval service in 1852, Mr. Haswell has been actively engaged in the professions of civil and mechanical engineering in his native city. He has been a Member and President of the Common Council of the city of New York; a trustee of the New York and Brooklyn bridge; Surveyor of steamers for Lloyd's and the Underwriters of New York, Boston and Philadelphia; Consulting Engineer for the Health Department, Quarantine Commission, and Department of Public Charities and Correction of New York; etc., etc. He designed and superintended the construction of the long crib at Hart's Island, and the filling in of Hoffman's Island and the erection of buildings on same; designed and superintended many commercial steamers, foundations for some of the heaviest buildings in New York, tests of water works plants, etc. One of his greatest works is the volume of rules and formula pertaining to mathematics, mechanics and physics, compiled in the engineer's handbook that bears his name, a book so invaluable that it has reached its fifty-ninth edition and has won the name of the "Engineer's Bible." Mr. Haswell is an honorary life member of the American Society of Naval Engineers; a member of the American Society of Civil Engineers; the Institution of Civil Engineers, and the Institution of Naval Architects of England; the Engineer's Club of Philadelphia, the New York Academy of Sciences, the American Institute of Architects, the New York Microscopical Society, etc., etc.

CHAPTER IX.

"Into the city of Kambalu,
By the road that leadeth to Ispahan
At the head of his dusty caravan,
Laden with treasures from realms afar.
Baldacca and Kelat and Kandahar,
Rode the great captain Alau."
—LONGFELLOW.

The Expedition to Japan and Treaty with That Country—Services of Engineers in the Expedition—Value of Steamers in Impressing the Japanese—Other Naval Affairs in the Far East.

THE opening of the ports of Japan to the world's commerce was one of the direct sequences of the settlement of California by citizens of the United States, for the latter event was accompanied with an immediate marine traffic in the Pacific and this in turn demanded the establishment of coaling ports, harbors of refuge, and other necessities to navigation on all the shores of that ocean. An extensive trade with China already existed, and the American whale fisheries in Asiatic waters gave employment to ten thousand men and represented an investment of seventeen million dollars. The march of commercial progress demanded that the veil of mystery and exclusiveness so long drawn over the Japanese islands be removed and the coasts of that country be opened and free to the world's shipping. The only port in Japan where foreigners were allowed to touch was Nagasaki in the southern part of the empire, where a Dutch trading station was permitted to exist under almost penal conditions, allowing annual visits from a single ship, bringing goods for exchange. To this place, any sailors who might be shipwrecked on the Japanese coast, and they were numerous, were conveyed and kept in close confinement until the time arrived for sending them out of the country by the Dutch merchantman.

In 1849, Commander James Glynn, U. S. Navy, in the brig *Preble* visited Nagasaki to demand the release of some American sailors known to be imprisoned there, and succeeded in his mission although not without much difficulty, as the authorities were very loth to have anything to do with a foreigner, other than the lonely dutch trader. While there, Glynn made a careful study of Japanese affairs and when he returned to the United States early in 1851 he represented to the Navy Department that the time was ripe for either forcing or flattering Japan into the brotherhood of nations, urging furthermore that he be sent on a diplomatic mission with that object in view. The idea was well received, but when steps were taken to organize a squadron sufficiently large to lend force and dignity to the expedition, Glynn found himself speedily outranked, and had to step aside for his seniors who commanded larger ships; to him, however, belongs the credit for beginning the movement which ended in the great triumph of Matthew C. Perry. In June, 1851, Commodore Aulick, commissioned by Secretary of State, Daniel Webster to negotiate a treaty with Japan, sailed for the East India station in the new side-wheel steamer *Susquehanna*, some of the details of this first voyage having been related in a former chapter.

Soon after arriving on the station; late in the year, Commodore Aulick was abruptly recalled, being temporarily relieved by Commander Franklin Buchanan of the flagship and later by Commodore M. C. Perry. The direct cause for Aulick's detachment was alleged violation of naval orders in having taken his son to sea with him as a passenger, and for having stated that he had been obliged to defray the expense of carrying the Brazilian minister, Macedo, from the United States to his own country. Commodore Aulick's friends asserted that Perry had deliberately undermined him, and the subject became one of those factional controversies which have from time to time become notorious in our naval annals. The fact that Perry had for some time been making a study of matters relating to Japan and its people, gave strength to the charge that he had sacrificed a brother captain to his own ambition, but it is also a matter of official record that he was at the same time an applicant for the command of the Mediterranean squadron and felt himself aggrieved when ordered to the Far East. His biographer publishes a long letter addressed to the Secretary of the Navy, dated December 3, 1851, in which Perry speaks of the command of the Mediterranean squadron as his fondest ambition, and objects to the proposed detail to Japan on the ground that it would be a degradation in rank for him to relieve Aulick who had served under him in a squadron some years before. This seems to clear Commodore Perry of any charge of double-dealing in the matter; at any rate the quarrel has no place in this book, and would not be referred to were it not necessary for the sake of thoroughness, to outline the steps leading up to, what may be fairly considered, the proudest achievement of the American navy.

On the 24th of January, 1852, Perry received orders to assume command of the East India squadron, and he at once began vigorously to make all necessary preparations for impressing the Japanese with the power and resources of the nation whose friendship they were asked to accept. His steam favorite the *Mississippi* was given for his flagship, and in compliance with his urgent request that he have more steamers, the *Princeton* and *Alleghany*, both then under extensive repairs, were promised. The mishaps to these vessels and their eventual failure to become part of the expedition are matters that have already been told. Perry had coal and ships' stores sent out in sailing vessels and by appealing to the mechanical industries of the country he made a vast collection of the implements of civilization with which to demonstrate to the Japanese the benefits they would derive from intercourse with foreign nations. Among other things he had a small locomotive and car, with rails to lay a circular track upon which to operate; agricultural machinery, telegraphic instruments, arms, sewing machines, printing presses, metal-working machinery, tools of various kinds, and all sorts of labor saving appliances. In a word, Perry drew upon the field of the engineer for his most potent arguments, and by that sign he conquered a peace that never could have been achieved by mere show of force or use of arms.

Wearied of delays, Perry finally sailed from Norfolk with only the *Mississippi* on the 24th of November, 1852, and proceeded to his station by way of Madeira and the Cape of Good Hope, arriving at Hong Kong on the 6th of April, 1853, and at Shanghai on May 4th. His flag was transferred to the *Susquehanna* on May 17, that vessel being the designated flagship of the squadron. Before going to the principal Japanese islands a visit was made to the Riu Kiu (also spelled Lew Chew and Loo Choo) and the Bonin islands. At Napa in Riu Kiu the telegraphic, photographic, and other appliances were tested to make sure that no failures would occur later. The artist, Mr. Brown, who had charge of the daguerrotype outfit, not being a specialist in that particular art, had some trouble in his preliminary work and called to his aid Third Assistant Engineer Edward D. Robie of the *Mississippi*, who from a love for scientific matters had made himself an expert in this art. He succeeded at his first attempt with the apparatus, and took what is supposed to be the first daguerrotype ever made in the far east; it being a picture of Commodore Perry standing at the gateway of a native temple. Perry was delighted with Robie's work and remarked to him, "I believe that you engineers can do anything."

Finally the squadron, then consisting of the steamers *Mississippi* and *Susquehanna* and the sailing sloops of war *Saratoga* and *Plymouth*, proceeded northward and on the 7th of July entered Yeddo Bay and came to anchor off the village of Uraga. Foreign ships were no curiosity in those waters even then. Seven years before, Commodore Biddle with the ship-of-the-line *Columbus* and sloop-of-war *Vincennes* had visited the same spot, in the hope of securing permission for his countrymen to trade, but was turned away with a positive refusal. Many whalers and merchant vessels had been there, sometimes seeking in vain for commercial intercourse with the people; sometimes driven in by stress of weather to be refused a harbor of refuge, and sometimes on errands of mercy bringing home Japanese waifs picked up adrift at sea in their junks. In 1848 foreign shipping in the seas about Japan had so increased that the fact was noted as a remarkable phenomenon by the native chroniclers, and in 1850 it had been made a matter of grave report to the great officials of the empire that no less than eighty-six of the "black ships of the *i-jin*" had been counted passing Matsumaé within the space of a single year.

If foreign ships were familiar objects, steamers were not, for Perry's two steam frigates were the first craft of the kind to be seen in Japanese waters and their appearance excited the utmost consternation among the intelligent; for the Japanese are of an investigating and mechanical turn of mind, and all who were above ascribing the movements of the mysterious ships without sails to the spirits of evil, immediately reasoned that they must have some motive power, to themselves unknown, but about which, it would be good to learn. The ignorant peasants supposed that the foreign barbarians had succeeded in imprisoning volcanoes in their ships, or, refusing to believe the evidence of their own eyes, comforted each other with the assurance that the uncanny spectacle was simply a mirage created by the breath of clams and would soon pass away.

Commodore Perry had thoroughly informed himself of the ceremonial customs of Japan, and used his knowledge of the extravagant etiquette observed by the people of that country to good and successful purpose. He secluded himself in his cabin and played Mikado and Sho-gun to perfection, first to the provocation, and finally to the amazement and awe, of the local officials of constantly increasing rank who visited the flagship, only to be snubbed by refusals to see the chief barbarian. Even the governor of the district learned to his mortification and dismay that he was not a personage important enough to be allowed to meet the mysterious power hidden behind the cabin doors. Orders to depart were met only by a movement of the ships further up the bay towards Yedo; offers to supply food and water in the hope that the unwelcome visitors would then leave were politely declined, and the natives were forced into accepting the proposal offered; namely, of designating an official of proper rank to meet the barbarian and listen to what he had to say. On the 14th of July, all arrangements having been completed, Perry first showed himself and went on shore with a large suite of officers and four hundred marines and sailors to meet the two commissioners appointed to deal with him. The whole affair was conducted studiously for theatrical effect to impress the natives with the grandeur and importance of the event, no detail of dress or ceremony likely to appeal to the sensibilities of the Japanese being omitted. A letter from the President of the United States to the "Emperor of Japan" asking that friendly relations between the two nations be established was delivered to the commissioners with all pomp and solemnity, but with few words, and the visitors withdrew, Perry saying that he would allow ample time for consideration and would return the following spring for an answer.

The vessels proceeded southward to Hong Kong, where the *Powhatan*, which had left the United States in March to join the squadron in place of the discarded *Princeton*, and some of the sailing vessels belonging to the station were met. Headquarters for the Japanese expedition were established at Macao, where a house was rented and facilities furnished the members of the expedition for developing their sketches and writing reports of their observations. A number of specialists were attached to the different ships with appointments as master's mates in order that they would be subject to naval discipline, thereby avoiding the friction always resulting from joint naval and civil enterprises afloat. Principal among these were Messrs. Heine and Brown, the water-color artists whose beautiful pictures so embellish Commodore Perry's report, and Mr. Bayard Taylor, the "landscape painter in words." Besides the specialists a number of officers belonging regularly to the navy contributed much valuable material for the report of the expedition, notable among these being Surgeon Daniel S. Green and Chaplain George Jones. A number of the most accurate drawings relating to Japanese boat building and marine affairs published in the report, were made by Third Assistant Engineer Mortimer Kellogg of the *Powhatan*.

In January 1854 the squadron again moved northward, consisting of the steamers *Powhatan*, *Susquehanna* and *Mississippi*, and the sloops-of-war *Macedonian*, *Vandalia*, *Plymouth* and *Saratoga;* the store-ships *Supply*, *Lexington* and *Southampton*, with coal and provisions for the ships, and presents for the Japanese government, were also in company. On the 11th of February the greater part of this force had assembled off Yedo Bay, anchoring on the 13th off Yokosuke, where the great navy yard of New Japan is now located. The mystery play began again by Perry retiring from public view and holding the visiting officials at a respectful and chilly distance. While the Japanese were exhausting their efforts to induce the foreigners to go away and leave them in peace, boats were kept busy sounding and surveying the adjacent waters and giving intelligible names to the prominent features of the region; one name thus bestowed, Mississippi Bay, so well known to all visitors to Japan, will serve for all time to perpetuate in a far country the name of the historical old steamer whose keel was the first of foreign build to disturb its waters.

The following is a list of the officers of the engineer corps serving in this squadron on the expedition which is the principal subject of this chapter:

OFFICE.	NAME.	SHIP.
Chief Engineer..................................	Jesse Gay.................	Mississippi.
" "	Samuel Archbold......	Susquehanna.
" "	George Sewell...........	Powhatan.
First Assistant Engineer....................	John P. Whipple......	Powhatan.
" " "	Robert Danby...........	Mississippi.
" " "	William Holland...	Mississippi.
" " "	George F. Hebard.......	Susquehanna.
" " "	Henry H. Stewart......	Susquehanna.
Second Assistant Engineer..................	John Faron...............	Powhatan.
" " "	George T. W. Logan..	Mississippi.
" " "	George Gideon, Jr......	Powhatan.
" " "	Edward Fithian.........	Susquehanna.
" " "	Eli Crosby.................	Susquehanna.
" " "	William Henry King..	Powhatan.
" " "	J. C. E. Lawrence.....	Susquehanna.
" " "	Wm. H. Rutherford...	Mississippi.
" " "	George W. Alexander.	Mississippi.
Third Assistant Engineer...................	Thomas A Shock.......	Susquehanna.
" " "	William S. Stamm.....	Powhatan.
" " "	Stephen D. Hibbert....	Susquehanna.
" " "	Mortimer Kellogg......	Powhatan.
" " "	Henry Fauth.............	Powhatan.
" " "	Edward D. Robie......	Mississippi.
" " "	LeRoy Arnold...........	Powhatan.
" " "	John D. Mercer.........	Mississippi.

On the 24th of February, Perry, to convince the Japanese that he was in earnest and would not be put off, moved six of the ships up the Bay to within hearing of the temple bells of Yeddo and anchored not far above Kanagawa. This move had the desired effect, for the Sho-gun's government sent word in post haste, "If the American ships come to Yeddo it will be a national disgrace. Stop them, and make the treaty at Kanagawa." Yokohama, a small fishing village across an arm of the bay from Kanagawa, was finally fixed upon as the place for the negotiations and there the Japanese erected the necessary buildings for the ceremony, the enclosure about them embracing the present location of the Custom House and British Consulate in the cosmopolitan city that Yokohama has now become.

On the 8th of March Perry landed with five hundred armed men, and a glittering staff of officers in full uniform, the same ceremonial display and scrupulous etiquette being observed which had so impressed the natives on the occasion of his former visit. The first formalities having been performed with becoming splendor and, dignity, the discussion of what was wanted was conducted more at leisure, the remainder of that month being thus consumed before a treaty was finally agreed to and signed. This treaty, which was signed on March 31st, conceded little to the Americans, but served as the thin end of the wedge for great possibilities thereafter. By its terms the Japanese agreed to treat kindly shipwrecked mariners; gave permission for ships to buy fuel, water, provisions, and other needed stores, and specified the ports of Simoda and Hakodate as places where foreign ships might anchor for repairs or to find refuge from storms. Trade in other than necessary ship supplies and permission to reside in the country were refused. These privileges, together with many others, and the opening of several treaty ports, followed in due time through the efforts of other diplomats.

While negotiations were going on at Yokohama the great collection of presents brought for the "Emperor," but by error given to the Sho-gun, was landed and displayed to the officials and people. The railway track, 369 feet in circumference, was laid by Chief Engineer Gay of the *Mississippi* and on it the little locomotive and car were daily operated, under the superintendence of Engineer Robert Danby of the same steamer, to the great interest and delight of the people. The telegraph line, a mile long, was another source of wonder and shrewd investigation on the part of the inquisitive and intelligent Japanese. This was in charge of two telegraphers named Draper and Williams, rated as master's mates, but was operated part of the time by engineers Alexander and Robie, whom Commodore Perry had sent ashore in New York in 1852 for a month, for the express purpose of learning telegraphy. A wealth of other useful articles—stoves, clocks, maps, books, and machinery of all kinds—were displayed, and their uses explained, this exhibition of mechanical appliances did more to win the people over to the fact that it would be beneficial to them to become neighbourly with other nations than all the arguments and bluster in the world. From the Japanese accounts of this most important event in their national history, it appears that the determining factors in Perry's success were his steamships and the machinery he brought with him. With a decided bent for the mechanic arts themselves, the Japanese were quick to see that the foreigners were far ahead of them in that respect, and they were willing to lay aside their ideas of exclusiveness for the opportunity of learning what the strangers had to teach.

The world at large knows of the wonderful results which sprung from the modest beginning above outlined, for the story of Japan is the most marvelous in all the histories of the nations. As Perry saw Japan, the people of that country were engulfed in the darkness and ignorance of a despotism fixed upon them by an unchanging and pitiless feudal domination of twenty centuries duration, a condition beside which the state of society existing along the banks of the Rhine in the middle of the Dark Ages would appear enlightened by contrast. From such a forbidding prospect the mind is dazed as it turns to look at New Japan with its railways, telegraph, post offices, factories, school-houses, and church-steeples, all as familiar objects to the people as they are to the dwellers in either Old or New England. The feudal system abolished; a parliamentary form of government established; the hundreds of thousands of idle and predatory knights deprived of their tyrannical prerogatives and transformed into industrious men, and the yoke of serfdom removed from the necks of four-fifths of the population of the empire are examples of the miracles that have been wrought in that wonderful land within the memory of men but little past middle age.

Having placed herself in the foremost rank of the civilized nations by making full use of the heritage of the ages conferred upon her, Japan has made herself the champion of modern enlightenment and assumed the task of breaking down Chinese conservatism and of introducing the methods of Western civilization by force into the greatest and most obstinate country that has ever been a barrier to the world's progress. By availing themselves of Western discipline, tactics and humane methods of warfare the brave little Japanese have been able to prevail against great numerical odds and by a series of victories, each more brilliant than its predecessor, have proceeded uninterruptedly on their mission of carrying enlightment and civilization into the Dark East. Great as may be the victory to Japan as a nation, its moral and far-reaching effects will be much greater for the well-being of the world. When New Japan has celebrated her victories and duly honored her great captains who achieved them, she cannot pay a more appropriate tribute to the first cause that made her modern power possible, than by erecting on the strand at Yokohama a statue of Matthew C. Perry, looking outward upon the water over which his steamers brought Western methods into Japanese history. And on the pedestal of that statue should be carved an image of a steamship, or some other symbol of the mechanic arts, as the true sign of the beginning of the greatness of New Japan; the sign by which she was conquered and by which she in turn has conquered.

Following the completion of negotiations in Japan, Perry's squadron began to disband, the Commodore himself proceeding home by way of Europe in a Peninsular and Oriental mail steamer—the *Hindustan*. The *Mississippi* left Hong Kong on the 12th of September and after touching at Simoda in Japan began the long voyage homeward by way of Honolulu and Rio de Janeiro. She arrived at New York the 23d of April, 1855, having circumnavigated the globe during her absence and placed herself on record as the second steam vessel of the United States navy to do so. The *Susquehanna* also returned home by way of the Pacific and South America, her arrival in Philadelphia on the 10th of March giving her the honor of being the first American naval steamer to make a cruise around the world.

The home-coming ships brought with them many presents, now in the Smithsonian Institution at Washington, illustrative of the skill of artists and artisans of Japan, consisting of bronze, ivory, porcelain, and other work. More appropriate even were the blocks of carved and inscribed stone from different parts of Japan given for the Washington monument and which may now be seen in the walls of that structure. From Napa in Riu Kiu came as a gift the large bronze bell which for so many years has hung in its little temple in the grounds of the Naval Academy. The date of founding inscribed on this bell corresponds to the year 1456, A. D., and part of the inscription on it, as translated by Giro Kunitomo, a Japanese student at the academy, reads as follows:

"This beautiful bell has been founded, and hung in the tower of the temple. It will awaken dreams of superstition. If one will bear in mind to act rightly and truly, and the Lords and the Ministers will do justice in a body, the barbarians will never come to invade. The sound of the bell will convey the virtue of Fushi, and will echo like the song of Tsuirai; and the benevolence of the Lords will continue forever like those echoes."

Regardless of the prediction thus written in brass, the barbarians not only came but carried the bell away with them.

The Tai-ping rebellion being in progress in China at the time now being dealt with, the United States vessels remaining in that region were kept actively employed in protecting the lives and property of American citizens. Piracy became rampant along the coasts and compelled much dangerous service in seeking out the piratical junks and capturing them in hand-to-hand conflicts, a chartered steamer of light draft, named the *Queen*, being especially active in this work. Referring to this disagreeable service, the Secretary of the Navy wrote in his annual report for 1855: "In these several encounters, the officers and men have conducted themselves gallantly, and honorable mention is made of Lieutenants Pegram, Preble, Rolando, E. Y. McCauley, and Sproston; Assistant Engineers Stamm and Kellogg; Acting Masters' Mates J. P. Williams and S. R. Craig; and Private Benjamin Adamson, of the Marine Corps, who was dangerously wounded. I deem this a proper occasion to suggest the purchase or building of one or two steamers of light draught, to be used in the Chinese rivers, as indispensable for the protection of the immense property belonging to citizens of the United States in China."

In July, 1855, while entering the harbor of Hong Kong, the *Powhatan* by accident had the starboard air-pump machinery so completely wrecked that the ship was seemingly disabled for an indefinite time. An international complication with Spain at the time made it probable that the next mail would bring news of a state of war, and the presence of a Spanish war vessel in Hong Kong harbor rendered the helpless condition of the *Powhatan* a source of most serious apprehension. In this emergency Mr. George Sewell, her chief engineer, rigged up a connection between the two engines, so that the port engine did the condensing of steam for the disabled starboard engine, the work being completed within forty-eight hours after the breakdown and the *Powhatan* made ready for any service, including battle if necessary. Officers of the British war-steamer *Rattler*, who attended a trial trip to test the success of Mr. Sewell's emergency makeshift, remarked that a chief engineer in their navy would be knighted for rendering service of such value in a similar emergency. An idea of the extent of the difficulty overcome by this ingenious engineer may be gained from the fact that ten weeks were consumed in permanently repairing the damages.

CHAPTER X.

"Our tall ships have souls, and plow with Reason up the deeps."
   OGILBY, *Translation of the Odyssey.*

End of the Experimental, and Beginning of the Creative Period of the American Steam Navy—The FRANKLIN—The MERRIMAC class of Screw Frigates—The NIAGARA—Services of Chief Engineer Everett in connection with the Atlantic Cable Laid by the NIAGARA—The HARTFORD class of Large Screw Sloops—Mr. Archbold succeeds Mr. Martin as Engineer-in-Chief—The MOHICAN class—The PAWNEE—The Paraguay Expedition—Small Steamers Purchased for the Navy—Project to Convert Old Line-of-Battle Ships into Steam Frigates.

ALL the vessels of the early steam period of our navy have now been described with the exception of the *John Hancock*, a small screw-steamer of 208 tons, built at the Boston Navy Yard in 1850, intended to serve the double purpose of a steam tug and water-boat for that station. Her length was 113 feet; breadth of beam, 22 feet; mean draft, 8 feet. The machinery was designed by Mr. Charles W. Copeland and built at the Washington Navy Yard by Mr. William M. Ellis, the civilian chief engineer of the yard. There were two oscillating non-condensing cylinders, 20 inches in diameter and 21 inches stroke, suspended over the shaft, and one iron return-flue boiler 22 feet long, containing 28 square feet of grate surface and 755 square feet of heating surface. The cost of the vessel was $20,550.72, of which sum $5,622.59 was charged to the engine and propeller, and $2,428.13 to the boiler and fittings. In 1851 the *Hancock* was used as a practice steamer for midshipmen at the Naval Academy, and later in the same year made a short cruise to the Gulf of Mexico.

In 1852 she was hauled into a ship-house at the Boston Navy Yard and remodeled, being cut in two and lengthened 38 feet, the change resulting in a trim bark-rigged steamer rated as of 382 tons burden. The engines were altered to low-pressure, with Pirsson's condenser, the stroke of pistons increased three inches, and the boiler replaced by two of the Martin vertical water-tube type, aggregating 70 square feet of grate surface and 2,280 square feet of heating surface. The alterations in machinery were made by Harrison Loring, Boston, from plans supplied by Chief Engineer D. B. Martin, U. S. Navy. When completed, the new steamer proceeded to the Pacific Ocean and was employed for about three years on surveying duty in the North Pacific, Bering and China seas, under the command of Lieutenant John Rodgers, Messrs. Elbridge Lawton and David B. Macomb being the senior engineers. After making a survey of Bering Sea the *John Hancock* was put out of commission at San Francisco and remained there as a receiving ship or in ordinary until 1865, when she was sold.

Reference has already been made to the fact that advocates of steam power for naval purposes were compelled to face a most discouraging argument based upon the unprotected condition of machinery in paddle-wheel steamers. Ericsson had proved with the *Princeton* that a ship could be driven by a submerged propeller, but his application of power was new, at least to the navy, and it was many years before the lesson of the *Princeton* was accepted by naval officers as conclusive. The Secretary of the Navy, Mr. Dobbin, had become thoroughly impressed with the necessity for building up a steam navy, and in his annual report for 1853 made an urgent appeal to Congress for authority to begin the immediate construction of six "first-class steam frigate propellers," using the following argument in support of his request:

"Steam is unquestionably the great agent to be used on the ocean, as well for purposes of war as of commerce. The improved system of screw-propellers, instead of side-wheels, is one of the grand *desiderata* to render the use of steam effective in naval warfare—the one being exposed to the shot of the enemy, the other submerged and comparatively secure. When the bayonet was added to the musket the invention was applauded, for placing in the hands of the soldier, at one time, two engines of *destruction;* and the introduction of the screw-propeller has been similarly appreciated, as combining, without confusion, two elements of *progress*— the sail and the steam-engine. Side-wheel steamers are much impaired in their capacity for sailing, and consume too much coal for distant cruises. Those now on hand can be made to answer well for short cruises and for despatch vessels. The screw-propeller, being upon a principle not so much interfering with the sailing

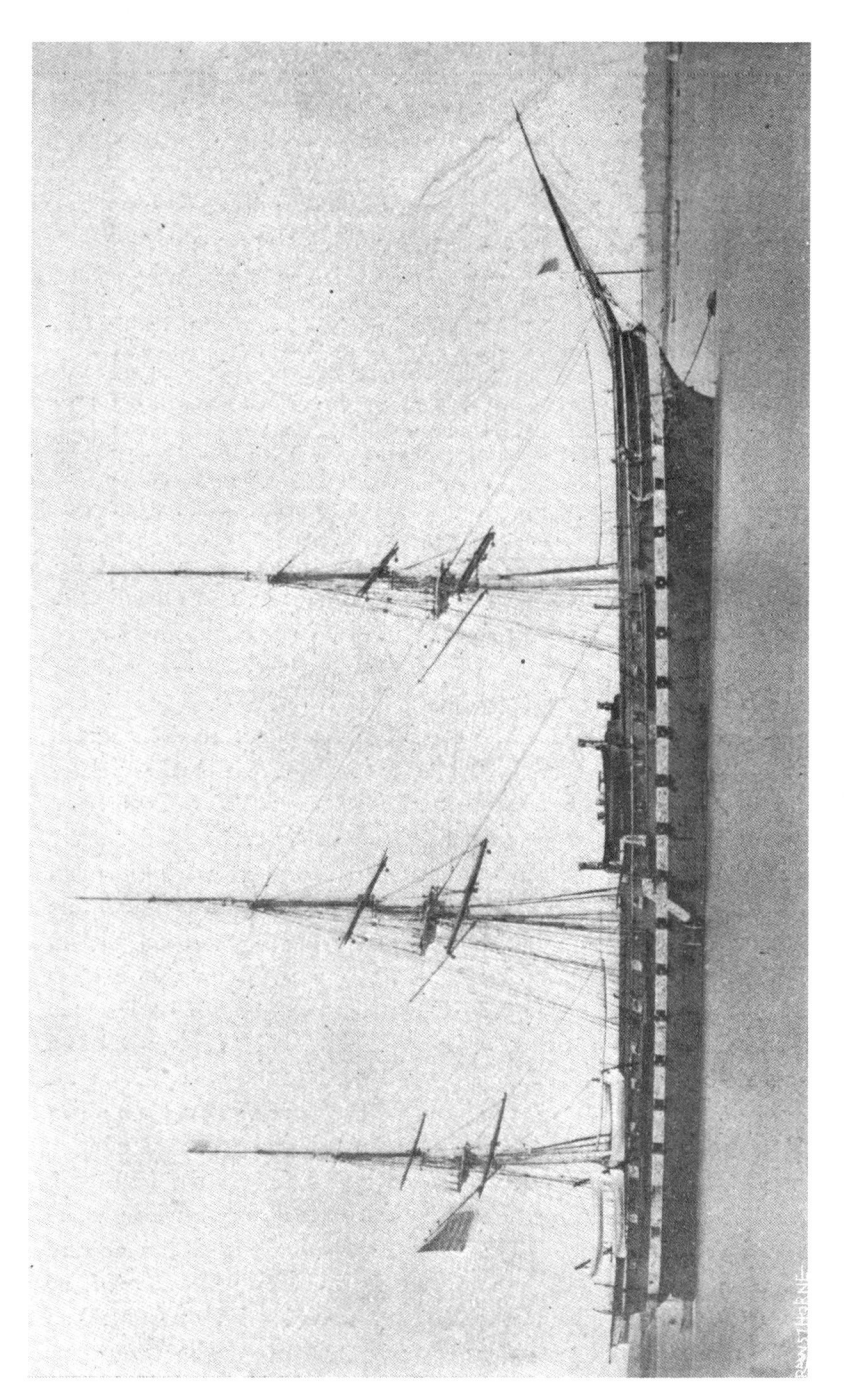

U. S. S. FRANKLIN.

Two telescopic smokepipes lowered below rail.

capacity, with the improved models of the present day, can be so constructed as to sail as well as the best clipper ships, and reserve the use of steam for emergencies when the greatest speed is required, or when, in a calm, a desirable position can be more promptly and surely taken. The great necessary expense incident to the expedition to Japan could have been materially, indeed, one-half curtailed, had it been in the power of the department to have supplied the squadron with screw-propellers instead of the side-wheel steamers, now costing so much from the consumption of coal."

In the same year, 1853, Mr. Dobbin had already begun one screw frigate by using his authority to repair old vessels, the one selected being the old ship-of-the-line *Franklin*, lying at the Kittery Navy Yard. Orders were issued to repair this ship and make such changes in her model as would fit her for a first-class steam frigate. The old ship *Franklin* was built in 1815 at Philadelphia, and was 188 feet long and 50 feet beam. The new *Franklin*, as finished, was 265 feet long on the load water-line, and 53 feet 8 inches beam, dimensions so entirely different from those of the original ship that the process of repairing evidently amounted in reality to building an entirely new hull out of the old material. As the amount of money available each year for repairs was small, work on the *Franklin* progressed slowly, and it was ten years before the condition of the hull warranted a contract for machinery, which will be described later in proper chronological order.

The recommendation of the department regarding steam frigates was favorably received by Congress, and a few months later an act, approved April 6, 1854, authorized the Secretary of the Navy to have constructed "six first-class steam frigates to be provided with screw propellers." These ships were all built by the Government at navy yards as follows: The *Merrimac* at Boston; the *Wabash* at Philadelphia; the *Minnesota* at Washington; the *Roanoke* and *Colorado* at Norfolk, and the *Niagara* at New York. The three first named were launched in 1855 and the three others early in 1856, they being, when completed, the superiors of any war vessels then possessed by any nation in the world. When the first of them went abroad they became objects of admiration and envy to the naval architects of Europe, and their type was quickly copied into other navies, notably that of England, which imitated their construction in the *Orlando*, *Mersey*, and others of that class.

Just at that period the American ship-building industry had reached its highest development; our architects had attained a skill in their profession which made their work famous throughout the world, and lent to the word American, when applied to ships, a peculiar significance, always an accepted guarantee of excellence. Some of the most eminent of the American ship-builders were members of the naval construction corps, which then included such men as Mr. Lenthal, the chief constructor of the navy; the two Delanos; Messrs. Pook and Hanscom, and several others, all famous in their line. To these gentlemen the navy was indebted for the designs which made our new ships the admiration of the world, and so elevated the standard and reputation of the American navy that every officer and man felt an accession of pride at being part of such an organization.

The first five of the ships named were frigate-built, with steam power that was merely auxiliary. They were full ship-rigged, the area of the ten principal sails being about thirty-two times the immersed midship section, which ratio is only slightly less than that observed in the practice of rigging sailing frigates. They were built of seasoned live-oak frames in stock in the navy yards and originally intended for use in old style sailing ships, an adaptation of material that exercised a controlling influence on the lines of the new ships from the necessity of so shaping them that the supply of frame timbers could be worked up without waste. The results, however, were entirely satisfactory as the ships proved to be fast and handy under sail alone, and their steam power was sufficient for the purpose intended—to steam in and out of port or across calm belts, and to lend additional manœuvering qualities in storms and battle.[1]

---

[1] Speaking of the building of these ships, the late Rear Admiral Edward Simpson, in an article published in Harper's Magazine, June, 1886, says: "There were those at that time who, wise beyond their generation, recognized the full meaning of the advent of steam, and saw that it must supplant sails altogether as a motive power for ships. These advocated that new constructions should be provided with full steam-power, with sails as an auxiliary; but the old pride in the sailing ship, with her taut and graceful spars, could not be made to yield at once to the innovation; old traditions pointing to the necessity of full sail-power could not be dispelled; it was considered a sufficient concession to admit steam on any terms, and thus the conservative and temporizing course was adopted of retaining full sail-power, and utilizing steam as an auxiliary."

U. S. S. MERRIMAC, 1856,

From a Lithograph made in London on the occasion of the visit of the *Merrimac* to Southampton. Loaned by Mr. Charles Schroeder, of Portsmouth, Virginia, who was a third assistant engineer on the *Merrimac* during her European cruise in 1856.

Of these vessels the *Merrimack* (or *Merrimac*, as the name is usually spelled), was the type, the others being only slight modifications of the original. The *Wabash* and *Minnesota* differed only from the *Merrimac* in having a few feet more length inserted amidships to give additional space for machinery and fuel, while the *Roanoke* and *Colorado*, exact duplicates of each other, differed from the others mainly in having about one foot more beam. The following table shows the principal dimensions of these frigates as originally built, from which the points of difference may be readily traced:

	MERRIMAC.	WABASH.	MINNESOTA.	ROANOKE.	COLORADO.
Length on load water line, feet and inches....................................	256.9	262.4	264.8½	263.8¼	263.8¼
Beam on same............................	51.4	51.4	51.4	52.6	52.6
Area of immersed midship section, square feet.....................	868.1	868.1	868.1	902.9	902.9
Displacement at load water line, tons......................................	4,635.6	4,774.3	4,833.4	4,772.2	4,772.2
Tonnage.................................	3,200	3,200	3,200	3,400	3,400

The *Merrimac* had two horizontal back-acting engines, the cylinders being on opposite sides of the ship and located at diagonally opposite corners of a rectangle circumscribing the engines, the jet condenser, air pump and hot-well of one cylinder being by the side of the other cylinder, the two piston rods of each cylinder striding the crank shaft. The cylinders were 72 inches in diameter by 3 feet stroke of piston and were designed to make about 45 double strokes per minute. A three-ported slide valve placed horizontally on top of the cylinder and actuated by a rock-shaft was used, expansion being obtained by the use of an independent cut-off valve of the gridiron type. There were four 4-furnace Martin's vertical water-tube boilers of iron, except the tubes which were brass; the grate surface of all boilers was 333.5 square feet and total heating surface 12,537 square feet. The single smoke-pipe was 8 feet in diameter, telescopic to avoid spoiling the appearance of the ship while in port, and stood 65 feet above the grate bars. Each boiler had a system of brass tubes underneath for a feed-water heater, the feed water being pumped through the tubes which were kept hot by the supersalted water being constantly blown off to keep down the saturation, according to the practice of those days. The propeller was a two-bladed Griffith's screw of bronze with spherical hub and blades, adjustable to different pitches, the mean pitch being 25 feet, and diameter of the screw 17 feet 4 inches. This machinery was designed by the contractor, Mr. Robert P. Parrot and built at his works at Cold Springs, New York, under the inspection of Chief Engineer Wm. H. Shock, U. S. Navy, who subsequently superintended its erection on board the vessel at Boston.

The maximum performance of the *Merrimac* in smooth water under steam alone is shown by the following figures:

Speed in knots per hour	8.87
Revolutions of screw per minute	46.7
Steam cut off in fraction of stroke	0.3
Steam pressure in boilers in pounds above atmosphere	13.5
Vacuum (mean) in inches of mercury	24.5
Total horse-power developed by engines	1,294.4
Pounds of coal per hour by square foot of grate	12.74
Pounds of coal per hour per horse-power	3.28

An abstract of the log of the *Merrimac* when under steam alone and in all conditions of wind and weather shows an average speed of 5.25 knots; 36.5 revolutions per minute; 12.8 average steam pressure; 20.4 average vacuum, and a consumption of 3,400 pounds of anthracite coal per hour. A similar set of averages under steam and sail combined shows 7.67 knots; 39.3 revolutions; 12.5 steam pressure; 21 inches of vacuum, and 3,392 pounds of coal per hour.

The *Merrimac* was put in commission in December, 1855, under the command of Captain F. H. Gregory, Mr. Shock being the chief engineer, and for a few months was on special duty on the home coast, going later to Europe where she visited Southampton, Brest, Lisbon, Toulon, and other naval stations, exciting everywhere the admiration of naval experts, for she is said to have been the most beautiful of all the ships of her class. In 1857 she went to the Pacific as the flagship and remained on that station until

1860, her chief engineer being first Mr. R. H. Long and afterward Mr. Alban C. Stimers. In 1860 she returned home and was laid up at the Norfolk navy yard for extensive repairs to her machinery, which was very unsatisfactory. Mr. Charles H. Loring, engineer-in-chief of the navy a few years since, who was the first assistant engineer of the *Merrimac* during the whole period of her service, has written the author regarding her machinery, that the steam log books of the cruise, "contained a record of efforts to overcome inherent defects of design, and of experimental work in different directions, that would be interesting even now, despite its being very ancient history." The arrival of this ship at Norfolk concluded her active career in the United States navy; later chapters dealing with the Civil War will relate the circumstances of her loss to the government, and her career in the hands of her captors.

The *Wabash* had two horizontal condensing cylinders 72 inches in diameter by 3 feet stroke, motion being communicated from the piston rods to the crank by means of a yoke or harp, the once popular steeple-engine form of connection; the piston rods were secured to the large end of the harp, from the opposite, or small end of which the connecting rod reached backward, the crank revolving inside the larger part of the harp, the bottom of the large end of the harp was fitted with a shoe which rode back and forth on a guide-plate. A jet condenser was employed. The steam valves, operated by a Stevenson link from a rock shaft, were flat slide valves with independent cut-off valves on the back of each; these latter were operated by separate eccentrics and consisted in each case of two blocks or plates adjustable by right and left hand screws, being in short, the well-known Meyer expansion valve, which from this application of it came to be generally known in our navy as the "Wabash valve." The boilers were the same in number and type as those of the *Merrimac*, differing slightly in outside dimensions but containing five furnaces instead of four, the grate area of each furnace being proportionately smaller and the total grate area practically the same. The same type of feed-water heater was used. The propeller was a two-bladed true screw of brass, 17 feet 4 inches in diameter and 23 feet pitch, made to disconnect and hoist up in a well in the stern. This machinery was built by Merrick & Sons, Philadelphia, from their own designs and was superintended while under construction by Chief Engineer James W King, U. S. Navy.

The *Wabash* was first commissioned in August, 1856, and served as the flagship of Commodore Hiram Paulding on the home station for about two years, then going to the Mediterranean with the flag of Commodore Lavallette, Mr. King being the first chief engineer and Benjamin F. Garvin the second. She returned home in 1859 and remained in ordinary until the outbreak of the Civil War, when she was put in commission and saw much active service, as outlined in the appendix.

The *Minnesota's* engines were built at the Washington Navy Yard from designs prepared by Engineer-in-Chief D. B. Martin, and furnish a third example of the engine practice of that day. There were two horizontal cylinders of the Penn trunk type, $79\frac{1}{2}$ inches in diameter and 3 feet stroke, the trunks being 33 inches in diameter. Unlike the usual Penn design, these engines had a separate slide valve for the cut-off valve, placed in advance of the main steam valve and working upon a fixed seat of its own. The steam valves were ordinary double-ported slides operated by link motion and located on the sides of the cylinders with faces vertical, while the cut-off valves were above them and horizontal, thus entailing the disadvantage of leaving a considerable space filled with steam after the cut-offs had closed. The boilers were in all respects duplicates of the Martin boilers described in the case of the *Merrimac*, and the propeller was exactly the same as that of the *Wabash*. The first service of the *Minnesota* was on the East India station in 1857–58 and '59 under the command of Captain S. DuPont, the *Mississippi* being the flagship of that squadron at the time.

The engines, boilers and screws of the *Roanoke* and *Colorado* were in all respects the precise duplicates of those of the *Minnesota*, the machinery complete for both ships being built by Anderson, Dulany & Co., (Tredegar Iron Works), Richmond, Virginia, under the superintendence of Chief Engineer W. W. W. Wood, U. S. Navy. The *Colorado* was prepared for sea when completed in 1857, but did very little service besides steaming to Boston, where she was laid up, before the beginning of the war. The *Roanoke* was flagship of the home squadron in 1858, 1859, and the first months of 1860, then being put out of commission and laid up until the war made her services again necessary. A dearth of enlisted men, and the increased cost of maintaining the steam frigates in

U. S. S. NIAGARA, 1857.

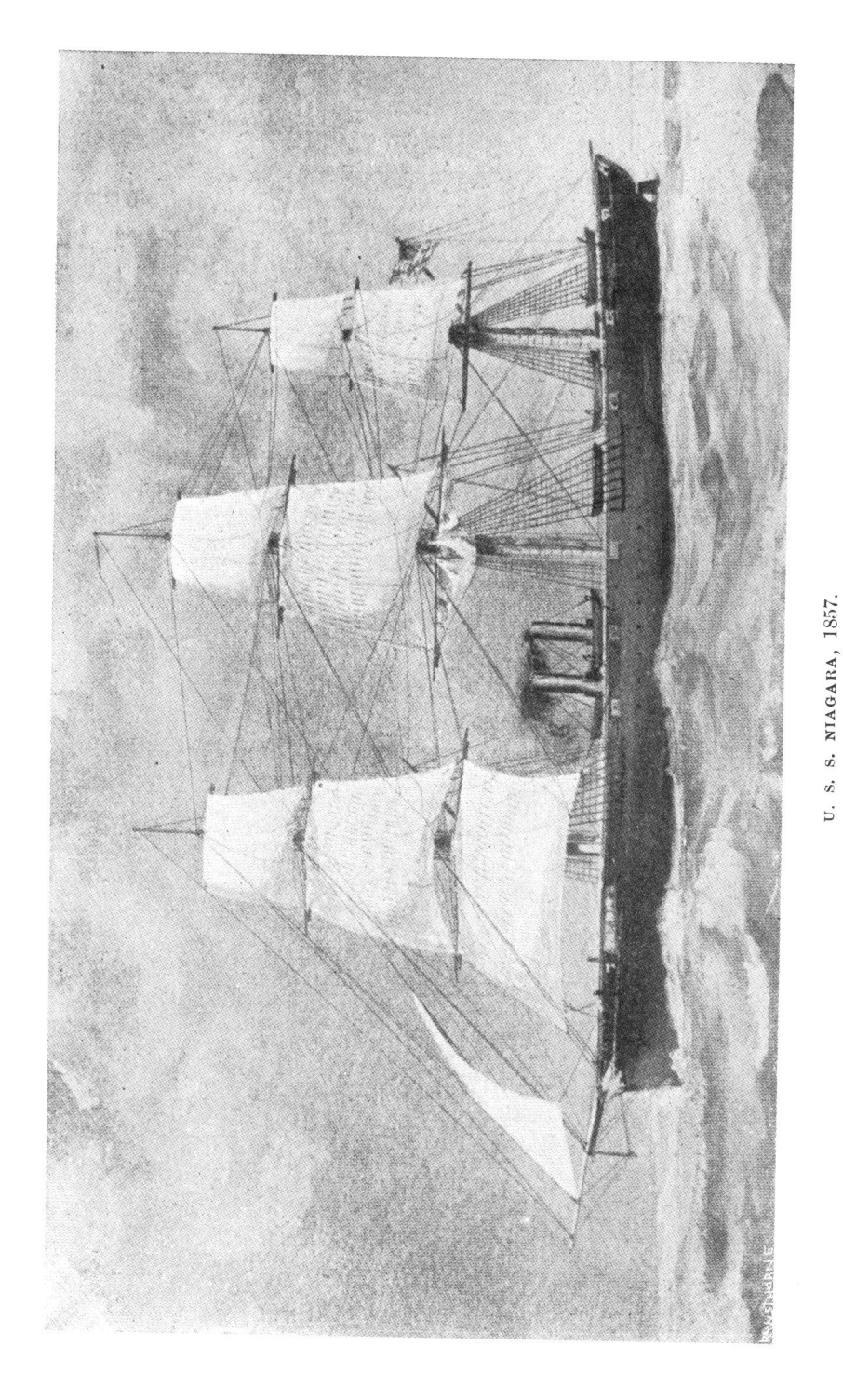

From a water-color by Clary Ray, Washington, D. C.

comparison with the cost of keeping sailing frigates in commission, were the reasons for the non-employment of these fine ships.

The *Niagara* is generally spoken of as a frigate, having been associated in building with the *Merrimac* class, but was in fact an exceedingly large sloop-of-war and not a frigate at all. The idea of speed was entertained in her case, and Mr. George Steers, an eminent ship-builder of New York, who had acquired fame as a designer of swift clipper-ships and yachts[1] was called upon for professional aid. Mr. Steers was given a temporary appointment as naval constructor, and during the two years he held that office he designed the *Niagara* and superintended her construction in the New York Navy Yard. The hull was designed with very sharp lines for speed, and her constructor was not restricted by any attempt to accommodate her model to the shape of frame timbers on hand; speed under sail was the primary quality sought, but speed under steam was not neglected, about fifty per cent. more power being provided than in the case of frigates. The dimensions of the vessel were unusually large for the time, length on the load waterline being 328 feet $10\frac{1}{2}$ inches; breadth at same, 55 feet; displacement, 5,540 tons, and registered tonnage (old measurement), 4,580.

The *Niagara's* engines consisted of three horizontal direct-acting cylinders 72 inches in diameter and 3 feet stroke, fitted with independent gridiron slide cut-off valves and jet condensers. The boilers were of the Martin type, the same as used in the five frigates, but were considerably larger, having six furnaces each and about fifty per cent. more grate and heating surface. No heating apparatus for feed-water was supplied. There were two telescopic smoke-pipes, and the propeller was of the same hoisting type used on the frigates. The machinery was designed and built by Pease & Murphy (Fulton Iron Works), New York, its construction being under the direction of Chief Engineer William H. Everett, who also had charge of the work of installing it in the vessel. The maximum speed in smooth water under steam alone was found to be 10.9 knots, and the average sea speed under steam and sail with varying conditions of weather, was 8.5 knots.

---

[1] Mr. Steers designed and built the famous yacht *America*, which won the Queen's cup in the regatta at Cowes, England, in 1851.

The *Niagara* was put in commission in the spring of 1857 under command of Captain Hudson, Mr. Everett being her chief engineer, and proceeded to England in April to undertake the work of laying the first Atlantic cable. One-half the cable (about 1,250 miles) was put in the hold of the *Niagara* and the other half in H. M. S. *Agamemnon*, the two ships leaving Valencia, Ireland, August 7th, 1857, the *Niagara* paying out her part of the cable. The U. S. S. *Susquehanna* accompanied the expedition to lend assistance if needed. Four days after leaving Ireland the cable broke through defects in the paying-out machinery and the enterprise was abandoned for that year, the *Niagara* returning home. Chief Engineer Everett had detected the faults in the cable machinery and submitted plans to remedy them which were considered so excellent that at the request of the cable company he was detached from the *Niagara* and granted leave of absence with permission to go to England to direct the construction of the mechanism proposed by him. In March, 1858, the *Niagara* returned to England and with the *Agamemnon* proceeded to the middle of the ocean, from whence each vessel started homeward, each paying out her section of the cable, Mr. Everett in his capacity of superintendent for the cable company directing the work from the *Niagara*. After a delay of about a month occasioned by a break in the *Agamemnon's* section three days after the work was begun, the ships had no further trouble and landed their ends of the cable successfully, the *Niagara* at Trinity Bay, Newfoundland, and the *Agamemnon* at Valencia, Ireland.

The engineers of the *Niagara* on this noteworthy voyage were, Joshua Follansbee, chief; John Faron and Wm. S. Stamm, first assistants; George R. Johnson and Mortimer Kellogg, second assistants, and Jackson McElmell, George F. Kutz, and Wm. G. Buehler, third assistants. They all received gold medals from the Chamber of Commerce of the city of New York in commemoration of the event. Chief Engineer Wm. H. Everett, whose genius made the undertaking successful, is said to have received $25,000 from the cable company for his services. After operating for two weeks and transmitting about four hundred messages, the cable ceased working on account of defective insulation, and was not replaced until 1866 when a much larger and better made cable was laid by the *Great Eastern*, that vessel having failed in an attempt the year before. After laying the cable in 1858 the *Niagara* spent the remainder of that year in a task which was neither agreeable or glorious. To meet a demand of public sentiment she was freighted with nearly three hundred destitute and savage negroes, who had been taken from a slaver named the *Echo* off the coast of Cuba, and transported them to Liberia on the west coast of Africa. Many of the negroes died on the voyage and the whole experience with them was intensely distasteful, and disagreeable.

In 1860 the *Niagara* conveyed to Japan by way of the Cape of Good Hope the embassy which had been sent to the United States by the Sho-gun of that country. The Civil War brought her home the next year and after undergoing extensive repairs she was sent on special service to Europe, her great size rendering her unfit for hostile operations along the insurgent coasts. The capture of the Confederate privateer *Georgia* in August, 1864, and refusing battle with the iron-clad ram *Stonewall* off the port of Coruna in April, 1865, were the chief incidents of this cruise, which was the *Niagara's* last. At the close of the war she was laid up in Boston and remained there until condemned and sold in 1885. In 1871-'72 the work of remodeling and repairing her was prosecuted for a time, but eventually abandoned.

A resolution of Congress, approved February 3, 1855, authorized the Secretary of the Navy " to provide and despatch a suitable naval or other steamer, and, if necessary, a tender, to the Arctic seas for the purpose of rescuing or affording relief to Passed Assistant Surgeon E. K. Kane, of the United States Navy, and the officers and men under his command." This resolution added one small vessel to the steam navy, the *Arctic*, purchased in 1855 and which rendered most efficient service and made the relief expedition successful through her ability as a steamer to " bore " through the ice-pack of Baffin's Bay. Lieutenant H. J. Hartstene in the bark *Release* commanded the expedition and succeeded after many trials and hardships in finding Dr. Kane and brought him and his party safely home. The officers volunteered for this service from the navy that being a requirement imposed by the congressional resolution, the only one now believed to be living, being Rear Admiral Joseph Fyffe,[1] who was a passed midshipman in the *Release*. First Assist-

---
[1] Since deceased.

ant Engineer Harman Newell and Acting Third Assistant Engineer Wm. Johnson went in the *Arctic*. In 1859 the *Arctic's* machinery was removed and the hull transferred to the light house board for a light-ship.

In the year 1855 also a somewhat larger screw steamer, the *Despatch* was purchased and sent to the Pensacola navy yard as a tender for that station, her tonnage being 558 and cost $139,088.17. In 1859 she was rebuilt at the Norfolk navy yard and enlarged to 694 tons, the name being at that time changed to *Pocahontas*, under which she performed much valuable service during the rebellion.

By an act of Congress approved March 3, 1857, authority was given for the immediate construction of five large screw sloops-of-war, the general size or class of the vessels being specified by the act. Four of them were at once placed under construction as follows: The *Pensacola* at Pensacola; the *Lancaster* at Philadelphia; the *Hartford* at Boston; and the *Richmond* at Norfolk. In order to incite a healthful rivalry between the naval constructors and civilian ship-builders it was decided to commit the building of the fifth sloop wholly to private enterprise, and advertisements were accordingly issued for competitive plans and specifications. Thirteen proposals were received in response, from which a board of officers selected the one submitted by Mr. Jacob Westervelt of New York, to whom a contract was awarded. The vessel thus brought into existence was the *Brooklyn*, the hull of which was built by Mr. Westervelt under the superintendence of Naval Constructor S. H. Pook, and the machinery by sub-contract by the Fulton Iron Works, superintended by Chief Engineer D. B. Martin, U. S. Navy.

Mr. Martin was the engineer-in-chief of the navy for a full term of four years beginning October 18, 1853, and was known as a thoroughly capable and painstaking engineer, familiar with the many branches of his calling so far as they were developed in his time. He was the inventor of the vertical water-tube boiler which for many years was the type of excellence in marine boiler work and was an improvement over the flue boilers that immediately preceded it. After being succeeded at the expiration of his term of office as engineer-in-chief by Chief Engineer Samuel Archbold, Mr. Martin performed duty as inspector of machinery for the *Brooklyn*, and as general inspector for some smaller sloops built

CHIEF ENGINEER DANIEL B. MARTIN, U. S. NAVY;
Engineer-in-Chief of the Navy from October 18, 1853, to October 17, 1857.

later, as well as serving on boards for the selection of types of new vessels authorized. He resigned from the service in 1859 and, like many other men who have occupied important public offices, expressed his weariness with the thankless world's work by returning to his native place and taking up the peaceful occupation of farmer.

The *Brooklyn* was 233 feet long on the load water line; 43 feet beam; 2,686 tons displacement, and of 2,070 tons burden. Her machinery consisted of two horizontal direct-acting cylinders 61 inches in diameter by 33 inches stroke. The steam valve was a three-ported slide fitted with the Meyer cut-off blocks on its back. A jet condenser was used. There were two Martin boilers with seven furnaces each, aggregating 250 square feet of grate surface and 7,788 square feet of heating surface, fitted with one telescopic smoke-pipe 7 feet in diameter and 50 feet high above the grate bars. The propeller was a two-bladed hoisting screw, $14\frac{1}{2}$ feet in diameter and 24.7 feet mean pitch. The total weight of machinery was 240 tons and of water in boilers, 64 tons. The vessel was completed in little more than a year after the date of contract and exhibited a speed of 9.2 knots under steam alone in smooth water, with 51 revolutions of the screw, 18 pounds steam pressure, 27 inches of vacuum, 878 developed horse-power, and 3.2 pounds of anthracite coal consumed per hour, per horse power. Her first service was in the home squadron in 1859-'60,'61.

The *Hartford*, built at the Boston Navy Yard, was slightly smaller than the *Brooklyn*, her principal factors being length, 225 feet; beam, 44 feet; tonnage (old) 1,900, and displacement, 2,550. Her machinery was built by Loring & Coney, Boston, under the supervision of Chief Engineer Jesse Gay, U. S. Navy, and consisted of a direct-acting two-cylinder jet condensing engine with cylinders 62 inches in diameter by 34 inches stroke, and two Martin boilers with 253 square feet of grate surface and 7,600 square feet of heating surface. The screw was of bronze, two-bladed, 14 feet diameter and 25 feet pitch. This was replaced in 1880 by a more efficient four-bladed screw and the original one diverted to a lasting and appropriate use by being melted and cast into the statue of Admiral Farragut, which stands in Farragut Square, Washington, D. C. The *Hartford* was launched early in 1859 and commissioned for sea the following summer, going to the East India station to relieve the *Mississippi* as flagship. Her maximum speed under steam alone in smooth water was found to be 9.5 knots, an average sea performance with sail and steam, 7.3 knots. In 1880 the *Hartford* was fitted with new machinery, the engines put in being a pair of the 60"x36" Isherwood engines built by Harrison Loring during the war for a sloop that was never finished—the *Kewaydin*.

The *Lancaster* was the largest of the ships of her class, being 235 feet 8 inches long, 46 feet beam, 3,290 tons displacement, and 2,362 registered tonnage. Her machinery was built by Reanie & Neafie, Philadelphia, under the inspection of Chief Engineer W. W. W. Wood, the engines and attachments being exactly like those for the *Brooklyn*. The boilers were of the same type, but about twelve per cent. larger in grate and heating surface than those of the *Brooklyn*. The contract price for the *Lancaster*'s machinery complete, was $137,500. Like the *Hartford*, she was eventually fitted with a pair of the 60"x36" Isherwood engines, built during the war. In 1879-80 the hull was thoroughly overhauled and remodeled with a ram-bow, making her a formidable appearing craft for our navy at that time. The *Lancaster* was launched in 1858 and went the following year to the Pacific station, where she remained as flagship until 1867, thus being deprived of an active part in the Civil War, in which her sister ships achieved so much glory.

The *Richmond* was built at the Norfolk Navy Yard and her machinery at the Washington Navy Yard, the latter being designed by Mr. Archbold, the engineer-in-chief. The principal dimensions of the vessel were: Length, 225 feet; beam, 42 feet; displacement, 2,604 tons, and registered tonnage 1,929. The machinery consisted of a two-cylinder direct-acting engine with cylinders 58 inches in diameter and 36 inches stroke of piston, fitted with single poppet valves and Sickles' cut-offs. The use of the poppet valves was forced upon the department by the political influence of two civilians who at that time had a contract for directing the construction of machinery for the *Pensacola*, and was found to be decidedly harmful to the efficiency of the ship. Much of the lighter engine work, pipe fittings, attachments, etc., was done at the Norfolk Navy Yard, but all the heavy work was done at Washington. In 1866, as soon as she could be spared from active service, the *Richmond* was fitted with a pair of the 60"x36" Isherwood engines built expressly for her

U. S. S. RICHMOND.

(*Brooklyn, Hartford, Lancaster, Pensacola.*)

at the Washington Navy Yard during the three preceding years. The *Richmond* was not launched until 1860, and in the latter part of that year went to the Mediterranean as flagship of the station; recalled by the outbreak of the rebellion the next year, she joined the West Gulf blockading squadron, and was a conspicuous factor in the varied operations which made Farragut famous.

The last of these five ships, the *Pensacola*, brought into the field of naval contention a new and unique character in the person of Mr. Edward N. Dickerson, who made the engineering life of the Navy Department exceedingly interesting for a number of years and enriched the annals of scientific experiment not a little, by injecting an element of novelty and humor into otherwise dry and technical matters. The *Pensacola* was built at the navy yard, Pensacola, Florida, and was 230 feet 8 inches in length; 44 feet 6 inches beam; 3,000 tons displacement, and 2,158 measured tonnage. Her greater displacement than the other ships of practically the same dimensions was due to the fact, that the machinery as originally installed weighed 540 tons, while that of the *Hartford* weighed only 200 tons, and of the larger *Lancaster* $246\frac{1}{2}$ tons. This machinery was built at the Washington Navy Yard by the Government from the designs, and under the supervision of two civilians, Messrs. Sickles and Dickerson.

Mr. Frederick E. Sickles was an inventor and engineer of ability and experience; he was the inventor of a cut-off mechanism for poppet valves, and at this time was engaged in fitting his patent to the engines of the *Richmond*, as previously mentioned. Mr. Dickerson was a New York lawyer who had become acquainted with Sickles through patent suits and from gaining a smattering of mechanical matters had become an enthusiast on the subject, entering into the study of engineering with all the zeal and blindness of a new convert. He appears to have become enamored of Mariotte's law regarding the relationship of volumes, pressures, and temperatures of gases, and from his faith in the infallibility of that law under all conditions came to the conclusion that his mission upon earth was to reform the engineering practices of the time, in which, as now, owing to material difficulties, the law of Mariotte when applied to the steam engine did not display its theoretical perfection. Mr. Dickerson is described as a man of graceful manners and appearance, and a most eloquent and persuasive speaker, capable of convincing almost anyone of the soundness of his theories.[1]

Having entered into partnership with Sickels, the new firm proposed to the Navy Department to design machinery for one of the new ships which would "produce the highest possible effect from a given amount of fuel, and with the least possible weight." The plans suggested were regarded by all engineers as very faulty and Mr. Toucey, the Secretary of the Navy himself, saw their impracticability. Engineer-in-Chief Martin and his successor, Mr. Archbold, both strenuously opposed the proposition, as did also engineers generally in the Navy and in civil life. Mr. Dickerson, however, was intimately connected socially and politically with Mr. Mallory of Florida,, then Chairman of the Senate Committee on naval affairs, and with Senator Yulee of the same state and a prominent member of the same Committee, through whose political influence, exerted with great energy, Mr. Dickerson eventually obtained the sought for contract. The opposition of the Secretary was overborne and he most unwillingly signed it. The date of this contract was April 3, 1858; by its terms Sickels and Dickerson agreed to design and superintend the building of the *Pensacola's* machinery and allow the Government to use their patents.

The drawings furnished by them are still on file in the Bureau of Steam Engineering, Navy Department, and exhibit by their brilliant coloring and crudeness of execution their amateur origin. Mr. Sickels apparently had allowed his good engineering sense to lie dormant and permitted his enthusiastic partner to revel unchecked in mechanical movements and designs. Cams, ratchets, bell-cranks, combination levers, etc., appear in profusion for the performance of the simplest functions, seemingly introduced for the purpose of indicating knowledge of mechanical motions rather than from any necessity of using them. The peculiarities of the machinery thus designed may be generally stated as follows:

---

[1] As a patent lawyer Mr. Dickerson enjoyed a national reputation. In 1855 he was counsel for McCormick before the Supreme Court of the United States in the great suit involving the question of infringement of patents on harvesting machinery. Associated with him in this famous case were William H. Seward and Reverdy Johnson, while the opposing counsel were Abraham Lincoln, Edwin M. Stanton and George Harding.

1. The use of large cylinders to work steam with a large measure of expansion.
2. The use of a peculiar condensing apparatus.
3. The use of an air tight fire-room.
4. The use of small boilers in proportion to the cylinders.

Four steam cylinders 58 inches in diameter and 3 feet stroke of piston were arranged in pairs on opposite sides of the ship, the cylinders being jacketed with steam belts 4½ inches in depth. The cylinders were directly opposite each other, but instead of two cranks, as was possible by the arrangement, the designer complicated matters by having *six*, in order to effect which, two of the connecting rods were made with forked ends to stride the crank of the opposite cylinder, each arm of the fork grasping a crank of its own. The intoxicating effect of this thing when in motion may be easily imagined. The four cylinders with their connections and gear made the engine plant of the *Pensacola* practically double in weight that of the other sloops, a fact that did not require an engineer to detect, and was fatal to the claim of the designers of minimizing weights. Two surface condensers with very small circulating pumps were supplied, the main dependence for effecting the circulation of water being scoops projecting from the ship's bottom, on the theory that the remarkable speed of the ship would drive water through the condensers, as is now done in practice on swift torpedo boats. The idea of the air-tight fire-room was not bad, but as the blowers were originally connected it was shown by experiment with a lamp that the air pressure obtained was actually negative, the flame of the lamp drawing inward from an open air-lock instead of being blown outward by the pressure within. Under this state of affairs the heat of the fire-room was so intolerable that men could not remain in it for any length of time. Two small 5-furnace horizontal fire-tube boilers and two 1-furnace auxiliary boilers of the same type were supplied, the total grate surface being 234 square feet and heating surface about 7000. Sickels' cut-off gear was of course used, the valves being set to cut off very early in the stroke, leaving Mariotte's law to do the rest. With this valve gear applied to steam and exhaust valves at each end of each cylinder, there was an array of lifting rods and dash-pots, decidedly bewildering.

The requirements of the department called for a 2-bladed hoisting screw of the type then in favor, and the designers projected such a screw with very fine pitch based upon a calculated engine speed of eighty revolutions per minute, but as the work progressed they lost faith in their calculations for speed and altered the screw by increasing its pitch to conform to *forty* revolutions per minute. This confronted them with a new and unexpected problem, for a corresponding increase in the surface of the screw followed as a necessity, to effect which the diameter was increased about four feet and four blades substituted for two. This destroyed the hoisting feature of the screw and necessitated throwing away all the costly brass castings for the hoisting apparatus, as well as the two-bladed screw already made. The hull had to be docked to alter the stern and deepen the keel to accomodate the new screw, and the ship's draft accordingly increased. This one blunder cost about $20,000, and is only one example of many, illustrative of what may be called the piece-meal manner in which the designing and fitting together of the different parts of the machinery was conducted. The result was, that when the machinery was at last pronounced ready for trial it had cost $308,460, or more than twice as much as that of any other ship of the *Pensacola* class.

Progressing in this tentative manner the work was necessarily slow and sometimes came to a complete standstill for lack of knowledge as to what to do next. The other ships of the class were completed and in service, the Civil War began, and still the *Pensacola* was unfinished; so slow and uncertain did the work progress that the designers were finally suspected of disloyalty and Mr. Sickels, who had charge of installing the machinery, was actually put under guard and not allowed to leave the vessel or his work. Finally Mr. Edward Faron, who had once been an engineer in the navy, was employed and put in charge of the work, his energy resulting in its completion and a trial trip on the Potomac the 3d of January, 1862. On this trial a maximum speed of 8.8 geographical miles per hour was developed, this costing five pounds of coal per horse power, or about 25 per cent. more than the *Hartford* or *Lancaster*, while the speed was 0.7 miles less.

The *Pensacola* was sent at once to join Farragut's fleet off the mouth of the Mississippi and arrived there in the course of time, after having been ashore for ten days on one of the Florida Keys, her machinery, and engineers as well, being in a condition of semi-collapse when she got in. She participated in the brilliant battle of the forts below New Orleans and the capture of that city in April, but was so uncertain under steam that she was thereafter used more as a floating battery than as a reliable cruising ship. In 1865 her entire machinery plant was taken out and replaced with new boilers and engines, the latter being a pair of the 60-inch Isherwood type built by Hazelhurst & Co., Baltimore, for a large sloop-of-war projected but never built, the name of which was *Wanalosett,*

Secession deprived Mr. Dickerson of his powerful Florida friends, but his persuasive eloquence about Washington had won him many more, with the support of whom he made himself a veritable thorn in the side of Engineer-in-Chief Isherwood, as well as a source of much trouble for the Secretary of the Navy. In spite of the object lesson furnished by the costly failure of the *Pensacola*, Mr. Dickerson was able to get other opportunities to experiment with his theories at public expense until his engineering career terminated with the complete failure of one of the finest ships ever built in this or any other country—the *Idaho*. The opportunity to make a grievance out of the *Pensacola* affair was not neglected by Dickerson, who had sufficient influence to have the matter made a subject for congressional investigation, the record of which (Report No. 8, 38th Congress, second session) is highly creditable to the engineering branch of the navy, and totally lacking in elements vindicating its instigator.

In 1864 Mr. Dickerson, as attorney in the case of Mattingly vs. the Washington and Alexandria Steamboat Company, had an opportunity to address a jury in the supreme court of the District of Columbia, on which occasion he launched forth upon a decidedly scholarly speech which he entitled "The Navy of the United States. An Exposure of its condition, and the Causes of its Failure." As an example of eloquent invective this speech is worthy of classification with the famous oration of Catiline, and its author was so proud of it, and so confident of its destroying the reputation of his archenemy, Isherwood, that he caused it to be published in pamphlet form and distributed broadcast. It turned out however to be a case of one's enemy writing a book and getting the worst of it. Mr. Isherwood was altogether too busy with a multitude of official cares to give any heed to this furious attack upon him, and, indeed, it disturbed him very little, for he had been too long and too prominent in public life to be super-sensitive to criticism. There were other members of his corps who had more leisure and who were capable of detecting in the Mattingly speech an opportunity for amusement at the expense of the author, and there soon appeared an illustrated booklet entitled "Uncle Sam's Whistle, and What it Costs," dealing with Dickerson, the trial trip of the *Pensacola*, and the famous speech, in a most entertaining and amusing manner. In it Dickerson and his theories were ridiculed so perfectly that instead of appearing before the public as the purifier and reformer of the Navy Department, he found himself suddenly transformed into a laughing-stock for the entire engineering and naval element of the country. The authorship of the book referred to, is somewhat in doubt; the caricatures and sketches were made by Second Assistant Engineer Robert Weir, and the text is generally credited to him, as he was equally handy with pen and pencil. At any rate, the little book was the most exquisite satire ever produced within the navy, and was entirely successful in its purpose of turning the tables upon the assailant of the head of the engineering branch of the service.[1]

In the annual report for 1857 the Secretary of the Navy reported progress on the five ships of the *Richmond* class and took occasion to say that they were too large for the performance of much of the service required of the navy on our own coasts, and especially in China. Ten steamers of "light draft, great speed and heavy guns" were recommended to meet the deficiency, to which Congress responded by an act approved June 12, 1858, authorizing the construction of seven screw-sloops and one side-wheel war steamer, the result of this legislation being the acquisition of a class of vessels whose names were familiar in the navy list for many years.

The side-wheel steamer, of only 453 tons, was built at the newly established navy yard at Mare Island near San Francisco and was named *Saginaw*. The machinery was designed and built by the Union Iron Works of San Francisco under the supervision of Chief Engineer George Sewell, and consisted of a 2-cylinder oscillating

---

[1] See Appendix C.

U. S. S. IROQUOIS, 1859.
(*Dacotah, Mohican, Wyoming*).

THE STEAM NAVY OF THE UNITED STATES.

engine with cylinders 39 inches in diameter by 48 inches stroke, and two 3-furnace Martin boilers aggregating 81 square feet of grate and 2000 square feet of heating surface. The water wheels were 20 feet in diameter with floats 6 feet in length. The *Saginaw* was completed in about a year, and in the latter part of 1859 went to the China Station for her first service, remaining on that station until 1862 when she returned to San Francisco. Thereafter she was constantly in commission attached to the Pacific squadron until October, 1870, when she was wrecked on Ocean island.

Of the seven screw sloops, four were specified to be of 13 feet draft when ready for service, and the other three of 10 feet draft. The following table exhibits the size, etc., of the four larger sloops, as well as the navy yard where each was built:

Name.	Displacement.	Tonnage.	Length.	Beam.	Immersed midship section.	Where built.
Mohican	1,461	994	198'- 9''	33'	363 sq. ft.	Kittery, Maine.
Iroquois	1,488	1,016	198'-11''	33'-10''	380 " "	New York.
Wyoming	1,457	997	198'- 5''	33'- 2''	366 " "	Philadelphia.
Dacotah	1,369	996	198'- 5''	32'. 9''	365 " "	Norfolk, Va.

The *Mohican's* machinery was built by Woodruff and Beach, Hartford, Conn., under the supervision of Chief Engineer D. B. Martin, and consisted of a 2-cylinder back-acting engine with cylinders 54 inches in diameter by 30 inches stroke, supplied with a Pirsson's condenser, and two Martin boilers. Pease & Murphy of New York built the machinery for the *Iroquois*, which was of the same type as that of the *Mohican*, the boilers being slightly smaller and the stroke of pistons 28 instead of 30 inches. The machinery for the *Wyoming* was by Merrick & Sons, Philadelphia, inspected by Chief Engineer Edward Whipple. The engines were direct-acting with two cylinders 50 inches in diameter by 30 inches stroke, and had a close surface condenser of Mr. Merrick's design. The boilers were of the same type but considerably smaller than those of either the *Mohican* or *Iroquois*. Murray & Hazlehurst of Baltimore built the machinery of the *Dacotah*, which was radically different from that of the other sloops. Two large direct-acting engines, 63 inches diameter by 36 inches stroke, drove a huge wooden-toothed gear wheel, which in turn drove a pinion keyed to the propeller shaft, the speed ratio being as 9 to 4. The engines were designed for a speed of 36 revolutions per minute, or 81 of the screw, which was about the same as the direct speed of the other vessels. The boilers of the *Dacotah*, two in number, were of the horizontal return fire-tube variety, instead of the Martin type then so generally used. Chief Engineer H. H. Stewart was the superintendent of construction of this machinery. The four vessels were all completed and in service by the end of 1859, the *Mohican* being on the coast of Africa, the *Iroquois* in the Mediterranean, the *Wyoming* in the Pacific, and the *Dacotah* on her way to join the Asiatic squadron. All of them showed a speed under steam alone in smooth water of about 11.5 knots per hour, and averaged 8 knots for general performance at sea.

The three smaller sloops were the *Narragansett*, *Seminole*, and *Pawnee*, all good and appropriate American names, like most of the names bestowed upon our war vessels in those days. The *Narragansett* was of 1,235 tons displacement and was built at the Boston navy yard, the machinery being built by the Boston Locomotive Works. She had a pair of direct-acting engines with cylinders 48 inches in diameter by 28 inches stroke of piston, driving a 4-bladed screw 12 feet in diameter. Pirsson's double-vacuum condenser was used. The boilers, two in number, were of the usual Martin type, containing 200 square feet of grate surface and about 6,150 square feet of heating surface. The *Narragansett* was completed and in commission by the end of 1859, sailing shortly thereafter for the Pacific station.

The *Seminole*, built at the navy yard, Pensacola, Florida, was a sister-ship of the *Narragansett* and similar to her in all principal dimensions. Her machinery was built by the Morgan Iron Works, New York, and consisted of a pair of back-acting horizontal engines with cylinders 50 inches diameter by 30 inches stroke, and two Martin boilers slightly smaller than those of the *Narragansett*. The *Seminole* went to the Brazil station in 1860 and was recalled in 1861 in time to take an active part in the battle of Port Royal in November of that year. Later she served in Farragut's West Gulf squadron and participated in the battle of Mobile Bay, going into action lashed alongside the *Lackawanna*.

The third of these sloops, the *Pawnee*, differed much from the other two in the form of her hull and in the feature of having twin screws. She was built by the government at the Philadelphia navy yard, but from the designs and under the supervision of a civilian ship-builder, Mr. John W. Griffiths of New York, who held a temporary appointment as a naval constructor while directing this work. It had been determined to arm the *Pawnee* with four XI-inch Dahlgren guns, and it was to demonstrate that this could be done without exceeding the specified draft of ten feet that Mr. Griffiths was employed. The resulting vessel was considerably longer and broader than the others of her class and of somewhat less than ten feet draft when armed and equipped for service, a fact that made her of great use with her heavy battery in the shallow rivers of the southern coast during the war. Besides having to carry the unusually large battery, the engines to drive the two screws

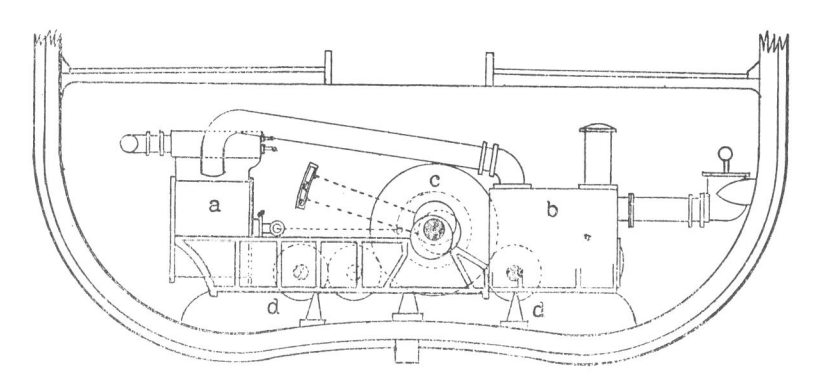

ELEVATION, LOOKING AFT, OF TWIN-SCREW GEARED ENGINES, U. S. S. PAWNEE.
a, cylinder. b, condenser. c, master-wheel. d-d, screw-shaft pinions.

were considerably heavier than in other vessels of the class, and this necessitated further calculation on the part of the constructor, who so modified the form of the hull that when the vessel was completed her bottom was actually concave.

The *Pawnee* was 221 feet 6 inches long; 47 feet beam; 1,533 tons displacement and rated at 1,289 tons burden. Chief engineers Wm. W. W. Wood and R. H. Long superintended the building of the machinery at the works of Reanie & Neafie, Philadelphia, there being two horizontal direct-acting cylinders 65 inches in diameter by 36 inches stroke, driving a large gear wheel 7 feet 3 inches in diameter, this driving two smaller wheels keyed to the two shafts, the small wheels or pinions being 2 feet 11 inches diameter of pitch circle. The master wheel was somewhat to port of the center line of the ship, as shown by the outline sketch of this unusual type of engine. There were two 7-furnace horizontal return fire-tubular boilers containing 133 square feet of grate surface each. The propellers were four-bladed, nine feet in diameter, and instead of being supported by struts under the counters, the shafts were prolonged to the stern post where they were upheld by a crossbar, the screws being at the ends of the shafts.

This vessel was launched in 1859 but was not completed for sea until the spring of 1861 when she at once became actively engaged in warlike operations along the Atlantic coast, her first important service being at the destruction of the Norfolk navy yard in April. During the same year she took part in the attack on Hatteras Inlet in August and in the battle of Port Royal in November. During the following years of the war she was attached to the South Atlantic blockading squadron and did much important service on the coast of Florida and elsewhere. After the war she made one cruise to the Brazil station and then became a hospital and store-ship at home, being finally sold out of the service at Port Royal in 1884.

In February, 1855, the *Water Witch*, which for years had been engaged in exploring La Plata River and its tributaries, was forcibly prevented from further prosecuting that work by being fired upon by a Paraguayan fort commanding the river, the man on duty at the wheel at the time being killed. Attempts to gain redress by diplomatic methods having been steadily repulsed by Lopez, the autocratic president of Paraguay, our government was finally forced to resort to a show of power, and late in the year 1858 a squadron of nineteen naval vessels carrying two hundred guns and twenty-five hundred men was assembled in the river under command of Flag Officer W. B. Shubrick. Nine of these vessels were sailing frigates, sloops-of-war and brigs, the other ten being small steamers capable of ascending the river. Two of the steamers, the *Fulton* and *Water Witch* belonged to the regular naval establishment; another was the revenue cutter *Harriet Lane*, named for the neice of

President Buchanan, and the others were merchant steamers chartered and armed for the occasion. Six of them were screw steamers varying from 220 to 550 tons burden and were named *Memphis*, *Atlanta*, *Caledonia*, *Southern Star*, *Westernport*, and *M. W. Chapin*, the seventh, the *Metacomet*, being a side-wheel steamer of 395 tons. Thirty-eight officers of the engineer corps were attached to these vessels.

All the steamers and such of the sailing vessels as were permitted by their draft of water were moved up the river to a point above Rosario, ready to act against Paraguay if necessary, and in January 1859 the Flag Officer and Mr. Bowlin, the special commissioner of the United States, proceeded in the *Fulton* and *Water Witch* to Assuncion, the capital of Paraguay. No difficulty was then experienced in gaining a respectful hearing and the object of the mission was fully and peacefully accomplished. A satisfactory apology was extended for firing on the *Water Witch*; an indemnity was paid on the spot for the benefit of the family of the seaman who had been killed, and the special envoy negotiated a new and advantageous commercial treaty with the Paraguayan government. Without the steamers the successful termination of this expedition would have been extremely difficult, if not impossible, Paraguay lying so far inland that natural obstacles would have prevented an approach by troops on land or by sailing vessels on the river except at an enormous outlay of life and money.

When the squadron returned to the United States the chartered steamers were purchased and added to the naval establishment, about one-half of their cost price being money already paid or due the owners for their charters. After purchase, the names were changed as follows: *Metacomet* to *Pulaski*; *Memphis* to *Mystic*; *Westernport* to *Wyandotte*; *Caledonia* to *Mohawk*; *Atlanta* to *Sumter*; *Southern Star* to *Crusader*; *M. W. Chapin* to *Anacostia*. The side-wheel vessel, the *Pulaski*, was kept on the Brazil station doing exploring and other river service until 1863, when she was sold at Montevideo. The smallest of the screw steamers, the *Anacosti*, became a navy yard tender and coastwise transport attached to the Washington navy yard, and the five other screw steamers were put on active cruising duty on the coasts of Cuba and Africa, in the suppression of the slave trade. All did good service during the

Civil War, and all were sold at its close with the exception of the *Sumter*, which had been sunk in 1863 by an accidental collision with the army transport *General Meigs*.

In the naval appropriation act approved June 22nd, 1860, a clause directed the Secretary of the Navy to have all the sailing vessels of the navy surveyed with a view to converting them into steamers. This duty was performed by a board composed of Captains George W. Storer and S. H. Stringham; Engineer-in-Chief Archbold and Chief Engineer Isherwood; Chief Constructor John Lenthal, and Naval Constructor B. F. Delano; the vessels which were abroad and therefore not accessible, were reported upon from their records and drawings in the department. The report of the board was, that it was not expedient to introduce steam into the brigs, sloops and frigates, but that it was desirable in the case of the ships of the line, which class was recommended to be razeed and converted into first-class steam frigates. The Secretary of the Navy transmitted this report to Congress with his annual report at the end of that year, and urged that the recommendation be carried out, on the ground that, "in the event of war no one of these line-of-battle ships, in the present state of steam navigation, could go to sea with a reasonable degree of safety." The work would undoubtedly have been authorized by Congress that winter had not events of startling magnitude intervened to split both Congress and the navy in twain, and made the problem of strengthening the steam navy one that could not be met by the make-shift of patching up old sailing ships.

CHAPTER XI.

"Ev'n now we hear with inward strife
A motion toiling in the gloom—
The spirit of the years to come
Yearning to mix himself with life."
ALFRED TENNYSON.

The Engineer Corps from 1850 to the Beginning of the Civil War—Congress Petitioned to Increase the Corps—Pay Increased by United Efforts of All Officers—Rank of Engineers Defined—Issue of New Regulations Governing Appointment and Promotion—Opinions of Chief Engineer Gay in Relation to Sails and Steam.

The membership of the engineer corps provided by the act of Congress of 1842 was based upon the number of steamers in the navy at the time, and made no provision for the performance of shore duty, except by the engineer-in-chief, thus compelling him to obtain technical assistance either from civilian engineers employed as clerks or draftsmen, or naval engineers who might be unemployed because of a steam war vessel having been put out of commission. The inspection work required of the engineer corps by the building of the *Powhatan* and other steamers at the same time, had with great difficulty been provided for; but had imposed upon the engineer-in-chief a vast amount of care and professional labor, greater in fact than one man could perform. In this dilemma the engineers petitioned Congress for relief, this memorial having been preserved in official form as Senate Miscellaneous Document No. 45, 32d Congress, 1st session, is herewith presented.

MEMORIAL
OF
ENGINEERS OF THE NAVY,
PRAYING
A REORGANIZATION OF THE CORPS TO WHICH THEY BELONG.

February 24, 1852.
Referred to the Committee on Naval Affairs
February 25, 1852.
Ordered to be Printed.

To the Senate and House of Representatives of the United States of America in Congress assembled:

The undersigned respectfully represent to your honorable bodies the utter inadequacy of the present organization of the engineer corps of the United States navy, and most earnestly solicit your attention to the following brief statement of facts in proof of this assertion, and in support of the propositions herewith submitted.

The law of Congress authorizing the present organization of the engineer corps was established in the very infancy of our steam marine—at the time of constructing our first steam ship as an experiment. At that date neither a rapid increase of steamers nor an enlarged sphere of duties for the naval engineers, such as has since taken place, was contemplated; and the organization was accordingly made on a basis to meet the limited duties, both in extent and kind, which were intended to be performed by the corps.

Those limited duties were to be entirely performed afloat on the *Atlantic* coast of the United States, and their sphere of action was to be confined to the management of the machinery of a few second class vessels, for *home* service exclusively, to which it was proposed to restrict our steam marine. It is scarcely necessary here to state that these expectations were never, even from the first, realized, and the engineers of the naval corps at once entered upon a wide and very responsible range of duties combining all of theory and practice known in the extensively ramified arts and sciences; making up a thorough knowledge of the principles and practice of marine steam engineering and steam navigation—a knowledge which it is believed will not be contested by any qualified to judge, to demand quite as much natural ability, united with as deep study and long practice, as are required for any other profession; certainly for any of those composing the various corps in the government service.

Some of the duties of the engineer corps are briefly stated as follows: they decide upon and design the various complex machinery of the government war steamers; furnishing, first, the working drawings in the most complete detail, then superintending its manufacture at the various establishments where it is contracted to be built, and afterwards its erection on board the vessels; finally they operate this machinery at sea.

The machinery so designed and constructed is of the largest, most complicated and costly description, frequently amounting in a first-class steam-ship to hundreds of thousands of dollars. It is manufactured by contract at the various works where the Navy department may direct, and naval engineers are the sole guardians of the public interest, where the expenditures constitute a formidable fraction of the naval appropriations. They furnish the only barrier to peculation on the government, and the fraudulent performance of contracts, if such were attempted.

The amounts and kinds of labor done are determined by and paid for wholly on the certificates of the superintending engineer and the engineer-in-chief.

Having thus shown, as we trust, to the satisfaction of your honorable bodies, the importance of having at all times in the country, on shore duty, a sufficient number of engineers of the higher grades to discharge the above mentioned responsibilities, we proceed to show that in this very particular the present organization is defective. The act of 1842 only provides for the appointment of a sufficient number of engineers of all grades to supply our war steamers, leaving no margin for sickness or other disability, and making no provision whatever either for the supply of the many steamers attached to the coast survey, or for the designing and superintending the construction of such new machinery as the continually increasing wants of the service may require. It therefore follows, as the necessary consequence, either that the duty afloat must be performed by an insufficient number of engineers—and those, too, taken from the lower grades, not possessing the requisite experience and knowledge for its proper performance—or the more important, and indeed paramount, shore duties must be neglected.

The Department has therefore preferred the former, rather than incur the loss and inconvenience of the latter. From the very commencement of the steam navy there has scarcely ever been a steamship in commission with the full complement of engineers. Those Engineers, therefore, who are ordered on duty *afloat*—a duty which tasks arduously their physical qualities—have thrown upon them a much greater amount than can fairly be performed with justice, either to themselves or the government. And if the latter alternative were preferred, and the service afloat *filled* with the prescribed number of Engineers, it would keep the whole corps at sea, continually absent from their families, and without the rotation of shore duty enjoyed by other officers of the navy.

The present organization allows one chief engineer, (commissioned by the President), two first assistant, two second assistant, and three third assistant engineers, for each *steamer-of-war.* All the assistant engineers hold their appointments by warrant of the Honorable Secretary of the Navy.

The present number of steamers-of-war actually in commission is *ten,* and in the course of four months *five* more will probably be added—making *fifteen,* in all, in commission by the first of June next.

The present organization authorizes the appointment of fifteen chief, thirty first assistant, thirty second assistant, and forty-five third assistant engineers. Now, by the first of June, next, twelve chief, twenty-seven first assistant, twenty-seven second assistant, and thirty-nine third assistant engineers will be required for service *afloat,* in naval steamers, leaving but *three* chief and *twelve* assistant engineers to perform the various shore duties, and engineer the *six* coast survey steamers. From this it will be seen how insufficient the present organization is, to provide for even a reasonable approximation of the requisite number.

Further: the original organization contemplating only a provision for the *management* of the machinery of the steam ships, provides merely for a chief engineer afloat as the highest grade; but, as has been before shown, the construction of this machinery has been also superintended by the engineers of the navy. Now, it is well known that designing and constructing machinery requires a much higher order of ability than its after management; and when the two duties are to be performed by the same Corps, those *distinct* offices should be performed by distinct grades—those of the highest talent being taken from the one to form the other.

The organization of 1842 is, therefore, insufficient, in not having this provision, and we suggest to your honorable bodies the propriety of adding another grade, formed from the present grade of chief engineers, (*without increase of pay*), to be called "*Inspectors of Machinery Ashore and Afloat.*" In the British Navy, the necessities of their largest steam marine have already compelled the organization here recommended, and from them the title of "Inspectors of Machinery" is borrowed.

Another reason for enlarging the engineer corps is furnished by the fact that a considerable extension of our steam marine must soon be made, and it is impossible to create good naval engineers as fast as it is possible to build steamships.

All other corps are sufficiently numerous to anticipate a considerable increase of the navy, while the engineers are too few even for the present service. Were a sudden enlargement of the steam marine now to be made, the Engineer Corps will have to be filled with such talent as could be immediately commanded—not such as would be desired—and the public interests would inevitably suffer as a consequence.

We would urge upon your honorable bodies the strong probability, which will scarcely be contested by any who have bestowed the proper reflection upon the subject, that in 20 years there will be no naval vessels unpropelled in whole or in part by steam. The introduction of steam for all marine war purposes will be compelled by necessity and the pressure of circumstances.

In conclusion, we, your memorialists, would state, that in our opinion the following additions to the present organization are necessary to render the engineer corps equal to the performance of the services required of it, viz:

The addition of the higher grade of Inspector of machinery ashore and afloat. An inspector of machinery ashore to be allowed for each of the *principal* navy yards, and a chief engineer for each of the other navy yards; also, an assistant engineer of each grade for each navy-yard. An inspector of machinery afloat to be allowed for each squadron containing two or more steamers.

The inspector of machinery for the Washington Navy Yard to be attached to the office of engineer-in-chief of the Navy and to perform such duties as the engineer-in-chief may require of him.

The inspectors of machinery to receive the same pay and be entitled to the same privileges and immunities in all respects as chief engineers, and to be commissioned in the same manner as Chief Engineers.

The inspectors of machinery *now* required to be selected by the

Hon. Secretary of the Navy from the present grade of Chief Engineers, but that thereafter all promotions to that grade to be made by examination by a Board of Inspectors of machinery.

Believing the above facts to be truthfully stated and relying on the wisdom and justice of your honorable bodies, we respectfully solicit for them a favorable consideration.

CHARLES B. STUART,
Engineer-in-Chief, U. S. N. Navy.

B. F. ISHERWOOD,
Chief Engineer U. S. N. for the
grade of Chief Engineer.

J. W. KING,
First Assistant Engineer U. S. N.
For the grade of Asst. Engineer.

A bill providing for more engineers on the lines of the petition was favorably reported by the naval committees of Congress, but like the great majority of naval bills, failed to reach a vote through lack of interest in Congress and external opposition. Soon afterward work was begun on the large screw frigates described in the preceding chapter, and this provided the opportunity of appointing engineers for them before they were completed, nearly fifty new members being added to the corps in the next three years and thirty more in the year 1857.

In 1856 the engineers joined with all other branches of the service in an organized effort to obtain an increase of pay from Congress; this effort is noteworthy from the fact, that probably it is the only instance on record where all the corps of the navy laying aside their rivalries and jealousies honestly worked together for a common purpose, also for the more especial and important reason that their united effort was successful.

The writer has been fortunate enough to have been given a copy of a circular letter prepared by the officers' committee in Washington and sent to all officers of the service, directing the manner to be observed in furthering their endeavor, which letter is here reproduced as an instructive example of the method of going about the difficult task of securing legislation for the navy.

"WASHINGTON, December, 8, 1856.

"SIR: At a meeting of Naval Officers, held in this city on the 6th instant, with the view of concert of action in advocating the necessity of a general increase of pay for the Navy, the following officers were unanimously appointed a committee, charged with the management of the memorial to which your signature is appended, viz:

W. W. Hunter, Commander.
Charles Steedman, "
Thomas B. Neille, Purser.
Maxwell Woodhull, Lieutenant.
Roger N. Stembel, "
Henry A. Wise, "
Joel S. Kennard, "
William G. Temple, "
John M. Brooke, "
A. W. Johnson, "
Robert Woodworth, Surgeon.
Mordecai Yarnall, Professor of Mathematics.
William Chauvenet, " " "
Joseph S. Hubbard, " " "
Montgomery Fletcher, First Assistant Engineer.
James C. Warner, " " "

"On the evening following, a sub-commiitee was appointed from this Body, under instructions to wait on the Hon. Secretary of the Navy, present the Memorial officially, make known the views of the memorialists, the action which had been already taken, and to consult with him as to the course most promissory of success.

"The Secretary suggested the presentation of the Memorial to Congress through the Chairman of the Naval Committees, and that if any suggestions as to the mode of increase were elicited from the Committee, the most simple should be offered; he has no objection to the exercise of whatever *personal* influence officers may possess with Members of Congress in furtherance of our object, but he will not approve indiscriminate approach to these gentlemen; indeed such action would not comport with the dignity of our position as members of the Naval profession.

"The Secretary, although sensible of the necessity and propriety of our application for an increase of pay, and willing to heartily second our efforts in that direction, is not disposed to favor per centage on sea-service; he is of opinion that such a mode of increase would not be strictly just in its operation on the higher grades of the service.

"At a subsequent meeting of the General Committee it was unanimously resolved: 'That, if our suggestions upon the subject were solicited by the Naval Committees, we should simply state, that, in our opinion, an addition of thirty per cent. to our present pay, all around, and *in each grade*, would not be taxing too much the liberality of Congress.'

"As a matter of course, the Naval Committees, should they require information upon this subject, will direct its enquiries to the Head of the Navy Department. So far as individual action of the officers is concerned, judicious management and unanimity of opinion is certainly necessary. It is with this view, and to prevent embarrassment, which might result in a defeat of the object contemplated, that we address to you this circular. This Committee, acting in the spirit of fairness and justice, would claim your confidence and earnest support.

"It is a well-known fact, that the expression of adverse views upon Naval matters before Congress tends to obstruct the action of that body, and we beg that in the exercise of whatever personal force you may be able to bring to the advancement and success of this measure, you will support the recommendation of your committee."

A bill entitled "A bill to increase and regulate the pay of the navy," was introduced and experienced the various vicissitudes of bills for two congresses, finally becoming a law on the 1st of June, 1860. By the terms of the act an increase of pay of about twenty-five per cent. in every grade and corps was provided for, and a longevity scale adopted, the majority of the grades being provided with four rates of pay increasing with length of service. The following rates were fixed for the engineer corps:

CHIEF ENGINEERS, (on duty).

For first five years after date of commission.........$1,800
For second five years after date of commission...... 2,200

For third five years after date of commission......$2,450
After fifteen years from date of commission.......... 2,600

On leave, or waiting orders.

For first five years after date of commission..........$1,200
For second five years after date of commission...... 1,300
For third five years after date of commission......... 1,400
After fifteen years from date of commission...... 1,500

First Assistant Engineers.

On duty..$1,250
On leave, or waiting orders............................ 900

Second Assistant Engineers.

On duty..$1,000
On leave, or waiting orders............................ 750

Third Assistant Engineers.

On duty..$ 750
On leave, or waiting orders............................ 600

In January 1859 Mr. Toucey, the Secretary of the Navy, issued the following general order conferring naval rank upon the officers of the engineer corps:

"Chief engineers of more than twelve years will rank with commanders.

"Chief engineers of less than twelve years with lieutenants.

"First assistant engineers next after lieutenants.

"Second assistant engineers next after masters.

"Third assistant engineers with midshipmen.

"This order confers no authority to exercise military command, except in the discharge of their duties, and no additional right to quarters."

This order was affirmed by Congress March 3, 1859, with the words "except in the discharge of their duties" stricken out, which omission merely served to emphasize the embarrassment of the engineers in controlling their own men aboard ship, where their authority was necessarily military, or else no authority at all.

Orders defining the rank of surgeons and paymasters, similar to the above, had been in existence for some time and the status thus conferred was generally satisfactory to the staff officers. That it was not satisfactory to others is shown by the fact that the department had to re-affirm the staff officers' rank by the following order, issued February 25, 1861:

"Surgeons of the fleet, surgeons, paymasters, and chief engineers of more than twelve years, rank with commanders. Surgeons, paymasters, and chief engineers of less than twelve years, rank with lieutenants. Passed assistant surgeons and first assistant engineers rank next after lieutenants. Assistant surgeons and second assistant engineers next after masters, and third assistant engineers with midshipmen.

"This rank is now established by law, and neither the department nor any officer in command has authority to withhold it, or the honors which belong to it.

"Commanding and executive officers of whatever grade, while on duty, take precedence of surgeons, paymasters and engineers, and the effect of this precedence is to elevate the former, but not to depress the latter, or to detract from the rank or the honors of the rank already secured to them. Commanders, while on duty as commanding officers, will have a corporal's guard. Lieutenants, while on duty as executive officers, will wear on the cuffs a gold embroidered star, one inch and a quarter in diameter, to be placed one half of an inch above the stripe of gold lace, and these will indicate the precedence to which they are by law entitled."

An entirely new schedule of requirements for admission and promotion of officers in the engineer corps was issued in 1859; the regulations in full are as follows:

REGULATIONS FOR ADMISSION AND PROMOTION IN THE ENGINEER CORPS.

Before persons can be appointed assistant engineers in the navy, they must have passed a satisfactory examination before a board of at least three engineers, designated at such times as the wants of the service require. Application for permission to appear before such board must be made in writing to the Secretary of the Navy, accompanied by satisfactory testimonials as to good moral character, correct habits, and sound constitution. The application will be registered, and when a board next meets, permission will be sent to the applicant, stating the time and place of the meeting of the Board.

In the examination for a *third assistant engineer*, the candidate must be able to describe all the different parts of ordinary condensing and non-condensing engines, and explain their uses and their mechanical operation; to explain the manner of putting engines in operation, how to regulate and modify their action, and the manner of guarding against danger from the boilers, by the means usually applied to them for that purpose. He will be expected to write a fair, legible hand, and to be well acquainted with arithmetic and the mensuration of surfaces and solids of the regular forms; to have worked not less than one year in a marine engine manufactory, and present testimonials of his mechanical ability from the director of the establishment in which he may have served. He must not be less than twenty nor more than twenty-six years of age.

Candidates for promotion to the rank of *second assistant engineer* must have served at least two years as third assistants in the management of steam engines in the navy in actual service, must produce testimonials of good conduct from the commanders and senior engineers of the vessels in which they may have served, and must pass a satisfactory examination upon the subjects, and to the extent prescribed for third assistants; they must likewise be able to explain the peculiarities of the different kinds of valves, the construction of expansion valves, the manner of their operation, the remedies which are usually resorted to, to check foaming in boilers; must possess a knowledge of the usual causes of derangement in the operation of air pumps, force pumps, and feed pipes, the proper preventives and remedies, and the mode of cleaning boilers when required. They must have a general knowledge of the mensuration of surfaces and solids.

Before promotion to the rank of *first assistant engineer* candidates must have been employed at least three years as second assistant engineers in the management of steam engines in actual service, and produce testimonials of character and good conduct from their former commanders and superior engineers; must pass a satisfactory examination upon the subjects prescribed for third and second assistants, the mechanical powers, the different kinds of deposits and incrustations to which boilers are exposed, and be able to furnish a working sketch or drawing of different parts of engines and boilers; to superintend their construction, and determine upon their accuracy and fitness for use.

Promotions to the grade of *chief engineer* are to be made after the candidate has served for two years as first assistant engineer in the management of steam engines in the navy in sea service, and has been examined upon any of the subjects specified for assistant, which the board may deem expedient, and after they shall have satisfied the board of their previous good conduct and character, of their sufficient knowledge of mechanics and natural philosophy, of the forms, arrangements, and principles of different kinds of steam engines, boilers, propellers, and their various dependencies, which have been successfully applied to steam vessels, and their alleged relative advantages, for sea or river service, and shall have attained 26 years of age.

Candidates for promotion who may fail to pass a satisfactory examination may be examined once again, and if they fail to pass at the second examination they shall be dropped from the list of engineers.

Candidates for admission or promotion will be required to furnish the board of examiners with evidence of their abilities in the execution of mechanical drawings, and their proficiency in penmanship.

The examining board will report the relative qualifications of the persons examined, and number them, giving the best qualified the lowest number.

When, in the opinion of the department, the wants of the service require the admission of engineers of any grade above that of third assistant, the same qualifications and restrictions as to times of service will be exacted as by the regulations required for promotion to the grade in question: *Provided*, that all appointments to the grade of second assistant shall be made between the ages of 21 and 28; and to that of first assistant, between 25 and 32; and to that of Chief engineer, between 28 and 35.

The assistants must employ all favorable opportunities for acquiring a practical knowledge of the fabrication of the different parts of steam engines and their dependencies, that they may be able to repair or replace such parts as the space and means for making and repairing can be furnished in steam vessels. When other qualifications are equal, candidates whose skill and abilities in these particulars are superior, will have precedence over others for admission or promotion, who may be considered equal in other particulars.

Isaac Toucey,

Secretary of the Navy.

Navy Department, May 7, 1859.

During this decade immediately preceding the Civil War the supremacy of steam power over sails as a means of marine locomotion came to be very generally admitted in the naval service, even by the most conservative, and the work of creating an efficient steam fleet was begun in earnest. Of the many opinions and reports originating in the navy about this time and dealing with the subject of steam *versus* sails, one of the most interesting and valuable that has been preserved is a letter by Chief Engineer Jesse Gay of the *Mississippi* which exhibits so much good practical sense in looking at the question, that it is here copied for the benefit of a younger generation of naval officers, some of Mr. Gay's views even yet being pertinent to naval economy.

U. S. Steamer Mississippi,

At Sea, November 8, 1851.

Sir: After long experience on board of this ship, a careful observation of the defects, with a wish to render her more efficient, I take the liberty to make the following observations, and suggest improvements, which, if adopted, will render the *Mississippi* more useful, efficient and safe.

The objects to be attained in a War Steamer are, first, weight of battery. Second, speed by steam, with an economical expenditure of coals. Third, to combine her steam and sails, so that one shall not be transported at the expense of the other. A ship of war, without guns, would be perfectly defenseless; a war steamer, with encumbrance on her steam power, is equally so. The sails of the

Mississippi are auxiliary to her steam; with her sails unaided by the engines, she is helpless; on the other hand her engines are sufficient to handle her without the assistance of sails. The conclusion is, therefore, that the less the engines are encumbered with the spars and sails, which are useless, the better for efficiency and safety. Again, if a ship is overburdened with sails, spars, steam engines, boilers, besides any useless weight, it deducts the same number of pounds from her battery, or immerses her to a dangerous depth in the water, obstructs her speed, and occasions a useless expenditure of coal, for which a small compensation is obtained.

The spars and sails of the *Mississippi* are too large; if they were reduced to the proper size, her speed would be augmented more than one knot per hour, allowing her to draw the same water. The engines not only have her vast hull to propel, but the great surface of spars, which are a great obstruction to the speed. It is supposed the larger the sails the more assistance they are capable of rendering. This is a mistaken idea, as experience abundantly has shown; a proper area of sails is unquestionably advantageous, but this area must not exceed a limit at which they would be an obstruction to speed by steam. When the winds are fair, a six knot breeze is required before the sails are of any use in propelling the ship conjointly with steam power; if the winds are strong a large spread of canvas is dangerous. In a storm, only a sufficient quantity is necessary to steady the ship, and this will of course be, fore and aft sails. With light fair winds, the power of the engines will bring light airs ahead; thus, a steamer will most of the time have light airs ahead, or occasionally aft, but not in sufficient force to make her sails effective; hence, it is clear that her great spars are an encumbrance to her speed under most of these circumstances; the mainsail cannot be carried—the main topsail has seldom been used—studding sails have been useless—fore topsail useful—top-gallant sails seldom—fore-topmast stay-sail and jib useful. The useful sails are fore and main trysails, fore topmast stay sail and jib, and occasionally the spanker with effect. With moderate or fresh breezes ahead, the top gallant sails are necessarily sent down; in strong head winds, lower yards and top masts are also sent down. In fine weather all these spars are again sent up to improve the appearance of the ship. All this has to be done at the expense of labor of the crew, while the very spars which are so often sent up and down are seldom of any use in propelling the ship. The ship may be propelled by the aid of her sails, but in a very awkard manner; the first difficulty, the crew is far too small to handle her immense sails with sufficient promptitude; in the second place, the mainmast is so far abaft the centre of motion that all the sails upon it, (except with a wind directly aft), are of but little or no use; the foremast is also too far forward. All these difficulties it is impossible to obviate; with sails alone she is a clumsy ship, hardly capable of handling herself; she never can be an auxiliary steamer with her masts in their present position, the most important of which cannot be moved (the main). But these are not all the difficulties; the great length of spars produce another difficulty of equal damage to her efficiency, which must exist with her great spars, viz: spare sails, spars and rigging must be put into the ship to the amount of many tons; this weight only adds to her immersion and reduces her speed; or, in other words, it requires a portion of her steam power to transport this useless weight, which does nothing to efficiency, speed or safety. As I before remarked, all the unnecessary weight put into a War Steamer, deducts the same from her general efficiency and safety. On two occasions she has been fitted for a cruise with all the spare material on board, which rendered her dangerously deep and almost unfit for sea, and I believe a very small proportion of these sails and spare spars have ever been used, for the purpose for which they were put on board.

To remedy the difficulties I have enumerated, I suggest that the spars, including lower masts, be reduced to a proper dimension, which would not exceed in weight more than one half the present ones; this would be a reduction of many tons, beside the reduction of weight of spare spars, sails and rigging, the saving to convert to more useful purposes room which it now occupies, and with this reduction the sails, rigging, etc., would be useful, where now it is so unwieldly as not to be used at all. Again, if this reduction was made, the sails and spars would be proportioned to her crews, and could then be worked with ease, where now they cannot.

Besides the reduction of spars, she requires a reduction in the weight of her anchors (she now carries four, which weigh 63 cwt. each; she only requires two, or if four, of much less weight than the present) this would also reduce the weight of chain. At no time during this cruise has she required more than two anchors; late in the cruise a much smaller one was substituted for one of the above weight; this has been found sufficient and much less labor to work it.

I am of the opinion that a steamer is more secure with two anchors (and not extremely heavy ones) than a sailing ship is with four. The engines themselves are a greater security than two anchors; hence, a steamer does not require so great weight of anchor.

If the forgoing suggestions were followed out the *Mississippi* could then carry two or four more guns, and draw less water than she now does; her speed would be augmented with the same expenditure of coal. She would have more room to berth her crew, which she much needs; her expenses would be reduced, and she would be more formidable; but if her present spars are retained, all of these qualities, which are so important in a war steamer, will be lost.

In submitting these views, which I have gathered from experience on board the *Mississippi*, I have felt some delicacy, knowing that I have ventured opinions which do not accord with theory. What I have submitted is based upon practical observations alone, for the correctness and verity of which I appeal to every experienced officer who has sailed in her any length of time. I have also had opportunity of seeing many foreign war steamers, particularly those of England and France; the difference between them and the *Mississippi* is, they carry less spars and more guns. I have not seen a war steamer of any nation carrying so heavy spars as the *Mississippi*, but I have frequently met with those of much less tonnage and power, carrying a much greater weight of battery.

I am very respectfully,
Your obedient servant,
JESSE GAY,
Chief Engineer.

Capt. JOHN C. LONG,
Com. U. S. Steamer *Mississippi*.

CHAPTER XII.

"There's a demon, and he dwelleth in the drum;
See the volunteers as down the street they come.
Proudly the procession marches,
Under bunting, under arches,
To the rattle, rattle, rattle,
Like a volley belched in battle,
And he saith:
I am Cain come again; on my forehead is the stain.
  Come,
  Come,
  Come, come, come—
    Unto Death."--FRANCIS Z. STONE.

THE CIVIL WAR.

IN Captain Collum's excellent history of the United States Marine Corps he prefaces his account of the services of the marines during the war of the rebellion with an extract from Lossing's "Civil War in America," which outlines most eloquently the services rendered by the navy to the nation during that gigantic struggle for life. So correctly is the arduous and baffling character of the naval operations indicated, and so gracefully is the praise due the navy accorded, that the author feels he cannot do better than introduce the same extract as a prelude to what he will have to say regarding the achievements of the naval engineers during that same trying period.

"In the spring of the year 1861 a civil war was kindled in the United States of America which has neither a pattern in character nor a precedent in causes recorded in the history of mankind. It appears in the annals of the race as a mighty phenomenon, but not an inexplicable one. Gazers upon it at this moment, when its awfully grand and mysterious proportions rather fill the mind with wonder than excite the reason, look for the half-hidden springs of its existence in different directions among the absurdities of theory. There is a general agreement, however, that the terrible war was clearly the fruit of a conspiracy against the nationality of the republic, and an attempt, in defiance of the laws of divine equity, to establish an empire upon a basis of injustice and a denial of the dearest rights of man. . . . . It was the rebellion of an oligarchy against the people, with whom the sovereign power is rightfully lodged.

"The services of the national Navy during the war, on account of their peculiarity, attracted less attention than those of the army, and were not appreciated by the people. They have an equal claim to the gratitude of the nation, so freely accorded to the other branch of the service. The Confederates having no navy, in a proper sense, and only flotillas here and there, and with some powerful 'rams' on rivers and in harbors, and not a ship on the ocean, excepting roving pirate vessels,—built, armed, furnished, and manned chiefly by the British, and cruising alone,—there were few occasions for purely naval battles. The whole force of the Navy Department was employed in the services of blockade, in assisting the attacks of the armies on fortifications along the rivers and on the borders of the Gulf and the ocean, or in chasing the pirates. In these fields of great usefulness the national vessels performed labors of incalculable value, and officers and men exhibited skill, valor, and fortitude unsurpassed.

"Never in the history of the world were there occasions for such exhausting labors and highest courage in service afloat as the American Navy was subjected to in its operations among the rivers and bayous of the southwestern regions of the Republic. Many a victory over which the people have shouted themselves hoarse in giving plaudits to the gallant army might never have been achieved but for the co-operation of the Navy. To the common observer it, in many instances, seemed to be only an auxiliary, or wholly a secondary force, when, in truth, *it was an equal, if not the chief, power in gaining a victory.* Without it, what might have been the result of military operations at Forts Henry and Donelson, Shiloh and all along the Mississippi River, especially at Vicksburg, Port Hudson, and New Orleans; what at Mobile, Pensacola, Key West, along the Florida seaboard, the sea-coast islands, Charleston and the borders of North Carolina, and even in holding Fortress Monroe and Norfolk?

"Notwithstanding the weak condition of the naval service, the decree went forth, in the spring of 1861, that all the ports of the

States wherein rebellion existed must be closed against commerce by a strict blockade. Foreign nations protested and menaced, *but the work was done.* There were no dock-yards or workmen adequate to construct the vessels needed for the service, yet such was the energy of the Department that an unrelaxing blockade was maintained for four years, from the Capes of the Chesapeake to the Rio Grande, while a flotilla of gunboats, protecting and aiding the army in its movements, penetrated and patrolled our rivers, through an internal navigation almost continental, from the Potomac to the Mississippi. Ingenuity and mechanical skill developed amazing inventions. That marine monster, the *Monitor*, was created and began a new era in naval warfare; and the world was suddenly enriched by new discoveries in naval service. Vessels of the merchant service were purchased and converted into strong warriors; and men from that service were invited to man them. Schools were established for nautical instruction; dock-yards were enlarged and filled with workmen; and very soon a large number of vessels were afloat, watching the harbors under the ban. No less than two hundred and eight war vessels were constructed, and most of them fitted out during the four years; and four hundred and eighteen vessels were purchased and converted into war ships.

"The blockading service was performed with great vigor and efficiency under the triple stimulus of patriotism, duty, and personal emolument. The British government professed to be neutral, but British merchants and adventurers were allowed to send swarms of swift-winged steamers, laden with arms, ammunition, clothing, and everything needed by the insurgents, to run the blockade. The profits of such operations were enormous, but the risks were equally so; and it is believed that a true balance-sheet would show no profits left, in the aggregate, with the foreign violators of the law. The number of such vessels captured and destroyed during the rebellion by the national Navy was fifteen hundred and four. The gross proceeds of property captured and condemned as lawful prize before the first of November following the close of the war amounted to nearly twenty-two millions of dollars, which sum was subsequently enlarged by new decisions. The value of the vessels captured and destroyed (eleven hundred and forty-nine captured and three hundred and fifty-five destroyed) was not less than seven million of dollars, making a total loss, chiefly to British owners, of at least thirty million of dollars.''

It is not believed that the distinguished historian from whose work the above is quoted has in the least overstated the value of the services rendered the nation by the navy during the Civil War. As the length of time increases since the conclusion of that struggle, we are getting to study its events more carefully and to be more critical in analyzing the exact relationship between causes and effects. An analysis that was quite impracticable in the years immediately succeeding the close of the war because at that time men's minds were filled with the magnitude and brilliancy of the achievements of an army numerically so enormous as to eclipse entirely the naval force, and in which a personal interest was compelled from the very circumstance of its greatness, which necessitated representation in its ranks of every family within the borders of the nation. The blockade of the sea coast alone, of the revolted territory, cannot appear now in any other light than a deciding factor in the ultimate conquest of the Confederacy. Had the Southern states been free to ship their cotton to Europe and exchange it for provisions and munitions of war, who is wise enough to say when the end would have come? Could the invasion of the South been possible had not the naval force, hovering over the coasts with ceaseless vigilance for more than three years, practically disarmed the Confederacy and starved its people into submission by depriving them of the benefits of commerce?

In telling the story of the maintenance of the blockade it is impossible to give too much credit for results to the naval engineers serving in the blockading squadrons. A great object in view was to keep the vessels in condition to remain on their stations, for the removal of even one steamer at a time meant the weakening of the line of watchers and might involve a breaking of the blockade, and this duty to a great extent fell upon the engineers, for without steam power—always ready—the ships were worthless. In hastily constructed gunboats, or commercial vessels as hastily equipped for war purposes, without an adequate supply of engineering stores and without proper tools or facilities for effecting repairs, the duties of the engineers were the most difficult and fretting that can be imagined; notwithstanding which, they, as a rule were found equal to the emergencies that confronted them and succeeded in keeping their ships and the blockade efficient, and this in spite of the fact that the engineering talent of every sea-port of Great Britain was arrayed against them in the effort to produce marine machinery that could over-endure that of the Federal vessels.

The author has been favored with a large number of letters from men who as regular or volunteer engineers performed their share in the labor of making a rigorous blockade possible, and from the recital of trials and hardships thus presented he cannot but marvel at the faithfulness, loyalty, and thoroughness of the services rendered. The engineers shared with other officers the dangers of battle, pestilence, and storm, as well as the hardships due to improper food and insufficient clothing, and in addition, they had to struggle constantly with the discouraging task of keeping old and worn-out, or new and badly adjusted, machinery in working order; a task that permitted no rest for either body or mind. A record of the make-shifts, alterations, inventions and substitutes to which these devoted men were compelled to resort from sheer lack of proper mechanical appliances to aid them in their labors, would prove a most interesting chapter in the history of man's ingenuity, and would be valuable to the engineers of to-day, even though our smallest gun-vessels now carry excellently equipped repair shops, and are supplied with a veritable mine of tools, fittings and spare parts.

Had the service been less arduous and afforded some opportunities for rest, the possibility of securing it was often wanting. Although absolutely essential to the well-being of the ship, in a degree scarcely approximated by any other class of officers, the engineer was too often precluded by the nebulous nature of his relative rank from occupying any but the merest leavings of the quarters in which he was supposed to have a share. One former member of the corps writes of an instance where an engineer attached to a small armed steamer was completely left out in the distribution of living space and for upwards of two years had no home on board whatever, except a piece of canvas in form of a tent under which he was allowed to sleep, summer and winter, on top of the deck house. Numerous other instances have been related to the writer of engineers unprovided with quarters being obliged to sleep in the hot drum-rooms over the boilers, or who constructed for themselves rough bunks in the engine rooms or shaft alleys. These cases of individual neglect and hardship fortunately do not stand as representative of the experience of all, for in many vessels there was room even for the engineers, but they serve to show what discouragements were encountered by a considerable number of an invaluable class of officers who inherited an official position vastly inferior to the value of their services or their real merits.

Under such circumstances it is remarkable that the engineers maintained their patriotism and devotion to duty as well as they did, the records of the war showing, however, that instances of defection or faint-heartedness among them were rare indeed. Soon after the war closed, Rear Admiral David D. Porter, writing to Chief Engineer W. W. W. Wood, thus referred to his experience with the naval engineers: " I have had more than two thousand engineers under my command during the Rebellion and I have never known them to shrink from any service." There were of course occasional instances of discouragement after prolonged and arduous duty where the engineer gave up in despair and declared his inability to keep his department longer in service, and there were also a very few cases where the engineer allowed a wearied and disgusted commanding officer to influence him into making such a report against his judgment. In either case the effort to get off the blockade and enjoy a respite from its toils at some Northern navy yard generally came to naught.

After the capture of Port Royal, early in the war, a naval supply and repairing station was maintained at that place, and there the broken-down ships from the blockade were usually sent for examination before being allowed to proceed North. The mechanical department of this station was presided over by veteran chief engineers of the old navy, who had long before lost all the nonsense of youth and were incapable of sympathy for their juniors who had tales to tell of what they *could not do*. To their minds, an engineer in charge of a steamer in the presence of the enemy ought to be able to do anything, and be resourceful enough to meet any emergency. If, upon examination, they decided that the reported defects in a vessel could have been repaired at sea the offending engineer whose report had taken the vessel off her station received very little mercy. A report to the commander-in-chief of the squadron meant a court-martial, and that in turn meant reduction in grade or summary dismissal from the service. This may seem harsh and uncharitable treatment of those whose duties at best were trying, but individuals have little right to consideration in great national operations, and their chief engineers, whose reports would have appeared cruel and savored of persecution in time of peace, were merely performing their proper part in the prosecution of the war. The service rendered by them in this manner, and in directing repairs to disabled ships, was of incalculable benefit to commanders of squadrons in carrying out the operations entrusted to them, a fact appreciated and very properly referred to by Rear Admiral Dahlgren, who wrote to the Department on the occasion of relinquishing command of the South Atlantic Blockading Squadron at the close of the war: "Fleet Engineer Danby has been for the last two years in charge of the mechanical steam department at Bay Point, where his industry and thorough knowledge of his business has alone enabled me to keep in active operation so many steamers; the first time, perhaps, that this power has been submitted to such a test."

To those who study the social and industrial conditions existing within the United States prior to the Civil War, conditions which contributed fully as much to the causes which made that war possible, as did the political questions generally supposed to have been its provocation, the fact that the mechanical element of the North, represented by the engineers of the navy, had such an important part in accomplishing the conquest of the Confederacy must appear as a most appropriate manifestation of retributive justice. An artificial state of society at the South, founded upon the institution of human slavery, had inculcated a genuine contempt for labor and the industrial arts, and resulted in the utter neglect of the vast mineral resources of that region, now one of its most important sources of wealth, simply because no one was so low in the social scale as to burden his mind with a knowledge of metallurgy, which involved practical experience. Had the South possessed the educated scientists, the skilled mechanics, and the innumerable mills and workshops that a higher order of progress has now given her, there is no telling when, or how the war might have ended.

As it was, when the war broke out there was but one establishment—the Tredegar Iron Works, of Richmond—within the limits of the Confederacy capable of making the very modest armor plates used on the *Merrimac* and *Albemarle*, while the total number of skilled artisans was probably exceeded by the number employed in any one of a score or more of Northern workshops busily engaged in making ships, engines and guns for the national navy. When the first supply of arms and tools had been exhausted, the South was unable to make others, nor could she receive them from abroad on account of the vigilance of the blockading ships, kept up to their work by the skill of the Northern engineers. As tersely expressed by Engineer-in-Chief Isherwood, in one of his official reports regarding the conduct of the war, "our antagonists had neither engineering skill nor resources in themselves, nor could they, owing to the efficiency of our navy, obtain them from others, and the want was fatal; they had despised the mechanical arts and sciences, and by those arts and sciences they fell."

CHAPTER XIII.

> " Mine eyes have seen the glory of the coming of the Lord;
> He is trampling out the vintage where the grapes of wrath are stored;
> He hath loosed the fateful lightnings of his terrible swift sword;
> His truth is marching on.
> JULIA WARD HOWE—*Battle-Hymn of the Republic.*

1861. The Civil War, continued—Engineers and Steam Vessels in the Navy at the Outbreak of Hostilities—Resignation and Dismissal of Officers—B. F. Isherwood Appointed Engineer-in-Chief of the Navy—Increase of the Engineer Corps—Qualifications of the Volunteer Engineers—Remarkable Career of Don Carlos Hasseltino—Vessels Added to the Fleet during the Year—The KEARSARGE and CANANDAIGUA Class of Steam Sloops—The Ninety Day Gunboats—The First Double-Enders.

AT the beginning of the eventful year 1861 the engineer corps of the navy consisted of twenty-eight chief engineers, forty-three first assistant engineers, twenty-nine second assistant engineers, and ninety-two third assistants, a total of one hundred and ninety-two. This number was established by adhering as closely as practicable to the provisions of the act of Congress of 1842, which authorized the appointment of one chief engineer, two first assistants, two second assistants, and three third assistants for each steam-vessel of war. The steam navy at the beginning of 1861 consisted of six great ships, of which the *Niagara* and *Colorado* were types, and which in their size, battery and beauty were the marvels of the maritime world at that day; six first-class screw sloops, every one of which was destned to become famous in the annals of the navy, and one of which—the *Hartford*—was to become a name synonymous with naval glory; four large side-wheel steamers, one of which was the *Powhatan;* eight second-class steam-sloops, represented in the modern navy by the *Iroquois;* five purchased screw steamers of about five hundred tons each, and five small side wheel gunboats, the *Michigan* of this class being still with us.

Twenty-seven of the members of the engineer corps were Virginians, and seven others belonged to the Carolinas, Alabama, and Florida, but the majority came from the New England and Middle States, Maryland and the District of Columbia being especially well represented. The Northwestern States, which now furnish so many naval engineers through the medium of the Naval Academy, then had but five representatives—two each from Ohio and Wisconsin and one from Illinois. Mr. Samuel Archbold was the engineer-in-chief of the navy at the beginning of the year, but in March he resigned that position and his commission as a chief engineer in the navy as well, going out of the service without any suspicion of disloyalty, as his motives for resigning were personal and not connected in any way with the political unrest of the times. He was succeeded by Mr. Benjamin F. Isherwood, who was selected by the President and appointed engineer-in-chief on the 26th day of March, 1861. Mr. Isherwood's name was the fifth in order on the list of chief engineers at the time, and he was recognized as the foremost man of his corps in professional ability and zeal, while his indefatigable energy and intense patriotism brought to the head of one of the most important executive branches of the Navy Department a man well fitted for the Herculean task that the next few years had in store.

In the spring of this year the political storm that had been gathering for so many years finally burst, and the officers and men of the navy were confronted with the desperate issue of choosing between two flags. Of the engineers from the Southern States five resigned and had their resignations accepted by the Department, but by that time resignations of officers of the army and navy had become epidemic, and President Lincoln directed that all such in the future be treated as proof of disloyalty sufficient to warrant summary dismissal from the service of the United States, which treatment was administered to seventeen of the naval engineers who sent in their resignations after it was too late. One of these, William P. Williamson, whose name had stood at the head of the list of chief engineers, became the engineer-in-chief of the Confederate navy; a few others continued their profession in the same service, while others went into the insurgent army, where some achieved considerable military distinction, and others were killed or crippled fighting against the flag under which they had acquired their first military ideas, and to which they would have remained loyal had they been inspired by that thoughtful good judgment supposed to be an attribute of all engineers by the virtue of philosophic nature of their calling.

CHIEF ENGINEER SAMUEL ARCHBOLD, U. S. N.
Engineer-in-Chief of the Navy from October 16, 1857, to March 25, 1861.

In July, 1861, Congress provided for a temporary increase of the navy "for and during the present insurrection," which act authorized the Secretary of the Navy to hire, purchase, or contract for such vessels as might be found necessary, to arm and equip them, and to appoint acting or volunteer officers for them. Under the operation of this law the navy grew rapidly both in ships and in *personnel:* such vessels as were bought outright or built on the order of the Navy Department became, of course, government war-vessels, and as such served to authorize a great increase in the regular engineer corps, a considerable increase being effected during the first year of the war, but not at all in proportion to the increase in the number of war steamers, as the officials of the Navy Department were wise enough to know that the rebellion would eventually be put down, and it was only a question of time before the navy would have to be re-established on a peace basis. Accordingly the majority of the new engineers held only acting appointments. At the end of the year 1861 the regular engineer establishment had increased to four hundred and four, of whom forty-eight were chief engineers; at the same time there were three hundred and sixty-four acting engineers distributed through the grades of first, second and third assistants. The increase in numbers went steadily on until, in January, 1865, there were four hundred and seventy-four regulars and eighteen hundred and three volunteers, of which numbers fifty-nine regulars and fifty- five volunteers were chief engineers.

In spite of all the hurry, excitement, and anxiety incident to the existence of a state of war, it is greatly to the credit of the officials at the head of the engineer corps that the careful system of examinations for admission to the regular service was rigidly adhered to throughout the war, thus preventing the acquisition to the permanent corps of any who were not professionally and morally fit for the service. In the case of acting appointments in the volunteer service little or no examination was required, the need for engineers being so great that almost any one who could show a letter of recommendation from a commander or chief engineer of a war-vessel, or from a civilian of prominence, could get an acting appointment. The majority of the acting engineers were men who were really engineers, many of them being of recognized ability and reputation in their line, who entered the service from motives of patriotism, and naturally chose the engineering branch of the navy in preference to wading through the mud, either with or without a sword, in the army.

Numbers of the volunteer engineers were men who belonged to the profession of civil engineering and were attracted to the engineer corps of the navy by the similarity of names, when they made up their minds to enter the military service of the government. These gentlemen, with possibly a few exceptions, began with no practical knowledge of marine machinery, but with their excellent training in matters relating to civil engineering they were quick to learn and in a short time became among the best acting engineers. Several of them entered the regular service by taking the prescribed examinations and, both during the war and since, have been professionally prominent in the corps. As was often the case in the army, many men of education and ability served in subordinate positions in the navy solely because they wished to serve their country in its day of need, and such men were generally appreciated and promoted to official positions after short periods of faithful service as subordinates. A case in point is that of Mr. P. J. McMahon, a civil engineer employed on the Boston and Worcester Railway, who was a personal friend of the chief engineer of the *San Jacinto*, and was very desirous of going to sea with him as an acting engineer. The plan was prevented by the *San Jacinto* hurriedly going to sea at a time when her complement was filled, with the exception of one coal heaver, but Mr. McMahon was determined to go, and accordingly took the vacant billet. He cheerfully did duty as a fireman, oiler and yeoman until, in about a year, he received the coveted warrant as an acting third assistant engineer; promotion to second assistant came not long afterward, and the close of the war found him a first assistant in charge of the machinery of the *Mahaska*.

Mr. McMahon's predecessor as engineer in charge of the *Mahaska* furnishes a curious example of motive, in seeking service in the volunteer engineer corps. The Atlantic Works of Boston did a tremendous business from the very beginning of the war in building ships and machinery for the navy, and when the owners found themselves getting rich by staying at home they came to the very proper conclusion that some one having a proprietary interest in the business must represent the patriotism of the firm by going to the

U. S. S. TUSCARORA.

Length, 198' 6''; beam, 33' 2''; disp., 1,457 tons.   (*Kearsarge*, *Oneida* and *Wachusett* same class.)

war. Accordingly, the proprietors cast lots and Mr. Philander S. Brown was elected to go to the front. He chose the engineer corps of the navy for his field of usefulness, asked for, and received a warrant as acting first assistant engineer, and served as chief engineer of the *Mahaska* until the war was over, when he resigned and returned to his home and business interests.

As might be expected, and as often occcurred in the other branches of the navy, some acting appointments were given to men who were unqualified for the duties they were expected to perform on board a war steamer. Adventurers who saw in the seven hundred and fifty dollars per annum of the "Acting Third" in the navy more attraction than was offered by thirteen dollars per month and found in the ranks of the Army of the Potomac; firemen recommended by their captains for some gallant or meritorious act; sons or friends of prominent military and civil officials; subalterns disgusted with the Chickahominy swamps, and many other classes too numerous to mention, all had their representatives in the volunteer engineer corps. As there were from four to ten engineers on each war steamer in those days, the presence of one of these inexperienced persons was not dangerous, as he was always under the eye of some one who was able to prevent disaster by interfering in case of necessity. When a number of them happened to get shuffled together, as sometimes occurred, and thus obliged to try to do something without being told how to do it, they generally came to grief, as is attested by innumerable tales in the service.

One of these stories relates to the wearing away of the valve faces and seats of the engine of one of the new sloops-of-war on one of her first sea trips. The acting engineer in charge of the machinery had been in the regular service and was a competent engineer, but, unfortunately for the vessel, he was confined to his room by illness on the voyage referred to. Of the four acting assistant engineers, one only had any experience with machinery and that was limited to fire-room work, he having been a fireman promoted as a reward for some act of bravery in an emergency; his scholastic attainments were extremely limited and stopped short at the problem of subtracting the hourly records of the engine-room counter and dividing the remainder by sixty to find the average revolutions of the engines per minute, a problem that he never mastered, and which finally drove him back into the fire-room, where he found more familiar tools to handle than pencils and paper. This case had numerous parallels in the line as well as in the engineer corps during the war, and is a good illustration of the folly of making officers of enlisted men simply as a reward for gallantry in battle, without any regard for the fitness of the person to perform the duties of the office to which he is advanced.

Another of the acting engineers was a village schoolmaster from the up-country of New Hampshire, whose knowledge of marine engines had been obtained from a picture of a condensing engine in Olmstead's "Principles of Natural Philosophy," at that time a favorite text book in the country schools of New England. The third one was a youth of about seventeen, who had been the schoolmaster's favorite pupil in the New Hampshire village, and who had joined him in the enterprise of suppressing the rebellion through the medium of the naval engineer corps. The fourth acting engineer had gained such engineering knowledge as he possessed by having been the captain of a tug boat. Although well meaning and inspired with a desire to do their best, these amateur engineers in some way managed to overlook in turn the necessity of having the steam chests oiled, and, as a result, the valves and seats at the end of the trip were found to be reduced to little more than a heap of iron filings, and the ship was kept from active service many weeks in consequence while damages were being repaired.

Another incident which occurred about the same time was not the source of any great amount of delight to the acting engineers directly concerned. A war steamer left New York for the seat of war one fine day, the commander and all hands indulging in high hopes of glory and prize money. After a few hours at sea the engine suddenly stopped, and then began running backward at a furious rate; do what they would, the engineers could not coerce the engine into going ahead again, and finally the captain had to ignominiously abandon his cruise and take his ship, tail first, back to New York, an object of surprise and derision to the watermen of that busy seaport. The navy yard was reached in the course of time, where a few vigorous remarks from the chief engineer of the yard and about two minutes work put everything to rights. The eccentric had slipped.

U. S. S. OSSIPEE.

Length, 205'; beam, 38'; disp., 1,934 tons   (*Adirondack*, *Housatonic* and *Juniata* in same class.)

The volunteer engineer who was not an engineer did not always get into trouble, as is shown by the successful experience of one Don Carlos Hasseltino, whose remarkable naval career is worthy of a little space in the history of the naval engineering of the rebellion. This gentleman was a native of the West Indies, but had graduated at a college in Ohio, and at the time of the outbreak of the war was reading law in Hamilton, Ohio. His sympathies being with the South, he went to Montgomery, Alabama, and entered the Confederate army, rising to the rank of lieutenant-colonel in about two years, when he fell into the hands of the enemy in the vicinity of Fort Donelson. Pretending to be a civilian and a foreigner, which he could easily do by his ability to speak French, he succeeded in getting a pass from the Union officer in command at Memphis, and went to St. Louis, not knowing just why he was going there or what he would do next.

In the streets of St. Louis he chanced to meet a former college mate who was an assistant engineer on one of the gunboats in the Mississippi River. This friend urged him to give up the Confederate cause and enter the navy as an engineer, to which proposal he demurred, as he said he "did not know a steam engine from a horse power," but his friend assured him that did not make any difference. Accordingly, and knowing that he would probably be hanged as a spy if his connection with the South were discovered, he studied some of the assistant engineer's books for a few weeks and then presented himself to the authorities as a candidate for the engineer corps. He made such a good impression that he was given an acting appointment as a first assistant engineer, and was ordered to duty on board the *Essex*, then the flag-ship of Rear-Admiral D. D. Porter.

According to Mr. Hasseltino's account of himself, his great fear at this time was that the *Essex* would be ordered to get under way to go somewhere, and he would consequently be called upon to do something with the machinery, which he knew he could not do, his mechanical knowledge being yet so imperfect that he thought the feed-pump was a contrivance for making the vessel go sidewise. But luck was on his side, for he had opportunities to talk with Admiral Porter, and so impressed that distinguished officer with his professional worth that he was put upon the Admiral's staff and assigned to important special duty in connection with the building and inspection of ironclads at various points on the Mississippi River. A report made by him to the admiral respecting the value of certain types of ironclads for river service was considered so meritorious that the admiral embodied it in his report to the Secretary of the Navy, and that official in turn transmitted it to Congress in his annual report.

In May, 1864, after less than a year's service, Mr. Hasseltino was made an acting chief engineer, in which capacity he continued on duty with the Mississippi flotilla; two years later, in May, 1866, he was honorably mustered out of the service. Subsequently he acquired the title of general and considerable wealth by engaging in various wars in Chile, Peru, and Cuba, but with this we need not deal here. Acting Assistant Surgeon J. M. Batten has written an interesting little volume of reminiscences of his service in the navy during the war, in which book occurs the following account of the person whose versatile career has just been described:

"Don Carlos Hasseltino was chief engineer of the United States monitor *Catawba*, but spent most of his time on board the United States monitor *Oneota*, and was one of the messmates of that vessel. I associated with him constantly from October 6, 1865, to January 16, 1866. He was a jolly, kind, sympathetic and intelligent associate. In height he was about six feet, and had a large, wiry frame. His hair and eyes were black; he wore a black mustache. He never gave offense to any one, but would not suffer himself to be insulted. He carried two Derringers in leather pockets buttoned to his pantaloons above the hips. He was very polite and chivalrous; woe to the person that gave offense or offered insult."

The progress made in increasing the fleet during the year 1861 was phenomenal. Mr. George D. Morgan of New York was appointed a special agent of the Navy Department with orders to buy every American merchant vessel found at all suitable for war purposes, in the selection of which he was aided by a board of officers of the navy—a constructor, a chief engineer, and an ordnance officer. This board had a small steamer in New York harbor and made a business of boarding and examining every American vessel within

U. S. S. CANANDAIGUA. (*Lackawanna, Monongahela, Sacramento, Shenandoah* and *Ticonderoga* in same class.)

Length, 225'; beam, 38' 4''; disp., 2,030 tons.

reach, a favorable report on any vessel making it obligatory on Mr. Morgan's part to buy the vessel at the best bargain he could make with the owners. As Mr. Morgan received a commission of two and one-half per cent. on his purchases this obligation to buy, was for him, a decidedly good thing. From the middle of July until the first of December there were purchased in this manner thirty-six side-wheel steamers aggregating 26,680 tons and costing $2,418,103; forty-three screw steamers aggregating 20,403 tons and costing $2,215,037, and one hundred and eighteen sailing vessels—ships, barks and schooners—at a cost of $1,071,898. Sixty of these latter were loaded with stone and sunk for the purpose of closing some of the southern ports; the others, and all of the steamers, were converted into war vessels and put into active service.

At the same time that merchant vessels were being pressed into service, the navy yards and private ship and engine building establishments were worked to their utmost capacity in building war vessels. By the end of the year, fifty-two such vessels were entirely completed and in service or were well along in construction. None of the navy yards were then equipped for the building of engines on a large scale, which work therefore had to be let out by contract to marine engine builders, the machinery specifications in the majority of cases being furnished by the Navy Department from designs of Engineer-in-Chief Isherwood. Excellent plants for building wooden ships existed at the navy yards and many of the hulls of these rapidly constructed vessels were built by the Government at the different yards while their machinery was under construction at neighboring machine shops.

The ship and engine building work of the Navy Department now assumes such magnitude that space forbids the practice previously observed in these pages of giving detailed information as to the designers and builders of the various vessels, their machinery, armament, cost, and subsequent naval careers, although it is hoped that the value of this work will be enhanced by its appendix, in which much of the information referred to is given in tabular form. Henceforth it will be necessary to refer to new vessels in general terms only, except in certain special cases where peculiarities of design or remarkable engine performance occasion so much interest from an engineering point of view that a more detailed history of their origin is desirable.

In February, 1861, Congress authorized the construction of seven sloops-of-war, and the Navy Department, to take advantage of the plans already in its possession of the sloops built in 1858, duplicated the *Iroquois* in the *Oneida*, the *Wyoming* in the *Tuscarora*, the *Mohican* in the *Kearsarge*, and the engines of the *Seminole* in the *Wachusett*. These vessels were of about 1,560 tons displacement. By subsequent action of Congress, at the special session, authority was granted to build other sloops of war, similar to those previously ordered, making fourteen in all, and work on them was begun in the early fall of the year. These sloops-of-war, besides those already named, were the *Juniata, Ossipee, Adirondack, Housatonic, Sacramento, Canandaigua, Lackawanna, Ticonderoga, Shenandoah*, and *Monongahela*. The first four named were of 1,934 tons displacement, and the other six, differing somewhat in size from each other, were of about 2,200 tons. The hulls of all fourteen were built by the Government at the navy yards, three each at Portsmouth, N. H., and Boston, and four each at New York and Philadelphia, the machinery being built by contract at various places in New England, New York and Philadelphia.

These fourteen steam sloops were large, handsome vessels and did much excellent service during the war and afterward. The only one still remaining in the service is the *Monongahela*, which, with her machinery removed, is used as a training ship in which naval cadets and apprentice boys acquire those arboreal habits supposed to be essential in the training of modern men-of-war's men. With the disappearance of this class of vessels we have suffered what the author regards as a most serious loss in the removal from the navy list of those sonorous and distinctively American names, like *Canandaigua, Oneida, Lackawanna, Tuscarora, Shenandoah*, and the like, which were sufficient in themselves to proclaim the nationality of the vessel bearing them, and at the same time precluded by their derivation from adoption by foreign navies, except inappropriately. Our *Ajax, Dolphin, Petrel, Vesuvius*, and others, always have their namesakes in other navies, and imply a poverty of resource on our part wholly undeserved in view of the great multitude of beautiful and euphonious words that have become part of our American language in the names the vanished tribes of aborigines gave to their hills and forests, rivers and lakes.

U. S. S. KATAHDIN, 1861.   Length, 158′ 4″; beam, 28′; disp., 691 tons.

Type of the Ninety-Day Gunboats.

Before work on the fourteen sloops heretofore named had been undertaken, the Navy Department, acting on its own responsibility in the emergency, without waiting for the sanction of Congress, issued proposals and entered into contracts with different builders for the construction of twenty-three small, heavily-armed screw gunboats, of about 500 tons burden, which, from the rapidity of their construction came to be known in the service as "ninety-day gunboats." The contracts were nearly all made during the first two weeks in July, and work was pushed to such an extent that four of them were in the battle of Port Royal on the seventh of November, and seventeen of them were in active service before the end of the year. Their names were: *Huron, Sagamore, Itasca, Sciota, Kennebec, Kineo, Aroostook, Chippewa, Cayuga, Chocura, Kanawha, Katahdin, Marblehead, Ottawa, Owasco, Pembina, Penobscot, Pinola, Seneca, Tahoma, Unadilla, Wissahickon*, and *Winona*.

The machinery of the first four named was constructed by the Novelty Iron Works, New York, which establishment duplicated in them the machinery it had previously put into two gunboats built for the Russian government. The machinery for the other nineteen was built by various contractors from designs and specifications furnished by Engineer-in-Chief Isherwood, and was somewhat similar to that of the first four, but with about sixty per cent. more boiler power. The hulls of all these gunboats were built by contract.

For service in shallow and narrow rivers a new and peculiar type of gunboat was developed in the "double-enders," twelve of which were begun during the summer and fall of 1861. These were pointed at both ends and had a rudder at each end, being thus freed from the necessity of turning around by being able to steam at equal advantage in either direction. Paddle wheels had become practically obsolete for war vessels, but the imperative demand for very light draft in these gunboats made it necessary to adopt side wheels for their propulsion. They were the *Maratanza, Mahaska, Sebago, Octorora, Sonoma, Conemaugh, Tioga, Genessee, Miami, Paul Jones, Port Royal*, and *Cimmerone*. They were of 850 tons burden. The engines were built by contract from Mr. Isherwood's plans, and were of the direct-acting inclined type. All had Bartol's vertical water tube boilers, except the *Paul Jones*, which had Mar-

MARTIN'S VERTICAL WATER TUBE BOILER.

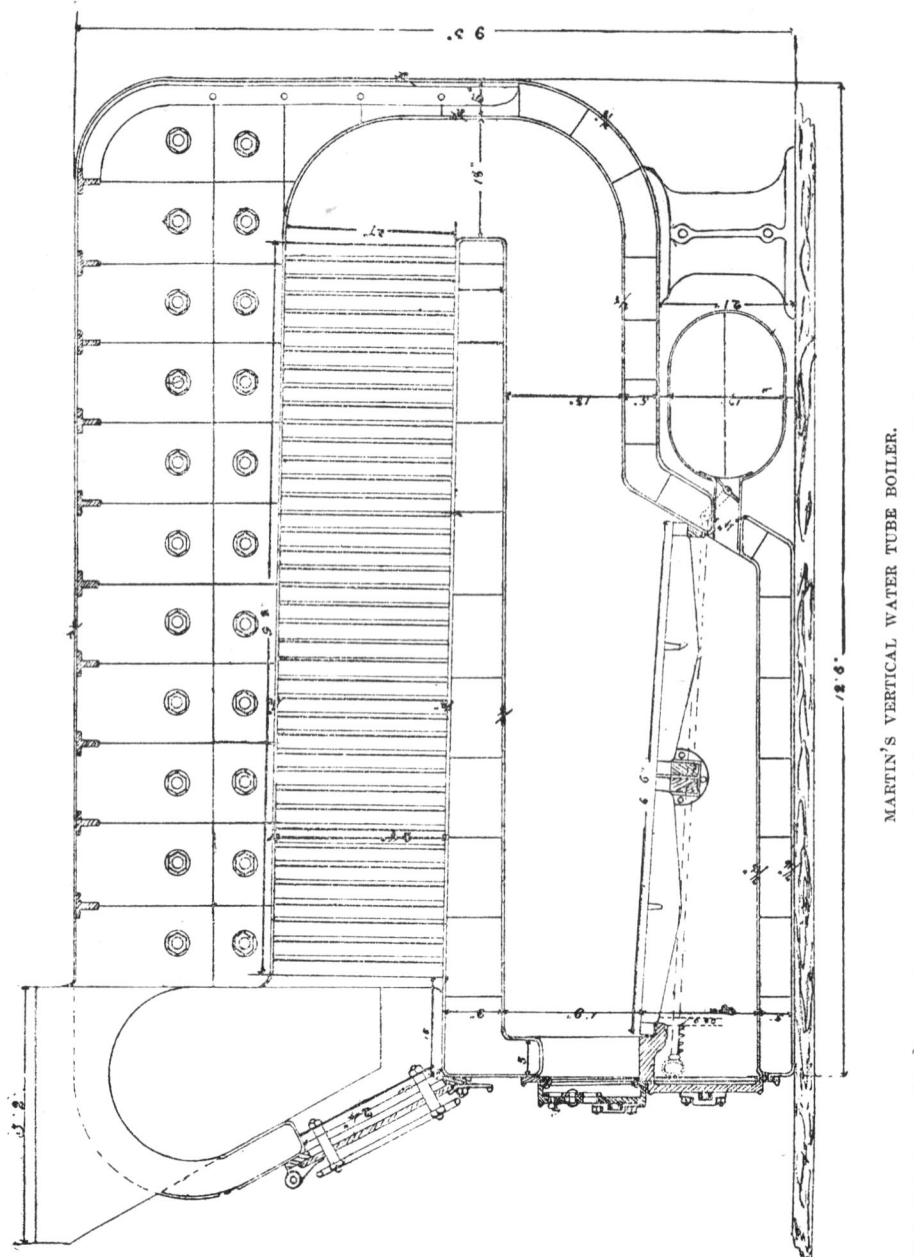

This Cut shows Air-duct and Arrangement for Ash-pan Forced-draft as Fitted to Boilers of the Ninety-day Gunboats, Many of the Double-enders, and Other Vessels Built During the War.

—11'3"—

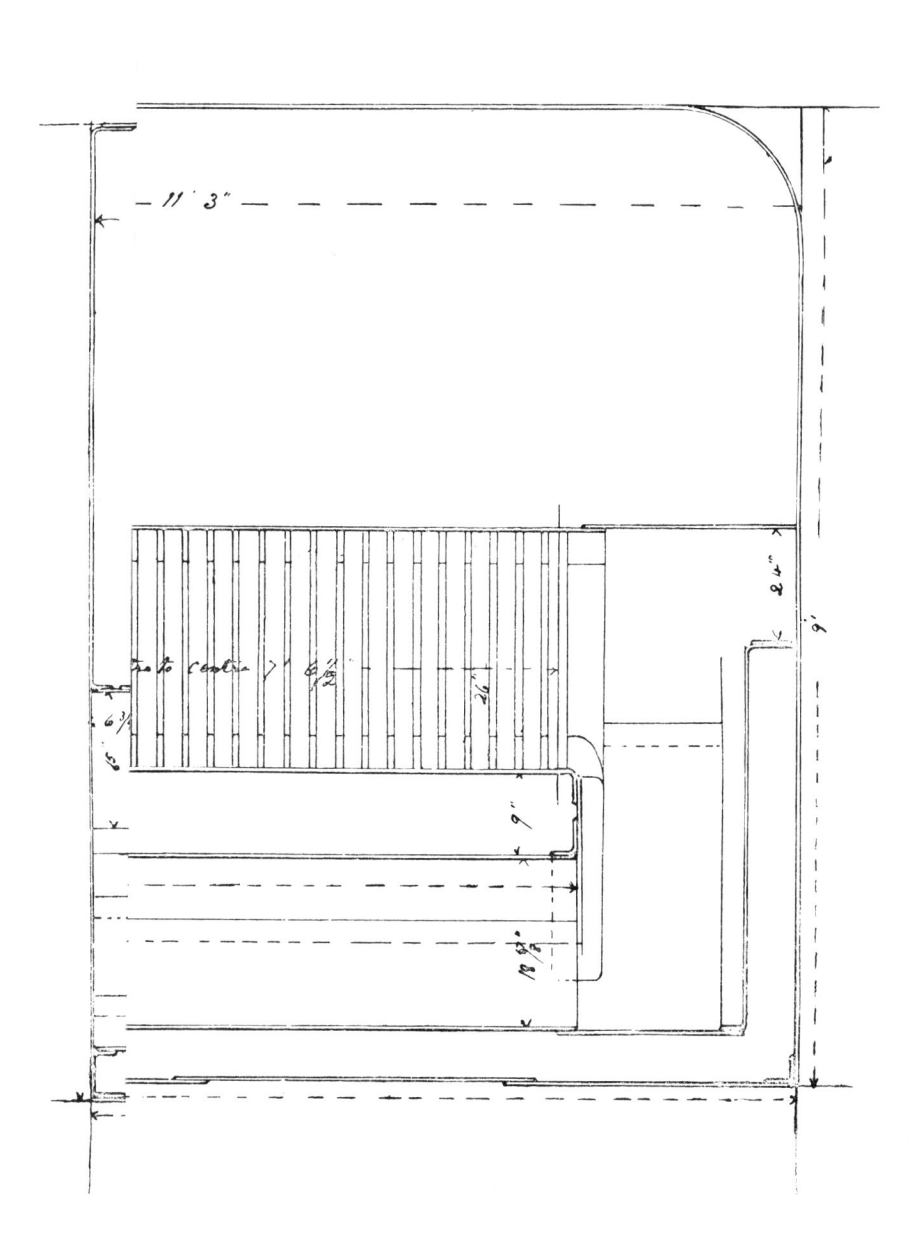

CHAPTER XIV.

"I have seen him in the watch-fires of a hundred circling camps;
They have builded him an altar in the evening dews and damps;
I have read his righteous sentence by the dim and flaring lamps;
His day is marching on."
JULIA WARD HOWE—*Battle-Hymn of the Republic.*

1861. The Civil War, Continued—The Norfolk Navy Yard—Attempt to Save the Frigate MERRIMAC—Endeavors of Engineer-in-Chief Isherwood—Destruction of the Yard—Attack on Hatteras Inlet—Destruction of the Privateer JUDAH at Pensacola.

WITH the exception of two events in the career of the frigate *Chesapeake* early in the present century, there are few incidents in our naval history more humiliating than the loss of several of our national vessels at the Norfolk navy yard at the beginning of the rebellion. So utterly lacking is this affair in redeeming features that it would be gladly passed over without comment were it not for the fact that the principal efforts to save the nation's honor and property on that occasion were the outcome of the zeal and patriotism of two naval engineers, and for that reason the story must be told as a necessary part of this history.

The navy yard at Norfolk, Virginia, at the beginning of 1861 was the largest and most important of the government navy yards. It was one of the oldest in date of establishment and the most completely equipped with wharves, docks, ship-houses, workshops, and store-houses. Great quantities of naval material and stores had been assembled there prior to the outbreak of the rebellion, among other war material there being about twelve hundred cannon of various types, mostly serviceable, although some of the guns were of very ancient patterns; fifty-two, according to the inventory made by the Confederates immediately after they took possession of the yard, were new nine-inch Dahlgren guns, at that time formidable pieces of ordnance.

At the beginning of April, 1861, the following named vessels were lying at the Norfolk Yard: the new steam frigate *Merrimac*, of forty guns; the sloops-of-war *Germantown* and *Plymouth*, of twenty-two guns each; the brig *Dolphin*, of four guns; the old ships-of-the-line *Pennsylvania*, *Delaware* and *Columbus*; the frigates *United States*, *Raritan* and *Columbia*; and the sloop-of-war *Cumberland*. An unfinished ship-of-the-line named the *New York* was on the stocks in one of the ship houses. The *Merrimac* was one of those large and beautiful steam frigates of which the Navy was then so justly proud. She had made one cruise, as flagship of the Pacific Station, and had been laid up in the Norfolk yard for an extensive overhauling of her machinery. The sloops *Germantown* and *Plymouth* were completely equipped for sea, but had no crews on board, and the *Dolphin* could have been made ready for sea in a few hours. The frigate *United States* was the same vessel, rebuilt, that had defeated and captured the British frigate *Macedonian* in 1812. The *Pennsylvania* was in commission as the receiving ship and was famous as being the largest ship-of-the-line ever built for our navy, mounting one hundred and twenty guns and being rated as of 3,241 tons, old measurement, which is little more than one-half the present rating by tons displacement. The other large battle ships of that time—the *North Carolina*, *Vermont* and others—carried eighty-four guns and were of about 2,600 tons. The *Cumberland* was the flagship of the home squadron and had just arrived at the yard after the usual winter cruise in Southern waters. She was saved from the destruction that followed, but less than a year later was destroyed by the *Merrimac*, which vessel by all rights should have been the one to have towed her and the other sailing vessels to a place of safety.

The navy yard was commanded by Captain Charles S. McCauley, a native of Pennsylvania, who, according to the custom then prevailing, was addressed as Commodore. The twelve other line officers associated with him were natives of southern states, seven of them being Virginians; three of the four medical officers were Virginians, and a majority of the other staff and warrant officers was likewise of southern nativity. These officers had been assigned to this station by the previous administration and the fact that the preponderance of southerners among them was so great makes it reasonably certain that there was more method than chance in their selection. The Chief Engineer of the yard, Mr. Robert Danby, was a native of Delaware and could be depended upon to stand by his colors, for the inhabitants of that little State have been distinguished for loyalty and patriotism ever since the "Blue Hen's Chickens," as the Delaware Regiment was called, made such an enviable record in the Continental Army.

One of the first acts of the new engineer-in-chief was to call the attention of the Secretary of the Navy to the possibility of getting the *Merrimac* away from Norfolk, and it is certain that had it not been for him no effort to that end would have been made. The Secretary's mind was engrossed with too many other important matters to give any thought to this particular subject unless it had been urged upon him and, indeed, it is more than probable, as he had been in office less than one month, and that month a most harrassing one, that he did not even know that the *Merrimac* was at Norfolk. Mr. Isherwood was familiar with the Norfolk yard and as the work on the *Merrimac's* machinery was an important detail of his office, the subject of saving the ship naturally suggested itself to his mind. By corresponding with chief engineer Danby, Mr. Isherwood had learned of the exact state of affairs, including the information that the Confederates counted surely on having the *Merrimac* as a nucleus for their future navy, which intention Mr. Isherwood determined to defeat if possible. With this knowledge he repeatedly urged Secretary Welles to order the removal of the ship and finally, on the 11th of April, orders were issued looking towards removing the *Merrimac* to Philadelphia, but about this time discouraging news came from Norfolk in the form of an official report saying that it would take a month to get her machinery in condition to move. This estimate of time was so different from the private information received from the chief of the yard that misrepresentation was evident and Mr. Isherwood at his own urgent request was ordered to go to Norfolk in person, take full charge of the *Merrimac*, and get her ready as soon as possible. He carried a peremptory order to Commodore McCauley to place the ship entirely in his hands, which order contained among other directions these words:

"The Department desires to have the *Merrimac* removed from the Norfolk to the Philadelphia Navy Yard with the utmost despatch. The Engineer-in-Chief, Mr. B. F. Isherwood, has been ordered to report to you for the purpose of expediting the duty,

CHIEF ENGINEER ROBERT DANBY, U. S. NAVY.

and you will have his suggestions for that end promptly carried into effect."

Mr. Isherwood arrived at the yard on Sunday morning, April 14th, and immediately, in company with Mr. Danby, made a most thorough examination of the *Merimac's* condition; the machinery was completely dismembered and many parts of it scattered about the shops, but nothing of importance was in such bad condition as to forbid its temporary use. The Navy yard employés had previously abandoned their places, but as many of the machinists and other mechanics were known to Mr. Isherwood and as Mr. Danby had been popular with them, those two officers succeeded that Sunday afternoon and evening in inducing a considerable number of them to resume work for a time. The force thus obtained began work Monday morning and worked night and day, being divided into three eight-hour gangs. Messrs. Isherwood and Danby relieving each other every twelve hours and exercising the most minute supervision over every detail, for they did not wish any mistakes to be made. On Wednesday afternoon Mr. Isherwood had the satisfaction of reporting to the Commandant that he was ready to get up steam. Commodore McCauley was seemingly startled by the suddenness of the preparation, after he had reported that a month's time would be necessary for the work that now appeared to have been done in three days, and when asked for authority to start fires hesitated and finally said, that the next morning would be soon enough, which order the engineers took the utmost advantage of by lighting the fires the very moment that midnight had passed. The following, from Boynton's history of the navy, gives an account of what followed with as much detail as is presented in any of the various historical accounts of this affair:

"About 9 o'clock on Thursday morning the report was made to Commodore McCauley that the vessel was ready to proceed, when he replied that he had not yet decided to send the steamer out. It was in vain that he was reminded of the peremptory nature of the order which Mr. Isherwood brought from the Secretary of the Navy, to get the Frigate out at the earliest possible moment and send her to Philadelphia; he only replied that in the course of the day he would let his decision be known. He seemed to fear that obstructions had been placed in the channel. He was told by those who were well informed that the obstructions already there would be easily passed by the *Merrimac*, but that every night's delay would increase the danger. All this produced no effect. Early in the afternoon Mr. Isherwood again called upon Commodore McCauley, who then said that he had decided to retain the frigate, and ordered the fires to be drawn. He was again reminded of the peremptory nature of the orders from the Navy Department, but it seemed to produce no impression; he had determined to retain her, and thus the noble frigate was lost."

The writer has been at great pains to get at the real truth of this event and with that object in view has made a careful study of the various official reports and documents relating to the case, as well as making use of numerous histories which treat of naval operations during the Civil War. More recently he has been favored with a thorough and most carefully written account of the affair from the pen of the chief actor—Chief Engineer Isherwood—which throws light upon some of the dark places found in the usual accounts, and which will be made use of as this narrative progresses. The principal officers concerned in the event were called upon to testify before the Senate Committee which investigated the Conduct of the War, and, while they told the truth so far as they went, they told no more than was necessary, for at that time it would not have been either patriotic or politic, to have made some of the details public; and this restriction applies to a considerable extent even yet.

Commodore McCauley's conduct appears highly inconsistent with the theory that he was loyal to the Government and anxious to defend his country's honor, notwithstanding which all the evidence shows that he was both loyal and patriotic. At the time of this trouble he had been *fifty-two* years in the Navy, having lived all through that long and uneventful period following the war of 1812, which may well be called the Dark Age of our naval history, during which midshipmen grew to middle age before becoming lieutenants, and then remained in that grade until old age was actually upon them, before they rose to a position of individual responsibility. He was surrounded by younger officers who, as we have already seen, were southerners and who systematically deceived him by false rumors and imaginary difficulties, but, upon whom the Commodore depended entirely, never doubting their loyalty to him, until they actually deserted their posts of duty.

In addition to the perplexities of the actual situation at the navy yard, the Commodore was hampered with political instructions from Washington which simply added to his bewilderment. - There was a false hope that Virginia would not secede, and President Lincoln was led to believe by arguments and influences that probably no one but himself ever knew, that an attitude of confidence and trust towards Virginia, on the part of the Federal Government would so conciliate the people that they would remain true to the Union. This in spite of the fact that Norfolk was full of armed men openly avowing their intention to seize upon the Navy yard, and that the Virginia authorities had begun obstructing the channels and placing guns to oppose the egress of any of the national vessels. So commodore McCauley was repeatedly cautioned not to do anything that might appear hostile, or provoking to the Virginians, and at the same time he was ordered to save the public property under his command by any means in his power.

All these contradictions and perplexities were too much for the Commodore to unravel, having spent the greater part of his life in a sphere where he only did what some one else told him to do, it is no wonder therefore, that the poor old man was unable to rise to the occasion. To his mind, long before narrowed to follow the one straight line of naval customs and precedents, the situation was most irregular and wholly inexplicable. His common sense told him that the information that his subordinates gave him could not be true, and yet he accepted it as truth because he himself had always been true to his superiors, and naval laws explicitly required such loyalty. Never before had he heard people talk of taking posession of a navy yard, a place sacred by every tradition of the service to the imperial sway of the commandant; never before had navy yard workmen been known to leave their employment and refuse to return except as hostiles; never before had the majesty of a navy yard been outraged by officers walking out of the gates without leave, and without written orders properly endorsed by the commandant as required by regulation. And then, as if to prove that all signs had failed, the infallible regulations themselves contained not a word of instruction as to what to do in case of insurrection and threatened seizure of a navy yard. The fault was not with Commodore McCauley, but with the system that had trained him.

Mr. Isherwood thus graphically describes the pitiful situation of the Commodore at this trying time:

"The Commodore was in a state of complete prostration. He sat in his office immovable, not knowing what to do. He was weak, vacillating, hesitating, and overwhelmed by the responsibilities of his position. He listened blandly, or seemed to listen, to what was said to him, but could not be made to give any order or take any action. I kept reporting to him what I was doing and what I intended to do. He looked vaguely at me, nodded his head, but said nothing. He behaved as though he were stupefied. He was a very good man, personally brave and loyal, perplexed in the extreme, deserted by his officers, and utterly unequal to the occasion. As a subordinate he would have done well; as a principal he was a wretched failure. I endeavored to advise him, to explain the object of the Department, and to make him understand the necessity of getting the *Merrimac* out at once, and I told him we could tow out at the same time several other vessels. I knew the Navy Yard would be in our possession but a few days longer, and wanted to save all the public property I could, as well as to diminish the force of the enemy by preventing it from falling into their hands. All was in vain. I could not get him to do anything. He never came near the vessel."

After getting up steam Thursday morning Mr. Isherwood kept the engines running at the dock all day as a visible sign that the Frigate was ready to go; he had got enough coal and stores on board by his own exertions (for no official of the Yard except Mr. Danby aided him by word or deed during all this time) to take the vessel as far as Newport News where she would be safe. Knowing that Commander Alden, who had been ordered to take command of the vessel after her machinery had been put in working order, was meeting with every obstacle that red-tapeism could suggest to prevent his getting men, Mr. Isherwood had inquired among his mechanics and found some who had been to sea, and these he detailed as wheelmen to steer the vessel. By lavish promises of pay he secured a sufficient number of the others to act as firemen, oilers, etc. and these men faithfully agreed to work the ship as far as Newport News, which promise they undoubtedly would have kept, as they needed the large sums offered them, and they were under many obligations to Chief Engineer Danby for liberal treatment when employed under him in the yard. Mr. Isherwood also on his own authority had the chain cables that secured the ship to the dock removed and replaced with rope hawsers and he had provided axes and stationed men with them to cut the hawsers when the word to go was given. Many other details of preparation were attended to by him and throughout the day the vessel was entirely ready to go out, which she could easily have done without a pilot as she was so light without coal, guns, or stores that she would easily have passed over the obstructions already in the channel. But the commandant would not say the word which would have authorized them to start.

It is pertinent to say just here, that the orders to Mr. Isherwood gave him full and absolute authority over the ship until the engines were in condition to drive her; then Commander Alden was by his orders to assume command and take the ship to sea. Had this authority been vested in Mr. Isherwood the *Merrimac* would have been saved and the carnage that Hampton Roads saw the following March would never have been heard of. As it was, Mr. Isherwood had to resist a very strong temptation to take charge of the ship himself, but he had been in the service too many years not to understand the full significance of the laws and regulations that declared staff officers not eligible to exercise command, and he felt that no meritorious result of such an assumption on his part, even if it were the saving of one of the finest ships in the Navy, would serve to excuse his encroachment upon the prerogatives held as belonging only to another class of officers. Mr. Isherwood himself writes as follows relative to this perplexing crisis:

"As I witnessed the gradual dying out of the revolutions of the *Merrimac's* engines at the dock I was greatly tempted to cut the ropes that held her, and to bring her out on my own responsibility. This would have been my destruction, for then, the disasters which followed her detention, and which are my justification for the desire to take the matter into my own hands, would not have happened."

The last act in this miserable affair, when the commandant finally refused to allow the ship to leave and directed her fires to be hauled, is told by Chief Engineer Isherwood in a letter to the writer, as follows:

"Although I could not get the Commodore to take any decisive action I kept the engines working at the dock all day in hopes that he might be persuaded to carry out the plain intentions of the Department. Late in the afternoon, at our last interview, he told me to draw the fires and stop the engines as he had decided to retain the vessel and meant to defend the yard. I looked at him with amazement, went over the case again, urged the orders and the desire of the Department, told him the inevitable consequences of his decision, tried to show him the utter absurdity of attempting to defend an unfortified navy yard without men or any military means at command, for by this time he was absolutely alone. But he was brave, had a high sense of honor and duty and considered himself bound to struggle to the last. If he had had the smallest force on which he could have depended he would have died gallantly, and I believe gladly, at its head, sword in hand against any odds.

"Finding that I could not move him and that he was growing impatient at my reiterated appeals I drew from my pocket the order of the Department to me, wrote upon it the usual indorsement that having completed the duty assigned me to return to Washington, and laid it before him. He understood the significance of the act, but signed the indorsement without a word. With great sorrow and chagrin I dismissed my men, waited until the engines made their last revolution, when I left the navy yard, and have never seen it since."

On Wednesday, the 17th of April, the State Convention of Virginia had passed the Ordinance of Secession, so there was no excuse whatever on Thursday, for maintaining a pacific attitude at the yard for fear of provoking the disloyal sentiment among the inhabitants into open rebellion; the rebellion was already declared and the time for temporizing had passed. Why the *Merrimac*, with her engines working and a sufficient number of men on board to handle her, did not that day tow out to safety the other vessels is one of those speculative questions that cannot be satisfactorily answered. Like many other controversies over sins of omission in the past, this question is important chiefly on account of the disasters that followed in the footsteps of the first error, the knowledge of which was of course hidden at the time that its possession would have incited action on the part of those whose failure it is now easy to criticise.

Mr. Isherwood's work on the *Merrimac* was known to all in Norfolk, and naturally, was greatly resented by the populace, as it was a menace to the prospects of possessing the ship. In fact, only a week before, the *Merrimac* had been moved under the shears of the ordnance wharf to have her guns placed on board, and this act had raised such a howl of protest that the commandant had stopped the work and moved her back, so we can readily understand the feeling when it was known that her machinery was being fitted for use. A plot to capture Mr. Isherwood and hold him as a prisoner of war was hatched, and it was only by chance that he escaped falling into the hands of his country's enemies. Fortunately for him, a civilian in the town, who knew of the plot was his warm personal friend and this gentleman warned him of his danger. The friend engaged a room on the Baltimore steamer in the morning, in his own name, and took possession of it with Mr. Isherwood's trunk, going later with a closed carriage to the hotel and conveying the unwelcome guest to the steamer, where he remained locked in the room until the boat was well out in Chesapeake Bay. A party of Confederates waited for hours on the wharf for him to arrive, and only knew by going to the hotel after the steamer had left, that their enemy had outwitted them and escaped. After his return to the Department Mr. Isherwood made a short written report of his connection with the *Merrimac*, and the Secretary and himself never exchanged a word about it. It was tacitly understood that the subject was to be ignored, as one not politic for the public to know in the existing state of high feeling and excitement, and it was ignored.

Following closely upon the events before narrated, came the order to abandon the navy yard. Captain Hiram Paulding, in the steam sloop-of-war, *Pawnee* with one hundred marines and a raw regiment of Massachusetts volunteers went up to the yard on April 20 and found the *Germantown, Plymouth,* and *Dolphin* scuttled and rapidly sinking, which prevented him from carrying out his intention to use those vessels to defend the channel. Feeling that the yard was hopelessly lost, and not wishing to let anything of value fall into the hands of the enemy, he ordered the destruction by fire of everything inflammable, and the work-shops, ship-houses, many of the ships, and numerous other buildings went up in smoke that night. The guns were spiked and many of them permanently ruined by knocking off the trunnions, but all efforts in this direction failed with the Dahlgren guns and they afterward became dreaded weapons in the hands of the enemy. The wild scene of destruction was of unearthly awfulness and sublimity utterly indescribable. The upper works of the *Merrimac* were burned away, but the submerged portion of the hull remained intact and was subsequently used with terrible effect.

As the morning of Sunday, the 21st, approached, the *Pawnee* took the *Cumberland* in tow and departed, leaving behind no vestage of the soverignty of the United States. The Confederates rushed in as the Union forces left, extinguished the train that was to blow up the granite dry dock, saved the officers' houses and some other buildings, and thus provided themselves with the nucleus for a great naval station. Thus was public property to the value of ten millions of dollars destroyed or lost to the Government. One of the vessels which escaped destruction that dreadful night was the historical old frigate *United States*, but her respite was brief, for, in May of the following year, when the Confederates in turn had to abandon Norfolk, she, too, notwithstanding the glorious memories that clustered about her, was burned to ashes.

In the latter part of August, 1861, an expedition planned by the Navy Department, and commanded by Flag Officer Stringham, proceeded from Hampton Roads to attack Hatteras Inlet, which place had been fortified and armed with guns taken from the Norfolk navy yard. Two transport steamers, carrying about nine hundred troops under the command of Major General Benjamin F. Butler, accompanied this expedition as a part of the combined attacking force. The naval vessels composing the squadron were the steamers *Minnesota, Wabash, Susquehanna, Monticello, Pawnee,* and *Harriet Lane,* and the sailing frigate *Cumberland.* About thirty engineers of the navy were attached to these vessels and in their appointed stations performed their duties thoroughly and well, keeping the motive power of their vessels in a constant condition of readiness and efficiency to meet any demand that the exigencies of the expedition might require.

The squadron arrived off Hatteras on August 28, and immediately landed the soldiers and marines to attack the fortifications from the land, in conjunction with the bombardment from the ships, which was maintained all the afternoon and resumed the morning of the 29th, ceasing only with the surrender of the enemy about 11 A. M. that day. The most exciting event connected with this affair was a bad quarter of an hour experienced by the *Monticello,* during which she narrowly escaped destruction. This small steamer, after assisting in landing the marines and soldiers, was supplied with a local coast pilot by the flag-ship and ordered to go in through the inlet to see what was going on inside. The pilot, either by design or through ignorance, took her into the wrong channel and she began to strike bottom when in dangerous proximity to the forts, the shoalness of the water finally obliging her to abandon her undertaking and to try to work out to sea again. Seeing the *Monticello* in this distress the large fort of fifteen guns, which had not molested her up to that time, opened on her with a furious cannonade, which was returned with the fire of such guns as could be brought to bear. By working the engines rapidly back and forth, to take advantage of the swell and eddying currents, the ship was finally turned around and worked out of her dangerous predicament, not, however, until she had suffered seriously from the merciless storm of shot and shell poured upon her. Her escape from destruction was due in large measure to the skill and ability of the engineers under whose alert charge the machinery responded instantly to every movement required. Commander John P. Gillis, who commanded the *Monticello* at the time, in reporting this experience expressed his indebtedness to the acting chief engineer of the ship—Mr. George M. Waite—"for his care and promptness in the management of the engine." The assistant engineers of the *Monticello* at this time were Messrs. Jonathan Thomas and Columbus L. Griffin.

On the night of September 13, the U. S. S. *Colorado*, lying off Fort Pickens, Florida, sent out an expedition in four boats against the navy yard at Pensacola then in possession of the Confederates, the objects of the expedition being the destruction of the schooner *Judah* fitting out at one of the docks for a privateer, and the spiking of a gun in battery at the southeast end of the yard. The party consisted of exactly one hundred officers, seamen and marines, the officers being Lieutenants Russell, Sproston, and Blake, Captain Reynolds of the marine corps; Assistant Surgeon Kennedy, Assistant Engineer George H. White, Gunner Boreton and Midshipmen Steece, Forrest and Higginson.

The attack was made on the morning of the 14th at half past three o'clock. Instead of surprising the enemy, the crew of the *Judah* was found awake and ready to receive the expedition, doing great damage with musketry fire as the boats approached, and not giving up their vessel until after a most desperate hand-to-hand combat on the deck. The schooner being captured and set on fire, and the gun spiked, the naval expedition withdrew, for by that time the yard was as busy as a hornet's nest and fully one thousand Confederates were swarming for an attack. The Union party had three men killed and twelve wounded, among the latter being Captain Reynolds of the marines and Midshipman F. J. Higginson, who had the end of his thumb shot off.

Assistant Engineer White's part in the exploits of the night is indicated by the following extracts from the official report of the affair:

"In the meantime the vessel was set on fire in several places. That which finally consumed her was lighted in the cabin by Assistant Engineer White and a coal-heaver Patrick Driscoll, who went as a volunteer."

"Assistant Engineer White brought down from the cross-trees of the schooner a man who had been seen to fire upon the boats, killing him instantly."

CHAPTER XV.

> "I have read a fiery gospel writ in burnished rows of steel;
> 'As ye deal with my contemnérs so with you my grace shall deal';
> Let the Hero, born of woman, crush the serpent with his heel;
> Since God is marching on."
> JULIA WARD HOWE—*Battle Hymn of the Republic.*

1861. The Civil War, Continued.—Expedition of Flag Officer Du Pont to Port Royal.—Loss of the *Governor*.—Naval Battle at Port Royal.—Killing of Assistant Engineer Whittemore on the *Mohican*.—The Affair of the *Trent*.

IN dividing the coast for convenience in maintaining the blockade proclaimed along the entire sea line of the insurgent states the limits of the South Atlantic blockading squadron were fixed at the boundary line between the Carolinas on the north and Cape Florida on the south. This region being far from any of the Union ports it became necessary to establish somewhere within its limits a harbor of refuge in heavy weather where a repair station and depot could be maintained. In order to seize such a place and hold it with a strong garrison a large combined army and naval expedition, commanded by Flag Officer Samuel F. DuPont and Brigadier General T. W. Sherman (not Wm. T. Sherman), was fitted out and sailed from Hampton Roads on the 29th of October. The frigate *Wabash*, Commander C. R. P. Rodgers, was the flagship, and the fleet, numbering forty-eight vessels including the troop ships, was the largest ever before assembled under our flag. A fleet of twenty-five schooners laden with coal was despatched the previous day under convoy of the sailing sloop of war *Vandalia* with orders to rendezvous at sea off Savannah.

On November 1st the fleet was scattered by a furious gale from the southeast, approaching a hurricane in violence, and some of the vessels fared very badly, especially the transports which had been hurriedly purchased or chartered and in some cases were actually unseaworthy. The steamer *Governor*, in which was embarked the fine battalion of marines, foundered, and the marines with seven exceptions were rescued by the frigate *Sabine* and the steamer

Isaac Smith, the latter vessel having been obliged to throw overboard her battery to save herself. The transport *Peerless* also went down and her people were taken off in boats under the most perilous circumstances by the crew of the *Mohican*.

The selection of the point to be captured was left entirely to the judgment of Flag Officer DuPont, who decided that Port Royal, South Carolina, was the best located and most suitable for a station for the blockading squadron. Accordingly as the vessels began to reassemble after the gale, the *Wabash* led them to the vicinity of that place and anchored off the bar during the day of November 4. All buoys and other aids to navigation had been removed by the enemy, which made it necessary to find, sound, and buoy the channel before any of the vessels could venture further, the bar being several miles off shore. This work was done under the direction of Mr. Boutelle the Assistant Chief of the Coast Survey, who was very familiar with the coast in this region and who was fortunately with the expedition in charge of a small steamer named the *Vixen*. Late in the afternoon the transports drawing less than eighteen feet of water and all the gun-vessels were sent to the anchorage in Port Royal roadstead, the gunboats having a brush with two or three Confederate steamers under command of Commodore Tatnall, of " blood is thicker than water " fame, and drove them under the shelter of the batteries on Bay Point and Hilton Head (Forts Beauregard and Walker).

The next morning, November 5, the grave responsibility of hazarding the noble frigate *Wabash* in crossing the bar was assumed by DuPont and that vessel, thanks to the careful work of Mr. Boutelle, was safely taken inside, followed by the side-wheel frigate *Susquehanna* and the deep-draught transports. Immediate preparation for action was made but various delays, among them the grounding of the *Wabash* after getting into the roadstead, occurred and night came on before the fleet was ready, while a southwesterly gale the following day again postponed the assault.

On the morning of November 7 the fleet got under way to attack the forts, the order of battle comprising a main squadron ranged in line ahead, and a flanking squadron to engage the enemy's vessels and prevent them from cutting off any of the vessels that might be disabled and fall out of action. The main squadron was made up of the *Wabash, Susquehanna, Mohican, Seminole, Pawnee, Unadilla, Ottawa, Pembina,* and the sailing-sloop *Vandalia* towed by the *Isaac Smith;* the flanking squadron was composed of the *Bienville, Seneca, Curlew, Penguin,* and *Augusta.* The battle was opened by a gun from Fort Walker at 9:26 A. M. and ended about 2 P. M.; the enemy abandoning his works with great zeal and precipitation. Commander C. R. P. Rodgers with a force of marines and blue jackets went ashore from the *Wabash* and took possession of Fort Walker and by nightfall a brigade of troops was landed and in possession. At sunrise the next morning Lieutenant commanding Daniel Ammen of the *Seneca* landed and hoisted the American flag on Fort Beauregard. The forts were badly damaged by the furious cannonading to which they had been subjected, the terrific nature of which can be understood from the fact that the *Wabash* alone fired nearly nine hundred shells, besides grape and shrapnel.

The foregoing briefly outlines the circumstances attending the taking possession of the forts by the Union forces, and is given in the usual form in which the event is recorded in history. The following extracts from Flag Officer DuPont's detailed report of the engagement furnish the foundation for the bestowal upon the distinguished Rodgers brothers of the honor of landing first and personally taking possession of Fort Walker:

"I sent Commander John Rodgers on shore with a flag of truce. The hasty flight of the enemy was visible, and was reported from the tops. At twenty minutes after two Captain Rodgers hoisted the flag of the Union over the deserted post. At forty-five minutes after two I anchored and sent Commander C. R. P. Rodgers on shore with the marines and a party of seamen to take possession, and prevent, if necessary, the destruction of public property."

"Commander John Rodgers, a passenger in this ship, going to take command of the steamer *Flag*, volunteered to act upon my staff. It would be difficult for me to enumerate the duties he performed, they were so numerous and various, and he brought to them all an invincible energy and the highest order of professional knowledge and merit. I was glad to show my appreciation of his great services by allowing him the honor to hoist the first American flag on the rebellious soil of South Carolina."

In large operations of this nature it is customary, and perhaps proper, to give credit for worthy deeds to the officer who commands, the acts of his subordinates being assumed to be his own. The actual details attending the landing at Fort Walker differ somewhat from the usual historical accounts, and have been learned by the author from some documents loaned him by Mr. Hillary Messimer, Superintendent of Motive Power of the Calumet and Hecla Mining Company, one of the most important papers being a letter written in 1883 by Rear Admiral C. R. P. Rodgers, then on the retired list.

It appears from these records that Third Assistant Engineer Hillary Messimer of the *Wabash*, hereafter referred to as having excited the admiration of his superior officers by his coolness and attention to duty during the action while stationed at the engine-room signal on the bridge, was selected by Flag Officer DuPont to take charge of an armed party of marines to land and spike the guns in the fort should the enemy show any signs of returning. Mr. Messimer's party took, besides the necessary tools, an American flag with which he landed and was inside the works with men stationed at the guns ready to spike them before Commander John Rodgers set his foot on the shore. The latter officer shoved off from the *Wabash* when Messimer's boat was almost on shore and his men about to jump overboard to land, in doing which a few moments later Messimer took care to be first, although followed closely by his men, and to him belongs the credit of being the first person from the Union force to land in this stronghold of the enemy. With his own hands, assisted by a marine corporal, Mr. Messimer hauled down the Confederate flags from the general and regimental headquarters, after which, leaving a sergeant in command of the spiking party, he went down to the beach to meet Commander C. R. P. Rodgers then landing with a force of men from the *Wabash*.

After receiving and approving Messimer's report of what he had done, Commander Rodgers ordered him to go off to the flagship and deliver to Flag Officer DuPont the captured flags and five Confederate prisoners whom he had taken, and then to return to the fort with the chaplain of the ship to bury the dead; all which was done. A sword carried on board the *Wabash* with the Confederate flags was afterward given to Mr. Messimer by Flag Officer DuPont with the complimentary remark, "You have earned it."

This engagement furnishes one of the many striking instances illustrative of the division of families over the issues which caused the Civil War. The Confederate commander of the works at Port Royal was General Drayton brother of Commander Percival Drayton of the Federal navy, whose vessel, the *Pocahontas*, was so disabled in the gale on the voyage down that he did not arrive in time to be assigned a position in the order of battle, but he succeeded in reaching the scene of action about noon and rendered gallant service by engaging the batteries on both sides in succession, and aided materially in driving his brother and his men out of the works.

Several of the vessels engaged were badly cut up by the fire from the forts and it was a matter of surprise, expressed at the time in the official reports, that the casualties under the circumstances were not greater than they were. These amounted to eight killed and twenty-three wounded, seven of the latter severely. The only officer killed was Third Assistant Engineer John W. Whittemore, of the *Mohican*, who was stationed on deck at the engine room telegraph where he was instantly killed by a solid shot coming through the hammock rail and driving before it a piece of an iron bolt or screw from the rigging which passed through his head. Mr. Whittemore was the son of a celebrated Universalist minister of Boston, and was a highly cultured and accomplished young gentleman, whose New England spirit of patriotism had impelled him to enter the naval service in a capacity where he felt he could serve his country most usefully. He had been in the service less than three months at the time of his death, but in that short time his many admirable qualities had greatly endeared him to all who were associated with him.

On the same vessel another assistant engineer, Mr. Mayland Cuthbert, narrowly escaped being killed while at his post of duty in the starboard gangway in charge of the fire division. A shot struck the main yard and cut the jack stay into pieces, one of which took an oblique direction downward, striking Cuthbert in the thigh and inflicting a frightful wound, in which the femoral artery was laid bare, but fortunately not cut. The vacancy on the *Mohican* caused by the killing of Whittemore was filled by transferring Assistant Engineer Absalom Kirby from the *Pocahontas*, which fact is mentioned because, by a curious coincidence, Mr. Kirby had narrowly escaped being killed in the action under the same circumstances leading to the death of Mr. Whittemore. He, also, was stationed at the engine-room bell, which on the *Pocahontas* was attached to the main mast, and while standing at his station a solid shot passed through the mast within a few inches of his head, showering him with splinters but doing him no serious harm.

Attached to the various steamers of the assaulting squadron were about seventy-five officers of the Engineer Corps, regulars and volunteers, all of whom acquitted themselves with great credit and by their skilful performance of duty, contributed very materially to the success of the undertaking. The chief or senior engineers of the different vessels engaged were the following: *Wabash*, J. W King; *Susquehanna*, Geo. Sewell; *Mohican*, E. D. Robie, *Seminole*, R. L. Harris; *Pawnee*, W. H. Rutherford; *Unadilla*, Edw. Marsland; *Ottawa*, W. W. Dungan; *Pembina*, Jefferson Young; *Isaac Smith*, J. Tucker; *Bienville*, W. H. Wright; *Seneca*, J. W. de Krafft; *Curlew*, George R. Emory; *Penguin*, M. P. Randall; *Augusta*, George V. Sloat. Mr. J. M. Hobby, who at a later period in the war signally distinguished himself as chief engineer of the *Sassacus* in battle with the ram *Albemarle*, was, on this occasion, the first assistant of the *Susquehanna*.

That one at least of the vessels was kept in action by the ability of her engineers is shown by the following extract from the report of the commanding officer of the *Curlew*:

"Messrs Emory, Swasey, McConnell, and Loyds engineers of the vessel, with great difficulties to contend against, in the general unfitness of engine, boilers and condensing apparatus, for such rough service, managed to carry us through the action, for which I was thankful.

Commander C. R. P. Rodgers of the flag ship reported as follows regarding the work of the engineers of that vessel.

"The engine and steam, during the whole action, were managed with consummate skill, which did great credit to Chief Engineer King and his assistants. Third Assistant Engineer Messimer, who stood upon the bridge by my side during the action, impressed me very favorably by his cool intelligence and promptness."

Flag officer DuPont also mentioned Mr. Messimer's excellence in his report of the battle, and in other reports of commanding officers occur references from which one concludes that the engineers were very necessary officials and a part of the combatant element of the fleet.

The affair of the *Trent*, on account of its international aspect, attracted probably more attention and wide-spread interest than any other single event connected with the operations of the Navy during the Civil War, and, as two officers of the engineer corps were prominently concerned, it is proper that a brief account be given in this work. The U. S. Steamer, *San Jacinto*, commanded by Captain Charles Wilkes, was employed the latter part of this year in cruising about the West Indies seeking for the Confederate privateer *Sumter*, which had committed numerous depredations in those waters; the last day of October the *San Jacinto* went into the port of Havana, where Wilkes learned that Messrs Mason and Slidell, commissioners from the insurgent states to England and France, were about to sail from that port for St. Thomas on their way to Europe in the British mail steamer *Trent*. These gentlemen with their families and secretaries had escaped from the blockade about Charleston in a famous swift blockade-runner, the *Theodora*, which had landed them at Cardenas in Cuba. Captain Wilkes was a grim, taciturn seaman of the old school, which had for its chief article of faith the celebrated sentiment of Stephen Decatur—"Our country! In her intercourse with foreign nations may she always be in the right; but our country, right or wrong,"—so when he learned of the proposed expedition of the Confederate emissaries to preach disruption of the Union abroad, there was, according to his lights, but one course of action to pursue, and that was, to intercept them, "right or wrong."

With this determination in his mind Captain Wilkes went to sea on the 2nd of November, after having coaled ship in Havana, and for a day or two cruised along the northern coast of Cuba looking for the *Sumter*; then he went over to Key West hoping to find the *Powhatan* to accompany him on his intended enterprise, but that ship had gone to sea the day before, thus making it necessary for the *San Jacinto* to watch for the *Trent* alone. The *Trent* was scheduled to sail from Havana on the 7th of November, and to make sure of her, Wilkes went down the coast some two hundred and forty miles to a place on the sea route to St. Thomas where the old Bahama Channel narrows to a width of fifteen miles; here the *San Jacinto* arrived on November 4 and laid in wait for her prey, with all the patience of a red Mohawk lurking sleeplessly on the trail over which his enemy might pass. About noon of November 8 the *Trent* ran into this fatal snare and was hove to by a shell thrown across her bows, after a shot had been disregarded.

The interesting details of what happened when the *Trent* was boarded are given hereafter in the copies of official reports of the boarding officers. For the present it is sufficient to say that Messrs. Mason and Slidell, after refusing to leave the mail steamer, were man-handled and put into the boats of the *San Jacinto*, taken aboard that vessel as prisoners, and ultimately incarcerated in Fort Warren, Boston Harbor. The *Trent* was allowed to resume her voyage after the commissioners had been taken. After a few weeks imprisonment Mason and Slidell were delivered to the British government in response to a demand not over gracious made by Earl Russel. Captain Wilkes made a mistake in allowing the *Trent* to escape, for the weight of precedent, established by decisions of the British admiralty courts, was largely on the side of the theory that neutral vessels knowingly carrying officials or despatches of the enemy were liable to capture and condemnation. No accepted principle of international law justified the act of taking the commissioners out of the vessel, and no nation but England had ever insisted upon such a right; indeed, in 1812, the United States had gone to war with the mother-country in opposition to the very doctrine involved in Wilkes' act.

It is not probable, however, that Wilkes' technical breach of international law in failing to take the *Trent* into port as a prize had any real effect upon subsequent events in the case; such a procedure would have been entirely in accord with the established rules of war, but the wave of popular indignation and rage which swept over England when the passengers of the *Trent* came home with their tale, is sufficient proof that considerations of abstract right would not have a determining part in the action taken by the

British Government. The United States, being fully employed in the task of suppressing the most gigantic rebellion that ever threatened a nation's life, could not engage in war with powerful neighbors disposed to seek it, and the demands made had to be acceded to whether agreeable or not. A few years later, when the rebellion was crushed, and the United States had a million armed men, hardened by years of campaigning both ready and willing for any service, and our navy, with five hundred vessels in commission, possessed the heaviest iron-clads and the swiftest cruisers in the world, another controversey between England and our country ended in the former swallowing her pride, and accepting the decidedly humiliating terms imposed by an arbitration commission. The two events, considered singly or together, are an excellent illustration of the truth of the principle, that might more frequently than right determines the actions of nations as well as of men.

The officers of the *San Jacinto* who boarded the *Trent*, although performing a duty in which they had no personal concern, were treated with great contempt and indignity on board that vessel, and exhibited in return a spirit of forbearance and dignity highly creditable to them, and the service which they represented. The details of their experience on board the *Trent* are usually eclipsed by the more important complications growing out of the event; they are, however, most interesting as showing what naval officers sometimes have to do in the line of their varied duties, and are here presented in the form of the reports made by the boarding officers.

UNITED STATES STEAMER SAN JACINTO,
At Sea, November 12, 1861.

SIR: At 1:20 p. m., on the 8th instant, I repaired alongside of the British mail packet in an armed cutter, accompanied by Mr. Houston, second assistant engineer, and Mr. Grace, the boatswain.

I went on board the *Trent* alone, leaving the two officers in the boat with orders to await until it became necessary to show some force.

I was shown up by the first officer to the quarter-deck, where I met the Captain and informed him who I was, asking to see the passenger list. He declined letting me see it. I then told him that I had information of Mr. Mason, Mr. Slidell, Mr. Eustis, and Mr.

McFarland having taken their passage at Havana in the packet to St. Thomas, and would satisfy myself whether they were on board before allowing the steamer to proceed. Mr. Slidell, evidently hearing his name mentioned, came up to me and asked if I wanted to see him. Mr. Mason soon joined us, and then Mr. Eustis and Mr. McFarland, when I made known the object of my visit. The captain of the *Trent* opposed anything like the search of his vessel, nor would he consent to show papers or passenger list. The four gentlemen above mentioned protested also against my arresting and sending them to the United States steamer near by. There was considerable noise among the passengers just about this time, and that led Mr. Houston and Mr. Grace to repair on board with some six or eight men, all armed. After several unsuccessful efforts to persuade Mr. Mason and Mr. Slidell, to go with me peaceably, I called to Mr. Houston and ordered him to return to the ship with the information that the four gentlemen named in your order of the 8th instant were on board, and force must be applied to take them out of the packet.

About three minutes after there was still greater excitement on the quarter deck, which brought Mr. Grace with his armed party. I however deemed the presence of any armed men unnecessary, and only calculated to alarm the ladies present, and directed Mr. Grace to return to the lower deck, where he had been since first coming on board. It must have been less than half an hour after I boarded the *Trent* when the second armed cutter, under Lieutenant Greer, came alongside, (only two armed boats being used). He brought in the third cutter eight marines and four machinists, in addition to a crew of some twelve men. When the marines and some armed men had been formed just out side of the main deck cabin, where these four gentlemen had gone to pack up their baggage, I renewed my efforts to induce them to accompany me on board—still refusing to accompany me unless force was applied. I called in to my assistance four or five officers, and first taking hold of Mr. Mason's shoulder, with another officer on the opposite side, I went as far as the gangway of the steamer, and delivered him over to Lieutenant Greer, to be placed in the boat. I then returned for Mr. Slidell, who insisted that I must apply considerable force to get him to go with me; calling in at last three officers, he also was taken in charge and handed over to Mr. Greer. Mr. McFarland and Mr. Eustis, after protesting, went quietly into the boat. They had been permitted to collect their baggage, but were sent in advance of it under charge of Lieutenant Greer. I gave my personal attention to the luggage, saw it put in a boat and sent in charge of an officer to the *San Jacinto*.

When Mr. Slidell was taken prisoner a great deal of noise was made by some of the passengers, which caused Lieutenant Greer to send the marines into the cabin. They were immediately ordered to return to their former position outside. I carried out my purpose without using any force beyond what appears in this report. The mail agent, who is a retired commander in the British navy, seemed to have a great deal to say as to the propriety of my course, but I purposely avoided all official intercourse with him. When I finally was leaving the steamer he made some apology for his rude conduct, and expressed personally his approval of the manner in which I had carried out my orders. We parted company from the *Trent* at 2:30 p. m.

Very respectfully, your obedient servant,

D. M. FAIRFAX,
Lieutenant and Executive Officer.

CAPTAIN CHARLES WILKES, U. S. N.,
Commanding *San Jacinto*.

UNITED STATES STEAMER SAN JACINTO,
At Sea, November 12, 1861.

SIR: In accordance with your instructions I submit the following: On November 8th, between 1 and 2 P. M., I was ordered by Lieutenant Breese, acting executive officer, to shove off with the third cutter and go alongside the English mail steamer, which was then lying-to under our guns. In the boat with me were Third Assistant Engineer Hall, Paymaster's Clerk Simpson, Master's Mate Dahlgren, one sergeant, one corporal, and six privates, of marines; four machinists and the crew, consisting of thirteen men, the whole party being well armed. When I arrived on the steamer, I was met on the guard by Mr. Grace, with a message from Lieutenant Fairfax (who had preceded me on board) to bring the marines on board and station them outside of the cabin, which I did; also to keep the spare men on the guard, and to have the boat's crew in readiness to jump on board if needed. As soon as the marines were stationed, I had the space outside and forward of the cabin kept clear of passengers, and assumed a position where I could see Lieutenant Fairfax, who was then engaged in conversation with persons in the cabin. He shortly came out and told me to remain as I was. He then went back into the cabin, and in a few minutes returned with Mr. Mason. He had his hand on his shoulder, and I think Mr. Hall had his on the other one. He transferred Mr. Mason to me, and I had the third cutter hauled up, into which he got. Shortly after Mr. McFarland came out and got into the boat; I think he was unaccompanied by any of the officers. About this time I heard a good deal of loud talking in the cabin, and above all I heard a woman's voice. I could not hear what she said. Mr. Fairfax appeared to be having an altercation with some one. There was much confusion created by the passengers and ship's officers, who were making all kinds of disagreeable and contemptuous noises and remarks.

Just then Mr. Houston came to me and said he thought there would be trouble. I told him to ask Mr. Fairfax if I should bring in the marines. He returned with an answer to bring them in. At that time I heard some one call out "shoot him." I ordered the marines to come into the cabin, which they did at quick time. As they advanced the passengers fell back. Mr. Fairfax then ordered the marines to go out of the cabin, which they did, Mr. Slidell at the same time jumping out of a window of a state-room into the cabin, where he was arrested by Mr. Fairfax, and was then brought by Mr. Hall and Mr. Grace to the boat, into which he got. Soon after Mr. Eustis came to the boat, accompanied by Mr. Fairfax. I then, by his order, took charge of the boat and conveyed the gentlemen arrested, viz: Messrs. Slidell, Mason, McFarland, and Eustis to the *San Jacinto*, where I delivered them over to Captain Wilkes. This was about 2 o'clock. I then returned to the steamer; when I reached her the baggage of the gentlemen was being brought up and sent to the *San Jacinto*. Soon after Mr. Fairfax told me to send the marines and spare hands on board, which I did. He then left me in charge of our party and went on board the *San Jacinto*. About 3 o'clock she ran under the *Trent's* stern; I was hailed and directed to come on board, which I did with all excepting Mr. Grace, Mr. Dahlgren and Mr. Hall, who came in another boat.

Very respectfully, your obedient servant,
JAMES A. GREER,
Lieutenant.

CAPTAIN C. WILKES,
 Commanding *San Jacinto.*

P. S. I desire to add that it was about 1.35 P. M. when I went alongside the *Trent*. There were but two armed boats used during the day; a third boat, the crew of which were unarmed, went alongside during the detention. When I first went on board with the marines, and at intervals during my stay, the officers of the steamer made a great many irritating remarks to each other and to the passengers, which were evidently intended for our benefit. Among other things said were: "Did you ever hear of such an outrage?" "Marines on board! Why, this looks devilish like mutiny." "These Yankees will have to pay well for this." "Thi is the best thing in the world for the South; England will open the blockade." "We will have a good chance at them now." "Did you ever hear of such a piratical act?" "Why, this is a perfect Bull's Run!" "They would not have dared to have done it if an English man-of-war had been in sight." The mail agent, (a man in the uniform of a commander in the royal navy, I think) was very indignant and talkative, and tried several times to get me into a discussion of the matter. I told him I was not there for that purpose. He was very bitter; He told me that the English squadron would raise the blockade in twenty days after his report of this outrage (I think he said outrage) got home; that the Northerners might as well give up now, etc., etc." Most all the officers of the vessel showed an undisguised hatred for the Northern people and a sympathy for the Confederates. I will do the captain of the vessel the justice to say that he acted differently from the rest, being, when I saw him, very reserved and dignified. The officers and men of our party took no apparent notice of the remarks that were made, and acted with the greatest forbearance.

Respectfully,
JAS. A. GREER.

UNITED STATES STEAMER SAN JACINTO,
At sea, November 13, 1861.

SIR: In obedience to your order of the 11th instant, I respectfully report: That upon going alongside of the English steamer *Trent*, on the 8th of this month, Lieutenant Fairfax went on board, ordering the boatswain and myself to remain in the boat. A few minutes after this my attention was attracted by persons speaking in a loud and excited manner upon the steamer's upper deck. While considering its meaning the noise was repeated, which decided me to join Lieutenant Fairfax immediately on board, and found him surrounded by the officers of the ship and passengers, among whom I recognized Messrs. Mason, Slidell, and Eustis. The confusion at this time passes description. So soon, however, as he could be heard, the mail agent (who was a retired lieutenant or commander in the British navy) protested against the act of removing passengers from an English steamer. Lieutenant Fairfax requested Mr. Mason to go quietly to the *San Jacinto*, but that gentleman replied that he would "yield only to force;" whereupon I was ordered to our ship to report the presence of the above-named gentlemen, together with Mr. McFarland, and ask that the remainder of our force be sent to the *Trent*, after which I returned to her, and entering the cabin, saw Mr. Fairfax endeavoring to enter Mr. Slidell's room, which was then prevented in a measure by the excitement which prevailed in and around that gentleman's quarters. The passengers (not including Mr. Mason, Slidell, Eustis or McFarland) were disposed to give trouble; some of them went so far as to threaten, and upon Lieutenant Greer being informed by me of this fact, he ordered the marines to clear the passage-way of the cabin, but as Mr. Slidell had now come out of his state room through the window, where we could get to him, the order to the marines was countermanded by Lieutenant Fairfax. Mr. Slidell was removed to the boat by Mr. Grace and myself, and no more force was used than would show what would be done in case of necessity. Mr. Mason was taken in charge by Lieutenant Fairfax and Third Assistant Engineer Hall. The two secretaries walked into the boat by themselves.

While we were on board of the *Trent* many remarks were made reflecting discreditably upon us and the government of the United

States. No one was more abusive than the mail agent, who took pains at the same time to inform us that he was the only person on board officially connected with her Brittanic majesty's government, who he said would, in consequence of this act, break the blockade of the southern United States ports. Another person, supposed to be a passenger, was so violent that the captain ordered him to be locked up. A short time before leaving the steamer I was informed by one of her crew that the mail agent was advising the captain to arm the crew and passengers of his ship, which I immediately communicated to Lieutenant Greer. About 3:30 P. M. we returned to the *San Jacinto*.

I am, respectfully, your obedient servant,
J. B. HOUSTON,
Second Assistant Engineer,
U. S. Steamer *San Jacinto*.

CAPTAIN CHARLES WILKES,
Commanding.

UNITED STATES STEAMER SAN JACINTO,
At sea, November 13, 1861.

SIR:—In obedience to your order of the 11th instant, I respectfully make the following report of what came under my observation on board the mail steamer *Trent* whilst hove-to under our guns on the 8th instant:

I boarded the steamer in the third cutter, under the command of Lieutenant Greer. Immediately on reaching the steamer's deck I stationed four men (an oiler, assistant oiler and two firemen) who accompanied me, in the port gang-way. I then went into the cabin, where I saw Lieutenant Fairfax, surrounded by a large number of passengers and the officers of the ship. He was conversing with Mr. Mason, and endeavoring to get him to come peaceably on board this ship. Mr. Mason refused to comply unless by force, and taking hold of Mr. Mason's coat collar, gave an order, "Gentlemen, lay hands on him." I then laid hold of him by the coat collar, when Mr. Mason said he would yield under protest. I accompanied him as far as the boat, which was at the port gang-way.

Returning to the cabin, Lieutenant Fairfax was at Mr. Slidell's room. After a short time Mr. Slidell came from his room through a side window. He also refused Lieutenant Fairfax's order to come on board this ship, unless by force. I, with several of the officers, then caught hold, and used sufficient power to remove him from the cabin. He was accompanied to the boat by Second Assistant Engineer Houston and Boatswain Grace. I then received an order from both Lieutenants Fairfax and Greer to retain the boat until Messrs. Eustis and McFarland were found. I remained in the gangway till Messrs. Mason, Slidell, Eustis and McFarland shoved off, Lieutenant Greer having charge of the gentlemen.

There was a great deal of excitement and talking during the whole time, the officers of the steamer endeavoring particularly to thwart Lieutenant Fairfax in carrying out his orders. They also used very harsh expressions toward us, calling us pirates, piratical expedition, etc., and threatened to open our blockade in a few weeks. At one time the officers and passengers made a demonstration, at the moment the marine guard came hastily in the cabin, but were immediately ordered back by Lieutenant Fairfax.

As far as I am able to judge, everything was conducted on our part in a peaceable, quiet and gentlemanly manner, and most remarkably so by Lieutenant Fairfax, who certainly had sufficient cause to resort to arms. I remained aboard the *Trent* till after the baggage belonging to the gentlemen had been sent, and finally returned to this ship with Lieutenant Greer.

Most respectfully, your obedient servant,

GEO. W. HALL,
Third Assistant Engineer, U. S. N.

CAPTAIN CHARLES WILKES,
Commanding U. S. Steamer *San Jacinto*.

Lieutenants Fairfax and Greer, who had such a conspicuous part in this affair, have both since made enviable records for distinguished services in the navy, and have both risen to the rank of rear admiral; the former was retired in 1881 and died in January, 1894. Rear Admiral Greer is also on the retired list now, having had the distinguished honor of being the senior officer of the navy for some months before his retirement. Second Assistant Engineer Houston served his country faithfully throughout the war and resigned from the naval service in July, 1865, to engage in business. He has been eminently successful, having been a director, vice-president and president of the Pacific Mail Steamship Company for a long period of years, and only recently gave up active business to enter into the quiet enjoyment of a fortune which his talents have enabled him to amass during his busy life. Third Assistant Engineer Hall served faithfully throughout the rebellion and resigned from the service not long after the close of the war.

The chief engineer of the *San Jacinto* was Mr. John Faron, who three years later was killed on board the *Tecumseh* with all five of his assistant engineers in the battle of Mobile Bay.

CHAPTER XVI.

"The man who goes into action in a wooden vessel is a fool, and the man who sends him there is a villain."—ADMIRAL SIR JOHN HAY.

1861. The Civil War, continued—The First American Iron Clads—The Stevens Battery Condemned by a Board of Naval Officers—Authority to Build Armored Vessels Conferred by Act of Congress—Report of Board on Iron-Clad Vessels—The GALENA, NEW IRONSIDES, and MONITOR—Armored Vessels in the Mississippi River.

AT the outbreak of the Civil War the United States had no armored war vessels, although the example of the unfinished Stevens' battery and the presentation of plans for an armored floating battery by the Swedish-American inventor John Ericsson to the Emperor Napoleon III. had resulted in the adoption of iron armor abroad to a limited extent. Three iron-plated floating batteries had been used by the French in the Crimean War, and at the beginning of the year 1861 that nation had *La Gloire* and three other large wooden steam frigates in commission, all sheathed with light iron armor, and fourteen others in process of construction. England also had entered the field and had at sea the *Warrior, Black Prince, Defense, Resistance* and *Royal Oak*, large armored steam-ships similar to *La Gloire*, with sixteen other armor-clads in various stages of construction. These British and French vessels were large full-rigged ships with auxiliary steam power, dependent upon the wind fully as much as upon steam for locomotion; their iron sides constituted the only feature wherein they resembled the Stevens' battery or the vessel suggested by Ericsson to Napoleon in 1854.

A joint resolution of Congress approved June 24, 1861, directed the Secretary of the Navy to appoint a board to examine the Stevens' battery and ascertain the cost and time necessary for its completion, and the expediency thereof. The board consisted of Commodores Silas H. Stringham and William Inman, Captain T. A. Dornin, Chief Engineer A. C. Stimers, and Joseph Henry, Esq., Secretary of the Smithsonian Institution. The report of this board, not made until the end of the year, was adverse to the completion of the iron battery, and the project was then dropped, so far as the government was concerned.

An extra session of Congress was assembled by presidential proclamation July 4, 1861, to which, the Secretary of the Navy made a report on the condition of the navy at that time. In this report the Secretary referred to the attention given by England and France to iron-clad war-steamers, and asked for authority to construct such vessels if an investigation by a competent board should show such construction to be advisable. Congress responded with liberality and promptness by an act, approved August 3, 1861, entitled "An Act to provide for the construction of one or more armored ships and floating batteries, and for other purposes," it being brief and to the point, as follows:

Be it enacted by the Senate and House of Representatives of the United States of America in Congress assembled, That the Secretary of the Navy be, and is hereby authorized and directed to appoint a board of three skilful naval officers to investigate the plans and specifications that may be submitted for the construction or completing of iron or steel-clad steamships or steam batteries, and, on their report, should it be favorable, the Secretary of the Navy will cause one or more armored or iron or steel-clad steamships or floating steam batteries to be built; and there is hereby appropriated, out of any money in the treasury not otherwise appropriated, the sum of one million five hundred thousand dollars.

SEC. 2. *And be it further enacted,* That in case of a vacancy in the office of engineer-in-chief of the navy the appointment thereto shall be made from the list of chief engineers.

August 7, the Navy Department issued an advertisement asking for bids from responsible persons for the construction of one or more iron-clad steam-vessels of war, either of iron or of wood and iron combined, for sea or river service, the advertisement giving in general terms the principal requirements. These were, that vessels proposed must be of not less than ten, nor more than sixteen feet draft; must carry an armament of from eighty to one hundred and twenty tons weight, with provisions and stores for from one hundred and sixty-five to three hundred persons, according to armament, for sixty days, with coal for eight days; must have two masts, with wire rope standing rigging for navigating the sea. The lighter draft of water, compatible with other requisites, was preferred. General descriptions and drawings of vessel, armor and machinery were required, as well as estimates of cost and time for completion of the whole. Twenty-five days from date of advertisement were allowed for the presentation of plans.

A naval board, composed of Commodore Joseph Smith, Commodore Hiram Paulding, and Commander Charles H. Davis, was appointed on the eighth of August to examine carefully all plans submitted and report upon the same. The report of this board, dated September 16, 1861, is both interesting and instructive from many points of view, showing as it does the opinions entertained by the naval men of that period regarding armor, and its probable utility; it also unfolds some of the rare schemes of inventors and patriots, who rushed to their country's succor. It follows in full:

REPORT ON IRON CLAD VESSELS.

NAVY DEPARTMENT,
Bureau of Yards and Docks, September 16, 1861.

SIR: The undersigned, constituting a board appointed by your order of the 8th ultimo, proceeded to the duty assigned to them, in accordance with the first section of an act of Congress, approved 3d of August 1861, directing the Secretary of the Navy "to appoint a board of three skilful naval officers to investigate the plans and specifications that may be submitted for the construction or completing of iron-clad steam-ships or steam batteries, and on their report, should it be favorable, the Secretary of the Navy will cause one or more armored or iron-clad or steel clad steamships or floating steam batteries to be built; and there is hereby appropriated, out of any money in the treasury not otherwise appropriated, the sum of one million five hundred thousand dollars."

Distrustful of our ability to discharge this duty, which the law requires should be performed by three skilful naval officers, we approach the subject with diffidence, having no experience and but scanty knowledge in this branch of naval architecture.

The plans submitted are so various, and in many respects so entirely dissimilar, that without a more thorough knowledge of this mode of construction and the resisting properties of iron than we possess, it is very likely that some of our conclusions may prove erroneous.

Application was made to the Department for a naval constructor, to be placed under our orders, with whom we might consult; but it appears that they are all so employed on important service that none could be assigned to this duty.

The construction of iron clad steamships of war is now zealously claiming the attention of foreign naval powers. France led; England followed, and is now somewhat extensively engaged in the system; and other powers seem to emulate their example, though on a smaller scale.

Opinions differ amongst naval and scientific men as to the policy of adopting the iron armature for ships-of-war. For coast and harbor defence they are undoubtedly formidable adjuncts to fortifications on land. As cruising vessels, however, we are skeptical as to their advantage and ultimate adoption. But whilst other nations are endeavoring to perfect them, we must not remain idle.

The enormous load of iron, as so much additional weight to the vessel; the great breadth of beam necessary to give her stability; the short supply of coal she will be able to stow in bunkers; the greater power required to propel her; and the largely increased cost of construction, are objections to this class of vessels as cruisers, which we believe it is difficult successfully to overcome. For river and harbor service we consider iron-clad vessels of light draught, or floating batteries thus shielded, as very important; and we feel at this moment the necessity of them on some of our rivers and inlets to enforce obedience to the laws. We however do not hesitate to express the opinion, notwithstanding all we have heard or seen written on the subject, that no ship or floating battery, however heavily she may be plated, can cope successfully with a properly constructed fortification of masonry. The one is fixed and immovable and though constructed of a material which may be shattered by shot, can be covered if need be, by the same or much heavier armor than a floating vessel can bear, whilst the other is subject to disturbances by winds and waves, and to the powerful effects of tides and currents.

Armored ships or batteries may be employed advantageously to pass fortifications on land for ulterior objects of attack, to run a blockade, or to reduce temporary batteries on the shores of rivers and the approaches to our harbors.

From what we know of the comparative advantages and disadvantages of ships constructed of wood over those of iron, we are clearly of opinion that no iron-clad vessel of equal displacement can be made to obtain the same speed as one not thus encumbered, because her form would be better adapted to speed. Her form and dimensions, the unyielding nature of the shield, detract materially in a heavy sea from the life, buoyancy and spring which a ship built of wood possesses.

Wooden ships may be said to be but coffins for their crews when brought in conflict with iron-clad vessels; but the speed of the former, we take for granted, being greater than that of the latter, they can readily choose their position and keep out of harm's way entirely.

Recent improvements in the form and preparations of projectiles, and their increased capacity for destruction, have elicited a large amount of ingenuity and skill to devise means for resisting them in the construction of ships-of-war. As yet we know of nothing superior to the large and heavy spherical shot in its destructive effects on vessels, whether plated or not.

Rifled guns have greater range, but the conical shot does not produce the crushing effect of spherical shot.

It is assumed that $4\frac{1}{2}$ inch plates are the heaviest armor a sea going vessel can safely carry. These plates should be of tough iron, and rolled in large, long pieces. This thickness of armor, it is believed, will resist all projectiles now in use at a distance of 500 yards, especially if the ship's sides are angular.

Plates hammered in large masses are less fibrous and tough than when rolled. The question whether wooden backing, or any elastic substance behind the iron plating, will tend to relieve at all the frame of the ships from the crushing effect of a heavy projectile, is not yet decided. Major Barnard says: "to put an elastic material behind the iron is to insure its destruction." With all deference to such creditable authority, we may suggest that it is possible a backing of some elastic substance (soft wood, perhaps, is the best) might relieve the frame of the ship somewhat from the terrible shock of a heavy projectile, though the plate should not be fractured.

With respect to a comparison between ships of iron and those of wood, without plating, high authorities in England differ as to which is the best. The tops of ships built of iron, we are told, wear out three bottoms, whilst the bottoms of those built of wood will outwear three tops. In deciding on the relative merits of iron and wooden-framed vessels, for each of which we have offers, the board is of opinion that it would be well to try a specimen of each, as both have distinguished advocates. One strong objection to iron vessels, which, so far as we know, has not yet been overcome, is the oxidation or rust in salt water, and their liability of becoming foul under water by the attachment of sea grass and animalcules to their bottoms. The best preventive we know of is a coating of pure zinc paint, which so long as it lasts, is believed to be an antidote to this cause of evil.

After these brief remarks on the subject generally, we proceed to notice the plans and offers referred to us for the construction of plated vessels and floating batteries.

It has been suggested that the most ready mode of obtaining an iron-clad ship of war would be to contract with responsible parties in England for its complete construction; and we are assured that parties there are ready to engage in such an enterprise on terms more reasonable, perhaps, than such vessels could be built in this country, having much greater experience and facilities than we possess. Indeed, we are informed there are no mills and machinery in this country capable of rolling iron $4\frac{1}{2}$ inches thick, though plates might be hammered to that thickness in many of our work-shops. As before observed, rolled iron is considered much the best, and the difficulty of rolling it increases rapidly with the increase of thickness. It has, however, occured to us that a difficulty might arise with the British government in case we should undertake to construct ships-of-war in that country, which might complicate their delivery; and, moreover, we are of opinion that every people or nation who can maintain a navy should be capable of constructing it themselves.

Our immediate demands seem to require, first, so far as practicable, vessels invulnerable to shot, of light draught of water, to penetrate our shoal harbors, rivers and bayous. We therefore favor the construction of this class of vessels before going into a more perfect system of large iron-clad sea-going vessels of war. We are here met with the difficulty of encumbering small vessels with armor, which, from their size, they are unable to bear. We nevertheless recommend that contracts be made with responsible parties for the construction of one or more iron-clad vessels or batteries of as light a draught of water as practicable, consistent with their weight of armor. Meanwhile, availing ourselves of the experience thus obtained, and the improvements which we believe are yet to be made by other naval powers in building iron-clad ships, we would advise the construction, in our own navy yards, of one or more of these vessels, upon a large and more perfect scale, when Congress shall see fit to authorize it. The amount now appropriated is not sufficient to build both classes of vessels to any great extent.

We have made a synopsis of the propositions and specifications submitted, which we annex, and now proceed to state, in brief, the result of our decisions upon the offers presented to us.

J. Ericsson, New York, page 19.—This plan of a floating battery is novel, but seems to be based upon a plan which will render the battery shot and shell proof. We are somewhat apprehensive that her properties for sea are not such as a sea-going vessel should possess. But she may be moved from one place to another on the coast in smooth water. We recommend that an experiment be made with one battery of this description on the terms proposed, with a guarantee and forfeiture in case of failure in any of the properties and points of the vessel as proposed.

Price, $275,000; length of vessel, 172 feet; breadth of beam, 41 feet; depth of hold, 11½ feet; time, 100 days; draught of water 10 feet; displacement, 1,255 tons; speed per hour, 9 statute miles.

John W. Nystrom, Philadelphia, 1216 Chestnut St, page 1.— The plan of (quadruple) guns is not known and cannot be considered. The dimensions would not float the vessel without the guards, which we are not satisfied would repel shot. We do not recommend the plan.

Price, about $175,000; length of vessel, 175 feet; breadth of beam, 27 feet; depth of hold, 13 feet; time, four months; draught of water, 10 feet; displacement, 875 tons; speed per hour, 12 knots.—

William Perine, New York, 2777 post office box, presents three plans. The specifications and drawings are not full. The last proposal (No. 3, page 2) for the heavy plating is the only one we have considered; but there is neither drawing nor model, and the capacity of the vessel, we think, will not bear the armor and armament proposed.

Price, $621,000; length of vessel, 225 feet; breadth of beam, 45½ feet; depth of hold, 15½ feet; time, 9 months; draught of water 13 feet; displacement, 2,454 tons; speed per hour, 10 knots.

JOHN C. LE FERRE, Boston, page 9.—Description deficient. Not recommended. Sent a model, but neither price, time, nor dimensions stated.

E. S. RENWICK, New York, 335 Broadway, presents drawings, specifications and model of an iron-clad vessel of large capacity and powerful engines, with great speed, capable of carrying a heavy battery, and stated to be shot-proof and a good sea boat. The form and manner of construction and proportions of the vessel are novel, and will attract the attention of scientific and practical men. She is of very light draft of water, and on the question whether she will prove to be a safe and comfortable sea-boat we do not express a decided opinion. Vessels of somewhat similar form, in the part of the vessel which is emersed, of light draught of water on our western lakes, have, we believe, proved entirely satisfactory in all weathers. To counteract the effect of the waves, when disturbed by the winds, by producing a jerk, or sudden rolling motion of flat shoal vessels, it is proposed to carry a sufficient weight above the center of gravity to counterpoise the heavy weight below, which is done in this ship by the immense iron armor. If, after a full discussion and examination by experts on this plan, it should be decided that she is a safe vessel for sea service, we would recommend the construction upon it of one ship at one of our dock yards.

The estimate cost of this ship, $1,500,000, precludes action upon the plan until further appropriations shall be made by Congress for such objects.

Time not stated; length of vessel 400 feet; breadth of beam, 60 feet; depth of hold, 33 feet; draught of water, 16 feet; displacement, 6,520 tons; speed per hour, at least 18 miles.

WHITNEY & ROWLAND, Brooklyn, Greenpoint, page 13; propose an iron gunboat, armor of bars of iron and thin plate over it. No price stated. Dimensions of vessel, we think, will not bear the weight and possess stability. Time, 5 months. Not recommended.

Length of vessel, 140 feet; breadth of beam, 28 feet; depth of hold, 13½ feet; draught of water, 8 feet.

DONALD MCKAY, Boston, page 6.—Vessel, in general dimensions and armor, approved. The speed estimated slow. The cost precludes the consideration of construction by the board.

Price, $1,000,000; length of vessel, 227 feet; breadth of beam, 50 feet; depth of hold, 26½ feet; time, 9 to 10 months; draught of water, 14 feet; displacement, 3,100 tons; speed per hour, 6 to 7 knots.

WILLIAM H. WOOD, Jersey City, N. J., page 14.—Dimensions will not float the guns high enough; not recommended.

Price, $255,000; length of vessel, 160 feet; breadth of beam, 34 feet; depth of hold, 22 feet; time, 4 months; draught of water, 13 feet; displacement, 1,215 tons; speed, not stated.

MERRICK & SONS, Philadelphia, pages 7 and 8—Vessel of wood and iron combined. This proposition we consider the most practical one for heavy armor. We recommend that a contract be made with that party, under a guarantee, with forfeiture in case of failure to comply with the specifications; and that the contract require the plates to be 15 feet long and 36 inches wide, with a reservation of some modifications which may occur as the work progresses, not to affect the cost.

Price, $780,000; length of vessel, 220 feet; breadth of beam, 60 feet; depth of hold, 23 feet; time, 9 months; draught of water, 13 feet; displacement, 3,296 tons; speed per hour, 9½ knots.

BENJAMIN RATHBURN, ———, page 20.—We do not recommend the plan for adoption.

Price not stated; length of vessel not stated; breadth of beam, 80 feet; depth of hold, 74 feet; time not stated; draught of water, 25 feet; displacement, 15,000 tons; speed not stated; specifications incomplete.

HENRY R. DUNHAM, New York, page 11.—Vessel too costly for the appropriation; no drawings or specifications; not recommended.

Price, $1,200,000; length of vessel, 325 feet; breadth of beam, 60 feet; depth of hold not stated; time, 15 to 18 months; draught of water, 16 feet; displacement not stated; speed per hour, 12 miles.

C. S. BUSHNELL & CO., New Haven, Conn., page 121.—Propose a vessel to be iron-clad, on the rail and plate principle, and to obtain high speed. The objection to this vessel is the fear that she will not float her armor and load sufficiently high, and have stability enough for a sea vessel. With a guarantee that she shall do these, we recommend on that basis a contract.

Price, $235,250; length of vessel, 180 feet; breadth of beam, — feet; depth of hold, 12⅔ feet; time, 4 months; draught of water, 10 feet; displacement, — tons; speed per hour, 12 knots.

JOHN WESTWOOD, Cincinnati, Ohio, page 17.—Vessel of wood, with iron armor; plan good enough, but the breadth not enough to bear the armor. No detailed specification; no price or time stated; only a general drawing. Not recommended.

NEAFIE & LEVY, Philadelphia, page 5.—No plans or drawings, therefore not considered. Neither price nor time stated.

Length of vessel, 200 feet; breadth of beam, 40 feet; depth of hold, 15 feet; draught of water, 13 feet; displacement, 1,748 tons; speed per hour, 10 knots.

WM. NORRIS, New York, 26 Cedar street, page 6.—Iron boat without armor—too small and not recommended.

Price, $32,000; length of vessel 83 feet; breadth of beam 25 feet; depth of hold 14 feet; time 60 to 75 days; draught of water, 3 feet; displacement 90 tons; speed not stated.

WM. KINGSLEY, Washington, D. C., page 10, proposes a *rubber-clad* vessel, which we cannot recommend. No price or dimensions stated.

A. BEEBE, New York, 82 Broadway, page 18.—Specification and sketch defective. Plan not approved.

Price, $50,000; length of vessel, 120 feet; breadth of beam, 55 feet; depth not stated; time 100 days; draught of water, 6 ft. displacement, 1,000 tons; speed per hour, 8 knots.

These three propositions recommended, viz: Bushnell & Co., New Haven, Connecticut; Merrick & Sons, Philadelphia, and J. Ericsson, New York, will absorb $1,290,050 of the appropriation of $1,500,000, leaving $209,750 yet unexpended.

The board recommends that armor with heavy guns be placed on one of our river craft, or, if none will bear it, to construct a scow, which will answer, to plate and shield the guns, for the river service on the Potomac, to be constructed or prepared by the government at the navy yard here for immediate use.

We would further recommend that the Department ask of Congress at the next session, an appropriation, for experimenting on iron plates of different kinds, of $10,000.

All of which is respectfully submitted,

JOSEPH SMITH,
H. PAULDING,
C. H. DAVIS.

HON. GIDEON WELLES,
Secretary of the Navy.

The first of the three plans accepted resulted in a contract dated September 27, 1861, with C. S. Bushnell & Co., of New Haven, Conn., for the armored gunboat that was named *Galena*. She was built at Mystic Bridge, Conn., from designs prepared by Mr. S. H. Pook, afterward a constructor in the navy, for $235,250, and was completed in April, 1862, being almost immediately thereafter in action and badly damaged at Drury's Bluff, on James' river. In form the *Galena* was similar to an ordinary gun-vessel, with the important difference that her sides tumbled home at an angle of nearly forty-five degrees and were covered with iron bars and plates, protecting a gun deck in which six large guns were mounted. She was rated as of 738 tons burden, and was rigged as a two-masted foretopsail schooner. There were two Ericsson vibrating lever engines, with horizontal cylinders forty-eight inches in diameter and three feet stroke, driving a four-bladed screw propeller, twelve feet in diameter and twenty feet pitch. Steam was supplied by two horizontal tubular boilers with three furnaces in each, two blower engines for fan blast being provided. The *Galena's* armor was about four inches in thickness and was so badly shattered at Drury's Bluff that she was not considered a success as an armor clad, although she continued in active service throughout the war, and, lashed to the unfortunate *Oneida*, was in Farragut's fleet in Mobile Bay. In the early '70's, under the guise of "repairing" her, the Department built the 1,900 ton sloop of war *Galena*, that was for many years a prominent figure in our wooden fleet.

The contract with Merrick & Sons of Philadelphia gave the United States navy the *New Ironsides*, beyond question the finest and most formidable example of a battle-ship in existence at the time she first took the sea. The hull was built of white oak at Cramp's shipyard in Philadelphia, Merrick & Sons building the machinery at their own works. The engines were of only about seven hundred horse power and could drive the ship scarcely six knots an hour, but that was regarded as fast enough for the service required of her, as it was not apprehended that she would be obliged to run away from anything then afloat. The contract price was $780,000. She was of 4,120 tons displacement; 232 feet long; 57½ feet beam, and mounted a very heavy battery, consisting of sixteen XI-inch Dahlgren guns, two 200-pounder Parrott rifles, and four 24-pounder howitzers.

The *New Ironsides* was large and decidedly ship-shape in appearance, with a projecting ram bow, the sides for the length of the main battery being sheathed with four inches of iron plate armor, the bow and stern sections being unarmored. The main battery was also protected with athwart-ship bulkheads, or walls, of the same thickness of armor as the sides, so she was really a case-mated ship. She was originally bark-rigged, but when sent to the seat of war she was stripped for fighting, the masts being taken out at Port Royal and replaced with light clothes-poles, with which rig her appearance was remarkably like that of a modern war-vessel. In 1863 the masts were replaced previous to a trip north for repairs, but were again removed, this time at Norfolk, before she again went into action.

Completed late in 1862, she proceeded at once to the front and was actively employed during the remainder of the rebellion, it being said of her that she was in action more days than any other vessel of our navy during the war. Mr. William S. Wells of New Haven, Connecticut, recently the Rear Admiral of the National Association of Naval Veterans, was attached to the *New Ironsides* as an assistant engineer during her entire period of war service, beginning with her first commission, and was the only officer who remained in her that length of time. To him Admiral Porter wrote long after the war that the *New Ironsides* had a record for having been hammered more thoroughly than any vessel that ever floated, and gave, with other interesting facts about the ship, the statement that in a series of engagements from July 18 to September 8, 1863, she had fired *four thousand four hundred and thirty-nine* eleven-inch projectiles. In one engagement with the batteries on Sullivan's Island she was struck seventy times within three hours, but aside from some temporary damage to the port-shutters, which the engineers quickly repaired, was in perfect fighting condition at the end of the action. On another occasion she very narrowly escaped being blown up by a torpedo. At the close of the war she was laid up at the League Island navy yard, where, on the night of December 15-16, 1866, she was burned to the water's edge, having taken fire in some unknown manner late at night and not discovered until the flames were beyond control.

The picture of this famous ship which appears in the text is a reproduction of a drawing made by Second Assistant Engineer William S. Wells, before referred to as having served in her throughout her war career, and represents the *New Ironsides* exactly as she looked in the battles in Charleston harbor in 1863.

The third proposal accepted resulted in the construction of John Ericcson's *Monitor*, probably the most famous and epoch-making craft that ever floated, unless we revert to very ancient history and except Noah's Ark. The contract for this novel iron-clad was made October 4, 1861, between John Ericsson and his sureties on one part, and Gideon Welles, as Secretary of the Navy, on the other. It provided that the parties of the first part should construct an iron-clad, shot-proof steam battery, of iron and wood combined, on Ericsson's plan; the length to be 179 feet; extreme breadth, 41 feet, and depth 5 feet, or larger if found necessary, to carry the required armament and stores. A sea speed of eight knots an hour, maintained for twelve consecutive hours was stipulated. The contract price was $275,000, to be paid in five instalments of $50,000 each and one of $25,000, payments to be made upon certificates of the naval superintendent of construction when in his judgment work had progressed sufficiently to warrant them. A reservation of twenty-five per cent. was withheld from each payment to be retained until after the completion and satisfactory trial of the vessel, not to exceed ninety days after she was ready for sea.

A clause of the contract provided that in case the vessel did not develop the stipulated speed or failed in other stated requirements, the contractors should refund to the United States the full amount of money paid them. This clause is the basis of the oft-

THE NEW IRONSIDES; 1862.

repeated statement that Ericsson and his sureties paid for the building of the vessel themselves; this was not the case, as all the payments, excepting the twenty-five per cent. reservation, were made before the *Monitor* left New York, although the contract would have required the contractors to pay for her had it not been for her fortunate encounter with the *Merrimac*, as her speed and some other qualities could not have been regarded as satisfactory. Her performance in Hampton Roads was regarded as a satisfactory test and the Navy Department paid the reservations within a week thereafter without insisting upon the full letter of the contract being carried out in minor particulars. A curious clause in the contract, which Ericsson ignored and the Department did not insist upon, indicates how reluctant the naval advisers of the Secretary were to authorise an entire departure from the method of marine propulsion which they had grown up to believe was the only reliable one. The clause referred to required the contractors to "furnish masts, spars, sails, and rigging of sufficient dimensions to drive the vessel at the rate of six knots per hour in a fair breeze of wind."

The adoption of the plan proposed by Ericsson was due to a train of accidental circumstances far more than to any percipience on the part of the board to which it was submitted. After being promised the contract for the *Galena*, Mr. C. S. Bushnell called upon Ericsson in New York for professional advice regarding some of the details of his plans, and during the interview Ericsson resurrected from a rubbish heap in the corner of his office the model that he had made for the French naval officials in 1854, and exhibited it as *his* idea of what an iron-clad should be. Bushnell instantly perceived the possibilities of the design, but could not induce Ericsson to submit it to the naval board, the inventor having already had a surfeit of experiences with the Navy Department in years gone by. He did succeed, however, in getting Ericsson's permission to take the model and submit it himself. Knowing that Secretary Welles, who was his personal friend, was then in Connecticut, Mr. Bushnell hastened thither and laid the plan before him, the Secretary being so impressed with its merits that he urged Bushnell to take it to Washington immediately, promising that he would, if necessary, order the board to extend the limit of time prescribed for the submission of plans.

Through influential friends Mr. Bushnell obtained a personal interview with President Lincoln and so enlisted his support by exhibiting the model and explaining the simplicity of operation of the ship it represented that the President voluntarily offered to accompany him to the Navy Department the next day. At the appointed time Mr. Bushnell and the President called on Assistant Secretary Fox and exhibited the model to him and a number of naval officers, including members of the iron-clad board. All were surprised with the simplicity and novelty of the plan, and some favored giving it a trial; others ridiculed it. The following day Commodore Smith convened his board and gave Mr. Bushnell an official hearing, that gentleman quitting the session with a hope that he had successfully presented his case; he was doomed to disappointment, however, for the next morning he found the interest of the previous day entirely gone, and the members of the board indifferent and skeptical. The two commodores told him that they would vote for a trial of the design if he could get Commander Davis to vote for it, Davis as the junior member of the board being evidently used as the executioner to administer the *coup de grace* to suspected "cranks." The latter officer, when appealed to by Bushnell, grew merry over what he regarded as the absurdities of the project and told Bushnell that he might "take the little thing home and worship it, as it would not be idolatry, because it was in the image of nothing in the heaven above or on the earth beneath or in the waters under the earth."[1]

Almost in despair, Mr. Bushnell resolved to play his last card by calling in the eloquent voice of Ericsson to explain his own invention, a difficult thing to do, for Ericsson had been so shamefully treated by the Navy Department in regard to the *Princeton* that he had often announced his determination never to set foot in Washington again. Bushnell proceeded to New York and by representing the state of affairs in much brighter colors than the actual facts warranted, induced Ericsson to go to Washington and appear before the board. Arriving there, he was coldly received and informed that his plan had already been rejected; mortified and indignant, he was about to leave, but a remark dropped by Commodore

---

[1] Letter from Mr. Bushnell to Hon. Gideon Welles; published in W. C. Church's Life of John Ericsson, Vol. I., page 250.

Smith to the effect that the cause for rejection was *lack of stability* excited his professional pride and he launched forth into a most masterful and eloquent defense of his model, convincing the members of the board in short order that he knew more of stability and ships in general than had ever been dreamed of in their philosophy. The impression he made gained him another audience with the board, the Secretary of the Navy, who had fortunately returned to Washington, being present on the second occasion; after Ericsson had charmed everyone in the room with his glowing description of what his vessel could do, Mr. Welles asked each member of the board in turn if he approved of a contract being made with Ericsson, and each in turn gently answered, "Yes, by all means." No more time was lost; the Secretary told Ericsson that he would be awarded a contract, and urged him to begin work at once without waiting for formalities, which he did with such vim that in the few days that elapsed before the contract was drawn up the keel plates of the *Monitor* were put through the rolling mill. Thus by the precarious train of happenings above related did Ericsson's model narrowly escape remaining for an indefinite time in the dusty oblivion of his workshop.

The name *Monitor* was given by Ericsson himself to his ironclad, his reasons for the selection being thus stated in a letter of his to Assistant Secretary Fox, dated January 20, 1862:

"SIR: In accordance with your request, I now submit for your approbation a name for the floating battery at Greenpoint. The impregnable and aggressive character of this structure will admonish the leaders of the Southern Rebellion that the batteries on the banks of their rivers will no longer present barriers to the entrance of the Union forces. The iron-clad intruder will thus prove a severe monitor to those leaders. But there are other leaders who will also be startled and admonished by the booming of the guns from the impregnable iron turret. 'Downing Street' will hardly view with indifference this last 'Yankee notion', this monitor. To the Lords of the Admiralty the new craft will be a monitor, suggesting doubts as to the propriety of completing those four steel-clad ships at three and a half millions apiece. On these and many similar grounds, I propose to name the new battery *Monitor*."

Every part of this wonderful vessel was designed by John Ericsson, and she was purely and wholly an engineers' ship, entirely free from the trappings and adjuncts pertaining to the seamanship of the period in which she was built. Hull, machinery, turrets, gun carriages, anchor hoists, everything, all were built from working drawings made by Ericsson's own hands. In order to hasten the work it was given out by sub-contracts to different establishments: the hull was built by Thomas F. Rowland at the Continental Iron Works, Greenpoint; the propelling engines and all auxiliary machinery by Delamater & Co., and the turret, built up of eight layers of one-inch iron plates bolted together, by the Novelty Iron Works. Chief Engineer Alban C. Stimers, U. S. Navy, represented the Government as the inspector of construction of the whole fabric. Within one hundred working days from the laying of the keel the *Monitor* was practically completed and her engines had been operated under steam. As built, her extreme length was 172

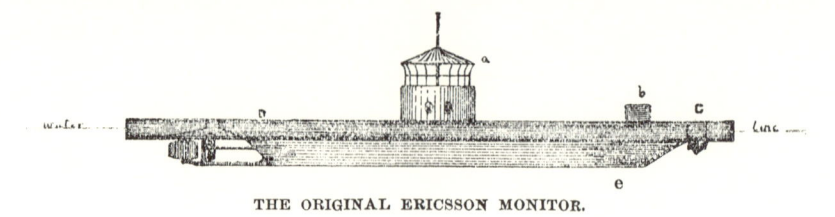

THE ORIGINAL ERICSSON MONITOR.

a. awning. b. pilot house of iron "logs." c. anchor well. d. wooden upper body or raft, armored on sides and deck. e. iron hull or under-body.

feet; breadth, 41½ feet; depth of hold, 11⅓ feet; draft of water, 10¼ feet; inside diameter of turret, 20 feet; height of turret, 9 feet. The deck was plated with iron an inch thick, and the sides of the upper body, or wooden cover of the iron hull as it may be called, were protected with five inches of iron armor. Two XI-inch Dahlgren guns were mounted in the turret. The engines were of Ericsson's vibrating-lever type, with cylinders three feet in diameter and twenty-six inches stroke, driving a propeller nine feet in diameter.

While the *Monitor* was being built, the Navy Department and Captain Ericsson were liberally ridiculed and abused by the public press for what was regarded as a fatuitous waste of public money, and Ericsson himself, in the midst of his overwhelming labors, had constantly to calm the doubts of Commodore Smith, who appears from his many letters full of foreboding to Ericsson, to have repented of his approval of this revolutionary design in naval architecture. In the midst of all this hostility and opposition, Mr. Secretary Welles, Captain Ericsson, the three gentlemen who became his sureties (Messrs. C. S. Bushnell, John A. Griswold, and John F. Winslow), and Chief Engineer Stimers remained steadfast in their faith in the new departure, and seem to have been about the only persons interested who did not regard the scheme as a crazy dream, doomed to utter failure. The performance of the *Monitor* in battle immediately after her completion caused a sudden change in sentiment, naval and civil, and many who had been loudest in jeering became

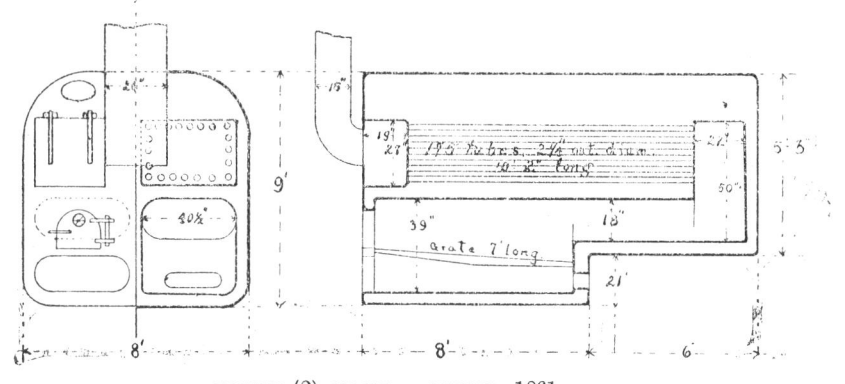

BOILER (2) OF THE MONITOR, 1861.

equally loud in praise, announcing their own prescience. Credit for the creation of the *Monitor* belongs largely to Mr. Secretary Welles for appreciating its possibilities and for his action in influencing the armor-clad board to approve the original plans; after him, the credit is probably fairly distributed in his own words as follows:

"To the distinguished inventor of this new-class vessel, to his sureties, to the board of naval officers who reported in her favor, to the vigilant and very able naval officer who superintended her construction, the Secretary has, on repeated occasions, tendered his obligations and his thanks for their patriotic services in coming to the assistance of the department and the government in a great emergency. Great praise and commendation are due to them respectively, but no one can be justified in attempting to arrogate to himself undue merit at the expense of others. The Navy Department, under great embarrassments, was compelled to enter upon a new field in naval warfare, and in this experiment it had the services and active and efficient co-operation of Captain John Ericsson, with that of the wealthy and deserving gentlemen who aided in the development of this new class of vessels, which have entered into the navy of the United States, and been elsewhere incorporated into the service of other governments."[1]

The year 1861 also saw the appearance of iron-clad steamers in the Mississippi River, built by the War Department for use in connection with the army. Seven of these iron-clads were built by the distinguished engineer of St. Louis, Mr. James B. Edes, under a contract dated August 7, 1861, and were mostly completed by the end of the year. They were 175 feet long, 50 feet beam, and were propelled by a huge paddle-wheel amidships near the stern, working in an opening 18 feet wide and 60 feet long fore and aft, the two parts of the after body of the vessel thus formed being joined abaft the wheel by a flying deck, known in river parlance as the "fantail." The wheel was 22 feet in diameter. Almost the entire deck was covered with a casemate, or superstructure, with sides sloping inward and upward at an angle of forty-five degrees, enclosing the battery, machinery and paddle-wheel. The expectation being to fight bows on as a rule, the front end of the casemate was plated with $2\frac{1}{2}$ inches of iron, backed with twenty inches of oak. The sides abreast the engines and boilers had the same thickness of iron without any oak backing, and the remainder of the surface was unprotected. The engines were of the usual high-pressure river type, and, with the boilers, were in constant danger from shot in action, the light draft of the boats making it impossible for the machinery to be placed below the water line. These Edes gun-boats were named *Cairo, Carondelet, Cincinnati, Louisville, Mound City, Pittsburgh*, and *St. Louis*, after towns in the Mississippi valley. They had two horizontal high-pressure steam cylinders, 22 inches in diameter and 6 feet stroke, and five cylindrical flue boilers, 3 feet in diameter and 24 feet long.

---

[1] Senate Ex. Doc., No. 86; 40th Congress, 2d Session.

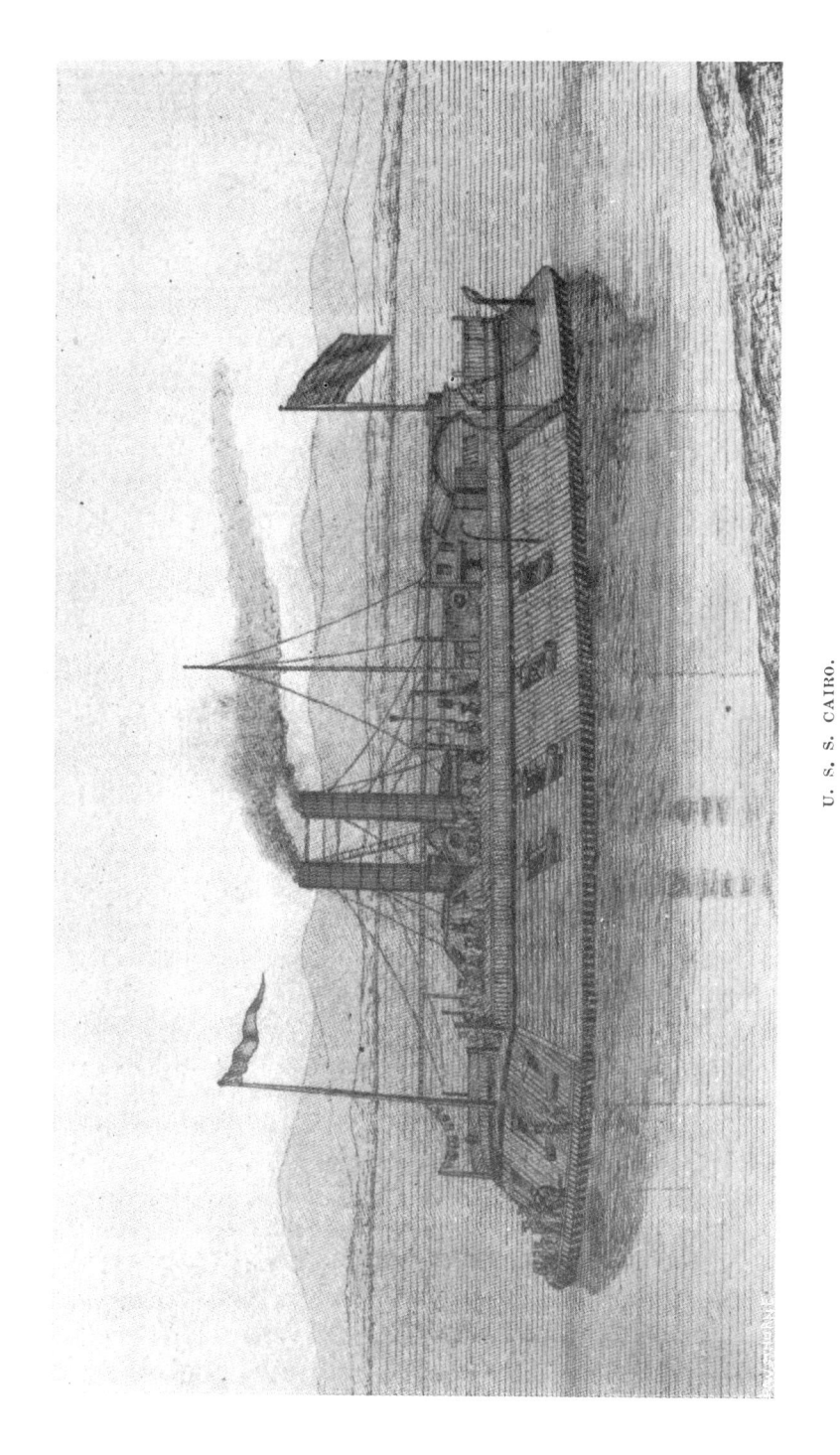

U. S. S. CAIRO.
Type of Western River Armored Gunboat.

Two other steamers—the *Essex* and *Benton*—nearly twice as large as the Edes' boats, were bought and converted into gunboats, the armor both iron and wood backing, being heavier than that of the seven contract vessels. A naval officer (Commander John Rodgers first, and Captain A. H. Foote a few months later) had general command of this flotilla under the army authorities, and officers of the regular navy were assigned to the command of the different steamers: the subordinate officers were volunteers, recruited chiefly from the captains, engineers, mates and pilots of the river, and the crews were decidedly mixed—soldiers, rivermen, men-of-war's-men from the East, and sailors from the Great Lakes. The naval commanders were of necessity junior by relative rank to the numerous generals and colonels doing duty about them, and this produced more or less friction, as the army officers had authority to give orders to the gunboats, or "interfere" with them, as Captain Foote expressed it. In July, 1862 this unpleasant state of affairs was done away with by the transferring of the entire river flotilla to the Navy Department.

CHAPTER XVII.

"Then, like a kraken huge and black,
    She crushed our ribs in her iron grasp!
Down went the Cumberland all a wrack,
    With a sudden shudder of death,
    And the cannon's breath
For her dying gasp."—LONGFELLOW.

1862. The Civil War, Continued. Capture of Roanoke Island and Elizabeth City. The MERRIMAC and her Raid. Destruction of the CONGRESS and CUMBERLAND. The MONITOR Completed and Commissioned. Her Chief Engineer, Isaac Newton. Voyage of the MONITOR from New York and her arrival in Hampton Roads.

AT the beginning of 1862 a large combined military and naval force under the command of Flag Officer L. M. Goldsborough and Brigadier General A. E. Burnside was fitted out at Annapolis for the purpose of entering the Sounds of North Carolina through Hatteras Inlet, and capturing the fortified positions of the enemy on Roanoke Island, the possession of which would give to the Union forces the military command of those waters. This expedition has passed into history as the "Burnside Expedition," but it might with much propriety be designated by Goldsborough's name, inasmuch as its character was essentially naval. Owing to the shoalness of water on the bulkhead at Hatteras Inlet and at many places in the Sounds, vessels of light draft were necessarily used, several of them being armed ferry-boats, and others were purchased tugs, river steamers, freight-boats, etc., not one of them having been built for war purposes. It should be remarked in regard to the ferry-boats that in spite of their uncouth appearance they were found remarkably useful for coast and river service, combining light draft with handiness in narrow places, being able to steam and steer equally well in either direction, while the broad overhanging deck furnished an excellent gun platform on which heavy batteries were habitually mounted.

Proceeding down Chesapeake Bay, the flotilla assembled in Hampton Roads and sailed thence the 11th of January, being then composed of one hundred and twenty-five vessels, about twenty of which belonged to the navy and the remainder were purchased or chartered army transports, carrying some twelve thousand soldiers, with horses, ammunition, provisions, and all the paraphernalia of war. With much tooting of whistles, waving of flags, and cheering of soldiers, the expedition moved out towards the Capes of the Chesapeake, being probably the most motley and piebald aggregation of craft ever afloat with warlike intent. The enthusiasm of the soldiers speedily subsided when the Atlantic was reached and the voyage down the coast was so devoid of pleasure that men who subsequently became hardened veterans of the Army of the Potomac now refer to that sea experience with more abhorrence than they exhibit in recalling the dreadful scenes of Chancellorsville and Gettysburg.

The fleet arrived off Hatteras January 13, and spent some two weeks in the very difficult task of working over the shoals inside the Sounds, the army transports not all getting inside until the 5th of February. Three of the transports were wrecked and a considerable number of horses, rifles, and ordnance stores were lost. One of the naval steamers, the *Whitehall*, was so injured in trying to get in that she had to return to Hampton Roads for repairs. As finally collected inside, the naval force consisted of nineteen vessels arranged in three divisions, commanded respectively by Lieutenant Reed Werden in the *Stars and Stripes*, Lieutenant A. Murray in the *Louisiana*, and Lieutenant H. K. Davenport in the *Hetzel*. A number of the army vessels were armed with one or more guns and were intended for fighting as well as transport purposes; these, bearing such names as *Picket*, *Lancer*, *Huzzar*,&c., were formed into a division under the command of Commander S. F. Hazard, of the navy. Mr Chas. H. Haswell, who has figured so prominently in the earlier chapters of this work, was attached to General Burnside's staff as fleet engineer, and Lieutenant D. W. Flagler, now brigadier general and Chief of the Ordnance Department of the army, was Burnside's chief ordnance officer. Flag Officer Goldsborough's flagship, the *Philadelphia*, not being suited for safe handling over the lumpy and uncertain bottom about Roanoke Island, did not participate in the ensuing engagement, Goldsborough temporarily transferring his flag and going, with his fleet captain, Commander A. L. Case, into action in the armed ferry-boat *Southfield*.

February 7th the fleet moved up and engaged the shore batteries and a small squadron of gunboats of the enemy with such good effect that by midnight Burnside had been able to land over ten thousand troops. The next day the attack was begun at daybreak and continued until the middle of the afternoon, when a bold charge of the military forces gained possession of the enemy's strongest positions and compelled his surrender. About three thousand Confederates were made prisoners, the remainder escaping in their gunboats to Elizabeth City near the Albemarle end of the Dismal Swamp canal.

The casualties in the fleet were small considering the character of the vessels and the severe bombardment they underwent, the total loss amounting to seven killed and sixteen wounded. Two of the killed were officers—Charles Harris, Master's Mate of the *Hetzel*, and Acting Second Assistant Engineer Stephen Mealius, senior engineer of the *Seymour*. Mr Mealius was struck in the hip by a 32-pound shot and so injured that he died about a week later, the same shot killing a coal-heaver at his side. These two were the only casualties on the *Seymour*. The unsuitability of the vessels for war service was shown by the fact that several of them were temporarily disabled during the attack by injuries to their machinery. The crosshead and one of the slides of the engine of the *Hunchback* were shot away, and the *Commodore Perry* was partly crippled by a shot which passed between the engine and boiler and destroyed the feed-water tank. A shell struck the upper deck of the *Ceres* and glancing downward from a beam in very curious flight passed through the lower deck and rolled into one of the ash pits where it exploded, hurling fire and grate-bars in all directions.

One episode of the fight brought Chief Engineer Haswell into enviable prominence for gallantry, the affair being thus related in Frank Leslie's Pictorial History of the War: "During her efforts to get near the fort, the *Ranger* got aground, and for a few moments was in great danger, being a stationary target for the rebel guns. Mr. Charles Haswell, Engineer-in-chief of the fleet, who was in command of the steamer *Tempest*, at this critical juncture went to the rescue, and taking her hawser, towed the *Ranger* out of danger into deep water again. The act was greatly applauded."

Immediately after the capture of Roanoke Island, Flag Officer Goldsborough despatched his second in command, Commander S.

C. Rowan, with fourteen of the steamers to Elizabeth City to attack the Confederate gunboats, all of which had taken refuge there with the exception of the *Curlew* which had been so badly damaged in the fight of the 7th that she had been set on fire and destroyed. February 10th Rowan's squadron attacked the enemy and destroyed all his vessels except one, the *Ellis*, which was captured in good condition and converted into a Federal gunboat, performing good service as such in the waters of the Sounds until her loss by stranding near the end of the year. At the time of her loss she was under the command of Lieutenant Wm. B. Cushing, then rising into prominence by virtue of a courage at once heroic and reckless. For exceptional excellence in the action at Elizabeth City Mr. John Cahill, second assistant engineer and acting chief of the *Underwriter*, was highly commended in the report of his commanding officer, Lieutenant William N. Jeffers, who praised Mr. Cahill's management of the engineer department and also his services in working the after gun during the fight. The same engagement furnished an instance of remarkable courage and presence of mind on the part of John Davis, gunner's mate of the *Valley City*, who, when the magazine was set on fire by a shell, deliberately sat down in an open barrel of powder and prevented its ignition until the fire division came to the rescue.

After the affair at Elizabeth City an expedition consisting of the *Shawsheen*, *Lockwood*, and two or three smaller vessels, all under the command of Lieutenant Jeffers, was sent to drive the enemy away from the mouth of the Chesapeake and Albemarle canal and to block up that water-way. On February 13, after shelling the position and driving the enemy back half a mile or more, a force of sailors and engine-room men under Acting Master Graves and Second Assistant Engineer John L. Lay, acting chief of the *Louisiana*, was landed and destroyed the machinery of a large dredging machine, afterward sinking it and some schooners in the canal, completely obstructing it. Mr. Lay, who afterward became prominent in the navy in connection with the torpedo service, was highly commended in the commanding officer's report for the thorough manner in which the work had been done.

The story of how the fine frigate *Merrimac* was lost to the Union has been told in a former chapter. After gaining possession of the

Norfolk navy yard the Confederates lost no time in making repairs and reaping the benefit of their enormous prize. Their most valuable booty consisted of the great number of guns, mostly uninjured, and the vast quantities of ordnance and equipment supplies that fell into their hands, but they gave attention also to the ships that had been scuttled. The *Germantown*, *Plymouth* and *Merrimac* were raised and the first two easily restored to a serviceable condition, but were not equipped for sea. The failure to attempt to make use of these two ships may be attributed to the fact that some of the most able and progressive officers of the old navy had joined the Confederacy and these gentlemen, from having studiously observed the tendencies of war-ship development, were ready to accept the inevitable and admit that the day of the sailing ship of war was over. They had discerned the growing shadow of coming events and in this regard were far ahead of their naval brethern at the North, who did not awake from the spell of old beliefs until the Southerners gave them a rude and terrible object lesson.

The upper works of the *Merrimac* had been burned as she sank but all the lower hull, as well as the machinery, was found in as good condition as could be expected after a month's submersion. A board, consisting of Engineer-in-Chief William P. Williamson, Lieutenant John M. Brooke, and Chief Constructor John L. Porter was assembled early in June to determine upon a plan for converting the *Merrimac* into an iron-clad battery, and a plan was adopted without any great delay. Lieutenant Brooke was given credit at the time in the newspaper and official reports for having originated the design adopted, and the question has been a matter of dispute and controversy ever since. Constructor Porter claimed the honor and he undoubtedly made the drawings from which the vessel was reconstructed, as that was a duty pertaining to his office, but he might have made them without originating them. In Scharf's History of the Confederate States' Navy the matter is gone over at length and Mr. Porter's claim very fully supported. Chief Engineer Thom Williamson, U. S. Navy, who is a son of the Confederate Engineer in-Chief, has informed the author that years before the war, when interest in the Stevens battery had directed the minds of naval men to the possibilities of iron armor, his father had made drawings of an iron-clad war vessel, and that the reconstructed *Merrimac* was in general design an exact reproduction of those plans. Williamson beyond doubt submitted his design and Porter developed it, the two men as representative ship engineers of the South being jointly entitled to the credit of having created the vessel which became the type and embodied the ideas of the engineers of the South of what an armored war-ship should be.

The damaged hull of the *Merrimac* was rebuilt up to the level of the berth deck and a huge cast iron spur was fitted on the bow about two feet below the water-line and projecting eighteen inches beyond the cutwater. When equipped for service, with coal and stores on board, it was designed that the vessel should float with her deck slightly submerged. On the central part of the deck extending one hundred and seventy feet fore and aft and the full width of the vessel athwartship was erected a citadel or casemate, with rounded ends, the sides sloping at an angle of forty-five degrees and extending some two feet below the water line along the sides, or *eaves*, as the lower edges have appropriately been called. This casemate was seven feet high in the clear, its flat top being covered with a wooden grating to let light and air inside, and forming the promenade or spar deck of the ship. The structure was built of pine, twenty inches in thickness, sheathed with four inches of oak planking and this in turn with two layers of 2-inch iron bars or plates, these being eight inches wide and about ten feet long. The first layer of these armor bars was put on horizontally like a ship's planking, the other, or outer course being up and down. Through-bolts, one and three-eighths inches in diameter secured inside fastened the armor to the wooden superstructure. The battery mounted in this floating stronghold consisted of a VII-inch Brooke rifle pivoted in each of the rounded ends and eight guns in broadside, four on each side, six of the latter being IX-inch Dahlgrens and two 32-pounder Brooke rifles.

The iron-clad approached completion early in March and was christened *Virginia*, but the name she had borne in the old navy stuck to her, probably on account of its alliterative affinity with *Monitor*, and as the *Merrimac* she will ever be known. On the 8th of March she got under way from the Norfolk navy yard and proceeded down the Elizabeth River accompanied by the gunboats *Beaufort* and *Raleigh*, mounting one gun each. Her crew of about three hundred men was composed mostly of volunteers from the troops about Richmond, and because of the crowds of workmen on board until the last minute had not been exercised at their stations. The engines, which had been a nightmare to the engineers of the old navy, had been thoroughly overhauled under the direction of Chief Engineer Williamson, but, with a raw force to manage them, were an object of apprehension rather than a reliable source of power. The Union force in and about Hampton Roads consisted of the large 40-gun firigates *Roanoke* and *Minnesota*, sister ships of the original *Merrimac*, some small armed tugs, the 50-gun sailing frigates *Congress* and *St. Lawrence*, and the 24-gun sloop-of-war *Cumberland*. The two steam frigates have been described in a former chapter, and were regarded as the climax of all excellence in war-ship construction, "yet," as remarked by Professor Soley, "it required but the experience of a single afternoon in Hampton Roads, in the month of March, 1862, to show that they were antiquated, displaced, superseded, and that a new era had opened in naval warfare."

"The *Congress* and *Cumberland* had been lying off Newport News for several months. Their ostensible duty was to blockade the James River; but it is not very clear how a sailing-vessel at anchor could be of any use for this purpose. Most of the old sailing vessels of the navy had by this time been relegated to their proper place as school-ships, store-ships, and receiving-ships, or had been sent to foreign stations where their only duty was to display the flag. Nothing shows more clearly the persistence of old traditions than the presence of these helpless vessels in so dangerous a neighborhood. Although the ships themselves were of no value for modern warfare, their armament could ill be spared; and they carried between them over eight hundred officers and men, whose lives were exposed to fruitless sacrifice."[1]

The *Merrimac* emerged from the river about 1 P. M and turned down towards Newport News where the *Congress* and *Cumberland* lay at anchor, already cleared for action. Three Confederate gunboats, the *Jamestown*, *Teazer* and *Patrick Henry* (or *Yorktown*), soon afterwards came out of the James River past the Federal batteries at Newport News and took part in the ensuing engagement, rendering much aid to the *Merrimac*. The story of what happened that

---

[1] Professor J. R. Soley: The Blockade and the Cruisers, page 61, chapter iii.

afternoon has been told so often that no detailed account of it will be repeated here. As the ram approached the sailing vessels she was furiously pounded by their broadside fire, but her sloping armor glanced the shot off like peas; passing the *Congress*, she deliberately rammed the *Cumberland* in the wake of the starboard forechains, tearing a great hole in her side, in which the cast-iron beak remained, it having been wrenched off in impact, Before reaching the *Cumberland* a broadside from that vessel put one or two shells into the forward gun port of the *Merrimac*, killing two and wounding five men,[1] but doing no serious damage to the ship itself. The first lieutenant of the *Cumberland*, Lieutenant George Upham Morris, who was in command in the absence of his captain, gallantly refused to surrender and fought his ship with a heroism not excelled in naval history, but in vain, for she sank in three-quarters of an hour, carrying down the wounded and many of the crew. The *Congress*, next assailed, was run on shore in hope of saving her, but the enemy got into easy range astern and tore her through and through with shot and shell, butchering her people without mercy. Unable to make any resistance, she surrendered, but the army force on shore, not understanding the situation, fired on the Confederate gunboats that had gone alongside to remove the prisoners, and drove them off. The *Merrimac* then set her on fire with incendiary shot, the survivors of the crew escaping to the shore in their boats or by swimming. The *Congress* burned until far into the night, when she blew up.

Meanwhile the *Minnesota* had got under way from Hampton Roads and approached the scene of action, but ran aground when still more than a mile distant; she was fortunately in such a position with regard to the deep-water channel that the *Merrimac* could not get within effective range of her, but the gunboats *Yorktown* and *Teazer* took comparatively safe positions off her bow and stern and did her much damage, besides killing three and wounding sixteen of her men. The *Roanoke* was unable to move under steam, having broken her shaft some months previously, and consequently had no more business in the presence of the enemy than had the sailing frigates. However, her gallant captain, John Marsden, as well as

---

[1] William Norris, a member of the *Merrimac's* crew; in Southern Magazine November, 1874.

Captain Purviance of the *St. Lawrence*, felt it to be duty to be in action, even in a forlorn hope, and they made desperate efforts to move their vessels from Hampton Roads with the aid of armed tugs, called gunboats, to the scene of action. The approach of night and the falling of the tide defeated the brave endeavors of these two captains, and their ships consequently did not become a prey to the invulnerable monster they hoped to destroy.

About 7 P. M. the *Merrimac* withdrew from action and anchored off Sewall's Point, intending to complete her work of destruction in the morning. Her captain, Franklin Buchanan, had been wounded by a rifle ball from shore; the muzzles of two of her guns had been knocked off, and her steaming ability, bad at best, had been considerably weakened by the loss of the smoke pipe above the casemate: otherwise she was entirely fit for action. Her people were jubilant over their success, and well they might be, for besides winning a sea-fight against great numerical odds they had proved their vessel to be absolutely in control of the situation with no apparent limit to the range of her conquests. Her performance that afternoon had been exactly what we have a right to believe would have resulted had the *Demologos*, nearly fifty years before, been completed in time to encounter a fleet of British frigates. The sound of the *Merrimac's* guns had rung the curtain down forever upon the most picturesque and romantic mode of sea fighting that the world has ever known: thenceforth the march of iron and the engineer would have to be recognized as all-important in naval warfare, and the picturesque must yield before a homely materialism.

Besides the loss of the *Congress* and *Cumberland*, the Federal navy suffered severely in men. The official reports show that the *Congress* lost in killed, wounded and missing one hundred and thirty-six men, or nearly one-third of her entire crew. Among her dead was her gallant commanding officer, Lieutenant Joseph B. Smith. The *Cumberland* lost one hundred and twenty-one, also about one-third of her crew, which numbered three hundred and seventy-six officers and men when the action began. The *Minnesota's* casualities, previously mentioned, were nineteen. On the gunboat *Whitehall* Third Assistant Engineer Andrew Nesbitt was instantly killed by a fragment of shell from the *Merrimac*, and another assistant engineer was wounded in the face in the same manner. Two of her men were killed. The *Whitehall* was a small New York ferryboat of 323 tons, purchased and armed in 1861, and has been mentioned before in this chapter as having been disabled in the Burnside Expedition. Her career ended the following night, March 9, by destruction by fire while lying at the wharf at Fortress Munroe, the chief loss involved being the breeching, tackles, and other gun gear of the *Minnesota*, together with a quantity of small arms and equipment, put on board her for safe keeping the night of the 8th when the destruction of the *Minnesota* seemed imminent. All the casualties due to the raid of the *Merrimac*, as above enumerated, amount to a total of two hundred and eighty. The Confederate loss, including casualities on their gunboats, was not more than one tenth of this figure.

Ericsson's *Monitor* was launched January 30, 1862, and by the middle of February was practically completed, going on a trial trip the 19th of that month. On this occasion the main engines, the steering gear, the turret turning mechanism, almost everything in fact, went wrong or refused to work; natural results of the lack of adjustment due to hasty construction, and needing only this trial to show what remedies were required. The newspapers that had indulged in endless jeremiads over "Ericsson's Folly" now redoubled their attacks and added greatly to the public mistrust of the vessel, but Ericsson himself and Chief Engineer Stimers maintained their faith unmoved and, ignoring the opportunities for controversy, patiently set to work to remedy the defects. February 25, the *Monitor* was put in commission under the command of Lieutenant John L. Worden, U. S. Navy, and on the 4th of March a final and successful trial trip was run, the guns being satisfactorily tried at this time and a favorable report regarding the vessel was made by a board of naval officers. On these trials and while adjusting the machinery Mr. Stimers made it his business to operate personally every piece of mechanism in the ship and to become thoroughly familiar with and master of every detail of every department, thus gaining knowledge without which the performance of the *Monitor* immediately thereafter would have been impossible and the events of the Civil War materially changed.

Escaping finally from the onslaughts of the press, the *Monitor* faced a new foe by putting to sea on the 6th of March, being convoyed by the gunboats *Sachem* and *Currituck* and in tow of the steamer

Seth Low, although she used her own steam as well. Two hours after her departure a telegraphic order arrived for her to proceed direct to Washington and this order was repeated to Captain Marsden at Hampton Roads. The failure of Worden to receive this order before leaving New York is referred to by naval historians as little less than providential, and so it seems in view of the ensuing events; at any rate the circumstance adds one more to the list of almost miraculous chances that united in making the *Monitor* possible and in shaping her career. The officers who went in her as volunteers for the more than hazardous experiment of taking her to sea were, besides Worden the commander, Lieutenant Samuel Dana Greene; Acting Masters John J. N. Webber and Louis N. Stodder; Acting Assistant Paymaster W. F. Keeler; Acting Assistant Surgeon Daniel C. Logue; First Assistant Engineer Isaac Newton; Second Assistant Engineer Albert B. Campbell, and Third Assistant Engineers R. W. Hands and M. T. Sundstrum. The commander, executive officer, and all the engineers were of the regular service and the other officers volunteers. The crew consisted of forty-three men who had volunteered from the receiving-ship *North Carolina* and the sailing frigate *Sabine*. Chief Engineer Stimers voluntarily went as a passenger to observe the working of the novel craft and to give her officers the benefit of his knowledge, he being, as stated by W. C. Church in his Life of John Ericsson, "The only man on board who thoroughly understood the characteristics of the vessel."

Mr. Isaac Newton, the acting chief engineer of the *Monitor*, was a genius in his way who deserves more than passing mention. His father, also named Isaac Newton, was a prominent North River steamboat builder and owner, and young Newton, besides getting an excellent education in the New York city schools, had grown up in his father's steamers and shops, so that by the time he reached manhood he was a thorough steamboat captain, pilot, engineer, boat builder, machinist, and all-around mechanic. In June, 1861, he volunteered for the war and selected the engineer corps of the navy for his place of best service, coming into the navy with letters of commendation from a number of the most prominent men in New York. His education enabled him to overstep the nominal requirements for the volunteer service, and by passing the required examinations he obtained an appointment as a first assistant engineer in the regular service. If his experience could have been augmented with the four or five years of military training so essential to service in the regular navy he would have been an ideal naval officer for a war-steamer: as it was, he won a fine reputation for ability as an engineer and for general usefulness. He resigned at the close of the war and associated himself with John Ericsson in his disastrous *Madawaska-Wampanoag* controversy with Engineer-in-Chief Isherwood; was later General McClellan's associate in the work of rebuilding the Stevens battery, and again, having embarked in politics, held the very important position of chief engineer of the Croton Aqueduct in the Public Works Department of the City of New York.

The first twenty-four hours of the voyage of the *Monitor* from Sandy Hook were uneventful, light winds and smooth water being encountered. The wind and sea then rose and the vessel was soon in great peril. Great quantities of water came in through the hawse pipes, due to "gross carelessness in going to sea without stopping them up," as claimed by Ericsson in a paper on the "Building of the *Monitor*," in Battles and Leaders of the Civil War. The turret was designed to slide on a bronze ring let into the deck at its base, this joint not being water tight nor intended to be, pumps being provided to remove the small quantity of water that would come in through this necessary crack. Before leaving New York, however, some "expert" at the navy yard, accustomed to the manifold uses of rope on shipboard, had caused the turret to be wedged up and had driven into the wide opening thus formed a plaited hemp gasket, the result being that when the sea began to break violently over the deck this gasket was washed out and water poured in cascades down the whole annular space sixty-three feet in circumference. The smoke pipes and blower supply pipes, were simply temporary trunks intended to be removed in action, projecting only about six feet above the deck, over which the seas broke and interrupted the action of the furnaces very seriously.

From getting wet, the belts of the blowers would not cling and the engine and fire-rooms soon became charged with poisonous gases to such an extent that life below became almost impossible. Messrs. Newton and Stimers, with the help of their assistants, struggled bravely to get the blowers in operation and kept at this task until they succumbed to the gas and were carried to the top of the turret, where they revived, though they were thought dead when dragged out of the engine room. Lieutenant Greene, the executive officer, a few days latter gave an account of the *Monitor's* experience in a letter written to his mother, which is regarded as the most graphic narrative of the event in existence, and which has been twice published in the United Service Magazine (In April, 1885 and October, 1893), in which he speaks of this incident as follows: "Our engineers behaved like heroes, every one of them. They fought with the gas, endeavoring to get the blowers to work, until they dropped apparently dead." In the meantime the fires had become so low from water and loss of air that the pumps stopped and loss by foundering became imminent. The tug was directed to steer shoreward and after four or five hours of constant peril smoother water was reached, the machinery started again, water pumped out, and danger for the time averted. It was then evening of the 7th, and for a time safe progress was made, but soon after midnight danger once more appeared as thus described by Lieutenant Greene in the letter to his mother:

"We were just passing a shoal, and the sea suddenly became rough and right ahead. It came up with tremendous force through our anchor-well, and forced the air through our hawse-pipe where the chain comes, and then the water would rush through in a perfect stream, clear to our berth deck, over the wardroom table. The noise resembled the death-groans of twenty men, and was the most dismal, awful sound I have ever heard. Of course the captain and myself were on our feet in a moment, and endeavored to stop the hawse-pipe. We suceeded partially, but now the water began to come down our blowers again, and we feared the same accident that happened in the afternoon. We tried to hail the tug-boat, but the wind being dead ahead they could not hear us, and we had no way of signaling them, as the steam-whistle which father had recommended had not been put on.

"We began then to think the 'Monitor' would never see daylight. We watched carefully every drop of water that went down the blowers, and sent continually to ask the fireman how they were going. His only answer was 'Slowly,' but could not be kept going much longer unless the water could be kept from coming down. The sea was washing completely over the decks, and it was dangerous for a man to go on them, so we could do nothing to the blowers. In the midst of all this our wheel-ropes jumped off the steering wheel (owing to the pitching of the ship), and became jammed. She now began to sheer about at an awful rate, and we thought our hawser would certainly part. Fortunately it was new, and held on well. In the course of half an hour we freed our wheel-ropes, and now the blowers were the only difficulty. About three o'clock Saturday A. M. the sea became a little smoother, though still rough, and going down our blowers somewhat."

By 8 o'clock the next morning smooth water was again found and the *Monitor* slowly and wearily pursued her voyage, entering the Capes of the Chesapeake about 4 P. M. Here they heard the sound of shotted guns, for the *Merrimac* was at that moment in the midst of her carnival of destruction, and the worn-out crew infused with new life cleared their novel and untried craft for action. A pilot-boat coming out told them of what was going on at Newport News but the tale of big frigates being helpless in the presence of any known form of enemy was so improbable that it was not believed until night came on and the pitiful spectacle of the doomed *Congress* loomed up in lines of fire against the dark sky. About 9 P. M. the *Monitor* anchored in Hampton Roads and Worden reported in person to Captain Marsden on the *Roanoke*.

In view of the events of the day it was decided without hesitation to disregard the order of the Department to send the *Monitor* direct to Washington, the occasion for which she was built being nearer at hand. The programme of the enemy for the morning so obviously would begin with an attack upon the grounded *Minnesota* that Worden was ordered to go up to Newport News to protect that vessel if he could, so the *Monitor* got under way again and about 2 A. M. came to anchor near the distressed frigate, her wearied crew spending the rest of the night in repairing damages wrought by the sea and in making ready for the struggle that they knew would come with the morning.

The stage settings were now complete; the curtain had fallen just before upon the last of a long series of glorious deeds performed under a slowly-fading system of seamanship that had many years before reached its culmination, and a new order of seamanship with a new type of sea warrior was about to appear upon the stage. The engineer's machine of John Ericsson was to face the fabric that represented the engineering ingenuity of the South, and the telegraphic tidings of their encounter would inflict an inconsolable fright upon the old romance of the sea, and in an hour reduce the masted navies of the world to mere collections of picturesque and useless relics.

CHAPTER XVIII.

> "The old must fall, and time itself must change,
> And thus new life shall blossom from the ruins."
>
> SCHILLER.

1862—The Civil War, Continued—First Fight of Iron-Clads—Effects of the Battle—Extraordinary Services Rendered by Chief Engineer Stimers—Attack on Drury's Bluff—The GALENA Badly Injured—Gallantry of Assistant Engineer J. W. Thomson.

THE morning of Sunday, March 9, dawned upon a peaceful scene in Hampton Roads. The *Roanoke* and *St. Lawrence* were lying at anchor near Fortress Monroe; the *Minnesota*, still aground off Newport News, overshadowed with her great hull the *Monitor* lying beside her, and off Sewall's Point, black and ominously still, was the *Merrimac*. The topmasts of the *Cumberland* sticking out of the water and blackened wreckage about the spot where the *Congress* burned were the only signs that anything unusual had happened or was likely to happen. Soon after daylight, volumes of black smoke appeared over the *Merrimac*, rising and spreading in the quiet morning air into a cloud that must have seemed a veritable embodiment of the Shadow of Death to the men in the Federal ships.

About 8 A. M. the *Merrimac* got under way and proceeded slowly up towards the Rip Raps in order to swing into the channel whence she could assail the *Minnesota*. Captain Buchanan's wound of the day before had proved so serious that he had been obliged to give up his command to the first lieutenant, Catesby Ap R. Jones, who was now taking the ship into action. Lieutenant Jones, upon whom the responsibility for the day's work rested, was about forty years of age and was a thoroughly trained naval officer, having seen twenty-five years' service in the old navy in the grades from midshipman to lieutenant. One cannot resist the temptation to pause a moment and speculate upon the possibilities that must have arisen before the mental vision of this young and ambitious officer as he moved his destroying machine slowly up to the place for action. The events of the day before left no doubt as to the outcome of the combat he was about to precipitate, and looking beyond his actual surroundings his mind's eye saw the cities of the North laid under ransom by his guns; the national capitol abandoned; the sovereignty of the South acknowledged; the war ended, and himself its central naval figure: he would be the admiral of the Southern navy; perhaps the president of the new nation of the South. It was indeed an hour of vast possibilities for him.

Turning leisurely down the main ship-channel the *Merrimac* headed for the *Minnesota* and opened fire when still a mile distant, the first shot striking the counter near the water line but doing no serious damage. Whatever dreams of conquest Lieutenant Jones may have indulged in earlier in the morning he was now giving all his attention to the material scene about him, and as he looked away to where the *Minnesota* lay stranded to see the effect of his shot, his eye fell on an unfamiliar object. The *Monitor* had moved out from behind the big frigate and was coming unflinchingly across the stretch of water to meet him. This movement of the *Monitor* excited the admiration of Captain Van Brunt of the *Minnesota*, who said in his official report that she ran "right within range of the *Merrimac* completely covering my ship as far as was possible with her diminutive dimensions, and much to my astonishment laid herself right alongside of the *Merrimac*, and the contrast was that of a pigmy to a giant."

On board the *Monitor* every preparation for battle had been made, but the officers and men were kept up by nervous excitement rather than by physical strength; almost without exception they had been without sleep for more than forty-eight hours, and on account of lack of facilities for cooking had had no proper food to sustain them. Worden had left a sick bed to go on board at New York and had suffered much on the voyage down. Newton, who had been at the point of death when dragged out of the engine-room on the occasion of the stoppage of the blowers, was confined to his bed and reported as being unable to do duty for at least a week; when the call to arms sounded, however, he got up and performed his part in the fight courageously and well. There was scarcely a man in the ship who would not have been in a condition of physical prostration had it not been for the excitement due to the presence of the enemy.

Worden took his station in the pilot house, Greene with sixteen men in charge of the guns in the turret, Stodder at the turret turning gear

CHIEF ENGINEER ALBAN C. STIMERS, U. S. NAVY.

and Webber had the small powder division on the berth deck. Stodder was disabled early in the action by the concussion of a shot striking the turret when he was touching it and Stimers took his place, he having volunteered at the beginning of the fight to go in the turret and show the people how to operate it. The pilot house, built log cabin fashion of iron beams or billets, 9 inches by 12 inches, with the corners dovetailed and bolted together, was far forward on deck with no means of communicating with the turret except by a speaking tube; this became disconnected soon after the fight began and communication between Worden and Greene then had to be maintained by passing the word along the berth deck, Paymaster Keeler and the captain's clerk doing this important service. The great error of separating the captain from the battery was remedied in the later monitors by simply placing the pilot-house on top of the turret, engineer Isaac Newton having suggested this arrangement immediately after the fight. As an offset to the wearied condition of the *Monitor's* men, the *Merrimac* was far from being in perfect fighting trim. Two of her guns were disabled by the loss of their muzzles, her ram had been wrenched off, and the upper part of the smoke-pipe was shot away. This last was her greatest injury for it so impaired the furnace draft that steam could not be maintained at anything like a proper working pressure, and her motions were consequently extremely sluggish. Speed is a word hardly applicable to either the *Monitor* or *Merrimac*, but by reason of the damage to the latter the great advantage of quicker movement rested with the *Monitor*.

The first shot fired at the *Monitor* missed her and the Confederates realized that they no longer had the big hull of a frigate for a target. Further enlightenment regarding the altered status of their antagonists came quickly in the furious impact of the heavy XI-inch solid shot of the *Monitor* against their casemate, knocking men down and leaving them dazed and bleeding at the nose, ears and mouth. It will be needless to repeat the circumstantial account of the combat, which has been told so carefully by so many writers. Neither vessel could penetrate the armor of the other, which prevented the question of their supremacy being definitely settled and left it open to dispute ever since. Each at different stages of the fight tried ramming, the *Monitor* with the most success as she struck her enemy fairly enough near the stern, having aimed to injure the propeller, but on account of the smoke and other obstacles to exact steering missed the vital spot by about three feet only. The *Merrimac's* attempt resulted in a harmless glancing blow, the superior speed of the *Monitor* making it an easy matter to elude her antagonist.

After about an hour of fighting, the *Merrimac* tried to give the *Monitor* up as a bad task and turned her attention again to the *Minnesota*, the first shell fired at the frigate passing "through the chief engineer's state-room, through the engineers' mess-room, amidships, and burst in the boatswain's room, tearing four rooms into one in its passage, and exploding two charges of powder, which set the ship on fire."[1] The second shell exploded the boiler of tug-boat *Dragon* lying alongside the *Minnesota*, and by the time the third shell was thrown the *Monitor*, not disposed to be ignored, had again interposed between the *Minnesota* and her assailant and thereafter she engrossed the entire attention of the enemy. Shortly after this diversion the ammunition in the *Monitor's* turret became exhausted and she had to go out of action to replenish it, the scuttle by which it was passed being impossible to use except when the turret was stationary and in a certain position. This circumstance greatly encouraged the Confederates who believed their opponent to be disabled from their fire, but in a quarter of an hour their hopes were dispelled by the *Monitor* resuming the fight more vigorously than ever.

Soon after 11 A. M. Lieutenant Worden, while looking through a sight-hole in the pilot-house, was disabled by a shell striking and exploding immediately in front of his eyes, he being temporarily blinded and his face terribly burned and cut by the flying grains of powder and bits of iron. The steersman was stunned for a few minutes by the concussion also and in that short space of time the *Monitor* without anyone in control of her ran off aimlessly towards shoal water away from the fight, for no one had signalled the engine-room to stop. This gave such an appearance of defeat that on the *Minnesota* all hope was abandoned and every preparation made for setting the ship on fire and abandoning her. In a short time, however, Lieutenant Greene learned of the casualty in the pilot-house and, leaving Stimers in charge of the guns, took command of the ship and turned upon his foe again. Then to the

---

[1] Official report of Captain Van Brunt of the *Minnesota*.

amazement of all the *Merrimac* suddenly gave up the fight and steamed away toward Norfolk. Catesby Jones reported afterward as a reason for withdrawing at this time that he believed the *Monitor* disabled and he was very desirous of crossing the Elizabeth River bar before ebb tide. There was no reason for believing the *Monitor* out of action and every reason for believing the contrary, for when she returned under the command of Greene, Stimers fired two or three shots against the *Merrimac*, which were the last guns of the encounter. Had the Confederates believed in their success to the extent of demanding the surrender of the *Monitor*, Greene could and very probably would have replied in the words used long before by John Paul Jones under similar circumstances—"We have not yet begun to fight."

Lieutenant Greene did not follow the retreating enemy, the orders under which the *Monitor* fought limiting her action to a defense of the Federal ships, the *Minnesota* especially. Greene was very young at the time and inexperienced in judging of the amount of discretion allowed a commanding officer in obeying orders in battle, so it was with many misgivings that he allowed the *Merrimac* to go unmolested while he returned to the side of the *Minnesota*, but the superior officers of both army and navy present sustained his action and assured him that he had done exactly the right thing. Curious as it appears, many able writers have indulged in much argument to prove which of the two iron-clads won the fight. The *Merrimac* won a most decided victory in her attack upon the wooden sailing vessels the first day of her appearance, but when all argument regarding the second day's fight is exhausted a few very pertinent facts remain undisturbed. When the *Merrimac* got up steam in the morning it was obviously for no other purpose than to destroy the Federal vessels in Hampton Roads, and she did not destroy anything. When the day was done she was not even in Hampton Roads herself. The *Monitor* was ordered to protect the wooden ships, and she protected them. When night came she was still on guard over them, grim, ugly, and ready to fight.

The *Monitor* was struck twenty-one times in the action and fired forty-one XI-inch solid shot. The most damaging blow she received was from the shell which disabled Worden, this having cracked one of the heavy iron logs of the pilot-house entirely through and forced the fractured ends inboard an inch and a half, besides knocking the loose cover of the pilot-house half off. The deepest indentation in her turret was two inches and the deepest score on her deck was only one-half inch. Two people in the turret were disabled by concussion and Chief Engineer Stimers was hurt in the same way, but his injuries were slight and he pluckily continued in the fight to the end. The *Merrimac* was struck ninety-seven times in the two days' fight, twenty of her shot marks being from the guns of the *Monitor*. Six plates of her outer layer of iron were penetrated but the inner layer was not broken. The XI-inch guns of the *Monitor* were new and large for their time and the Bureau of Ordnance was suspicious of them, having issued orders not to use more than fifteen pounds of powder for their charge; otherwise their shot would probably have broken into the casemate of the *Merrimac*. At a later period greater confidence regarding these guns was entertained and thirty, and even fifty pounds of powder were safely used in charging them. Engineer Isaac Newton, who was very level-headed about such matters, testified before the Congressional Committee on the Conduct of the War that he believed the failure of the *Monitor* to destroy her antagonist was due entirely to the low powder charges prescribed. He also testified to his belief that, "But for the injury received by Lieutenant Worden, that vigorous officer would very likely have badgered the *Merrimac* to a surrender." The *Merrimac* having been hastily equipped and not expecting to meet any but wooden ships had nothing but shell on board; had she been provided with solid shot the effect upon the *Monitor* might have been different.

The success of the *Monitor* completely changed the aspect of the opening military operations of the year and raised the North from a depth of apprehension to a pinnacle of hope and jubilation. No single event of the Civil War so thoroughly aroused the enthusiastic admiration of the loyal North as did this Sunday duel in Hampton Roads, and the *Monitor* and her crew became the great and almost only subject for public discussion and applause. The world is prone to sing the praises of the warrior who destroys, and to neglect the honors due to him who makes the soldier's success possible by providing him with his armor and his weapons, but in this case the patient toiler reaped the greater glory, and the name and fame of John Ericsson went to the uttermost parts of the earth. Worden, Greene, Stimers and Newton were all heroes in the public estimation and saw their pictures and the story of their deeds in the public prints for many a day, but all the applause showered upon them was little compared to the perfect avalanche of honors heaped upon Ericsson the Engineer. The reason for this unusual sentiment is easily found. Ericsson had been for several months held up to ridicule and abuse to such an extent by the press that he and his work were known to all men, and when his hour of triumph came, that innate sense of sympathy for the " under dog " in a fight manifested itself joyously at seeing him suddenly and unexpectedly come uppermost. Ericsson's enemies had so overdone the matter of persecution that in the end he owed much of his fame to their acts.

Abroad, the news of the battle created a profound sensation and more than one naval power whose commercial interests or thirst for foreign conquest had led to the point of seriously preparing to assail the American Republic in the day of its distress, now paused to take a sober second thought and ultimately concluded to check their designs. "Probably no naval conflict in the history of the world ever attracted as much attention as did the battle in Hampton Roads, between the *Monitor* and the *Merrimac*. It revolutionized the navies of the world, and showed that the wooden ships, which had long held control of the ocean, were of no further use for fighting purposes. Commenting upon the news of that event, the *London Times* said: ' Whereas we had available for immediate purposes one hundred and forty-nine first-class war-ships, we have now two, these two being the *Warrior* and her sister *Ironside*. There is not now a ship in the English navy, apart from these two, that it would not be madness to trust to an engagement with that little *Monitor*.' England and all other maritime powers immediately proceeded to reconstruct their navies, and the old fashioned three and four-decker line-of-battle ships were condemned as useless. Not only in ships, but in their armament, there was rapid progress, and so great has been the advance in marine artillery that the *Monitors* of 1862, and the subsequent years of the American war, would be unable to resist the shot from the guns of 1880-'87."[1]

---

[1] Thomas W. Knox;—Decisive Battles since Waterloo.

On March 28, by joint resolution, Congress passed a vote of thanks to Ericsson for his "enterprise, skill, energy, and forecast" in the design and construction of the *Monitor*, and he was the recipient of similar honors from the Legislature of the State of New York and from innumerable civil organizations and societies. Lieutenant Worden was tendered the thanks of Congress by a resolution approved July 11, 1862, and in the following February was given more substantial recognition for his great service by a second resolution authorizing his advancement one grade, that is, to the rank of captain, he having been promoted to commander in the meantime. Ericsson steadily maintained that Stimers and not Worden was the real hero of the *Monitor*, because he alone of all on board knew how to operate the various mechanisms of the vessel, without which knowledge she would have been utterly useless in the face of the enemy. At a banquet given him by the New York Chamber of Commerce Ericsson made a point of asserting in his speech that he regarded the success of the *Monitor* as "entirely owing to the presence of a master-mind (Mr. Stimers)," a belief which he defended at length and with an indisputable array of facts.

This public laudation of Stimers, not confined by any means to Ericsson, greatly disturbed Lieutenant Worden and his friends, and Worden, as late as two years after the fight, waited upon Mr. Griswold, a Member of Congress and a friend of Ericsson, having been one of his sureties in the enterprise of building the *Monitor*, to complain of the fancied injustice done him by Ericsson. Of this interview Mr. Griswold wrote to Ericsson: "I have just had a call from Captain Worden. He thinks you did him injustice in your Chamber of Commerce remarks for the sake of complimenting Stimers, and says the 'master-spirit' had nothing at all to do with the affairs of the *Merrimac*, was not consulted, and was in no special way tributary to the result of that combat."[1] In spite of this assertion, the great weight of testimony goes to show that Stimers was consulted and was in a special way "tributary" to the result of the action. Assistant Secretary of the Navy Fox, who saw the fight, telegraphed the Navy Department as soon as he

---

[1] W. C. Church;—Life of John Ericsson, Vol. I, p. 298.

THE MONITOR-MERRIMAC DUEL.

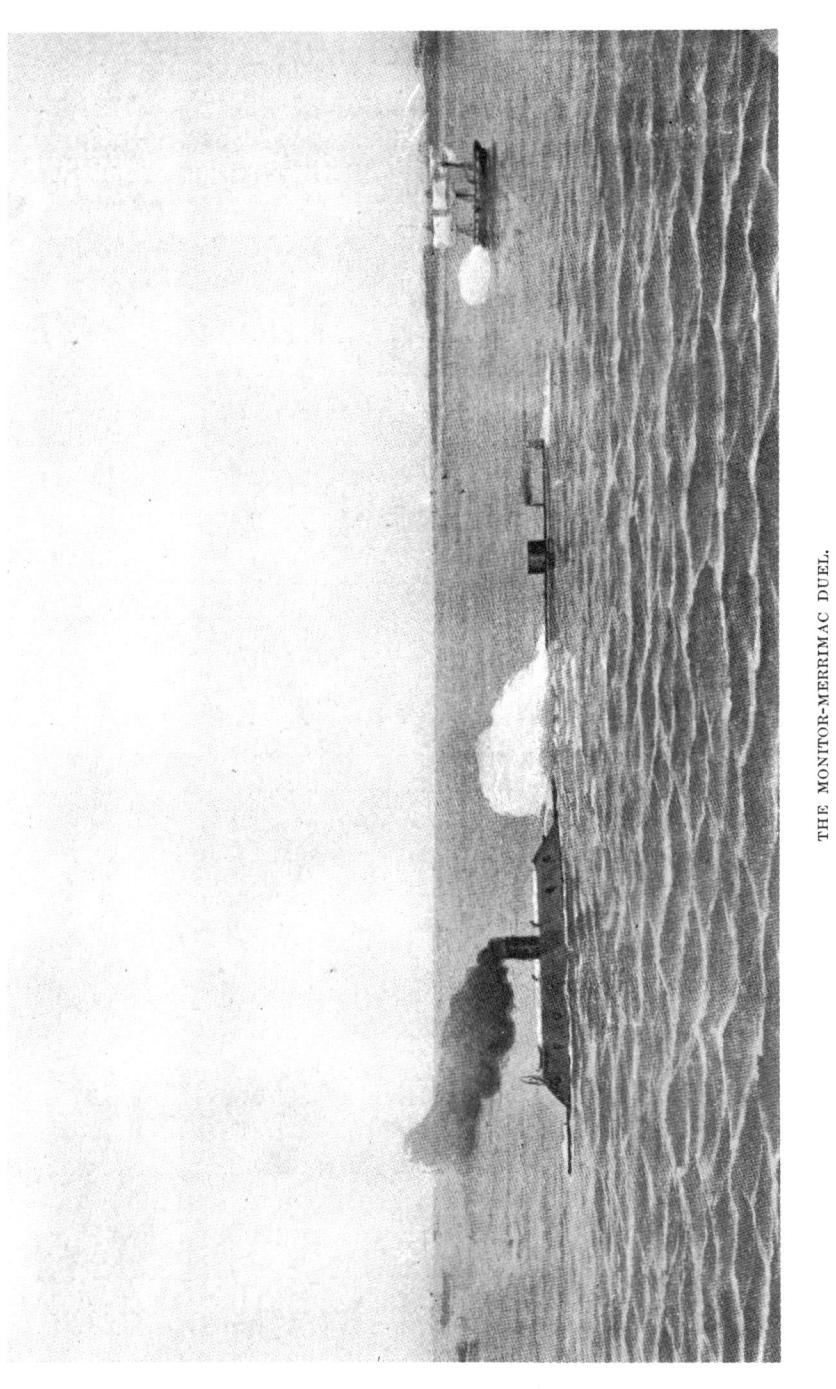

From a copyrighted photograph of a painting by Mr. B. A. Richardson of Norfolk, Va., the use of which is kindly allowed by him.

could learn particulars that "Lieutenant Worden, who commanded the *Monitor*, handled her with great skill, and was assisted by Chief Engineer Stimers." He could have had no other object in mentioning Stimers' name, to the exclusion of the other officers, in this message except the wish to have the Department understand who, next to Worden, deserved credit for the victory of the *Monitor*.

Lieutenant Greene in the letter to his mother before quoted from in these pages, and which for obvious reasons is more apt to reveal unvarnished facts than a formal official report that would become a public document, says in regard to the officers' stations for battle: "Acting Master Stodder was at the wheel which turns the tower, *but as he could not manage it*, he was relieved by Stimers." The italics are the author's.

Mr. W. C. Church, who cannot be accused of partiality for Mr. Stimers, says in his Life of John Ericsson: "During the passage from New York, the working gear of the turret was permitted to rust for want of proper cleaning and oiling, and it worked with so much difficulty during the engagement with the *Merrimac* that, but for the energy and determination of Engineer Stimers, it might not have revolved at all."

Proofs like the above may be multiplied, but these are sufficient for every logical purpose. The writer has no desire to magnify the services of Mr. Stimers, especially as it will become a duty as this history progresses to narrate certain mistakes of that officer whereby the naval engineer corps suffered the most serious reflection upon its professional competence that it has ever experienced, but from an impartial review of all the facts connected with the *Monitor-Merrimac* battle the conclusion is plain that Chief Engineer Alban C. Stimers was the one person on board the *Monitor* who thoroughly knew how to use that vessel and her weapons, and but for his presence the result of the combat would in all probability have been very different, and most disastrous to the *Monitor*, to the reputation of Lieutenant Worden, and to the cause of the Union.

The day after the fight of the iron-clads, the *Minnesota* was floated and soon restored to serviceable condition. Immediately thereafter the Union fleet in Hampton Roads began receiving additions almost daily, for the naval occupation of this position was an important element in the grand campaign against Richmond then in movement by the Army of the Potomac. The *Merrimac* retired to Norfolk where she was docked by Constructor Porter, her plating repaired and strengthened, and a new spur fitted to her bow. The rough-and-ready old commodore, Josiah Tatnall, was placed in command and great things were expected. On two occasions—April 11 and May 8—she went into Hampton Roads and looked at the *Monitor* and the Federal fleet, but no fight occurred at either time. From the reports of the Federal commander-in-chief, Goldsborough, and of Tatnall it appears that each party earnestly desired a conflict and that the other was afraid, or at least avoided hostilities.

Military operations compelled the surrender of Norfolk to the Union forces on the 10th of May, and Tatnall endeavored to save the *Merrimac* by taking her up the James river, but finding her to draw several feet too much water for the river he reluctantly set her on fire and abandoned her. Early on the morning of May 11 the fire reached her magazine and she blew up. This event occasioned such a wild outburst of public grief in Richmond that for a time it was feared the governmental departments of the Confederacy would be attacked by a mob. The *Merrimac* had been proudly called the "iron diadem of the South," and had been so confidently relied upon for the defense of the James River that after her destruction serious thoughts of surrendering Richmond were entertained. The men of the *Merrimac* were utilized to man a battery up the river at Drury's Bluff, where a few days later they again encountered their old foes of the *Monitor*.

Immediately after the destruction of the *Merrimac*, Flag Officer Goldsborough took possession of the lower part of James River with his flagship, the *Susquehanna*, and a number of smaller vessels, sending Commander John Rodgers with the *Galena*, *Monitor*, *Aroostook* and *Port Royal* on an expedition up the river. The *Galena* had just come from the builders' works at Mystic, Conn., and will be recalled as the iron-clad gunboat built in accordance with the report of the board on armored vessels of the previous year. The *Monitor* was now commanded by Lieutenant William N. Jeffers. The *Aroostook* was one of the ninety-day gunboats and the *Port Royal* was one of the first lot of double-enders. Accompanying them was the vessel fitted out by the Stevens brothers to demonstrate the excellence of their system of protective armor, this vessel being referred to indiscriminately in the official reports as the *Naugatuck* and the "U. S. revenue steamer *E. A. Stevens*;" she was commanded by a revenue marine lieutenant named D. C. Constable.

The morning of May 15 this squadron came up to Ward's, or Drury's Bluff, eight miles below Richmond, where the river was found obstructed with piles and sunken vessels and defended by a heavy battery mounted about two hundred feet above the water. The *Galena* and *Monitor* anchored about six hundred yards from the battery and the unarmored vessels about twice that distance, all opening fire upon the enemy's works. The *Monitor* soon had to remove to a greater distance on account of being unable to elevate her guns sufficiently. She was struck only three times during the attack and had no casualities. The 100-pounder Parrott gun of the *Naugatuck* burst early in the action and disabled that vessel as it was the only gun she had, the accident resulting eventually in the discouragement of the efforts of the Stevens brothers to induce the government to accept their unfinished battery.

The *Galena*, at anchor and with her broadside sprung towards the enemy's battery, proved a fine target and was very roughly used by the plunging shot from the bluff, which struck her sloping side armor almost at right angles. In the plain words of her commander, John Rodgers, "We demonstrated that she is not shot proof." Thirteen shot penetrated the side armor, several coming clear through and doing great damage to the crew by scattering splinters and fragments of the iron plating, while others stuck in the wooden backing after passing through the plating. One shell made a clean passage through the side and exploded in the steerage, setting the ship on fire. The spar deck was badly splintered and broken through in some places. All along the port side, which was the one exposed, knees, planks, bulkheads, and beams were splintered and started out of place. Although exposed to this terrible riddling, Commander Rodgers kept his ship in action for more than three hours and only withdrew when his ammunition was nearly expended. The *Galena* had thirteen men killed and eleven wounded; the *Naugatuck*, two wounded, and the *Port Royal* had her commander, George Morris, wounded.

The following extracts from the official report of Commander Rodgers of the *Galena* refer to meritorious services performed by members of the engineer department of that vessel:

"Mr. J. W. Thomson, first assistant engineer, coolly repaired some of the valve gear which broke down, under fire, and under his direction a fire in the steerage, caused by an exploding shell, was extinguished before the regular firemen reached the place."

"Mr. T. T. Millholland, third assistant engineer, in charge of the steam fire department, was active and efficient; as a sharpshooter he did good service."

"Charles Kenyon, fireman, was conspicuous for persistent courage in extracting a priming wire, which had become bent and fixed in the bow gun, and in returning to work the piece after his hand, severely burnt, had been roughly dressed by himself with cotton waste and oil."

The *Wachusett* being at City Point in the James River the 19th of May, it was represented to her captain that there were no physicians in the town and that some of the people, mostly women and children, were in great need of medical attendance. The enemy's lines were believed to be about eight miles from the town, so there was apparently no danger in answering this appeal. Assistant Surgeon G. D. Slocum volunteered to go on shore and minister to the distressed people if some of his shipmates would go with him, he not caring to be entirely alone in an enemy's town, and Assistant Paymaster L. S. Stockwell, Chief Engineer Charles H. Baker, and Lieutenant DeFord of the army signal corps agreed to accompany him. On shore, while visiting the sick, a detachment of Confederate cavalry suddenly appeared and made prisoners of the officers and two of the boat's crew with them, carrying them off to Petersburg. At that place the commander of the district, General Huger, apologized to them for the stupidity of his men and said he would have them released, as they had been captured while rendering humane aid to citizens of Virginia, and, furthermore, were unarmed with the exception of side arms when taken.

The Richmond authorities refused to release the prisoners on General Huger's recommendation and they were accordingly taken to a military prison at Salisbury, North Carolina, and confined in that place. The peculiar action of the Richmond government in this case was due to the fact that there was talk at the North of treating some Confederate officers captured on privateers as pirates, and the Southerners wished to hold some Federal naval officers as hostages to insure their own officers being treated as prisoners of war. After a detention of twelve weeks in Salisbury, Mr. Baker and some of the others were transferred to Libby prison in Richmond, and about a week later were allowed to enter the Union lines on parole. On the 24th of September Chief Engineer Baker was exchanged for a Confederate army captain and resumed duty under his own flag.

CHAPTER XIX.

> " He has sounded forth the trumpet that shall never call retreat ;
> He is sifting out the hearts of men before his judgement-seat ;
> Oh! be swift, my soul, to answer Him ; be jubilant, my feet ;
> Our God is marching on."
> JULIA WARD HOWE—*Battle-Hymn of the Republic.*

1862—The Civil War, Continued—Naval Operations in the Mississippi River—Battles Below New Orleans—Catastrophe to the MOUND CITY—Attack on Vicksburg—Warfare on the Atlantic Coast—Wreck of the ADIRONDACK—Loss of the MONITOR—Peril of the PASSAIC—Heroism of Assistant Engineer H. W. Robie.

AS soon as a sufficient number of iron-clad steamers in the Mississippi were completed, Commodore Foote hastened to make use of them, the first hostile movement being an attack upon Fort Henry, which was captured Februry 6th after a closely contested action of little more than one hour. The attacking force consisted of the iron-clads *Benton,* (Foote's flagship); *Essex, Carondelet,* and *St. Louis,* and the wooden gunboats *Conestoga, Tyler,* and *Lexington.* The attack was planned as a joint army and navy enterprise by General U. S. Grant and Commodore Foote, but owing to the wretched condition of the roads the army was delayed and consequently did not share in the honor of the capture, the fort having surrendered to the naval force. From Fort Henry, Foote moved with his flotilla to Fort Donelson, which place he attacked February 14th. Here he met with much more vigorous opposition than had been experienced at Fort Henry, and in the course of an hour and a half two of his vessels were temporarily disabled, and the attack was discontinued for the night. The next morning, upon resuming the bombardment, the enemy was found considerably demoralized and after a feeble resistance surrendered.

A naval movement on a far greater scale was already on foot, having for its object the opening of the Mississippi River from its mouth. Captain David G. Farragut was selected for the command of this expedition and in his flagship, the *Hartford,* arrived on the 20th of February off the mouth of the great river where he was to make his name famous. The vessels ordered to this station assembled one by one at the Southwest Pass and the entire month of March was consumed in the task of getting the heavier ships into the deep water of the river inside, which labor was finally accomplished with the exception of the *Colorado*, which vessel could not be lightened enough to make her entrance possible. Her commander and a large number of her officers and men went as volunteers in other ships of the fleet. As finally assembled in the river at Pilot Town the fleet proper consisted of seventeen vessels of the classes and armament exhibited in the table following. The *Varuna* was a merchant steamer purchased in 1861 for $135,000, but all the others will be recognized as being regularly built war-vessels and all, with the exception of the *Mississippi*, of a type then modern.

NAME.	TONS.	GUNS.	COMMANDING OFFICER.	CHIEF ENGINEER.
Screw Sloops				
Hartford......	1990	24	Capt. D. G. Farragut.[1] Capt. H. H. Bell.[2]	Chief Engr. J. B. Kimball.
Pensacola.....	2158	23	Capt. H. W. Morris.[3]	Chief Eng. S. D. Hibbert.
Brooklyn	2070	22	Capt. T. T. Craven.	Chief Eng. Wm. B. Brooks.
Richmond....	1929	24	Com. James Alden.	Chief Eng. John W. Moore.
Oneida.........	1032	9	Com. S. P. Lee.	Chief Eng. F. C. Dade.
Varuna.........	1300	10	Com. Chas. S. Boggs.	Act. 1st. A. Eng. R. Henry.
Iroquois......	1016	7	Com. John DeCamp.	1st Asst. Eng. John H. Long.
Side Wheel.				
Mississippi ..	1692	17	Com. M. Smith.	Chief Eng. E. Lawton.
Ninety-day gunboats				
Cayuga........	507	2	Lieut. N. B. Harrison.	2d. Asst. Eng. G. W. Rodgers.
Itaska..........	507	2	Lieut. C. H. B. Caldwell.	2d. Asst. Eng. J. H. Morrison.
Katahdin. ...	507	2	Lieut. Geo. H. Preble.	2d. As. Eng. T. M. Dukehart.
Kennebec.....	507	2	Lieut. J. H. Russell.	2d. As. Eng. Henry W. Fitch.
Kineo...	507	2	Lieut. G. M. Ransom.	2d. As. Eng. S. W. Cragg.
Pinola	507	2	Lieut. Pierce Crosby.	1st As. Eng. John Johnson.
Sciota..........	507	2	Lieut. E. Donaldson.	2d. A. Eng. Chas. E. Devalin.
Winona........	507	2	Lieut. E. T. Nichols,	2d. A. Eng, Jas. P. Sprague.
Wissahickon	507	2	Lieut. A. N. Smith.	2d. A. Eng. T. S. Cunningham.

[1] Flag Officer, commanding fleet.

[2] Fleet-Captain. Commander Richard Wainwright actually commanded the *Hartford* during the ensuing operations.

[3] Owing to Captain Morris' defective eyesight, the executive officer, Lieutenant F. A. Roe, was in practical charge of this ship.

In addition to this force there was also a flotilla of twenty schooners under the command of Commander David D. Porter, each schooner mounting one XIII-inch mortar. These vessels were mostly commanded by their former captains, who had entered the naval service as acting masters and were excellent examples of that large and courageous class of practical seamen who contributed so largely to the success of the naval arms during the rebellion. Their character and services were well understood by Porter, who thus refers to them in a report written by him in July, 1862:

"Again, sir, I have to mention favorably the divisional officers, and the acting masters commanding mortar vessels. Anchored at all times in a position selected by myself, more with regard to the object to be accomplished than to any one's comfort or safety; knowing that they will have to stay there without a chance of getting away till I think proper to remove them, (no matter how thick the shot and shell may fly) there has always existed a rivalry as to who shall have the post of honor (the leading vessel) almost certain to be struck, if not destroyed.

"They know no weariness, and they really seem to take delight in mortar firing, which is painful even to those accustomed to it. It requires more than ordinary zeal to stand the ordeal. Though I may have at times been exacting and fault-finding with them for not conforming with the rules of the service (which requires the education of a life-time to learn) yet I cannot withhold my applause when I see these men working with such earnest and untiring devotion to their duties while under fire."

Six steamers accompanied the mortar fleet to move the schooners about and to protect them in a measure from attacks that their peculiar armament could not oppose, these steamers being the *Owasco*, *Miami*, *Harriet Lane*, *Westfield*, *Clifton*, and *J. P. Jackson*. The *Owasco* was a ninety-day gunboat; the *Miami* one of the first lot of double-enders; the *Harriet Lane* a side-wheel revenue cutter transferred from the Treasury Department, and the other three were large and heavily-armed side-wheel ferry-boats.

After the fleet had stripped for action and left at Pilot Town all spars, sails, rigging and unnecessary boats, it moved up to the desperate undertaking of attacking and passing the two forts, Jackson and St. Phillip, most advantageously located at a bend on opposite banks of the river. A short distance below the forts the river was barred with a combination of large log rafts and schooners at anchor, supporting heavy chains reaching from bank to bank. Auxiliary to the forts and above them in the river was a flotilla of Confederate vessels, consisting of four naval steamers, six gunboats of the local River Defense Fleet, and two armed steamers belonging to the State of Louisiana. The most formidable of the Confederate naval vessels was the ram *Manassas*, which the previous October had been in action with the *Richmond* in the Southwest Pass and had somewhat damaged that vessel. She was originally a large sea-going tug-boat named *Enoch Train* and had been converted into a ram by being arched over with timber and plated with old-fashioned railroad strap iron, about an inch thick. She had twin screws and carried one 32-pounder gun pointing right ahead. Another of the naval vessels was the *Louisiana*, a large armored river steamer similar to the Federal iron-clad *Benton* described in a previous chapter; she had sixteen heavy guns, nine of them being VI and VII-inch rifles, and would have been a formidable antagonist had it not been for the fact that Farragut made his attack before her machinery was quite finished. The other naval vessels and the River Defense boats were river steamers mounting from two to seven guns each, lightly armored forward, and the two State vessels were small sea-going steamers, also armored on their bows, and mounting two guns each.

The mortar flotilla was moved up to within about three thousand yards of Fort Jackson and rendered almost indistinguishable by dressing the masts with bushes and foliage, the vessels lying close to the bank with a background of trees. On the 18th of April they opened fire upon Jackson and for nearly six days maintained an almost uninterrupted bombardment, doing the enemy's works much damage and receiving some in return, one of the schooners being sunk at her anchors by a shell dropping completely through her. To divert the fire of the forts from the mortar fleet, a sloop of war and two or three gunboats were each day advanced into the zone of fire and effected the object satisfactorily by moving about near the head of the line of schooners and firing on the forts at the same time. The *Oneida*, just out of the shipyard where she was built, was the first of the sloops to go into this fire and she demonstrated that in spite of her pretty name of the beautiful lake of the Iroquois she was to be ruled by an evil star, for her baptism of fire cost her many ugly hits and nine men badly wounded. Thenceforth her career was one of misfortune, until finally in a far-distant sea she went to the bottom with the greater part of her crew.

While the mortars were thus furiously engaged, Farragut was making all ready for the attempt to run past the forts. One interesting expedient adopted by him was the shifting of weights on board all the vessels so that they were down by the head about one foot, the object being to prevent the swift current from swinging them head down stream in case of taking the bottom, as would have resulted had they grounded with the usual trim of the greatest draft aft. All unnecessary top-hamper had been previously dispensed with, and now five of the gunboats removed even their lower masts. Chain cables were stopped up and down the ships' sides to protect the machinery, and the vessels were rendered difficult to see on the muddy water by daubing them over with the yellow mud of the river. These last two expedients were due to the ingenuity of engineers on board the *Richmond*. The use of chain cable for armor is said by several officers who were attached to the *Richmond* at the time to have been suggested by First Assistant Engineer Eben Hoyt of that vessel and was proposed to the commanding officer by the chief engineer, Mr. John W. Moore. From Farragut's detailed report of the battles below New Orleans the following relating to this point is quoted:

"Every vessel was as well prepared as the ingenuity of her commander and officers could suggest, both for the preservation of life and of the vessel, and, perhaps, there is not on record such a display of ingenuity as has been evinced in this little squadron. The first was by the engineer of the Richmond, Mr. Moore, by suggesting that the sheet cables be stopped up and down on the sides in the line of the engines, which was immediately adopted by all the vessels."

Under the date of October 16, 1862, Chief Engineer Moore,

writing from the *Richmond*, then at Pensacola, addressed the Navy Department in regard to a change which had been made to his disadvantage in the arrangement of the list of chief engineers. On the original of this letter, now on file in the Department, in Admiral Farragut's own handwriting is the following endorsement:

"Respectfully forwarded. Mr. Moore is the gentleman whom I mentioned in my official letter as the originator of cladding the ships with their chain cables and has always been spoken of by his Commander as a man of great merit both in and out of his profession.

"Very respectfully,
D. G. FARRAGUT."

The commanding officer of the *Richmond* in forwarding Mr. Moore's protest took occasion to write the following letter, which certainly is conclusive as to whether or not the expedients referred to originated with members of the engineer corps:

"SIR:—I have the honor to enclose herewith a remonstrance of Chief Engineer Moore of this vessel against the action of a Board of Examiners which has evidently done him great injustice. Being more or less interested in the welfare of all those serving under my command and feeling it a duty to come to their aid when they require it, I trust that I shall be excused for thus trespassing on your valuable time and will proceed at once to the point. *Imprimis* then, Mr. Moore's professional standing has been fixed at the highest point by the several Boards before which he has appeared, and to my mind he is justly entitled to that distinction; but I wish now to show the Department that he has besides that other claims to consideration. They are as follows: About this time last year I arrived at the Southwest Pass in the *South Carolina* pretty nearly broken down in machinery. Our main shaft was all adrift and neither the *Niagara* and *Colorado* could do anything for us. Mr. Moore, who was on board this ship at the time at the head of the passes, hearing of our trouble came down and very soon decided that he could make us all right again, and in less than three days we were, by his individual exertions, fully and efficiently repaired and off for our station. Again, the idea of mailing our vessels' sides, which was adopted by all the ships of the squadron, with chain cables, is his. We know that it saved this ship's as well as the *Hartford's* machinery from serious injury and consequently the vessels from destruction, the armor on both having been struck by solid shot in that vital locality. After the passage of the forts two-thirds of a 32-pounder shot, which had broken its way through parts of the chain, was found embedded in our side. The Captain of the *Brooklyn* says in his official report, in speaking of the ram *Manassas*: "His efforts to damage me were completely frustrated, our chain armor proving a perfect protection to our sides." Subsequent examination showed, however, that the ship had received serious damage and that *nothing but the armor saved her from destruction.*

"The idea of painting the ships with the mud of the Missisippi on that memorable occasion so as to screen them as much as possible from observation, a color now adopted by the Department as national, is also Mr. Moore's.

"Regretting my inability to state this case properly in fewer words, I am, Respectfully, Your obedient servant,

"JAMES ALDEN, Commander.

"HON. GIDEON WELLES, Secretary U. S. Navy, Washington, D. C."

The night of the 20th of April, Lieutenant Caldwell in the *Itaska* most gallantly boarded one of the schooners supporting the barrier chain and, finding its ends bitted on board, slipped them and thus created a gap in the line of obstructions. The night of the 23rd Farragut made all final preparations for passing through the gap and running the batteries of the forts. A detailed account of the event that followed would fill a book the size of this if properly dealt with, and is, moreover, a story of our navy to which sufficient justice has never yet been done by historians, it being one of the greatest and most desperate engagements in our naval annals. Briefly, at 2 A. M. the 24th, the signal—two blood-red lights at the peak of the *Hartford*—was made for the movement to begin and the leading division, after some delay on account of difficulty in managing the anchors in the strong current, moved up through the opening and into furious action with the forts. This division was led by Captain Theodorus Bailey in the gunboat *Cayuga*, followed by the *Pensacola*, *Mississippi*, *Oneida*, *Varuna*, *Katahdin*, *Kineo*, and *Wissahickon*, in the order named, and was under orders to proceed along the left, or east, bank of the river, engaging Fort St. Phillip with the starboard batteries. Captain Bailey belonged to the *Colorado* and had hoisted his division flag on the *Cayuga* through the kindness of Lieutenant Napoleon B. Harrison commanding that vessel, the commander of the *Oneida* having previously objected to being overshadowed by the presence of a divisional officer on board his vessel, which objection cost him the honor of having his ship lead the first column.

Behind Bailey's division came Farragut with the *Hartford*, *Brooklyn* and *Richmond*, forming what was called the center division, and this was followed by Fleet Captain Bell, leading the third division of six vessels, in the gunboat *Sciota*. The second and third divisions were to follow up the western bank and engage Fort Jackson with the port batteries.[1] The steamers attached to the mortar flotilla moved up near the forts as the fleet got under way and in conjunction with the mortar schooners opened a terrific cannonading against the works, greatly augmented by the firing from the passing ships. In the heavy smoke that soon settled over the river it became impossible for signals to be read and much confusion resulted, each vessel being obliged to fight out its own destiny. With the air filled with bursting shells and obscured by smoke, the roar of heavy guns, the shouts of command, the screams of mangled men, and the river covered with fire rafts and burning wreckage, the scene was most awful and unearthly, and justified the brief comment made by Farragut in his official report: "Such a fire, I imagine, the world has rarely seen."

The vessels suffered severely from damages and casualties, but within an hour and a quarter after the *Cayuga* had passed the gap in the barrier the fleet with the exception of three gunboats of the last

---

[1] The order of battle herein described is derived from the supplemental report published in the annual report of the Secretary of the Navy for 1869, which was intended as an official correction of numerous inaccuracies that had appeared in several naval histories.

division—the *Kennebec, Itasca* and *Winona*—had passed above the forts and appeared in the Confederate flotilla, "like dogs among a flock of sheep," as Captain Mahan expresses it in his account of the battle in "The Gulf and Inland Waters." The three last gunboats had to bear the brunt of the fire from the forts after the other vessels had passed out of range and were very roughly used; the *Itasca* was wholly disabled by a shot through her boiler, two firemen being severely scalded as a result, and the other gunboats suffered so severely that the attempt to run the batteries appeared not only foolhardy but impossible. They rejoined the fleet a few days later.

The first vessels to break into the enemy's fleet were the *Cayuga* and *Varuna*, both of which fared badly until more vessels came up. The *Varuna* was rammed by two of the Confederate boats and so damaged that her commander ran her ashore, where she sank, the crew escaping previous to the disaster with the exception of three men killed and nine wounded. The *Cayuga* was badly cut up, being struck forty-two times, but she remained in action and individually received the surrender of three of the enemy's vessels. The ram *Manassas* struck the *Richmond* on the starboard side and so crushed in her planking that she must have been destroyed had the blow been slightly heavier; as it was, the chain armor saved her. The *Manassas* also rammed the old side-wheel frigate *Mississippi* and nearly stove in her side, but the blow being a glancing one the break did not extend entirely through the side. These acts of the *Manassas* were committed while the vessels were in action with the forts. When the Federal fleet had passed up, the *Mannassas* was seen quietly following, and Captain Melancthon Smith of the *Mississippi*—a good fighter and a good Christian—asked and obtained permission by signal to go back and attack her. The ram seemed unwilling to try conclusions with the heavy old ship coming straight down upon her with the swift current, and just before the impending collision she shied high up into the river bank, where her crew made hurried preparations for her destruction and abandonment, and then took to the shore. As soon as possible a boat was sent from the *Mississippi* to see what could be done with her late antagonist, First Assistant Engineer William H. Hunt being in the boarding party to take charge of the machinery. The boat soon returned, reporting that it was impracticable to save the *Manassas*, which had been set on fire and disabled, and Mr. Hunt on his part reported that the piping through the hull had been cut, the water run out of sight in the boiler, the fires kept raging in the furnaces, the safety valves shored down, and the steam guage showing 136 pounds (a frightful pressure in those days), —"with a tendency hellward." The *Mississippi* therefore returned up the river to rejoin the fleet. Later, the water coming in through the cut pipes, depressed the stern of the *Manassas*, floated her bow off the bank, and the current carried her down to Porter's mortar fleet, where her appearance created considerable consternation, but she soon faintly exploded and sank.

According to Flag Officer Farragut's report eleven of the enemy's steamers were destroyed during this morning fight, which practically annihilated their fleet. The Federal fleet remained at anchor one day to rest the men and repair damages and on the morning of the 25th, Captain Bailey in the *Cayuga* still leading, proceeded up the river, had a sharp skirmish with the Chalmette batteries, and at noon anchored off the City of New Orleans. The city was taken possession of and held by the naval force under very strained and trying circumstances until May 1, when General B. F. Butler arrived with a large force and assumed military control of the place, the fleet soon after proceeding on its mission of conquest up the river. Commander Porter continued the bombardment of the lower forts with his flotilla until the 28th of April, when they surrendered to him. The casualties in the fleet during the battle of the 24th, as reported by the fleet surgeon, amounted to thirty-seven killed and one hundred and forty-seven wounded, a record that makes this one of the bloodiest naval battles of the rebellion. Two officers, both midshipmen, were killed and eleven were wounded; three of the latter—Second Assistant Engineer S. Wilkins Cragg, acting chief of the *Kineo*; Third Assistant J. C. Hartley of the *Pensacola*, and Acting Third Assistant Frank R. Hain of the *Colorado*, serving as a volunteer on the *Iroquois*—were of the engineer corps, all injured by gunshot wounds.

The reports of many of the commanding officers of vessels engaged in this battle referred in terms of praise to the zeal and ability displayed by the engineers and their men in keeping the machinery in efficient operation under trying conditions. Captain Bailey, in describing the battle afterward, on the occasion of a banquet given him at the Astor House in New York, is credited with having made the modest statement that, "the engineers ran the ships and all we had to do was to blaze away when we got up to the forts." Assistant Engineer Hartley of the *Pensacola* was most highly referred to in the official reports for the courage he exhibited; he was stationed at the engine-room bell and was wounded in the head by a piece of shell, and, although urged to go below for treatment, refused to leave his station, remaining there all through the action.

On the 28th of May Chief Engineer James B. Kimball of the *Hartford*, while ashore in Baton Rouge with a boat's crew on duty was suddenly fired upon by the enemy and himself and two of the men badly wounded. Mr. Kimball was struck in the head, face and neck with slugs and most painfully hurt, although he recovered.

A frightful disaster befell a squadron of the Mississippi flotilla in June of this year. The gunboats *Mound City*, *St. Louis*, *Lexington*, and *Conestoga*, under Commander Augustus H. Kilty of the *Mound City*, were sent into White River to convoy some troop transports and assist in an attack upon some Confederate batteries at St. Charles, Arkansas. The attack was made June 17 and resulted in the capture of the enemy's fortifications, but during its progress a shot penetrated the casemate of the *Mound City* just above a gun port, killed three men in its flight, and exploded her steam drum. The immediate result was horrible; nearly eighty men were scalded to death by the steam which filled the casemate, and forty-three others were drowned or shot by the enemy after leaping overboard. Of one hundred and seventy-five officers and men only twenty-five escaped uninjured, the number killed or who subsequently died being one hundred and thirty-five. Commander Kilty was so scalded that his left hand had to be amputated. Among the killed were Chief Engineer John Cox; Second Assistant Engineer John C. McAfee, and Third Assistant G. W. Hollingsworth.

Early in the morning of June 28th, Admiral Farragut with the *Hartford*, *Richmond*, *Iroquois*, *Oneida*, *Wissahickon*, *Sciota*, *Winona*, and *Pinola* ran the batteries at Vicksburg, assisted by

Commander Porter with his mortar flotilla. The military importance of this move is not apparent, as the batteries were not destroyed, and in the nature of things could not be materially harmed by ships, located as they were on bluffs high above the water From Farragut's report it seems that the move was largely experimental, for he says:

"In obedience to the orders of the department and the command of the President, I proceeded back to Vicksburg with the *Brooklyn*, *Richmond*, and *Hartford*, with the determination to carry out my instructions to the best of my ability."

And again:

"The department will perceive from this (my) report that the forts can be *passed*, and *we have done it*, and can *do it again as often as may be required of us.* It will not, however, be an easy matter for us to do more than silence the batteries for a time, as long as the enemy has a large force behind the hills to prevent our landing and holding the place."

One of Porter's steamers, the *Clifton*, was disabled in this affair by a shot through her boiler which killed six men by scalding. The total casualties of the morning were fifteen men killed and thirty wounded, about one-third of the number being on the flagship. Farragut himself and Captain Broome of the Marine corps appear on the surgeon's report of casualties as having suffered from contusions on the *Hartford*. The report of Commander S. P. Lee of the *Oneida* says: " One 6-inch rifle shell came through the starboard after pivot port, killing S. H. Randall, a seaman, at the after pivot gun, severely wounding Richard Hodgson, third assistant engineer, at the engine bell, and, passing through the coamings of the engine-room hatch, picked up three loaded muskets, (each lying flat on the deck, on the port side of that hatch) and burst into the bulwarks, over the first cutter, which was lowered to near the water's edge, drove the muskets through the open port there, and severely wounded William Cowell, seaman, who was in the boat sounding, and slightly wounding Henry Clark, chief boatswain's mate . . . . . A second 8-inch compound solid shot carried away, amidships, the keel of the launch, (which was partly lowered) and, entering on the starboard side, struck the steam drum, and, glancing, fell into the fire-room."

On the 5th of July when the iron-clad *Lexington* was proceeding along the White River, Arkansas, her chief engineer, Mr. Joseph Huber, was shot dead by guerillas lurking along the banks.

On the Atlantic coast after the remarkable fight of the ironclads in Hampton Roads there were no very important naval engagements during the year. The unromantic and wearying work of maintaining the blockade along that coast employed the greater number of the sea-going vessels and kept them extremely active, while in the rivers, bays and sounds the smaller steamers were engaged in a ceaseless border warfare with the armed vessels and shore batteries of the enemy. This latter employment furnished a fine field for adventure and, although on a small scale, gave opportunity for the development of a class of intrepid and self-reliant young officers, of which class Lieutenant-commander C. W. Flusser and Lieutenant Wm. B. Cushing were brilliant examples. Two or three incidents will suffice to indicate the dangerous nature of this litteral warfare.

On the 14th of August Lieutenant George B. Balch in the *Pocahontas* proceeded up Black River, South Carolina, some twenty-five miles looking for a Confederate steamer said to be in hiding there. Meeting with more resistance than expected from the enemy along the banks he finally turned back and as the neighborhood had become aroused the *Pocahontas* had to run the gauntlet for over twenty miles of riflemen concealed in the thickets on both banks, she replying all the distance with grape and cannister and smallarm fire. By keeping the men behind breastworks of hammocks and lumber she escaped with only one casualty, that being reported by Lieutenant Balch as follows: "At 3:40 P. M., whilst under a very sharp fire of the enemy, Acting Third Assistant Engineer John A. Hill was wounded by a Minie ball, and I regret to report that his wound is very dangerous; as yet, however, I am rejoiced to state that his symptoms are all favorable; it is a penetrating wound of the abdomen, the ball having passed entirely through his body. I need not say that he is receiving the most assiduous care of Dr.

Rhoades, and he has been removed to the open deck under the poop, that he may have the benefit of the cooler atmosphere; and I am satisfied that if skill and attention can avail his life will be saved."

Mr. Hill furnished an example of remarkable recovery, for he survived his wound, served faithfully throughout the war and, as a first assistant engineer, was honorably mustered out in December, 1865.

September 9th, the *Shawsheen* had a similar experience, she being ambushed off Cross' Landing in the Chowan River, North Carolina, and escaped with one casualty, also an assistant engineer; this officer, John Wall by name, was shot in the thigh and wrist and dangerously wounded, but ultimately recovered.

The morning of October 3d, Lieutenant Commander Flusser with the *Commodore Perry*, *Hunchback*, and *Whitehead* went up the Blackwater River to co-operate with Major General Dix in an attack on Franklin, Virginia. When near the town the vessels were suddenly attacked by a large force lying in ambush in the woods and on high bluffs, and suffered severely, not being able to use their ordnance to advantage in reply. After fighting for three hours under these conditions and getting no support from the army, which did not appear, the steamers returned down the river, being obliged to force their way with a heavy head of steam through obstructions made by the enemy felling trees into the narrow stream. The affair cost four men killed and fifteen wounded, twelve of the casualties being on Flusser's steamer, the *Commodore Perry*. One of the killed was an officer—Master's Mate John Lynch. The following instances of gallantry are mentioned in Flusser's report:

"I desire to mention as worthy of praise for great gallantry, Lieutenant William B. Cushing, who ran the field-piece out amid a storm of bullets, took a sure and deliberate aim at the rebels, and sent a charge of cannister among them, that completely silenced their fire at that point. Mr. Lynch assisted Mr. Cushing, and here met his death like a brave fellow, as he was.

"Mr. Richards, third assistant engineer, who had charge of the powder division, also assisted with the howitzer, and showed great courage. Mr. Anderson, the paymaster, was of great assistance in bringing in the wounded from under the fire."

Upon the receipt of this report Acting Rear Admiral Lee, commanding the squadron, directed that Acting Third Assistant Engineer George W. Richards be examined for promotion on account of his conduct in the fight, and he was shortly afterward advanced to the grade of acting second assistant engineer.

The fine screw-sloop *Adirondack*, fresh from the New York navy yard where she was built, while proceeding to the Gulf of Mexico struck on a reef near Little Abaco Island the morning of August 23rd, and became a total wreck, the engineer of the watch stating that when she struck he saw the jagged points of the reef sticking up through her bottom into the fire-room. At daylight the commanding officer, Captain Guert Gansevoort, ordered all hands to go to the island, about five miles distant, and said that he would remain on board. The boatswain, Mr. William Green, and Second Assistant Engineer Henry W. Robie elected to stay with him and soon had to defend the ship with hatchets and revolvers against a boat load of villainous-looking black wreckers who came off to board her, but were successfully driven off. The two officers named finally prevailed upon the almost distracted captain to abandon the ship, her salvage being hopeless, and with him went ashore to join the rest of the crew. All hands lost everything they owned except the clothing they had on at the time of stranding, as the ship filled with water immediately and settled down on the reef until her spar deck was almost awash. The shipwrecked men remained on Little Abaco about two weeks, when they were taken off by the U. S. S. *Canandaigua*. The members of the corps who shared in this misfortune were Chief Engineer Alexander Henderson, First Assistant Engineer George J. Barry, Second Assistants Louis J. Allen and Henry W. Robie, and Third Assistants T. M. Mitchell, J. G. Greene and Thomas Crummey.

Mr. Robie was a brother of Chief Engineer E. D. Robie, a prominent member of the corps until his recent retirement, and from his unfortunate adventure in the *Adirondack* went to the new monitor *Passaic*, where a more dangerous experience was in store for him. The *Passaic* and the *Monitor* left Hampton Roads the afternoon of December 29th, 1862, to join the blockading fleet off Charleston, the former being towed by the *State of Georgia* and the latter by the *Rhode Island*, but both using their own steam as well. Captain Percival Drayton commanded the *Passaic* and Commander J. P. Bankhead the *Monitor*, the senior engineers of the vessels respectively being First Assistant Engineer George Bright and Second Assistant Joseph Watters. The evening of December 30 the sea became rough, and the *Monitor* began making heavy weather of it, taking in quantities of water through the hawse pipes and under the turret, and generally renewing the experience of her first voyage from New York. The water gained steadily and soon impaired the fires by rising into the ash pits and swashing against the grate bars, until the falling steam pressure showed too plainly that the engines and pumps must soon stop. At 10:30 P. M. signals of distress were made to the *Rhode Island* and that vessel undertook the extremely dangerous and difficult task of removing the *Monitor's* people in the heavy sea by means of boats, but before the work was completed the *Monitor* sank. This happened shortly after midnight of the morning of December 31, about twenty miles S. S.-W. of Cape Hatteras. With her perished acting ensigns Norman Atwater and George Frederickson; third assistant engineers R. W. Hands and Samuel A. Lewis, and twelve enlisted men. In Commander Bankhead's report of the disaster he asserted his conviction that a serious leak had been sprung by the pounding of the sea separating the iron hull from the wooden upper body, and this seems very probable.

In the meantime the *Passaic* was having a similar experience, water gaining in her bilges steadily on account of lack of strainers on the suction pipes of the pumps which resulted in the pump valves soon choking with dirt and ashes. This absence of a very essential fitting was caused by the vessel having been hurried away from the contractors' works by the naval authorities before the engine-room details were completed. About midnight the last pump gave out and as the water threatened to reach the fires and extinguish them, the fire-room was abandoned and the crew assembled on top of the turret. The chief engineer was confined to his room by illness before the vessel left Hampton Roads, leaving Mr. Robie in charge, and he now proved himself equal to the emergency. With a second class fireman named Richards, who volunteered to stay below with him, he put on the bilge injection and for two or three hours stood over it, almost submerged in water, keeping the mouth of the pipe clear and opening or closing the valves as required, while the fireman attended to the fires. Captain Drayton waded into the fireroom during this time and gave the not very cheering information that the *Monitor* had just gone down. Eventually the pump gained on the water and confidence was restored. The story of Mr. Robie's heroism is more fully set forth in the following affidavit made by the surgeon of the vessel:

"Newark, N. J., May 1st., 1890.

"To whom in the interest of patriotism and justice it may concern, be it known that I, Edgar Holden, formerly Surgeon of the monitor *Passaic*, actuated by a desire to see atonement made by a great government for the unmerited neglect of a brave fellow-officer, to whose heroism and fortitude were due the safety of the monitor *Passaic*, and through this the consummation of the plan for placing the monitor ironclads in southern waters during the late war, do certify to the following facts; said facts being not matters of memory but drawn from notes made at the time in my private journal and in large part published in the year 1863 in Harpers Monthly Magazine, October, 1863.

"To-wit: That when in that awful night in which the original *Monitor* was lost, officers and men had toiled for hours at the seemingly hopeless task of throwing overboard shot and shell and bailing the sinking ironclad with buckets passed from hand to hand, and when from exhaustion and despair we fell at times to rise again to the futile task, and when from the engine-room came the report that one after another the pumps had given out, and that the water was knee deep in the fire-room, swashing against the fire bars with every lurch of the ship, and when finally the report came 'the last pump has failed' and we threw down our buckets to die, that Assistant Engineer H. W. Robie stood alone at his post and succeeded in starting the pumps known as the bilge injections, and frequently submerged to the neck in water, worked the valves with his hands, his head held by myself or his fireman, while the task seemed puerile to the despairing men on deck. That he stood for hours under the platform around the engines to prevent the entrance of chips and floating debris from entering and clogging the valves which were without the usual strainers. That these pumps were the only ones that could be so cleared, the others having suction pipes passing in some way that I have forgotten through an iron bulkhead and making it impossible to free them. That Mr. Robie thus stood at his post after all but one fireman had left the engine rooms. That further it was my conviction, as well as that of all who knew at the time of his heroism, that to his fidelity alone was due the safety of the *Passaic*.

"And I would further certify that only of late have I been made aware that this unsurpassed devotion to duty has never been acknowledged by the Navy Department or the Government, and that the facts were not made known at the time, probably through a patriotic desire to conceal the bad sea-going qualities of the monitors, and were certainly omitted from my published journal solely on this account.

"I would further state that this gallant officer is, as I am credibly informed, ill and in straitened circumstances, and that any action tending to show a just appreciation of his invaluable services should be taken promptly.

(Signed,)
"EDGAR HOLDEN, M. D., PH. D.
"Medical Director Mutual Benefit Life Insurance Co., Fellow and Vice President American Laryngological Society, Member American Medical Association, etc., etc.; formerly Assistant Surgeon U. S. N."

"Personally appeared before me this 2d day of May, 1890, Dr. Edgar Holden, of the city of Newark and county of Essex, known to me to be a physician and surgeon in good standing, formerly an officer of the United States Navy, who certifies that the above statements are just and true.

(Signed,)
"F. K. HOWELL, Notary Public, N. J."

Heroism and devotion to duty of the order described have won promotion and reward in innumerable instances where the degree was less than in this case, but there is no record of Mr. Robie having received either for his signal services. One considerable recognition which he did receive, and which he said well repaid him for his experience, occurred shortly before the battle in Mobile Bay, when Captain Drayton introduced him to Admiral Farragut with the remark, "Mr. Robie saved the *Passaic* the night the *Monitor* was lost."

CHAPTER XX.

"When the temple at Jerusalem was completed, King Solomon gave a feast to the artificers employed in its construction. On unveiling the throne it was found that a blacksmith had usurped the seat of honor on the right of the king's place, not yet awarded. Whereupon the people clamored and the guard rushed to cut him down. 'Let him speak!' commanded Solomon. 'Thou hast, O King, invited all craftsmen but me, yet how could these builders have raised the temple without the tools I fashioned?' 'True,' decreed Solomon, ' the seat is his of right. All honor to the ironworker.'"—*Jewish Legend*.

1862—The Civil War, Continued—Increase of the Navy—Steamers Purchased Mississippi Flotilla Transferred to the Navy Department—Steam Vessels of War Placed Under Construction—The PASSAIC Class of Monitors—The DICTATOR and PURITAN—The MIANTONOMOH Class—Other Monitors—The KEOKUK—The DUNDERBERG—Legislation Regarding the Navy—Retired List Established—Creation of the Bureau of Steam Engineering—Pensions.

DURING 1862 the naval force both in ships and men was largely increased. About fifty steamers from the merchant service were bought during the year and converted into armed vessels, and a similar number of vessels was added to the naval establishment by the transfer of the Mississippi flotilla in July from the army and by the transfer of some revenue cutters from the Treasury Department. Several vessels captured from the enemy in action, or while attemptiug to run the blockade, were found suitable for use as war steamers, prominent among these being the powerful iron-clad ram *Tennessee* captured at New Orleans while still unfinished, and the steamer *Eastport* taken by Lieutenant Phelps in the Tennessee River.

This year witnessed a remarkable awakening of public interest in naval ship construction; an interest that took the form of practically dictating to the Navy Department the types of war ships the country needed, and was so powerful that it entirely overcame and consigned to the background the practices and prejudices which had long been fundamental in the naval service relative to the same subject. As a result all the old theories based upon the supposed unreliability of steam, the alleged necessity for sail-power on war-vessels, and the doubted utility of iron as a material for ship construction, were cast aside, and with the prestige resulting from the performance of the *Monitor* and the failure of the old type of ships in Hampton Roads the engineer was allowed free scope to develop his ideas and build ships embodying them. It was, in fact, one of those occasions which recur from time to time when society is forced by unusual circumstances to admit its dependence upon the iron-worker, and in its distress to fall before him humbly begging for succor. The result of all this was that the greater part of the constructive activity of the year was devoted to the building of engineers' warships,—mastless vessels dependent entirely upon steam and mailed with iron.

If public opinion sustained and demanded this revolution in naval architecture, the same cannot be said of naval opinion. With the exception of engineers, who saw in the change a development of their own specialty. the general sentiment of the navy, as exhibited by a multitude of letters, reports and opinions, all items of public knowledge through the medium of Navy Department and Congressional publications, appears to have been one of mistrust, if not positive opposition to the new development. Thus it was that the engineer corps, with a few prominent exceptions in other branches of the service, had to bear the brunt of incessant attacks upon the probable utility of the new class of vessels; a strife that was well maintained against great odds at first and finally terminated in an historical controversy between a prominent representative of each naval faction, from which controversy the engineer and the principles championed by him emerged signally victorious.

It is unnecessary to introduce any of the opinions of the old school naval officers, breathing hostility to the engineers' ships, for a proper respect for the intelligence and patriotism of the officers of our navy as a class is sufficient warrant that such of those opinions as have been preserved are not indicative of the belief of the whole service. That belief, however, while not actually hostile, was far from being favorable, and cannot be more truthfully presented than by quoting from an opinion respecting iron-clads submitted to the Navy Department in February, 1864, by Rear Admiral L. M. Goldsborough, an officer of more than fifty years service, of great prominence and recognized professional ability, and as progressive and liberal-minded a representative of this class as could well be found.

"Their absolute worth, however, in these particulars, (offensive and defensive properties), I cannot regard as entitled to the extravagant merit claimed for it, induced, I apprehend, in a great measure by conclusions drawn from the encounters of the first *Monitor* and *Weehawken* with the *Merrimack* and *Atlanta*, without a sufficient knowledge of the facts attending them, and without any (or more than an unwilling) reference to the cases of opposite results, as, for instance, the Ogeechee, and the repeated displays before Charleston. That the charm of novelty in construction, or quaintness in appearance, had anything to do with the matter, I will not undertake to assert, although I may, perhaps, be allowed to indulge suspicion as to probable effect. Popular opinion is not always right on such subjects, nor do I know that it is apt to be when it runs counter to popular naval opinion. At any rate, I do know that the latter is not likely to be very wrong in relation to professional matters of the kind."

Before the original *Monitor* was launched, Secretary Welles had become convinced of the extraordinary merits of that type of fighting ship, and in his annual report, in December, 1861, he recommended the immediate construction of twenty iron-clad steamers. The House of Representatives acted quickly on this recommendation and passed a bill authorizing the Secretary of the Navy to cause to be constructed not exceeding twenty-one iron-clad steam gunboats. The Senate, more conservative, delayed action on the bill until February, when the Secretary of the Navy, forseeing that the country would suffer from longer inaction, addressed the chairman of the Senate naval committee on the subject, with the result that the bill was soon passed. In its final form it authorized the Navy Department to expend $10,000,000 for armored vessels, and this appropriation was greatly augmented by subsequent legislation.

Under date of March 31, the Department entered into contract with John Ericsson for the construction, hull and machinery complete, of six single-turreted monitors, slightly larger than his first vessel and possessing improvements that experience had shown to be desirable. Chief among the changes was the locating of the pilot house on top of the turret, and the installation of a permanent smoke-pipe. Chief Engineer Alban C. Stimers was detailed as general superintendent of the building of these vessels. Encouraged by his happy selection of the name of the *Monitor*, Ericsson proceeded to name these six, *Impenetrable, Penetrator, Paradox, Gauntlet, Palladium,* and *Agitator,* but the Department very properly disapproved of these polysyllables and gave the vessels good American names—*Passaic, Montauk, Catskill, Patapsco, Lehigh,* and *Sangamon,*—under which they did the state good service and with which four of them are still on the navy list, and a fifth, the *Sangamon* with her name changed to *Jason,* also remains with us. The *Patapsco* was lost in January, 1865. Besides these six, there were four others of the *Passaic* class, built by other contractors from Ericsson's general designs, these being the *Nantucket,* built by the Atlantic Works, Boston; the *Nahant,* by Harrison Loring, Boston; the *Weehawken,* by Z. and F. Secor, New York, and the *Camanche.* The contract for this last vessel was given to Donahue, Ryan & Secor of San Francisco, Cal. and the actual work of building the ship was done at the ship yard of the Secor brothers in Jersey City: when the different parts were all completed a sailing ship, the *Aquila,* was freighted with them and proceeded to San Francisco by way of Cape Horn, having the misfortune to sink at the dock soon after arriving at her destination. After these delays, the *Camanche* did not appear as a completed monitor until 1865. There is perhaps no more eloquent tribute to the genius of John Ericsson than the fact that of the thirteen single turreted monitors that remain in our navy as the survivors of the many vessels of that type built during the war, eight are members of the original ten of the *Passaic* class.

On the 28th of July a contract was made with Ericsson for two large and high-powered monitors, which he named *Puritan* and *Protector,* the first name being accepted by the Department and the second changed to *Dictator.* The following table exhibits the main features of the Ericsson monitors of 1862 compared with the original *Monitor,* the data given being with reference to the vessels as actually built and not according to their dimensions as altered by subsequent rebuilding or repairs. The table is from Church's Life of John Ericsson.

U. S. MONITOR, NANTUCKET, 1862.

Typical of the *Passaic* class; length, 200 feet; beam, 46 feet; displacement, 1,875 tons. The flying-bridge, with hammock-boxes, etc. Shown abaft the turret is a peace-time convenience that was not built upon the monitors during the war.

	Monitor.	Passaic & class 6.	Dictator and Puritan.
Contract price, each	$275,000	$400,000	$1,150,000
Extreme length, feet	172	200	312 and 340
Extreme breadth, feet	41½	46	50
Depth of hold, feet	11⅓	...	21⅜
Draft of water, feet	10½	10½	20
Diam. of turret, inside, feet	20	21	24
Thickness of armor, inches	8	10½	15
Diameter of propellers, feet	9	12	21½
Diam. steam cylinders, inches	36	40	100
Length of stroke, inches	24	22	48
Side armor, inches	4½	5	6
Weight of guns, pounds	44,000	84,000	84,000 and 220,000
Coal capacity, tons	100	150	300 and 1,000
Displacement, tons	987	1,335	4,438 and 4,912
Tonnage	776	844	3,033 and 3,265
Midship section, square feet	321	392	777

The story of the troubles and delays experienced in the building of the two large monitors is too long to go into. Ericsson was much hampered and annoyed by the numerous changes in his designs forced upon him by the Department acting on the advice of naval officers with and without experience in monitors. One considerable modification in the *Dictator* was in dispensing with the forward overhang of the upper hull, which Ericsson regarded as an essential as it afforded a perfect protection to the anchors when under fire. Officers in command of the smaller monitors while the *Dictator* was building generally condemned that feature and believed it had been the cause of the loss of the *Monitor*, their opinions ultimately leading to the modification referred to. When the *Dictator* went into service at the end of 1864 her commander, Captain John Rodgers, complained of the absence of the forward overhang, which complaint angered Ericsson on account of the source of the influence that had forced him to make the change. Writing to the Secretary of the Navy regarding the criticisms to which the monitors were subjected by the commander of one of them, he said: "I trust that neither he nor the officers of the turret vessels, all of whom are admitted to be as skilful in their profession as they are brave, will take offense at my remarks. I have only the single object in view—the triumph of the service which their skill and valor has raised so high in the public estimation. I beg, earnestly, however, to call their attention to the fact that they have entered on a new era, and that they are handling not ships, but floating machines, and that, however eminent their seamanship, they cannot afford to disregard the advice of the engineer."

With all his engineering ability, Ericsson made some mistakes himself right in the line of his own profession, and as he was so stubborn by nature and so confident of his own powers his errors were seldom corrected until too late, for he would take advice of no man. Chief Engineer E. D. Robie, U. S. Navy, was the naval superintendent of the construction of the *Dictator*, and, without claiming to be a genius or a remarkable inventor, he was a better marine engineer than Ericsson, for he had the invaluable knowledge gained by long experience with engines at sea which Ericsson lacked, and without which no engineer, no matter how accomplished, can intelligently design marine engines. Several faults in design were pointed out by Mr. Robie, who knew to a certainty that they would result in trouble at sea, but Ericsson would listen to nothing, his favorite reply to these suggestions, which was both egotistical and incorrect, being that he had built successful engines before Robie was born.

One fault alone which Ericsson scorned to recognize resulted in defeating the hopes of the Department regarding the first operations of the *Dictator*. Her main shaft was nineteen inches in diameter, an enormous size even for this day, and the main bearings as designed were disproportionately short for the size of the shaft they were to support. This was strenuously objected to by Robie, but without avail, and the result was that when the *Dictator* started to join the fleet for the first assault on Fort Fisher, her first employment, the bearings wore down three-eighths of an inch in going twenty miles and the shaft became so loose as to endanger the ship. Upon Chief Engineer Robie's report, she was turned back to port, and for many weeks she had to lie idle under Robie's charge while he had longer brasses made and brackets fitted to support them. This was a most lamentable failure when the Department was expecting so much of the ship, and Ericsson afterward admitted in conversation with Mr. Robie that for once he had made a mistake in not listening to the opinions of another engineer.

U. S. S. MIANTONOMOH;

Photographed in Europe in 1866. Length, 257 feet; beam, 52 feet 10 inches; disp., 3,401 tons. (*Agamenticus, Monadnock, Tonawanda,* in class.)

Against Ericsson's wishes the *Puritan* was provided with twin screws, and it was also directed that she be fitted with two turrets ; to this latter modification of his plan Ericsson vehemently objected, and finally arranged a compromise of one huge turret to mount two twenty-inch guns, but these changes and counter changes amounted to nothing, for the end of the war found the *Puritan* still unfinished. The *Virginius* excitement in 1874 induced the Navy Department to take steps towards her completion, but she cannot be said to be finished yet, for now (1896) the work of converting her into a coast defense battle-ship is still going forward. Very little of Ericsson's ship remains in the new *Puritan*. The *Dictator* was put in service and sent to Key West at the time of the *Virginius* affair and proved to be an excellent sea boat, but very expensive to operate. In 1883 she was sold to A. Purves & Son of Philadelphia for $40,250, the government having expended up to that time about $260,000 for her preservation and repair, in addition to her original cost.

Besides the twelve Ericsson monitors already referred to, twenty-eight other armored vessels, the majority of which were of the monitor type, were placed under construction during the year. Four of these were large double-turreted vessels designed to carry four XV-inch guns each and were undertaken by the government at the navy yards as follows: *Miantonomoh* at New York; *Tonawanda* (afterward *Amphitrite*) at Philadelphia; *Monadnock* at Boston, and *Agamenticus* (*Terror*) at Kittery, Maine. Machinery for these vessels was contracted for with various builders in New York and Philadelphia, that for the first two named being designed by Engineer-in-Chief Isherwood and that for the other two by John Ericsson. The turrets, side armor, deck plating, stringers, etc. were obtained by contract with different iron manufacturers. The *Onondaga*, also two-turreted, was contracted for, hull and machinery complete, with George Quintard of New York and was built for him by T. F. Rowland at the Continental Iron Works, Greenpoint. Four other two-turreted monitors were placed under construction in the Mississippi Valley, the contracts for them, dated May 27th, being with the following builders: Thomas G. Gaylord, Cincinnati, Ohio, for the *Chickasaw*; G. B. Allen & Co., St. Louis, for the *Kickapoo*; James B. Edes, St. Louis, for the *Milwaukee* and *Winnebago*. These western craft were modifications of Ericsson's monitor, their decks instead of being flat were so much crowned that they were known as "turtle-backs," and the guns were mounted in turrets built from Edes' designs on the disappearing principle.

In September, nine single-turret monitors, somewhat larger than the *Passaic* class were contracted for as follows: With Harrison Loring, Boston, for the *Canonicus;* Swift, Evans & Co., Cincinnati, for the *Catawba* and *Oneota;* Z. & F. Secor, New York, for the *Mahopac, Manhattan* and *Tecumseh;* Albert G. Mann, Pittsburgh, for the *Manayunk;* Harlan & Hollingsworth, Wilmington, Delaware, for the *Saugus*, and Miles Greenwood, Cincinnati, for the *Tippecanoe*. Two very small single-turret vessels, the *Marietta* and *Sandusky*, were contracted for May 16th with Hartupee & Co., Pittsburgh, and during the same month contracts were signed with James B. Edes, St. Louis, for the *Neosho* and *Osage*, having one turret and recessed stern wheels, and with George C. Bestor, Peoria, Ill., for a similar vessel, the *Ozark*. Joseph Brown of St. Louis by contracts signed May 30th, built three small iron-plated casemate vessels named *Chilicothe, Tuscumbia* and *Indianola*. These vessels had side wheels far aft working independently to facilitate turning in close quarters, and had also twin screw propellers.

One or two novel plans for armored war-vessels were accepted during the year as the aftermath of the crop of designs submitted to the iron-clad board of 1861. One remarkable vessel originating in this manner was the *Keokuk*, built according to the terms of the contract made with Charles W. Whitney of New York on the 25th of March. This contract called for an iron-plated, shot-proof steam battery, 159 feet long, 36 feet beam, 13 feet 6 inches depth of hold, to carry two XI-inch guns mounted in towers. Low-pressure condensing engines capable of driving the vessel ten knots per hour for twelve consecutive hours were specified. The contract price was $220,000. The peculiar feature of the *Keokuk* was in the disposition of armor, the sides being built of alternate horizontal strata of wooden timbers and iron bars, each layer being about five inches wide. Like the *Galena*, this conception came to grief when subjected to the fire of the enemy, and in worse degree, for she sank from the effects of the puncturing she received, as will be related in a subsequent chapter regarding naval operations off Charleston.

Another iron-clad of quite different type was the *Dunderberg*,

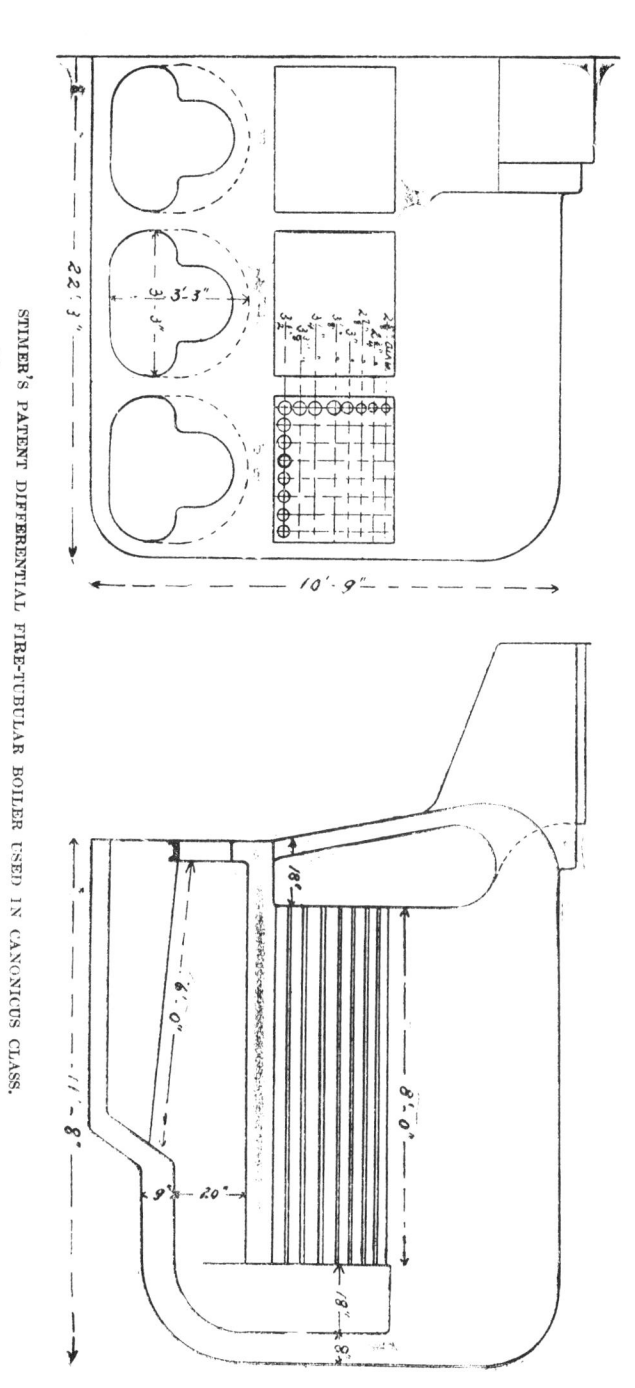

STIMER'S PATENT DIFFERENTIAL FIRE-TUBULAR BOILER USED IN CANONICUS CLASS.
Six surfaces in each boiler; 117 square feet grate surface in each boiler.

contracted for with W. H. Webb of New York city, July 3rd, 1862. This vessel, described as an "ocean-going iron-clad frigate ram," was a remarkable step in advance of the war-ship construction of the time, but was not put to the test of battle as her great size and huge pieces of iron work to be made so delayed her building that she was not launched until July 22, 1865. The tendency in armored ship construction after the affair of the *Monitor* and *Merrimac* was to accept Ericsson's circular turret as the proper protection for guns, and this plan, modified and improved by changing conditions and better appliances for perfecting mechanical work, still remains and may be seen in one form or another in almost every armored vessel of the present day. The *Dunderberg*, however, departed most radically from the favorite practice of her year, and instead of the features of the *Monitor* her construction presented an almost faithful reproduction, in a greatly improved form, of the general characteristics of the *Merrimac*. That is, she consisted essentially of a low hull surmounted with a sloping-sided armored casemate protecting a very heavy battery. Great engine power, calculated to give a sea speed of fifteen knots an hour, and an enormous ram fifty feet long were important factors in her war-like make up. The hull, of unusually heavy timbers, was built in Mr. Webb's shipyard, foot of Sixth Street, East River, and the machinery was built by John Roach & Son at the Etna Iron Works near by. Chief Engineer Wm. W. W. Wood, U. S. Navy, was the general Superintendent of construction and Second Assistant Engineer Wilson K. Purse was the resident inspector at the Etna Iron Works. The contract price for the vessel complete was $1,250,000.

The following table exhibits the general dimensions of the ship and machinery, and shows her to have been an unusually huge craft for her day.

Extreme length	380 feet	4	inches.
Extreme beam	72 "	10	"
Depth of main hold	22 "	7	"
Height of casemate	7 "	9	"
Length of ram	50 "		
Draft when fully equipped for sea	21 "		
Displacement		7,000	tons.
Tonnage		5,090	"
Weight of iron armor		1,000	"

U. S. S. DUNDERBERG.

Diameter of steam cylinders (two) ....100 inches.
Stroke of pistons.. 45   "
Boilers—Six main and two auxiliary.
Depth of boilers..13 feet.
Height of boilers......................................17 feet 6 inches.
Front width of boilers, each....................21 " 5 "
Weight of boilers......................................450 tons.
Total heating surface...............................30,000 square feet.
Grate surface..1,200   "   "
Cooling surface in condensers.................12,000   "   "
Diameter of screw propeller....................21 feet.
Pitch of propeller...................................27 to 30 "
Weight of propeller................................34,580 pounds.
Capacity of coal bunkers........................1,000 tons.
Horse-power of main engines................5,000

This "Thundering Mountain" of the navy, as her size and armament as well as the translation of her name caused her to be called, embraced a number of features in construction now regarded as essential but which in 1862-3 were thought unimportant or were almost unheard of. She had a double bottom, collision bulkheads, and a system of transverse longitudinal and water-tight bulkheads extending up to the spar deck. The engine and boiler spaces were entirely enclosed with water-tight bulkheads. Her air and circulating pumps were independent of the main engines and she had also a pair of independent wrecking pumps. The smoke-pipe, thirteen feet in diameter, had armor gratings fitted inside it, as is now universally practiced, to prevent injury to the boilers by grenades or heavy debris. The engines were horizontal back-acting in arrangement, designed to run at an ordinary speed of sixty revolutions per minute, with intention to work up to eighty revolutions for full power. The main shaft was 118 feet long and 18 inches in diameter, and was supported by bearings 40 inches long cored for water circulation The air and circulating pumps each had two steam cylinders 36"x36", which in themselves were engines nearly as large as the propelling engines of the *Canandaigua* class of sloops of war.

Not being completed until after the Civil War was over, the naval authorities had no desire to receive this splendid specimen of war-ship into the service, the policy then being to get rid of as many vessels as possible instead of adding to the number. At Mr.

Webb's request the vessel was released to him under the terms of a special act of Congress approved March 2, 1867, he refunding to the government the sum of $1,092,887.73, which had been paid to him on account. He immediately sold her to the French government, and under the name of *Rochambeau* she was for many years regarded as one of the most formidable vessels in the navy of that country. The effect of the presence in the French navy of the *Dunderberg* is still visible in the exaggerated ram bows and home-sloping top sides so generally designed by French naval architects. Mr. Edward Marsland, who had been a first assistant engineer in the navy during the war, went across the Atlantic in the *Dunderberg* as her chief engineer and found the sea-behaviour of both ship and machinery admirable. The same day that Congress authorized the release of the *Dunderberg* to Mr. Webb another private act was passed releasing the *Onondaga* to Mr. Quintard, who refunded the money he had been paid and received the vessel, although she had

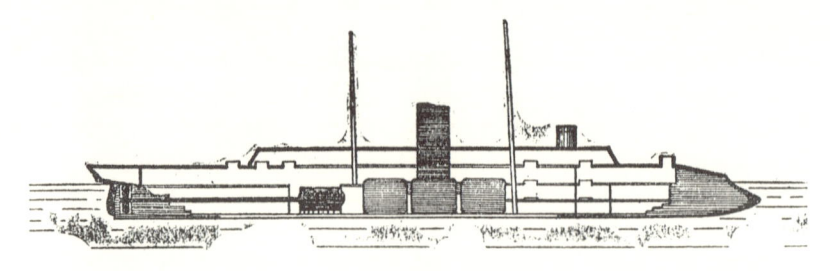

Longitudinal section of the *Dunderberg*, showing backing of ram, arrangement of machinery, disposition of armor, etc.

been completed and in active service the last eighteen months of the war. She also was sold to the French and still appears on the navy list of that country as an armored coast-defense turret ship.

From the lesson of Hampton Roads the Navy Department attempted one modification of a war vessel that was not especially successful. In 1862 work was begun on the frigate *Roanoke* of cutting her down as the *Merrimac* had been, and on the low deck resulting three Ericsson turrets were fitted by the Novelty Iron Works, New York. Although employed about a year in the North Atlantic squadron, the modified *Roanoke* was not found satisfactory. The

U. S. S. IOSCO, 1862.

Type of the *Sassacus* class; length, 240 feet; beam, 35 feet; disp., 1,173 tons.
In general appearance, without regard to dimensions, this vessel well represents the *Octororo* class of 1861 and the *Mohongo* class of 1863, as well as its own class of double-enders.

great weight of the three turrets made her rolling dangerous and the hull was not found to be strong enough to properly carry them, the thrust of the turret spindles on the keel when the turrets were being keyed up for action always threatening to force out the bottom.

The twelve double-ended gunboats begun in 1861 proved so useful that in the autumn of 1862 contracts were made for twenty-seven others, considerably larger than the first lot. From the name of one of these that became especially famous they came to be known as the *Sassacus* class, their names being as follows: *Agawam, Ascutney, Chenango, Chicopee, Eutaw, Iosco, Lenapee, Mackinaw, Massasoit, Mattabessett, Mendota, Metacomet, Mingoe, Osceola, Otsego, Pawtuxet, Peoria, Pontiac, Pontoosuc, Sassacus, Shamrock, Tacony, Tallahoma, Tallapoosa, Wateree, Winooski,* and *Wyalusing.* All were built of wood with the exception of the *Wateree*, which was of iron. They were all rated as of 974 tons burden. One other wooden vessel of this class—the *Algonquin*—was delayed on account of controversy as to the machinery to be fitted in her and was not put under construction until March, 1863. A few of the hulls were built at navy yards, but the majority of them and the machinery for all were built by contract, the engineer-in-chief furnishing the machinery designs except for the *Algonquin*. The *Sassacus* was built at the navy yard, Portsmouth, New Hampshire, by Naval Constructor Isaiah Hanscom, and her machinery by the Atlantic Works, Boston.

Near the close of the year a class of small screw sloops, about 100 tons larger than the ninety-day gunboats, was begun at navy yards and contracts let for their machinery. These were the *Kansas, Maumee, Nipsic, Nyack, Pequot, Saco, Shawmut,* and *Yantic.* With the exception of the *Kansas* all were under construction by the 1st of January, 1863.

Important changes in naval organization and administration were brought about by Congressional action during the early part of of the Civil War. During the special session of the 37th Congress in the summer of 1861, to go a little back of the year with which this chapter is dealing, an act, approved August 3, 1861, created a naval retired list by providing that any officer of the navy who had been forty years in the service of the United States might be retired upon his own application; the same act provided that officers of the navy found incapacitated for active service by reason of wounds or

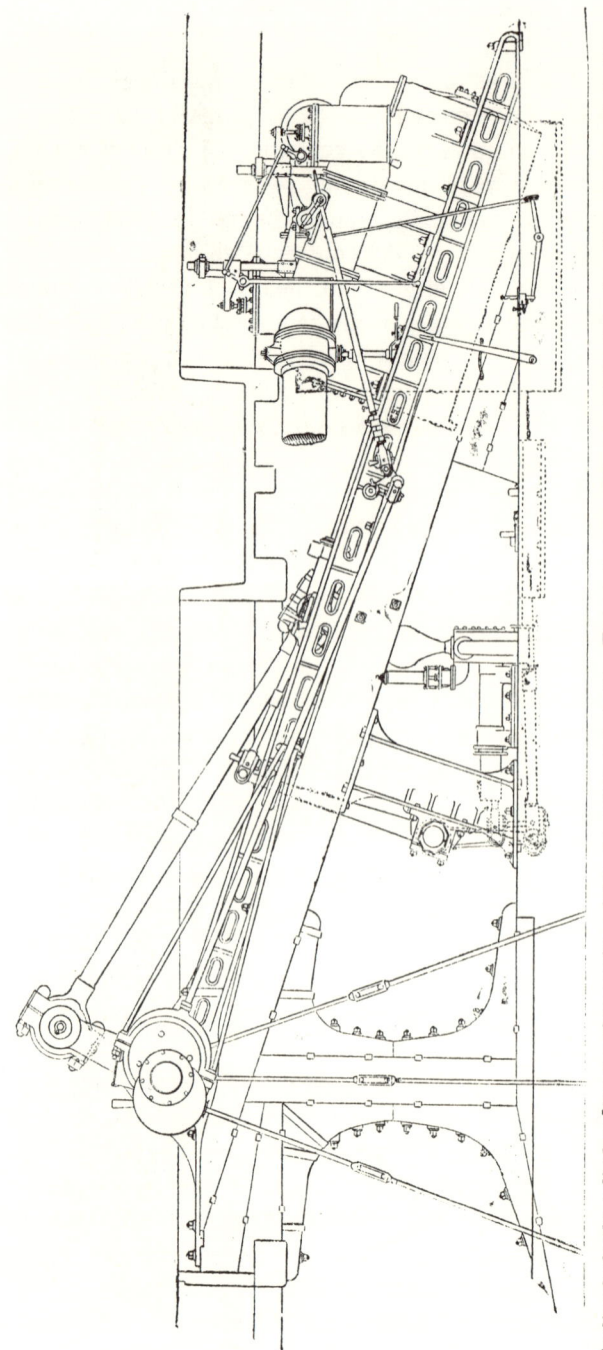

Inclined single-cylinder direct-acting engine of the *Agawam* and class. The same arrangement obtained in the other classes of double-enders and in numerous other vessels that have been described in this book.

U. S. S. SHAWMUT, 1863.

Type of the *Kansas* class; length, 179 feet 6 inches; beam 30 feet; disp., 836 tons.

other disability incurred in the line of duty should be placed on the retired list, and the officer next in rank promoted to the place of the retired officer according to the established rules of the service. Early in the first regular session of the same Congress, an act, approved December 21, 1861, made the retirement of naval officers compulsory after forty-five years' service, or upon arriving at the age of sixty-two. A number of old officers of the line and medical corps were immediately retired in accordance with this legislation, and it was due only to the presence on the active list of these superannuated officers, unable to perform their duties in time of war, and at the same time deserving of all consideration for past services, that the navy received the inestimable, though deserved, gift of the retired list.

An act to reorganize the Navy Department was approved July 5th, 1862, which created the Bureau of Steam Engineering as a separate executive branch of the department and provided that the chief of that bureau should be a skillful engineer selected from the list of chief engineers of the navy. The same act created the present bureaus of Navigation, Equipment, and Construction, the two last named and the bureau of steam engineering being obtained by dividing up the old bureau of Construction, Equipment and Repair, the business of which under the demands of war having grown to the extent of making its division a business necessity.

The present schedule of pensions for disability incurred in the naval service was established by an act of Congress approved July 16th, 1862. Other acts approved the same day directed the transfer of the western gunboat fleet built by the War Department to the Navy Department, and reorgnized the grades of line officers of the navy; the last act referred to added the grades of commodore and rear admiral to the line establishment and created within it the additional grades of lieutenant-commander and ensign. A new pay table was also established.

CHAPTER XXI.

" When sorrows come, they come not single spies,
But in battalions."
—*Hamlet; Act IV. sc. 5.*

1863—The Civil War Continued—Disasters at Galveston—Loss of the *Columbia*—Raid of Rebel Rams off Charleston—Loss of the *Isaac Smith*—The *Florida*, and Her Pursuit by the *Sonoma*—Investment of Washington, North Carolina—Assembling of Ironclads off Charleston—Remarkable Breakdown and Repairs to the Machinery of the *Weehawken*—Attack on Fort McAllister—First Attack on Fort Sumter—Destruction of the *Keokuk*—The *Atlanta-Weehawken* Duel—Protracted Investment of the Charleston Forts by the Monitors—Sinking of the *Weehawken*.

NAVAL operations during the year 1863 were conducted on a greater scale than before and were in the main successful, the enemy's coasts being more rigorously invested and the lines of the blockade made more and more impassable. A number of misfortunes to vessels engaged in more or less important undertakings which occurred with considerable regularity from month to month served, however, in connection with the first unfortunate demonstration of the ironclads at Charleston, to distract public attention from the real service being done by the navy and to give the general impression that the operations of that arm for the year were largely unsuccessful.

The series of disasters to the navy began the first day of the new year with an extremely humiliating affair at Galveston, Texas. That place was in partial possession of the Union forces and was occupied by 260 men of the 42d regiment, Massachusetts volunteer infantry, camped on a wharf, a blockade of the approaches to the harbor being maintained to seaward by the steamers *Westfield*, *Clifton*, *Harriet Lane*, *Owasco*, and *Sachem*, and the schooner *Corypheus*. About 3 A. M. the morning of January first a large force of Confederates appeared in the town and made an attack upon the soldiers on the wharf, the latter being supported by the fire from some of the vessels lying nearest to them. At dawn two large river steamers crowded with troops and well protected by barricades of cotton bales attacked the *Harriet Lane*, or rather were attacked by her, she being under way at the time and moving up into range of the fight going on ashore, and effected her capture by boarding in overwhelming numbers. Her captain, Commander J. M. Wainwright, and Lieutenant Commander Edward Lee, were both killed, as were also three enlisted men, and fifteen people were wounded, the survivors of the ship's company, amounting to about one hundred, being made prisoners of war. The officers of the engineer corps who fell into the hands of the enemy on this occasion were M. H. Plunkett, second assistant engineer; C. H. Stone, second assistant engineer; and John E. Cooper, R. N. Ellis and A. T. E. Mullen, third assistant engineers.

An interesting incident illustrative of considerate forethought under trying conditions is related of Assistant Engineer Mullen on this occasion. After Commander Wainwright had been killed and the loss of the ship appeared inevitable, Mr. Mullen threw away his own sword and put on that of the captain with the hope of preserving it for Wainwright's relatives; a most generous undertaking which is said to have been successful, as it was a custom on both sides to return side-arms to captured officers after their surrender was complete.

The gunboat *Owasco* went to the relief of the *Harriet Lane* but was driven off by an incessant musketry fire to which she could make scarcely any reply, the narrowness of the channel preventing her from getting into a position to use her guns. She had fifteen men killed and wounded. Her experience deterred the *Clifton* from making the same attempt and that vessel's fire was accordingly directed against the shore batteries. The *Westfield*, lying a considerable distance out, had got underway and gone hard and fast aground early in the morning when the first movement of the enemy's steamers had been observed. About 7:30 A. M. a Confederate officer bearing a flag of truce boarded the *Clifton* and informed her commander that the Massachusetts troops and the *Harriet Lane* had surrendered and that the steamers, three more of which had appeared, were about to move upon and overwhelm the Federal vessels in detail. As an alternative he proposed the surrender of all the Federal vessels but one, which would be allowed to leave the harbor with the crews of all.

Lieutenant Commander Law of the *Clifton* did not favor this proposal, but agreed to carry it to Commander Renshaw of the *Westfield*, the senior officer present, it being promised that the flags of truce should fly for three hours to give him time to go and return. Commander Renshaw of course refused to accept the terms and ordered Law back to his ship with instructions to get the vessels under way and take them out of the harbor at all hazards, saying also that as the *Westfield* could not be floated he would blow her up and escape with her crew in the army transport *Saxon* lying near him. Finding upon his return to the *Clifton*, that the enemy had made many changes to their advantage in the position of their steamers and batteries, Law felt under no obligation to observe the truce and immediately got under way with all the vessels and went out of the harbor under a heavy fire, abandoning the blockade for the time being by going to New Orleans. Two barks laden with coal for the steamers were left behind and fell into the enemy's possession with the *Harriet Lane*.

Through some terrible blunder in firing the *Westfield* her magazine blew up before the people were out of her with the result that fourteen persons were killed and sixteen wounded, among the killed being commander William B. Renshaw; Lieutenant C. W. Zimmerman, and Acting Second Assistant Engineer William R. Greene, the senior engineer of the ship. Mr. Greene had acquired an excellent reputation for professional and personal worth and his untimely taking off was a source of much regret in the corps. In July of the previous year when the *Westfield* was employed in the operations about Vicksburg, Commander Renshaw had reported to the Department in the following highly favorable terms regarding him: "The engineer in charge, Mr. William R. Greene, with his assistants, Messrs. George S. Baker and Charles Smith, have been untiring in their exertions to keep the engine in repair, and have exercised so much judgment and care that since leaving the United States there has never been a day that the machinery has not been in perfect working order."

The Confederates recovered the large main shaft of the *Westfield* from the wreck and manufactured from it a 60-pounder rifled gun. This in due course of time found its way to the Annapolis Naval Academy and has rested in the grass of the gun-park there for many years as a trophy of war.

THE HARRIET LANE.

Immediately after the arrival of the *Clifton* at New Orleans with the news of the disaster at Galveston, Admiral Farragut sent Commodore Bell with the *Brooklyn* and six gunboats to re-establish the blockade off that port. The afternoon of January 11th a strange sail was seen off Galveston and the iron steamer *Hatteras*, Lieutenant Commander H. C. Blake, was sent in pursuit. After running from the *Hatteras* until dark, the stranger ceased steaming and allowed her pursuer to approach close alongside, replying to the hail that she was "Her Britannic Majesty's ship *Vixen*." The *Hatteras* lowered a boat to board her, when she suddenly fired a broadside at point blank range, accompanying it with the announcement that she was the Confederate steamer *Alabama*. The *Hatteras* returned the fire at once and for several minutes a sharp fight ensued, in which the Federal vessel was speedily disabled. She was a commercial steamer originally named *St. Mary*, purchased in Philadelphia in 1861 for $110,000, and was wholly unfit for a contest with a regularly built vessel of war. Her overhead walking beam was shot away immediately and another shot struck and destroyed the main engine cylinder, either of which blows was sufficient to deprive the ship of her motive power and prevented her commander from carrying out his intention of closing with the *Alabama* and boarding her. Shells striking the *Hatteras* near the water line tore off whole sheets of iron and caused her to fill as rapidly as a perforated tin pan. In this fatal predicament she surrendered and her crew was taken off by the victors, who had barely time to save them before the *Hatteras* sank. The boat's crew that had been called away to board the stranger escaped and carried the news of the disaster to Galveston.

In this engagement the *Hatteras* had two men, both firemen, killed and five wounded. The prisoners were taken to Kingston, Jamaica, all except the officers being kept in irons on the voyage of nine days to that place. At Kingston they were put on the beach in a most pitiable condition without money or adequate clothing, having lost everything they owned in the *Hatteras*. In spite of their unfortunate condition the treatment accorded them by the British residents of Kingston was such as to cause the following comment to appear in the report of Lieutenant Commander Blake: "Landed on an unfriendly shore, in a state of abject destitution.

that should have commanded the sympathy of avowed enemies, we felt keenly the unkind criticisms of those who profess to have no dislike for our government or its people." The engineers of the *Hatteras* who shared in the resulting hardships were Acting First Assistant A. M. Covert, and acting third assistants Jos. C. Cree, Jacob Colp and Benjamin C. Bourne.

On the evening of the 14th of January, the steamer *Columbia*, a purchased vessel attached to the North Atlantic Blockading Squadron, while on duty off Marlboro Inlet, North Carolina, got ashore on an unknown bar. The gunboat *Penobscot* went to her aid the following day and succeeded in taking off about thirty of her crew by means of a surf-line, but night coming on and the sea increasing compelled the abandonment of the effort at rescue. The second day the enemy mounted some guns on the shore and opened a heavy fire on the distressed vessel, then practically a wreck, which forced her to surrender; the commander, Acting Lieutenant J. P. Couthouy, with his remaining officers and men going on shore and delivering themselves up as prisoners of war after having spiked and thrown overboard the battery. The wreck was burned by the captors. The officers all belonged to the volunteer service and included George M. Bennett, first assistant engineer; W. W. Shipman and Samuel Lemon, second assistants, and J. H. Pelton and W. H. Crawford, third assistants. They were confined first at Salisbury, North Carolina, and later in Libby prison until May 5th, when they were sent north for exchange. The surgeon, by some curious mental operation on the part of the Confederates, was declared a "non-combatant" and was released on parole, but it did not occur to anyone that the paymaster and engineers were entitled to like consideration. Perhaps in an actual state of war there was no doubt about their military status.

Early in the morning of January 29th, the British steamer *Princess Royal*, from Halifax by way of Bermuda, attempted to run the blockade off Charleston and nearly succeeded, being headed off at the last moment by the gunboat *Unadilla*, whose shots forced the captain of the blockade runner to run his ship ashore. Acting Master Van Sice and Third assistant Engineer R. H. Thurston with two armed boat-crews took possession of the prize and labored all day of the 29th in lightening her preparatory to hauling her off, which was accomplished about dark by the combined efforts of her own engines and those of the light-draft vessels of the squadron. When afloat, the prize was anchored close to the *Housatonic*, acting as flagship in the absence of the *Powhatan* and *Canandaigua* gone to Port Royal for coal, and preparations were carried forward for sending her north with a prize crew. The *Princess Royal* had a very valuable cargo of rifled guns and marine engines for some Confederate rams building at Charleston; a great quantity of shoes for the army, small arms, armor plates, medicines, canned provisions, hospital stores, etc., all worth many times their money value to the Confederacy. When adjudicated in the prize court at Philadelphia the sum of $342,005.31 was declared available for distribution, shares of which made some of the officers of the *Unadilla* almost wealthy. The vessel had powerful engines with two cylinders 49 inches diameter and 39 inches stroke, geared to the screw shaft in the ratio of five to two. She was converted into a gun vessel and performed excellent duty on the blockade during the remainder of the war.

While the people of the *Unadilla* and the fleet were exerting themselves to get the *Princess Royal* afloat, the Confederates were making equally strenuous efforts to prevent it, horses and men in large numbers being engaged throughout the day in dragging siege guns from Fort Moultrie through the sands of Sullivan's Island into a position to fire upon the stranded steamer, but about the time their battery opened fire she was floated and taken out of range. Baffled in this attempt, they made on the morning of the 31st, the *Princess Royal* still lying by the *Housatonic*, a most desperate effort to wrest her from her captors. At 4 A. M. two rams—the *Chicora* and *Palmetto State*—came down from Charleston and about daylight assailed the blockading squadron, superior to them in numbers in about the proportion of four to one. Without any desire to detract from the gallantry of this attack, it should be stated that with the exception of the *Housatonic* and *Unadilla* the blockaders in the vicinity were all purchased merchant vessels wholly unfit for fighting at close quarters, their unsuitability being fully demonstrated by the event.

The Federal vessels were lying at wide intervals apart, a circumstance that further reduced the seeming disparity in force, and owing to the morning mist that lay over the water did not discover the approach of the enemy until he was close aboard. The first vessel attacked was the *Mercedita*, a purchased screw-steamer of about 800 tons that had cost $100,000 in 1861. She was struck a glancing blow on the starboard quarter by one of the rams and at the same time was disabled by a heavy rifle shell which passed diagonally through her, penetrating the steam drum of the port boiler in its passage and filling the ship with hot steam. The ram lay so low in the water that the guns of the *Mercedita* could not be depressed to bear upon her and the latter vessel, being thus both helpless and defenseless, accepted the summons to surrender, the executive officer going on board the ram and pledging his word of honor for the parole of the crew. Nothing was said regarding the vessel and as she was not taken possession of by the enemy she was retained in the squadron after the fight was over. Her gunner, who was in his room at the time, was killed by the shell, and she had three men killed and three wounded by scalding; with the exception of one ordinary seaman slightly scalded at the engine-room hatch these unfortunate men all belonged to the watch on duty in the engine-room.

Leaving the *Mercedita* to her fate, to sink or not, the ram next joined her consort in an attack upon the *Keystone State*, a large sidewheel merchant steamer of nearly 1,400 tons that had cost $125,000 in 1861, and did her great damage with shells, one of which set her on fire in the fore-hold and another exploded the steam chimneys or drums of both boilers. About one-fourth of her crew was instantly prostrated by the escaping steam, among them Assistant Surgeon Gotwold who was scalded to death while in the act of rendering aid to the wounded; several men had been killed or wounded by the shells and of the latter a number met death from the steam. The total number of casualties was forty, of which twenty-six were due to scalding. In this critical condition of the *Keystone State* her captain, Commander (afterward Rear Admiral) William E. LeRoy, ordered her flag hauled down in response to a summons to surrender, resistance or flight being apparently impossible. The chief engineer, Acting First Assistant Archibald K. Eddowes, did not stop the engines at this juncture but hastened on deck and informed Commander LeRoy that they would run for fifteen or twenty minutes on their vacuum and that that time should suffice to get out of the enemy's reach or obtain assistance from other vessels already beginning to engage the rams. Upon this representation the captain ordered the colors hoisted and the ship moved away from her assailants, being soon taken in tow by the *Memphis* and in that manner was saved to the United States government through the fidelity and knowledge of her chief engineer.

Mr. Eddowes was subsequently promoted to be an acting chief engineer and had the honor of serving for a time as chief engineer of the big frigate *Minnesota*. Being in the volunteer service, he was honorably discharged at the close of the war and disappeared from naval cognizance for many years. In the summer of 1894 the hard times compelled him to write to the Navy Department asking to be admitted to the Naval Home in Philadelphia, his letter stating that he was old, broken in health, out of employment, and homeless. Although not eligible for admission to the institution mentioned under a strict interpretation of the law, it is a gratifying fact that his case was considered in a liberal manner and his prayer was granted. Although now cared for in that manner, there remains in the story an undercurrent painfully suggestive of the concluding lines of Mr. Kipling's reproachful verses concerning the survivors of the charge of the Light Brigade:

"O thirty million English that babble of England's might,
Behold, there are twenty heroes who lack their food to-night;
Our children's children are lisping 'to honor the charge they made,'
And we leave to the streets and the workhouse the charge of the Light Brigade."

Besides the two vessels so badly used by the rams, the *Quaker City* was considerably damaged by a shell exploding in her engine-room, which fortunately did not kill anyone, and the *Augusta* also received a shell through her side without loss of life. While the fight was in progress Mr. Thurston on the *Princess Royal* by almost superhuman exertions got up steam from cold water and the vessel was taken out seaward for safety. About 7.30 A. M. the *Housatonic* and other vessels having reached the scene and attacked the rams, they gave up the fight and retreated up the channel to the vicinity of Fort Moultrie; late in the afternoon they got under way and returned to Charleston.

"It was this incident which led to the famous dispute in which it was asserted by General Beauregard and Commodore Ingraham, on the one side, that the blockade had been broken, and that, under the accepted interpretation of international law, it could not be reestablished until after three months' notice, that time at least being thus permitted to free trade, by foreign nations, with the Southern Confederacy; while, on the other hand, it was unanimously certified, by the officers of the National fleet, that, on the contrary, the blockade had not been broken, the fleet had not been driven off, and that it had only been the more closely drawn in around the harbor of Charleston by the action with the iron-clads. This, which was the finally accepted version of the affair, was certainly correct, as those of us who were in the action well know. The whole affair was over before breakfast, and at 9:30 A. M., our prize was on her way to report to Admiral DuPont, at Port Royal, convoyed by the injured vessels, which were sent there for repair."[1]

On January 30th the purchased screw steamer *Isaac Smith* was sent up the Stono River, South Carolina, to make a reconnoissance. When near Legareville she was suddenly attacked by three batteries of heavy guns concealed on the banks, and was soon compelled to surrender, having been entirely disabled by getting a shot through her steam drum. Before surrendering she had nine people killed and sixteen wounded, the only officer killed being Acting Second Assistant Engineer James S. Turner, who was struck in the breast and thigh by pieces of shell. Acting Third Assistant Engineer Erastus Barry was wounded, as was also Acting Lieutenant Conover, who was in command, and the paymaster, Mr. F. C. Hills, the latter being in command of the powder division. The survivors, including First Assistant Engineer Jacob Tucker and Third Assistant William Ross, became prisoners of war.

On the 15th of January the commerce-destroyer *Florida* ran out from Mobile through the blockading fleet and entered upon a devastating career in the waters of the West Indies, adding to the terror already inspired by the known presence of the *Alabama* in those waters. In September of the preceding year the *Florida* had run into the port of Mobile past the blockade under circumstances that made the exploit one of the most daring of any performed

---

[1] Dr. R. H. Thurston, in Cornell Magazine, March, 1890.

afloat during the war. Built in Liverpool as a copy of a class of gun-vessels in the Brit'sh navy designed for swift despatch boats, this vessel had proceded out to the West Indies late in the spring of 1862 and had spent the summer of that year with a small and disheartened crew wandering about from place to place trying to procure men and equipments sufficient to allow her to enter upon her intended mission of destruction against American commerce. Eventually her commander, Maffitt, with only about twenty men on board fit for duty on account of the ravages of yellow fever, was driven to the extremity of seeking a port in the Confederacy where he could procure a crew and also acquire nationality for his vessel.

The *Florida* being exactly like some of the British gun-boats cruising about the Gulf coast, Maffitt resolved to put on a bold front and take the chances of a deliberate rush into the line of blockaders in broad daylight, which desperate resolve was carried out the afternoon of September 4th. The blockading squadron off Mobile consisted of the *Susquehanna*, *Oneida* and about half a dozen gunboats, but it happened by mere chance that on the day of the *Florida's* appearance all the steamers but the *Oneida* and *Winona* were away from the immediate vicinity, having gone for coal or on other errands in the neighborhood. The approach of the *Florida* was not regarded with much suspicion, as her appearance and the white English ensign she displayed made it reasonably certain that she was a British gun-vessel that would stop and communicate according to custom before proceeding through the lines. As she came on with no slacking of speed, however, the *Oneida* already cleared for action as required by regulation under the circumstances fired three shots across her bow in rapid succession, and as these produced no sign of her stopping a broadside was fired into her, followed by a general cannonading from the *Oneida* and from the *Winona* and gun-schooner *Rachel Seamen* some distance away. But the ruse was successful; the *Florida* had advanced so far and was running at such speed that she passed on and was soon under the protection of the guns of Fort Morgan, having received a "frightful mauling," to use Maffitt's own words, and lost twelve men in killed and wounded. When thoroughly repaired, manned and equipped, she came out in January, 1863; ran the blockade successfully, and began her career as before mentioned.

A flying squadron commanded by Captain Wilkes of *San Jacinto* fame was kept busy scouring the West Indies in search of the commerce-destroyers. On the first day of February the double-ender *Sonoma* of this squadron, while near the southern end of that body of water lying between Andros Island and Nassau known to sailors as the Tongue of the Ocean, discovered a strange sail about six miles to the northward and gave chase, the stranger being identified when examined with the marine glasses as the much-sought-for *Florida*. The pursuit was kept up with varying prospects of success for thirty-four hours, during which time no one on the *Sonoma* slept nor ate a regular meal; after traversing the length of the Tongue of the Ocean and the Providence Channel the pursued vessel stood out on a northeast course into the open sea, where her superior sea qualities enabled her to draw away from the *Sonoma* and escape. The episode is not especially important except for an engineering question involved, which is the reason for its introduction.

The chief engineer of the *Sonoma* was Acting First Assistant Engineer Henry E. Rhoades who demonstrated his capability and zeal as an engineer by remaining on duty continuously during the chase and urging the boilers to their utmost capacity under forced draft, even going to the extent of burning hams and bacon to add to the fierceness of the fires. That he was able to keep a vessel like the *Sonoma* for more than thirty hours close astern of the *Florida*, built with special reference to speed, is sufficient proof of his ability as an engineer, although in doing it he well knew that he was inflicting fatal injury upon his own machinery. The commanding officer of the *Sonoma*, Commander T. H. Stevens, published in the Cosmopolitan Magazine for December, 1890, a very interesting account of this chase, from which narrative the following extracts are made: "Orders were at once given to the engineer to make all possible steam, the sails were cast loose, and the *Sonoma* sprung ahead in pursuit." . . . "Renewed orders were given to the engineer to crowd all steam and use every possible effort to increase the steam by the use of blowers or through any other means." . . . "Two or three times the engineer reported that the extreme pressure upon the boilers if kept up would cause an explosion, to which reply was finally made, 'Your duty is to obey orders, mine to capture or destroy the *Florida* at any risk.''

This latter sentiment is an eminently proper one from a military standpoint, for more than one commander or final judge of expedients in a camp or on board an armed vessel can only result in confusion and failure through crossing of authority, but the principle should in all cases be double-acting to the extent of holding the determining authority alone responsible for the results of his judgment, both in success and failure. The last reference to the *Sonoma* in the magazine article from which quotations have been made says : " Shortly afterward, upon receiving orders to take the *Sonoma* to New York, we proceeded thither and immediately after our arrival there the vessel was put out of commission. The long chase of the *Florida* made extensive repairs essential." The vessel arrived at New York about the middle of June and a survey showed that her cylinder had been damaged by overwork and that her boiler tubes were so nearly burned out that they would have to be entirely renewed. The story is concluded by the following letter sent to Mr. Rhoades under date of July 25th : " Sir : A report of the examination of the machinery of the gunboat *Sonoma* shows that it has been seriously injured in consequence of your neglect of duty. You are therefore dismissed the service, and will, from this date, cease to be regarded as an Acting First Assistant Engineer in the navy.

Very respectfully,

GIDEON WELLES, Secretary of the Navy."

The town of Washington some distance up the Pamlico River from Pamlico Sound had been taken and occupied by the Federal naval force in the North Carolina Sounds since early in 1862. During the first two weeks of April, 1863, the enemy cut off water communication by occupying some works below the town and made a determined though unsuccessful attempt to recapture it, the two or three naval vessels thus cut off being forced to severe and prolonged exertions to retain possession of the place and preserve themselves. The following extracts from official reports regarding the investment refer to valuable services performed by members of the engineer corps.

From the report of Acting Rear Admiral S. P. Lee :

"The *Louisiana*, *Commodore Hull*, and an armed transport

called the *Eagle*, under charge of Second Assistant Engineer Lay and Paymaster W. W. Williams, of the *Louisiana*, as volunteers, were almost constantly engaged with the enemy's batteries opposite Washington."

" . . . Acting Second Assistant Engineer H. Rafferty, Acting Third Assistant Engineer John E. Harper, . . . are recommended to especial notice for their good conduct and bravery in battle."

From the report of Commander R. T. Renshaw of the *Louisiana*:

"Second Assistant Engineer John L. Lay and Assistant Paymaster W. W. Williams volunteering to take charge of the guns on board transport *Eagle*, I directed them to do so; they have done good service, and acted to my entire satisfaction."

"Acting Third Assistant Engineer Thomas Mallahan, of the *Ceres*, while attempting to land in one of her boats, was killed by a musket ball."

From the report of Acting Lieutenant Graves of the *Lockwood*:

"Late in the afternoon my boiler commenced leaking to such an extent as to put out the fires. I ordered the engineers to blow out the water and repair it temporarily with all possible despatch, and my thanks are due to Acting Second Assistant Engineer J. T. Newton and and Acting Third Assistant John I. Miller for the energy and promptness they displayed in complying with my orders. At 9 P. M. had steam again."

As early as May, 1862, the Navy Department had informed Flag Officer DuPont confidentially of its intention to attempt the capture of Charleston, and in January, 1863, orders were sent to him to carry the plan into execution, the iron-clads as fast as completed being ordered to report to him for the undertaking. One of the first to arrive, the *Montauk*, Captain John L. Worden, distinguished herself the 28th of February by going under the guns of Fort McAllister in the Ogeechee River and destroying with her shells the Confederate steamer *Nashville* which had been discovered aground about 1,200 yards up the river, the *Montauk* receiving a severe fire from the fort without material damage while shelling the *Nashville*. On the third of March, DuPont, to test the mechanical appliances of the monitors and give the men practice in firing the guns, sent the *Passaic, Patapsco* and *Nahant* to attack Fort McAllister. The monitors stood the test well and received no serious damage beyond dents in the turrets and side armor, while the few defects in turret turning mechanism, gun mounts and machinery that existed were discovered and remedied. The *Weehawken* while on her way to join the fleet broke down February 7th off Port Royal and was completely disabled. The trunk of one of her engines broke short off at the piston, canting the latter to the extent of cracking the cylinder beyond repair. It happened that the cylinders of the *Comanche* were completed in Jersey City and were made from the same patterns and in the same shop where the *Weehawken* was built, so by use of the telegraph and the chartering of a vessel the cylinders of the latter with all their attachments were hastened to Port Royal and installed in the disabled vessel in a remarkably short space of time.

On the 7th of April DuPont made an unsuccessful attack upon Fort Sumter with the *New Ironsides, Montauk, Weehawken, Catskill, Passaic, Nahant, Patapsco, Nantucket and Keokuk*. The iron-clads were in action less than two hours and were then withdrawn by signal from the flagship. A quartermaster was killed in the pilot house of the *Nahant* by a flying piece of bolt from the armor and Commander Downes and five others were injured in the same manner on that vessel. The *Keokuk* with her curious striped armor fared badly, being struck ninety times in thirty minutes and pierced through at and about the water-line nineteen times, while her turret was penetrated and the ship generally riddled. Fifteen of her crew were wounded, some of them seriously. She was kept afloat during the ensuing night, but when the water became rough in the morning she sank, her people being taken off just in time to save their lives. Rear Admiral DuPont made a discouraging report to the Navy Department respecting the monitors, and Chief Engineer Stimers, who had been sent down from New York with a company of machinists and ship-smiths to repair injuries to the iron-clads, reported very favorably regarding them, the two reports being the beginning of a famous controversy that will be dealt with in a separate chapter.

The iron-clads did not again engage the Charleston forts while under DuPont's command, but in June an event took place that did much to redeem the reputation of the monitors. In November, 1861, an English iron steamer named *Fingal* ran the blockade into Savannah and after discharging her cargo was sold to the Confederate government and converted into an armored vessel of war by alterations practically the same as those adopted in the case of the *Merrimac*, with the addition of a heavy armor belt of timber about the water-line and a torpedo spar fitted on the bow. She was armed with two $6\frac{4}{10}$ inch and two 7 inch Brooke rifles, the latter pivoted for bow and stern as well as broadside fire, and had a crew of one hundred and forty-five officers and men. These preparations consumed much time and it was not until 1863 that she was ready for service, the blockaders in the meanwhile having maintained a vigilant watch over all channels whereby she might get to sea. In June it became definitely known that the *Atlanta*, as the *Fingal* had been re-named, had crossed over into Wassaw Sound south of Savannah and might be expected to make a raid on the blockaders thereabouts. The double-ender *Cimmerone* being the only vessel just then off Wassaw Sound, Admiral DuPont immediately despatched thither the monitors *Weehawken* and *Nahant*, the senior officer being sturdy John Rodgers in the *Weehawken*.

Early in the morning of June 17th, the anniversary of Bunker Hill, the *Atlanta* came down to give battle to the monitors, being accompanied by two steamers said to have been filled with excursionists expecting to witness an easy victory. Owing to the narrowness of the channel the *Nahant*, having no pilot, had to follow the *Weehawken* and was unable to fire a gun in the action which ensued. At 4.55 A. M. the *Atlanta* opened fire without effect, which was not returned until twenty minutes later when Rodgers with deliberate precision began using the *Weehawken's* guns, one of which was a XI-inch like those of the original *Monitor*, and the other a XV-inch. In fifteen minutes the *Atlanta*, then aground and badly damaged, hauled down her colors and surrendered. Four of the five shots fired from the *Weehawken* had struck her, one of the XV-inch, the first fired, having broken through the armor and wood backing, strewed the gun-deck with splinters and prostrated forty men by the concussion, one of whom died ; the other XV-inch shot knocked off the top of the pilot-house and disabled both pilots and the man at the wheel, which accounts for the vessel going aground. One of the XI-inch shots did no damage beyond breaking a plate or two at the knuckle, but the other one carried away a port-shutter and scattered its fragments about the gun-deck. Lieutenant Commander D. B. Harmony of the *Nahant* was put in charge with a prize crew, Acting First Assistant Engineer J. G. Young of the *Weehawken* taking charge of the engines. The prize was found fully equipped with ammunition and stores for a cruise and was appraised as follows by a board of naval officers:

Hull	$250,000.00
Machinery	80,000.00
Ordnance, ordnance stores &c	14,022.91
Medical stores	20.00
Provisions, clothing and small stores	1,012.85
Equipments and stores in the master's, boatswain's, sailmaker's, and carpenter's departments	5,773.50
Total valuation	$350,829.26

The above amount, less $789.30 costs of trial, was subsequently declared by the prize court as available for distribution.

Three hours after the surrender the engine of the *Atlanta* was reversed by engineer Young and the vessel backed off into deep water, proceeding later under her own steam without convoy to Port Royal where she was repaired and enrolled in the naval service of the United States. Captain Rodgers' report of the engagement contains the following: "The engine, under the direction of First Assistant Engineer James G. Young, always in beautiful order, was well worked. Mr. Young has, I hope, by his participation in this action, won the promotion for which, on account of his skill and valuable services, I have already recommended him." On the 5th of July Mr. Young received his promotion to the grade of acting chief engineer.

The outline sketches of the *Atlanta* here following are reproduced from drawings made at the time of her capture by Second

Assistant Engineer P. R. Voorhees of the *Wabash*, and were forwarded as part of the official report of the capture. In a general way they serve to illustrate the type of armored vessels which lack of iron building material forced the constructors and engineers of the South to resort to.

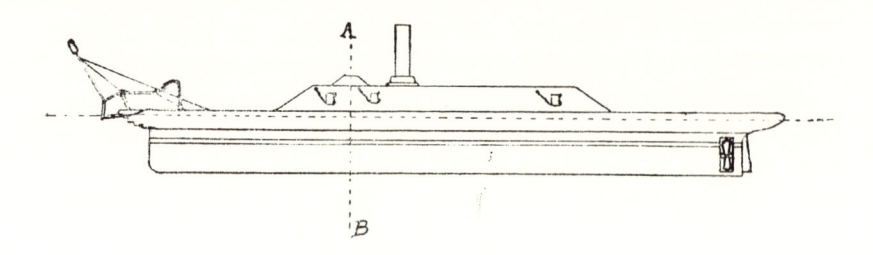

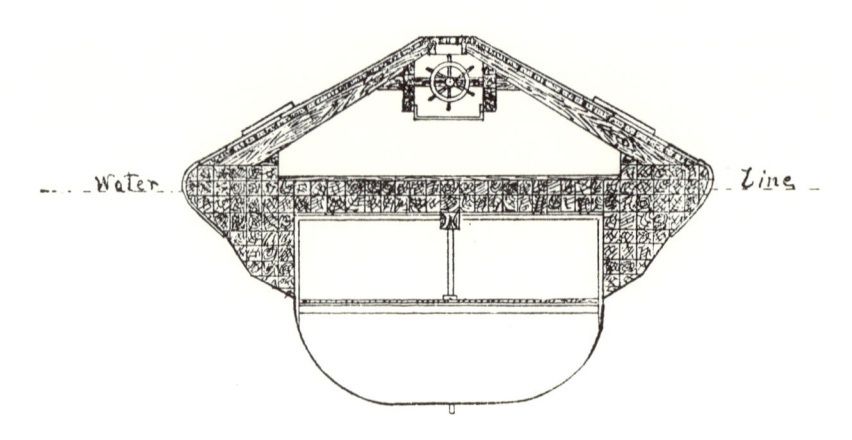

CONFEDERATE IRON-CLAD *Atlanta*, CAPTURED BY THE *Weehawken*.
Enlarged section on A-B showing framing, wooden armor, etc.

Rear Admiral John A. Dahlgren relieved Rear Admiral DuPont on the 6th of July and immediately began a determined and prolonged struggle, in conjunction with the army, for the possession of Charleston Harbor, partial success being achieved by the capture of Morris Island and its formidable fort, Wagner, on the 6th of September. Fort Sumter was steadily assailed for months and by the end of the year was little more than a heap of ruins, though the enemy retained possession of it. A noteworthy casualty of the siege occurred on the *Catskill* while engaged with Fort Wagner on the 17th of August. A shot from the fort struck the top of the pilot-house and shattered the inner lining of it, pieces of which killed Commander George W. Rodgers and Assistant Paymaster J. G. Woodbury, and wounded a pilot and a master's mate, all of whom were in the pilot-house. It is claimed by the friends of the monitor type of ships that these two unfortunate officers and the quartermaster killed on the *Nahant* were the only persons who were killed on the monitors by cannon fire during the whole course of the war. The constant employment of the monitors during these months of siege entailed much hard work and suffering upon the engine-room force, the reports of commanding officers containing frequent reference to a prostration of engineers and firemen from the intense heat of their stations.

Immediately after the evacuation of Morris Island by the enemy an unsuccessful attempt was made to take Sumter by assault, a landing party of about four hundred men from the fleet being sent on shore the night of September 8th for that purpose. While landing from the boats a number of casualties occured from the enemy's fire and the party was driven off after a sharp fight with the loss of about one hundred and twenty officers and men made prisoners, Third Assistant Engineer J. H. Harmony of the *Housatonic* being one of the latter. The night of October 5th a most daring attempt to blow up the *New Ironsides* was made by Lieutenant Glassell, Assistant Engineer Toombs, and a pilot, who went out to her in a small and almost submerged cigar-shaped craft and exploded a torpedo close alongside the big iron-clad. The explosion started some beams and knees in the side of the iron-clad but did no serious injury. A mass of water fell upon the deck and also extinguished the fires of her assailant. Lieutenant Glassell took to the water and was captured; the engineer and pilot stuck to their disabled boat and afterward got up steam and returned to Charleston the same night. For this Mr. Toombs was made a chief engineer.

In the operations of this protracted seige the resisting and aggressive qualities of the monitors were well tested and demonstrated. An idea of the hard knocks they gave and took during the summer may be gained from the following tabular statement of their services, as reported to the department by Admiral Dahlgren:

	NUMBER SHOTS FIRED JULY 10-SEPT 7, 1863.		HITS.	HITS, APRIL 7; FIRST ATTACK ON SUMTER.	HITS AT FT. MCALLISTER.
	XV in.	XI in.			
Catskill	138	425	86	20	......
Montauk	301	478	154	14	46
Lehigh	41	28	36	......	......
Passaic	119	107	90	35	9
Nahant	170	276	69	36	......
Patapsco	178	230	96	47	1
Weehawken	264	633	134	53	......
Nantucket	44	155	53	51	......
New Ironsides	......	4,439	164	......	......
Totals	1,255	6,771	882	256	56

The limited operations of the *Lehigh* were due to the fact that she did not arrive at Charleston until August 30, and consequently was engaged only about a week of the period dealt with.

About the middle of the afternoon of Sunday, December 6, the *Weehawken* sank at her anchorage off Morris Island. The cause of this disaster as determined by a court of inquiry appears to have been altering her trim by stowing an unusual quantity of shot and shell in the bow compartments and leaving the forward hatch open when water was breaking on board. Ordinarily all water ran aft and was thrown out by the pumps in the engine-room, but with the changed trim this did not occur until a large quantity of water had accumulated forward, bringing her more and more down by the head, and rapidly increasing through new leaks started by the unusually heavy load forward. This condition was not discovered until ten or fifteen minutes before she sank, and the desperate attempts then made to relieve her were unavailing; her limit of buoyancy, which was only 125 tons, was reached before the pumps began gaining on the water, and she went down. Four officers and twenty-six men perished in her, the entire watch on duty in the engine and fire-rooms being lost. The four officers drowned were all third assistant engineers—Messrs. Henry W. Merian; Augustus Mitchell; George W. McGowan, and Charles Spangberg. Two of these were on duty and the other two heroically went to the engine-room to try to render assistance instead of saving themselves, as they might have done. The engineer in charge, Mr. J. B. A. Allen, acting second assistant, whose duties obliged him to go on deck at intervals to report to the executive officer, was saved.

CHAPTER XXII.

"For Southern prisons will sometimes yawn,
And yield their dead unto life again;
And the day that comes with a cloudy dawn
In golden glory at last may wane."

KATE PUTNAM OSGOOD.

1863—The Civil War, Continued—The War on the Western Waters—Passage of Port Hudson—Destruction of the Frigate MISSISSIPPI—Minor Operations in the West—New Vessels Placed Under Construction—The Light-Draft Monitors—Iron Double-Enders—Large Wooden Frigates and Sloops-of-War—The First Swift Cruisers—The KALAMAZOO Class of Monitors—Assimilated Rank of Staff Officers Raised—New Regulations Governing Promotion in the Engineer Corps Issued.

THE naval force in 1863 on the western rivers was engaged in a ceaseless and baffling warfare under conditions that were very difficult and often disheartning. Great annoyance was experienced from the development by the Confederates of the torpedo, and another danger, equally unassailable, existed in the guerrillas or "bushwhackers" who infested the swamps and forests along the river banks in such unseen numbers that no man's life was safe on a passing steamer. David D. Porter, still a commander, but holding an acting appointment as rear admiral, was now in general command of the Mississippi fleet, which had been increased by a number of regularly built war vessels in addition to the mortar boats and make-shifts previously spoken of. On the 4th of July Porter was commissioned a rear admiral in recognition of his services before Vicksburg, which place succumbed to the combined army and naval forces on that date. Besides Porter's fleet, vessels of Farragut's West Gulf blockading squadron also operated in the river, the most noteworthy battle of the year in this region being fought by a division of that squadron.

The night of March 14-15 Farragut attempted to run past the formidable batteries at Port Hudson, Louisiana, his object in wishing to get above them being to cut off the enemy's supplies from the Red River region and also to recover if possible the iron-clad casemated gunboat *Indianola,* which had been captured by four Confederate steamers on February 24th. Farragut's fleet consisted of his flagship *Hartford,* three large ships and three gunboats. To provide for keeping the large vessels going ahead in case of injury to their machinery they were each ordered to lash a gunboat alongside on their port sides, that being away from Port Hudson which is located on the east side of the river. The *Mississippi* had no consort; not from any sentiment that the old sea-veteran could fight her battles better alone, but because there was no gunboat for her and her overhanging paddle-boxes would have made the arrangement difficult if not impossible had there been another gunboat available. The iron-clad *Essex* and some mortar boats of Porter's fleet were also present and did good service bombarding the forts, as they had done before at the forts below New Orleans.

Shortly before midnight the squadron moved up the river and received a terrible fire from the batteries on shore, the ships being brought into bold relief by the light of burning buildings and bonfires on the banks. Farragut in the *Hartford,* with the *Albatross* lashed alongside, succeeded in running the batteries and gained a position in the river above, but all the other vessels failed in the attempt. The *Monongahela* grounded on a spit in front of the principal battery and for half an hour was a stationary target for a most severe fire which killed six and wounded twenty-one of her crew, Captain McKinstry being among the wounded. Her escape from this almost fatal predicament was due largely to the exertions and courage of her chief engineer, Mr. George F. Kutz, and his assistants, the senior one of whom was Mr. Joseph Trilley, now a chief engineer in the navy. To work the engines to their utmost in the endeavor to back off, these officers took the desperate risk of doubling the steam pressure in the boilers and with the added power thus obtained and the assistance of the consort *Kineo* the ship was finally floated. This extraordinary power worked through the engines resulted in heating the forward crank pin, the brasses of which were slacked off during a momentary stop, and the engines thereafter kept running at full speed by playing a stream of water from the fire hose on the hot pin until the ship was off the bottom. By that time the pin was so burned and cut that the engines were disabled and the *Monongahela* and *Kineo* had to drop down the river out of action. While the engineers were struggling with the crank-pin adjustment an 80-pounder rifle shot came into the engine-room and broke into pieces by striking the end of the reversing shaft.

The reports made by the commanding and executive officers ascribed the failure of the *Monongahela* to get past the batteries to the failure of the engines, but Chief Engineer Kutz was able to prove to the satisfaction of Admiral Farragut that the casualty to the engines occurred while unusual exertions were being made to back off the spit, and not after the vessel was again afloat, as had been charged.

The *Mississippi* following astern of the *Monongahela* also went aground and for thirty-five minutes made heroic endeavors to get off and escape from the galling cross fire of three batteries concentrated upon her. The chief engineer, Mr. Wm. H. Rutherford, increased the steam pressure from thirteen to twenty-five pounds and backed the engines with all their power without avail. The fire of the enemy finally became so accurate and deadly that Captain Melancthon Smith deemed it "most judicious and humane," as he expressed it in his report, to abandon the vessel, and then followed a task that must have been most repugnant to those who loved the old ship and respected her historical associations. Her battery was spiked; the small arms thrown overboard; the engineers and their men broke and destroyed the vital parts of the machinery; fires were kindled in several places between decks, and after the sick and wounded were brought up the ship was left to her fate. Sixty-four of her crew were reported killed and missing and two hundred and thirty-three as saved, a number of the latter being wounded from the enemy's fire, among them Mr. J. E. Fallon, third assistant engineer. In this disaster and its sequence Third Assistant Engineer Jefferson Brown was the subject of one of those incidents of resurrection from supposed death which occurred a number of times during the Civil War and turned mourning into rejoicing for a number of families both North and South. Mr. Brown was reported drowned when the *Mississippi* was lost, and in collecting material for this book the writer found his name still inscribed in the list of the dead in the casualty-book of the rebellion kept by the bureau of Medicine and Surgery, Navy Department. Some months after the disaster, when an exchange of prisoners was effected, Mr. Brown appeared among the captives given up, and has lived to be at present a chief engineer on the retired list of the navy.

The following spirited description of the final scene in the career of the *Mississippi* is taken from a paper read before the District of Columbia Commandery of the Military Order of the Loyal Legion by Chief Engineer Harrie Webster, U. S. Navy, who as an assistant engineer on board the *Genesee* witnessed the tragedy.

"As the smoke slowly drifted to leeward we caught sight of the old frigate *Mississippi*, hard and fast aground, apparently abandoned, and on fire.

"When we first discovered her the fire was already crawling up the rigging.

"From every hatch the flames were surging heavenward, and it seemed but a question of minutes when the good old ship must blow up.

"Every mast, spar, and rope was outlined against the dark background of forest and sky, and it was a sad, and at the same time, a beautiful spectacle.

"While all hands were speculating on the causes of the disaster the staunch old craft, which had braved the gales of every clime, slowly floated free from the bank, and, turned by an eddy in the current, swept out into the river and headed for the fleet as though under helmsman's control.

"As the burning ship neared the ships at anchor in her path, her guns, heated by the flames, opened fire, one after another in orderly sequence, and as their breechings had been burned away the recoil carried them amidships, where, crashing through the weakened deck, they fell into the fiery depths, showers of sparks and fresh flames following the plunge.

"Fortunately for us, her guns had been trained on the bluffs, so her shots flew wide of the fleet and sped crashing into the forest below the batteries of Port Hudson.

"Majestically, as though inspired with victory, the ship, which by this time was a mass of fire from stem to stern, from truck to water-line, floated past the fleet, down past Profit's Island, down into the darkness of the night.

"Suddenly, as if by magic, her masts shot into the air all ablaze, a tremendous tongue of flame pierced the sky for an instant, and amid the muffled thunder of her exploded magazine the *Mississippi* disappeared in the stream whose name she had borne so bravely and so long."

The *Richmond*, with the *Genesee* alongside, was the second in line following the flagship, and was disabled at the turning point in the river opposite the batteries by a shot carrying away both her safety valves and letting off the steam, which obliged her to drop down stream, the *Genesee* being unable to carry her up against the strong current. She had three men killed and twelve wounded, the majority of the casualties occurring among the marines, a gun's crew of whom were nearly all swept away by a single shot. Commander James Alden of the *Richmond* in his report of the battle said, "To Mr. Moore, our chief engineer, great credit is due for his management throughout the fight, and particularly after the accident to the safety-valve chest." The *Genesee* was considerably damaged by shot and had three wounded; her commander reported, "I also bring to special notice the efficient manner in which Mr. John Cahill, senior engineer, and the assistant engineers, Charles H. Harreb, Michael McLaughlin, Christopher Milton and Harrie Webster, with the firemen and coal heavers attached to this department, worked the engine and supplied the furnaces during the action."

The state of affairs in the engine department of the *Richmond* was most critical after the destruction of the safety valves, the engine and fire-rooms being filled with steam, which obliged the most heroic devotion to duty in order to save the boilers by hauling the fires. Mr. Eben Hoyt, the first assistant engineer, was conspicuous in this work, as described by the following from the official report of Chief Engineer John W. Moore:

"I consider it my duty to bring to your notice the valuable assistance rendered me by First Assistant Engineer E. Hoyt, who, during the whole engagement, was actively employed wherever most required, until after having penetrated the steam several times, while superintending the hauling of the fires, trying to ascertain the extent of injury, &c., he was finally led away completely exhausted and fainting."

In forwarding this report to the Secretary of the Navy, Commander Alden sent the following letter:

"SIR: I have the honor to enclose herewith the report of the chief engineer of this vessel setting forth the injuries done to our machinery on the night of the 14th instant. It would have been sent with the others, but Mr. Moore's attention has been so entirely engrossed in the personal superintendence of the repairs that it was found impracticable.

" In my general report of our proceedings, at the time referred to, I had occasion to speak of Mr. Moore's services, and would again call the attention of the department to his merits as an officer. All that he says of his assistants I can endorse most fully, and would beg leave to mention here what I regret was from some oversight omitted in my first report, namely, that Third Assistant Engineer Weir, who was stationed at the bell-pull on the bridge, was of the greatest assistance to me in pointing out the location of the different batteries, and although knocked down and injured by splinters, recovered himself immediately and continued unflinchingly at his post."

In order to communicate with the admiral above Port Hudson, Commander Alden directed the commander of the *Genesee* to fit out an expedition from his vessel for that purpose. As the undertaking was one of great peril, volunteers were called for from among the officers, and three or four responded: from these Commander Macomb selected Acting Third Assistant Engineer Harrie Webster, although he was the only staff officer who had volunteered; put him in command of a boat's crew, and started him off on his dangerous mission. Mr. Webster successfully took his boat through the six or eight miles of intervening swamps and lagoons, delivered his despatches to Admiral Farragut, received others from him to Commander Alden, and returned to the *Genesee* the same night. On the way back he landed and examined a signal station of the enemy, and, finding about it the fresh trail of a horseman, he took his party in pursuit, eventually overhauling and capturing at the point of his revolver a Confederate lieutenant with his horse, accoutrements, and important despatches. The exploit was one of remarkable nerve and daring, performed as it was in the gloomy fastnesses of the enemy's country.

On the 22nd of March while Rear Admiral Porter with some mortar-boats and small steamers was trying to work through the thickets of Steele's Bayou and thus get into the Yazoo River, he was attacked by a large force of the enemy concealed in the woods; two of his men were severely wounded and Acting Third Assistant Engineer Henry Sullivan of the *Dahlia* was struck by a rifle ball and killed.

On March 28th the purchased gun-vessel *Diana*, Acting Master T. L. Peterson commanding, was sent into Grand Lake from the Atchafalaya River to make a reconnoissance. When on her return she was attacked near Berwick Bay from shore by field pieces and sharp-shooters, and was forced to surrender after a fiercely fought contest lasting nearly three hours. The commanding officer and two master's mates next to him in rank were killed before the surrender, and Acting Assistant Engineer James McNally was also killed, the latter's death being instantaneous from a Minie ball in the head.

About the middle of July while a detachment of vessels of the Mississippi flotilla was up the Yazoo River destroying Confederate steamers that had taken refuge there, the armored gunboat *Baron de Kalb* ran upon two torpedoes and was sunk in twenty feet of water. Her hull was so damaged that no effort was made to raise her, but her guns, stores, and parts of the machinery were removed, and her armor plates were taken off to prevent them from becoming of use to the enemy. The *Baron de Kalb* was originally the *St. Louis*, the name having been changed about the time she was transferred to the Navy Department, and she was the third of the seven original Edes iron-clads to be destroyed by the enemy. The *Cairo* was sunk by a torpedo in the Yazoo River in December, 1862, and the *Cincinnati* was sunk by the Vicksburg batteries, May 27th, 1863. These disasters were unattended with loss of life except in the case of the *Cincinnati*, which had nineteen people killed or drowned and fourteen wounded, First Engineer Simon Shultice being one of the latter.

An unfortunate and unsuccessful attack was made September 8th by a combined army and navy force upon a fortified position at Sabine Pass, Texas. The force consisted of 1,200 troops in transports, convoyed by the naval steamers *Granite City*, *Arizona*, *Sachem*, and *Clifton*, all purchased vessels of inferior resisting powers. In the engagement the two last named were both disabled by shots exploding their boilers, and were compelled to surrender. The *Sachem* had two engineers and seven men killed and a considerable number wounded, the two unfortunate engineers being John Frazer, acting second assistant engineer, and John Munroe, acting third assistant. The executive officer, Acting Master Rhoades, and seven men of the *Clifton* were killed and a number, mostly soldiers, wounded; her chief engineer, Mr. Bradley, was wounded and was afterward reported by the Confederate captors of the survivors as having died of his injuries.

In October the commander of the ironclad *Osage*, of the Mississippi squadron, having received information that a Confederate steamer was tied up to the bank in the Red River, sent out an expedition under command of Acting Chief Engineer Thomas Doughty, with Assistant Engineer Hobbs as his lieutenant, which expedition captured and destroyed the steamer and another one, took a number of prisoners, and returned without loss to the *Osage*. Mr. Doughty's report of the affair, dated October 7, 1863, follows:

"SIR: In obedience to your order, I, with a party of twenty men, with the assistance of Mr. Hobbs, started for Red River this morning. Arriving at Red River, I could see no signs of a steamboat. I divided the party, sending eight men down the river to look into the bend below, and with twelve started up the river. When we had traveled about half a mile I saw the chimneys of a steamer. The woods were found so dense that we could not penetrate them, and the only alternative was to advance in sight. The steamer was on the opposite side of the river, and I feared those on board might see us in time to escape before we were near enough to use our rifles. No one saw us, and I chose a spit opposite her, where we could see any one who attempted to escape. I hailed her; two men were seen to run forward and disappear; I directed three files on the right to fire. The fire brought the men out, and at my command they brought to my side of the river two skiffs which belonged to the boat. I was about to embark a party to burn her, when I heard a steamboat descending the river. I ordered the men out of sight behind a large log and some bushes, and in two minutes I saw a steamer round the point above. I waited until she was within four hundred yards, and showed myself, and ordered her to stop. She did so, and I found myself in possession of nine prisoners and two steamboats. I knew I could not get them out of the river, and I ordered the destruction of the first one captured, the *Argus*, and embarked on board the second, the *Robert Fulton*, and steamed down to the landing where I first struck the river, where I ordered her to be set on fire, and in a few minutes she was one mass of flame. She was the better vessel of the two, and was valued by her owner at seventy-five thousand dollars. Neither of them had any cargo on board. I captured all the officers of the boats, one first lieutenant in the Confederate army, and three negroes."

Admiral Porter in reporting this affair to the Department said, "This is a great loss to the rebels at this moment, as it cuts off their means of operating across that part of Atchafalaya where they lately came over to attack Morganzia. This capture will deter others from coming down Red River. The affair was well managed, and the officers and men composing the expedition deserve great credit for the share they took in it."

During 1863 the navy was increased by about one hundred and thirty vessels of all kinds acquired by purchase or capture, and lost thirty-two in battle or by accidental destruction. Fifty-eight vessels of war were placed under construction during the same period. The first of these were twenty light-draft single-turreted monitors, contracts for the construction of which were distributed among a dozen different cities from Portland, Maine, to St. Louis, Missouri, during the spring months of the year. The general plans for these monitors were furnished by John Ericsson and the entire control and supervision of their building was entrusted to Chief Engineer A. C. Stimers. They were designed to draw six feet of water and were intended to operate in shallow rivers and other inland waters where guerrillas had made the service of other types of light-draft boats extremely perilous and of doubtful success. For causes that will be referred to later, these monitors failed to fulfill

U. S. STEAM FRIGATE GUERRIERE.

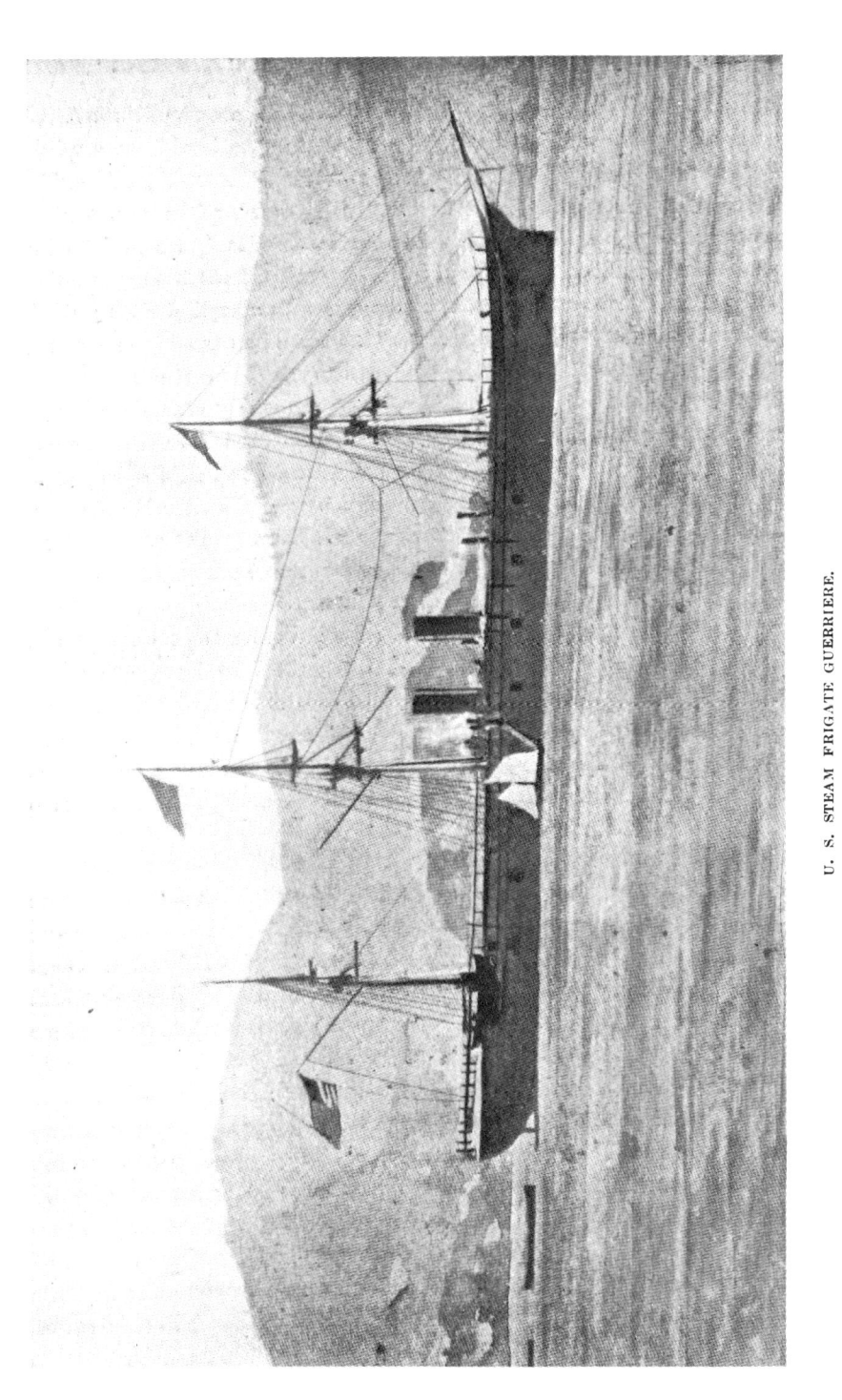

Length, 312 feet 6 inches; beam, 46 feet; disp., 3,953 tons.

(From a photograph taken in Rio de Janeiro, loaned by Chief Engineer John L. Hannum, U. S. Navy.)

their mission and never rendered any service of value to the government. Their names were, *Casco, Chimo, Cohoes, Etlah, Klamath, Koka, Modoc, Napa, Naubuc, Nausett, Shawnee, Shiloh, Squando-Suncook, Tunxis, Umpqua, Wassuc, Waxsaw, Yazoo,* and *Yuma.*

In June and July contracts were made with various ship-builders for seven iron double-enders, somewhat larger than those of the two classes previously built; each had a single inclined low-pressure engine from designs furnished by the engineer-in-chief. They were of 1,370 tons displacement and were named *Ashuelot, Mohongo, Monocacy, Muscoota, Shamoken, Suwanee,* and *Winnipec.*

In order to provide for a fleet that would be useful for general cruising purposes when peace should be restored, the Department had plans prepared by the Bureau of Construction during the summer for a number of large wooden frigates and sloops-of-war, and began the construction of a number of them at the different navy yards. Unfortunately the supply of seasoned timber had been so drawn upon by the unusual amount of ship-building of the preceding years that much green material had to be used in these vessels and as a consequence those that were eventually finished were very short-lived. Being long and narrow, they were strengthened with diagonal iron bracing amounting almost to an enormous iron basket woven over the hull, and this held them together long after the decay of the timbers and would have caused them to fall in pieces.

Eight of these ships were gun-deck frigates of 4,000 tons displacement and full ship-rigged. They were about 310 feet long between perpendiculars and forty-six feet extreme beam. Their names were, *Antietam, Guerriere, Illinois, Java, Kewaydin, Minnetonka, Ontario,* and *Piscataqua.* Two other gun-deck frigates, the *Hassalo* and *Wautaga,* somewhat larger than these eight, were projected at the same time, but their hulls were never built. In addition to the frigates, ten large sloops-of-war of what was known as the *Contoocook* class were ordered. They were of about 3,050 tons displacement and were named *Arapahoe, Contoocook, Keosauqua, Manitou, Mondamin, Mosholu, Pushmataha, Tahgayuta, Wanalosett,* and *Willamette.* Of these only four—the *Contoocook, Manitou, Mosholu* and *Pushmataha*—were ever built, and they, with the new names of *Albany, Worcester, Severn,* and *Congress* respectively, fell into decay after not many years' service. All twenty of the ships above named were to have two-cylinder back-acting engines of the Isherwood type, the cylinders being sixty inches in diameter and three feet stroke of piston; boilers for each vessel were specified to have not less than 546 square feet of grate service. Late in the fall Mr. Isherwood, acting for the Department, entered into contracts with eleven different machinery firms for the engines and boilers of these ships, the contract price for machinery for each ship being $400,000, except the *Ontario* which contract was awarded to John Roach of the Etna Iron Works for $385,000. Owing to the non-completion of the hulls of many of the ships, the matter of making settlements and compromises with the machinery contractors became a vexed problem for the bureau of steam engineering to struggle with after the war.

The swift cruiser came into existence this year also by the beginning of work on seven vessels in which speed was to be the most important element. The Secretary of the Navy in explaining the need of having such vessels said in his annual report for that year, "Besides the turreted vessels for coast defense and large armored ships for naval conflict we need and should have steamers of high speed constructed of wood, with which to sweep the ocean, and chase and hunt down the vessels of an enemy." One of these cruisers, the *Idaho*, was the child of Mr. E. N. Dickerson, who had secured sufficient influence to obtain this opportunity of experimenting on a large scale with his theory of perfect expansion of gases when applied to the steam engine. With the *Idaho* the Bureau of Steam Engineering had nothing to do, the contract for hull and machinery complete being made by the Bureau of Construction in May, 1863, with Paul L. Forbes and E. N. Dickerson, the contract price being $600,000. The hull was built by the famous shipbuilder, Steers, of New York, and the machinery by the Morgan Iron Works from designs prepared by Mr. Dickerson; there were two pairs of engines driving twin screws, the cylinders having the very remarkable dimensions for marine engines of eight feet stroke and thirty inches diameter. The *Idaho* was 298 feet long, $44\frac{1}{2}$ feet beam, and of 3,240 tons displacement.

John Ericsson also availed himself of this opportunity to try engineering conclusions with Engineer-in-Chief Isherwood. It was

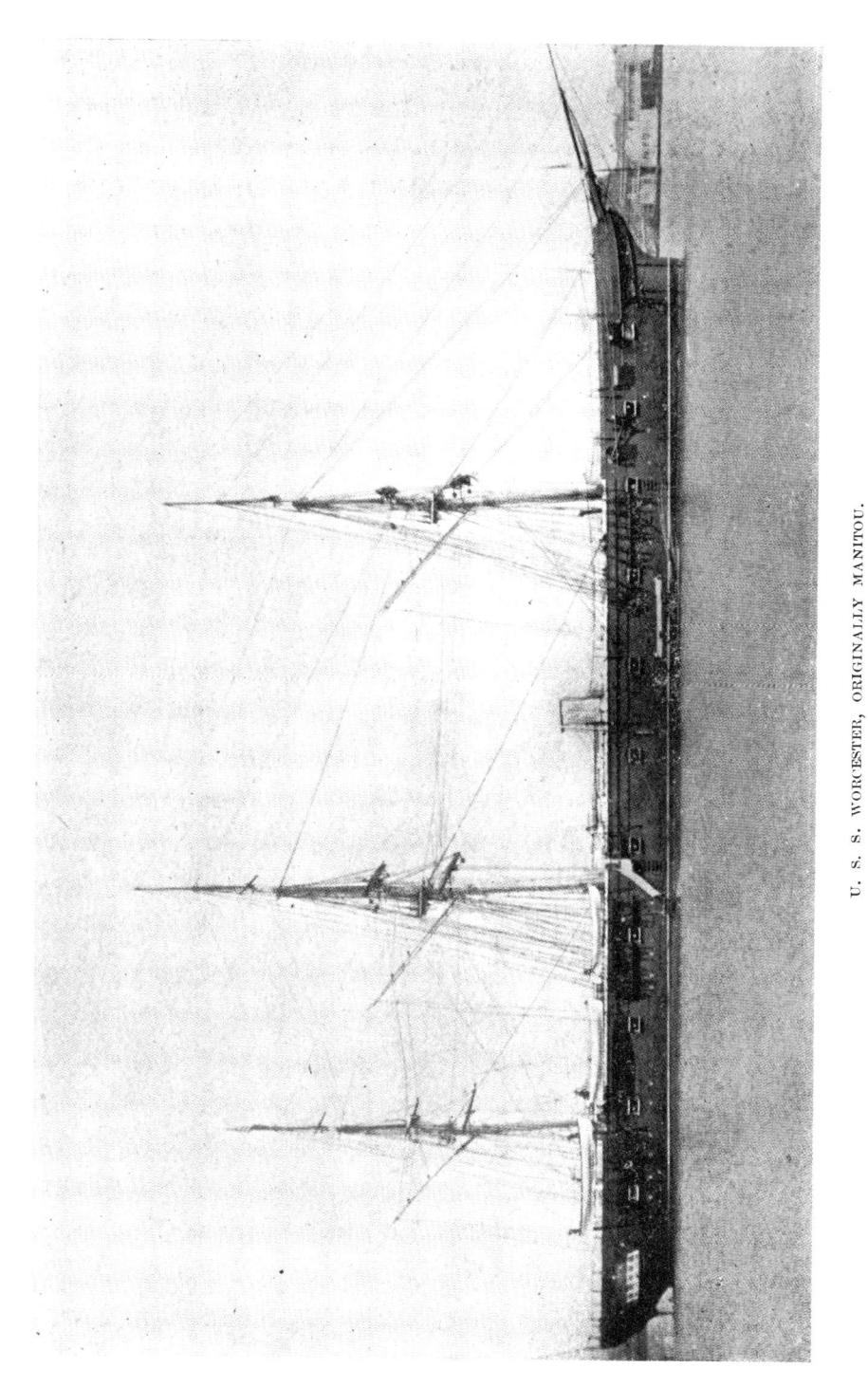

U. S. S. WORCESTER, ORIGINALLY MANITOU.
Typical of the *Contoocook* class of screw sloops.

arranged that two ships exactly alike should be built, one to be fitted with Isherwood's engines and the other with Ericsson's. The ships were the *Madawaska* and *Wampanoag*, built side by side in the Brooklyn navy yard by that master-builder, Naval Constructor B. F. Delano; they were 335 feet long, 45.2 feet beam, 4,200 tons displacement, and rated at 3,281 tons burden. Their boilers and all auxiliaries were the same. Isherwood's engines consisted of a pair of cylinders 100 inches in diameter and four feet stroke, arranged by means of huge wood-toothed gear wheels to make one double stroke of the piston for every 2.04 revolutions of the propeller shaft. Ericsson's cylinders were the same in number and dimensions as Isherwood's, but their arrangement was according to his patented vibrating lever type, connecting directly with the shaft. Ericsson's engines for the *Madawaska* were built at the Allaire Iron Works, New York, and Isherwood's for the *Wampanoag* at the Novelty Iron Works in the same city, the contract price in each case being $700,000.

Still another ship entered into this competition for speed was the *Chattanooga* by the Cramp & Sons Ship Building Co. of Philadelphia, which firm built the hull at their own yard and obtained the machinery by sub-contract from Merrick & Sons. The *Chattanooga* had a pair of back-acting engines, 84 inches diameter by 42 inch stroke, and 980 square feet of grate surface; her length was 315 feet; breadth 46 feet, and displacement 3,040 tons. The contract price for the vessel complete was $600,000. The three other cruisers not yet mentioned were the *Pomponoosuc*, *Ammonoosuc*, and *Neshaminy*, all of which had Isherwood engines precisely like those of the *Wampanoag*, and which cost $700,000 for each of the first two named and $680,000 for the *Neshaminy*. The machinery for the *Pomponoosuc* was built by the Corliss Steam Engine Co. of Providence, Rhode Island; that for the *Ammonoosuc* by George Quintard at the Morgan Iron Works, New York, and that for the *Neshaminy* by John Roach, New York. The *Ammonoosuc* was built at the Boston Navy Yard and the *Neshaminy* at the Philadelphia navy yard, these two being sister ships, and of about 4,000 tons displacement each. The *Pomponoosuc* was somewhat larger than the other two, but was never completed: under the name of *Connecticut* she stood in frame on the stocks at the Boston navy yard for many years and was finally broken up. The completion and speed trials of these cruisers did not occur until some time after the close of the war; the trials of some of them demonstrated a new possibility in war-ship building and were the occasion for one of the most remarkable professional triumphs ever achieved by an engineer, for which reasons the subject will be taken up in detail hereafter.

Towards the end of the year it was decided to build four double-turreted monitors to be heavily armed and armored and adapted to ocean cruising; battle-ships, in fact. These were big vessels (5,660 tons displacement) with big names—*Quinsigamond, Passaconaway, Kalamazoo*, and *Shackamaxon*. The hulls were put under construction at four different navy yards, wood being used, and all deck-plating, side armor, turrets, etc., obtained by contract with iron masters. In December the Bureau of Steam Engineering made contracts for their machinery, the contract price for that for the *Quinsigamond* and *Kalamazoo* being $580,000 each, and $590,000 each for the other two. The contracts called for twin screws, each screw shaft to be actuated by a pair of direct-acting horizontal engines with cylinders 46½ inches in diameter and 50 inches stroke; horizontal tubular boilers of not less than 900 square feet of grate surface for each vessel were specified. Designs for this machinery were furnished the contractors by Mr. John Baird, engineer, of New York city. None of the hulls were ever completed, but under changed names they stood on the stocks for a number of years and were eventually broken up. The following table shows the place of building of the ships and machinery:

OLD AND NEW NAME.	WHERE BUILT.	
	HULL.	MACHINERY.
Quinsigamond, (Oregon)..	Boston Navy Yard.	Atlantic Works, Boston,
Passaconoway, (Mass.).....	Kittery Navy Yard.	Delamater Iron Works, N.Y
Kalamazoo, (Colossus)......	New York Navy Yard.	" " " "
Shackamaxon, (Nebraska)	Philadelphia Navy Yard.	Pusey, Jones & Co. Wil'n Del.

In November of this year Mr. Isherwood entered into a contract with the Atlantic Works of Boston for a complete outfit of machinery for the big frigate *Franklin*, still unfinished at the Kittery navy yard. The contract called for a pair of back-acting engines with cylinders 68 inches in diameter and 42 inches stroke; four vertical water-tube boilers; two superheating boilers; a Sewell's surface condenser, and a detachable hoisting screw. The contract price was $440,000.

Under the old naval organization the ranks of line officers as established by law were, midshipman, master, lieutenant, commander, and captain. Staff officers held assimilated rank with these up to the rank of commander, as directed by Secretary Toucey's order of January 13, 1859. In 1862, as has been noted, the line ranks were increased by adding commodore and rear admiral at the top and inserting the intermediate ranks of ensign and lieutenant-commander, no change in the assimilated rank of the staff being made at that time. To remedy the practical reduction in rank of the staff thus occasioned the Secretary of the Navy issued an order, dated March 13, 1863, re-grading the relative rank of the staff corps, that part of the order especially interesting to engineers reading as follows:

"*Third Assistant Engineers* to rank with Midshipmen.

"*Second Assistant Engineers* to rank with Ensigns.

"*First Assistant Engineers* to rank with Masters.

"*Chief Engineers* to rank with Lieutenant Commanders for the first five years after promotion; after the first five years, with Commanders; and after fifteen years date of commission, to rank with Captains.

"*Fleet Engineer* to rank with the Captain.

"The *Fleet Captain* to be called the 'Chief of Staff,' and to take precedence of the Staff Officers of every grade.

"*Chiefs of Bureaux* of the Staff Corps to rank with Commodores, and to take precedence of each other according to their dates of commission as Surgeons, Paymasters, Naval Constructors, and Engineers, and not according to the date of appointment as Fleet Officer, or Chief of Bureau.

"*Fleet Staff Officers* to take precedence of Executive Officers."

August 11th, 1863, the Navy Department issued a circular directing that thereafter no more appointments of engineers for acting or volunteer service should be made until the applicant had passed satisfactory examinations before the chief engineer and surgeon of the navy yard where application for appointment was made.

The following is an extract from a general order issued by the department under date of September 16, 1863:

"Engineers will hereafter understand that the condition of the machinery under their charge on the arrival of the vessel from a cruise will be considered as a test of their efficiency and fidelity in the discharge of their duties; and that the result of the examination then made will determine whether they have discharged their duties in such manner as to deserve commendation, or have been so grossly negligent or incompetent as to render their expulsion from the service an act of justice to the public."

On the 22nd of December a new schedule of examinations for promotion of engineers in the regular service was promulgated by circular order, the standard being raised considerably above the requirements of the regulation on the subject issued in 1859. This order was specified to apply temporarily only, during the war, and to the examination of engineers in the squadrons.

CHAPTER XXIII.

> "Beware
> Of entrance to a quarrel; but being in,
> Bear't that the opposed may beware of thee."
> *Hamlet: Act 1, Sc. 3.*

1863—The Civil War, Continued—Controversy as to the Efficiency of Iron-Clads—Rear Admiral DuPont Reports Adversely to Them—Chief Engineer Stimers Reports in Their Favor—Rear Admiral DuPont Prefers Charges Against Chief Engineer Stimers—The Case Investigated by a Court of Inquiry.—Vindication of Mr. Stimers.

THIS history of the steam ships and engineers of the American navy would be incomplete without some reference to an internal strife in the service in the year 1863, growing out of the introduction of mastless war-vessels; a controversy that produced much ill feeling at the time, and one that would gladly be passed over in silence were it not for the fact that it was a matter of national interest and importance while it lasted and reduced itself to a clean-cut issue between the old and the new. It was in fact a struggle for existence almost on the part of the engineers and their machinery, opposed by the older, more picturesque, and more conservative sentiments that had formed the traditions and institutions of the old navy and sought to preserve them unchanged, regardless of the progress in all other things being effected through the agency of the steam engine.

The attack made upon Fort Sumter April 7th by Rear Admiral DuPont with a squadron of iron-clads has been described in a former chapter, and the fact that the Navy Department expected unqualified success from these vessels has been mentioned. Great, therefore, was the disappointment in Washington when DuPont's report of the engagement arrived with his announcement that he had determined not to renew the attack, as in his judgment it would convert a failure into a disaster. In a later report he enlarged upon what he considered the bad qualities of the monitors and said they could not be depended upon for protection against the armored vessels the Confederates were known to be fitting out at Charleston. It is possible that an element of distrust entered into the disappointment felt in Washington, for immediately after the receipt of the news from Charleston President Lincoln telegraphed DuPont to hold his position inside the bar near Charleston, or to return to it if he had left it and hold it until further orders. Beginning in this way a correspondence was opened between Rear Admiral DuPont and the Navy Department, gradually increasing in acerbity, and terminating in the admiral being relieved of his command and deprived of any further participation in the war.

The whole story of this affair was given to the public more than thirty years ago by the publication in book form, by virtue of a joint resolution of Congress, of five thousand copies of the documents in the case together with other interesting letters and reports relating to armored vessels. In the present chapter the author will confine himself almost entirely to the records as preserved in the public form referred to, not being disposed to enter upon any expression of his own views as to the motives and interests involved.

Chief Engineer Alban C. Stimers, as the general inspector of all iron-clad vessels of the Ericsson type built or building for the government, made frequent visits to the fleet off Charleston for purposes of examination and to direct repairs in case of damage. He was present at the first attack on Fort Sumter and made a visit of inspection to each of the monitors immediately after they came out of action. Returning to his office in New York a few days later he made, on the 14th of April, a detailed and critical report to the Secretary of the Navy of the result of his observations, his views as to the offensive and defensive properties of the monitors being very favorable to them and quite at variance with the opinions expressed in Rear Admiral DuPont's despatches. For this he was thereafter involved in the growing controversy and appeared in it to excellent advantage as the defender of the new type of war ship. Besides exercising an oversight upon the iron-clads, he had attempted while at Charleston on this occasion to induce the authorities to use an "obstruction remover" invented by Ericsson and with which Stimers had made some satisfactory experiments in the still waters of New York harbor. This was a huge raft, called by the sailors a "boot-jack" on the account of its form, intended to be pushed by a monitor and carrying an enormous elongated shell or torpedo at its forward edge designed to destroy by explosion any piling or other obstacles that might be encountered. Mr. Stimers referred with much regret in his report to the lack of success he had had in trying to convince the naval captains of the utility of this invention. It received a fair enough trial from Captain John Rodgers of the *Weehawken* soon afterward and was found so unmanageable in the rough water in which it had to operate that it may be put down as one of Ericsson's inventions that was more successful on a sheet of drawing paper than it was in actual practice afloat. Chief Engineer E. D. Robie, one of the most ingenious and capable engineers of the war period, was diverted from his regular duty as resident inspector of the building of the *Dictator* to go to Charleston to try to make this torpedo raft a success, and his failure to do so is good proof that it was impracticable.

On the 22nd of April Rear Admiral DuPont sent a long letter to the Navy Department complaining most bitterly of an account of the battle of April 7th which had been published in a Baltimore newspaper and in which it was stated that the weapons at DuPont's disposal were not used to advantage through disinclination induced by a dislike to Ericsson and his naval innovations. The complaint closed with the statement that the newspaper mentioned "seems to have had its own hostile proclivities heightened by an association with an officer of the service whose name appears frequently and prominently in its report in connexion with the repairs upon the iron-clads and in relation to the torpedoes and the rafts; I mean Mr. A. C. Stimers, a chief engineer in the naval service of the United States." The reply of Secretary Welles to this letter reminded the rear admiral that the press of the country had been generally lenient and indulgent toward him, and the censures, under a great disappointment, had been comparatively few. It told him that his suspicions regarding Mr. Stimers did that officer much injustice, and concluded with the comment:

"It has not appeared to me necessary to your justification that the powers of assault or resistance of our iron-clad vessels should be deprecated, and I regret that there should have been any labored effort for that purpose."

Rear Admiral DuPont replied at much length to this letter, making an especial point of objecting to the use of the word "lenient" as applicable to the opinions entertained by the public toward him; and so the matter went on; every letter written by each of the distinguished gentlemen tending more and more to estrange them. On the 22nd of May the Department sent the rear admiral an item cut from a Charleston newspaper in which it was stated that the guns of the *Keokuk* had been removed by the Confederates and taken to Charleston, and requested information regarding it. DuPont replied curtly that he knew nothing of it other than the statement of the newspaper; that he had little doubt of its truth; that the work must have been done in the night, and that he had offered Chief Engineer Robie every facility to blow up the *Keokuk*, with Mr. Ericsson's raft, but that officer found it too dangerous to use. This called forth an equally curt retort from Secretary Welles, who wrote, "The duty of destroying the *Keokuk*, and preventing her guns from falling into the hands of the rebels, devolved upon the commander-in-chief rather than on Engineer Robie. I do not understand that the operations were necessarily limited to Mr. Ericsson's raft, of which such apprehensions appear to have been entertained. The wreck and its important armament ought not to have been abandoned to the rebels, whose sleepless labors appear to have secured them a valuable prize."

In the latter part of June Rear Admiral Andrew H. Foote, who had achieved such success while commanding the Mississippi flotilla, was ordered to relieve DuPont, but being seized with a fatal illness the orders were transferred to Rear Admiral John A. Dahlgren, who took over the command of the South Atlantic blockading squadron on the 6th of July from DuPont, who was placed on waiting orders. The protracted siege of the Charleston forts at once inaugurated by Dahlgren has already been described.

Previous to this, on the 12th of May, Rear Admiral DuPont had requested the Navy Department to arrest Chief Engineer Stimers and send him to Charleston to be tried on the following charges:

Charges and Specifications of Charges Preferred by Rear Admiral Samuel F. DuPont, Commanding South Atlantic Blockading

Squadron, against *Chief Engineer Alban C. Stimers*, United States Navy.

CHARGE FIRST: Falsehood.

"*Specification.*—In this: that between the eleventh and fifteenth days of April, eighteen hundred and sixty-three, the said Alban C. Stimers, a chief engineer in the United States navy, being then on board the steamship *Arago*, by the authority and direction of Rear Admiral Samuel F. DuPont, commanding the South Atlantic blockading squadron—the said *Arago* being on her passage from Port Royal, South Carolina, to New York City, via Charleston bar—did, at the table of said steamer, in the presence of officers of said steamer and other persons, a number of whom were correspondents of the public press, and at divers other times during the passage of said steamer, falsely assert, knowing the same to be untrue, that he was told by one or more of the commanders of the iron-clad vessels engaged in the attack upon the forts and batteries in Charleston harbor, on the seventh day of April, eighteen hundred and sixty-three, that the attack of that day ought to have been renewed; and that they did further state to him that the said iron-clad vessels were in fit condition to renew it; and the said Alban C. Stimers did further falsely assert, knowing the same to be untrue, that several of the commanders of the said iron-clad vessels had said to him in his presence and hearing that they, the said commanders, were, after the attack aforesaid, ' hot for renewing the engagement,' or words to that effect.

" CHARGE SECOND: Conduct unbecoming an officer of the navy.

"*Specification.*—In this: that between the eleventh and fifteenth days of April eighteen hundred and sixty-three, the said Alban C. Stimers, a chief engineer in the United States navy, being then on board the steamship *Arago*, by the authority and direction of Rear Admiral S. F. DuPont, commanding South Atlantic blockading squadron—the said *Arago* being on her passage from Port Royal, South Carolina, to New York City *via* Charleston bar—did, at the table of said steamer, in the presence of officers of the said steamer and other persons, a number of whom were correspondents of the public press, and at divers other times during the passage of the said steamer, with the intent to disparage and injure the professional reputation of his superior officer, Rear Admiral S. F. DuPont, criticise and condemn, in terms unbecoming the circumstances and his position as an officer of the navy, the professional conduct of his superior officer, Rear Admiral S. F. DuPont, in the attack upon the forts and batteries in Charleston harbor on the seventh day of April, eighteen hundred and sixty-three, and did, with the like intent, knowingly make false statements, using, among other improper and unfounded expressions, words in substance as follows: 'That the monitors were in as good condition on Wednesday, the eighth day of April, eighteen hundred and sixty-three, after they had undergone some slight repairs, to renew the attack, as they had been to commence it the day before; that they could go into Charleston in spite of guns, torpedoes, and obstructions, and that Rear Admiral DuPont was too much prejudiced against the monitors to give them a fair trial.'

Instead of sending the accused officer to DuPont for trial by court-martial the department convened a court of inquiry at the Brooklyn navy yard to investigate the truth of the charges and report regarding them. This court was composed of Rear Admiral Francis H. Gregory, Rear Admiral Silas H. Stringham, and Commodore William C. Nicholson, all old and distinguished officers, but by training and professional associations more apt to lean towards DuPont's side of the issue than to feel any sympathy for Stimers and the mechanical innovations represented by him. Mr. Edwin M. Stoughton was named as judge advocate, but that gentleman refused to act, and appeared in the case as counsel for Stimers. Judge Edward Pierrepont of New York was next appointed judge advocate, and he too refused to accept the office, which was then conferred upon Mr. Hiram L. Sleeper. The list of witnesses named by the prosecution included the officers and a number of passengers of the *Arago* and the commanders and some other officers of the rron-clads off Charleston.

The court met at the Marine Barracks, Brooklyn, June 5th, and continued in session for more than four months, with some lengthy adjournments to allow of the taking of testimony of witnesses on duty with the fleet at Charleston, which was done by means of written interrogatories and cross-interrogatories according to the terms of a formal stipulation between the judge advocate and the counsel for the accused which was spread on the pages of the record. The testimony presented by the prosecution was generally favorable to Mr. Stimers and failed to substantiate the charges and specifications made against him. As printed in the public document before referred to as the source of information for the facts presented in this chapter it is too long to admit of an analytical review in this place, which review is therefore omitted in favor of the careful one made by Chief Engineer Stimers in his written defense; a most manly and straightforward argument which was submitted to the court on the 19th of October and is here reproduced in full:

"*May it please this honorable court:*

" The testimony introduced by the Judge Advocate to sustain the charges made against me by Rear Admiral DuPont is now closed. Acting in view of the proof thus placed before the court I deem it wholly unnecessary to offer evidence in reply. The very foundation on which these charges must rest is wanting, and hardly an attempt has been made to supply it. They were carelessly, if not recklessly, made by a high officer of the Government, willing to give them the sanction of his name, apparently without inquiring whether they were capable of proof, or founded upon worthless rumor. Much time has been uselessly spent in apparent efforts to prove them; but anyone attentively reading the evidence discovers that the real purpose has been not to establish the charges in question, but to justify their author in failing effectively to use the formidable means for destroying the defences of Charleston, which our Government in its confidence and hope had lavished upon him. That I am not unjust or uncharitable in making this suggestion will be manifest from an examination of the charges and proof which I will now proceed to make."

"1st. The first specification charges me with having, whilst on board the steamer *Arago*, on her voyage from Charleston to New York, at table, in presence of her officers and other persons, a number of whom were correspondents of the public press, falsely asserted, knowing the same to be untrue, that I was told by one or or more of the commanders of the iron-clads engaged in the attack on Charleston that it ought to have been renewed; that the vessels were in a fit condition to renew it; and that several of the commanders had said to me that they were hot for renewing the engagement.

"A person observant of Christian precepts, considerate of his duty towards a fellow man, or actuated by self respect, would, before deliberately framing a charge calculated to consign a brother officer to disgrace and infamy, have inquired carefully into its truth, and the means of establishing it. Indeed, he would hardly have been content to make it before conversing personally with those capable of proving it; and then a just man would have withheld the accusation, so painful for a gentleman to bear, until satisfied that his witnesses were entitled to full credit. The course which my accuser has seen fit to pursue presents a wide departure from the path thus indicated. The names of persons who were on board the *Arago* during the voyage were appended as witnesses to the charges made, and most of them have been examined. It appears that I sat at the public table of the steamer in the immediate neighborhood of several other persons, all no doubt accessible to my accuser, or to those seeking to support the charges. If, therefore, I, during the voyage, used the language imputed to me, it was susceptible to easy proof. Not a particle of testimony to that effect has, however, been furnished. No one pretends I ever said that any commander of the iron-clads had stated to me either that the attack on Charleston ought to have been renewed, or that the iron-clads were in a fit condition to do so, or that their commanders were hot for renewing the engagement. No language bearing the least resemblance to that charged is proven to have been uttered by me at any time; and I am bound to assume that neither of the witnesses named ever stated otherwise than they have sworn here. If not, then upon what information could the charges in question have been framed? Was it believed that they could be proven? And if not, were they wantonly made, so that upon pretense of sustaining them, the naval inactivity, painful to a whole nation, might be justified by proof quite irrelevant to the charges being tried, and therefore quite likely to pass uncontradicted by me?

"2d. The second charge made against me is for conduct unbecoming an officer of the navy, and specifies, in substance, that at the table of said steamer, and elsewhere on board of her, during the passage, I criticised and condemned, in terms unbecoming the circumstances, the professional conduct of Rear Admiral DuPont, by stating that the monitors were in as good condition on the 8th day of April, 1863, after they had undergone some slight repairs, to renew the attack, as they had been to commence it the day before. That they could go into Charleston in spite of guns, torpedoes and obstructions; but that Admiral DuPont was too much prejudiced against the monitors to give them a fair trial.

"Now if, under the circumstances, I had stated all that is charged, it would, in my judgment, have been no more than I was authorized to say. I had been charged by the government with the important duty of inspecting the construction and armament of the vessels whilst they were being made. They were new in the history of the world; but in the contest between the *Monitor* and *Merrimac* although the latter on the day previous had defied a fleet of our largest frigates, carrying an armament fifty times greater than the *Monitor*, destroying some and threatening all with the same fate, yet the *Monitor*, working her two eleven inch guns behind an invulnerable shield, tested her powers, offensive and defensive, by so terrible an ordeal that intelligent and unprejudiced men here and in Europe from that hour saw that naval supremacy must be maintained, if at all, by abandoning wooden ships and adopting those which the genius, engineering skill, and ripe, practical knowledge of their author had taught the world how to construct. My knowledge of this class of war vessels had been acquired not only by watching and inspecting their construction step by step, but under the orders of the government I had enjoyed the good fortune of participating in the contest to which I have referred, and which had developed the capacity of the *Monitor* system to sustain unharmed the fire of heavy guns at short range, and at the same time to inflict deadly injuries upon an adversary's ship of great power heavily sheathed in iron. With an experience thus gained I might, as I think, have justly claimed the right to express an opinion as to the value and capacities of the monitors, even had this differed from the views entertained by Rear Admiral DuPont, whose knowledge concerning them was probably derived from casual inspection and the reports of others. Moreover, I was charged by the Government with the duty of proceeding to Charleston to watch and report the performance of these vessels in action, to assist in maintaining them in readiness for battle, and afford to the officers having them in charge such information as might be needful.

"In addition to all this it may here be proper to say that at a great expense shells had been devised by Captain Ericsson, the author of the Monitor system, which, in connexion with rafts to be attached to the bows of vessels, were to be used for removing by means of explosive force, obstructions within the harbor, and by firing torpedoes supposed to be sunk by the enemy in the track of our advancing fleet. The effectiveness of these shells had been so tested by me, before they were sent to Admiral DuPont, as to make it clear to my mind and to that of the government that they would be practically safe and capable of clearing the track of battle. I strongly urged Admiral DuPont to use these shells, and requested permission to participate in the action of the 7th, on board a monitor which should be thus armed. The privilege was denied to me, and although in view of supposed obstructions, I had expressed to Admiral DuPont and to his officers the opinion that the monitors could successfully pass them, my confidence in expressing it was greatly strengthened by, and somewhat founded upon, the assumption that these shells were to be employed, and this the Admiral knew. He nevertheless declined to order their employment and thus was lost to the government and nation a powerful means of penetrating to the cradle of this great rebellion.

"Under these circumstances, and well aware that the government had expected much from the attack upon Charleston with the abundant means furnished to the rear admiral commanding, I was greatly disappointed that the important instruments I have mentioned were not used by him, especially as I believed (an as an earnest of my conviction had offered to hazard my life and limb) that with shells attached to the monitors they could pass all obstructions and hold the city of Charleston at their mercy.

"All this was certainly calculated to awaken in my mind criticism upon the conduct of Rear Admiral Dupont, which, as the evidence shows, I refrained from expressing, maintaining a reserve, not merely respectful to him, but calculated to defend him from the censures freely and openly cast upon him for failing to renew the attack of the 7th of April.

"I will now briefly examine the proof introduced to maintain the second charge, the mere reading of which will show that even if I had said all that is charged against me, it was but the statement of views which, if honest, I had a right in common with all other persons to express. Entertaining the opinion, and officially reporting it as I did to Rear Admiral DuPont, that the monitors were on the 8th substantially, for practical purposes, as fit to renew the attack as they had been to make it on the day previous. I was bound neither by courtesy nor by any rule of the service with which I am acquainted, to withhold or conceal it; and believing, as I certainly did, that the monitors, with the rafts and shells attached, could have gone into Charleston in spite of guns, torpedoes and obstructions, I was equally entitled to state, in respectful language, that opinion also; and, moreover, I think the disrespect, if there be any, in imputing to Rear Admiral DuPont prejudice against the monitors, was so slight that his self-respect can hardly have been increased by noticing it. Indeed, whilst there is no proof in the case that I ever charged him with entertaining this prejudice, and whilst by asserting that I did, he, by implication at least, denies the existence of the prejudice so imputed, the evidence introduced on his behalf very clearly established that he was prepossessed against them, for Captain Drayton in substance declares *he don't think Admiral DuPont had a high opinion of the monitors, and that he could not have had after reading his (Drayton's) reports concerning them, made before the fight.*

"What these reports were does not appear, but that the witness believed he had succeeded in instilling into the admiral's mind his own unfavorable opinion is quite clear.

"The proof, however, fails to show that I made the statement charged against me. The evidence on this subject consists of the testimony of Captain Gadsden, of the *Arago*, and of several other persons who were on board of that steamer during her voyage from Charleston to New York. He says in substance that I stated that the monitors had received no serious injury; that they could be repaired in a few hours; that the trial ought not to condemn them; that they had not had a fair trial; that with the shells attached to them they could go in. He further swore that I said the *officers* of the navy were prejudiced against the monitors, but that I mentioned no one in particular, and did not reflect upon Admiral DuPont.

"The purser of the *Arago* testified that I said the officers of the navy were rather prejudiced against them, but that I spoke of Admiral DuPont personally in the highest terms. Mr. Colwell swore that those on board the *Arago* were much excited about the fight at Charleston, and condemned the admiral for his failure; but he did not intimate that I took part in such conversation, stating only that I said the monitors were very little injured, and were repaired in about five hours; that I was respectful in my remarks concerning Admiral DuPont; and although this witness said he at one time was under the impression that I had said the admiral was prejudiced against the monitors, he afterwards stated that I might not have said so, but that as the passengers generally united in condemning him, the witness may have confounded their statements with mine.

"Mr. Fulton, in his testimony, states that my conversations with him on the subject of the attack were private, and in an undertone, and that I said I had sometimes retired to my stateroom to avoid being questioned; that I said the attack was not an earnest one, and expressed disappointment that the shells were not employed, but did not say the monitors could have entered the harbor without them, nor that the admiral was prejudiced against the monitors, but that I did say he would have renewed the attack but for the influence of some of those who were.

"Mr. Mars, a passenger, testified that I appeared not to wish to speak on the subject of the attack, and that although he sat opposite to me at the table, he did not hear me say that the admiral was prejudiced.

"Having thus failed to prove that I had uttered any of the language as charged, and it appearing upon the evidence that I had spoken of Rear Admiral DuPont in high terms, studiously refraining from talking upon the subject of the attack, it appeared to me remarkable that the prosecution, instead of acknowledging the injustice of these charges, should persist in calling witnesses to prove that the monitors were seriously injured in their attack upon the forts, and could not have renewed it without probable disaster.

"Whilst this attempt has signally failed, it has nevertheless disclosed the real purpose of this prosecution to have been, not an inquiry into any language or conduct of mine, but, under that pretext, an effort to justify the failure by Rear Admiral DuPont, which had attracted the observation of the world, by condemning as inadequate the instruments which a liberal government had placed in his hands.

"His desire to justify himself was natural, but that he should have been willing to achieve even his own vindication by making and persisting in prosecuting unfounded charges against a brother officer, is extraordinary. How utterly he has failed to accomplish this a brief examination of the proofs will show.

"It appears from these that before the attack was made it was supposed by Admiral DuPont that torpedoes had been placed in the channel along which his fleet must pass. That network had been suspended from buoys designed to entangle the propellers and thus prevent their action, and that for some purpose piles had been placed across the middle ground to obstruct the entrance of monitors from that direction. It moreover appears, especially from a careful reading of the deposition of Commander C. R. P. Rodgers, the admiral's fleet captain, that no additional information upon either of these subjects was obtained by means of the attack. After that was over, the existence of torpedoes, of network and the purpose of the piles were shrouded in the same mystery as before. It was ascertained, however, that if torpedoes lurked in the channel, they were probably harmless, for none had been exploded; and that they were incapable of being fired is shown by the letter referred to by this witness, written by a rebel officer in Fort Sumter, stating that the effort to explode a torpedo whilst directly under the hull of the *Ironsides* had failed.

"We must therefore accept it as established, that as no information was obtained during the conflict which could be used to strengthen the surmises before existing as to the character of these obstructions, their supposed existence could not have afforded ground for declining to renew the engagement which was not equally good as an objection against having made it at all; and this being so, we must look for some other reason for the failure of the admiral to offer battle on the 8th, in pursuance of his declared intention, when he gave the signal for the monitors to haul off on the previous day.

"It is true that some of this testimony conveys the impression that the fear of encountering these supposed obstructions was a controlling element in the admiral's mind in forming the determination not to renew the attack; but in this there is evident mistake, for a brave and intelligent commander would hardly be so fearful of obstructions which might or might not be real, as to abandon a great enterprise without practical effort to learn whether obstacles to its achievement existed or not. Against such a suspicion I feel disposed to defend Admiral DuPont, and hence am constrained to look elsewhere for some reason why he failed to renew an attack which, if persisted in, might have succeeded. His witnesses on this subject next point to the injuries sustained by the monitors, and to their alleged inability to withstand a repetition of the terrible fire to which they were subjected on the 7th. A glance at the testimony will show how utterly unfounded is this effort at an excuse, whilst it will also establish to the satisfaction of intelligent and unprejudiced men that the capacity of the monitors to resist unharmed the most terrible fire from guns and rifles of the heaviest calibre, has never been overstated. It appears from the testimony of the fleet captain that the fire to which they were exposed was by far more terrific than that which he or anyone connected with the fleet had ever before seen. From fifty to one hundred rebel guns, of heavier calibre than were ever before employed against ships-of-war, were brought to bear upon the monitors at the same time, and probably many more. The *Patapsco* was struck by fifty-one shots, twenty-one of which hit the turret, and fifteen or more of these—all heavy ball—struck it within the period of five minutes, and yet at 8:30 o'clock on the evening of the 7th she was in a fit condition to renew the engagement.

The *Nantucket* was struck fifty-three times; and although the mechanism which worked her XV-inch gun was disordered, this was repaired on the 8th. Captain Drayton states that the top of the pilot house of the *Passaic* was raised up by a shot, but it is quite evident, from his account of it, that this in no manner disabled the vessel, whilst it hardly increased the chances of danger to those within. It sufficiently appears that the *Weehawken* was fit to have renewed the engagement on the following day, although she was struck several times on her side armor in nearly the same place.

"Without following this subject further in detail, it is sufficient to state, what appears from the proof, that each and all of the monitors were in fighting condition within twenty-four hours after they came out of battle, whilst the injuries received by them were so trifling, when the terrible means employed for inflicting them were considered, that they may be pronounced substantially invulnerable to the strongest artillery. But one life was lost on board of them during the conflict; and whilst one or two of the turrets were by the impact of shot partially prevented from turning until repaired, it should be remembered that, turning by their rudders, each could at all times present her guns to the enemy at pleasure. Indeed, it was partly by this means that the guns of the *Monitor* were brought to bear on the *Merrimac* in that first engagement of ironclads to which I have before referred. One of the witnesses has suggested that if other shots had struck in the same place as previous ones, the armor might have been endangered. Entertaining, as I do, the opposite opinion, I would suggest that even if the witness was correct, he anticipates a hazard too remote to be much apprehended: for it is well known that the chances that one shot will strike exactly where a previous one had hit, are very slight.

"The *Keokuk*, an ironclad vessel, but not built upon the plan of the monitors, was almost immediately disabled, having fired but three guns at the enemy; and the *Ironsides*, a much stronger and better armed ship, although she escaped serious injury, no doubt owed this to the temporary means employed to strengthen her before going into action, and to the care exercised in keeping her at a great distance from the enemy's guns.

"That this distance was maintained is apparent from the testimony of the fleet captain, who stated in substance, that when the order was signalled for the monitors to retire from the conflict they *all passed the Ironsides in moving out*. This shows that they were inside of her and much closer to the enemy's batteries; and how much nearer may be inferred from his cross-examination, in which he states that twenty minutes may have elapsed before the last of the monitors passed by. They engaged the batteries within six hundred yards, and it need hardly be suggested, that no ship not constructed upon their plan could have lived under the heavy fire to which, at that distance, they were subjected.

I here close what I have thought it well to say concerning this attempt by Rear.Admiral DuPont to justify his inaction and failure by attacking that system of war vessels which has already, in my opinion, given us a more effective fleet than is possessed by any other nation. A judicious use of these vessels might have transmitted his name with honor far into the future. An assault upon the system can but recoil upon the assailant. From me it needs no defense. Time and battle will but confirm the opinions I have expressed concerning it, whilst its adoption by the nations of the world will bear unfailing testimony to the great skill and foresight of its contriver.

"With these remarks I submit my case to the just consideration of this honorable Court.

"Very respectfully,
(Signed) "ALBAN C. STIMERS,
"Chief Engineer, United States Navy.
"Naval Lyceum, New York, October 19, 1863."

The next day, October 20, the court met for its last session and added the following finding to its record :

"The court having diligently and fully inquired into the matters embraced in the specifications of charges in this case, hereby report that, in their opinion, there is no necessity or propriety for further proceedings in the case."

Rear Admiral DuPont was an eminent and capable naval officer of the old school, but of too long service and of too fixed ideas to yield before a development that entirely upset all the naval methods of his lifetime, and by standing in the way of the march of progress, instead of gracefully stepping aside and admitting the competence of a mechanical generation, he was run over and humiliated by a power more potent than he had imagined. In a time of peace when the public is indifferent to the navy and its advancement the conservative opinions of its veteran officers usually prevail and prevent changes in methods or *material* that involve any great departure from what has existed so long as to become custom, but in time of war sentiment and dogma must yield to practical utility, and the irresistible power of public opinion will always force this submission. Assistant Secretary of the Navy, Fox, was from his own training probably the most competent official connected with the Navy Department during the war to judge of the characteristics of the officers of the navy. In a letter written by him to John Ericsson in 1864 he summed up in the following manner the actual attitude of Rear Admiral DuPont towards the new iron-clad war-vessels:

"He is of a wooden age, eminent in that, but in an engineering age behind the time. You were always opposed to attacking forts, but DuPont despised the vessels and the brain that conceived them."

The "old school" of navalism means a great deal unknown to the officers of the present generation if all the testimony of the past may be depended upon. A very curious condition of affairs was allowed to grow up in our navy during that long period of comparative inactivity, interrupted only by the Mexican War, which intervened between the end of the last war with Great Britain and the outbreak of the rebellion. "The commodore of the period was an august personage who went to sea in a great flag-ship, surrounded by a conventional grandeur which was calculated to inspire a becoming respect and awe. As the years of peace rolled on, this figure became more and more august, more and more conventional. The fatal defects of the system were not noticed until 1861, when the crisis came, and the service was unprepared to meet it."[1] Surrounded thus with much of the pomp and dignity of a court and invested with what some of the admirers of that old *regime* have been pleased to call "kingly power," it is no wonder that the average commodore lost sight of his true relation to the civil head of the navy and, unconsciously perhaps, came to regard him as merely a secretary, in fact as well as in title, interposed somewhat unneces-

[1] Professor J. R. Soley, in Battles and Leaders of the Civil War: Vol. I, p. 623.

sarily between himself and the chief executive. Instances are not lacking of commanders-in-chief of squadrons abroad ignoring or mis-interpreting orders sent them from the department, and there is at least one case on record of a commodore issuing an order, upon taking command of a squadron in a remote part of the world, abolishing all regulations of the Navy Department except such as had been approved by the President.

Under these influences and surroundings Samuel F. DuPont had acquired step by step his naval education and beliefs through all the monotonous years from a midshipman in 1815 to within two numbers of being the senior rear admiral in 1863. The sentiments expressed by him in his correspondence with the Secretary of the Navy are therefore not surprising, although they would be actually startling if attempted at the present day. When the court of inquiry had finally disposed of the Stimers case, DuPont, under date of October 22nd, broke the silence that he had observed since being detached from his command and sent a letter to the department that is one of the most instructive documents ever made public, its expressions providing us with a perfect mirror of the mind of the old navy. A few of them are repeated as illustrative examples.

"It is with profound regret that I perceive in your despatch of the 26th of June a reiteration of the charges and reproaches of previous despatches and in your silence since, during a period of three months, a resolution not to recall them. My last hope of justice at the hands of the department is therefore extinguished.

"If I have failed in my duty I am liable to trial, but insulting imputations in official despatches are grave wrongs, perpetrated on the public records to my permanent injury.

"The remedy which the law would afford me against a superior officer indulging in the language of your despatches does not exist against the civil head of the department.

"I was aware of the visit of the Assistant Secretary to Charleston, but I learn with surprise from your despatch that, without a commission in the navy, he *commanded* the expedition which witnessed the bombardment of Sumter without relieving it.

"I have no desire to question the power of the department to relieve me at its discretion, but its order of the 3d of June assigns causes which do not exist, and ascribed to me opinions which I had neither expressed nor entertained."

Secretary Welles, after a delay of about two weeks, replied to this letter without resentment, reviewing the whole subject at great length and giving reasons in justification of the course pursued by the department that were considerate, even if not necessary. The general tone of the communication impresses one as conveying fatherly sorrow rather than the expression of offended authority, the only passage in it that may fairly be considered harsh being the following review of DuPont's operations at Charleston :

"You disapproved of the occupancy of the harbor, yet I am not aware that you ever caused or attempted to have a reconnoissance of the obstructions or any examination of the harbor made before the attack, nor am I aware that you have ever offered an excuse for this omission. After the attack was made you were dissatisfied with the *Ironsides*—dissatisfied with the monitors—dissatisfied with Chief Engineer Stimers, against whom you prepared charges and desired that he might be arrested and sent to you for trial, he having expressed his surprise that you should abandon the assault on so brief an effort—dissatisfied with Surgeon Kershner, whom you court-martialed for a similar offense—dissatisfied with Mr. Fulton, the special agent of the Post Office Department, for his criticisms on your movements and acts—dissatisfied with the President for his telegram, and dissatisfied with the department for not more promptly and formally acknowledging and publishing your reports.

"If these complaints and reports, wherein the admiral of the squadron devoted so large a portion of his time to his personal matters and so little towards marshalling his force for the occupation of the harbor of Charleston and the capture of the city, were not received with the patience to which they were entitled, it was my misfortune. I do not deny that it would have been more acceptable to the department to have witnessed the zeal manifested in hunting down newspaper editors, engineers, and surgeons, directed against rebel enemies and to the destruction of their works."

This correspondence terminated the controversy and also concluded Rear Admiral DuPont's active participation in the executive administration of the operations of the Navy Department, for he remained unemployed, on waiting orders, until his death, which occured in June, 1865, soon after the close of the war. It was the fault of the system under whose influence his life had been passed rather than from any personal short-coming of his own that the last years of his life were embittered. "There was no more accomplished officer in our naval service than Admiral DuPont, no man of nobler personality, but he was the very incarnation of naval exclusiveness and prejudice against innovation, and the introduction of the monitors into our navy gave a shock to his sensibilities from which they never recovered. It may be that he was expected to accomplish with them more than was possible in his attack upon Charleston, but he was disposed to exaggerate their deficiencies and to criticise them in a spirit of unfriendliness that arrayed against him the active hostility of their champions."[1]

---

[1] W. C. Church, Life of John Ericsson; Vol. II., p. 64-65.

CHAPTER XXIV

"In the beauties of the lilies Christ was born beyond the sea,
With a glory in his bosom that transfigures you and me;
As he died to make men holy, let us die to make men free;
While God is marching on."
JULIA WARD HOWE; *Battle-hymn of the Republic.*

1864.—The Civil War, Continued—Confederate Successes in the Use of Torpedoes—Blowing up of the Sloop-of-War HOUSATONIC—Minor Naval Operations—Boiler Explosion on the CHENANGO—The KEARSARGE-ALABAMA Fight—The Great Battle in Mobile Bay—Loss of the TECUMSEH—Capture of the Privateer FLORIDA by the WACHUSETT—The Gunboat OTSEGO sunk by a Torpedo—First Attack on Fort Fisher.

NAVAL operations during 1864 were marked by a number of minor disasters and by several decisive victories, the general results of the year being most favorable to the reputation of the service. The first mishap of the year occurred to the small side-wheel steamer *Underwriter*, prominently identified with the service of holding possession of the North Carolina Sounds during the two preceding years. About 2 A. M. February 2nd this vessel, while lying at anchor in the Neuse River near Newburn, was boarded in the dark by a force of over one hundred men in boats and overpowered after a resistance of fifteen minutes in which her commander, Acting Master Westervelt, was killed, and the crew, numbering only forty people all told, became prisoners of war. After taking off the prisoners and plundering the vessel she was set on fire and destroyed. Acting Third Assistant Engineer George E. Allen and twenty-two of the men escaped in a peculiar manner due to the haste of the enemy and the courage and presence of mind of Mr. Allen. They were all driven into one boat, the last to shove off from the *Underwriter*, and were soon surprised to hear the guard in charge of it hailing the boat ahead for assistance, it appearing that in their hurry to get away from the ship the Confederates had all embarked in the first boats, leaving only two to go in the last one, in which were over twenty prisoners. Quickly realizing the situation, Mr. Allen snatched the cutlass from the belt of the guard near him and thus made himself master of the boat, the other guard jumping overboard and swimming for another boat which had turned back. By hard pulling on the part of the men, Mr. Allen safely conducted his captured boat to the Federal fortifications at Newbern and at daylight reported with his party on board the *Lockwood*, lying at that place. The other officers and the remainder of the crew became prisoners of war.

About 9 o'clock the evening of February 17th a Confederate "david," as the nearly immersed cigar-shaped torpedo boats of the enemy came to be called from the name of one of the first of them, just as monitor became a generic term, approached the sloop-of-war

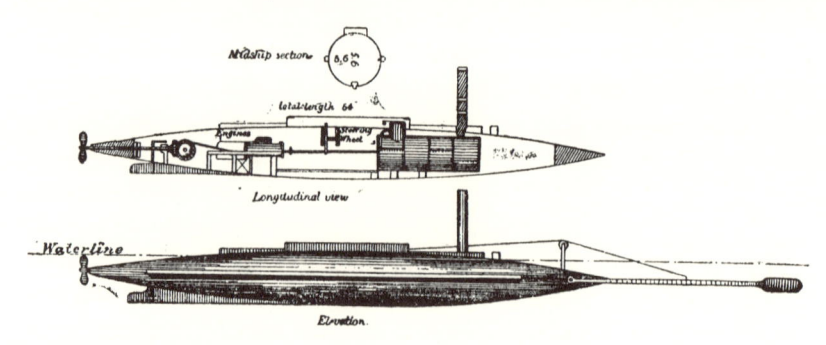

Confederate "david," or torpedo boat. From a drawing by Second Assistant Engineer W. S. Smith for a report of Rear Admiral Dahlgren.

Housatonic, lying on the outer blockade off Charleston, and was not discovered until so close as to explode a torpedo under the *Housatonic*, sinking her. Ensign Hazeltine, Captain's Clerk Muzzy, and three men were drowned, all others of the ship's company saving themselves by taking to the rigging, which remained above water, the boats of the *Canandaigua* rescuing them soon afterward. The torpedo boat itself also went to the bottom. This disaster was due to the excellence in the use of torpedoes which had been arrived at by the Confederates, they, in the absence of ships to carry on naval operations, being forced to wage war with these weapons then novel and unusual. The use of torpedoes was by no means a new thing, but it was a practice rather abhorrent to the minds of trained fighting men, and owed its development by the naval officers of the South to necessity rather than desire.

One of the first successful uses of the torpedo in the Civil War was the blowing up of the iron-clad gun-boat *Cairo* in the Mississippi River in 1862, by a Confederate naval officer who had been taught less furtive methods of warfare in the old navy, and who was so doubtful of the propriety of the mode of attack directed by him that he described his feelings, when he saw that the *Cairo* was actually going to sink, as much the same as those of a schoolboy at seeing serious results follow from something begun in sport. The sentiment in the navy regarding torpedoes at that time is well shown by some comments of Rear Admiral Farragut, who, reporting to the department in May, 1864, that he intended to make use of them to be on an equality with his enemy, felt it necessary to excuse himself by explaining:

"Torpedoes are not so agreeable when used on both sides; therefore I have reluctantly brought myself to it.

"I have always deemed it unworthy of a chivalrous nation, but it does not do to give your enemy such a decided superiority over you."

In the hands of the Confederates torpedo warfare was considerably advanced and torpedoes became the most formidable weapon against which our naval vessels had to contend, as well as the cause of the greater part of the disasters suffered by the Federal navy during the rebellion. The present high development of torpedoes as a weapon for naval warfare may be directly traced to the impetus gained by its successes during the Civil War, which not only illustrated its great possibilities but also overcame any chivalric objections to its use which may have been formerly entertained by naval officers.

The evening of April 18th another "david" passed through the iron-clad blockade line off Charleston and made for the big frigate *Wabash* lying in the outer line. In this case, however, it was discovered in time for the *Wabash* to get under way and man the battery, her fire either destroying or driving off the small but much-feared adversary. On the sixth of May the ferry gunboat *Commodore Jones* while near Four Mile Creek in the James River ran upon a moored torpedo and met with utter destruction, about one-half of her crew being either killed or wounded. The next day the gunboat

Shawsheen while searching for torpedoes near Turkey Bend in the same locality fell a victim to exposed machinery and was destroyed by a battery suddenly unmasked in the woods, the first shots from which disabled her by exploding the steam drum and breaking the walking-beam of the engine. The officers and crew became prisoners and the vessel was burned by her captors.

A daring expedition, although on a small scale, was conducted in March by Acting Master Champion of the *Pawnee*, who, with the tug gunboat *Columbine* commanded by Acting Ensign Sanborn, and a party of volunteers from the *Pawnee*, proceeded up the St. Johns River in Florida, captured two steamers, a large quantity of cotton, provisions, and army supplies, and returned safely to the ship after having been for two weeks in the enemy's country and penetrated the river over two hundred miles. The volunteer party from the *Pawnee* consisted of Second Assistant Engineer Alfred Adamson, Third Assistant Engineer Arthur Price, an acting master's mate, and twelve men, all embarked at first in a launch towed by the *Columbine*, but transferred the second day to a steamer, the *General Sumter*, they had captured in Great Lake George. Two days later the *Sumter* encountered and captured the steamer *Hattie* in Deep Creek and converted her into a transport for carrying cotton, machinery, and other contraband of war seized at the river stations visited. When taken, the *Hattie* was found disabled by the Confederates, who in abandoning her had carried off all the valves of the feed and other pumps about the engines and boilers, but the ingenuity of Messrs. Adamson and Price overcame this defect and soon restored the steamer to a useful condition. Without any means of doing better, they hastily made valves of wood which were found to answer the purpose and enabled the vessel to do service until time permitted more permanent repairs.

Two months' later in the same river the *Columbine* met the fate that had overtaken so many of the purchased steamers with exposed machinery and fell into the hands of the enemy. She was attacked by a battery hidden in the underbrush along the bank and almost at the first fire rendered helpless by a shot cutting the main steam pipe, her surrender following as the natural result of her inability to move into a position to use her guns or get out of the range of fire. Her people were taken prisoners and the enemy burned their prize without taking time to remove anything of value. The senior engineer of the *Columbine* was referred to in the following complimentary manner in the commanding officer's report of the disaster: "I take great pleasure in recommending to your favorable notice the conduct of Acting Third Assistant Engineer Henry J. Johnson, who coolly performed his duty until the engine became disabled, when he rendered me the most valuable assistance on deck." Mr. Johnson and his assistant, Mr. George Whitney, acting third assistant engineer, had a most miserable time for several months after capture, being moved about to various prison pens, jails and workhouses, and forced to mix with felons imprisoned for all sorts of crimes.

A frightful disaster occurred on board the new double-ender *Chenango* when she first sailed from the city where she was built. This vessel, on the 15th of April, left New York, under the command of Lieutenant Commander T. S. Fillebrown, bound for Hampton Roads; while passing between Forts Hamilton and Lafayette her port boiler suddenly exploded blowing up the deck, killing twenty-five of the crew and wounding ten others, all four of her engineers being among the killed. A court of inquiry held at the Brooklyn navy yard found that the disaster was caused by a defective vein in the iron in the boiler, and that no blame or want of vigilance could be ascribed to any officer of the vessel. The chief engineer, Mr. Joseph N. Cahill, first assistant engineer, U. S. Navy, was particularly exonerated, he being known as one of the most careful and cautious officers in the service. The *Shenango* belonged to the *Sassacus* class of double-enders and was built by J. Simonson, Greenpoint, Long Island, the engines and boilers being supplied by the Morgan Iron Works, New York. The boilers were of the Martin vertical water-tube type and may have been defective in bracing as well as material, as another of them had exploded with fatal results on the *Lenapee* of the same class when steam was raised in it at the contractor's works.

Besides the naval court of inquiry as to the accident, it was also investigated by a coroner's jury which found the cause to be defective material and fixed the blame upon the person or persons responsible for the construction of the boilers. The responsibility narrowed down to Second Assistant Engineer S. Wilkins Cragg, who as an assistant to a general engineer superintendent had been stationed at the Morgan Works in special charge of the *Chenango's* machinery, and he was dismissed the service by the Secretary of the Navy, who cited the finding of the coroner's jury as the reason for his action. Owing to the haste with which vessels were built in those days and the constant pressure always bearing upon the contractors to hurry their work along, Mr. Cragg proved that he was unable to control the nature of the work under his inspection and that his dismissal was unjust. About two years later he was restored to the navy, and a few years afterward resigned. In after years he was a prominent figure in Paris in connection with the street improvements of that city.

On the morning of June 2nd the U. S. Steamer *Victoria* chased ashore, captured and set on fire a large British steamer named *Georgianna McCaw* trying to run the blockade into Wilmington, on which occasion an engineer officer of the *Victoria* greatly distinguished himself, as shown by the following extracts from the report of the commanding officer:

"I immediately ordered the first and second cutters to board and fire her—the former under command of Acting Master's Mate William Moody, the latter under charge of Acting Third Assistant Engineer Thomas W. Hineline.

"On their arrival on board they found that two boats with their crews had escaped to the shore. They, however, succeeded in capturing twenty-nine of the crew, including the captain and most of the officers, together with three passengers. They fired her in several places, and she continued to burn until 10 a. m., when she was boarded from the shore.

"At daylight Fort Caswell and the adjacent batteries opened fire upon our boats with shot and shell, which compelled them to return without accomplishing her destruction.

"I would add, sir, that too much credit cannot be awarded to Acting Master's Mate William Moody and Acting Third Assistant Engineer Thomas W. Hineline for their perseverance and energy displayed, and their cool and gallant conduct while under fire of the enemy."

For this exploit the acting master's mate was made an acting ensign, and Mr. Hineline advanced to the grade of second assistant engineer, the following letter being sent him by the department on the 22nd of July, 1864:

"SIR: For your cool and gallant conduct under fire of the enemy as mentioned by Acting Master Everson commanding U. S. S. *Victoria* in his report of the attempt to destroy the blockade-runner *Georgianna McCaw*, you are hereby promoted to the grade of acting Second Assistant Engineer in the navy of the United States, on temporary service.

"Very respectfully,
"GIDEON WELLES."

The capture of the *Water Witch* in Ossabaw Sound on the 3rd of June, 1864, has been referred to in an earlier chapter, but is worthy of further comment on account of a peculiar question regarding the conduct of her chief engineer in the affair. The *Water Witch* was boarded while lying at anchor by a large force of the enemy, who, in the extreme darkness of the night, got close aboard before being discovered and gained the deck before the crew could be assembled to repel them. The commander of the vessel, Lieutenant Commander Austin Pendergrast, reported afterward that his crew showed no disposition to defend the ship and gave as a reason for this very remarkable behavior that the men were dissatisfied because the most of them were kept on board after their time of enlistment had expired. Such defense as was made was against great numerical odds by a few of the men and some of the officers, the hero of the occasion and most formidable combatant being Acting Assistant Paymaster Luther Billings, who was subsequently recognized by promotion for his gallantry.

With the hope of swamping the enemy's barges alongside, the ship's engines (side-wheels) were started, but soon stopped at the demand of a Confederate officer who enforced his order with a revolver. Lieutenant Commander Pendergrast referred to this in his report as an exhibition of cowardice on the part of the engineers and charged the loss of the ship against them in the following words: "Had they obeyed my orders to work the engine, the enemy would have been unable to board us; but, so far from fighting the rebels, they surrendered at the first summons, and thereby lost the ship." The engineers on their part called attention to the fact that they were unarmed and claimed that the appearance of the enemy in the engine-room led them to believe that the deck had been already carried. Just how an unarmed man, engineer or not, is to resist an order given by an armed enemy in battle is not at all apparent. Instead of charging the disaster to the cowardice of the engineers it seems that a more liberal and logical view of the matter would place the blame upon an organization that compelled them to go into action unarmed, when the nature of their duties were such that they might at any moment be called upon to fight and when their inability to do so might result in the loss of the ship, as the commanding officer reported was the case in this instance.

Besides the misbehavior charged against him at the time of the capture, the senior engineer of the *Water Witch*, Samuel Genther, acting first assistant engineer, was reported by his commanding officer for "disgraceful conduct" while held as a prisoner of war, in that he asked to be released from confinement on the ground that he did not fight and as a non-combatant should not be made to suffer the consequences of war. Mr. Genther was a volunteer officer of less than two years' service, the greater part of which had been passed on the *Water Witch*, and it may be that he had been led to believe that he, as a staff officer, was simply a civil employe and a non-combatant, and he may have been sincere in asserting his claim to release from captivity. It was unfortunate for him, however, that he could not have had a time of peace in which to pronounce himself a non-combatant, for it availed him nothing under the living conditions of war: the enemy refused to liberate him, and the Navy Department, as soon as he was exchanged, summarily dismissed him from the service for his part in the surrender of the *Water Witch* and for "un-officer-like conduct" while held as a prisoner of war.

The duel between the U. S. sloop-of-war *Kearsarge* and the Confederate war-steamer *Alabama* on Sunday the 19th of June, 1864, was one of the most gratifying events of the Civil War, not alone from the fact that it resulted in removing from the surface of the ocean the scourge and terror of American commerce, but because circumstances made it practically a competitive test to destruction of the systems of ship, engine and gun building and management in the American and British navies. The two ships were as evenly matched in size, armament and crew as could possibly be expected of vessels built and armed in different countries, their relative proportions being as follows:

	ALABAMA.	KEARSARGE.
Length over all	220 feet	214 feet 3 inches.
Length on water-line,	210 "	198 " 6 "
Beam	32 "	33 " 10 "
Depth of hold	17 "	16 "
Tonnage	1,150	1,031

The *Alabama* was full bark-rigged with very lofty spars, her main especially being so tall that it had come to be recognized as a sign of danger to American skippers in all seas, and this gave her the appearance of being a much larger vessel than the *Kearsarge*, which at that time was fitted with disproportionately low and small masts and carried no spars above the topsail yards. The armament of the *Alabama* consisted of one VII-inch Blakely rifle; one VIII-inch shell-gun, and six long 32-pounders; all British guns. That of the *Kearsarge* was two XI-inch smooth-bore guns; one 30-pounder rifle, and four short 32-pounders; all American guns. The *Alabama* went into action with 149 officers and men in her crew, a majority of her men being British subjects, and the *Kearsarge* had 163 all told. With the exception of eleven persons of inferior ratings this ship's company was composed of native-born citizens of the United States, the most of them being seamen and mechanics from the coast and workshops of New England.

The magnificent discipline and courage displayed by the *Kearsarge's* men; the question of the chain armor; the conduct of the British yacht *Deerhound;* the wild firing of the *Alabama* and the deadly precision of that of the *Kearsarge*, with other familiar and often-told incidents of the fight need not be gone over here, but instead a few comments will be made upon some other features of the combat not usually brought into prominence in the historical accounts. One of these points is the assumed superiority of the gunners of the *Alabama*, her commander, Semmes, being quoted in the *London Times* a few days after the fight as saying that he expected his trained British gun-captains to make short work of the volunteers of the *Kearsarge*. It is true that the gun's-crews of the

Federal ship, divisional officers as well as men, were volunteers, but they were anything but recruits as the term usually signifies. The *Kearsarge* had been in commission for more than two years under a well organized and liberally administered system of naval discipline, that length of time being more than sufficient to convert almost any class of recruits into thorough men-of-war's-men. The material in this case happened to be of intelligence to start with, and after thirty months of constant training aboard ship had arrived at a state of competence and familiarity with their duties that left absolutely nothing to dread from the products of British or any other system of naval training. Just such volunteers as these manned our ships in the war of 1812, and will man them in the next naval war.

The circling tactics observed by the two ships during the fight were forced by Captain Winslow of the *Kearsarge* to prevent his antagonist from approaching the neutral three-mile limit off shore. His ability to thus determine the order of battle was due to the superiority of his engineer's department, and to that alone, for had the *Alabama* possessed the greater speed she could have compelled the fight to be maintained on parallel courses leading shoreward, as pointed out in Winslow's report of the battle. The *Alabama* was built with special reference to speed both as a steamer and as a sailer and was supposed to be much the superior of the *Kearsarge* in both capacities, Captain Semmes, again, being authority for the statement that he expected to have a decided advantage in the matter of speed when he went into action. With the weaker motive power, the *Kearsarge* owed her superior performance to her engine-room force which was made up of intelligent and capable young American mechanics, who had been trusted to carry out the details of their duties without captious interference, and who consequently had arrived at a point so near perfection that when the hour of battle came the performance of the machinery exceeded all previous records and made the *Kearsarge* the better ship.

The *Kearsarge's* machinery was built by the well-known firm of Woodruff & Beach, Hartford, Connecticut, the contract price for it being $104,000. The ship itself was built at the navy yard, Kittery, Maine. The machinery was well made and excellent for its kind, although not designed with any special reference to speed, and its fine condition after thirty months of service is the best possible proof of the zeal and capability of the engineers who had charge of it. An Englishman, Mr. Frederick Milnes Edge, who published a pamphlet account of the battle soon after it occurred, was so impressed with the evident care exhibited by the condition of the machinery of the *Kearsarge* that he wrote:

" I have not seen engines more compact in form, nor apparently in finer condition—looking in every part as though they were fresh from the workshop, instead of being, as they are, half through the third year of the cruise."

Mr. Cushman, the chief engineer of the ship, was a veteran of the old navy well qualified to train the new hands which the war had brought into the service; the four assistant engineers belonged to the regular service but had entered on account of the existence of war and consequently had no more naval experience than the volunteer deck officers of their ship, but that, as the event showed, was quite sufficent for both classes. The *Kearsarge* went into action with her fires raked perfectly clean and bright, the furnace draft forced by artificial means, and the safety valves lashed down, under which conditions she fought at her utmost speed throughout the engagement, her decks trembling under the feet of the crew from the vibration of the engines and the roar of the fires. The senior assistant engineer, Mr. Badlam, was stationed in charge of the engines; Mr. Miller, the next engineer in rank, had charge of the boilers; Third Assistant Engineer Sidney L. Smith was on the spar deck with the fire-hose company, and the junior, Mr. McConnell, was stationed at the engine-room signal-bell. In the report of the chief engineer the conduct of these four officers and of the men of the engine-room force was especially referred to as being cool, self-possessed and efficient. The same was true of the whole ship's company, for the action was fought with the same deliberation and lack of excitement that had characterized the daily drills.

The detailed report of the conduct of officers and men contains the following relative to the engineer's department :

"The engineer's division was admirably and efficiently con

ducted, under the command of Chief Engineer W. H. Cushman. Sidney L. Smith and Henry McConnell, third assistant engineers, were stationed on deck, and their conduct came immediately under my observation. It was distinguished by coolness and vigilance. The other assistants, Mr. W. H. Badlam and Mr. F. L. Miller, were on duty in the engine and fire-rooms, and, judging from the prompt manner in which the orders from the deck were executed, I know that their duties were creditably performed."

The *Alabama* fired about three hundred and seventy times but only twenty-eight of her shots struck the *Kearsarge*, and they did her no serious harm; only three of her men were wounded, one of whom, William Gowin, subsequently died. The *Kearsarge* fired one hundred and seventy-three times, the most of her projectiles finding the mark: about forty men were killed and wounded on the *Alabama*, and the ship was dreadfully cut to pieces before she sank. Her engines were disabled by a shell which exploded in a coal bunker, completely blocking the engine-room with coal and wreckage and wounding two assistant engineers. Another shell alone was reported by prisoners to have killed and wounded eighteen men and disabled a gun. Ten of the shots fired from the *Kearsarge* were from a 12-pounder howitzer and performed no part in the sinking of the *Alabama*.

"Two quartermasters were put in charge of this gun with instructions to fire when they were ordered; but the old salts, little relishing having nothing to do when their shipmates were all so busy commenced peppering away with their pea-shooter of a piece, alternating its discharges with vituperation of each other. This low-comedy by-play amused the ship's company, and the officer of the division good-humoredly allowed the farce to continue until the single box of ammunition was exhausted."[1]

One other incident of the fight cannot be told too often to correct a popular error regarding the supposed narrow escape the *Kear-*

---

[1] From a popular account of the battle by Mr. Henry McConnell, cashier of the Kensington National Bank of Philadelphia; Mr. McConnell was the assistant engineer of the *Kearsarge* stationed at the engine-room signal bell.

sarge had from destruction. A 100-pounder shell was found lodged in her stern-post after the battle and has been exhibited at one of the navy yards ever since with a section of the stern-post, where it has been regarded with awe by a whole generation of visitors. At the World's Columbian Exposition this same piece of the stern-post with the shell still lodged in it was one of the most attractive exhibits on the model battle-ship and was seen by upwards of three million people. It is currently believed that if this shell had exploded, the *Kearsarge* and not the *Alabama* would have gone to the bottom of the English Channel, and people, according to their degree of piety, ascribe the miraculous escape to luck, Providence, or the direct intervention of the Almighty. The truth is, however, that this shell struck the counter of the *Kearsarge* at least twenty feet from the stern-post and would have exploded then, where the damage would have been slight, had it possessed any explosive power, for it was a percussion shell. After striking, it glanced, scoring the planking for about ten feet, then passed through the air some ten feet more and finally embedded itself in the stern-post, its final impact doing some damage by starting the transom frame and binding the rudder so that four men were required thereafter to work the wheel.

The most sanguinary and important naval battle of the Civil War was the battle in Mobile Bay the morning of August 5, 1864. The fleet under command of Rear Admiral Farragut stripped for action much the same as was done more than two years before preparatory to passing the forts below New Orleans. Superfluous boats, spars, etc., were taken out of the ships and anchored off shore or left at Pensacola, some of the ships thus disposing even of their lower yards and topmasts. The plan of lashing a small vessel to the unexposed side of a larger one to carry her past the fort in case of serious damage was again adopted, and at daylight the morning of the 5th the vessels designated for the attack moved up the bay to their work, the pairing and order of advance, together with the names of commanding officers and chief engineers being as follows:

{ *Brooklyn*, Captain James Alden; Chief Engineer Mortimer Kellogg.
Octorora, Lieutenant Commander C. H. Greene; Acting First Assistant Engineer W. W. Shipman.

{ *Hartford* (flag), Captain Percival Drayton ; Chief Engineer Thomas Williamson.
Metacomet, Lieutenant Commander Jas. E. Jouett ; First Assistant Engineer James Atkins.

{ *Richmond*, Captain Thornton A. Jenkins ; Chief Engineer Jackson McElmell.
Port Royal, Lieutenant Commander B. Gherardi ; First Assistant Engineer Fletcher A. Wilson.

{ *Lackrwanna*, Captain J. B. Marchand ; First Assistant Engineer Jas. W. Whittaker.
Seminole, Commander Edward Donaldson ; Acting First Assistant Engineer Claude Babcock.

{ *Monongahela*, Commander J. H. Strong ; Chief Engineer George F. Kutz.
Kennebec, Lieutenant Commander Wm. P. McCann ; Second Assistant Engineer L. W. Robinson.

{ *Ossipee*, Commander Wm. E. LeRoy ; Acting Chief Engineer James M. Adams.
Itaska, Lieutenant Commander George Brown ; Second Assistant Engineer John L. D. Borthwick.

{ *Oneida*, Commander J. R. M. Mullany ; Chief Engineer William H. Hunt.
Galena, Lieutenant Commander Clark H. Wells ; First Assistant Engineer William G. Buehler.

Four monitors, two of the Ericsson type and two of the Edes Mississippi "turtle-back" type, were already inside the bar and near Fort Morgan with orders to move along with the head of the column between the leading ships and the fort, in the following order :

Tecumseh, Commander T. A. M. Craven ; Chief Engineer John Faron.
Manhattan, Commander J. W. A. Nicholson ; Acting Chief Engineer C. L. Carty.
Winnebago, Commander T. H. Stevens ; Acting Chief Engineer Simon Shultice.
Chickasaw, Lieutenant Commander Geo. H. Perkins ; Acting Chief Engineer Wm. Rodgers.

Six small gunboats, the *Pembina, Pinola, Sebago, Tennessee, Bienville,* and *Genesee,* were advanced into the shoal water off Mobile Point somewhat to the rear of Fort Morgan for the purpose of disconcerting by their fire the batteries of that fortification, but owing to some confusion of orders or misunderstanding they anchored so far away that their fire was ineffective and they are not usually credited with having participated in the battle.

About 6.30 A. M. the line was well up towards the fort, the four monitors being close into the shore, and the formation for battle was being perfected, the first shots at the fort being fired at that time by the *Tecumseh.* A few minutes past seven the fort opened on the leading ship, the *Brooklyn,* and immediately thereafter the action became general between the fort, the leading ships and the monitors. In this firing the *Tecumseh* did not take part, for after having fired the first two shots to scale her guns she had loaded with steel bolts and the heaviest charges of powder allowed, to be in readiness to engage the iron-clad ram *Tennessee* then emerging from behind Fort Morgan. At 7.30 A. M. the *Tecumseh* was the foremost vessel in the line, being off the starboard bow of the *Brooklyn,* and was steadily advancing, intent only upon getting into action with the *Tennessee,* when her destruction came with awful suddenness by the explosion of a torpedo underneath her, from the effects of which she went to the bottom with her gallant commander and the greater part of her crew within less than half a minute. The swiftness of her destruction may be comprehended from the following extract from a lecture by an eye-witness, Chief Engineer Harrie Webster, U. S. Navy who as an assistant engineer was in the turret of the *Manhattan* in charge of its turning gear, only two hundred yards distant from the *Tecumseh.*

"A tiny white comber of froth curled around her bow, a tremendous shock ran through our ship as though we had struck a rock, and as rapidly as these words flow from my lips the *Tecumseh* reeled a little to starboard, her bows settled beneath the surface, and while we looked, her stern lifted high in the air with the propeller still revolving, and the ship pitched out of sight, like an arrow twanged from her bow."

The *Tecumseh* went into action with seven line officers, including the commander, six engineers, one surgeon, one paymaster, a pilot, and ninety-eight enlisted men. Of these, three line officers, the pilot, and seventeen men were saved, all others losing their lives by drowning or concussion. With the exception of one coal-heaver the entire engine-room force of six officers and thirty-seven men was annihilated, the majority probably by shock, as the survivors reported that the torpedo exploded under the middle of the ship and blew the bottom about the machinery spaces to pieces. The chief engineer, Mr. John Faron, had left a sick bed in the hospital at Pensacola at his own urgent request to go on board his vessel to take part in the battle. He had been in the regular navy since 1848 and was a popular and capable officer whose death, resulting from his own devotion to duty, was greatly deplored. The engineers who perished with him were F. S. Barlow, Elisha Harsen, and H. S. Leonard, all second assistants in the regular service, and Thomas Ustick and Henry Ritter, acting third assistants.

The tragedy of the *Tecumseh* occasioned some confusion in the fleet, during which the *Brooklyn* faltered and Farragut went ahead of her with the *Hartford* and led the fleet successfully past the fort, but not without great loss, the fire from the fort and from the Confederate gunboats lying above doing great injury to several of the ships. The broadside fire of the larger vessels was so terrific that it eventually practically silenced the fort and the column was able to pass almost unmolested after the first vessels had gone by. Last in the line came the evil-starred *Oneida*, and by the time she arrived abreast of Morgan the gunners had returned to their batteries and opened upon her with great fury. Able naval critics say it was a mistake to put a small vessel last in line, for had one of the large broadside ships like the *Richmond* or *Brooklyn* brought up the rear she could have successfully protected herself by her own fire and forced the enemy to again abandon his guns. As it was, the *Oneida* was roughly handled.

" A rifled shell passed through her chain armor, and entering the starboard boiler exploded in it, causing sad havoc among the firemen and coal-heavers of the watch below, all of whom were either killed outright or fearfully scalded by the escaping steam. Another shell, exploding in the cabin, cut both wheel-ropes, while a third set fire to the deck above the forward magazine; yet, encouraged by the chivalric bearing of their commander, and the fine example set them by the executive officer and the chief engineer of the ship, the crew of the *Oneida* behaved splendidly. The relieving tackles were instantly manned, the fire put out, and connection between the starboard and port boiler cut off; and the *Oneida*, assisted by the *Galena*, went on as if nothing unusual had happened on board of her, her guns never for a moment ceasing to respond to the really terrific fire of the enemy."[1]

The chief engineer of the *Oneida*, Mr. Wm. H. Hunt, was badly scalded in both arms but remained at his post and succeeded in restoring order from the frightful scene following the explosion of the shell in the boiler, his gallantry being so conspicuous that it was made a subject of special reference in the report of the commanding officer. Mr. Fitch, the senior assistant engineer of the ship, was severely scalded and likewise distinguished himself by his gallant behavior, the chief engineer reporting of him in the following terms: "Too much praise cannot be accorded to First Assistant Engineer R. A. Fitch, who, at the time of the injury to the boiler, displayed the utmost courage and coolness, remaining at his station in the execution of his duties until he was so badly scalded by the escaping steam as to be rendered almost helpless." Acting Third Assistant Engineer Nicholas Dillon was also commended in the official reports for extraordinary services, he having undertaken the duties of Mr. Fitch when that officer succumbed to his injuries.

After getting past the fort with the assistance of the *Galena*, the *Oneida* came up to the scene of a fierce combat between the *Monongahela* and some of the other Union vessels and the *Tennessee* just in time to be assailed by the latter, which, by chance rather than design, got under the *Oneida's* stern and raked her fore and aft with a broadside, destroying boats and rigging, dismounting a gun, crippling the mainmast, and injuring some of her people, among them Commander Mullany, who lost an arm. At this stage of the

---

[1] Commodore Foxhall A. Parker, U. S. Navy—The Battle of Mobile Bay; page 31.

fight the Confederate gunboats had become so annoying that Farragut signaled his own small vessels to cast loose from their consorts and attack them; to which order the *Metacomet, Port Royal, Kennebec* and *Itaska* at once responded. The first named, under Lieutenant Commander (now Rear Admiral) James A. Jouett, got off first and captured the *Selma* which she singled out and pursued. One of the enemy's gunboats, the *Morgan*, escaped to Mobile; the other, the *Gaines*, was run on shore in a sinking condition near the fort, set on fire by her own people and abandoned. The *Tennessee* withdrew from the fight and anchored under the guns of the fort, still practically uninjured and without a man in her crew disabled. The Federal vessels proceeded about four miles up the bay and anchored, piping to breakfast after hastily clearing away the wreckage and other more dreadful evidences of the conflict.

Scarcely had the men gathered about their mess-cloths when the *Tennessee* was observed to be under way, standing up the bay for another fight. The struggle that ensued between her and the whole Federal fleet was a desperate one and lasted more than an hour before the *Tennessee* was literally worried into a surrender. She was pelted with the broadsides of the large ships, which, however, did her little damage, and was rammed in succession by the *Monongahela, Lackawanna* and *Hartford*. The three monitors, especially the *Chickasaw*, hung close aboard her and with their heavy projectiles succeeded in crushing her casemate armor, jamming her port-shutters, and finally reduced her to the necessity of surrendering. Her admiral, Franklin Buchanan, lost a leg; two of her men were killed; two assistant engineers, the pilot, and five men were wounded. The *Selma* in her fight with the *Metacomet* had eight men killed and seven wounded before she surrendered. The Confederate loss in Fort Morgan was not known.

The last shot fired by the *Tennessee* entered the berth deck of the *Hartford*, exploded and killed five men and wounded eight, one of the latter being Third Assistant Engineer William G. McEwan, stationed there in charge of the fire-hose company, who lost his right arm. The sword which he wore was torn from him and hurled across the deck, the sword-belt being driven under a mess-chest where it was found several days later. Mr. McEwan was a volunteer officer, and as he had distinguished himself in the earlier part of the engagement,

Admiral Farragut made a special report of his case, recommending that he be rewarded by transfer to the regular service, which was done and a comfortable pension assured him for life by his being placed on the retired list.

The *Tennessee* was the largest and most formidable war vessel built within the limits of the Confederacy during the war, her length being 209 feet; extreme beam 48 feet, and average draft of water 14 feet: her general design was like the *Atlanta*, of which a sketch has appeared in a former chapter, except that her hull was built wholly of wood. The casemate was of the same form but heavier, the wooden backing of yellow pine and oak being $22\frac{1}{2}$ inches thick, sheathed with 5 inches of iron plating on the sides and after end and 6 inches forward. This iron plating, it is worthy of remark, was made from the ore at the iron furnaces in Atlanta, the Southerners having begun when too late to pay attention to the mechanic arts so necessary for prosperity in peace and absolutely vital in war. The *Tennessee* was built at Selma, Alabama, from timber that was standing at the time the work was begun in 1863, and was gotten down the Alabama river and into Mobile bay only by overcoming many difficulties. Her battery of six Brooke rifles was also of southern manufacture. Her weak point was the machinery, which was not built for her and was wholly unfit for a war vessel: it was taken out of a river steamer named *Alonzo Child*, and consisted of two high-pressure engines with cylinders 24 inches in diameter by 7 feet stroke placed fore and aft in the vessel and driving an idler shaft by means of spur gearing; this shaft in turn driving the screw-shaft through the medium of cast iron bevel-gears. Steam was supplied by four horizontal return-flue boilers 24 feet long, placed side by side with one furnace under the whole of them. The vessel was found by a board of survey immediately after capture to be fit for service, and was taken into the navy at the appraised value of $595,000. Admiral Farragut's original report of his prize was accompanied with some excellent drawings and sketches of her, made by second assistant engineers Isaac DeGraff of the *Hartford* and Robert Weir of the *Richmond*, from whose sketches and the accompanying description the data of this paragraph have been obtained.

Fort Morgan surrendered to the combined army and naval

forces about two weeks after the battle, the other fortifications in Mobile Bay having surrendered or been abandoned within a day or two after the Federal fleet forced its way in.

The casualties in the fleet during the morning battle were as follows:

	KILLED.	WOUNDED.
Hartford	25	28
Brooklyn	11	43
Lackawanna	4	35
Oneida	8	30
Monongahela	0	6
Metacomet,	1	2
Ossipee	1	7
Richmond	0	2
Galena	0	1
Octorora	1	10
Kennebec	1	6
Tecumseh	92	0
Total	144	170

The above list of casualties does not include two men killed and two wounded immediately after the battle on the small armed steamer *Phillippi* which rashly attempted to follow the fleet in and was destroyed by the guns of the fort.

The loss in the British fleet at the battle of Copenhagen, somewhat similar in character to that of Mobile, was 253 killed and 688 wounded.

Early in October the U. S. sloop-of-war *Wachusett*, Commander Napoleon Collins, was in the harbor of Bahia, Brazil, in company with the Confederate privateer *Florida*, which vessel the *Wachusett* was seeking. Determined to seize or destroy her, even if the neutrality of the port had to be violated, Collins assembled some of his officers and announced he was going to get under way with the apparent intention of going to sea and when near the *Florida* to suddenly change the course, run into and sink her, or carry her by boarding. To this plan the chief engineer objected on the ground that the shock of the collision might start the boilers from their seatings and create ruin by rupturing the steam pipes and boiler connections; an objection that appeared so reasonable in the absence of anyone with experience in ramming that the intention would probably have been abandoned had not one of the assistant engineers announced that he would voluntarily take charge of the machinery, allow everyone else to leave the engine and fire-rooms just before the collision and remain there alone himself to take the consequences of an accident and to reverse the engines if required after the shock. The *Florida* was run down according to the plan of the commander but owing to some error in handling the *Wachusett* the blow struck was a glancing one and did no great damage to the privateer beyond carrying away her mizzen mast and main yard; a few volleys of small arms were exchanged, and upon the discharge of two of the *Wachusett's* broadside guns the *Florida* surrendered and was towed out of the harbor by her captor, the Brazilian forts firing upon the *Wachusett* as she went out. A serious complication grew out of the affair, ending in an apology made by our government to Brazil and an agreement to return the *Florida* to the port where she had been captured. While preparing at Hampton Roads for the voyage to Brazil the *Florida* sank, apparently by accident, and the return was never made.

The assistant engineer who courageously volunteered to risk his life in the engine-room of the *Wachusett* when ramming was first proposed was George Wallace Melville, who was destined to make his name famous at a later period by the exhibition of heroism and fortitude of such superior quality as to extend far beyond his own individuality and reflect world-wide honor upon the naval service and the nation to which he belonged. Previous to the capture of the *Florida*, Mr. Melville, knowing that his commander was desirous of gaining information as to the battery of the enemy's ship, attempted to get on board of her in civilian's clothing in the guise of a visitor, but was suspected and driven off when he went alongside; this act in itself was far from commonplace, for the penalty for being in the enemy's country or on board an enemy's ship in plain clothes in time of war was well known by him.

The evening of December 9th the double-ender *Otsego*, of the *Sassacus* class, ran upon two torpedoes near Jamesville in the Roanoke river and was sunk, no lives being lost, she being at the time a member of a flotilla sent up the river to attack a battery at Rainbow Bluff. Lieutenant Commander H. N. T. Arnold, the commanding officer, in his report of the disaster expressed his indebtedness to the senior engineer, Mr. Samuel C. Midlam, who had advised and rigged a torpedo net over the bow which had saved the *Otsego* on two occasions by picking up torpedoes, but was unavailing against those that finally destroyed the vessel, they being struck when she had rounded to preparatory to anchoring and were not under the bow.

Towards the close of the year a great fleet was assembled under commander Rear Admiral Porter to co-operate with General B. F. Butler in an attack upon the immense fortification known as Fort Fisher on Federal Point at the mouth of Cape Fear River, North Carolina. An unusual method of making war was attempted on this occasion, the result of which exposed both Porter and Butler to considerable ridicule, although General Butler is said to have been the instigator of the plan. An accidental explosion of a powder magazine in England not long before had done so much damage to the neighborhood that the idea was conceived of adopting the same means to "paralyze" the enemy or destroy his works by concussion. Accordingly the purchased screw gun-vessel *Louisiana*, which had cost only $35,000 in 1861 and which was pretty well worn out by constant service in the North Carolina Sounds, was converted into a torpedo on a huge scale by being loaded with an enormous quantity of powder arranged in cells to facilitate its simultaneous explosion. The crew of this dangerous floating mine consisted of Commander A. C. Rhind, Lieutenant S. W. Preston, Second Assistant Engineer Anthony T. E. Mullen, Master's Mate Paul Boyton, and eleven enlisted men, all volunteers from Rhind's vessel—the *Agawam*. Admiral Porter referred to the mission in his report of the attack as "the most perilous adventure that was, perhaps, ever undertaken," and recommended that the officers be promoted, adding that no one in the squadron expected them to survive their expedition.

The night of December 23rd the powder vessel was towed by the *Wilderness* to a position close to Fort Fisher where she was cast off, and, though literally a powder-magazine from stem to stern, proceeded under her own steam to within three hundred yards of the beach under the walls of the fort, trusting to her disguise as a blockade runner to escape being fired into. Having anchored unmolested, the fuzes and fires for causing the explosion were lighted, these having been arranged, as stated in Commander Rhind's report, by Engineer Mullen. The crew then left her by boat and boarded the *Wilderness*, that vessel going at full speed to join the fleet lying twelve miles off shore to be beyond reach of the catastrophe that was supposed would occur. The explosion took place about 1.30 A. M. and resulted in nothing; the men in Fort Fisher were disturbed in their sleep, but no one was paralyzed and no earthworks were jarred down, while the sound was scarcely heard by the people in the fleet intently listening for it. The reward extended to Mr. Mullen for his share in this perilous enterprise was very considerable, he receiving a week later the following letter from the Secretary of the Navy:

"SIR: As a recognition of your gallant conduct while attached to the *Louisiana* you have permission to present yourself to Chief Engineer Newell, at the navy yard, Philadelphia, for examination for promotion."

Mr. Mullen at the time was number ninety-two on the list of second assistant engineers and his advancement to the foot of the list of first assistants, which occurred immediately after his examintion, is belived to be the most substantial reward for distinguished service conferred upon any staff officer during the war.

On the 24th of December Admiral Porter gave the fort a terrific battering and silenced its fire for the time being, but no important results followed, as General Butler with the troop-ships was not present to follow up the advantage. Porter's attacking force consisted of thirty-seven war-vessels, ranging in size from the *New Ironsides*, *Wabash*, *Colorado* and *Powhatan* down to the double-enders *Sassacus* and *Mackinaw* and the ninety-day gunboats *Unadilla* and *Chippewa*, lying in semi-circular formation about one mile distant from the fort. The monitors *Monadnock, Mahopac, Saugus* and *Cunonicus* were in this line of battle and did great execution with their heavy guns, they and the *New Ironsides* lying a considerable distance inside the one-mile circle. Besides the fighting line, a reserve division of nineteen vessels, all purchased merchant steamers, laid further out and did not take part in the attack.

The army transports came the next day (Christmas) and the

attack was renewed, General Butler landing some of his troops under cover and with the assistance of about twenty of the gun-vessels. He, however, gave up the plan of attack and began re-embarking his men after a few thousands had landed, an act that was the beginning of a bitter controversy between him and Admiral Porter, prosecuted by both as long as they lived. During the two days the vessels suffered slightly from the fire of the fort, their chief losses resulting from the bursting of their own guns, about forty-five officers and men being killed or wounded by the bursting of 100-pounder Parrott rifles. On the *Juniata* Lieutenant Wemple and four men were killed and Paymaster Caspar Schenck and seven men wounded in this manner; the *Ticonderoga* had eight killed and eleven wounded in the same way, and similar casualties, but with less loss of life, occurred to the *Mackinaw*, *Yantic* and *Quaker City*. An idea of the magnitude of the bombardment may be gained from the fact that the *Colorado* alone fired 1,569 heavy shot and shell the first day, and 1,226 the second day.

CHAPTER XXV.

"And in this faith all went to their posts, prepared to obey the regulations and 'fight courageously'; for in a fleet where a single shell, exploding in the boiler of a vessel, might subject the engineers and firemen to the fate of Marsyas, or a torpedo or infernal, exploding under her bottom, send all hands journeying *ad astra*, no one could properly be considered a non-combatant.
"Commodore FOXHALL A. PARKER—*Battle of Mobile Bay.*"

1864. The Civil War, Continued—Naval Operations in the North Carolina Sounds—The Ram ALBEMARLE—Sinking of the SOUTHFIELD and defeat of the MIAMI—The Naval Battle of May Fifth—Disaster to the SASSACUS and Heroism of Her Chief Engineer—Daring Attempt of Enlisted Men to Destroy the Ram—Her Destruction by Lieutenant Wm. B. Cushing—Battle and Capture of Plymouth—Prize Money Distributed on Account of the ALBEMARLE.

MENTION has been made in former chapters of the capture of the fortified posts of the enemy on the large sounds lying along the coast of North Carolina, and of the constant warfare waged thereafter by the national war-vessels to keep possession of what had been gained. This region, remote as it was from the battle-grounds of the war, was not of direct importance to the Federals as its occupation could have little influence upon the strategical combinations being attempted by the armies in distant fields, but from the Confederate point of view the situation was very different: to them possession of these waters and ports meant a source of supply from Europe, through the medium of blockade-runners, of clothing, medicines, arms, and other war supplies, and an almost perfect facility for the distribution of such articles by the many rivers and water-ways flowing into the sounds. Thus it was that Federal policy required the seizure and retention of the entire region, while Confederate necessity dictated a ceaseless struggle for the recovery of what had been lost early in the war.

The theatre of operations for the naval force assigned to this region was geographically small compared with the vast extent of coasts and rivers on which the navy had to operate, but it was large enough to afford very active employment, and to require the most untiring vigilance on the part of the small force there charged with the task of maintaining Federal supremacy. The vessels sent into these waters were called gunboats by courtesy, but as a rule they were a sorry lot, being generally purchased steamers, tugs, or ferry-boats, armed and protected as well as the nature of their construction would allow; owing to the shallowness of the waters in which they had to operate they were necessarily small, until the naval authorities had had time to build light-draft gunboats, when some side-wheel vessels of considerable size, built expressly for war purposes, found their way into the Sounds. The officers and men aboard these vessels were a fair average of the naval *personnel* of the period; mostly volunteers, with a sufficient sprinkling of the "old navy" both before and abaft the mast to keep alive the traditions and maintain the rigid rules of the service. Volunteer officers commanded some of the smaller vessels, and the subordinate officers, almost without exception, were of this class; the larger vessels were generally commanded by regular officers, usually lieutenants and lieutenant-commanders. Chief among these C. W. Flusser and W. B. Cushing, whose exploits read like romance as well as history. They were young: Flusser, who at times was the ranking officer in the Sounds, was about thirty, while Cushing was barely of age, yet these young men accepted responsibilities and dealt with questions of policy, the gravity of which in these days would be regarded great enough to warrant consideration by a board of admirals.

The conditions of service were vastly different from the ideal naval life of the period; the lofty frigate shortening sail and clearing for action under the blue sky far out in the open sea was then the symbol of naval glory, but no such spectacle cheered the eyes and exalted the patriotism of the seamen in the Carolina Sounds. The vessels were small and smoky, redolent of engine oil and innocent of snowy canvass and glistening spars; instead of the bright blue sea of nautical romance, one saw the muddy, shallow flood of the far-reaching inland waters, stained and poisoned by the ooze and vegetable decay swept down by numberless rivers and creeks from the surrounding swamps. The great peninsula between Pamlico and Albemarle Sounds was a vast miasmatic swamp; stretching northward from Albemarle Sound lay the deadly and forbidding morass known as the Dismal Swamp, the character of which was the type of all the region lying adjacent to the Sounds. Thomas Moore, who visited this country early in the present century, described the physical characteristics of more than one locality in verse that will live as long as our language lasts, and in his beautiful ballad called "The Lake of the Dismal Swamp," narrating the legend of the youth who sought the firefly lamp and white canoe of his dead sweetheart in the depths of the Dismal Swamp, occurs the two following verses that describe the nature of the region far better than can any prose description:

"Away to the Dismal Swamp he speeds,—
 His path was rugged and sore;
Through tangled juniper, beds of reeds,
Through many a fen where the serpent feeds,
 And man never trod before!

"And when on earth he sank to sleep,
 If slumber his eyelids knew,
He lay where the deadly vine doth weep
Its venomous tear, and nightly steep
 The flesh with blistering dew!"

Such, then, were the surroundings of the Federal naval force and the material with which it had to operate; both doubtless very different from what the officers would have wished. But the country was at war, and whatever came to each man's hand that was he expected to do with all his might; so these gentlemen abandoned the dreams of romantic adventures at sea acquired by reading Cooper and the "Naval Monument," took off their white gloves, folded away their finely starched linen, and went to work.

Frequent attempts by the Confederate land forces to recapture the sea-ports of the Sounds came to naught, principally on account of the persistent presence of the little gunboats and their wicked habit of throwing large quantities of shells into the woods where the attacking forces were making their approaches; while boat attacks and guerilla warfare from the shore directed at the gunboats simply served to provoke Flusser and the other commanders to more vigorous hostility, and to teach the enemy that the gunboats would have to be assailed with some more powerful weapon than had yet been used against them if they were to be defeated. The fruit of this lesson was the *Albemarle*. She was built in the woods at Edward's Ferry on the Roanoke River, some forty miles above Plymouth, by Mr. Gilbert Elliot, from designs prepared by John L. Porter, who was the chief constructer of the Confederate navy, and who had been a naval constructer in the United States navy before the war. The hull was shallow, or "flat," built of eight-inch by ten-inch frame timbers sheathed with four-inch planking; near the water-line the sides were protected by a belt of several courses of squared logs bolted on longitudinally, and corresponding in some degree to the armor belt worn by modern battle-ships; the bow was developed forward into a solid oaken beak plated with two-inch iron and tapered to an edge. On the water-line the craft was one hundred and twenty-two feet long (which is sixteen feet less than the length of our modern torpedo boat *Cushing*), and the breadth of beam was forty-five feet. On the central part of the deck the full width of the boat and sixty feet in length fore and aft stood the superstructure or casemate; this was of heavy squared timbers inclined at an angle of almost sixty degrees to the vertical, sheathed with heavy planking and two layers of two-inch iron plates; the timbers at the forward part of the casemate were carried up above the flat top high enough to form the framing of a conning-tower of truncated pyramidal form. The corners of the main central structure were cut off, making its deck plan an oblong octagon. Inside the casemate at each end was mounted a 100-pounder rifled gun, one a Brooke, the other a Whitworth; each gun was pivoted to fire out of its end port and out of a port on each broadside. The vessel had twin-screws, each screw driven by an engine of only two hundred horse-power. The draft of water when ready for service was eight feet. From this description the *Albemarle* will be recognized as a typical Confederate war-vessel, differing from the *Merrimac*, *Atlanta* or *Tennessee* in no important particular except that of size.

In the spring of 1864 the *Albemarle* was ready for service, and on April 18 she dropped down the Roanoke River to within about three miles of Plymouth; her engine-power was so feeble and her steering qualities so bad that it was found impossible to keep her in the channel when going ahead with the current, so she came down the river backward dragging chains from her bows. The commanding officer was Captain J. W. Cooke, of the Confederate navy, whose name stood at the head of the list of lieutenants of the old navy when the war broke out in 1861. After anchoring, a lieutenant was sent out to explore the river in the vicinity of Plymouth, he returning in about two hours with the report that the river was so obstructed with piles, sunken vessels, and torpedoes that it would be impossible to pass down. Fires were then banked and port watches set. Mr. Elliott, the builder of the vessel, was on board as a volunteer aide to the captain, and he seems to have been more anxious to see his fabric get into a fight than was anyone else connected with her; he took the pilot, two seamen, and a small boat and proceeded to examine the obstructions with a long pole, finding to his great delight that there was a place near the middle of the river, wide enough for the ram to pass through, where there was ten feet of water; this was due to a remarkable freshet, the water being higher in the river that night than it had been known to be for many years. He returned to the *Albemarle* about one o'clock in the morning and reported his discovery to the captain, who immediately resolved to go out. All hands were quietly called, fires spread, and when all was ready she proceeded slowly down the river, being fired on in the darkness by the Union batteries about Plymouth as she passed.

Meantime, Flusser, in command of the *Miami*, with the *Southfield*, *Ceres*, and *Whitehead* in company, had been in action all day of April 18, aiding the garrison of Plymouth in resisting the attack of a large body of Confederates. The *Miami* was a paddle-wheel gunboat of about seven hundred and thirty tons, carrying six IX-inch guns, one 100-pounder Parrott rifle, and one 24-pounder howitzer; the *Southfield* was a ferry-boat, but had a very respectable battery (five IX-inch guns, one 100-pounder rifle, and one 12-pounder howitzer); the *Ceres* and *Whitehead* were merely armed tug-boats of less than one hundred and fifty tons each. The *Miami* and *Southfield* anchored for the night below Plymouth, the two smaller vessels lying higher up to watch for the ram, which was known to be abroad. In reporting the result of the day's fighting, Flusser wrote that night that he expected the ram down at any moment, and that he thought he could whip her. This was his last letter: he had already come within the range of vision of the

Fates, and she of the open shears was about to close them and sever the thread of his life.

With the dawn came the *Albemarle*. During the night the *Miami* and *Southfield* had been lashed together, and with the first warning of the coming of the foe, which was given by the *Ceres* at 3:45 A. M., they got under way and steamed up the river at full speed with the intention of ramming. The advantage of this combination is not manifest, although the majority of naval writers who have described this affair pass over it without comment, apparently accepting it as a proper arrangement. Admiral Ammen, in his book regarding the naval operations on the Atlantic coast, says that he is at a loss to understand the *rationale* of lashing two vessels together and using them as a ram. The *Albemarle* avoided the attack by running close in to the southern shore, and then, turning towards mid-stream, taking advantage of the swift current, and using all the steam power she had, she rushed at her antagonists, striking the *Miami* a glancing blow on the port bow and crushing into the starboard side of the *Southfield* so far that her beak appeared in the fire-room. The *Southfield* immediately sank, dragging the bow of the *Albemarle* which was tangled in her side, down so far that the forward deck of the ram was deeply submerged, and water poured in torrents through the port-holes in the forward part of the casement. When the *Southfield* touched bottom she rolled over away from the ram, and this disentangled the vessels and allowed the latter to resume an even keel. While this was taking place the *Albemarle*, being partially between the two Union vessels, was fiercely assailed by the great gun and small-arm fire of both, but she did no firing herself except with small arms. The projectiles fired at point-blank range struck fire on the sloping sides of the *Albemarle*, and flew harmlessly off high up into the air, or were broken in pieces to fly back on the decks of the vessels whence they came. From the engagement of the previous day the guns of the *Miami* were loaded with shell, and this circumstance proved fatal to her commanding officer. With his usual zeal and courage this officer had personally taken charge of his battery and fired the guns himself, being instantly killed and badly mangled by pieces of the third shell he fired, it having rebounded from the enemy's side and exploded.

The pressure of the ram between the two Federal vessels had parted the forward lashings, and as the *Southfield* was sinking the after lashings were cut or cast adrift, leaving the *Miami* unencumbered. After getting clear of the wreck of the *Southfield* the *Albemarle* backed off preparatory to striking the *Miami*, which vessel, at the same time, having swung around to starboard, began backing her engines to straighten herself in the current and keep off the bank.

Acting Volunteer Lieutenant C. A. French, who had been in command of the *Southfield*, and who with six officers and about thirty men had come aboard the *Miami* over the stern as his own vessel sank, had now assumed command of the *Miami*, and knowing that it would be folly to further resist the ram when the fire of his guns had no effect upon her armor, and where there was not room to avoid her terrible beak, he withdrew to the open water at the mouth of the river, the *Albemarle* doggedly following for some distance and receiving the fire of the *Miami* with unconcern.

Besides the people of the *Southfield* who got on board the *Miami*, a few others escaped by boat and were picked up by the *Ceres* and *Whitehead;* the remainder got ashore, where some fell into the hands of the enemy, and some ultimately escaped by hiding in the swamps. Flusser was the only person killed on the *Miami;* but that vessel had one ensign, two assistant engineers, and nine enlisted men wounded, mostly by pieces of her own shells. In the engagements of the two previous days the *Ceres* had one fireman killed and three assistant engineers, one master's mate, and four men wounded.

The *Albemarle* having thus obtained command of the river, preparations were at once made by General Hoke for assaulting the Federal fortifications about Plymouth, which assault was successfully made the next day (April 20), but not without severe loss, Ransom's brigade alone leaving five hundred killed and wounded men on the field in front of the breastworks east of the town. All day long the *Albemarle* held the river front and poured shell into the Federal intrenchments. Thus far the *Albemarle* was a success. She had accomplished the first act of her mission to wrest the waters of North Carolina from the invader, and within the limits of her intended field of operations she was the symbol of what men call the dominion of the seas. Of the places remaining liable to her attack, Newbern was by far the most important, as the Union forces had recently been making it an important depot and supply station, and even as early as the time with which we are dealing stores were being assembled there in anticipation of the last stages of the grand movement of Sherman's army through Georgia, and then northward through the Carolinas. So the capture of Newbern was a move of vast importance to the Confederacy, and one to be prevented by the Federals at any cost.

News of the disaster at Plymouth traveled quickly, and the Navy Department made all haste to get a sufficient force into the Sounds to resist the progress of the *Albemarle* towards Newbern. One of the vessels hurriedly ordered to the scene of hostilities was the *Sassacus*, whose movements we will now follow. Lieutenant-Commander (now Rear Admiral) F. A. Roe was in command. The *Sassacus* left Hampton Roads just before midnight of Friday, April 22, and anchored at Hatteras Inlet at 6 the following evening; on Monday, the 25th, she crossed Hatteras bar, and soon after went aground on a sand-bar a mile inside known as the "Bulkhead," where she was delayed about twelve hours, and was disabled for a time by the condenser being filled with sand. Once inside the Sounds, she first visited Newbern, then the post on Roanoke Island, and finally, on May 3, went with other vessels up to the vicinity of Plymouth in the western end of Albemarle Sound.

Captain Melancthon Smith had been selected by the Navy Department to assume command of the naval forces in the Sounds, with special orders to devote his energies to the destruction of the *Albemarle*. The force he now had with him in Albemarle Sound consisted of the double-enders *Mattabessett*, Commander Febiger; *Sassacus*, Lieutenant-Commander Roe; *Wyalusing*, Lieutenant-Commander Queen, and *Miami*, Acting Volunteer Lieutenant French; the armed ferry-boat *Commodore Hull*, Acting Master Josselyn, and the little gunboats *Ceres* and *Whitehead*, commanded by Acting Master Foster and Acting Ensign Barrett respectively. The *Mattabessett* was the flag-ship. In Captain Smith's order of battle, issued on May 2, the *Mattabessett*, *Sassacus*, *Wyalusing*, and *Whitehead*, in the order named, were constituted the first or right line of steamers, the *Miami* being the leader of the second column. A council had been held on board the flag-ship when the vessels were in the vicinity of Roanoke Island and the methods of attacking the ram discussed; the Department and Rear-Admiral S. P. Lee, who was in command of the North Atlantic blockading squadron, seem to have favored ramming, but Captain Smith was doubtful of this mode of attack, chiefly because of the peculiar construction of the "double-enders," they having an enclosed rudder in the bow as well as one at the stern. Captain Smith was hopeful of disabling the ram by paying out seines about her, to be caught and wound up in her propellers. In the order of battle it was directed that the vessels should pass alongside the ram as close as possible and pound her with their broadsides, then round to for a second discharge. The *Miami*, which had a torpedo fitted to her bow, was to seek every opportunity to use it. All vessels were to be ready to throw powder and shell down the ram's smoke-pipe, and also to have the fire-hose ready for throwing water into the smoke-pipe should it be found so capped as to prevent the introduction of powder and shell. Ramming was doubtfully referred to, and was left to the discretion of the commanding officers. Rear-Admiral Roe told the writer recently that he took the *Sassacus* into the action that ensued with the firm intention of ramming, saying that under the circumstances he believed it would be a good trade if he could disable the enemy by "expending his vessel, his crew, and himself."

At "turn to" after the men's dinner hour on May 5 the *Miami*, *Commodore Hull*, *Ceres*, and army transport *Trumpeter* got under way from their station in Edenton Bay, and steamed across the end of the Sound with the intention of planting torpedoes in the mouth of Roanoke River. When within a short distance of the buoy at the mouth of the river the *Albemarle* was discovered coming down, accompanied by the steamer *Cotton Plant* laden with troops, and the captured army gunboat *Bombshell* with coal and stores. The *Trumpeter* was dispatched as a herald in haste to give warning to the squadron lying about ten miles down the Sound, and the *Miami* and consorts, in accordance with previous instructions, slowly retired before the foe to take their places in the plan of battle as the second line as before described.

It was a beautiful day, clear and still, and as the *Albemarle* emerged from the river and moved slowly down the bay she presented a spectacle of concentrated, deliberate power that was viewed by the anxious watchers in the fleet with anxiety and and misgiving, but not with fear. Her iron plates had been covered with grease, and shone and glistened in the sun like the scales of a dragon. Formidable as the *Albemarle* seemed, it appears that the *Boombshell* was at first regarded with even more apprehension. She was a steam canal-boat, long and flat, formerly in use on the Dismal Swamp Canal, but had been converted into a river gunboat by the army authorities, and had fallen into the hands of the Confederates at the time they captured Plymouth. Her sides were notched or indented for the reception of a large number of small field pieces, and in the refraction caused by the slanting rays of the hot afternoon sun on the shimmering water this novel craft appeared magnified, distorted, and unreal to the Union naval officers, few of whom had ever seen her before.

As soon as the ram appeared in the Sound the vessels of the squadron began getting under way to form order of battle to meet her, and in this a delay of about half an hour occurred on account of the unreadiness of the flagship. The chief engineers of all vessels in the squadron had received orders to keep their fires in readiness for steaming at a moment's notice, which order had been supplemented later by another enjoining economy in the use of coal, schooners with a supply of the latter having failed to appear when due. The two orders were successfully reconciled by all the chief engineers, upon whom their execution devolved, except in the case of the *Mattabessett*, on which vessel an allowance of coal had been fixed by authority superior to the engineer and, as it proved, so small as to prevent the maintenance of the fires in a condition for use. The result was that when the enemy did appear, the *Mattabessett* was found wanting, and was indebted only to the slow speed of the enemy for being able to get into her position at the head of the first column before the ram was upon them. After the engagement the chief engineer of the *Mattabessett*, Mr. John T. Hawkins, was suspended from duty for the delay that had occurred, but as he had written a letter to his commanding officer informing him of the insufficiency of the coal allowance, he had reason to believe himself unjustly treated, and his view was supported by a court of inquiry which acquitted him of all blame in the matter.

At 4.40 P. M. the *Albemarle* opened the battle by firing a Brooke shell, which tore the launch of the *Mattabessett* into splinters and wounded several men, following it quickly by a second, which did considerable damage to the rigging. The *Albemarle* being headed directly for the *Mattabessett* with the intention of ramming, that vessel starboarded her helm and circled around the ram to port, giving her a broadside at very close range as she passed, afterward putting her helm to port to come on around the enemy's stern. As she crossed the wake of the *Albemarle* she came close up to the *Bombshell*, fired into that vessel and received her surrender, according to the official reports. Failing to strike the *Mattabessett*, the ram turned on the *Sassacus*, and that vessel narrowly escaped being rammed as she followed the lead of the flag-ship, she pouring in her fire against the iron sides of the enemy as she passed; then, with a port helm, she rounded the stern of the *Albemarle*, and fired a broadside into the *Bombshell* still lying there, which vessel in answer to a hail said she surrendered, at the same time hauling down the Confederate flag. The *Wyalusing* coming on next in line made a move to ram the *Bombshell*, learning only just in time to avoid striking that luckless craft that she had surrendered.

There was a controversy afterward as to whether the *Bombshell* had surrendered to the *Mattabessett* or the *Sassacus*, but the weight of evidence from the official reports, viewed at this distance by one who has no interest in the dispute beyond a desire to get at the facts, points to the conclusion that the *Sassacus* was the captor. When the battle was over, the crew of the *Bombshell* was on board the *Sassacus*. The engine-room log-book of the *Sassacus* records the fact that in the eight to twelve watch that evening an assistant engineer and some engine-room men went on board the prize to take charge of the machinery. Lieutenant Hudgins, who had commanded the *Bombshell*, when asked about the matter and not knowing that there was any dispute about it, replied readily that he had surrendered to the *second* in line, which was the *Sassacus*.

As the first column of vessels passed around the starboard side of the *Albemarle* that vessel kept turning towards them with her helm aport until by the time the *Mattabessett* and *Sassacus* had gotten well across her wake she had turned almost around and was headed in the opposite direction, that is, towards the mouth of the river whence she came. This turn brought the *Mattabessett*, which vessel had continued on in her circling course, constantly firing, almost astern, while the *Sassacus*, thrown considerably out of line by her affair with the *Bombshell*, was almost abeam of the ram, and at a distance given at from three hundred to five hundred yards in the various reports. Roe saw the chance for which he hoped, and shouted to his navigator, "Can you strike her?" "Yes," answered Boutelle. "Then go for her!" As before stated, Commander Roe intended to ram if he got a chance, and this intention he had communicated to his officers. Mr. Boutelle, as the navigator or sailing-master, had entered into an understanding with Mr. Hobby, the chief engineer, to inform him should the attempt be made. Accordingly, after ringing the signal for full speed and laying the course for the enemy, he went to the engine-room skylight and shouted down to Hobby that the time had come.

There was then a pressure of thirty pounds in the boilers, which was ten pounds, or about fifty per cent., more than usually carried; the steam valves were set to cut off at about half stroke. In order to utilize the full force of the steam, the chief engineer resorted to an expedient known as "gagging" the engine, the hand working-gear being called into play to hold the steam valves open after their automatic closing had been effected by the toes on the rock-shaft. This was a task requiring a quick eye, good judgment and a high order of courage and self-reliance, for an error in working the valves of a fraction of a second at either end of the stroke would have defeated the object and destroyed the power of the engine by opposing pressure on both sides of the piston, while the danger of disaster in thus driving a heavy engine at an abnormal pressure was great. Mr. Hobby, however, had sufficient self-confidence and nerve to assume all risks involved, and imposed upon himself this dangerous post in order to get the greatest power from his machine and consequently the greatest speed from the ship. He thus became the active agent in driving the ship onward, just as an oarsman urges forward a racing boat, except that in his case the power of eight hundred horses followed up each motion of the lever that he controlled, and instead of moving a small boat he was giving momentum to a projectile weighing nearly twelve hundred tons with which to strike the enemy.

ACTION BETWEEN THE SASSACUS AND ALBEMARLE.

May 5th, 1864.

The *Sassacus* struck the *Albemarle* squarely abaft her starboard beam, and in line with the after end of the casemate, with a speed of nine or ten knots, the engines making twenty-two revolutions with thirty pounds of steam. The force of the blow drove the bronze stem of the *Sassacus* several feet into the timber belt of her antagonist and in all probability started her to leaking. The ram heeled considerably over towards the side on which she had been struck, so much so in fact that a quantity of large stones lying on her after-deck, probably to weigh her down to bring her knuckle into the water, fell overboard, making a great racket as they tumbled and slid across the deck. Hoping to ride her enemy down, the *Sassacus* kept her engines running ahead at full speed while in contact (about thirteen minutes), a furious fire of small-arms being maintained during that period. The constant pressure against the ram considerably abaft her centre of gravity tended to swing her around, which tendency was overcome to some extent by her own motion in going ahead, but eventually the resultant of these two forces so changed the angle between the ships that the starboard battery of each could be used, which advantage was quickly availed of by both; as soon as the *Sassacus* came under the range of the *Albemarle's* guns the after one was fired, its shot passing diagonally through the berth-deck, but doing no material damage; this shot was immediately followed by a similar one from the forward gun, which shot, entering the *Sassacus* abreast of the foremast four feet above the water on the starboard side, crushed obliquely through the side, cutting throught the back of a hanging-knee and leaving the inside of the ceiling about seven and one-half feet abaft where it first struck on the outside. From thence it passed through the throat of the next hanging-knee, through the dispensary and bulkhead, starboard coal-bunker, passing on through the starboard boiler, and, keeping on through the engine-room, cut in two a three-inch stanchion, thence through steerage and wardroom bulkheads, smashing doors and sideboard, cutting through magazine-screen, when, striking an oak stanchion,—which it splintered,—it glanced at right angles and lodged in one of the starboard state-rooms.

The havoc wrought in the engine-room by this shot is best told by the engine-room log for the first dog-watch of that eventful day:

"About 6 P. M. she succeeded in getting clear of us and fired a solid shot, which passed through the berth-deck and forward coal-bunker, then entering forward end of starboard boiler seven feet from front and fourteen inches from top, passing out the after end three feet from front and fourteen inches from top, cutting away in its passage stays, T-irons, and dry-pipe and steam and exhaust-pipes for Woodward pump; then passed the length of engine-room between cylinder and condenser, cutting away a three-inch stanchion and discharge-water thermometer, and badly bending exhaust unhooking gear; thence through after bulkhead. The rush of steam was instantaneous, driving all hands out of the engine and fire-room, killing Thomas Johnson, coal-heaver, instantly and severely scalding First Assistant Engineer J. M. Hobby and the following men." Then follow the names of fourteen firemen and coal-heavers, and some other information, including the statement that the engines continued to run on a vacuum until 6.35 P. M.

Pandemonium then reigned. The howl of the escaping steam from the overcharged boilers completely drowned all other sounds, even the discharge of the guns, while the steam gathered in a dense cloud over the ship, shutting off her vision so completely that the enemy close alongside could not be seen. The men on deck were bewildered by the sudden calamity and demoralized at the horrible spectacle of their scalded comrades rushing up from below frantic and screaming in agony. Order was finally restored by the officers leading the men to repel boarders on the starboard bow, although there is no record that any attempt was made by the enemy to board. The men being thus reorganized were returned to their guns, and began firing again as soon as the ram could be seen, the first proof to the on-lookers in the surrounding ships that the *Sassacus* was not destroyed being the bright flash of her guns bursting out of the cloud that hung over her. The annals of naval warfare contain few instances of persistence and dauntless courage in adversity that can match this exhibition made by the *Sassacus*. The interval during which the engines continued to run was availed of to get the ship clear of the enemy and out of the way of the other gunboats so they would be free to attack: in getting clear the starboard paddle-wheel rode over the stern guard of the *Albemarle* and was "tangled up

APPEARANCE OF BOW OF "SASSACUS" AFTER THE BATTLE.

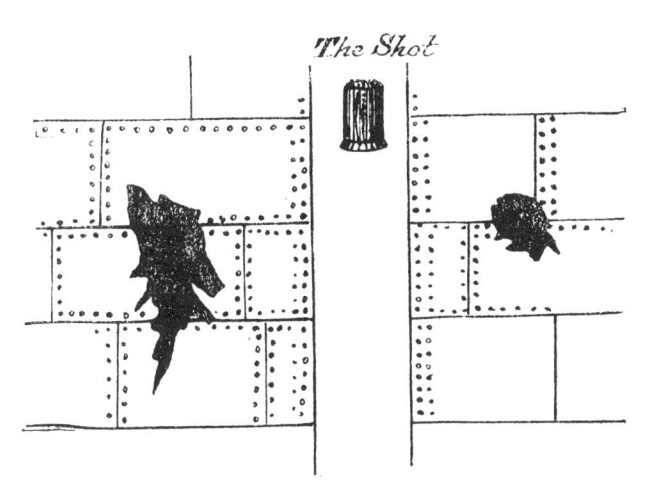

The Shot

EXIT OF SHOT FROM BOILER.   ENTRANCE OF SHOT IN BOILER.

like a cobweb," as Admiral Roe expressed it to the writer. The false stem of the *Sassacus* was so bent out of line that she steered very badly, and on her subsequent voyage to Hampton Roads she was obliged to steam backward in consequence.

In the midst of all the horrors before described, the chief engineer, although badly scalded, stood with heroism at his post; nor did he leave it until after the action was over, when he was brought up helpless to the deck. For some reason, which is not clearly stated in any of the reports, it was impossible to cut off the connection between the two boilers, so that steam from the port boiler, rapidly generated by the fierce fires in its furnaces, continued to pour out of the holes in the other boiler, thus maintaining the cloud that hung over the ship and embarrassing her movements; in this emergency Mr. Hobby saw that the fires must be hauled, not only to stop the out-rush of steam, but also to prevent the complete disabling of the ship by burning the sound boiler, not to mention the danger from its possible explosion. By his voice and example, injured as he was, he rallied some of his men and led them into the fire-room, where the necessary work was done, he doing a good part of it personally with his scalded hands. So modest was this brave man that in his official report of the engagement he dismisses this incident with the following words: "The steam so filled the engine and fire-rooms that it was with the greatest exertions on the part of the engineers that the fires were hauled." In those days of war, when all on board a ship were equally exposed to danger, and when all contributed to the fighting qualities of the ship as a unit, it was customary to accord credit for duty well done to all deserving it, irrespective of corps: accordingly we find in the reports of the commander of the *Sassacus* that praise for the conduct of Mr. Hobby which is always accorded by one brave man to another who has shared the danger and assisted to his utmost in an endeavor common to both. In the hurried report made at midnight after the battle occurs the following: "The chief engineer, Mr. Hobby, is badly scalded, but most nobly and heroically remained at his post, and saved us from a worse disaster, of explosion to the other boiler and of being helpless."

In the fuller and more complete report made by Lieutenant-

Commander Roe the following day, he speaks highly of all his officers, and of the chief engineer in the following terms:

"To the heroism and devotion of First Assistant Engineer J. M. Hobby the government is probably indebted for the preservation of the *Sassacus* from a worse disaster. While every one who could was forced to seek safety by flight from the scalding clouds of steam, Mr. Hobby stood at his post by the machinery, and though fearfully scalded himself, he cared for his machinery until the engine finally stopped. If it were possible to promote this officer, I earnestly and devoutly beg it may be done, for I consider that it has been amply and professionally won."

The medical journal of the *Sassacus* shows that Mr. Hobby was on the sick list for his injuries about three weeks, and that four of the scalded firemen subsequently died. The surgeon attributes the comparatively quick recovery of Mr. Hobby from injuries that were almost as serious as those of any of the men to the rare presence of mind shown by him in covering his burns with oil the moment he received them. A very simple remedy, and one that is well worth remembering.

As soon as the *Sassacus* was well clear of her antagonist the engagement again became general, and the ram was furiously assailed, especially after the order of battle had been restored and the vessels thus enabled to operate without danger of injuring each other. Shot and shell were poured upon the slooping sides of the enemy; seines were paid out almost encompassing him, but without success, and the *Miami* tried in vain to use her torpedo, being thwarted in this endeavor by her own slow speed and bad steering qualities. Finally, as twilight approached, the *Albemarle* headed up the Sound and proceeded slowly to the mouth of the Roanoke River, which she entered never again to emerge from. The extent of her damages has never been satisfactorily known, but it is certain that she was so much injured as to be glad to withdraw from the fight, and unwilling to renew it on another day. That the blow from the *Sassacus* did her considerable damage cannot be doubted; the muzzle of one of her guns was knocked off, although she pluckily continued to use it; several shot and shell were believed to have entered her ports, and her plaiting was observed to be much injured. An idea of the terrible pounding she received can be gained from the fact that over four hundred and sixty shot and shell were hurled against her at close range, this number not including the expenditures of the *Sassacus*, which are not given in the official reports.

The casualties on the *Albemarle*, if any, have never been known. Those of the Federals were confined to the three largest double-enders, and were: *Mattabessett*, two killed, six wounded; *Sassacus*, one killed, nineteen wounded; *Wyalusing*, one killed. Included in the number of wounded here given are the four firemen of the *Sassacus* and one man of the *Mattabessett* who subsequently died of their injuries.

The *Albemarle* returned unmolested to her fastness in the river at Plymouth, and, although she was not conquered, the result of the engagement may be regarded as a Federal victory, inasmuch as the object of the *Albemarle* was defeated: she had failed to win the supremacy of the Sounds, and Newbern remained safe from her attack. That all of the vessels in Captain Smith's command that were in the engagement performed their share in effecting this result is evident from the official reports; but as the details of this struggle become dim with the lapse of years since the roar of hostile cannon has been heard in Albemarle Sound, there is one point that rises above all others and becomes more and more prominent, and that is that the *Sassacus* was the ship that issued boldly forth from the line of battle and threw down the gage of single combat to her powerful antagonist. If praise is due to one ship more than to another we cannot help awarding it to the brave little *Sassacus*.

As soon as possible after the *Sassacus* had dropped out of the fight her engineers set to work to repair damages as far as circumstances would permit. Her engine-room log-book shows that the necessary alterations in the steam connections were completed, water run up in the port boiler, and fires started again in that boiler at 10.45 the same evening, and that at 3.30 the next morning, only about nine hours after the shot had passed through her boiler, the engines were reported ready for service. With the repairs effected by her engineers' force the ship remained in the Sounds on active service for more than a month, always steaming with one boiler, and finally steamed north and went on duty in James River without any more extensive repairs.

When the reports of this engagement had been received and considered in Washington, many of the officers of the *Sassacus* were commended by the Navy Department and promoted for gallantry in battle. Acting Masters Muldaur and Boutelle were appointed acting lieutenants; Acting Ensign Mayer, who had personally fought the forward pivot rifle, and whose shot was supposed to have been the one that knocked the muzzle off one of the enemy's guns, was made an acting master, and Acting Assistant Paymaster Barton, who had served as signal-officer and aid to the commander during the engagement, was appointed an assistant paymaster in the regular service. Lieutenant-Commander Roe was advanced *five* numbers in his grade. After reading of the advancement of a number of officers of a whole grade, one naturally wonders that their commanding officer who had led them in the fight, and whose bravery had made their promotion possible, received no greater reward than this; but on this matter the records contain nothing beyond the mere statement of fact.

The chief engineer, who had been freely voted the hero of the occasion by his associates, was overlooked in the distribution of awards and it was not until a year and a half after the battle, the war then being many months ended, that he received the recognition that was his due and was advanced in his grade in accordance with the following notification sent him by the Secretary of the Navy:

"SIR: By and with the advice and consent of the Senate you are hereby advanced thirty numbers in your grade, to take rank next after First Assistant Engineer Finney, for distinguished conduct in battle, and extraordinary heroism as mentioned in the report of Lieutenant Commander Francis A. Roe, commanding the U. S. steamer *Sassacus* in her action with the rebel ram *Albemarle* on the 5th of May, 1864. I have the pleasure to transmit herewith your warrant, the receipt of which you will acknowledge to the department.

"Very respectfully,
"GIDEON WELLES,
"*Secretary of the Navy.*"

The *Albemarle* remained at Plymouth, inactive but a constant menace to the Federals and making necessary the maintenance of a large naval force in Albemarle Sound in anticipation of her again attempting to dispute the supremacy of those waters. A daring attempt to destroy her was made the night of May 25th by some of the enlisted men of the *Wyalusing*, who conceived an excellent plan of attacking her with torpedoes, and were allowed to try the experiment without any official oversight or direction. The plan, briefly stated, was to get in the river above the ram and float down upon her two large torpedoes joined by a line or bridle, these after getting across her bows—one on either side— to be exploded by means of a hauling line in the hands of a man hidden on shore. The torpedoes, containing 100 pounds of powder each, were carried by the men on a stretcher through the swamps until a proper position was reached, when they were connected and one of the men, Charles Baldwin, coal-heaver, assumed the really heroic task of swimming down the river with them to guide them upon the *Albemarle*. The programme was accidentally interrupted by fouling a schooner, and when Baldwin finally got within a few yards of the ram he was discovered and fired upon, this thwarting the attempt and obliging the men to hide in the depths of the neighboring swamps to avoid capture. Three of them got off to their ships the second day and the other two, two days later, all having suffered much from exposure and hunger. The names of these gallant men were John W. Lloyd, coxswain; Allen Crawford and John Laverty, firemen, and Charles Baldwin and Benjamin Lloyd, coal-heavers. All received the medal of honor prescribed by Congress for bravery.

Late in October Lieutenant William B. Cushing arrived in Albemarle Sound with a large steam launch fitted with a spar torpedo, he having some time before been selected on account of his reputation for intrepidity for the perilous undertaking of assailing the ram with this instrument of destruction. The launch with the torpedo and all attached gear had been carefully fitted out at the New York navy yard by Chief Engineer William W. W. Wood and First Assistant Engineer John L. Lay, the torpedo being known in the service by the name of the latter, although it is well known that the perfection of its details was the work of Mr. Wood. The crew of the picket launch, besides Lieutenant Cushing, consisted of W. L.

Howarth, acting master's mate; William Stotesbury, acting third assistant engineer; Samuel Higgins, first class fireman, and Lorenzo Dening, Henry Wilkes and Robert H. King, landsmen. When ready for the attack this crew was increased by volunteers from the ships of the squadron as follows: Francis H. Swan, acting assistant paymaster; Charles L. Steever, acting third assistant engineer, and Thomas S. Gay, acting master's mate, from the *Otsego;* William Smith, Bernard Hartley and E. J. Houghton, ordinary seamen, from the *Chicopee;* Richard Hamilton, coal-heaver, from the *Shamrock;* and John Woodman, acting master's mate, from the *Commodore Hull.* With these additions the crew numbered fifteen all told.

The night of October 27th Cushing set out on his mission, having the second cutter of the *Shamrock* with a crew of eleven men and two officers in tow, this boat being taken along with the ambitious design of capturing the ram by boarding and bringing her out of the river uninjured. When near the ram this part of the programme was frustrated by discovery and the cutter was cast off and sent back, her crew boarding the wreck of the *Southfield* on the way down the river and taking as prisoners therefrom four Confederate pickets whose neglect of duty had permitted the boats to pass up close by them without discovery. Without answering the repeated hails from the *Albemarle* and ignoring the fire of musketry opened upon him and by which Paymaster Swan was wounded, Cushing steamed up the river past the ram, swept around in a circle, and rushed at her bows on, the impact being sufficient to breast in a boom of logs about the vessel and reach near enough to use the torpedo, which was trained into position and the firing line pulled by Cushing, standing on the bow of his boat, just as one of the *Albemarle's* guns directly overhead was depressed and fired. A large hole was blown in the side of the ram and she sank at her moorings in a short time.

Refusing the summons to surrender, Cushing told his men to look out for themselves and with them took to the water as their launch swamped from the effects of the explosion. Acting Master's Mate Woodman and Fireman Higgins were drowned; Cushing and Houghton, after much suffering and hardship, regained the squadron, and the others were made prisoners. In Lieutenant Cushing's report he made special reference to the coolness and gallantry of

Master's Mate Howarth and Engineer Stotesbury. This daring achievement led to the capture of Plymouth a few days later, removed all apprehension as to the safety of government supplies at Newbern, and released for service elsewhere the large squadron of vessels that had been kept so long in Albemarle Sound to guard against another raid of the ram. Cushing himself received the thanks of Congress and was promoted to be a lieutenant commander, he being at that time only twenty-one years of age, and all the officers who shared the expedition with him were advanced one grade for conspicuous gallantry; the enlisted men were advanced in ratings and all received the medal of honor for distinguished service and bravery.

Immediately after Cushing's return with the tidings of the sinking of the *Albemarle*, Commander Macomb, in command of the squadron known as the Naval Division of the Sounds of North Carolina, moved against Plymouth, but because of sunken vessels in the Roanoke River could not approach close enough to deliver the attack successfully. He then took his vessels by way of a branch outlet into the river above Plymouth and on the 31st of October descended upon that place and captured the enemy's batteries after a severe and well-fought engagement. Besides Macomb's vessel, the *Shamrock*, the attacking force consisted of the *Otsego*, Lieutenant Commander Arnold; *Wyalusing*, Lieutenant Commander Earl English; *Tacony*, Lieutenant Commander W. T. Truxton, all double-enders, and the armed ferry-boat *Commodore Hull*, Acting Master Josselyn. The tugs *Whitehead*, *Bazley*, and *Belle* were lashed to the unengaged sides of the three first named double-enders in accordance with the tactics established by Farragut at Port Hudson and Mobile. To guard against the distressing casualties and disablement of ships that had occurred in other engagements from boilers being struck by shot, steam was blown off the boilers on the engaged sides of the double-enders and fires in those boilers kept low banked to keep the water warm so that steam could be quickly raised when wanted. All these vessels, and others generally throughout the navy, were fitted by their engineers with appliances for closing the boiler stop-valves from deck, the affair of the *Sassacus* having demonstrated the necessity for such precaution.

The battle at Plymouth took place early in the morning of

October 31st, and, as before stated, resulted in the capture of the enemy's batteries, the town of Plymouth, and the partly submerged ram *Albemarle*. The latter was eventually raised and taken to Norfolk, where the material of which the vessel was built was sold for the benefit of the Navy Department. In this battle Commander Macomb's squadron suffered a loss of six men killed and nine wounded, the senior engineer of the *Shamrock*, Mr. W. H. Harrison, being one of the latter. The control of the ships while under way and in action in the narrow and intricate river put a difficult and responsible duty upon the engineers, which was performed with credit, as shown by the following complimentary references in the reports of commanding officers:

Shamrock: "The engineers' department, under Second Assistant Engineer W. H. Harrison, was very efficient."

Otsego: "The precaution taken by Acting First Assistant Engineer Samuel C. Midlam (in charge of this vessel's engines) to meet any mishap that might have occurred to her boilers or engine merits my approbation, and the prompt manner in which the whole engine corps performed its duty during the engagement was most satisfactory and creditable to it."

Wyalusing: "In conclusion, I cannot refrain from mentioning the handsome manner in which the engine was worked, under the supervision of Chief Engineer H. H. Stewart, through the whole engagement, and likewise on the day previous, while passing the narrow bends in Middle river."

Tacony: "The engineer's department, under its very efficient chief, First Assistant Engineer Thomas M. Dukehart, performed its duties in the most satisfactory manner."

The reward received by Cushing and his crew in the form of prize money was very considerable, as the prize law directed that when the captured vessel was of superior force to the one making the capture, as was the case in this instance, the whole of the prize money should be distributed among the captors. In 1865 the Navy

Department fixed the value of the *Albemarle* at a little less than $80,000, probably very near her true value, which amount was distributed to the crew of the picket boat or their heirs, but it afterward transpiring that property, acquired as a result of Cushing's exploit, of the net value of $282,856.80 had been applied to public use, the case was re-opened by direction of a special act of Congress and by virtue of the reappraisal Congress appropriated $202,912.80, the difference between the former award and the new appraisal, which was distributed in 1873.

The case became very much involved, Cushing being paid on the basis of his salary instead of being awarded one-tenth of the whole as commander of the capturing vessel, and he and some of the other officers had their shares computed upon the rates of pay of the higher grades into which they were promoted after the event, while others received only the share to which their rate of pay entitled them, this latter being the proper apportionment as provided by law. As a result of the illegal method followed, some of the beneficiaries were very much overpaid, while others suffered in consequence and received less than their true shares. The matter finally got before Congress in the form of a bill which was favorably reported by the Naval committee, but never became a law, and as the original appropriation had been distributed those who were wronged got no redress. An interesting item connected with the last Congressional investigation of the matter was the testimony of Admiral Porter before the naval committee, he stating that the *Albemarle* had cost the Confederates $1,500,000, and could not have been built and equipped as she was, in Northern shipyards, for less than $800,000, which opinion shows that a man may become eminent in a profession without being familiar with the practical business details upon which it is founded. The following table, taken from the report of the naval committee (Report No. 97; 45th Congress, 2d Session) exhibits the actual distribution of this prize money, with the amount received by each officer and man, or their heirs, and the amount that each was over or underpaid.

Rate of Pay Adopted.	True Rate.		DISTRIBUTION MADE.			True Shares.	Overpaid.	Underpaid.
			1865	1873	Total.			
$1,875	$\frac{1}{20}$	Admiral Porter	$3,864.93	$9,791.82	$13,656.75	$13,656.75		
	$\frac{1}{100}$	Commander Breese	772.98	1,958.37	2,731.35	2,731.35		
	$\frac{1}{50}$	Commander Macomb		5,462,70	5,462.70	5,462.70		
2,342	$\frac{1}{10}$	Lieutenant Cushing	15,112.50	} 38,103.69	56,056.27	27,313.51	$28,742.76	
		Same afterwards as Commander						
1,200	$480	Master's Mate Howarth	2,840.08	24,394.17	35,887.50	16,745.48	19,142.02	
1,500		Same afterwards as Master	9,194.66					
1,200		Master's Mate Gay	2,298.67					
	480	Paymaster Swan	3,868.81	24,841.19	28,710.00	16,745.48	11,964.52	
	1,300	3rd Asst. Engr. Stotesbury	10,477.97	20,624.53	31,102.50	45,352.32		$14,249.82
	1,000	" " Steever	8,060.00	15,865.00	23,925.00	34,886.40		10,961.40
	1,000	Master's Mate Woodman	8,060.00	15,865.00	23,925.00	34,886.40		10,961.40
	480	Fireman Higgins	3,868.81	7,615.19	11,484.00	16,745.48		5,261.48
	360	Coal-heaver Hamilton	2,901.50	5,711.51	8,613.01	12,559.10		3,946.09
	240	Ordinary seam'n Houghton	1,934.41	3,807.60	5,742.01	8,372.73		2,630.72
	192	" " Harley	1,547.53	3,046.07	4,593.60	6,698.20		2,104.60
	192	" " Smith	1,547.53	3,046.07	4,593.60	6,698.20		2,104.60
	192	Landsman King	1,547.53	3,046.07	4,593.60	6,698.20		2,104.60
	168	" Wilkes	1,354.09	2,665.31	4,019.40	5,860.93		1,841.53
	168	" Deming	1,354.09	2,665.31	4,019.40	5,860.93		1,841.53
	168		1,354.09	2,665.31	4,019.40	5,860.93		1,841.53
		Amount for distribution	81,960.18	191,174.91	273,135.09	273,135.09	59,849.30	59,849.30
			77,298.70	195,836.39				
		Difference	4,661.48					

CHAPTER XXVI.

"An examination of facts is the foundation of science."
CHAS. H. HASWELL.

1864. The Civil War, Continued—New Ships and Machinery Begun—The SERAPIS Class—The RESACA Class—Competitive Machinery of the QUINNEBAUG and SWATARA—The STROMBOLI, or SPUYTEN DUYVIL—The Light-Draft Monitors —Petition of the Engineer Corps Addressed to Congress and its Results.

THE work of building a great steam navy, so vigorously prosecuted during the three preceding years, went forward in 1864, but with a less number of new vessels projected, and of these still fewer ever reached completion. One more of the large swift cruisers of the *Wampanoag* class was ordered and the machinery at once begun at the Washington navy yard, the keel of this vessel, which was given the name of *Bon Homme Richard*, was never laid, and the ship, therefore, never existed except on paper; but the engines, of the 100-inch geared type, like those of the *Wampanoag*, were carried to completion in the course of about four years, and remained in store at the Washington yard for many years, being finally broken up and the material used for various purposes.

Eight screw-sloops of 2,400 tons displacement, slightly larger than the *Shenandoah* class, were projected in 1864, and named *Algoma, Confiance, Detroit, Meredosia, Peacock, Serapis, Taghkanic,* and *Talledaga*. Of these only one, the *Algoma*, built at the Kittery navy yard, was ever constructed, she being launched in 1868, and continued in the service, the name being changed in 1869 to *Benicia*, until 1884, when she was sold at Mare Island for $17,000. The Bureau of Steam Engineering, carrying out its instructions, undertook the work of building engines for these ships at the navy yards, several of the yards being by this time supplied with suitable tools, and four sets of the engines required were commenced at each of the yards at Boston and New York. They were of the usual Isherwood back-acting type, the cylinders being 50 inches diameter by 42 inches stroke. One pair of these was erected in the *Benicia*, and three pairs went into some vessels built in 1868—the *Alaska*,

Omaha and *Plymouth* (originally named *Kenosha*); the other four sets were converted into compound engines for vessels built or re-engined in 1872–1880.

Six smaller screw-sloops, of what was known as the *Resaca* class, were also projected this year, and four of them were launched eventually at navy yards as follows: The *Swatara* at Philadelphia, May, 1865; the *Resaca* at Kittery, November, 1865; the *Quinnebaug* at New York, March, 1866; and the *Nantasket* at Boston, August, 1867. The other two, named *Alert* and *Epervier*, were never built. The four completed were each 216 feet long and about 12 feet mean draft, the *Nantasket* and *Resaca* being 31 feet beam and 1,129 tons displacement, and the other two 30 feet beam and 1,113 tons displacement. The engines of the *Swatara*, *Resaca* and *Nantasket* were of the Isherwood design, with cylinders 36"x36", and were built at navy yards, the two former at Washington and the latter at Kittery. By direction of Assistant Secretary Fox the engines for the *Quinnebaug* were contracted for in England, with Jackson & Watkins, of London, the object of this unusual proceeding being to subject the machinery designed by the Bureau of Steam Engineering to a competitive test with that produced by the best English practice. The *Quinnebaug's* model was altered for the reception of twin screws to suit the English machinery, which consisted of two pairs of two-cylinder engines with cylinders 38 inches in diameter by 21 inches stroke of piston. The grate surface of the boilers was 114 square feet, while that of the other sloops of the class was 210 each. The English engines were designed on the high expansion principle, the valves cutting off at one-fourth stroke, while Isherwood's engines cut off at six-tenths of the stroke.

The machinery for the *Swatara*, the sister-ship of the *Quinnebaug*, was nearly completed when the contract for the machinery of the latter was made, and the contractors were informed of the exact dimensions and arrangement of the machinery against which they were to compete. They believed, however, that with twin screws and the high rate of expansion adopted, their area of grate surface would give better results in speed and economy than the Bureau's design. The result was greatly to the disadvantage of the English engines. The *Swatara* on her steam trial near Hampton Roads made twelve geographical miles per hour, while the *Quinnebaug's* best effort in New York harbor was seven geographical miles, both vessels burning the same kind of coal and having the same conditions of trial as nearly as possible. The *Quinnebaug* made one cruise of about three years' duration on the Brazil station and was then laid up; she subsequently was rebuilt and received a pair of the 50"x42" Isherwood engines, converted into compound engines.

The *Alert* and *Epervier* were never built, but the Bureau of Steam Engineering carried out the Department's order and constructed machinery for them, that for the *Alert*, built at Kittery, being exactly like the machinery of Bureau design put into the other ships of the class. The *Epervier's* engines were of the same back-acting type but the proportional dimensions of the cylinders were changed, they being 36 inches in diameter and 48 inches stroke; they were built at the Washington navy yard and were of remarkably excellent workmanship and quality, the forged parts of them being of steel, which was the first use of that material for such purpose in our navy or in the engine practice of the country. In 1870 these engines were prepared for erection in the *Quinnebaug* in place of the defective English engines, but before the work of altering the vessel to receive them was completed it was determined to fit her with compound engines, and the *Epervier's* engines were soon after shipped to the Norfolk navy yard for stowage. In 1876 they were exhibited at the Centennial Exposition in Philadelphia as an example of excellence in navy yard work, and were thereafter stowed at the Norfolk yard until as late as 1894, when an order was reluctantly given by the engineer-in-chief to break them up and make use of the material, the changes in marine engine practice having precluded the possibility of their ever being made use of.

At the time Mr. Fox ordered a contract made for the engines of the *Quinnebaug* in England, a pair of 36" x 36" Isherwood engines for that vessel were practically completed at the Washington navy yard; there being thus no ship for this pair of engines they were sent to the Naval Academy in 1866 and erected in the new department of steam engineering at that institution, where they have remained ever since, a valuable object lesson originally to the cadet engineers of much that was excellent in marine engineering, but eventually transformed by the changing years into relics of what has been and is no more.

U. S. S RESACA, 1865.

Contracts were made this same year for the *Pinta* class of large iron sea-going tugs, designed to carry two guns and to be of general usefulness in the operations of war. The class embraced nine vessels in all, six being built by James Tetlow, Boston; two by Reany & Archbold, Chester, Pa., and one, the *Triana*, by Wm. Perrine, New York. Their cost complete varied from $84,640 to $128,000 each. The principal dimensions were, length, 137 feet; beam, 26 feet; displacement, 420 tons, and registered tonnage 350. Three of these steamers—the *Fortune*, *Mayflower*, and *Standish*—in after years became familiar and not especially beloved objects to the youth of the engineer corps as practice vessels for summer cruising from the Naval Academy. Two smaller tugs, the *Pilgrim* and *Maria*, of 170 tons each, were also built in 1864 by contract, and several other smaller ones were undertaken at navy yards, the events of the war having shown the value of such vessels in carrying on warlike operations.

Continued Confederate successes with torpedoes finally forced the Navy Department to give attention to that weapon, on the principal of fighting the devil with fire, and proposals were issued inviting inventors to submit plans for boats and torpedoes to use with them. Many designs were submitted, from which those of Chief Engineer W. W. W. Wood and First Assistant John L. Lay were accepted and the work of constructing the boats and torpedoes begun under the direction of these engineers in the spring of 1864. Wood and Lay's plans embraced two projects; one of fitting large steam launches with a torpedo on a spar, and the other of building a regular armored torpedo boat like a small monitor and equipping it with a torpedo on the end of a long bar operated by steam, both of which plans were accepted. A number of steam launches were fitted out and supplied with torpedoes by Wood and Lay during the the summer of 1864 and one of these was the boat placed at the disposal of Lieutenant Cushing and with which he sank the *Albemarle*.

The spar was carried in suitable supports or crutches alongside the boat and could be run forward and the end submerged to the desired depth by attached ropes. The torpedo consisted of a cylindrical copper case held in a scoop at the end of the spar and so overlooped by a line that it could be thrown out of the scoop when desired. It was only partly filled with powder, the remainder of the case being an air chamber separated from the powder by a partition, the two parts being so proportioned that the specific gravity of the whole was slightly less than that of water. Running down from the air-chamber end was a tube with a fulminate cap in its lower end near the bottom of the powder space and provided with a grape-shot held in the upper end by a pin working through a stuffing box, and to which a hauling line was attached. When used, the spar and torpedo were lowered under or near the object to be attacked and the torpedo thrown forward from the scoop by means of the first line. Its construction then caused it to float with the air end uppermost and with a tendency to rise to the surface or against the bottom of the attacked vessel. By pulling the second line the pin could then be withdrawn, causing the grapeshot to fall upon the cap and explode the charge of powder. Besides the torpedo these picket boats were armed with one 12-pounder boat howitzer mounted on the bow.

The other plan resulted in the building of a torpedo boat by contract with Samuel H. Pook of New Haven, Conn., which was first named *Stromboli* but soon afterward changed to *Spuyten Duyvil*. To this vessel Lieutenant Commander Barnes, writing a treatise on submarine warfare, in 1868, referred to as "the most formidable engine of destruction for naval warfare now afloat of which the public have any knowledge." The contract for this boat, dated June 1, 1864, required that "for the consideration hereinafter mentioned, he will construct upon the plan of Mr. Wm. W. W. Wood, Chief Engineer, U. S. Navy, a torpedo vessel in accordance with specifications herewith attached, of the following dimensions, viz: length of keel, 75 feet; breadth of hull, $19\frac{1}{2}$ feet; depth of hold 9 feet more or less." As actually built the boat was 84 feet 2 inches long; 20 feet 8 inches extra beam; 7 feet 5 inches draft, and of 207 tons displacement. The total cost was $45,036.29.

When going into action the draft was increased to about nine feet by admitting water into sinking tanks, thereby lessening the exposure above water. The deck was covered with three inches of iron; the sides with five inches, and the pilot-house with five inches. The torpedo was the same in principle as the one fitted to the picket boats, but was so much larger that it was worked by machinery which ran the torpedo-bar out through a water-tight box and gate-valve in the bow, the detachment and firing of the torpedo being automatic when the extreme reach of the bar was attained, and at the same time the return motion of the bar was begun. When the bar had returned to its inboard position the gate-valve was closed, the water-box pumped out, which could be done in a few seconds, and everything was then ready for attaching another torpedo. The weight of the torpedo handling machinery was ten tons while that of the motive engine was only two and one-half tons.

The *Spuyten Duyvil* was in service in the James River during the last months of the war and had the honor of taking President Lincoln to Richmond when he visited that city after its abandonment by the enemy. She subsequently made extensive use of her torpedoes by blowing up the obstructions that had been placed in the river by both Union and Confederate combatants. After the war she remained for many years at the New York navy yard and was subjected to many improvements by her inventors, as well as serving for a series of experiments in torpedo warfare upon which much of our modern torpedo practice and knowledge is founded.

The twenty light-draft monitors undertaken in 1863 began arriving at completion in 1864 and immediately revealed defects so serious as to destroy their usefulness. The history of these vessels is as unfortunate a chapter of errors as the annals of our navy during the war afford, involving as it does an account of much public money expended for which the nation received no benefit. So little attention had been given to the displacement of the vessels that it was found they would float with only three inches of freeboard instead of fifteen, as intended, a difference that practically ruined their efficiency. Various causes contributed to this result and none of the officials connected with their construction was entirely blameless, but the principal responsibility fell upon Chief Engineer A. C. Stimers, the general inspector of iron-clads, who had been given free scope by the Department to have the monitors built according to his own ideas.

The matter was so serious that it became the subject of an investigation by a committee of the House of Representatives and also by the joint Congressional Commission on the Conduct of the War: the latter investigation occupies 124 pages in volume III of the 1865 series of that committee's report, and is a useful document to the historian and biographer, because by judiciously selecting extracts from it, as some writers have already done, it is easy to prove credit or culpability indifferently in the case of any individual concerned. As the object of this book is to call spades by their right names within the bounds of propriety and to tell the truth so far as it can be ascertained, the following outline of this unhappy story is given as the most probable version deducible from the mass of conflicting and in some cases decidedly spiteful testimony. In arriving at conclusions the author has given especial weight to the testimony of Assistant Secretary of the Navy Gustavus V. Fox, who was an official superior to the contractors and officers connected with the building of the vessels, was less apt to have any personal grudges or rivalries to ventilate.

The need for light-draft armored vessels, especially for service on the Mississippi River and its tributaries, impressed itself upon the Navy Department during the summer of 1862. Mr. John Ericsson was appealed to for designs and he decided that the proposed draft of water (four feet) was incompatible with impregnability. He afterward furnished the Department with general plans for monitors of the required type, but of six feet draft, which he pronounced the least possible for vessels of the desired size, armor and battery. Ericsson being engrossed with the *Puritan* and *Dictator* and the *Passaic* class, as well as with the *Canonicus* class then being built from his designs, had little time for new work and his plans were turned over to Chief Engineer Stimers to be developed. Mr. Stimers was directed to establish an office in New York adjacent to that of Ericsson for convenience in consultation, and was given practically unlimited power in the matter of designs, inspection, authority to make changes, etc., the Secretary of the Navy ordering him verbally not to trouble the Department with letters on technical matters but to judge and act for himself.

Mr. Stimers proceeded on the line of his instructions so literally as to lose the benefit of advice from the heads of the two mechanical bureaus of the Department—construction and steam engineering—neither of whom he consulted except informally when visiting Washington at intervals, and both of whom naturally felt aggrieved that a subordinate officer should be permitted to direct extensive work pertaining to them without being in any way under their control. Stimers in fact ruled a combined construction and engineering bureau of his own with a staff of assistants, draftsmen and clerks that was, as testified before the Congressional committee, almost as numerous as the total office force of all the bureaus of the Navy Department, and he was subject to no authority less than that of the Department. Rear Admiral F. H. Gregory, who was on the retired list, was on duty in New York as general superintendent of all ship and engine work being done by contract along the Atlantic coast for the navy and all correspondence had to be forwarded through his office, but as his naval service dated from 1809 it is not probable that he exercised any technical direction over steam vessels or steam engines. In fact, when the contracts for the light-draft monitors were made Admiral Gregory received an order from the Department informing him "very laconically," to quote from his testimony, that Mr. Stimers would have entire charge of all vessels building on the Ericsson plan. The admiral succeeded after a number of months in getting this order so modified that Stimers had to forward all communications through him and obtain his approval, but, to depend upon the admiral's testimony again, Stimers went right on ordering changes and writing letters over his head. Mr. Stimers probably thought that in busy times action was more important than red tape, and there is no doubt whatever that he had the tacit consent of the Department to hasten matters along by communicating directly with the contractors in all technical matters.

To add to the difficulty arising from Stimers' relations with the construction and engineering bureaus he fell out with his friend Ericsson about this time and this so nearly concluded their intercourse that Ericsson's opinions were thereafter seldom sought and never volunteered. The occasion of the estrangement was the unsympathetic manner in which Stimers had tested Ericsson's friction gear on the *Canonicus;* a trifling matter for middle-aged men to quarrel about, but sufficient to cause Ericsson, proud, stubborn, and imperious as he was, to avoid his former friend and protégé and leave him to his own resources.

Many changes were made in Ericsson's original plans and many of these changes were of a nature to increase the weight and draft of the vessels. Instead of the boilers proposed by Ericsson a different type with differential tubes, designed by Stimers himself,[1] were adopted, and these, in the opinion of Ericsson, were twice as large and heavy as the size of the engines required, although Stimers claimed that they were designed to furnish steam for all the main and auxiliary machinery in the ship should the unlikely occasion of using it all at the same time arise. The engines were considerably reduced in size, being finally made with cylinders 22 inches in diameter and 30 inches stroke of piston, one engine being placed on each side of the ship, inclined upwards, and driving a screw-shaft on the opposite side, the vessels all having twin-screws. After the first fight of the iron-clads with Fort Sumter it was decided to fit all the monitors then building with heavy base rings around the turrets, and this, in the case of the light-drafts, increased their weight about eighteen tons each, and also added much to the cost, the most of them being under contract before the change was ordered. The pilot-houses were also made thicker and heavier as a result of the experience gained in the Fort Sumter fight.

The most important change was in fitting large tanks along the sides inside the vessels for carrying water to increase the draft purposely; this was ordered by the Department on the urgent recommendation of Rear Admiral Joseph Smith, chief of the Bureau of Yards and Docks, the idea being that when the vessel grounded in shallow and little-known rivers, as would necessarily occur sometimes, she could be quickly floated by pumping out these tanks. The intention was excellent, but the application of the idea to vessels of only 15 inches freeboard was of doubtful propriety as it involved much extra weight for the tanks, piping, valves, and pumping engines, not to mention the weight of water to be carried.

A serious mistake involving additional weight was made in Stimers' office in calculating the weight of the oak deck and side timbers, of which latter especially there was an enormous mass. It appears from the testimony that the weight of seasoned white oak timber formed the basis for the estimates, no allowance being made

---

[1] These boilers had the same differential sizing of tubes as those of the *Canonicus* class illustrated in a former chapter, but the structural design was different. To make the boilers low enough to go into the shallow hulls, the tube boxes were placed *between* the furnaces, two of the latter being at each end of the boiler.

U. S. S. MAYFLOWER.

Fitted as a Practice Steamer for Cadet Engineers.

for the fact, then well enough known, that green timber would have to be used on account of the supply of seasoned oak ship timbers at the North being completely exhausted. The result of all the changes and errors was that when the first of the light-draft monitors —the *Chimo*—was launched she was found to draw about a foot more water than was intended, leaving her deck almost awash. The certainty that others of the class would possess the same fatal defect was a startling discovery to the Department and a cause of chagrin to Mr. Fox who had selected Chief Engineer Stimers for their superintendence and who was chiefly responsible for the conferring upon him of power superior to the bureaus under whose cognizance their building properly belonged. The crying need for light-draft armored vessels in the Western rivers and the great things that had been promised from these monitors were well known to the public, and this made the failure more notorious and disappointing.

Mr. Fox went immediately to New York and held a consultation with Mr. Ericsson and Chief Engineers King and Wood as to what should be done, his desire being to remedy the defects if possible and get monitors with which to make war, rather than to waste time in speculating as how the mistake had been made or who was to blame for it. It was decided that the only remedy was to build the vessels up about twenty-two inches, thereby still further increasing their draft with the added weight and lessening their usefulness for service in shallow waters, but which would give the country monitors that could be made of some use. This was done with fifteen of them at an additional cost of from $55,000 to $115,000 each, varying with the degree of completion when the change was ordered. The water-tanks with their pipes and pumps were taken out of nearly all of them. This work of raising the sides of the vessels so delayed their completion that they were not finished in time to be of any service before the war came to an end, and their cost was therefore practically thrown away.

The officer in command of the North Atlantic blockading squadron having asked for light-draft armored vessels to be used as torpedo boats in the North Carolina Sounds and James River, it was decided to equip five of these monitors for that purpose without their turrets and without building their decks up, which was done with those nearest completion when the fault in displacement was dis-

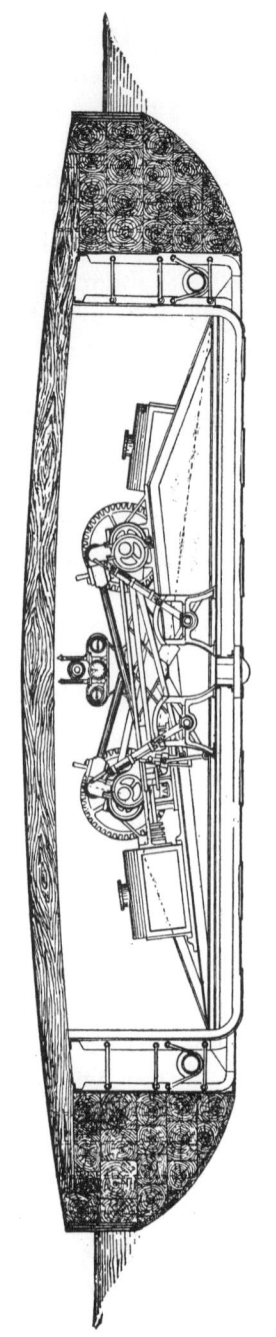

LIGHT DRAFT MONITOR. SECTION THROUGH ENGINE ROOM.

covered, they being fitted with spar-torpedo gear of the Wood–Lay invention. They had a gun mounted on deck forward without any protection for the men who would work it, a serious objection for service in narrow rivers within easy gunshot of the banks, and their speed was barely five miles an hour, which made their use as torpedo boats almost ludicrous. These five were in active service for several months before the end of the war, but their employment was of little use to the government. The others after being built up became reasonably good monitors for coast service and were seaworthy, as appears from a report made by Acting Lieutenant Commander H. A. Gorringe, an excellent sea-officer, relative to a voyage of the *Waxsaw* from Hampton Roads to Philadelphia in January, 1866, although it was asserted by the opponents of Mr. Stimers that they would be worthless even after modification.

Mr. Gorringe says: "We experienced during the whole passage fresh northerly winds, and a heavy swell from the southeast, which gave us an opportunity of testing the sea-worthiness of this class of monitor. I beg leave to add that the behavior of this vessel during the passage has increased the confidence I already had in the ability of this class of monitor to ride out safely a gale of wind."

The responsibility for this deplorable failure and waste of public money rests largely upon Chief Engineer Stimers, though not by any means so completely as the enemies of that officer charged. The added weights due to the heavy base-rings around the turrets, the water-ballast equipment, and increased armor on the pilot-houses, were not by his direction. The testimony before the joint Committee on the Conduct of the War developed the fact that the error in computing the weight of timber was committed by a draftsman in Stimers' office and that Stimers had not personally verified the calculations. In this he was of course to blame as the responsible official, in precisely the same manner that the commander of a ship is responsible for disasters due to the mistakes of the navigator or other subordinate officer. Although officially culpable, there is no evidence to show that the blunder resulted from personal incompetence on the part of Mr. Stimers, and there is much to prove that physical impossibility and not negligence was the cause of his failure to critically examine the work of his subordinates.

Besides the twenty light-draft monitors, Mr. Stimers had under his general direction the building of a number of other iron vessels, the *Canonicus* class especially, and he was required to be absent from his office in New York much of the time visiting ship and engine works in many cities where these vessels were under construction. In the spring of 1863, just at the time when the plans for the light-drafts were being completed and the contracts being awarded, he was sent as superintending engineer to the iron-clad fleet off Charleston and was absent on that duty for two months. For four months during the summer of 1863 when his whole time should have been given to the new monitors his attention was largely occupied with the court of inquiry investigating the charges preferred against him by Rear Admiral DuPont, which in itself was sufficient to distract his mind from his legitimate duties, as his reputation and commission in the navy were at stake. The report made by Senator Wade, the chairman of the Committee on the Conduct of the War, states the difficulties under which Mr. Stimers labored, and that report does not specifically fix the responsibility for the failure upon him.

The Department detached Mr. Stimers from his duty as general inspector and put the work of completing the monitors in other hands; but beyond this nothing was done to punish him for his part in the affair. Assistant Secretary Fox wrote: "I cannot be too hard upon Stimers, who helped us in the first *Monitor* with so much zeal and courage." The shortcomings of Mr. Stimers in connection with these vessels may properly be charged to an excess of ambition. His connection with the *Monitor* had made his name well known throughout the country, and his subsequent responsible connection with the building of armored vessels had still further extended his fame and associated his name with that of Ericsson as an exponent and champion of the new order of war ships. When, therefore, he was trusted by the Department with almost absolute power in the construction of the light-drafts, from which so much was expected that the whole country knew of them, he sought to achieve all the honor for their success by refusing advice from older and wiser men than himself, and in attempting too much came to disaster. His professional reputation was so well established, however, that it was not overthrown by this failure, and at the close of the war he received such inducements as to resign his commission and enter upon practice as a consulting engineer in New York under the most favorable and prosperous circumstances. Not long thereafter he fell a victim to an epidemic of small-pox and lost his life.

As John Ericsson stood before the country as the inventor and sponsor of the monitor type of war-ship, and as his name was linked with the light-drafts and all other monitors, he received much public censure for their failure; a censure that was almost entirely undeserved. When asked by the joint committee in what relation he stood to the twenty light-draft monitors, he replied: "I have nothing whatever to do with those twenty monitors, directly or indirectly." He did, however, furnish the original plans and some of his details were carried out; in his own testimony further on he said that the turrets were arranged very nearly according to his principle and instructions, and from his testimony and that of others it is proved that although he ceased intercourse with Stimers the draftsmen from the latter's office frequently consulted him as to different details. It is true that he disapproved of almost everything shown him, but the fact admitted by himself that he was consulted is proof enough that he had some connection with the work, for no one who has any conception of his devotion to work and intolerance of interruption can believe that he would have given a moment of his time to anything that did not concern him. There is no doubt whatever that he knew that Stimers was supposed to be working under his direction, and the fact that a quarrel between them should have prevented the one from seeking advice and the other from insisting upon giving it, is not at all creditable to either.

Although busily employed with the duties compelled by war, the naval engineers found time at the beginning of 1864 to prepare and submit to Congress a memorial asking for legislation in their interests in certain directions. This document was neatly gotten up in pamphlet form with a decorative cover embellished with engravings of the *Monitor* and *Wampanoag* and a wreath made up of weapons of war and engineer's instruments—the *arms* and the *tools* symbolical of the naval and military engineer's calling. The memorial asked for an increase of pay commensurate with that received by other officers of the navy and dwelt at length upon the desirability of establishing some regular system of education and training for the future engineers of the navy. Both objects were attained. Congress passed a bill, which received Presidential approval July 4, 1864, establishing the course of instruction for cadet engineers at the Naval Academy and fixing a new rate of pay for engineer officers, amounting to an increase for all grades of about twenty-two per cent., the new rate being shown by the following extract from the act:

"SEC. 6. *And be it further enacted*, That the number of chief engineers shall not exceed one for each first and second rate vessel in the navy, with such first, second, and third assistant engineers, or those acting as such, as the wants of the service actually require. And that from and after the passage of this act the annual pay of the engineer officers of the navy, on the active list, shall be as follows: Every chief engineer on duty, for the first five years after the date of his commission, two thousand two hundred dollars. For the second five years after the date of his commission, two thousand five hundred dollars. For the third five years after the date of his commission, two thousand eight hundred dollars. After fifteen years after the date of his commission, three thousand dollars. Every chief engineer on leave or waiting orders, for the first five years after the date of his commission, one thousand five hundred dollars. For the second five years after the date of his commission, one thousand six hundred dollars. For the third five years after the date of his commission, one thousand seven hundred dollars. After fifteen years after the date of his commission, one thousand eight hundred dollars. Every first assistant engineer on duty, one thousand five hundred dollars. While on leave or waiting orders, one thousand one hundred dollars. Every second assistant engineer on duty, one thousand two hundred dollars. While on leave or waiting orders, nine hundred dollars. Every third assistant engineer on duty, one thousand dollars. While on leave or waiting orders, eight hundred dollars."

CHAPTER XXVII.

"And the long mountains ended in a coast of ever-shifting sand,
And far away the phantom circle of a moaning sea.
There the pursuer could pursue no more,
And he that fled no further fly the king;
And there, that day when the great light of heaven
Burn'd at his lowest in the rolling year,
On the waste sand by the waste sea they closed."

ALFRED TENNYSON.

1865. The Civil War, Concluded—Loss of the SAN JACINTO—Second Attack on Fort Fisher—The PATAPSCO Destroyed by a Torpedo—Charleston Abandoned by the Confederates—The Monitors MILWAUKEE and OSAGE Sunk—Loss of the SCIOTA and ADA—Restoration of Peace—Some Naval Lessons of the War—Armed Merchant Vessels Unsuited for Operations of War—Casualities of the Engineer Corps During the Rebellion.

THE last year of the great war began with a naval disaster, though one not due to the action of the enemy. The old and troublesome screw-steamer *San Jacinto*, under command of Captain R. W. Meade, father of the present rear admiral of the same name, at 1.30 A. M. January 1st, struck on a reef between Green Turtle and No Name Keys and became a wreck, her guns and a considerable quantity of stores and equipment being saved by the crew, who camped on No Name Keys until taken north by the *Tallapoosa*. The *San Jacinto* had been attached to the East Gulf blockading squadron during the greater part of the war and had not had an occasion to achieve any particular distinction after the *Trent* affair in 1861. In 1863, while under repairs at New York, she had been made valuable use of by being turned over to a board of naval engineers for a competitive test of boilers, she having one each of the two types then standard—vertical water-tube and horizontal fire-tube. Similar experiments had been conducted with her boilers in 1858, and the knowledge gained on the two occasions was of quite as much benefit to the country as any achievement in war by a vessel of her class could have been.

On the 13th, 14th, and 15th of January, Rear Admiral Porter, acting in conjunction with Major General Terry and 10,000 troops, made a second and successful attack upon Fort Fisher, the adjacent fortifications on the river and Wilmington itself falling not long afterward as results of the victory. The naval force under Porter's command was the largest that has ever been in action under the American flag, as well as the most powerful fleet in men and guns that has been assembled for a hostile purpose in modern times. The main force consisted of forty-four war steamers, including almost all the largest vessels of war built for the U. S. Navy from the *Powhatan* and *Susquehanna* period down to that of the *New Ironsides* and *Monadnock*, they being ranged in a line about a mile distant from and parallel to the fortified shore line, upon which a continuous fire from hundreds of the heaviest guns then known was concentrated. Outside the line of battle lay a reserve division of fourteen smaller steamers not engaged in the bombardment but made use of in assisting and covering the landing of troops and in carrying despatches. The *New Ironsides* and the four monitors named in a previous chapter as participating in the first attack upon this fort were stationed within about half a mile of the shore, from which position they used their heavy guns with terrible effect. The nearness of their station made them targets for small arm as well as great-gun fire, but they suffered no damage except of a temporary nature to their light upper works and had very few casualties. On the *Canonicus* two men were wounded during the bombardment and Second Assistant Engineer John W. Saville was shot through both thighs by a grape-shot that had passed over the heads of the assaulting party on shore and came aboard the vessel. On the *Saugus* one man only was injured, and he by the bursting of a XV-inch gun; another XV-inch gun burst on the *Mahopac* but without injuring anyone.

On the 15th, fourteen hundred sailors and marines were landed from the fleet to assault the sea face of Fort Fisher while the troops attacked from the land side, the combined assault resulting in the capture of the enemy's works about ten o'clock that night. The naval brigade was obliged to land on a sand beach with no shelter or protection whatever and suffered severely without being able to gain the objective point, although its attack diverted the enemy from resisting in force the assault of the troops. The total loss of the navy was 309—74 killed; 213 wounded; 22 missing, or nearly as many as at the battle of Mobile Bay. About one-third of these casualties occurred the morning of the 16th, after the fort had been taken possession of, by the accidental explosion of a powder magazine, the paymaster and an ensign of the *Gettysburg* being killed at this time. Assistant Surgeon William Longshaw, who had on a previous occasion greatly distinguished himself by gallantry in the monitor fleet off Charleston, was killed in the assault of the 15th, he being shot while in the act of ministering to a wounded marine. Altogether seven officers were killed and about fifteen wounded in the Fort Fisher battle.

The few following extracts from reports of commanding officers are selected from many of like tenor and will be sufficient to show that the engineer corps bore its full share in the battle both afloat and ashore.

From the report of Commodore S. W. Godon of the Susquehanna:
"Chief Engineer Johnson, with his entire department, are also entitled to my thanks; they not only performed their duties with proper spirit, but, in the absence of the portion of my crew forming the landing party, assisted at the guns as far as lay in their power."

From the report of Commander E. G. Parrott of the Monadnock:
"Acting Chief Engineer J. Q. A. Zeigler, by faithfully watching for symptoms of failing of the turret and other gear, and the application of timely and rapid repairs, enabled us to come out of the action in perfect order."

From the report of Lieutenant Commander T. C. Harris of the Yantic:
"At 10.30 sent a landing party on shore, composed of forty-two (42) men, in command of Acting Ensigns J. C. Lord and S. T. Dedener, and Acting Third Assistant Engineer George Holton, with orders to report to Lieutenant Commander K. R. Breese, (fleet captain). . . .
. . . "Acting Third Assistant Engineer Holton was also a volunteer, and had charge of the entrenching party. I have learned that he was always in the advance, cheering the men on, and exposing himself in the most gallant manner. I think that he may be made a Third Assistant Engineer in the regular service."

From the report of Lieutenant Comander D. L. Braine of the Pequot:
" To Second Assistant Engineer (in charge) A. H. Fisher I am much indebted, for without his skill and perseverance the ship would not have been in a condition to enter action without being towed."

News of the victory of Fort Fisher was carried by a despatch vessel to Hampton Roads and thence telegraphed to Washington and the country. The senior officer at Hampton Roads, Commander E. T. Nichols, selected Second Assistant Engineer David P. Jones (now chief engineer, retired) to carry the information to General Grant at City Point, the dangerous journey up the James River, both banks of which were infested with outlying parties of the enemy, being performed at night and the despatches delivered in person by Mr. Jones to General Grant. For this important and extremely hazardous service Mr. Jones was highly complimented in personal and official letters by his commanding officer, and he might have received promotion for it had not his youthful modesty and ignorance of the methods of naval administration prevented him from following up his advantage with a claim for recognition.

The night of January 15, the same day that the naval brigade was assaulting Fort Fisher, the monitor *Patapsco* was destroyed by a torpedo with great loss of life in the harbor of Charleston. That night the *Patapsco* was on duty as picket vessel in advance of the investing line of iron-clads and was engaged, as was the practice, in drifting with the tide up to a point abreast of Fort Sumter, then steaming back to station to again drift up. She had torpedo nettings rigged out and was preceded by picket boats dragging for torpedoes, but when arrived at her station after the third excursion a torpedo exploded under her about thirty feet from the bow, from the effects of which she sank in about thirty seconds. Five officers and thirty-eight men, the most of whom were on duty and therefore awake, were saved by boats from the *Lehigh* and in one of their own; the remainder of the crew, numbering sixty-two officers and men, went down with their ship. The engineer of the watch, Mr. DeWitt C. Davis, was lost, the official report of the captain, Lieutenant Commander S. P. Quackenbush, saying that, " Third Assistant Engineer D. C. Davis remained nobly at his post when the ship went down." The officers saved were the captain, the executive officer and the officer of the deck, all whom were on duty on deck, and two engineers who happened to be on deck at the time of the disaster; those lost were three volunteer line officers, three engineers, the surgeon, and the paymaster, two of the engineers and the surgeon being of the regular service. The executive officer, Lieutenant W. T. Sampson, is now a captain and at present chief of the Bureau of Ordnance, Navy Department.

First Assistant Engineer Reynolds Driver, senior engineer of the ship, distinguished himself by unusual heroism in the disaster, he, after persistently jeopardizing his life by remaining on the sinking ship trying to open the hatches to allow those below to escape, no less than twice while in the chilly water gave up pieces of wreckage on which he was afloat to men more exhausted than himself, and was finally picked up under the walls of Sumter, after having previously refrained from making an outcry when relief was near at hand lest the drowning should be neglected while he was yet able to swim. Afterward, when he appeared on the deck of the rescuing vessel, his conduct being known, he was greeted with cheers from the men and expressions of admiration from the officers, and thereafter was treated with marked deference and respect by all with whom he was associated. He died at his home in New Castle, Delaware, the year following the war.

On the 18th of February the enemy abandoned Charleston as a military post, Rear Admiral Dahlgren taking possession of the city which he had besieged so long, and began at once directing from thence naval operations against the neighboring positions of the enemy. With the fall of Charleston and Wilmington the downfall of the Confederacy was assured, and it became only a question of short time before the end would come.

Although in the last ditch, the rebellion showed itself dangerous to the end against the navy by the successful use of torpedoes. The river-built monitors *Milwaukee* and *Osage* were sunk in Blakely River, flowing into Mobile Bay, on the 28th and 29th of March by these weapons, the former without loss of life but the latter with the loss of three men killed and eight wounded. On the 1st of April the "tin clad" *Rudolph* met with destuction in the same river and by the same means, four of her men being killed and ten seriously wounded by the explosion. The ninety-day gunboat *Sciota* was sunk in Mobile Bay in the same way on the 13th of April with a loss of ten men killed and wounded. She was subsequently raised, repaired, and sold out of the service. The tug gunboat *Ida* was blown up the same day in Mobile Bay by a torpedo which exploded her boiler, killed the senior engineer, Mr. Sanford Curran, and two firemen, and wounded two others. This list of disasters was due to the extraordinary activity of the enemy in making use of this mode of warfare, the waters about Mobile Bay being literally full of these infernal machines, and to the slowness of the Federals in appreciating the need of guarding against them.

Richmond was abandoned the 4th of April and was immediately occupied by the military and naval forces, the surrender of General Lee's army soon afterward putting a practical end to the war. Although not a matter of historical importance, it is a fact that the first representative of the navy to enter Richmond after its surrender was a member of the engineer corps. Mr. Clark Thurston, now Vice President of the American Screw Company of Providence Rhode Island, was at that time a third assistant engineer attached to the James River torpedo service under charge of Chief Engineer Alexander Henderson, and being fired by a youthful love of adventure left his post of duty at Dutch Gap when he heard of the fall of Richmond and proceeded alone in a skiff to the city, spending a day there without knowing how to account for himself, before the arrival of Admiral Porter with President Lincoln. Mr. Thurston subsequently spent two weeks under arrest for being absent without leave but that does not detract in the least from his distinction of having been the first of the navy to enter the enemy's capital.

When peace was assured, the Navy Department at once set about disbanding the great navy that had been called into existence; all new ship and engine building work was stopped; volunteer officers and men were discharged as fast as possible and returned to the industries of peace, while immediate steps were taken to effect the sale of all vessels purchased for naval purposes as well as many that had been built expressly for the navy. All the better class of purchased steamers readily found buyers, for with peace came a revival of our shipping industry hastened in no small degree by the return to civil pursuits of a large sea-faring element, it not being unusual for the volunteer officer to take advantage of the bargains offered to provide himself with a vessel with which to begin life again. Of the steamers built expressly for war purposes the double-enders, and especially the ninety-day gunboats, were found to be well adapted to commercial purposes, they being of a size and draft of water suitable for river and coastwise traffic, and the most of them were readily sold. Although generally preserved as steamers, some of the gunboats were converted into sailing vessels and employed in the ocean carrying trade; one famous little gunboat, the *Kennebec*, was altered into a bark and was lost on her first voyage.

Some of the naval lessons of the Civil War are quite as pertinent to-day as they were thirty years ago and will be valuable if heeded when the next war comes. It is sometimes claimed that war-ships and naval methods have so changed within the past generation that we cannot hope to again get officers and men from the merchant marine who will as easily adapt themselves to naval conditions or become as efficient as did the men of 1861, but this is an imaginary rather than a real source of anxiety. The changes in appliances and construction of war-vessels have had their counterpart in commercial steamers and the two classes of vessels bear to-day the same relation that existed between them thirty years ago, while the officers and men of both services have developed in parallel lines to meet the altered conditions: to claim, therefore, that the master, mate or seaman of the present time is incompetent to learn the gunnery drill and routine of a modern man-of-war is equivalent to charging our sea-faring citizens with intellectual deterioration since the war, or is an attempt to obscure with difficulty and mystery the administration of rather every-day and commonplace duties about which there can be no secrets.

If the man-of-war's-man has put away the marline-spike and serving-mallet and taken up the monkey-wrench and coal-shovel in their stead, as is admitted with regret or satisfaction according to the point of view, by all attentive to naval matters, the very same change has come over the merchant sailor, and by every commonsense reason he is fully as fit for the duties of a man-of-war as was his predecessor fit for the naval life of his time, and our war showed that that fitness was sufficient. Furthermore, the changes in appliances on board war-ships is such that a much broader field is now open for the recruiting of a suitable enlisted personnel than formerly existed, when activity aloft and familiarity with ships' rigging were the necessary attributes of a seaman. On the modern war-vessel the machinist, the blacksmith, the boiler-maker, the copper-smith, and craftsmen of many other mechanical trades, can all find more to do and be infinitely more useful than the men whose usefulness is based upon ability to furl sails and splice ropes. Thus, instead of being limited to the merchant marine for a supply of seamen, the navy now has the whole vast field of the mechanic arts open and preferable for the purpose.

There is no mystery about the modern rifled gun, the torpedo, or the rapid-firing machine-gun; all are purely and simply machines constructed upon ordinary mechanical principles, a knowledge of which can be more easily acquired by a man who is already a mechanic than by one who is a sailor. Nor can it be claimed that the use of these modern appliances is more difficult to learn than was that of the older and ruder type of gun, for it is a matter of common remark by naval officers that the gunnery drill of to-day is in every respect more simple than it was twenty or even ten years ago. An ideal fighting crew for a modern ship would be composed of young mechanics from the machine shops and engine works of the country, enlisted as soldiers or marines if the application of the name of seaman to them is too violent an encroachment upon ancient traditions, drilled with the weapons they are to use until they become familiar with them, and habituated to the sea life by going to sea, just as other men get used to it, sea-sickness and all, for a year or two. Such men would handle their machine weapons with intelligence and precision, and would be able to repair and re-adjust them in the days following a battle, instead of looking on while the engineer's force does the work for them.

For officers in case of another great expansion of the navy in sudden emergency we will have to turn as we did before to the merchant marine, for however desirable the mechanic may be as an operative of machine weapons, the men who are to handle ships and control their propelling machinery must be found among those who have had long experience in such work. The masters, mates and engineers of our commercial steamers will be found in the next war quite competent to carry on their vocations in the navy and doubtless as willing to do it as were their predecessors. The surroundings on a man-of-war may be somewhat more formal and theatrical than those to which they are accustomed on their own ships, but their duties will not be so much more difficult as to be impossible. The writer does not claim that such officers would be as perfect in all things as those who have been trained from youth for the naval service, for training and experience in any calling tend toward perfection, but he submits as a belief derived from the record of the volunteer element in the navy during the Civil War that they would be found sufficiently capable both above and below decks to guarantee an honorable and worthy guardianship of their country's flag.

Satisfactory as was the behavior of the officers and men drawn into the navy from the merchant marine during the rebellion, the same cannot be said of the vessels obtained from the same source. Indeed, if any one point in naval warfare is sharply emphasized by the events of that war, that point is that vessels built for commercial purposes are unsafe and absolutely unfit for war operations. In the foregoing chapters a few only of very many disasters to ships in action have been mentioned ; the most casual reader must have noticed, however, that the cause of disaster has been in almost all cases the same—namely, unprotected machinery. One of the most humiliating incidents of the war was the quick destruction of the *Hatteras* by the *Alabama*, and that event is an excellent illustration of this point. After confidently chasing an unknown vessel until lured beyond the reach of help from her consorts the *Hatteras* was suddenly turned upon and at once disabled by a shot striking her walking-beam, poised in the air apparently as a target and a temptation for attack by a weaker foe. With the ability to move taken from her, she fell an easy prey to the enemy, and her fate is simply one of many provoked by similar vulnerability.

With the change in building material, the increase in speed, etc., the commercial steamer has about kept pace with the development of the gun, so that now, when no slow wooden steamers with overhead beam engines would be thought of for use in war, the relation between the ship and the gun is practically the same as it was in 1861–65. We may therefore expect to see our merchant steamers reasonably efficient as cruisers or blockaders when again called into service, but almost certainly doomed to destruction when obliged to fight with a properly built and armed vessel of war.

Our armored cruisers and protected cruisers of the present day do not furnish a complete safeguard for their vitals against the fire of modern guns, but in that respect they may be said to be quite as safe, probably more so, than were the regularly built vessels of the war period. Such casualties to machinery as occurred to the *Richmond*, the *Sassacus*, and the *Oneida* were exceptions with naval vessels, although the rule with commercial steamers when brought within range of the enemy's guns, and in another war we may look for such disasters occasionally to protected and armored cruisers in spite of their protection. The curved protective deck over engines and boilers as now supplied may be relied upon for protection against the fire of any except heavy guns, but a shot or shell from the latter must be expected to break through this shield, and then we will experience a disaster like that of the *Oneida* at Mobile, and in more frightful degree. In fact, a dread of the intensely horrible makes one shrink from speculating as to what would happen in a modern closed fire-room when a boiler or steam pipe is pierced.

Not long since public attention was quite generally drawn to a discussion as to the relative merits in war of swift naval cruisers and armed merchant steamers, a considerable party, including even naval officers of experience, claiming that the latter were the most desirable, being faster, and, as was claimed, capable of carrying batteries sufficiently heavy to be able to fight the cruisers on equal terms. An examination of the structural differences of the two classes, considered in connection with the actual experience in war of the prototypes of each, should be conclusively convincing of the absolute superiority of the cruiser. Neither vessel is expected to carry very heavy guns, but in this respect the cruiser will in all probability have the advantage, being built in the first instance to carry guns rather than passengers and freight. Admitting, however, that a typical vessel of each class will have the same battery, the cruiser would still have a marked advantage in the structural protection to her vitals, the machinery of her antagonist being not only unprotected but, in the case of the engines at least, so much higher as to be well above the water-line and a target which none but a blind gunner could well miss.

This point cannot be better emphasized than by a few diagrams in illustration. Figures 1 and 2 represent transverse sections of

Fig 1.

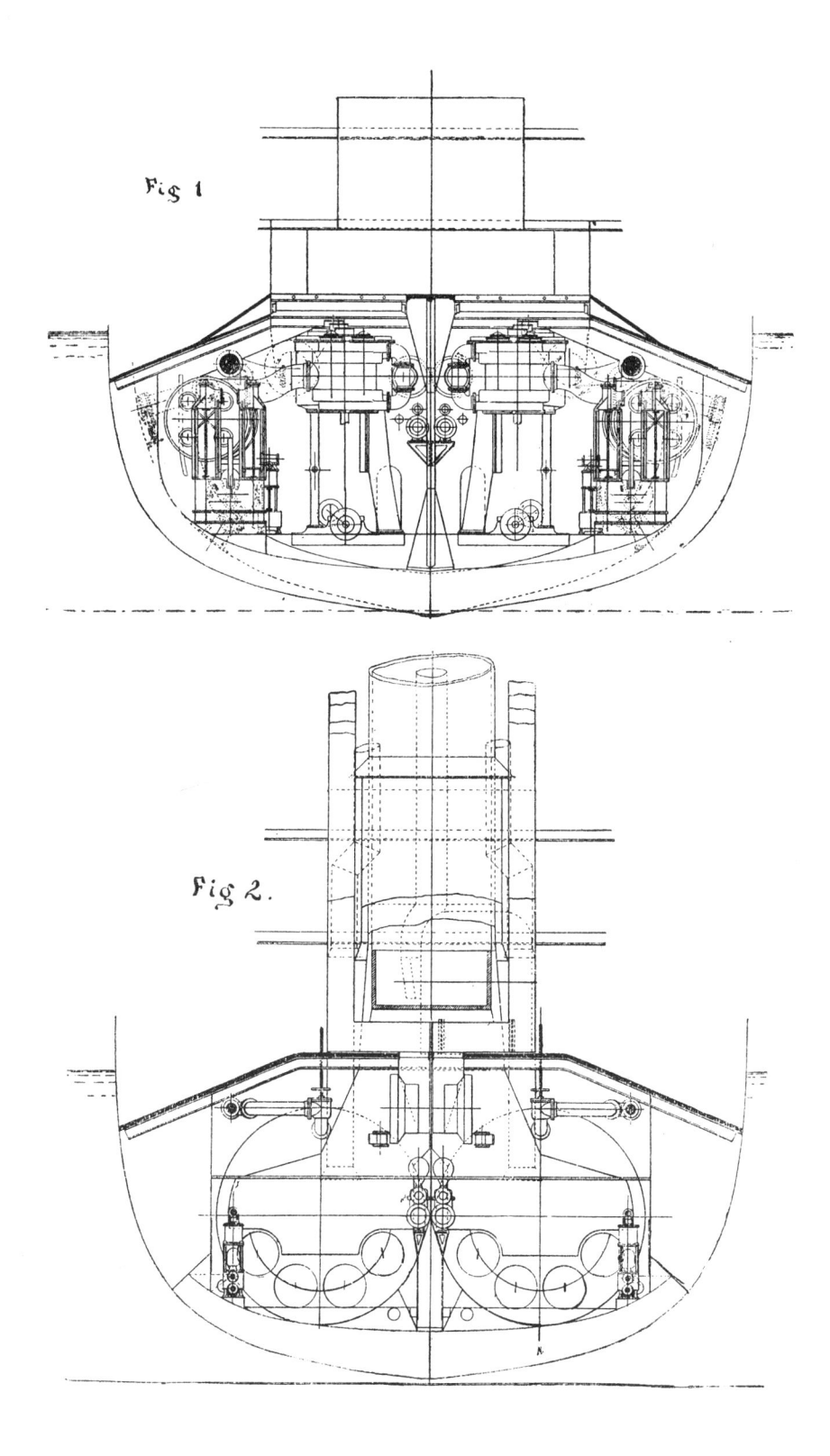

Fig 2.

the cruiser *Columbia,* an excellent modern instance of a swift naval cruiser, showing the location of her engines and boilers with reference to the water-line and the steel protective deck. Figure 3 shows the same, minus the protective deck, for the English-built ocean "greyhound" *Paris* of the International Navigation Company, which may be taken as typical of the arrangement common in a great number of fast mail steamers of different lines. A different and more recent arrangement is that of the latest steamers of the North German Lloyd's, adopted also in the *Campania* and *Lucania* of the Cunard line, which economizes fore-and-aft space by placing the

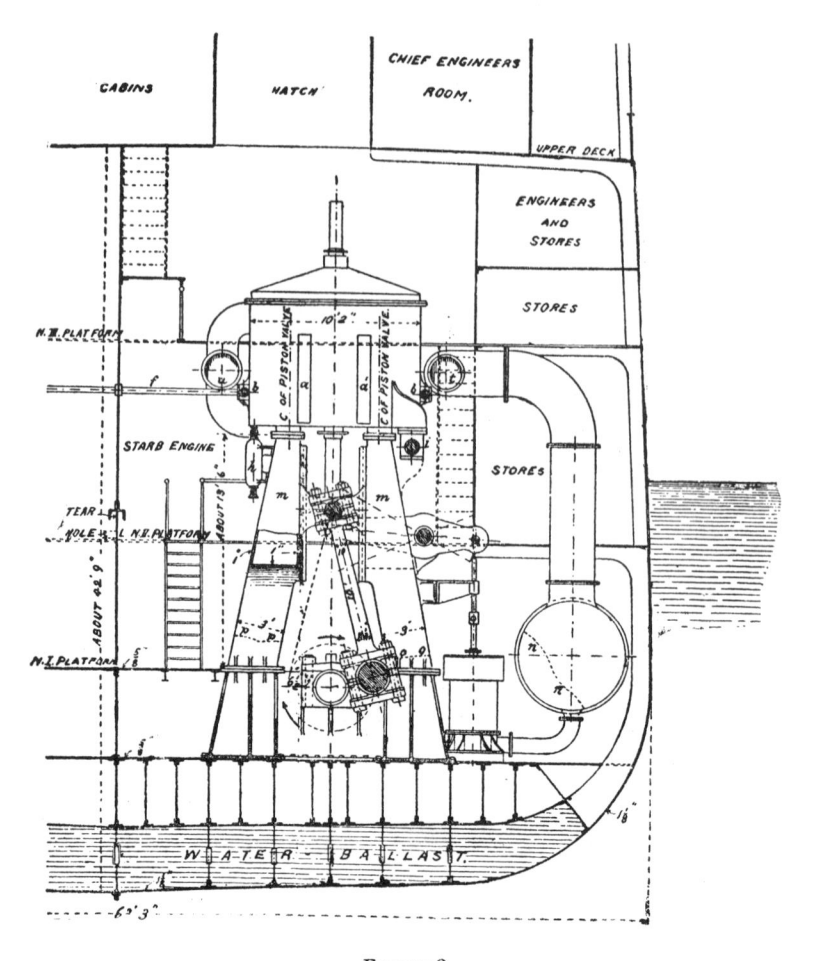

FIGURE 3.

high-pressure cylinders over the low-pressure. The large Cunarders named have five cylinders to each engine, the intermediate pressure in the center and a tandem pair of high and low pressure cylinders at each end; the height of these engines from bed-plate to top of high-

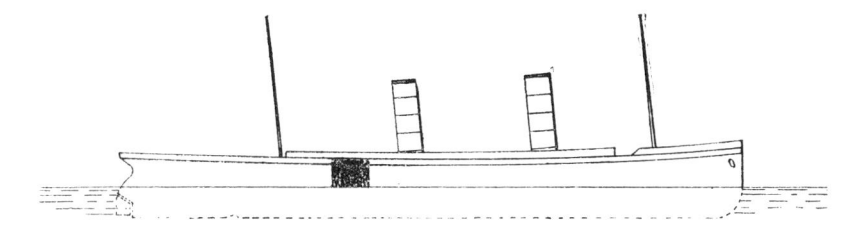

FIGURE 4.

pressure cylinders is forty-seven feet, and the foundation framing under them is eight feet in depth. Therefore they stand, when the ship is drawing thirty feet of water, to a height of twenty-five feet above the water-line, making with their fore-and-aft extent a target 25x34 feet in any part of which a shot or shell would most surely

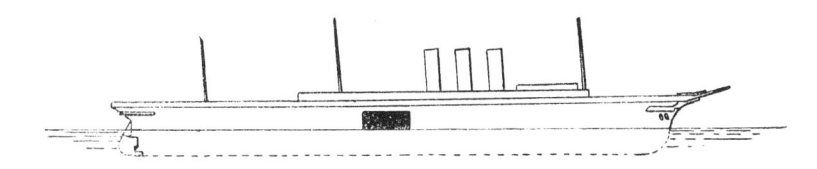

FIGURE 5.

disaable one engine and probably both; this, furthermore, without reckoning the danger to steam, exhaust and receiver pipes leading to and from the cylinders. The same target in the case of the *Paris* would be 38x16 feet, both graphically illustrated in figures 4 and 5. The boilers of these steamers are below the water line, but without any protection for themselves or their pipe connections against glancing shot or bursting shells.

It is hardly necessary to match the *Columbia* against the typical swift merchant steamer in this argument; a much smaller cruiser with protected machinery—the *Baltimore* for example—might be expected to disable her quite as easily if engaged; and she probably would be engaged if sighted at all, for it would require a degree of moral courage far greater than most men possess to run away from her with a ship three or four times her size which happened to be speedier. The *Baltimore* or other cruiser might be expected to suffer severely in her upper works and *personnel* from the quick-firing guns of the mail steamer, but the chance of her receiving a disabling blow before giving one would be so remote as not to deserve consideration.

Such protection to machinery as could be furnished by temporary expedients on board the merchant steamer cannot be relied upon as any more useful against modern guns than were similar efforts available against the guns of the Civil War period. The *Keystone State* was a fine example of the better class of merchant vessels armed for naval service in 1861, and for the better protection of her steam drums barricades were built about them, in addition to which it was customary to stow coils of hawsers, bales of cordage, and other material abreast of the drum-rooms. In spite of all this protection it will be recalled that a single shot from a Confederate ram penetrated the drums, scattering death and destruction in its wake and so crippled the ship that she nearly surrendered, being saved from that misfortune only by the zeal and professional knowledge of her chief engineer.

The instances of invaluable professional and military services rendered by the officers of the engineer corps, regular and volunteer, during the Civil War that have been mentioned in the foregoing chapters are a few only of the many on record in the official reports in the Navy Department, but it is hoped that they are sufficient to redeem from error every fair-minded person who may have been led to believe from partisan arguments that the engineer officers of the navy occupy a non-combatant status, or that the engineer corps is not a necessary and essentially military arm of the naval service. The truth of this must be known even to those who imagine it to be to their interest to deny it ; it was freely admitted by scores of commanding officers who had experience in war and who did not hesitate to do honor in their official reports to whom it was due irrespective of corps. Its frank admission now would relieve the engineer corps from an aspersion under which its members have smarted much too long, and would amount to nothing more than a generous admission of a truth unquestioned by the great majority of the citizens of this republic.

During the four years of the war one hundred and fifteen officers of the engineer corps are recorded as having died in the service, the majority of them being killed in battle or died from wounds or exposure incident to their duty. In proportion to the numbers employed it is believed that no other corps suffered so severely. The actual deaths and injuries of engineers inflicted by violent means during the same period are given in the following table, which has been compiled from the casualty book of the rebellion kept in the office of the Surgeon General of the navy, and which is generally very accurate, although the author's attention has been called to a few casualties that are not recorded in the book referred to :

Name.	Grade.	Vessel.	Date of Injury
John M. Whittemore	3d Asst. Engr.	Mohican.	November 7, 1861.
Mayland Cuthbert	3d Asst. Engr.	Mohican.	November 7, 1861.
Stephen Mealius	2d Asst. Engr.	J. N. Seymour.	February 8, 1862.
Samuel Brooks	2d Asst. Engr.	Carondelet.	February 14, 1862.
Sidney Albert	2d Asst. Engr.	Narragansett.	February 16, 1862.
Andrew Nesbitt	3d Asst. Engr.	Whitehall.	March 8, 1862.
Walter Bradley	Act. 3d Asst. Engr.	Henry Andrews.	March 22, 1862.
Frank R. Hain	Act. 3d Asst. Engr.	Colorado.	April 24, 1862.
S. Wilkins Cragg	2d Asst. Engr.	Kineo.	April 24, 1862.
John C. Huntley	3d Asst. Engr.	Pensacolo.	April 24, 1862.
Eugene J. Wade	Act. 3d Asst. Engr.	Daylight.	April 25, 1862.
J. D. Williamson	Act. 2d Asst. Engr.	Delaware.	May 3, 1862.
Jas. B. Kimball	Chief Engr.	Hartford.	May 28, 1862.
Jackson McElmell	1st Asst. Engr.	Octorora.	June 14, 1862.
John Cox	Act. Chief Engr.	Mound City.	June 17, 1862.
John C. McAfee	Act. 2d Asst. Engr.	Mound City.	June 17, 1862.
G. W. Hollingsworth	Act. 3d Asst. Engr.	Mound City.	June 17, 1862.
Richard M. Hodson	3d Asst. Engr.	Oneida.	June 28, 1862.
Joseph Huber	Act. Chief Engr.	Lexington.	July 5, 1862.
W. J. Reid	3d Asst. Engr.	Katahdin.	July 22, 1862.
John A. Hill	Act. 3d Asst. Engr.	Pocahontas.	August 15, 1862.
John Wall	Act. 3d Asst. Engr.	Shawsheen.	September 9, 1862.
Francis C. Dade	Chief Engr.	Oneida.	September 17, 1862.
Wm G. Smoot	Act. 2d Asst. Engr.	Dragon.	November 15, 1862.
Albert W. Morley	3d Asst. Engr.	Richmond.	December 16, 1862.
R. W. Hands	3d Asst. Engr.	Monitor.	December 31, 1862.
Samuel A. Lewis	3d Asst. Engr.	Monitor.	December 31, 1862.
Nicholas Meislang	Act. 3d Asst. Engr.	Laurel.	December 31, 1862.
A. B. Campbell	2d Asst. Engr.	Monitor.	4th quarter.
W. R. Green	Act. 2d Asst. Engr.	Westfield.	January 1, 1863.
Wilbur F. Fort	3d Asst. Engr.	Pocahontas.	January 14, 1863.
Erastus Barry	Act. 3d Asst. Engr.	Isaac Smith.	January 30, 1863.
Jas. S. Turner	Act. 2d Asst. Engr.	Isaac Smith.	January 30, 1863.
J. E. Fallon	3d Asst. Engr.	Mississippi.	March 14, 1863.
Henry Sullivan	Act. 3d Asst. Engr.	Dahlia.	March 22, 1863.
John Huff	Act. 2d Asst. Engr.	Carondelet.	March 25, 1863.
Wm. Wright	Act. 3d Asst. Engr.	Peterhoff.	March 19, 1863
James McNally	Act. 3d Asst. Engr.	Diana.	March 28, 1863.
Bobt. Laverty	Act. 3d Asst. Engr.	Catskill.	April 7, 1863.
Thos. Mallahan	Act. 3d Asst. Engr.	Ceres.	April 16, 1863.
John Healy	Act. 3d Asst. Engr.	Mt. Washington.	April 20, 1863.
Simon Shultice	Act. 1st Asst. Engr.	Cincinnati.	May 27, 1863.
John Brooks	Act. 3d Asst. Engr.	New London.	July 10, 1863.
F. I. Bradley	Act. 3d Asst. Engr.	Clifton.	September 8, 1863
John Frazer	Act. 2d Asst. Engr.	Sachem.	September 8, 1863
John Munroe	Act. 3d Asst. Engr.	Sachem.	September 8, 1863.
Samuel T. Strude	Act. 3d Asst. Engr.	Nansemond.	October 15, 1863.
Chas. J. Morgan	Act. 3d Asst. Engr.	Queen.	October 21, 1863.
John B. Edwards	Act. 2d Asst. Engr.	Stettin.	November 14, 1863.
Wm. G. Pendleton	1st Asst. Engr.	Lehigh.	November 16, 1863.
H. W. Merriman	3d Asst. Engr.	Wehawken.	December 6, 1863.
Aug. Mitchell	3d Asst. Engr.	Wehawken.	December 6, 1863.
Geo. W. McGowan	Act. 3d Asst. Engr.	Wehawken.	December 6, 1863
Chas. Spangberg	Act. 3d Asst. Engr.	Wehawken.	December 6, 1863

NATURE OF INJURY.	RESULT OF INJURY.	REMARKS.
Gunshot.	Death.	Killed instantly ; cannon shot.
Gunshot.	Recovery.	Splinter from cannon shot.
Gunshot.	Death, Feb'y 20.	Cannon shot ; fracture of thigh-bone.
Gunshot.	....	In action ; Fort Donelson.
Fracture.	Recovery.	Arm broken ; on shore.
Gunshot.	Death.	Killed instantly ; fragment of shell.
Gunshot.	....	Shot in forehead ; boat expedition, Mosquito Lagoon, Fla.
Gunshot.	Recovery.	On board Iroquois, in action Forts Phillip and Jackson.
Gunshot.	Recovery.	Wound of face and lip, in action Forts Phillip and Jackson.
Gunshot.	Recovery.	Fragment of shell in scalp, in action Forts Phillip and Jackson.
Gunshot.	....	Fracture right arm, splinter; in action, Fort Macon, Ga.
Fracture.	Recovery.	Both bones right leg, by falling.
Gunshot.	Recovery.	Buckshot and slugs in head, face and shoulder.
Internal scald.	Recovery.	Inhaled hot steam while examining boiler.
Scald.	Death.	Boiler exploded by shell, in action, St. Charles, Ark.
Scald.	Death.	Boiler exploded by shell, in action, St. Charles, Ark.
Scald.	Death.	Boiler exploded by shell, in action, St. Charles, Ark.
Gunshot.	....	Severe, of left leg ; in action, Vicksburg.
Gunshot.	Death.	Shot by guerrillas from shore ; White River, Ark.
Gunshot.	Recovery.	Fragments of shell in scalp and groin ; in action, Grand Gulf.
Gunshot.	Recovery.	Musket shot in abdomen ; boat expedition, Black River, S.C.
Gunshot.	Recovery.	Left thigh and wrist ; in action, Chowan River, N. C.
Laceration.	Recovery.	Right hand caught in machinery.
Spinal contusion.	Recovery.	By fall on machinery.
Contusion.	Recovery.	Leg caught in machinery.
Drowning.	Death.	Perished in the vessel.
Drowning.	Death.	Perished in the vessel.
Gunshot.	Death.	Compound fracture, right thigh, expedition Yazoo River.
Contusion.	Recovery.	Of knee.
G'npowd'r explos'n	Death.	Destruction of vessel in action, Galveston, Texas.
Contusion.	Amputation,	Three toes of right foot crushed ; on duty in engine-room.
Gunshot.	Recovery.	Shot in thigh ; in action, Stono River, S. C.
Gunshot.	Death.	Pieces of shell ; in action, Stono River, S. C.
Gunshot.	Recovery.	In action, Port Hudson.
Gunshot.	Death.	Killed by rifle bullet ; Yazoo River.
Gunshot.	Death.	Thigh fractured ; expedition to Deer Creek, Miss.
Contusion.	Recovery.	Hand crushed in machinery.
Gunshot.	Death.	Shot through head ; in action, Atchafalaya River, La.
Gunshot.	Recovery.	Shot in leg ; in action, Charleston, S. C.
Gunshot.	Death.	Killed by rifleman from shore ; Pamtico River.
Fracture.	Death.	Instantly killed ; head crushed by crank while on duty.
Gunshot.	Recovery.	In action ; Vicksburg.
Gunshot.	....	Wound of r. thigh and scald ; in action, Donaldsonville, La.
Gunshot.	....	In action ; Sabine Pass, Texas.
Gunshot.	Death.	In action ; Sabine Pass, Texas.
Gunshot.	Death.	In action ; Sabine Pass, Texas.
Drowning.	Death.	In line of duty ; breaking of boat davit.
Hernia.	....	Left inguinal.
Hernia.	....	While removing condenser.
Gunshot.	Recovery.	Right arm ; in action with Fort Moultrie.
Drowning.	Death.	By sinking of vessel at anchor, Charleston.
Drowning.	Death.	By sinking of vessel at anchor, Charleston.
Drowning.	Death.	By sinking of vessel at anchor, Charleston.
Drowning.	Death.	By sinking of vessel at anchor, Charleston.

Name.	Grade.	Vessel.	Date of Injury.
E. R. Clemens	Act. 1st Asst. Engr.	Mound City.	January 22, 1864.
Cicero B. Curtis	Act. 2d Asst. Engr.	Galatea.	February 12, 1864.
Fred'k E. Brown	2d Asst. Engr.	Niagara.	March 22, 1864.
Jos. A. Cahill	1st Asst. Engr.	Chenango.	April 15, 1864.
Albert Murray	2d Asst. Engr.	Chenango.	April 15, 1864.
Frank R. Root	Act. 2d Asst. Engr.	Chenango.	April 15, 1864.
John White	Act. 3d Asst. Engr.	Chenango.	April 15, 1864.
Geo. W. Dean	Act. 3d Asst. Engr.	Ceres.	April 17, 1864.
John A. Frank	Act. 3d Asst. Engr.	Ceres.	April 17, 1864.
Jos. R. Sherwood	Act. 3d Asst. Engr.	Ceres.	April 17, 1864.
D. Harrington	Act. 3d Asst. Engr.	Miami.	April 19, 1864.
Wm. Moran	Act. 3d Asst. Engr.	Miami.	April 19, 1864.
Jos. Griffin	Act. 2d Asst. Engr.	Prairie Bird.	April 22, 1864.
Chas. P. Parks	Act. 2d Asst. Engr.	Cricket.	April 26, 1864.
	Temporary Engr.	Champion No. 3.	April 26, 1864.
	Temporary Engr.	Champion No. 3.	April 26, 1864.
	Temporary Engr.	Champion No. 3.	April 26, 1864.
D. A. Lockwood	Act. 1st Asst. Engr.	Saugus.	April 27, 1864.
John T. English	Act. 3d Asst. Engr.	Covington.	April 27, 1864.
Jas. M. Hobby	1st Asst. Engr.	Sassacus.	May 5, 1864.
Horace Whitworth	3d Asst. Engr.	Commodore Jones.	May 5, 1864.
T. McCarthy	Act. 2d Asst. Engr.	Commodore Jones.	May 5, 1864.
J. R. McKenzie	Act. 3d Asst. Engr.	Commodore Jones.	May 5, 1864.
Wm. Wilson	3d Asst. Engr.	Wave.	May 6, 1864.
M. F. Fitzpatrick	Act. 2d Asst. Engr.	Wave.	May 6, 1864.
Wm. H. G. West	2d Asst. Engr.	Nahant.	May 16, 1864.
Samuel Lockwood	3d Asst. Engr.	Stockdale.	May 24, 1864.
Wm. McEwan	Act. 3d Asst. Engr.	Hartford.	August 5, 1864.
R. H. Fitch	1st Asst. Engr.	Oneida.	August 5, 1864.
Wm. H. Hunt	Chief Engr.	Oneida.	August 5, 1864.
John Faron	Chief Engr.	Tecumseh.	August 5, 1864.
F. S. Barlow	2d Asst. Engr.	Tecumseh.	August 5, 1864.
Elisha Harsen	2d Asst. Engr.	Tecumseh.	August 5, 1864.
H. S. Leonard	2d Asst. Engr.	Tecumseh.	August 5, 1864.
Thos. Ustick	Act. 3d Asst. Engr.	Tecumseh.	August 5, 1864.
Henry Ritter	Act. 3d Asst. Engr.	Tecumseh.	August 5, 1864.
H. McMurtrie	2d Asst. Engr.	Juniata.	September 1, 1864.
Wm. H. Harrison	1st Asst. Engr.	Shamrock	October 31, 1864.
Geo. W. Parks	3d Asst. Engr.	Tulip.	November 11, 1864.
John Gordon	3d Asst. Engr.	Tulip.	November 11, 1864.
Wm. S. Dobson	2d Asst. Engr.	Bigonia.	November 15, 1864.
Wm. H. Crawford	Act. 3d Asst. Engr.	Eutaw.	November 24, 1864.
Thos. McNellis	Act. 2d Asst. Engr.	Banshee.	November 25, 1864.
Chas. F. Fowler	2d Asst. Engr.	Atlanta.	2d quarter.
J. P. Phillips	Act. 3d Asst. Engr.	Little Ada.	4th quarter.
P. J. Murphy	Act 3d Asst. Engr.	Little Ada.	4th quarter.
Geo. L. Palmer	Act. 2d Asst. Engr.	Patapsco.	January 15, 1865.
DeW. G. Davis	3d Asst. Engr.	Patapsco.	January 15, 1865.
B. R. Stevens	3d Asst. Engr.	Patapsco.	January 15, 1865.
J. W. Saville	2d Asst. Engr.	Canonicus.	January 15, 1865.
John Fulcher	Act. 3d Asst. Engr.	Dai Ching.	January 26, 1865.
W. S. Thompson	Act. 1st Asst. Engr.	Atlanta.	April 6, 1865.
Sanford Curran	Act. 3d Asst. Engr.	Ida.	April 13, 1865.
Alpheus Nichols	Act. 2d Asst. Engr.	Rose.	2d quarter.

Nature of Injury.	Result of Injury.	Remarks.
Hernia.	....	In line of duty, from fall.
Fracture.	Recovery.	Hand caught in machinery.
Subluxation.	Recovery.	Left ankle, by jumping from wharf into boat, on duty.
Scald.	Death.	Explosion of boiler; New York harbor.
Scald.	Death	Explosion of boiler; New York harbor.
Scald.	Death.	Explosion of boiler; New York harbor.
Scald.	Death.	Explosion of boiler; New York harbor.
Gunshot.	Capture.	In action off Plymouth, N. C.
Gunshot.	Recovery.	In action off Plymouth, N. C.
Gunshot.	Double internal hernia.	In action off Plymouth, N. C.
Gunshot.	Recovery.	In action off Plymouth, N. C.
Gunshot.	Recovery.	In action off Plymouth, N. C.
Gunshot.	Recovery.	From fragment of casemate, in action; Yazoo River.
Gunshot.	Death.	In action near Alexandria, Red River, La.
Scald.	Death.	By shot piercing boiler in action, Red River, La.
Scald.	Death.	By shot piercing boiler, in action, Red River, La.
Scald.	Death.	By shot piercing boiler, in action, Red River, La.
Hernia.	....	
Gunshot.	Recovery.	Of right arm.
Scald.	Recovery.	By shot piercing boiler; in action with ram Albemarle.
Contusions.	Recovery.	Blowing up of vessel by torpedo in James River.
Contusions.	Recovery.	Blowing up of vessel by torpedo in James River.
Contusions.	Recovery.	Blowing up of vessel by torpedo in James River.
Starvation.	Death.	Captured with vessel; died in prison pen, Camp Groce.
Starvation.	Death.	Captured with vessel; died in prison pen, Camp Groce.
Gunshot.	Recovery.	Back torn by splinters in action.
Gunshot.	....	Wounded in head and captured; boat expedition, Fla.
Gunshot.	Amputation r. arm.	Fore-arm shattered in action by shell; Mobile Bay.
Scald.	Recovery.	Shell exploded in boiler in action, Mobile Bay.
Scald.	Recovery.	Shell exploded in boiler; in action, Mobile Bay.
Drowning.	Death.	Vessel sunk by torpedo; in action, Mobile Bay.
Drowning.	Death.	Vessel sunk by torpedo; in action, Mobile Bay.
Drowning.	Death.	Vessel sunk by torpedo; in action, Mobile Bay.
Drowning.	Death.	Vessel sunk by torpedo; in action, Mobile Bay.
Drowning.	Death.	Vessel sunk by torpedo; in action, Mobile Bay.
Drowning.	Death.	Vessel sunk by torpedo; in action, Mobile Bay.
Hernia.	Disabled.	By over-exertion on duty.
Gunshot.	Recovery.	Of neck and arm, in action; Plymouth, N. C.
Scald.	Death.	Explosion of boiler, Potomac River.
Scald.	Death.	Explosion of boiler, Potomac River.
Hernia.	Resigned.	Not in line of duty.
Gunshot.	Recovery.	Not in line of duty.
Contusion.	Recovery.	Of back; by fall while on duty.
Hernia.	Discharged, disabled.	
Contusion.	....	To Norfolk hospital; no details.
Fracture.	....	Of right thigh-bone.
Drowning.	Death.	Destruction of vessel by torpedo.
Drowning.	Death.	Destruction of vessel by torpedo.
Drowning.	Death.	Destruction of vessel by torpedo.
Gunshot.	Recovery.	By grape-shot; in action, Fort Fisher.
Gunshot.	Recovery.	In action, Combahee River, S. C.
Gunshot.	Death.	By torpedo; James River.
Gunshot.	Death,	Fracture of thigh-bone; torpedo; Mobile Bay.
Fracture.	Recovery.	Hand caught in machinery; on duty.

CHAPTER XXVIII.

"Let not him that girdeth on his harness boast himself as he that putteth it off."—OLD TESTAMENT.

Competitive Trials of Steam Machinery—The NIPSIC and KANSAS—Failure of the SACO—The Famous ALGONQUIN-WINOOSKI Controversy—Performance of the IDAHO—Her Success as a Sailing Ship—Trial Trip of the CHATTANOOGA—Trial of the MADAWASKA—Comparative Table of Results of Trials of the IDAHO, CHATTANOOGA, MADAWASKA and WAMPANOAG—Subsequent Career of the MADAWASKA, or TENNESSEE.

FREQUENT reference has been made in former chapters to vessels built during the rebellion, with machinery designed by the contractors for the purpose of competing with the designs of the Bureau of Steam Engineering, and in some cases with the avowed intention of proving by practical test certain faults alleged to exist in the practice of the Bureau. The record of these competitions is a very interesting chapter in the history of naval engineering in the United States and will now be taken up in some detail as one of the engineering lessons of the war.

The first instances of competitive machinery in vessels built after the beginning of the war occur in the small gun-boats of the *Nipsic* class placed under construction about the end of 1862. The machinery of three of these—the *Nipsic*, *Shawmut*, and *Nyack*—was designed by Mr. Isherwood and consisted in each case of a two-cylinder back-acting engine with cylinders 30 inches in diameter by 21 inches stroke of piston, fitted with ordinary slide valves and Stephenson link motion. The boilers, two in number, were of the Martin type aggregating in each vessel 198 square feet of grate surface and 4,950 square feet of heating surface. The machinery of the five other vessels in each case was of special design. The gun-boats were all of wood, built by the government at different navy yards, and were of the following general dimensions: Length, 179 feet 6 inches; beam, 30 feet; displacement, 836 tons; tonnage, 593.

In the cargo of the blockade-runner *Princess Royal*, captured off Charleston in January, 1863, was found a complete marine engine of English manufacture, intended for a Confederate ram, and this engine was placed in the *Kansas*, one of the gun-vessels of the class under description, then building at the Philadelphia navy yard. The engine was direct-acting with two cylinders 42 inches in diameter and 24 inches stroke, designed for working steam at a high rate of expansion. Two straight-way boilers were supplied the *Kansas*, their dimensions differing from those of the Isherwood gunboats to suit the different type of engines. The screw propellers of the vessels were precisely alike. The first opportunity of testing the *Kansas* with one of the Bureau vessels occurred in January, 1866, when she happened to meet with the *Nipsic* in the Brazil squadron and a

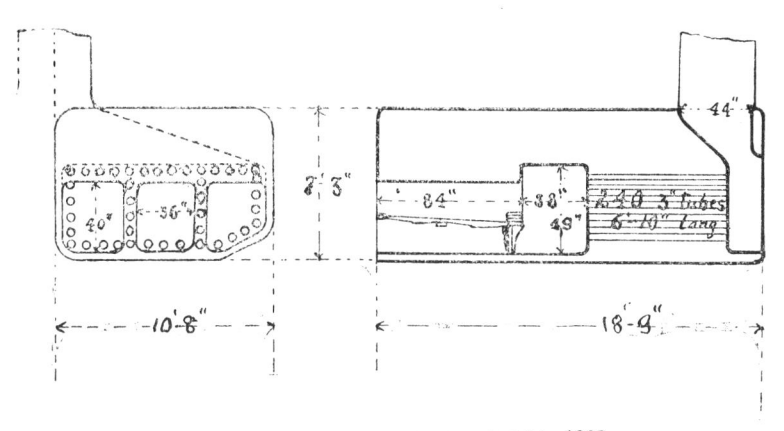

STRAIGHT-WAY BOILER, U. S. S. KANSAS, 1863.
Grate surface, 54 sq. ft.   Heating surface, 1,539 sq. ft.

competitive trial was ordered by Rear Admiral Godon, who hit upon an unusual but rather excellent basis for the test. Each vessel was allowed the same amount of coal per hour (1,600 pounds) and ordered to make the best speed possible for twelve hours with that allowance: both throttles were kept wide open; the Isherwood engine of the *Nipsic* cut off at six-tenths of the stroke and the English engine of the *Kansas* at one-fourth of the stroke. The result of the competition was decidedly in favor of the American practice, the *Nipsic* averaging eleven knots an hour for the twelve hours, while the *Kansas* averaged only eight.

The machinery of the *Saco* was built by the Corliss Steam Engine Co. of Providence, Rhode Island. The engine was of the vibrating lever type with two cylinders, of the same dimensions as the cylinders of the Isherwood engines in the same class of vessels; the valve gear used was the well-known Corliss type of automatic cut-off so successful in stationary engine practice. The boilers were return fire-tubular, designed with the object of stowing below the water line and thus being protected from shot. This machinery failed when tried, the fault resting principally with the boilers, which were not designed to use salt water and were quickly ruined by chemical action. The *Saco* was towed to the Washington navy yard, the machinery removed at the expense of the contractor, and new machinery of Bureau design substituted, the cost of the latter being charged against the Corliss Company and collected by deducting it from bills due on account of some large engines that company was building by contract.

The three other vessels of this class with special engines were fairly successful, but in no case were as fast or efficient as the Isherwood gunboats. The best one of them—the *Maumee*—had machinery designed by John Ericsson and built by the Stover Machine Company, of New York, the engine being of Ericsson's favorite vibrating lever type. The *Yantic* had a direct-acting two-cylinder engine designed and built by Merrick & Son, Philadelphia. The *Pequot* had a remarkable variation from the usual marine engine practice, her engine being of the Wright segmental type, built by Woodruff & Beach, Hartford, Connecticut. The cylinders, if they may be so called, were segmental or bent, as shown in the outline sketch,

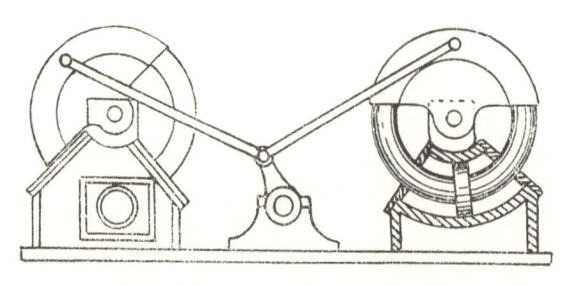

WRIGHT'S PATENT SEGMENTAL ENGINE.

the piston rods being in the form of rings as represented. The *Pequot* did some service in the North Atlantic blockading squadron but was never in commission after the war closed and was sold out of the service in 1869.

The most famous machinery competition in the annals of the steam navy was that of the double-enders *Algonquin* and *Winooski* of the *Sassacus* class. Mr. E. N. Dickerson, the devotee of Mariotte's law, had won the confidence of Mr. Paul S. Forbes, a responsible business man of New York, and induced that gentleman to take contracts for naval machinery. In this manner Dickerson became the designer of the machinery of the *Algonquin*, which included a type of boiler of his own patent, illustrated further along, and one inclined engine with a cylinder 48 inches in diameter by 10 feet stroke, this machinery being built by sub-contract by the Providence Steam Engine Company, of Providence, Rhode Island. The machinery of all other vessels of this class consisted of Martin boilers and large inclined engines, the cylinder being 58 inches diameter and 105 inches stroke. The *Algonquin* was built in the Brooklyn navy yard and her machinery was installed in 1865, about two years after the expiration of the contract time. When completed and ready for trial, one of the steamers of the class was selected to compete with the *Algonquin*, the one selected as being most available being the *Winooski*, named after a river in Vermont. The hull of the *Winooski* was built at the Boston navy yard and the machinery by contract at the same shops where Dickerson's machinery for the *Algonquin* had been constructed.

So little engineering knowledge entered into the machinery designs of the *Algonquin* that when it was all placed on board it was found to make the vessel so lop-sided that a dead weight of about sixty-nine tons had to be applied to keep her on an even keel. By the time the vessels were ready for trial Dickerson's theories and his assertion that the engineer-in-chief was violating all the rules of good practice in his machinery designs had become so well advertised that public attention was very generally drawn to the rivalry between the two ships, much space being given to it by the newspapers in England as well as in our own country. In this notorious controversy it is a remarkable fact that the expression of public sentiment was almost wholly favorable to Mr. Dickerson and hostile to Mr. Isherwood; this in spite of the facts that the former was not an engineer and had no naval record to refer to except the fiasco of the *Pensacola*, while the latter stood at the head of his corps and had the engines of at least one hundred successful war-vessels to point to as proofs of his skill.

Mr. Dickerson's eloquent tongue and facile pen were largely contributory to the creation of this sentiment and Mr. Isherwood himself aided indirectly in strengthening it. That officer had found himself placed at the head of an executive branch of the Navy Department formerly rather looked down upon as of slight importance but which had risen at one bound under the pressure of war to a place of first rank, and upon him fell the task of governing the gigantic system thus suddenly created. In doing this he entirely absorbed his own interests in those of the government and proceeded about his duty without fear or favor, insisting upon the exact letter of the law from every politician, naval officer, or contractor with whom he came into official contact. He thus made scores of enemies simply because he did his duty, and few friends; of the latter, indeed, he has written that he had none, and did not wish any. He exercised official authority and power never before conferred upon a member of his profession in this country, and with a full knowledge of the elements that resented that authority and grudged him the official power accorded him he felt himself capable of maintaining himself against all opposition.

When the war closed and there was more time for personal jealousy and dislike to assert themselves, all the disappointed contractors, all the naval officers whose official toes had been trodden upon, and all the politicians whose favorites had failed to retain positions for which they were unfit, banded together and for two or three years filled the pages of the newspapers with tales of the incompetence of the engineer-in-chief and assertions as to the uselessness of his machinery. Through this prolonged storm of abuse Mr. Isherwood passed unconcerned, neither depressed by slander nor exhilarated by success; he had calculated upon both, and was never disappointed. The attack centered upon the trial trips of the vessels built to compete with those of Bureau design, for it was confidently predicted that their results would be so to the disadvantage of the Bureau practice that the chief of that Bureau would be overthrown and buried in the wreck. When these events had all passed by and the competing ships had made records of failure, complete in some cases, while Isherwood's machinery had been wonderfully successful, there was little left for the hostiles except surprise and chagrin.

The claim of the contractors for the *Algonquin's* machinery was that it would propel a given hull at a certain speed, or a certain distance, more economically than could the Bureau engines; that is, with a less expenditure of coal. With equal allowances of coal they expected to develop more power and speed. In an open letter to the Department written by Mr. Forbes, that gentleman expressed Dickerson's belief as follows: "The engineer on whose skill I rely, is of opinion that, with equal amounts of coal supplied to both vessels, the *Algonquin* can go as far and as fast as the *Winooski*—both vessels running at economical rates of speed—and then tow her home after her coal is exhausted; and that, tied stern to stern, the *Algonquin* can tow the *Winooski* backward across the North River in twenty minutes as a measure of power." In order that an impartial method of conducting the trial be prescribed the Secretary of the Navy appointed a board of civilian experts, composed of eight of the most prominent marine engineers in New York city, and requested them to prepare the instructions to be followed on the trial. This board agreed that a dock trial for power would be the fairest possible test, directing that the paddle-wheels of the two vessels be made of exactly the same width and immersion that they might act as equal dynamometers: each vessel was to burn as much coal as desired, taken from the same pile and weighed on the same scales on the wharf between them, the amount of coal consumed in the specified time (ninety-six hours) compared with the number of revolutions of the engines to be the measure of economy.

To this method of trial the contractors for the *Algonquin* objected, although it was more favorable for showing the truth of their claims than a trial in free route would have been. One of their objections was that the *Algonquin* had no circulating pump, a scoop, or "mud shovel" as it was irreverently called, being depended upon to throw water into the condenser by the motion of the ship; another objection was that the smaller boilers could not burn as much coal as those of the *Winooski*, the latter having 200 square feet of grate surface to 132 in the *Algonquin*, but this objection was inconsistent with the claim that they could produce a given power with a much less expenditure of fuel. The press generally sided with Dickerson and ridiculed the idea of a dock trial, one of the leading illustrated papers of the country coming out with a caricature representing Secretary Welles mounted on an ordinary-looking donkey labeled "Winooski," the tail of which was hitched to a post, while Mr. Dickerson in the garb of Uncle Sam pranced near by astride of a fiery animal bearing the name "Algonquin" on its collar. The legend underneath this picture ran as follows:

"ALL'S WELL, THAT ENDS WELL(ES)!

"*Uncle Sam* (*Dickerson*)—Now Grandaddy, my little donkey, Algonquin, is ready to run agin yourn.

"*Granny Welles*—Well, I'm ready too—just tie your animal's tail to the post, as mine is, and whose tail comes off first wins the race."

During the autumn months the competitive dock trial of the rival engines was twice undertaken, and twice discontinued by Mr. Dickerson, who personally supervised the running of the *Algonquin's* machinery. The first stop was occasioned by an alleged defect in the steam pipe of the *Algonquin*, under the pretext of repairing which a delay of six weeks resulted, and the second stop, made after both engines had been run about seventy hours, was without other cause than that Dickerson was dissatisfied with the progress of the trial, in which his vessel was steadily losing ground. The *Winooski* completed the specified ninety-six hours without stoppage or hitch of any kind, her performance steadily improving and giving better results the last twelve hours than at any time before. The following extracts from the report of the board of chief engineers which conducted the trial give the main conclusions:

"The trial was conducted in exact conformity with the instructions of the board of civilian experts, consisting of Messrs. Everett, Copeland, Baird, Hibbard, Coryell, Bromley, and Wright.

"At the time the *Algonquin's* engine was stopped it was falling rapidly behind the *Winooski's*, the difference in the performance being nearly one revolution of the wheels per minute.

"The stoppage, in our opinion, was caused by this fact, and was wholly unauthorized, unwarranted, and unjustifiable, and was done in open defiance of our prohibition.

"With regard to the economical results, they are as follows, according to the two methods of determining them:

"By the first method, taking the cubes of the number of revolutions made per minute by the paddle-wheels for the measure of power, we find the power with the *Algonquin's* machinery to cost about two and one-tenth per cent. more in fuel than the power with the *Winooski's* machinery.

"By the second method, taking the indicator results for the measure of power, we find the power with the *Algonquin's* machinery to cost about ten and six-tenths per cent. more in fuel than the power with the *Winooski's* machinery.

"By both methods, the economy of fuel is in favor of the *Winooski's* machinery, and the difference in the results given by the two methods is probably due to the difference in the effects of the tide on the paddle-wheels of the two vessels."

The following is an abstract of a table of comparative data which accompanied the report of the trial board:

	Winooski.	Algonquin.
Date of commencement, October 23d, P. M.	4:23	4:22
Duration of experiment in hours and minutes	96.	69.8
Totat number of revolutions	85,884	62,407
Average steam pressure in steam pipe	19.64	71.63
Average point of cutting off steam	0.619	0.132
Average vacuum in condenser in inches of mercury	27.80	20.54
Average revolutions per minute	14.91	15.045
Average indicated pressure on piston	26.276	31.60
Average indicated horse power	545.485	517.317
Pounds of coal per hour per ind. horse-power	2.905	3.113
Temperature on deck	53.6	53.6
Temperature in fire room	98.	108.9
Temperature in engine room	66.8	70.1

After this trial, the Department ordered the contractors, through Rear Admiral Gregory, to prepare the *Algonquin* for another dock trial, to be a complete one as to time. To this order Mr. Forbes refused, his letter to Admiral Gregory containing the following comments:

"In former communications I have protested against a dock trial as unfair, and consequently improper. I now reiterate that protest. My engine, I had, perhaps, ignorantly imagined, was built to navigate the sea, and not to strain hawsers and pull docks. I consequently decline to run it again at the dock; but whenever the Navy Department or Mr. Isherwood is ready to run the vessels at cruising speed (say about eight knots), for comparative economy of fuel, and afterward at full speed, for development of power, you will find me ready and anxious. It was for this that the engine was built.

"The experts, who adhere with so much tenacity to the dock trial, have failed to convince me or the scientific world that it is a fair trial * * * "

It is needless to follow out in detail the controversy that followed. The Navy Department ultimately abandoned its determination to insist upon a complete dock trial and it was finally agreed to make a last comparative test of the two vessels by racing them eight times consecutively over a course from Execution Rock to and around the light on Faulkner's Island and return, the total course being something less than one thousand miles. The race began about 3 p. m. February 13th, 1866, and terminated the night of the 14th on account of a severe storm, less than one-half of the course at that time having been traversed by either vessel.

When the vessels first got under way the sky was clear, with a light breeze from the north north-east, and as they proceeded up Long Island Sound the *Winooski* quickly began to widen the distance between the two, she being four and one-half miles ahead when Stratford light-ship was reached, forty miles from the starting point. She rounded Faulkner's Island about 8 p. m. and half an hour later met the *Algonquin* going toward the island, she being then about thirteen miles behind. At 1 a. m. next morning the *Winooski* reached Execution Rock, having completed one-eighth of the whole course, and having run one hundred and twenty miles in ten hours and seven minutes. She was here retarded to some extent by fields of floating ice, but suffered no damage and her machinery was in excellent working order. At 5.48 that morning she again turned Faulkner's Island and shortly after seven met the *Algonquin* steering for it and thirty miles behind. At 10.37 a. m. she once more worked through the ice about Execution Rock and stood up the Sound, forty miles ahead of her rival, meeting and saluting the latter about noon. At five minutes past eight that evening the *Winooski* completed her third round voyage and the race was given up on account of the weather, she being then seventy miles ahead, which was regarded as sufficient to establish the relative merits of the two ships.

The official report of the trial board thus condemned the *Algonquin*: "In every point guaranteed by the contractor for the *Algonquin's* machinery he has failed, and we are of the opinion that it is totally unfit for the naval service." By the terms of the contract the contractors were required in case of failure to remove their machinery from the *Algonquin* and replace it with machinery like that of the competing vessel, and this the Department called upon Forbes and Dickerson to do, at the same time withholding from them the last payment on the contract and a final payment in the shape of a percentage reservation. The contractors refused to carry out this requirement of the contract, informing the Department that they had appealed the matter to Congress, and so it rested for two or three years: the contractors eventually received the withheld payments and the *Algonquin*, after lying in ordinary at the New York navy yard until 1869, was sold. Mr. Dickerson offered no reason in defense of the failure of his expectations; in fact he is said to have appeared quite unconcerned about the matter and less disposed to discover any element of personal defeat in it than was any one of a great number of newspaper editors who had been defending him. The hope of retrieval that follows failure is frequently more comforting than success with its accompanying weariness, and this was true in this case, for the Dickerson party turned with renewed hope and marvelous predictions to the *Idaho*, then approaching readiness for her steam trials.

The principal dimensions of the *Idaho*, the names of her builders and the unusual proportions of her steam cylinders have been given in a former chapter. The contract required that she make an average of fifteen knots per hour for twenty-four consecutive hours under the usual conditions of sea weather with the wind not more favorable than abeam. The extreme to which the expansive theory of steam was carried by Dickerson in the designs for this machinery is shown by the scanty provision for generating it, her boilers aggregating only 396 square feet of grate surface, or less than one-half as much as the practice of that day demanded for vessels of her size and proposed speed. These boilers were of Dickerson's own patent and had inclined water tubes with a superheating chamber in the top, as shown in the accompanying sectional view. The large removable plates in the wake of the tube-boxes were of *cast-iron* although compelled to withstand the full steam pressure of the boilers, and this was one of many departures from sound practice which the construction of the engines and boilers revealed. One of the officers assembled on board for the steam trial was Chief Engineer E. D. Robie, U. S. Navy, than whom no one had a better reputation for nerve and professional acumen, or was freer from suspicion of hysteria. After critically examining the machinery in all its details, he, without taking counsel with anyone, quietly went on shore, insured his life for a large sum for the benefit of his family, and then returned ready to perform his duty and face any possible consequence, an incident which illustrates the curiosities of design embodied in the construction of the *Idaho's* machinery much better than the same can be conveyed by any technical description.

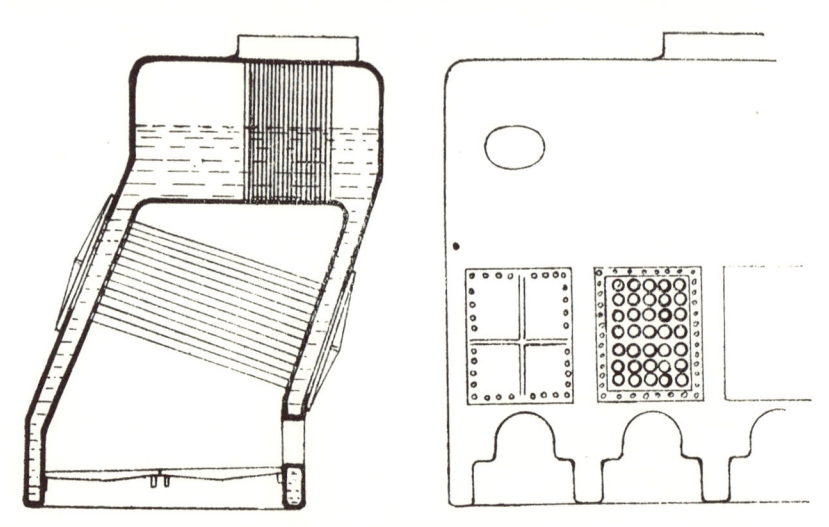

DICKERSON'S PATENT BOILER.

On the 15th of May, 1866, the *Idaho* got under way from New York harbor and proceeded seaward with the intention (on the part of her designers) of breaking the record of speed at sea under steam and of so completely vindicating the theory of extraordinary expansion that the scoffing Isherwood would be forced to hide his ruined reputation in the depths of professional oblivion. After getting to sea the trial run was repeatedly interrupted by casualties to machinery and it was not until the evening of May 20th that a consecutive steaming period of twenty-four hours without break-down had been secured, the course run over being in smooth water up and down the coast of New Jersey. The performance of the machinery was the maximum that the contractors' engineers could coax from it, but the result was forcibly suggestive of the Esopian tale of the mountain and its offspring. Instead of the contract requirement of fifteen knots, or the far greater speed predicted, the average for the twenty-four hours was *eight and twenty-seven one hundredths knots per hour!*

The story of this trial trip is appropriately concluded by quoting the following endorsement put on the report of the trial board by Rear Admiral Gregory, and by reproducing the report of a board that surveyed the *Idaho* a few months later:

"SIR: Respectfully transmitted herewith are the reports of the board of officers appointed to carry out the orders of the Bureau for the sea trial of the steamer *Idaho*. These records show conclusively that the *Idaho* has not in any particular been fitted and equipped in accordance with the obligations of the contract, and that her performances, particularly in speed, show that she is unfitted for the service, and should be condemned and rejected as totally unfit for service in the navy.

"I am, sir, very respectfully, your obedient servant,

"F. H. GREGORY,
"*Rear Admiral.*

"JOHN LENTHAL, ESQ.,
"*Chief Bureau Construction, Washington.*"

"NEW YORK NAVY YARD, August 22, 1866.

"SIR: Agreeable to your orders of the 9th instant we have examined the *Idaho*, and have respectfully to report as follows:

"The vessel is not in conformity with the contract, inasmuch as she is not an efficient vessel of war, with the proper conveniences of capacity and stowage, and her machinery is worthless as a motive-power; it also occupies much of the space in the vessel which should have been appropriated to other purposes.

"The board does not consider the vessel a desirable one, or proper to be retained in the service.

"The board is of the opinion, if sold at public auction (exclusive of the sails, cables and anchors, and other property belonging to the government) that the vessel should bring one hundred and twenty-five thousand ($125,000) dollars.

"We are respectfully, &c.,

"F. H. GREGORY, *Rear Admial.*
"JOHN L. WORDEN, *Captain.*
"B. F. DELANO, *Naval Constructor.*
"J. W. KING, *Chief Engineer.*
"G. W. RANSOM, *Commander.*
"H. H. STEWART, *Chief Engineer.*
"E. D. ROBIE, *Chief Engineer.*

"JOHN LENTHAL, ESQ.,
  "*Chief of Bureau of Construction, Washington, D. C.*"

Mr. Dickerson took no part personally in the speed trials of the *Idaho*. A bright and accomplished man in many respects, he appears to a student of his dealings with the Navy Department to have been not a charlatan but a monomaniac on the subject of engineering; without much professional knowledge of that subject but able to discourse upon it in such manner as to win a reputation as an eminent engineer and to enlist for himself the enthusiastic support of newspaper editors, politicians, and capitalists. With the failure of the *Idaho* Mr. Dickerson's connection with the Navy Department came to an end and he ceased from troubling with his visionary theories and vexatious political influence. With the severance of that connection this strange and fantastic figure passes beyond the horizon of the present work and these pages will know him no more.

Although condemned in the positive manner indicated by the official reports copied above, fate decreed that the *Idaho* should occupy for a brief period a place in the American navy and become

THE IDAHO AS A SAILING SHIP.

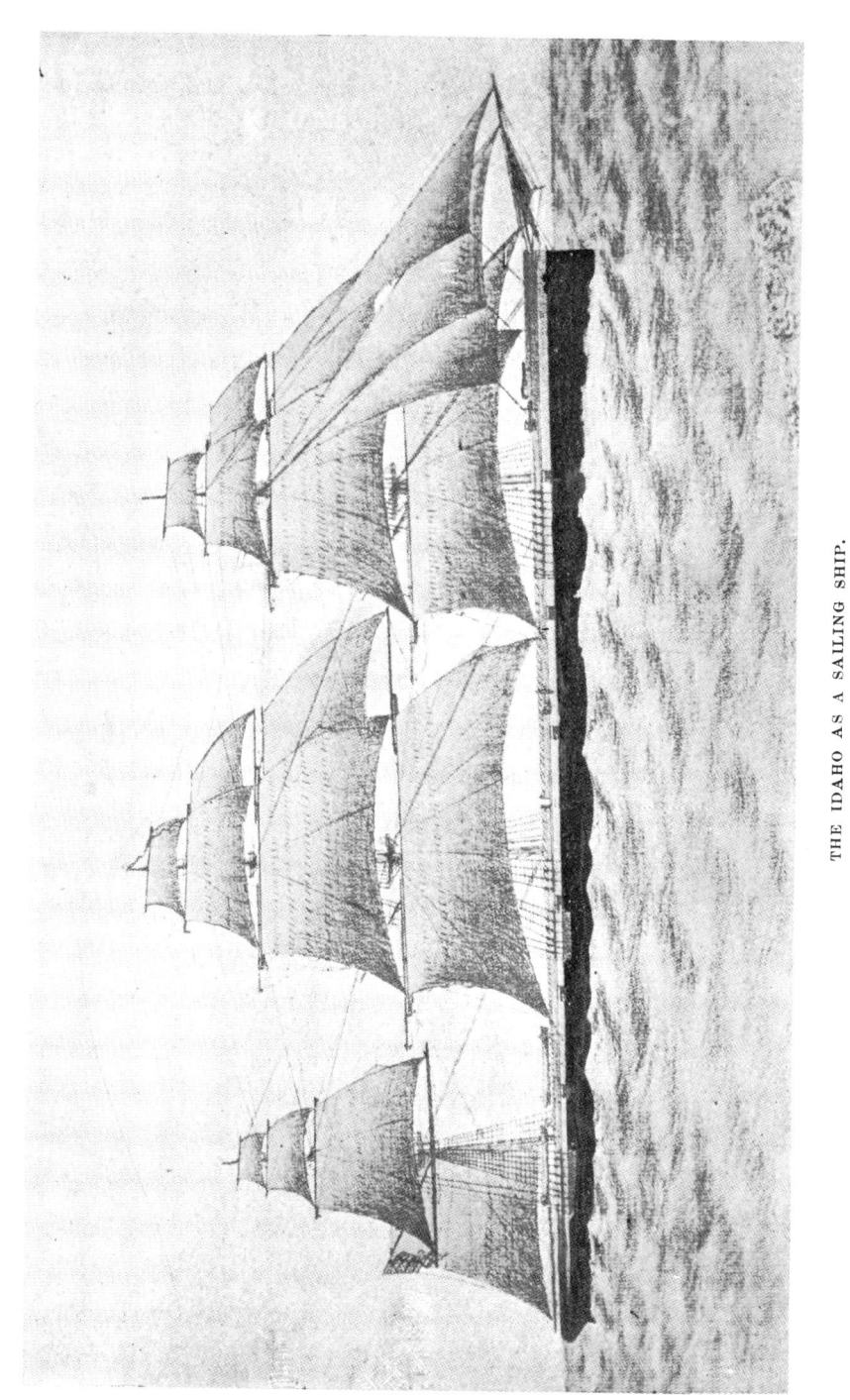

the central figure in an ocean tragedy as unusual and thrilling as as any in our naval history. When the Navy Department refused to accept her, Mr. Forbes, who had much influence by virtue of his prominence and high standing among men, appealed to Congress for relief and obtained it almost immediately. A joint resolution, approved February 18, 1867, forced the vessel upon the government by directing the Secretary of the Navy to accept her at the price of $550,000 already paid Mr. Forbes, this being $50,000 less than the contract price. As the hull had been built by Mr. Steers, the most eminent ship-builder of the day, and was considered faultless in model and construction, it was decided not to sell it at the low figure necessarily commanded by condemned government property. Accordingly, after the machinery had been removed, the vessel was fitted up as a full-rigged sailing ship and ordered to proceed to the Asiatic station, the intention being to make use of her as a store-ship at the naval depot established at Nagasaki by permission of the Japanese government.

The *Idaho* sailed from New York for Japan the first day of November, 1867, under the command of Acting Volunteer Lieutenant Commander Edward Hooker, her watch officers also being from the volunteer service. From her unfortunate experience as a steamer the ship had a bad name and those who embarked in her did so with many misgivings, but when she got into the open sea she most nobly did justice as a sailer to the genius that had shaped her beautiful lines. With the wind well ahead and her yards braced almost sharp up she logged hour after hour $14\frac{1}{2}$ knots, and in one watch of four hours made sixty-five knots; later in the voyage, when in the Southern Indian Ocean, on one occasion with a fair wind she ran all the log-line off the reel, marking $18\frac{1}{2}$ knots, before the sand had entirely run out of the glass, when the ship was probably making 20 knots through the water. In spite of these fine performances, the *Idaho*, perhaps the fastest sailing ship in the world, made one of the longest passages on record, being so baffled by head winds and calms in the latter part of her voyage that when she reached Nagasaki she was two hundred days out from New York.

The reports of her wonderful qualities as a sailing ship and the remonstrances of her officers against laying up as a hulk such a splendid example of naval architecture finally induced the Navy Department to recall her and she was ordered to Yokohama to prepare for the voyage home. On this trip her speed was not remarkable, the bottom being foul from having swung at anchor for fifteen months in Nagasaki harbor, but she maintained her right to be considered the queen of sailing ships by weathering without the loss of a spar a typhoon that wrecked many vessels in the harbor of Yokohama and destroyed large buildings in that city. When all preparations were completed, the *Idaho* started for home by way of Hong Kong, being ordered to sail from Yokohama the 20th of September, 1869, although a typhoon was then brewing and the delay of one week would have assured her fair monsoon weather. The start was propitious, with a favoring wind and good speed, but the next day, the 21st, the weather became squally and the barometer fell steadily. About sunset the full fury of the first semicircle of the most awful circular storm that a ship has ever survived burst upon the devoted *Idaho* and for several hours her crew had an experience the like of which few other men have lived to tell of. The main yard, ninety-eight feet long and seven feet in circumference, broke in three pieces and fell on deck, following which disaster the sails, even those snugly furled, were torn away, and one by one the yards and masts came crashing down until the ship was merely a hulk held down almost on her beam ends by the force of the hurricane. At the climax of this hellish scene the barometer reached the almost unprecedented reading of 27.62.

With a final wild, unearthly howl, the wind suddenly dropped to a dead calm and those on board the *Idaho* who were familiar with the laws of storms knew that they had passed into the vortex or center of the cyclone, but this brought no release from danger, for the sea, previously planed smooth by the terrific power of the blast, now rose on all sides to mountainous heights, as though boiling in a huge caldron, and great masses of water began toppling into the hapless ship, while her rolling and plunging became indescribably violent. On one occasion she shipped huge volumes of water at the same moment over both bows, both quarters, and the starboard waist, from which she nearly went down, but finally rose slowly and wearily with four feet of water on her spar deck. Under this ordeal, stanchions, beams and timbers broke and were carried away, the decks opened, bolts drew out, and nothing but certain destruction appeared to be the prospect for the unfortunate crew. And in all this, it must be remembered, it was night, and a Cimmerian darkness brooded over the deep, so intensely black and unnatural that the world seemed shrouded in the shadow of the pinions of the angel of death.

When the other side of the revolving storm came on with all its terrific fury it found nothing to destroy but a battered unmanageable wreck, in which the helpless crew crouched miserably together waiting for the death that seemed unavoidable. By one of those strange fatalities in which a quality of mercy on the part of natural elements, even of the sea, seem manifested, the *Idaho* remained afloat when the storm had passed on. Jury masts were rigged and the vessel and crew, thus miraculously preserved, worked slowly back to Yokohama, making the distance in eight days that had been covered on the way out in one. A curious matted mass of sail, cordage and lightning rod, so compactly woven together that men were unable to undo it, was preserved as a memento of this struggle for life and as an illustration of the power and capriciousness of the Storm King.[1]

The ruined hull of the *Idaho* remained in Yokohama harbor until 1874, when it was sold to the highest bidder for almost nothing.

In August, 1866, three months after the trial trip of the *Idaho*, the *Chattanooga*, built by the Cramp Company for the swift cruiser competition, was reported ready for her speed trials. There was nothing novel or fantastical about this ship's machinery, engines and boilers being of types well known and in general use, and were designed and built by Merrick & Sons, an engineering firm of long experience and excellent reputation. The *Chattanooga* began her trial trip at 9 A. M., August 17th, and was kept up to full power for twenty-four hours without difficulty, the course, in dead smooth water, being nine times back and forth between the lights on Cape

---

[1] This brief account of the tragedy of the *Idaho* is based upon an article entitled "A Night in a Typhoon," written by a survivor, Medical Director A. S. Gihon, U. S. Navy, which in the humble opinion of the author is the most thrilling and graphically-told tale of the sea that has ever appeared in print. It was published originally in the *Atlantic Monthly* for March, 1870, and was reprinted in the *United Service Magazine* for April, 1884.

Henlopen and the Brandywine shoals, and then out to sea for fifteen hours. The average speed for the twenty-four hours was a little short of 13½ knots per hour, this being a knot and a half less than required: the report of the engineer trial board was decidedly favorable to the machinery, with the exception of the circulating pump driven by independent oscillating engines, which was pronounced unreliable, and the failure of the ship to meet the speed requirements was charged against the agent of the contractors, who had entire control of the machinery, and who was accused in the report of entirely ignoring the stipulations of the contract.

A subsequent examination showed that the brasses, bearings, and some other parts of the engines had suffered to some extent from the severe trial to which they had been subjected, but no serious damage was discovered. The engines were not able to work off all the steam the boilers could produce, for which reason the trial board recommended the replacing of the screw with a larger one of coarser pitch. Some minor defects were recommended to be made good and after considerable correspondence between the Cramp Company and the Department the *Chattanooga* was accepted, the engineer-in-chief and other competent engineers being satisfied that she could make the required speed, if properly handled, after these alterations had been effected. The desired modifications were not all made, but the vessel was accepted and performed some service in the North Atlantic squadron and on the Fishing Banks. She was then laid up in ordinary at the League Island navy yard, where she remained until December, 1871, when she sank at the dock from having her side cut through by running ice. The wreck was sold a month later for $45,700. Her total cost, including original contract, charges for alterations, cost of trial trips, repairs, etc., amounted to $950,159.31.

John Ericsson's machinery in the *Madawaski* received its sea test in January, 1867, and to the great surprise of the admirers of that distinguished engineer, failed by over two knots to drive the vessel at the required speed of fifteen knots per hour. She went to sea the 14th of January from New York, under command of Commander F. A. Roe, and remained out for one week, during which she steamed about one thousand miles, finally returning when her supply of coal was exhausted. Stormy weather was experienced, and

U. S. S. CHATTANOOGA, 1865.

From an india ink drawing loaned by Mr. Charles H. Cramp.

for fifty hours during the latter part of the week a hurricane with the force of the wind as high as eleven at times continued. A trial performance of forty-one hours was obtained by aggregating three periods of best performance under fair conditions, the longest period thus selected being sixteen hours; the data derived from this trial is given in tabular form hereafter.

With all his knowledge and mechanical ability there is no doubt that Captain Ericsson made a very serious mistake in putting direct-acting engines of the size and type he selected into a vessel of the class represented by the *Madawaska*. He had, it will be remembered, many years before when the science of marine engineering was young, overthrown the fallacy that gearing was necessary for driving screw shafting in vessels, but the genius that had seen the falsity of the logic of the earlier engineers seems to have failed to realize that the very conditions formerly feared and which he knew did not exist had at last come to pass as a reality in the effort to concentrate power in an abnormally slender hull. Engineer-in-Chief Isherwood, on the other hand, observed the danger which Ericsson in his self-confidence overlooked, and by providing his swift cruisers with geared engines guarded against the risk of racking the hull and the equally dangerous reflex action of a yielding foundation upon the operation of the engines.

It must not be understood that Ericsson's engines in the *Madawaska* were wholly bad, for they were excellent of their kind and with no radical fault except the one, unfortunately fatal, of being unsuited to the surroundings in which they were placed. In one of the staunchly-built armor-clads, or in the rigid steel fabrics of the present day they would have given satisfaction and undoubtedly have driven the vessel at the speed on which Ericsson counted. Although the average speed attained by the *Madawaska* during the trial was less than thirteen knots, it is due in the interest of history to say that for a short time the required speed was reached, and at one heaving of the log was exceeded by one knot. Commander Roe states in his report of the trial trip that from 10:30 p. m. to midnight of January 16th the ship logged $15\frac{1}{2}$ knots per hour, and in the midwatch immediately following attained a speed of 16 knots and made $60\frac{1}{2}$ knots for the four hours. This report of the commanding officer closes with the following complimentary reference to the machinery : "Her machinery is as perfect as it need be. It has undergone the severest test and not once been found wanting. She is the fastest ship I have ever seen." The report of the board of engineers also spoke highly of the strength and workmanship of the machinery. Its great fault seems to be that it was put into the wrong ship.

Owing to the practical cessation of all government work at the close of the war it was not until early in 1868, a year after the trial of the last of the competing contract cruisers, that the first of the Isherwood cruisers was ready for a sea trial, the *Wampanoag* running her trial trip in February of that year and the *Ammonoosuc* in June. Both these ships so far exceeded the sea speed of anything then afloat that their trial trips, especially that of the first—the *Wampanoag*—may fairly be regarded as a most important event in the history of marine engineering, and constituted such a glorious triumph for the American naval engineers that the story will be fully told in a separate chapter. The *Wampanoag* was the pioneer of the class of swift ocean steamers that in our own day has completely changed the tactics of naval warfare, and so promoted the possibilities of maritime commerce that the interests of all great nations are now so closely woven together that great wars between them are almost impossible. It was the fate of the *Wampanoag* to live too soon, before the world was ready for the era which her creation heralded, and for that reason she has been almost forgotten ; it is therefore due to her and to the genius that made her possible that her story be told for the benefit of the present generation. For convenience of comparison the data yielded by the sea trial of the *Wampanoag* is printed with that derived from the trials of the *Idaho*, *Chattanooga* and *Madawaska* here inserted in this chapter :

The *Madawaska* was accepted by the Navy Department after her trial trip and was promptly laid up in ordinary. In 1869 her name was changed to *Tennessee* at the same time that many other names peculiar to the Civil War period were changed to others that in most cases were certainly not more appropriate. The history of the *Tennessee* in the navy is interesting and peculiar; to quote from the report of the Secretary of the Navy for 1887, "She had a short life, but, as a consumer of money, a brilliant one." Her total original cost for hull, engines, and equipment was $1,856,075.81, and between 1869 and 1871 she was repaired at a cost of $576,799.61, only $73,000 of which was spent on the machinery. One-half of her boilers were removed at this time, and a deck was built, converting her into a gun-deck frigate. She then made a special cruise of three months conveying United States commissioners to the island of San Domingo, and soon after her return home was turned over to Mr. John Roach to be fitted with new machinery and receive general repairs. This work was done during the three following years at a cost of $801,713.60 in addition to the value of the Ericsson machinery which was given to Mr. Roach; of this enormous sum the records of the Bureau of Steam Engineering show that about $350,000 was charged to the new engines and boilers.

The contract for this new machinery was dated October 3d, 1871, and names $300,000 as the price of engines, boilers, and fittings complete. This contract is especially interesting from the fact that it marks the first appearance in our steam navy of the compound engine. The engineer-in-chief, Mr. J. W. King, was at that time absent in Europe on special duty investigating the question of compound engines, which had recently appeared in the engineering practice of some of the European navies, but the contract with Mr. Roach was made by order of the Secretary of the Navy, Mr. Robeson, upon Mr. Roach's own representations before any reports from Mr. King had been received. The new machinery of the *Tennessee* consisted of two horizontal back-acting compound engines placed side by side with the cylinders arranged tandem, the high-pressure cylinders outboard. The contract required the high-pressure cylinders to be 40 inches in diameter, the low-pressures to be 76 inches in diameter, and the stroke 42 inches, but when it was

DATA AND RESULTS OF THE SEA TRIALS AT MAXIMUM SPEED OF THE COMPETITIVE STEAMERS "IDAHO," "CHATTANOOGA," "MADAWASKA," AND "WAMPANOAG," UNDER STEAM ALONE.

	Idaho.	Chattanooga.	Madawaska.	Wampanoag
Date of commencing the trial	May 19, 1866	Aug. 17, 1866	Jan. 14, 1867	Feb. 11, 1868
Duration of the trial in consecutive hours	24.	24.	41.	38.
Length of the vessel on load water line from forward edge of rabbet of stem to after side of sternpost, in feet and inches	298.	315.	335.	335.
Extreme breadth of the vessel on load water line, in feet and inches	44.6	46.	45.2	45.2
Mean draught of the vessel during the trial, in feet and inches	17.1	14.11½	18.2	18.6
Greatest immersed transverse section of vessel at her mean draught during the trial, in square feet	606.44	535.	725.47	740.52
Displacement of the vessel at her mean draught during the trial, in tons	3,240.58	3,043.	4,105.17	4,215.54
Ratio of the length to the breadth	6.697	6.848	7.417	7.417
Ratio of the displacement to its circumscribing parallelopipedon	.509	.537	.566	.566
Number of square feet of grate surface in the boilers	396.	980.	1,128.	1,128.
State of the sea	Smooth.	Smooth.	Rough.	Rough.
Kind of wind	Light breeze.	Light breeze.	Moderate.	Strong breeze
Angle from ahead made by the wind with the vessel's keel, in degrees	90.	90.	90.	132.
Number of pounds of coal consumed per hour	4,905.	10,700.	11,042.683	12,670.606
Number of pounds of coal consumed per hour per square foot of grate surface	12.386	10.918	9.790	11.232
Temperature of the feed-water in degrees of Fahrenheit	101.	92.	128.	138.
Number of double strokes of engines pistons made per minute	35.93	50.45	46.234	31.265
Steam pressure in the boilers, in pounds per square inch above the atmosphere	37.90	27.52	29.84	32.43
Proportion of throttle valve open	1.	.18	.224	1.
Fraction of stroke of piston completed when the steam was cut off	.13	.52	.600	.66
Vacuum in condenser in inches of mercury	26.	19.34	24.33	24.
Steam pressure, per indicator, per square inch of piston	13.4	14.4	11.92	34.2
Indicated horse-power developed by the engines	645.415	1,696.131	2,085.188	4,048.84
Horse-power developed by the auxiliary engines supplying the condensing water, (estimated)	....	40.823	57.532	....
Total indicated horse-power developed	645.415	1,736.954	2,142.72	4,048.84
Pounds of coal consumed per hour per indicated horse-power	7.500	6.160	5.170	3.129
Speed of the vessel per hour in geographical miles	8.27	13.375	12.732	16.758

found that the length of the engines cramped the passage-way outboard of the high-pressure cylinders the stroke was reduced to 40 inches and the diameter of the low-pressure cylinders increased to 78 inches, with which dimensions the engines were built. There were ten return-tubular cylindrical boilers, six of them being in one fore and aft fire-room forward of the engines and the others in a similar fire-room abaft the engines. The vessel was ship-rigged.

This overhauling of the *Tennessee* is one of the most remarkable transactions in the history of the Navy Department, and one about which there has always been more or less mystery; no direct legal authority for incurring the great cost of the changes appears to have existed and it is a fact that the Ericsson machinery of the ship, which had originally cost $700,000, had never been condemned by a board of officers, nor had its value ever been fixed by a government board; yet it was turned over to Mr. Roach in barter as old iron at a stated value of $65,000. At the time the contract for the new machinery was made with Mr. Roach there was stored at the Washington navy yard a complete and entirely new set of 100-inch geared engines built for the *Bon Homme Richard* and exactly like the engines that had driven the *Wampanoag*, the sistership of the *Tennessee*, seventeen knots an hour, yet it was deemed proper to contract for a complete new outfit of machinery, and that of an experimental nature, for, as has been observed, the compound engine was then an unknown thing in our naval practice. In 1872 a Congressional committee, of which Hon. Austin P. Blair was chairman, was appointed to investigate certain charges against the Navy Department and took 420 printed pages of testimony [1] about the *Tennessee* transaction and some other matters, but failed to make any definite discoveries; in view of which failure the writer will not undertake the hopeless task of seeking to unravel the mystery.

After the *Tennessee* had received her new machinery and had failed by about four knots to make the speed promised for her she was sent, in 1875, to the Asiatic station as flagship. In 1879, having returned home the previous year and been again repaired, she was commissioned as flagship of the North Atlantic squadron

---

[1] Miscellaneous Document No. 201 ; 42d Congress, 2d Session.

and continued as such until 1887 when she was condemned by the Statutory Board as unseaworthy and was sold that same year by public auction for $34,527. Including nearly $600,000 spent on her for repairs between 1875 and 1887 her total cost to the government had been in round numbers $3,800,000.

During the first two years of this vessel's service on the North Atlantic station the writer, then fresh from the Naval Academy, gained on her decks and in her engine-room his first practical ideas of the naval customs and practices of his country. The *Tennessee* was then the largest vessel in commission in the American navy and the era of mastless steel cruisers was yet so far away that she was not suspected, by the youngsters at least, of being obsolete and stood as the type of all that was excellent and majestic in ship construction. And the routine and discipline observed in the daily life of the ship was in perfect accord with the era her type represented, which period is commonly designated as that pertaining to the old navy. The admiral lived in stately splendor in spacious apartments far aft on the gun deck, into which few but his orderlies and servants ever ventured to intrude, and his appearance abroad in the world of the ship's life always produced the bustle and commotion incident to a great and unusual event. The captain, an officer of magnificent physique, whose fame from the Civil War clothed him in the eyes of his subordinates with all the attributes of heroism, was likewise surrounded with all the ceremonials of a court, and, like the admiral, did not walk forth into his kingdom except at times when something was going to happen. Even the ward-room was a semi-sacred and exclusive precinct; it was separated from the junior officers' space by only a thin pine partition, but that to all intents and purposes was more impassable and impervious than the heavy steel water-tight bulkheads of the present day.

All the punctillious etiquette of the old régime was religiously followed: the direction of the wind determined which side of the spar deck and which side of the gun deck might properly be used as a thoroughfare; the junior, or "steerage," officers knew only the port gangway and had their own liberty boats, two boats being necessary to take officers on shore even though there would be but one from the ward-room and one from the steerage to go; no enlisted man ever risked his freedom by venturing to windward of an

U. S. STEAM FRIGATE TENNESSEE, ORIGINALLY THE CRUISER MADAWASKI.

Length on l. w. l., 335 feet; beam, 45.2 feet; displacement, 4,840 tons.

officer. The arrival of eight bells in the morning and of sunset in the evening marked the unfailing and unvarying performance of certain rites with boats, masts and spars. No steam capstan gave warning with its rapid rattle of the coming of a power more potent and trustworthy than the brawn of men, and in consequence the function of getting under way approached the sublime in its gravity; when the grizzled old boatswain and his troop of weather-beaten mates gathered about the main hatch and made the ship echo with their shrill calls and hoarse shout in unison, "All hands up anchor!" it meant all hands; none could look on. The great cable came in link by link laboriously keeping time to the measured tramp of more than four hundred men walking around on the capstan bars and urged meanwhile to more rapid exertion by the rollicking strains of " Rory O'More " and " Lannigan's Ball " from the band. In all the memories of that long-vanished cruise nothing lingers with more vividness than the echo of the voices of those boatswain's mates and the rhythmic tremble of the decks beneath the tread of the men tramping round and round about the capstans; and it is good to have had an experience of such things, for they were picturesque and typical of a system that most excellently served its purpose in its own time, and has now passed away.

The ship was huge and roomy, affording ample space for all except the junior officers, who were herded into two narrow and noisome dens on the berth deck, hot in summer, cold in winter, unlighted save by candles or dim, smoky lamps, and unventilated except by two or three very small bull's eyes so nearly awash that they could not be opened except in dead smooth water or in a drydock. Those were the days of an unlimited number of midshipmen, cadet midshipmen and cadet engineers, not to mention a bountiful supply of ensigns and staff officers of that grade, so these steerages were always densely populated; more so than those of other ships probably from the circumstance of the *Tennessee* being on the home station and easily reached without any great outlay for mileage on account of officers ordered to join her.

The average number of young officers crowded into those darksome dens was about twenty-five, and there they stowed their clothes, performed their ablutions, wrote their letters and notebooks, ate, and as many as possible slept. Had an equal or a considerably smaller number of Chinese attempted to live in a cellar in any American City under precisely similar sanitary conditions they would have been promptly jailed; still, the young gentlemen survived their surroundings and without any cares worth worrying about managed to have a reasonably good time. The writer, for one, is rather glad at this distance of having had the experience and the opportunity, then almost the last one, of learning by actual contact just what the life and habits of the old navy were. Nevertheless, he thinks that the youth of the new navy are to be congratulated on the practical impossibility of such a condition of naval affairs ever returning.

U. S. S. WAMPANOAG, 1868.

CHAPTER XXIX.

"I consider the 'Wampanoag,' as a ship, to be faultless in her model, and, as a steamship, the fastest in the world."
Captain J. W. A. NICHOLSON, official report.

The Trial Trip of the WAMPANOAG—Remarkable Speed Developed—Official Reports of Commanding Officer and Board of Chief Engineers—Attempt of the Press to Discredit Her Performance—Her Success Verified by the Trial of the AMMONOOSUC—The Real Reasons for Building Swift Cruisers During the Civil War—The WAMPANOAG Condemed by a Board of Naval Officers—Her Subsequent Career.

THE delay after the war in completing the government-built cruisers was made great use of by the anti-Isherwood party, and the press of the country teemed with charges that the ships were held back to permit time for radical changes or even renewal of their machinery; that Isherwood was afraid to trust them in competition with the record made by the *Madawaska*, or even the *Idaho;* etc., etc. One example will be sufficient to show the intensity of this feeling, which is presented by the following extract from an editorial which appeared in a prominent service newspaper only two weeks before the sea trial of the *Wampanoag:*

"We speak . . . very severely of Mr. Isherwood's practice. But we have done so from mature, profound and complete conviction that he is ruining the navy by his untenable steam delusions. If we have utterly condemned his theories, we have done so only upon a basis of irrefragable facts—facts which we have set forth in array before that gentleman and before our readers in an elaborate series of articles, and to which, despite their bold challenge of refutation, never has there been even attempted a reply. We are free to say that there is no such monument of mechanical incapacity as the steam machinery of the *Wampanoag* class to be found in the annals of marine engineering.

" . . . We find, as a result of this short-sighted restriction, a man presiding over the Engineering Bureau who would not be allowed to plan, on the principles he employs for our whole new screw fleet, a hundred dollars' worth of machinery in any private establishment in the country.''

Early in 1868 the *Wampanoag* was pronounced completed and with a full complement of officers and men and her battery and stores on board was ordered to proceed to sea for her steam trials. She went out from New York the 7th of February and was first experimented with under sail, the propeller being uncoupled, and then ran under steam for twenty-five hours at a speed of as near eleven knots as could be approximated, for the purpose of ascertaining the amount of coal necessary for that speed. Heavy weather and damage to her rigging then drove her to seek shelter inside of Sandy Hook, where she remained one day, standing out to sea again at sunset on February 11th. At 9 P. M. that same night she began her full power steam trial, starting from a point north by east of Barnegat light and heading to the southward in the dark and wintry sea. Her great engines performed beautifully and at midnight the ship had worked up to a speed of seventeen knots, then unprecedented in steam navigation, and a source of surprise to all on board. Throughout the night and all the following day this high speed was closely adhered to, and when night again fell upon the stormy waters the people on the *Wampanoag* realized that they were participating in a remarkable event and experiencing a new sensation. The ''monument of mechanical incapacity'' was the master-piece of the age and the sovereign of the seas. The engineers were delighted, despite fatigue and nerve-tension incident to vigilant watching about the ponderous engines, and went about their second night's duties with the zeal and elation of victory, for this was an engineer's ship and the record she was rolling up was one to make every engineer proud of his calling and ambitious for the future of steam at sea which that record would make possible. All that long winter night the *Wampanoag* drove ahead, rolling deeply in a heavy irregular sea and keeping well up to her first established speed, the light of morning finding her still rushing through the tall seas like some huge sea-creature instinct with furious life.

At 11 A. M. that day, thirty-eight hours after the beginning of the trial, the engines were stopped to permit an adjustment to be made, although this was reported by the trial board as not absolutely necessary, and the full speed was not again resumed on account of the increasing heavy weather, the exhaustion of the fire-room force, and the satisfaction of all in authority with the performance of the ship and her machinery. When the record-breaking run was terminated the *Wampanoag* was off Savannah, Georgia, having run in the thirty-eight hours from Barnegat the distance of 630 knots, or 728 statute miles, 467 statute miles having been passed over during the first twenty-four hours of the run. This achievement was so far ahead of any record made by any sea-going commercial vessel or war steamer as to make comparisons almost impossible and render the *Wampanoag* peerless as a swift ocean cruiser.

The full details of this famous steam trial appear in the official reports of the commanding officer and board of chief engineers, which reports are here reproduced in the form in which they were originally published shortly after the trial.

REPORTS OF THE TRIAL TRIP

OF THE

United States Steamer Wampanoag,

At sea, (armed and equipped,) February 7 to February 17, 1868.

HULL.—Constructed at the New York navy yard, from designs of Naval Constructor B. F. DELANO. *Dimensions.*—Extreme length of spar deck, 342 feet 8 inches; extreme breadth, 45 feet 2 inches; depth of hold, 23 feet 6 inches; draught of water, 19 feet; tonnage (old measurement), 3,281 tons.

MACHINERY.—Constructed at the Novelty Works, New York, from designs by Chief Engineer B. F. ISHERWOOD, Chief of Bureau of Steam Engineering. Two geared direct-acting engines, with one surface condenser to both engines; two cylinders 100 inches in diameter, with four-feet stroke of piston; propeller nineteen feet diameter; eight vertical tubular boilers for main engine, with four super-heating boilers; aggregate grate surface of all the boilers 1,128 square feet; aggregate of the water-heating surface 30,578 square feet.

REPORT OF THE COMMANDING OFFICER.

UNITED STATES STEAMER WAMPANOAG, (1ST RATE,)
Hampton Roads, Va., February 18, 1868.

SIR: I have the honor to make the following report of results obtained during the experimental trial of this vessel at sea:

On the 7th instant I tried the ship under top-gallant sails, jib and course, propeller disconnected, wind fresh abeam, sea smooth, speed ten and one-half (10.5) to eleven knots per hour, propeller making twenty-nine (29) revolutions, the ship steering easily, helm amidship, no sail on mizzenmast.

On the 9th instant I began trial under steam to obtain a continuous speed of eleven (11) knots, with the least consumption of coal. I was obliged to end this trial in twenty-five (25) hours, and heave the ship to during a heavy gale from SE. to SW., with a topping sea.

During these twenty-five hours we ran two hundred eighty-two five-tenths (282.5) knots, consuming not quite forty-seven (47) tons of coal. This gives an average of about forty-five tons per day for an hourly speed of eleven and three-tenths (11.3) knots.

During this gale, which blew hard for twenty hours, we sustained some damage to our spars, owing to iron bolts carrying away. We lost one whisker, and our port bee. The F. T. mast stay with the staysail were blown to leeward, but finally secured. The parral eye-bolt in jaws of F. topsail yard broke, and sheet hook in foretopsail also. Before the yard and sail could be secured the foretop mast was chafed severely.

Owing to the weather being intensely cold, and the heavy sea, we could do nothing more than temporarily secure our spars.

As the gale moderated, I determined to run in and anchor under Sandy Hook, and there repair damages.

Received a New York pilot at 9 P. M., and at midnight anchored; at daylight commenced repairs, made new whiskers and bees, secured spars, stays, etc., and at sunset stood to sea. I would here remark, that in my opinion iron is used too much in rigging our ships. It would be more preferable to have the old-fashioned rope parrals to topsail yards, than to have either "tubs" or "jaws."

Iron cannot be trusted at any time, and is especially dangerous in extremely cold weather.

At 9 P. M. on the 11th I commenced a trial of the full steaming power; this trial continued through a period of thirty-eight hours, until 11 o'clock A. M. of the 13th instant. At this time a rubber washer in after crank working loose, endangered the heating of that journal. I therefore stopped the engines to have the washer replaced. This having been accomplished, at 2 o'clock the engines were again started, the ship going fourteen knots. At 3 P. M., as the sea was heavy, with appearance of bad weather, I determined, after consulting with Chief Engineer Zeller, presiding officer of the board of engineers, that it was unnecessary to work the engines up to full power again, as it had already been proved that an average speed of nearly *seventeen* knots could be continuously maintained during good weather.

During the first twenty-four hours of the trial we logged 405.375 knots, equal to 467.53 statute miles. During the thirty-eight hours we logged 630.875 knots, equal to 727.61 statute miles, an average of 16.6 knots, or 19.14 statute miles for each and every hour of the trial. Greatest speed obtained 17.75 knots, or 20.47 statute miles. I append a statement of the hourly speed made during thirty-six hours, arranged in six hours' tables for convenient reference. The speed and courses are copied from ship's log. The remarks are my own, made from personal observation. I add that the logging of the ship and distance run were verified by observation. We having started from a point twenty miles north by east from Barnegat light, passing Cape Hatteras at about a distance of twenty miles, and ceasing the run in latitude 31° 42' north, longitude 80° 24' west, 29 miles southeast half east of Tybee lighthouse.

The results of all trials in abstract are as follows:

We steamed seventeen knots with full boiler power on a consumption of five and three-fourths tons of coal per hour.

We steamed eleven to twelve knots per hour with a consumption of one seven-eighths (1.875) tons of coal half boiler power.

We steamed nine (9) knots with one-fourth boiler power, on a consumption of one and three-eighths ton of coal per hour.

Under sail, with a fresh breeze, she steers well and sails fast, but in light breezes not well, as she needs to move four to five knots through the water to turn the propeller. Under steam and sail she "lies to" well, shipping no seas.

Under all circumstances she steers perfectly easy. At fourteen knots speed she turned in nine minutes forty-five seconds, the sea heavy and wind fresh. At ten knots speed, fresh wind, smooth sea, turned in twelve minutes.

Under all sail by the wind, with a moderate breeze and smooth water, we logged seven to eight knots, propeller disconnected, making 21.5 revolutions.

Under sail it requires a speed of from four to five knots to turn the propeller, but once started it turns very easily.

I have had no fair opportunities for exercising under sail alone.

I consider the "Wampanoag," as a ship, to be faultless in her model, and, as a steamship, the fastest in the world.

If at any time it should be contemplated to alter the vessel by reducing her power, her forward boilers could be dispensed with, giving increased room for storage, and then she would be a twelve knot steamship.

I would recommend that a light spar-deck be built on the vessel, and that she be rigged as a ship. The addition of a light spar-deck will not require any alteration in her spars. The accommodations with this additional deck would be ample for her crew, and it would also give room for storage. In both these particulars the ship is at present cramped.

I neglected to state that at a trial with one-half boiler power and all sail, with a moderate wind abeam, we logged fourteen knots.

I am, sir, very respectfully, your obedient servant,

J. W. A. NICHOLSON,
Captain.

Hon. GIDEON WELLES,
Secretary of the Navy, Washington, D. C.

UNITED STATES SHIP WAMPANOAG.

Tabular statement full power steam trial.

Hours.	Knots.	Fathoms.	Course.	
				FEBRUARY 11, 9 P. M.
10	8	1	S. by W. ½ W.	Commenced full power steam trial from latitude 40° 6' north, longitude 74° 1' west. Wind light, northward and westward. Sea smooth. Ship rolling 3° to 4° each way. Compass deviation ¾ point west.
	8		S. by W.	
11	16	6	...do.	
12	16	4	...do	
1	17	4	S.SW.	
2	17	4	...do.	
3	17		...do	
Total...	101	3		Average speed per hour during six hours, 16.896 knots.
				FEBRUARY 12, 4 A. M.
4	17		S.SW	These six hours wind from northward and westward to northward and eastward. Sea increasing. Ship rolling as previously. Compass deviation ¾ west.
5	17		...do	
6	16	6	...do	
7	17		...do	
8	16	2	...do	
9	17	2	...do	
Total...	101	2		Average speed per hour during six hours, 16.875 knots.
				FEBRUARY 12, 10 A. M.
10	17		S.SW	These six hours wind fresh from the northward. Sea heavy, ship rolling to 6° each way.
11	17		SW	
12	16	4	...do	
1	8	2	...do	
2	8	6	S.SW	
3	16	6	...do	
	16	4	...do	
Total...	100	6		Average speed per hour during six hours, 16.79 knots.
				FEBRUARY 12, 4 P. M.
4	17	2		Wind fresh from northward to light E.SE., thence back to a moderate northward breeze. Sea heavy. Ship rolling as before.
5	17	2		
6	17			
7	17			
8	17			
9	16	4		
Total...	102			Average speed per hour during six hours, 17 knots
				FEBRUARY 12, 10 P. M.
10	16	6	W.SW	Wind fresh N.NE. to east. Heavy, irregular sea. Ship rolling deeply.
11	16	6	...do	
12	16	4	...do	
1	16	2	SW	
2	16	4	...do	
3	16	2	SW by W	
Total...	99			Average speed per hour during 6 hours, 16.5 knots.
				FEBRUARY 13, 4 A. M.
4	16	2	SW. by W	Wind very variable, but fresh. The sea irregular and heavy. Ship rolling 12° each way.
	7	2	...do	
5	9	4	W.SW	
6	16	6	...do	
7	15	4	...do	
8	16		...do	
9	15	4	...do	
Total...	96	6		Average speed per hour during six hours, 16.125 knots.

REPORT OF THE BOARD OF ENGINEERS.

UNITED STATES STEAMER WAMPANOAG,
Hampton Roads, Virginia, February 17, 1868.

SIR: We have the honor to report that we have completed the trial of the machinery of the "Wampanoag" at sea, with the vessel driven at the maximum speed, under steam alone, during $37\frac{1}{2}$ consecutive hours; and at the speed of 11 nautical miles per hour, under steam alone, during 25 consecutive hours; the latter performance being to ascertain with what consumption of coal per hour the speed of 11 knots can be maintained at sea.

The average performance during the $37\frac{1}{2}$ consecutive hours of maximum speed was as follows:

Average speed of vessel per hour in nautical miles... 16.71
Average speed of vessel per hour in statute miles... 19.265
Average number of the revolutions of the engines per minute............................. 31.06
Average number of the revolutions of the screw per minute................................ 63.673
Average steam pressure in boilers in pounds per square inch............................. 31.97
Average position of the throttle valves open... wide.
Average consumption of coal in pounds per hour... 12,690

There was a fresh breeze abaft the beam, with a moderate sea most of the time on the quarter; the latter part of the trial the sea was heavy. During the above maximum performance the vessel averaged, for 24 consecutive hours, 16.97 nautical miles, or 19.566 statute miles, per hour. During 12 consecutive hours, 16.98 nautical miles, or 19.577 statute miles, per hour; and during 6 consecutive hours, 17.25 nautical miles, or 19.89 statute miles, per hour.

The greatest distance run in any one hour was 17.75 nautical miles, or 20.465 statute miles; the latter speed was obtained and logged four separate half hours, and it is only necessary that the men shall be properly drilled at their duties in the fire-room and coal bunkers to maintain that speed continuously in smooth water.

The average performance during the 25 consecutive hours, with the intended speed of 11 nautical miles per hour, was as follows:

Average speed of the vessel in nautical miles per hour.. 11.39
Average speed of the vessel in statute miles per hour... 13.13

Average number of revolutions of the engine per minute.................................. 21.36
Average number of revolutions of the screw per minute.................................... 43.78
Average steam pressure in the boilers in pounds per square inch...................... 20.69
Average position of the throttle valves open... $\frac{6}{10}$ of 1 hole.
Average consumption of coal per hour in pounds.. 3,474

There was a light wind and sea ahead for six hours, and a light breeze and moderate sea abaft the beam during nineteen hours of the trial, when it was suddenly interrupted by a gale.

The main valves, gearing, and all other parts of the machinery worked smoothly and in a satisfactory manner, and every journal of the engines, during their entire performance at sea since leaving the navy yard on the 4th instant worked perfectly cool until the 38th hour of the maximum speed trial, when the crank-pin of the after engine began to warm; the speed of the engines was then reduced by throttling, the first and only time for any requirements of the machinery. The warming of the crank-pin did no injury whatever, nor would it have been the cause of a non-completion of the 48 hours' trial at maximum speed. There was no foaming or priming in the boilers, and the performance of the whole machinery was excellent, and it returned to this port in a condition for any service without requiring repairs.

The maximum performance can be easily maintained during a passage across the Atlantic, or for any required service, and we are of opinion that it is not equalled for speed or economy by that of any sea-going screw vessel of either the merchant or naval service of any country.

Very respectfully, your obedient servants,
THEO. ZELLER,
Chief Engineer U. S. N.
JNO. S. ALBERT,
Chief Engineer U. S. N.
JOHN H. LONG,
Chief Engineer U. S. N.

Hon. GIDEON WELLES,
Secretary of the Navy, Washington, D. C.

The return of the *Wampanoag* to port with the report of her wonderful performance was a sad blow to the writers who had been assailing the engineer-in-chief and his engine practice, and proved an effective quietus to the most of them; some continued the war by disparaging the published reports and insinuating that they were incomplete, inaccurate and unreliable, while a few stood their ground and openly denied the truth of the reported performance. Chief in this latter class were some of the engineering journals of England which had the mortification of seeing all their theories and contentions swept away by the occurrence of what they had vociferously proclaimed impossible, and had the further provocation of seeing a rival nation suddenly become possessed of a naval weapon with which British pride could be humbled, British wealth destroyed, and all classes of British subjects distressed in case of war by the complete capability of that weapon to take possession of the seas and reduce the vast over-sea commerce of England to floating masses of smoking rubbish. Probably no engineer ever experienced a professional triumph of the magnitude of this one, nor had greater cause for rejoicing over his opponents, but Mr. Isherwood is said to have manifested little elation at the result; with much knowledge and experience to sustain him, he had not been working in the dark and so far as human certainty goes he had known what the result would be all the time.

With the higher rates of sea speed now familiar to all connected with steam navigation it is not easy for us to comprehend the greatness of the achievement of the *Wampanoag* without considering the state of steam at sea in her day. The fastest ocean steamers then were the *City of Paris* of the Inman line and the *Ville de Paris* of the French line which were competing for the championship in the trans-Atlantic trade and in which rivalry each had made the westward voyage at an average speed of about $14\frac{1}{2}$ knots, though this was considerably more than the general average of either. The famous old side-wheeler, *Adriatic*, originally built for the Collins line, had made a record of 15.91 knots as the average of four runs of one mile each over a measured course, but this was about two knots more than her sustained sea speed. The *Warrior, Black Prince* and some other steamers of the British navy were classified as being of 14 knots speed; but then, as now, the measured mile fallacy existed in that service and the speed attained by a vessel running a mile after gathering headway and bottling up her steam bore no more relation to the speed she could maintain at sea than does the record achieved by a college athlete in a hundred yards foot-race indicate the rate he is able to travel on foot over ordinary roads for a day or a week. Two paddle-wheel steamers of abnormal proportions for that day (327 feet long; 35 feet beam; 1,900 tons displacement; 336 square feet greatest immersed midship section; 677 square feet of grate surface) engaged in carrying the royal mails between Holyhead and Dublin, a distance of about fifty-seven sea miles, were then regarded as the best examples of swift steamers in existence, although not strictly speaking ocean steamers, and they had made some remarkable runs under favoring conditions, but their average speed for a great number of trips was only 14.51 knots.

From all the foregoing it appears that $14\frac{1}{2}$ knots was an unusual sea speed for even the Atlantic "Greyhounds" of that day, and sufficient to entitle the vessel making it to the championship in the struggle for speed. The record in that race is now (1895) led by the *Lucania* of the Cunard line, which, in September, 1894, ran from Sandy Hook light-ship to Daunt's Rock, a distance of 2,810 knots, in 5 days, 8 hours and 38 minutes, or an average of 21.84 knots per hour for the whole voyage. From the above figures and 16.758 knots, the average sustained sea speed of the *Wampanoag*, a proportion may be formed from which is derived 25.24 knots as the sea speed of an ocean cruiser of the present day that would parallel the performance of the *Wampanoag* in 1868. The speed of 23 knots recently achieved by the triple-screw cruiser *Minneapolis* is justly regarded as a signal triumph for the distinguished engineer whose brain conceived her machinery and for the mechanics whose skilful hands constructed it, but her performance was relatively inferior to to that of the *Wampanoag*. And it must be remembered also that while the *Minneapolis* won her laurels in a smooth summer sea and was only four hours in the ordeal, the *Wampanoag* made her record by a long struggle with a mid-winter gale.

The importance of speed as a factor in naval warfare, although demonstrated by many events of the Civil War, was disputed, or at least not admitted, as soon as that war was over, and the element that disparaged the *Wampanoag* type of war vessel by referring to them as "engine carriers" and "run-aways" succeeded so well in checking naval development in this direction that it was more than twenty-one years after the triumph of the *Wampanoag* before her speed was again reached in our navy; the first vessel to equal it being the steel cruiser *Charleston* on the occasion of her four hours' trial trip in smooth water in September, 1889. The British, more progressive and less hide-bound in naval matters than ourselves, arrived at the speed of the *Wampanoag* in their navy in 1879 with the large despatch vessels *Iris* and *Mercury*. In commercial life, speed at sea has always been a prime factor and the most flattering circumstance in the whole story of the *Wampanoag* is that with all the rivalry for speed between the great trans-Atlantic steamship lines and with all the engineering talent of two continents at work upon the problem it took more than eleven years to produce an ocean steamer that was her equal, this steamer being the *Arizona* of the Guion line, which in June, 1879, crossed the Atlantic at an average speed of 16.6 knots, only slightly less than the rate established by the *Wampanoag;* this remained the fastest Atlantic passage for more than two years when the *Arizona* herself lowered it by about two hours in the whole time of crossing. The first steamer to land passengers at New York on the same day of the week after leaving Europe was the *Alaska*, also of the Guion line, in 1882, and her best day's run on that voyage was 419 sea-miles, not much in excess of the 405 knots made by the *Wampanoag* during the first twenty-four hours of her trial trip, and probably not as much when allowance is made for difference in time due to the *Alaska's* westing.

Besides the cry of fraud raised against the *Wampanoag*, it was also charged that she was a freak; that is, the hostiles reluctantly admitted that she had actually made the remarkable speed reported, but asserted it to be the result of a chance combination of circumstances verging upon the miraculous that could not be repeated, and was in no way due to the machinery or creditable to the engineer who had designed it. This contention held well for a few months but was overthrown by the performance of the *Ammonoosuc*, the only other one of the swift cruisers with Isherwood's machinery that was ever entirely completed. This ship left New York June 15th, 1868, for Boston with orders to make a full speed trial on the passage, but was prevented from carrying out the order on account of fog over a considerable portion of the course. Full speed rates were obtained for two short intervals which, as reported by the captain, Commander Wm. D. Whiting, and chief engineer, Mr. John S. Albert, actually exceeded the performance of the *Wampanoag*, although they cannot be fairly compared with the latter on account of the shortness of the runs and the smoothness of the water. They prove conclusively enough however that the *Wampanoag* was not a freak or a miracle, but rather the carefully considered production of a master engineer.

One of the runs of the *Ammonoosuc* on which the speed at full power was ascertained was from a bearing off Sandy Hook lighthouse to the light-house on Fire Island, and the other was from the Highland light on Cape Cod to Fort Warren in Boston harbor. The principal data of these two performances are given in the following table, which is a summary of Chief Engineer Albert's report:

	Sandy Hook to Fire Island.	Cape Cod to Fort Warren
Distance run in nautical miles	30	49.8
Time of making the run	1 hr. 47 min.	2 h. 54½ min.
Average speed per hour in knots	16.82	17.11
Average speed per hour in statute miles	19.36	19.89
Average number revs. of engine per minute	31.35	32.68
Average number revs. screw per minute	64.27	67.00
Average steam pressure in boilers, lbs	32.12	31.66
Average position of throttle valves	wide open.	wide open.
State of the sea	smooth.	smooth.

Regardless of this fine showing, the *Ammonoosuc* was laid up in ordinary as unsuited for the naval service and for many years remained at the Boston navy yard a prey to wind and weather, her name in 1869 being changed to *Iowa*. In September, 1883, she was sold by inviting proposals, for $44,605. Her original cost was $1,261,250.27, of which sum $729,565.00 was for machinery.

At this day when we are accustomed to seeing the navies of all nations striving for speed as a determining element in warfare it is decidedly odd to know that the strongest argument used in condemning our first fast cruisers was the very fact that they were fast.

Some of the old and experienced officers recognized and deferred to the exigency which called these peculiar ships into being, but naval opinion in general was decidedly against them because they were steamers pure and simple, full of machinery, and the naval mind was not then ready to accept any advance in construction that involved the subordination of sail power to steam for ocean cruising. No one can justly condemn the opinions of the older officers of that day, for every man is entitled to his own beliefs, and when those beliefs are founded upon a long and illustrious professional career their possessor can hardly be expected to suddenly throw them overboard in deference to some new thing, even if that new thing is an evident improvement over old methods. The logic, arguments, and opinions of that older day are extremely curious and in some respects almost ridiculous in the light of present knowledge, but they are interesting nevertheless.

For international political reasons it was not expedient for the Secretary of the Navy to inform Congress in public reports of the exact object in view in building these swift cruisers, and they were therefore referred to as designed to hunt down the vessels of the enemy, the only open enemy at the time being the Southern Confederacy. No one can imagine that the Navy Department projected so many large ships at such great cost for the sole purpose of intercepting blockade-runners and hunting down the two or three armed cruisers of the enemy, and we consequently know that a much more important object must have been in view. At that period of the war (1863) the probability of European interference in our domestic affairs was imminent and under cover of building cruisers to chase blockade-runners the Navy Department was really arming itself to resist such interference with the best possible weapons to use against a commercial enemy. The ships thus created never had an opportunity to prove themselves in actual war, but they played a silent, though forceful, part in the negotiations that brought about a peaceful settlement of the quarrel over the *Alabama* depredations. The possession by the United States in 1868 of the *Wampanoag* and *Ammonoosuc*, with the ability to quickly fit for service two or three other commerce-destroyers like them did more to convince Great Britain that arbitration was better than war than did all the arguments of statesmen expended upon that controversy.

CHIEF ENGINEER B. F. ISHERWOOD, U. S. NAVY,
Engineer-in-Chief of the Navy, March 26, 1861, to March 15, 1869.

The military value of vessels like the *Wampanoag* in a war with a nation whose very life depends upon its ocean commerce is manifest and it is a curious fact in connection with the building of that class of vessels that their military uses were better comprehended by the naval engineers, a corps sometimes charged with being of a civilian character incompetent to deal with military questions, than they were by many members of the naval corps whose functions are supposed to be military. The Engineer-in-Chief, Mr. Isherwood, conceived the idea of building these ships for the object above stated, asserted his ability to provide them with power that would make them the fastest in the world, and by persistent argument convinced the Navy Department of the soundness of the policy of constructing them. Political pressure for the distribution of government work and the rivalry existing between private ship-building and marine engine manufacturers and designers induced the Department to contract for some of these cruisers on competetive conditions, as has been told, while others were constructed by the government at navy yards and engined by contract from Mr. Isherwood's designs.

As the originator both of the military policy of building these ships and of the means of making the successful ones go, Mr. Isherwood is the best authority as to the purposes of their creation and his explanation, given after the danger of foreign war had passed, will be repeated as a straightforward statement in which the objects are clearly set forth and no disguise as to the name of the nation for whose discomfiture the ships were designed attempted. Shortly after the trial trip of the *Wampanoag* she was ordered to make a short voyage at sea with a board of three commodores— Melancthon Smith, Thornton A. Jenkins, and James Alden, who were to report upon the qualities of the vessel. In the order to the president of this board Secretary Welles reminded him that the ship was intended for fast ocean cruising and stated that the Department wanted an opinion as to whether or not she was efficient in view of that object. The report of the board, signed by two members, stated that—"The original purpose of providing a vessel of the greatest attainable speed, with a sufficient armament for destroying the enemy's commerce, and for self-defense in case of need, has been attained." The junior member of the board, Commodore Alden, differed from his associates and submitted a minority report severely condemning the steam machinery of the *Wampanoag* and instituting unfavorable comparisons between it and the machinery of the *Minotaur*, a British iron-clad built for a totally different purpose. This report was referred to Engineer-in-Chief Isherwood for an opinion, which he wrote out at considerable length ably defending the *Wampanoag* and leaving very little of Commodore Alden's argumentative fabric intact.[1] In explanation of the ship's being in existence Mr. Isherwood offered the following:

"The commodore could have stated in his report that the construction of the *Wampanoag's* machinery was commenced in 1863, during the war, under a guarantee by the contractors that it should be completed in one year; that the vessel was designed for an exceedingly fast ocean cruiser, fast enough to capture any British mail or merchant steamer, as at that date a rupture with Great Britain was imminent, and we were wholly unprepared with any steamers that could be used against her commerce; that the career of the *Alabama* had shown the necessity of such vessels in war; and, finally, that in constructing the *Wampanoag* other qualities were to be necessarily sacrificed in a greater degree than usual to obtain unprecedented speed, as upon speed alone depended her utility, of which it was the direct measure. The speed was to be so great as to make any attempt to exceed it hopeless. This required a very large vessel, and much of it to be devoted to the machinery and fuel; the battery being made only what was sufficient for the special service intended. The vessel itself, constructed of live-oak frames, would be the most formidable projectile that could be devised when hurled as a ram at her enormous speed against the sides of a slow antagonist, though armed with a three-fold battery. She was planned with a special view to that use, for which purpose even the bowsprit was to be omitted. In the design of such a vessel the sails were a secondary consideration, the first being the

---

[1] All the correspondence in this matter, as well as official reports of the trial trips of the *Wampanoag, Madawaska, Idaho, Ammonoosuc, and Chattanooga,* is printed in Executive Document No. 339, House of Representatives, 40th Congress, 2d Session, from which document the greater part of the material presented in this and the preceding chapter has been obtained.

durability, simplicity, and reliability of the machinery, combined with maximum power to be exerted continuously as long as the fuel lasted, and with extreme economy of fuel in the development of that power. It was proposed to construct a vessel having a greater speed by several miles per hour than any other ocean steamer; which should be able to go to the British coast in case of hostilities, and burn, sink, and destroy every vessel of inferior force, naval or merchant, that might be found there. Nothing she pursued could escape her, and nothing she fled from could overtake her. The more heavily armed but slower cruisers of the enemy could only follow her by the flames of the burning wrecks she left behind her. She would obtain a plentiful supply of coal, water, provisions, and other stores from her prizes for an indefinite length of cruising, and would neutralize the large number of naval steamers required to form a cordon around the British coast for the protection of its commerce from her depredations. Her speed would enable her to enter and leave any port despite the most vigilant blockade. In fact, the destruction made of the enemy's resources and the military advantages of breaking up his communications and obtaining the quickest intelligence of his movements, due to the employment of one such vessel, are incalculable. Modern naval warfare includes much more than a yard-arm to yard-arm fight in mid-ocean. These are the ideas that would naturally have occurred to any naval officer, and without comprehending the purpose for which the vessel was built, it is impossible for any one to properly criticise it. It must be judged as to how successfully the design has been carried out, and not as to whether the vessel is adapted to wholly different uses."

The year after the completion and trial of the *Wampanoag* her name was changed to *Florida* and she was condemned for naval purposes by a board of officers which examined and reported upon all steam machinery afloat at the different navy yards. That board consisted of Rear Admiral R. M. Goldsborough, Commodore Charles S. Boggs, Chief Engineers E. D. Robie and John W. Moore, and Mr. Isaac Newton, the latter an ex-naval engineer whose connection with the *Monitor* is well known. He was an anti-Isherwood man, a fact that is said to have had something to do with his selection for service as a civilian member of the board. The report of this board condemned many of the vessels of the navy, because they possess qualities now regarded as essential, and its pages reveal a sentiment of opposition to the spirit of progress that in our day has replaced sails on war vessels with steam and made the safety of ships at sea a matter of scientific control instead of the chance sport of the winds. To the student of steam navigation the report of this board is a veritable curiosity of professional literature, more than worth reading, and may be found printed in full in the annual report of the Secretary of the Navy for the year 1869. It is proper to say in connection with it that the two naval chief engineers, Robie and Moore, submitted a minority report dissenting from many of the expressions and opinions of the other members of the board. Some of the faults found with the *Wampanoag* by this board were compared with modern essentials by Passed Assistant Engineer Ira N. Hollis, U. S. Navy, in a lecture on marine engines delivered in 1892 at the Naval War College, Newport, as follows:

"It was a stroke of genius which put geared engines with slow reciprocating parts and rapid rotating screw into a ship that would have been racked to pieces by the engines we construct to-day. She was condemned in 1869 by a board of naval officers for various reasons, among them the following : ' Excessive weight of machinery and coal.' The *Minneapolis* has 3,971 tons devoted to this purpose, about the displacement of the *Wampanoag*. ' Enormous coal consumption.' She burned 136 tons of coal a day, while our latest cruiser will burn 360 tons for her sustained speed. ' Because her grate surface was 1.53 times the midship section.' ' Relative length to breadth said to cause inordinate rolling and dangerous straining of ship.' The latter cruiser has about the same relative dimensions and a lower coefficient of fineness. ' Carried coal enough to last only five or six days at maximum power.' The *Minneapolis* has the same endurance. ' Four-bladed screw nullified the use of canvas.' ' The substitution of a two-bladed screw recommended, and the removal of several boilers for the purpose of giving her full sail power.' Her later sister carries no sails at all. Her speed was superior to that of most of our cruisers, and we have gained between two and three knots by building a ship of twice her size. Nobody thought of the fact that she had no water-tight subdivision, and would fill from one hole in her side or bottom."

The board recommended the removal of four of the *Wampanoag*'s boilers to do away with two of the smoke-pipes, and advised that the other two pipes be made telescopic; the superheating boilers were declared of no benefit and two of them were recommended to be removed; to re-arrange the masts so that the vessel could be rigged as a ship it was seriously suggested that one of the gang of driving gear wheels and pinions of the main engine be taken out to make room for the step of the mainmast. Various other changes were advised, but after all had been enumerated the report adds:

"Although the *Wampanoag's* arrangements may be modified as just stated, yet in truth but little, comparatively, will be gained by it, considering the expense that will have to be incurred, and, above all, the condition in which she will still be left. It is, in short, utterly impracticable to render her a vessel of war worthy of our navy. Her case is so bad as to be beyond cure, and to make palliatives appear as though they were labor lost.

"It nevertheless may serve, like most others of the sort, as a source from which important lessons can be drawn, and among them it impresses the expediency of consulting, instead of ignoring, experienced and intelligent naval minds as to the properties to be secured in the construction and arrangements of a vessel of war."

A few comments relative to other high-powered vessels which this report contains are worth quoting, as serving to show how utterly different from the present were the naval beliefs of only a quarter of a century ago and how far away the era of the steam war-vessel was even then. Thus, with reference to the *Madawaska* we find the following:

"The case of this vessel is essentially that of the *Wampanoag*. They are twin ships—both the unfortunate offspring of an irretrievable blunder *ab initio*.

"The boilers are the same in number, size and type, as those on board the *Wampanoag*, and they are as bountifully provided with smoke-pipes of a standing order."

With regard to the *Neshaminy* the following is remarked:

"The predominent idea in getting her into existence seems to have been the production of a sort of overgrown Indian canoe in shape and lightness, and thus to obtain speed at all hazards, no matter what might become of other indispensable qualities; and the result has been, as it were, scarcely anything less in effect than—pardon the expression—a slunk foal.

"Her designer, a man of marked ability as a naval architect, and, indeed—without meaning to be invidious—certainly at the very head of his profession in this country, was, no doubt, pressed to yield his own solid judgment, as to her model and construction, to the importunity of others, and in a way difficult, if not almost impossible, to resist. He is not, therefore, in common fairness, to be held to a strict accountability for her palpable, terrible failure in embryo.

"The real source of the difficulty in her case, and in that of others of similar size and shape, is to be traced to the egregious error of assuming the want of vessels of their type, and the possibility of their production to answer the ends of efficient vessels of war, and this never proceeded from his clear and ample brain."

With reference to the *Mosholu*, or *Severn:*

"This vessel, in hull, may be regarded as having the *Wampanoag* or *Madawaska* as an archetype, except that she is rather better as to relative breadth, and rather worse as to relative depth, whether the later be compared with her length or breadth; but she has about the same extravagant running off at the ends. Essentially she is a diminished pattern of the same tribe, but yet not loaded perhaps with steam appliances to quite the same exorbitant degree.

"In all, therefore, the number of furnaces amounts to thirty, and their grate surface amounts to 585 square feet, which exceeds the area of the vessel's immersed section, the proportion being : : 1.083:1; which, although in the same exceptional way as in the case of the *Wampanoag* or *Madawaska*, is not carried to the same extravagant extent."

The *Wampanoag* was not altered into what the board regarded

THE LAST OF THE WAMPANOAG.

as a vessel of war worthy of our navy, but remained in ordinary at the New York navy yard for about five years and was then, in 1874, taken to New London, Connecticut, and used as a receiving and store ship at the naval station there; in this unworthy employment the finest war-steamer ever built, all things considered, remained for over ten years rusting and rotting away, unknown and almost unappreciated except by the young cadet engineers of the Naval Academy who on their annual practice cruises made pilgrimages to this spot to see what had been accomplished by the engineers before their day, and to acquire a spirit of emulation that in after years with better facilities and with a less stubborn generation to deal with enabled many of them to aid most materially in making the swift cruisers of our new steam navy so successful that they are the admiration and envy of officers of all navies.

In February, 1885, thé *Wampanoag*, or *Florida*, was sold for $41,508.00, which is less than three per cent. of her original cost of $1,575,643.84. She disappeared from naval surroundings soon after the sale when a swarm of screeching New York tug boats gathered about the battered and disheveled relic and dragged it away, like a band of ants tugging at the carcass of a big beetle; and in this ignoble fashion ended the career that had begun so gloriously.

CHAPTER XXX.

*"Give me the ocular proof ;—
Make me see't ; or, at the least, so prove it,
That the probation bear no hinge, nor loop,
To hang a doubt on."*

Othello ; Act III, Scene 3.

Some Naval Events After the Civil War—The Voyage of the MONADNOCK to California—The MIANTONOMOH Visits Europe—The MOHONGO in a Pampero—Loss of the NARCISSUS—Yellow Fever on the KEARSARGE and MUSCOOTA—Wreck of the SACRAMENTO—Earthquakes and Tidal Waves—Wreck of the SUWANEE—The Affair of the FORWARD—Loss of the ONEIDA—Wreck of the SAGINAW.

IMMEDIATELY after the close of the war it was determined to send one of the monitors to the Pacific coast, partly to provide a coast guard ship for that region, but more especially to give a convincing object lesson to the great multitude of doubters in and out of the navy, at home and abroad, as to the ability of this type of vessel to make a voyage of any length at sea. Assistant Secretary Fox appears to have been the prime mover in this determination and he had in the navy, besides the great majority of the engineers who naturally favored the monitor type, a most able and influential supporter in the person of Commodore John Rodgers, the hero of the *Weehawken-Atlanta* duel. Perhaps none of the older class of naval officers had a better right by reason of length of service and family traditions to be prejudiced against the introduction of the new form of war-ship to the disadvantage of the old than had John Rodgers, and the fact that an officer of his distinction was capable of subordinating his natural predilections to a development in the line of naval progress is not only creditable to his name, but was most beneficial by example to the naval service.

The iron-clad selected to make the voyage was the *Monadnock*, one of the four large twin-screw, double-turreted wooden monitors placed under construction at navy yards in 1862. She was built at the Boston yard from designs of Naval Constructor Isaiah Hanscom and had two pairs of Ericsson's vibrating lever engines, the latter built by Morris, Towne & Co., Philadelphia. The turrets were made by the Atlantic Works, Boston. Her length was 259 feet; beam, 52 feet; draft, 12 feet, and displacement about 3,300 tons when fully loaded for sea. She left Hampton Roads the 2d of November, 1865, in company with the *Vanderbilt*, *Powhatan*, and *Tuscarora*, and arrived safely at San Francisco the 22d of June, 1866. Her commander was Lieutenant Commander Francis M. Bunce and chief engineer, Mr. J. Q. A. Zeigler. Commodore John Rodgers in the *Vanderbilt* commanded the squadron and kept a watchful eye on the behavior of the monitor.

The *Vanderbilt* is worthy of passing notice. She was a large side-wheel steamer (3,360 tons burden), built in 1855 at a cost of $800,000 by Mr. Cornelius Vanderbilt, of New York, and used by him as a passenger steamer between New York and Havre in competition with the French line. In 1857 she had made a run from New York to the "Needles," off the Isle of Wight, in nine days and eight hours. Not being able to break up the French line, Mr. Vanderbilt withdrew his competition in 1861 and presented the steamer *Vanderbilt* to the War Department, whence she was transferred to the naval service about September, 1862. The chief event in her naval career was the long and fruitless search for the *Alabama*, thwarted by Commodore Wilkes diverting her from her mission for use as his flagship. In 1873 she was sold out of the service to George Howes, of San Francisco, for $42,000. Her machinery was removed by the purchaser and under the name of *Three Brothers* she became one of the largest and fastest sailing ships in the world. As an illustration of the wonderful ship-building materials of the Pacific coast it is told that in fitting the *Vanderbilt* out as a sailing ship the mainmast and bowsprit were made from the same stick. She is now, or was a few years ago, a coal hulk in the harbor of Gibraltar.

The experience of the *Monadnock* on her long voyage may be best told by the following extracts from official reports made by the officers most directly concerned in her management:

From Report of Commodore Rodgers written at St. Thomas:

"The *Monadnock* has behaved so well at sea as to inspire her officers not only with confidence but with enthusiasm at her performance as a sea boat. They do not doubt her ability to go anywhere. Her fire-room, however, is very hot. Eight men were carried out in a state of collapse during the passage to this place. I am putting some ventilators upon her through holes previously made for the purpose, which I hope will in great part remedy the evil. A board of surgeons has recommended a spirit ration to her firemen while under way. I shall approve it and order the recommendation carried out."

From report of Commander Bunce written at St. Thomas:

"The engines have not stopped except in obedience to the bell.

"She has made an average speed of 5.85 knots per hour, the greatest distance run in one day being 162 ; the least, 79.5."

From report of Commander Bunce written at Salute Island:

"The temperature of the fire-room has been from 120° to 140° during the passage. Sixteen of the firemen and coal-heavers have been removed from the fire-room in a state of insensibility ; they soon, however, recovered, and returned to duty. A spirit ration of half a gill has been served out to the firemen and coal-heavers at the expiration of each watch and drank mixed with oatmeal and water.

"A call for volunteers from the crew to serve in the fire-room in case of emergency, with the inducement of forty cents additional pay, made during the passage from Hampton Roads to St. Thomas, produced three men willing to serve. A similar call during this passage, the additional incentive of the whisky ration being understood, brought out seventeen."

From report of Commodore Rodgers written at Rio de Janeiro:

"I have the honor to inform the Department that the Emperor of the Brazils visited the *Monadnock* this morning, on board which I hoisted my broad pennant to receive him. He examined the vessel, and, as far as we could judge, seemed well pleased with his visit."

From report of Commander Bunce written at Panama:

"Since crossing the equator the weather has been very hot. The temperature of the fire and engine-rooms very high. The firemen, however, more accustomed to their work, have not suffered from the extreme exhaustion experienced in the same latitude before."

From the report of Commodore Rodgers written at San Francisco:

"The *Monadnock* found no weather in her voyage from Philadelphia to this place which seemed to touch the limit of her sea-going capacity.

"In a gale off Point Conception, on the coast of California, two successive waves rose which interposed between my eye and the masthead light of the *Monadnock*. Upon inquiry I found that the light was elevated seventy-five feet above the water, my own eye being about twenty-five feet above the sea level. In this sea, according to the testimony of her officers, she was very easy. While it blew the hardest, and the sea was the most violent, she twice parted her tiller ropes in quick succession. Thus, without the use of her rudder, she hove to with the double screw propellers, lying dry and comfortably in the storm.

"The engines have performed as satisfactorily as the hull, and have arrived in complete order.

"The *Monadnock* has not been towed, nor while at sea, during the entire voyage, has she received any assistance whatever.

"The success of the voyage amply vindicates the judgment of the Department in undertaking it; and the hopes of the most sanguine of 'monitor' people are fulfilled in this crucial experiment."

From reports of Chief Engineer Zeigler written at San Francisco:

"The engines of this vessel are in good working condition,

having been thoroughly tested in the long, heavy sea during the passage from Magdalena Bay to San Diego, and more so during a gale of fifty hours' duration which we encountered off Cape Conception, between San Diego and this port, which tried not only the engines and machinery, but the ship generally, more than any time since leaving Philadelphia. They have worked admirably. giving the utmost satisfaction.

"I also take pleasure in reporting that I have had no occasion to use any of the spare brasses or extra machinery during the entire cruise from Philadelphia to San Francisco, it having been a long and severe test to the engines.

"The boilers are also in good working condition and repair, The blow and part of the feed pipes are entirely worn out and will require new ones.

"With these trifling exceptions the engines and boilers are fit for immediate service, and ready to return to Philadelphia.

"The passage on the Atlantic side, from Hampton Roads to Bahia, was severe and trying to the men, many of them giving out from exhaustion, caused by the extreme heat in a tropical climate, making it difficult for the department to get along.

"The passage from Callao to Acapulco, on the Pacific side, was also a severe one on the department, several of the engineers being sick, besides a number of the firemen giving out, the thermometer standing at times as high as one hundred and fifty degrees in the fire-room.

"The cruise has been a long and severe test to the engines, and a hard and arduous one on the engineer's department."

The *Monadnock* was laid up at the Mare Island navy yard for a few years and was then pronounced unseaworthy, her wooden hull being badly decayed in many places. Mr. Phineas Burgess took her in hand at his ship-yard in Vallejo and repaired her by building a complete iron hull; before the new ship was completed, complications arose which caused the government to take possession of her and remove her to the Mare Island navy yard, where she has after many years been finished. New engines (triple expansion) and a new battery of boilers have also been built for her at the same yard, so the *Monadnock* of to-day possesses little but the name that belonged to the old *Monadnock* of the war period.

The successful voyage of the *Monadnock* from the Atlantic to the Pacific convinced American skeptics of the seaworthiness of well built monitors, but murmurs of doubt still came from across the Atlantic. A prominent naval and engineering journal of London sturdily maintained its contention that monitors could not swim and afterward, when convinced by seeing an American monitor in British waters, explained its previous doubts by saying editorially: "Although we knew that monitors had within the last year or so gone on moderately long voyages, the details of those voyages never reached England. The only information to be had was gleaned from the pages of the American press, and we regret to say the standard of Yankee journalism is so low that it was difficult to take even the meagre statements made as being positive truths." An unsuccessful attempt to assassinate the Czar gave our government an opportunity to express its appreciation of Russia's friendly attitude toward us during our domestic strife by sending a special envoy bearing a message of congratulation, Assistant Secretary of the Navy Fox being selected as the envoy and the monitor *Miantonomoh* as his conveyance.

That vessel belonged to the same class as the *Monadnock* and was of the same general dimensions: she was built at the New York navy yard by Naval Constructor Delano and engined by the Novelty Works of that city, the engines being of Mr. Isherwood's design. Of course her sea voyage furnished an excellent opportunity for controversy over the relative merits of Isherwood and Ericsson machinery by comparing the *Miantonomoh* and *Monadnock* and that well-worn contention came again to the fore in the newspapers, but as the performances of the two ships were almost identical and each eminently satisfactory it is hardly worth while to revive the rivalry at this date. One point of difference, however, should be noted, and that is in the matter of engine and fire-room temperatures. The *Monadnock*, as shown by the reports quoted, was very hot, while the fire-room of the *Miantonomoh* ranged from 106° to 115°, the engine-room being about ten degrees less. This difference was partly due to the difference in latitude in which the two vessels cruised, but was more especially a result of difference in design: Mr. Isherwood with many years of actual experience at sea knew the disadvantages of hot working places and would naturally think of them and arrange his machinery to avoid them, while Ericsson had no such experience and no means of detecting hot places from an engine or fire-room plan on a sheet of drawing paper.

The policy of sending an iron-clad to England was much criticised by the press, the weight of opinion being that it was not incumbent upon the United States to convince its maritime rival of the advantages of the monitor system, especially as the English newspapers, lay and scientific, and even debaters in the English parliament, were engaged in declaring the inability of monitors to go to sea and laughing at the idea of one of them ever appearing in British waters. The opinion of the American public on the question may be fairly shown by the following extract from an editorial in a New York newspaper devoted to military and naval affairs:

"Now, having satisfied ourselves on this point, why should we so itch to prove it practically to Englishmen? With tremendous stupidity, they have insisted year after year that the monitors could not go to sea. Argument has been pooh-poohed, facts denied, and official reports made the subject of ridicule by two-penny London wits. . . .

"For all that, as we have said, we think it best, in a national point of view, not to insist on forcing open the eyes which an enlightened British public persists in keeping shut. When they have exhausted all their appropriations for iron-clad navies, then is the time to send over a monitor."

Notwithstanding public objection, the *Miantonomoh* proceeded on her mission, sailing from New York May 6, 1866, under the command of Commander J. C. Beaumont, Mr. Wm. A. R. Latimer being her chief engineer. The iron double-ender *Ashuelot* and the purchased side-wheel steamer *Augusta* accompanied her. To guard against any Yankee trick, presumably, as to the method of getting her across the ocean, the British naval attaché was allowed to go in her as a passenger. After touching at Halifax and St. John's, the *Miantonomoh* proceeded directly across the Atlantic without mishap of any kind, arriving at Queenstown in perfect order less than eleven days after leaving St. John's, as appears from the following extracts from the report of the commanding officer of the *Augusta*, who as senior officer commanded the squadron:

"I have the honor to report the arrival of this ship, the *Miantonomoh* and *Ashuelot* at this port, having performed the trip across the Atlantic in ten days and eighteen hours, without accident of any kind.[1]

"Our progress was uniform, the longest day's run being 176 miles, and the shortest 137; average 168.

"A great portion of the way (1,100 miles) the *Miantonomoh* was in tow of the *Augusta*, as a matter of convenience and precaution more than necessity, the *Miantonomoh* consuming a fair proportion of coal.

"I think she could have crossed over alone. The weather generally was very good, the only strong winds being from the westward. Heavy weather does not appear to materially affect the speed or rolling of the monitor, for while the other vessels were lurching about, and their progress checked by heavy seas, she went along comparatively undisturbed or unchecked."

Assistant Secretary Fox made an elaborate report to the Department detailing the behavior of the vessel at sea and discussing her qualities from a military point of view in such manner as to set the American public at rest so far as any fear of our ability to defend ourselves at sea then existed.

From Queenstown the *Miantonomoh* went to the great British naval station at Portsmouth and by allowing free inspection convinced the naval and editorial minds of England that she was a ship built for war, capable of making it near the shore or on the high seas, and, according to the surprised comments of the English press, rather superior as a fighting machine to anything then possessed by that country. Like the *Wampanoag*, she later played a quiet but impressive part in bringing about a change of heart on the part of England as to the settlement of the *Alabama* claims. No one can now regret that the *Miantonomoh* went to England when she did, for the story of her peaceful conquest of a nation's prejudice is one of the most pleasing incidents in the annals of our steam navy and is fully as worthy of being a source of national pride as would

---

[1] Time estimated by the sun; by the watch it would be four hours less, or ten days and fourteen hours.

have been the career of destruction of which the *Miantonomoh* was capable.

From England the *Miantonomoh* and *Augusta* went to Cronstadt and the monitor and her officers received such a reception that it is an event still told of in St. Petersburg, gay as that capital is, and has become traditional in our navy; the interesting details of this affair are foreign to the subject of this book, which deals with men, iron, and steel, rather than with softer material. The *Miantonomoh* subsequently visited many of the chief seaports of Europe, admired everywhere by naval officials, and probably accomplished more than any vessel we ever possessed in spreading abroad a knowledge of the power of the United States and the skill of our mechanics.

An incident illustrative of the general usefulness of a skilled engineer on board ship occurred during the voyage of the *Mohongo* from New York to join the Pacific squadron in the fall of 1865. After leaving Montevideo and when about the center of the wide and shallow gulf at the mouth of the river La Plata the vessel was caught in a pampero, a furious wind peculiar to that region, and was brought to anchor to ride out the gale, the sea being so heavy and so much water boarding the ship that about sixty tons of coal had to be thrown overboard to keep her from foundering. During the night the working of the rudder was so violent as to break the tiller off near the head of the rudder-stock, and this was followed by the breaking of the yoke-bolts and quadrant below deck, rendering the steering gear useless. All efforts to repair this damage were unavailing owing to the constant swinging of the rudder under the blows of the sea, and three days of anxiety and hard work were passed in futile attempts to secure the rudder by appliances from the outside, the ship being battened down all the time and extremely uncomfortable as well as in much peril.

The senior assistant engineer of the vessel, Mr. B. F. Wood, had remarked to others who were lamenting the plight they were in that he could secure the rudder if given a chance to try, and his remark was finally carried to the captain with the suggestion that it was his duty in the emergency to give the engineer an opportunity, as the salvation of the ship seemed to depend upon getting the steering gear repaired and getting under way. After some hesitation Mr. Wood was told to do anything he saw fit, and within twenty minutes he had the rudder fast and was at work readjusting the gear below, completing the latter work within three hours, when the ship got under way and struggled back to Montevideo for permanent repairs. Mr. Wood took aft a section of the bow chain and wound it about the rudder-head until the mass furnished sufficient leverage to allow a deck tackle hooked in each side to hold it fast. The largest steamship ever built—the *Great Eastern*—had had an exactly similar break-down in mid-ocean and had not only secured the rudder in the same manner but had actually been steered to port by means of the tackles hooked in the mass of chain. This is not an especially bright expedient after one knows of it, but in the case of the *Mohongo* no one but Mr. Wood appears to have been able to think of it, or to have had it stowed away in his mind, after reading of the *Great Eastern's* mishap. The captain of the vessel, Commander J. W. A. Nicholson, often remarked to naval officers afterward in telling the story that "Ben" Wood saved the *Mohongo* by his ingenuity.

The only instance in the history of the American navy of a steam vessel being lost with all on board occurred at the beginning of 1866. The unfortunate vessel was the *Narcissus*, a small purchased steamer that had been in service in the West Gulf squadron as a gun-boat and had been in bad luck there, having been sunk by a torpedo in Mobile Bay in December, 1864, without any loss of life, however. She had been subsequently raised and repaired for use as a tug and despatch vessel at the Pensacola navy yard. On the first day of January, 1866, she left Pensacola for Key West, under the command of Acting Ensign J. S. Bradbury, and was wrecked in the surf on Egmont Key, near Tampa, Florida, the night of January 2nd, the entire ship's company of thirty-two officers and men perishing with her. Among the lost was the chief engineer, Acting Second Assistant Engineer Francis R. Shoemaker, and three acting third assistants—Messrs. Edward A. Hopkins, Joshua Halsall, and George Anderson.

In March, 1866, yellow fever appeared on the sloop-of-war *Kearsarge*, at sea at the time making a passage from Monrovia, Liberia, to Lisbon, and seven officers, including the surgeon, Dr. Benjamin Vreeland, and seven men died. Four of the unfortunate officers were members of the engineer corps—Messrs. Joel A.

Bullard and Joseph Hoops, second assistant engineers, and Richard F. Edwards and E. R. Tyson, third assistants.

In August of the same year the iron double-ender *Muscoota* doing service on the coast of Mexico also suffered from the same dread disease, losing one officer and a number of men and was forced to proceed to a home port for help as the deceased officer was the surgeon, Dr. J. Wesley Boyden. When the *Muscoota* arrived off Pensacola in distress she had over seventy cases on board and was wholly unable to proceed further on account of all the engineers but one—Acting Third Assistant Engineer Jos. P. Mickley—and the greater part of the fire-room force being down with the fever. It being imperative that she should go to a northern climate, volunteers were asked for the perilous service and a sufficient number cheerfully offered themselves to take the ship to Portsmouth, N. H., where she was put out of commission. Acting Passed Assistant Surgeon S. P. Boyer, Acting First Assistant Engineer Thomas Dobbs, Acting Third Assistant Engineer J. V. Horne, and a sufficient number of firemen to run the *Muscoota*, all volunteered from the special service steamer *Newbern* then at the Pensacola navy yard. Other volunteers were Acting Ensigns A. J. Iverson and R. Hunter. To offer one's self for service of such deadly peril as this in time of peace requires courage of a lofty order and it is a pleasure to know that these gallant men received an appropriate expression from the Navy Department of its appreciation of their heroism. The following is a copy of a letter sent to Acting Engineer Dobbs, and is the same in terms as others sent to the other officers who came forward so nobly in the distressing emergency:

"Navy Department,
"Washington, Sept. 7th, 1866.

"Sir: The Department has learned through Commodore Winslow, commanding the Gulf squadron, and Commander Pattison, commanding the U. S. Steamer *Muscoota*, of your heroic conduct in volunteering for service on that vessel when her complement of officers and men had been reduced and weakened by death and disease from a contagious fever then raging, there being at the time seventy-five cases on board.

"Your conduct on the occasion deserves commendation and is appreciated by the Department.

"Very respectfully, &c.,
"WM. FAXON,
"*Acting Secretary of the Navy.*
"Act. 1st Asst. Engineer THOMAS DOBBS,
"*U. S. S. Muscoota, Portsmouth, N. H.*"

The screw-sloop *Sacramento*, of the *Canandaigua* class, while making a special cruise in the East Indies was wrecked on the 19th of June, 1867, on the reefs near the mouth of the Godavery River on the Coromandel coast of Hindustan. The vessel was a total loss together with all the effects of the officers and men, but no lives were lost. In attempting to get on shore by the use of rafts constructed on the wreck, one raft with twenty-nine officers and men was swept out to sea by the tide and currents and its occupants would have perished but for their chance discovery and rescue the following day by a passing steamer—the *Arabia*, of the British India Company. After a succession of privations on a sterile coast the shipwrecked crew reached Madras and subsequently proceeded to the United States in a chartered British ship, the *General Caulfield*. The executive officer, Lieutenant Commander P. C. Johnson, and Chief Engineer Wm. B. Brooks were left behind to guard the interests of the United States in disposing of the wreck. The other engineers who shared in this unpleasant experience were F. L. Miller, John D. Ford, James Wylie, and David M. Fulmer, all second assistant engineers, and third assistant Robert D. Taylor.

An earthquake in the West Indies on the afternoon of November 18th, 1867, followed by a tremendous tidal wave, dragged the U. S. sloop-of-war *Monongahela* from her anchorage in the harbor of Frederiksted, St. Croix, and carried her over the warehouses into the streets of the town; the reflux wave left her stranded on a reef at the water's edge practically uninjured and almost on an even keel. Only three of her men, who were on duty as boatkeepers at the time, were lost. Her chief engineer, Mr. J. Q. A. Zeigler, was enthusiastic over a project to launch her and he was sent to the United States with drawings and plans to explain his plan to the

Department officials, the result being that the bark *Purveyor* was fitted out at the New York navy yard with all the material deemed necessary by Mr. Zeigler and with a force of twenty-six shipwrights under charge of Naval Constructor Thomas Davidson proceeded to the scene of the disaster. After an infinite amount of labor for more than three months in building launching ways and strengthening the ship she was successfully floated and thus preserved for many years of active naval service. Constructor Davidson in reporting upon his work expressed his indebtedness to Chief Engineer Zeigler who was indefatigable in his exertions, and to whom the success of the undertaking was largely due. Mr. Zeigler then held only an acting appointment as a chief engineer continued over from the war time, and for this service, in connection with his management of the machinery of the *Monadnock* on her voyage to California, he was rewarded with a commission as a chief engineer in the regular navy.

A much more terrible earthquake on the west coast of South America the 13th of August, 1868, almost completely destroyed the city of Arica, Peru, and hurled to destruction the U. S. storeship *Fredonia*, her annihilation being so complete that no vestige of her remained when the waters subsided. Her commanding officer, the surgeon, the paymaster, and two men, who happened to be on shore, survived, but the remainder of the crew amounting to twenty-eight officers and men perished. The U. S. S. *Wateree*, the first built of the iron double-enders, was also in the harbor of Arica and was removed from the navy list, though not destroyed. She was carried inland by the tidal wave and deposited almost uninjured about one-fourth of a mile beyond high water mark, where she is yet unless her remains have been very recently removed, the nature of her surroundings being such as to make the cost of floating her by means of ways or digging a trench much more than her value. Incredible as it seems, she lost only one man in the remarkable experience.

Another of the iron double-enders came to grief in the same ocean about a month before the disaster to the *Wateree*. While bound for Alaska from Victoria, B. C., the *Suwanee* ran upon a rock in Shadwell Passage, Queen Charlotte Sound, and became a total wreck, the tide leaving soon after she struck causing her to break up. Her people were taken off by Her Majesty's steamer *Sparrowhawk*, and were able to save many of their effects, as the water was smooth. A coast pilot was in charge at the time of the wreck and the rock on which she struck was previously unknown.

On the 17th of June, 1868, six armed boats from the U. S. S. *Mohican* under command of Lieutenant W. H. Brownson, the executive officer of that vessel, were sent up the Teacapan river, Mexico, for the purpose of cutting out the piratical steamer *Forward* which had been guilty of depredations in that region. A sharp fight ensued, resulting in the capture and destruction of the *Forward*, but the American force suffered the loss of Ensign J. M. Wainwright and one enlisted man killed, and three wounded, one of the latter being Second Assistant Engineer F. W. Townrow, who was shot from shore while in one of the boats and severely injured.

The sloop-of-war *Oneida*, having completed a cruise on the Asiatic station, sailed from Yokohama homeward bound late in the afternoon of January 24th, 1870. Less than two hours later when about ten miles from Yokohama she was run down by a heavy iron mail steamer inward bound—the *Bombay* of the Peninsular and Oriental line—and sank fifteen minutes later. Of 24 officers and 152 men but two of the former and fifty-seven of the latter escaped death, the surviving officers being Master I. I. Yates and Surgeon James Suddards. The entire starboard quarter of the *Oneida* was cut off down to below the water line and her sinking was so obviously a question of brief time that the *Bombay* was hailed for assistance, signal guns were fired and the whistle blown constantly: regardless of which the *Bombay* proceeded on her way to Yokohama, her master, Eyre, testifying later that he heard no signals, although the guns of the *Oneida* were distinctly heard in Yokohama, more than nine miles away.

The frightful loss of life on the *Oneida* was due to lack of boats, the gig being crushed in the collision and one of the cutters destroyed by the smoke-pipe falling on it shortly before the ship went down; three other boats had been lost in a gale not long before and had not been replaced. Had the *Bombay* sent her boats to the rescue nearly all would have been saved. The *Oneida* had been very popular on the station and the circumstances of her taking off were such that public feeling in the foreign settlement at Yokohama was intensely bitter against the master of the *Bombay;* so bitter in fact that serious thoughts of lynching him were entertained. A sailor can commit no more grievous crime against his fellows than to sail away from a sinking ship. A court of inquiry composed of the British consul at Yokohama, two commanders of British war vessels, and the masters of two British merchant ships, subsequently punished Captain Eyre by suspending his master's certificate for six months! Much has been said about this verdict and about the tragedy generally, and much might be said about it even now, though perhaps it is better to pass the opportunity by.

In her lonely and terrible ending in Yedo Bay the *Oneida,* unfortunate from the day of her birth, furnished examples of devotion to duty, self-sacrifice and true manhood as glorious to our navy and nation as any deeds in war, and proved that heroism and nobility in the American sailor had not ended with the war in which she took such a conspicuous part. Her people went to their stations on deck and below when the alarm was given and coolly performed their allotted duties without murmuring or panic, though they knew that death was very near. The sick were put into the only boat that could be lowered and with the surgeon in charge shoved off from the doomed vessel without a word of protest or an attempt on the part of any man to get into it, when the only hope of all of that ship's company left behind lay in a single cutter lying in chocks on the deck. Commander Williams refused the entreaties of officers and men to try to save himself, and went down standing on the bridge of his ship where he said he belonged. The last official act on the *Oneida* was performed by the navigator, Lieutenant Commander Alonzo W. Muldaur, who at the last moment saluted the captain as calmly as at Sunday inspection and reported the condition of the ship. He was the same officer who, as an acting master, received commendation and promotion for his conduct in the *Sassacus-Albemarle* fight, and whose brilliant career as a volunteer officer during the war had won him a commission in the regular navy. These are but a few of the many instances of heroism related by the survivors. The engineers of the ship died at their stations, and were the following : First Assistant Engineers N. B. Littig (acting chief), and Haviland Barstow; Second Assistant Engineers C. W. C. Senter and John Fornance.

In August, 1870, the U. S. steamer *Palos*, having been altered into a small gunboat, was sent to the Asiatic station for service in the rivers of China and passed through the Suez canal the 11th, 12th, and 13th of that month, the fact being sufficiently important to mention because she was the first vessel of the American navy to make use of that canal.

The act making appropriations for the naval service, approved March 1, 1869, appropriated $50,000 for beginning the work of deepening the entrance to the harbor of Midway Islands in the North Pacific ocean to afford a harbor of refuge for naval and merchant vessels of the United States in those remote waters. The work was undertaken by a contractor and the side-wheel steamer *Saginaw* detailed to assist therein. No appropriation being made the following year to pursue this desirable improvement, it had to be abandoned, the *Saginaw* collecting the contractor's men and tools and departing for San Francisco the 28th of October, 1870. Before proceeding on his course, Commander Sicard determined to run down to Ocean Island, about one hundred miles to the westward, to rescue any sailors who might be wrecked there; a fatal act of kindness, for at three o'clock the next morning the *Saginaw*, running slowly in the darkness, struck and was wrecked on a reef projecting from the island she was seeking. The people got ashore without loss of life and succeeded in saving from the wreck a scanty supply of provisions estimated as sufficient to last for three months on one-fourth rations, just enough to sustain life.

Accounts of previous wrecks on the same dangerous spot reported the existence of a spring of fresh water, but all efforts to find it failed and the men began to suffer terribly from thirst, only two small breakers of water having been brought on shore. Men were set digging for water all over the islet, but no fresh water could be found, the supply in the breakers being husbanded in the meantime by serving it out at the rate of two table-spoonsful three times a day. This was but an aggravation and the men sought relief by keeping their clothes soaked with sea water, many of them, as they waded out into the water for this purpose, thinking of suicide by drowning as a last alternative to the more terrible death from thirst. In this extremity the chief engineer of the *Saginaw*, First Assistant Engineer James Butterworth, who is described as having been foremost in all efforts to recover necessary articles from the wreck in the dangerous surf, discovered a small boiler, that had belonged to the contractor and had rolled off the deck, lying submerged near the reef. Knowing the use he could make of it he carefully noted its position, and after reporting his discovery returned with boats and men and succeeded in getting it ashore after great labor. Stowed inside the paddle-box of the wreck was a coil of iron pipe with a section of hose attached to it, and this Mr. Butterworth secured at much risk, though quickly, as he knew just where to look for it. With the coil immersed in the sea and connection made from it with the hose to the boiler set up on the beach a distiller was extemporized that would produce ten gallons of water an hour, and the danger of death by thirst was past. The spring of fresh water was found after the party had been three weeks on the island.

The prospect of rescue by being discovered by a passing vessel was very remote in those unfrequented waters, and the executive officer, Lieutenant John G. Talbot, volunteered to go for assistance in the whale-boat to the Hawaiian Islands, about fifteen hundred miles distant. This being the only hope, though a desperate one, he was allowed to go, departing from Ocean Island with a volunteer crew of four men on the 18th of November, and after experiencing much privation and difficulty arrived, on the 19th of December, off one of the Hawaiian Islands. In attempting to land, the boat was capsized and all drowned but one man—Wm. Halford, coxswain. The details of this distressing event are too well known to need repeating, though it is proper to say that the simple mural tablet in memory of Lieutenant Talbot which is in the chapel at the Naval Academy tells of as noble an example of heroism as any of the imposing shafts throughout the world that preserve the deeds of the great. A small steamer was dispatched as soon as possible to Ocean Island and the shipwrecked men rescued early in January, 1871, they having at that time nearly completed a small schooner in which to attempt their own rescue.

But one sextant was saved from the *Saginaw* and this of course had to go with Talbot in the whale-boat. As the odds were great that this boat would never reach her destination, another sextant became a necessity to those left behind who might remain to perish on their sand heap without the means of making another attempt to cross the sea, and this other sextant was supplied by the ingenuity of Assistant Engineer Herschel Main, a graduate of the Naval Academy of the class of 1868. Without proper tools and in absolute lack of material it seems an impossible feat to make an instrument of precision like a sextant, but the task was well done and the result, a curious instance of what patience and ingenuity may accomplish, is still preserved in the engineering department at the Naval Academy, where the maker acquired the knowledge that made his labor possible.

The dial plate of a vacuum gauge washed ashore was used for the body of the instrument, screws and other fittings for it being made from some brass curtain rods found in the wreckage. The moving arm was made from a copper bolt cut out of a piece of ship timber and laboriously hammered flat and filed into shape. A fortunate find was made on the beach of a gauge cock with a taper hole in it for the plug, this hole being smaller than the curtain rods and the cock therefore available for the material from which to make the accurate pivot on which the moving arm was to swing. The material for the mirrors was a small oval shaving glass such as sailors use, and the only one in camp. From dread of breaking this precious mirror, each edge was first filed almost half through before attempting to break it to shape, and these filings were carefully treasured for use in grinding in the taper pin made from a curtain rod to fit the pivot sleeve formed from the gauge cock. The frames for the mirrors were made from two brass bureau-drawer locks. The shade glasses were spare ones taken from the saved sextant. A piece of sheet zinc cut to shape and scoured with ashes served for a scale plate, the scale being transferred to it from the sextant by marking with the point of a knife, and the vernier was made in the same way. Rivets made from copper tacks taken from the sheathing of a boat held the scale plate to the arc of the extemporized sextant. Pieces of curtain rods were used for legs and a handle was formed by burning a hole through a piece of wood and mounting it on a piece of curtain rod, with brackets made of drawer-lock plates.

The most difficult part of the undertaking was making the tangent and thumb screws, there being no die plate with which to cut the threads. Mr. Main had a small tap with which he tapped some holes in a piece of sheet iron and then used the holes for dies, the threads being first filed nearly to shape, using the tap as a model. The tools at the disposal of this young engineer were a hammer, a chisel, two small taps, four or five half-worn and ill adapted files, a pocket knife, a drill brace, and some pieces of steel wire from which he made drills and a small chisel. When finished and adjusted, the instrument was found equal to the work for which it was intended, and accurate to within one minute as compared with observation, made with the other sextant.

A noteworthy act of bravery on the part of an engineer is told by the following official letter:

"NAVY DEPARTMENT,
"WASHINGTON, June 12, 1872.

"SIR: The Department takes pleasure in informing you that it has received from your commanding officer, Captain Crosby, a report highly honorable to you as an officer, and giving you claims to public respect and esteem as an individual. It refers to the courage and humanity displayed on the 27th ultimo by yourself and also by Ordinary Seaman Henry Couch, and Landsman George W. Cutter, in leaping overboard from the *Powhatan* in order to save the life of Seaman James Mitchell, who had fallen from aloft, and was so injured by the fall as to be unable to help himself. This act of true heroism will make a part of your history and reputation in in the service, and give you a record well worth preserving unblemished.

"Medals of honor will be prepared for Ordinary Seaman Couch and Landsman Cutter, and you are at liberty so to inform them.

"I am respectfully your obedient servant,
"GEO. M. ROBESON,
"*Secretary of the Navy.*
"2d Asst. Engineer GEORGE COWIE, JR., U. S. N.,
"*U. S. S. Powhatan, Norfolk, Va.*"

CHAPTER XXXI.

"Their names were counted on the day of battle; but they were overlooked in the division of the spoil."—*Gibbon.*

Condition of the Engineer Corps after the War—Resignations—The Question of Brevet Rank—First and Second Assistant Engineers Become Commissioned Officers—Chief Engineer J. W. King Appointed Engineer-in-Chief—Sweeping Reduction in Rank of Staff Officers—Use of Steam Discontinued on Ships of War—The Pay Act of 1870—The Act of 1871.

THE Navy Register issued in January, 1865, contains the names of 474 regular and 1,803 volunteer engineers, of whom 59 regulars and 55 volunteers were chief engineers, and the total number was about the same four months later when the war, so far as the navy was concerned, was practically over. The sale of vessels no longer needed and the stoppage of work on those building made it advisable to dispense with the services of many of these officers and the process of disbanding the volunteer force began at once, although it was several years before all the acting engineers disappeared. In the case of all volunteer officers the custom was to grant about three months' leave with pay prior to discharge and to give an ornamental discharge paper embellished with the great seal of the Navy Department as a suitable and appropriate souvenir of military service. The wording of this discharge was complimentary to the recipient, and as follows:

"The war for the preservation of the Union having, under the beneficent guidance of Almighty God, been brought to a successful termination, a reduction of the Naval force becomes necessary.

"Having served with fidelity in the United States navy from the . . . day of . . . . ., 186 . . to the present date, you are hereby honorably discharged with the thanks of the Department."

The regular engineers who remained in the navy were rather more unfortunate than their volunteer brethren who, without any claim for retention, could not object to being discharged and returned to civil life with an honorable record of duty well done, and with all the possibilities of the reviving industries of the country before them. The number of regulars was fixed by the act of July 4, 1864, which limited the number of chief engineers to one for each first and second rate steam vessel of war and the number of assistants to the very indefinite "actual needs of the service." With the rapid diminution in the number of ships and the certainty that the number of first and second rates could not in time of peace equal the number of chief engineers already in the service came discouragement over the hopelessness of their prospects and the engineers began to resign. Within four years no less than one hundred and fifty-five, or about one-third of the whole corps, left the service in this manner.

The futility of hoping for promotion was not the only source of discouragement to the engineers, for they had excellent reasons for feeling themselves slighted in the distribution of rewards for war service. They knew perfectly well the invaluable character of the services rendered by them as a corps and as individuals, and when they saw other officers being advanced as a reward for similar service and themselves passed by without notice it is no wonder that they became heart-sick. The history of our naval *personnel* for the few years succeeding the Civil War is anything but pleasant. Rivalry, jealousy, and strife for preferment were rampant, not only between corps, but between individuals and factions within separate corps. The columns of the service newspapers at the time were literally flooded with letters from officers urging the claims of some individual or party, or assailing some other interest. In former chapters some reference has been made, especially in connection with the competitive trials of machinery, to the war within the engineer corps between what may be called the Isherwood and anti-Isherwood factions, and this on a small scale represents the greater strifes raging throughout the navy.

Although line and staff had just emerged with equal credit from a long and weary war in which they had shared common dangers and striven side by side for the salvation of their country and the glory of the navy, the relation now existing between them was far from the ideal bond of comradeship. One side was obliged to seek official recognition for service well done, and the other just as energetically opposed the endeavors and denied the claims of its comrades in arms. Without going into this controversy at any length, it will be instructive to touch upon one of the many issues quarrelled over, as we may in this way obtain an idea of the feeling then existing, the example selected being the question of brevet rank in the navy.

When the war was over and the great army disbanded, every officer of the regular army who had at all distinguished himself was given the somewhat empty, but nevertheless gratifying, honor of an advance in rank by brevet, no distinction of corps being made in the distribution of this honor, all—cavalry, infantry, engineers, medical department, all arms and branches—sharing alike in the reward. Brevets were not confined to the regular army, volunteers of distinguished and faithful service receiving the same honor, in consequence of which thousands of captains were mustered out as majors, hundreds of majors as colonels, and scores of colonels as brigadier generals; all which did no harm and justly honored the recipients. With this example before it, the navy was not long in seeking the same recognition for its war service and the subject of conferring additional rank by brevet upon all naval officers whose record of service was meritorious soon became a question of general and favorable public consideration. As in the army, the question of corps or of line and staff had no place in this proposition, the inherent capability of a man to be brave, zealous, and faithful remaining the same whether he serve on foot or on horse-back, whether above or below decks, or whether he be called a colonel, a commander, or a surgeon: unhappily, however, this issue was soon dragged into the discussion, as appears from the following extracts from letters published over assumed names in the correspondence columns of one of the service newspapers:

. . . "Why should brevets be confined to the army? In that service, general, field, staff and line, have been breveted—even doctors have been made colonels, brigadiers and major generals, but no one in the navy has been found worthy of the honor. Surely the boon craved has been richly earned by the work performed at New Orleans, Wilmington, and Mobile. Brevets in the army never produce a conflict of authority. Cavillers on that ground may be assured that the *regularly educated* naval officer is possessed of too high *a tone* ever to allow his brevet rank to affect the discipline of the service. It would be absurd to confer brevets on the staff, for, with all due respect for these gentlemen, it is believed that *line officers* are only fairly entitled to them, beside which, the line have been already sufficiently humiliated to claim exemption from further inroads on their prerogative. The navy is in a state of transition, and queer changes are taking place. Time-honored class distinctions are ruthlessly swept away, and, if the 'steerage be fleeted aft,' and bulkheads knocked down, then good-by to peace and comfort in every *dignified* ward-room." [1]

Another correspondent adds the following fuel to the brightly-blazing controversy:

"There is frequent complaint by staff officers that *their* rank stops at captain, while a *line* officer may get to be an admiral; is not the contrast which their position offers to that of their army brethren sufficient to show them that *non-combatants* can not and ought not to look for such high rank?"

Of course staff officers were foolish enough to reply to these aspersions, citing many cases of gallant service performed by "non-combatants" upon whom it would be "absurd to confer brevets." Instances were brought up of engineer officers whose heroism and devotion to duty, at the risk of their own lives, had saved the ships in which they served and the lives of all on board, line and staff; of the paymaster who, sword in hand, fought like a lion on the deck of his ship against an overwhelming boarding party and rescued from death his commanding officer; of the assistant surgeon who carried a line through a storm of shot and shell to a disabled vessel while other officers looked on: but nothing came of it all. The navy got no brevets for either line or staff.

Under the Welles order of March 13, 1863, first and second assistant engineers held rank with masters and ensigns respectively, but as they did not hold commissions from the President they presented the absurdity of warrant officers ranking with commissioned

---

[1] "Bogus" in Army and Navy Journal, June 16, 1866; page 681.

officers, but constrained on ship-board to the status of warrant officers. This anomaly was removed by Congress in 1866, an act approved July 25th of that year providing "That naval constructors and first and second assistant engineers in the navy shall be appointed by the President and confirmed by the Senate, and shall have naval rank and pay as officers of the navy." Even this did not assure to the engineers the enjoyment of privileges pertaining to their improved official status, for lack of room on ship-board was given as a reason for not improving their messing and living accommodations, and a year later, in July, 1867, the Department issued a circular order saying:

"First and second assistant engineers, being now commissioned, are no longer regarded as steerage officers. For want of sufficient ward-room accommodations, they will room and mess in conformity with existing regulations, but they are entitled to all other privileges of commissioned officers with whom they have relative rank."

The act of July 25, 1866, was a most important one for the navy in many respects. It fixed the number of line officers in each rank, making the total number on the active list 857 commissioned officers, which was more than twice as many as the number then in the service. To fill the vacancies thus created in the different ranks it was provided that promotions be made by selection from the rank next below of officers who had rendered the most efficient and faithful service during the war. It also provided that a certain number of vacancies in the different grades from ensign to lieutenant commander both inclusive, and amounting in the aggregate to 150, might be filled by the appointment of volunteer officers who had served not less than two years, and in this way a number of these very deserving men were rewarded for their war services.

The flow of promotion resulting from this act was simply feverish, in many cases youths going from the position of midshipmen through the lower grades and receiving commissions as lieutenant commanders within less than three years. This rapid advance in rank was by comparison somewhat of an injury to the staff officers, for whom the act provided no promotion, and who consequently stood still while their former juniors went far ahead of them.

This overlooking of the interests of the staff was especially galling to a number of the most capable members of the engineer corps who had been on duty as instructors at the Naval Academy and who, upon going to sea at the expiration of their details, found themselves junior in rank to youngsters who a short time before had been their pupils: the navy lost the services of some of these able gentlemen, for with such a practical demonstration of neglect they became disgusted and resigned; one of them, Mr. John T. Hawkins, first assistant engineer, giving his reasons as above in an open letter to the Secretary of the Navy. Another of them, Mr. Robert H. Thurston, now Director of Sibley College, Cornell University, is recognized as one of the foremost scientists in the United States and by achieving such a position has proved the folly of the policy that drove his talents out of the navy.

With an apparent wish to do justice to the volunteer engineers the Department offered them an opportunity similar to the one provided by Congress for the volunteer line officers, and all who so desired were given permission to appear before a board in Philadelphia for examination for admission into the regular service. As the number of regular engineers then in the navy exceeded the actual needs of the service there was no possibility of making room for more, so little attention was given to the findings of the Philadelphia examining board and only one volunteer engineer, so far as the writer has been able to discover, received an appointment in the navy by virtue of having passed that examination. To provide rapid promotion for line officers and create vacancies for worthy volunteers that branch was increased far beyond the needs of the fleet, and it would not have been an intolerable burden upon the country to have similarly increased the engineer corps and thus rewarded in the same manner the regular and volunteer members of an equally loyal and deserving arm whose energetic performance of duty contributed so much to the success of the navy in the war.

One of the first acts of the administration that came into power in the spring of 1869 was to relieve Mr. Isherwood from his office as engineer-in-chief, his successor being appointed on the fifteenth of March, a few days before his term of office would have expired by limitation. Mr. Isherwood needs no eulogy from one who has grown up in the service long since his day. His eight years occupancy of the office of engineer-in-chief were the most exacting and important in the history of the steam navy, during which time every demand made upon that office was promptly and efficiently met and the standard of naval engineering in the United States, despite the cries of those personally hostile to him, raised to an enviable height. Ever watchful over the welfare of his corps and a fearless defender of its rights, he missed no opportunity to advance its interests and laid aside the duties of his office as the head of the corps with the satisfaction of knowing that more progress had been made under his stewardship than had been accomplished in all the years before.

Chief Engineer James W. King, U. S. Navy, was appointed to succeed Mr. Isherwood. His name has occurred frequently in the preceding pages and he was at this time one of the best known engineers in the service, having been trusted by the Department with the execution of many important duties. He had been fleet engineer of the naval force that captured the forts at Port Royal in 1861, and later, in 1863, was detailed as superintendent of the hulls of all iron vessels and their machinery building west of the Alleghanies, a duty that involved constant travel over a region about eight hundred miles in extent and embraced the superintendence of the construction of vessels costing in the aggregate nearly seven million dollars. In 1864 he was sent on a special mission to Europe to collect information to be used in equipping some of our navy yards for building iron ships and manufacturing marine machinery and armor plates. The boiler explosion on the *Chenango* and some minor casualties having convinced the Department that the government was being imposed upon by some of the contractors it was determined to subject all work under contract to a rigid special examination and Mr. King, in December, 1864, was selected for this very responsible duty, his orders containing the following paragraph:

"It is deemed best that an engineer of approved integrity, and rigid and critical ability, should visit in detail every place outside of the navy yards, where contract work is being executed for the navy, and, after a personal and careful examination, report the condition of all such work, and whether it is equal in every respect to the specifications of the contracts. You are hereby selected for this important duty, on which you will enter the 2d prox. You will make separate reports for every contract, and address them to the Secretary of the Navy."

Under this order Mr. King examined and reported on the condition of the hulls of twenty light and four deep draft monitors, and their machinery, nine iron screw tugs and machinery, twenty-seven pairs of marine screw engines, boilers, etc., for wooden ships, and three sets of engines for paddle-wheel ships. In all 117 marine engines, 245 marine boilers, and the hulls of 33 iron vessels, in different localities from Portland, Maine, to St. Louis, Missouri.

Mr. King was especially well known among engineers as the author of an excellent text book on marine engines, which first appeared in 1860. His book is now out of date, but for many years was regarded as the best American work of the kind and had a greater sale than any book ever written by a naval officer up to the appearance of Captain Mahan's work on Sea Power in 1893, nineteen editions of it having been disposed of before it was supplanted by more modern books on the same subject.

Mr. King held the office of engineer-in-chief for one term of four years, his position being one of much difficulty as the aim of the administration at that time was to reduce expenses to a minimum, and the appropriations granted by Congress for the engineering department were barely sufficient to provide for the repair of machinery already afloat. He also fell heir to the vexing task of straightening out the many claims against the government for machinery contracted for during the latter years of the war and for which the ships were never built. The principal professional event of his administration was the introduction of the compound engine into the navy, he having been sent to Europe in 1871 to collect data regarding the subject and in his report recommended the adoption of the new type for all naval vessels.

Within a month after the advent of the new administration the naval engineers and all other staff officers suffered a severe blow in the publication of General Order No. 120, dated April 1, 1869. This order annulled the order of Secretary Welles of March 13, 1863, quoted in Chapter XXII. of this work, which raised the

CHIEF ENGINEER JAMES W. KING, U. S. NAVY.
Engineer-in-Chief of the Navy from March 15, 1869, until March 20, 1873.

assimilated rank of staff officers, and restored to operation the act of March 3, 1859, which has also been quoted.

General Order No. 120 read as follows:

"The Attorney General having advised the Department that Congress alone can fix the relative rank of line and staff officers in the navy, and the only officers whose relative rank has been thus legally established being those below mentioned, the order of March 13, 1863, and the Navy Regulations, Article II., paragraphs six to twenty-eight (both inclusive), are hereby revoked and annulled.

"Surgeons of the fleet, paymasters of the fleet, and fleet engineers; and surgeons, paymasters, and chief engineers of more than twelve years, rank with commanders.

"Surgeons, paymasters, and chief engineers of less than twelve years, and the Secretary of the Admiral, and the secretary of the Vice Admiral, rank with lieutenants.

"Passed assistant surgeons and first assistant engineers rank next after lieutenants.

"Assistant surgeons, assistant paymasters, and second assistant engineers rank next after masters.

"Third assistant engineers rank with midshipmen."

The practical effect of this order upon the standing of officers of the engineer corps may best be shown by figures. Prior to its issue the corps had, under the operation of the Welles order, five members ranking with captain; forty-three with commander; one with lieutenant commander; ninety-one with lieutenant; one hundred and twelve with master, and thirty-three with midshipman. When the change was made only the eight senior members of the corps ranked with commander; the next forty with lieutenant; those who had before ranked with lieutenant were put down as ranking "next after" that grade, and their next juniors appeared as ranking "next after" masters. In other words, every engineer in the service with the exception of three who remained in the grade of commander was reduced one rank, and forty who were in the commander's grade were degraded two ranks, that is, to the rank of lieutenant. The phrase "ranking next after" was simply another way of saying that the rank was of the grade below, and to make sure that this be understood the general order was followed six weeks later by a circular letter to commanders of stations and squadrons as follows:

"The Department is informed that certain officers of the navy are wearing the uniform of a rank above them. Those officers ranking by order and the law of Congress 'next after' certain grades will be considered as ranking with the next lower grades. For example, a staff officer ranking next after lieutenant will rank with master, and one ranking next after master will rank with ensign, and will wear in each case a corresponding uniform. Commanders of stations, navy yards, and squadrons will see this order carried out."

No change in pay was involved in this degradation in rank, but the humiliation was complete as it was, entailing as it did the removal of stripes and other insignia of rank from the uniforms and the substitution of the marks of inferior grades. Severe as this was upon the engineer corps it is proper to say in regard to it that it bore much harder upon the medical corps, which, as a much older establishment, had a greater proportion of its members in the higher grades by virtue of age and length of service. Of the eighty surgeons fifteen had ranked with captains; thirty-nine with commanders, and twenty-six with lieutenant commanders. The new arrangement gave twenty-one of them the rank of commander and the other fifty-nine the rank of lieutenant, with corresponding reductions among the assistant surgeons. The pay corps also suffered more severely than the engineers, but not so much as the medical corps.

The *personnel* of the engineer corps being suppressed by this means, attention was given to the *material*, the performance of such ships as the *Wampanoag* and *Monadnock* having given a hint that steam was becoming a military arm and a more reliable agent for power than sails or oars. A general order dated June 11, 1869, directed that "Hereafter all vessels of the navy will be fitted with full sail power. The exception to this will be the tugs and dispatch vessels not fitted with sails. Commanders of squadrons will direct that constant exercises shall take place with sails and spars." Then follows in the order a long list of exercises in which proficiency would be required, from which a few may be quoted as examples:

"Sending up and down top-gallant masts, lower yards, and top-masts at one time."
" Shifting top-sail yards."
"Getting under way from single anchor with all sail set."
"Coming to single anchor and taking in all sail, together."
" Shifting three top-sails at one time."

Although issued only a quarter of a century ago, it is a pleasing sign of the progress made in that time that this order sounds as archaic to-day as though it were the translation of an inscription from the columns of the temple of Karnak.

A week later, on June 18, the above order was followed with another enjoining strict economy in the use of coal and directing the commanders of fleets, squadrons, and vessels acting singly to do all their cruising under sail alone, which, it was stated, "will not only have the effect to economize coal and save expense, but will also instruct the young officers of the navy in the most important duties of their profession." Other provisions of the order were:

"Regulations, soon to be issued, will determine the number of times it will be desirable to get up steam for the purpose of turning the engines.

"Commanders are not to make dispatch an excuse for using coal except under the most urgent circumstances.

" They must not be surprised, if they fail to carry out the spirit of this order, if the coal consumed is charged to their account."

The promised regulation to establish the frequency of getting up steam to turn the engines did not materialize, as a change came over the control of the Navy Department about that time. Mr. A. E. Borie, appointed Secretary of the Navy by President Grant at the beginning of his administration, continued his residence in Philadelphia where he had large business interests and gave only interrupted attention to the duties of the Department, leaving the latter to the vice admiral of the navy and the bureau chiefs. In June Mr. Borie, finding himself unable to do justice to his office without neglecting his own affairs, tendered his resignation and was succeeded on the 26th of that month by Mr. George M. Robeson of New Jersey. The latter gentleman, having nothing more important to engross his time, took up his residence in Washington and assumed personal charge of the Navy Department. He was a self-willed man, fond of power, somewhat inclined to be dictatorial, and disposed to govern his department himself, the result of which was an immediate change in the frequency and character of the general orders issued.

Important legislation was embodied in the first naval appropriation bill passed by the 41st Congress and approved July 15, 1870. This act provided a new schedule of pay for all branches of the navy, the rates established being practically the same as those now (1896) in effect, with the exception of the pay of passed assistant engineers which has since been modified. The new pay table amounted to an increase for all officers of about twenty-five per cent., the pay of the admiral being raised from $10,000 to $13,000 per annum; that of captains from $3,500 to $4,500; lieutenants from $1,875 to $2,400; fleet surgeons, paymasters, and engineers from $3,300 to $4,400; first assistant engineers from $1,500 to $2,000, and so on for all the different grades and corps. As an offset to this increase all officers were deprived of a previous commutation for quarters on shore duty amounting to thirty-three per centum of their pay; so while benefitting in sea pay the navy in general lost greatly in shore pay, where the higher rate is usually the most necessary.

The same act reduced the number of lieutenant commanders from 180 to 80, and increased the number of lieutenants from 180 to 280: the numbers of masters and ensigns, fixed by the act of July 25, 1866, at 160 each, were by this latter act reduced to 100 each and ensigns were designated as steerage officers unless assigned to duty as watch and division officers. The title of cadet midshipman was substituted for that of midshipman as the designation of students at the Naval Academy, and the grade of third assistant engineer was declared abolished, its occupants being transferred to the list of second assistants. Thus for the first time in its history all the members of the engineer corps became by law commissioned officers.

The question of staff rank in the navy also came before the 41st Congress. The sea-going staff corps had patiently witnessed the elevation of their comrades of the war and the coincident neglect of their own claims for the same service, but when they were suddenly struck down by the order depriving them of the assimilated rank given them during the war as a reward for duty well done, patience ceased to be a virtue and they combined in an appeal to Congress for redress. A bill regulating staff rank, introduced in the House of Representatives by the Hon. A. F. Stevens of New Hampshire and ably championed by him, went through the usual stages of a bill and after an exhaustive debate, in which the position of the naval staff was presented in a masterful manner by Mr. Stevens, it reached a vote in the House in January, 1871, and was passed by a large majority. The avowed object of this bill was to define the rank of staff officers in the navy in precisely the same manner that the law defined staff rank in the army, and the bill passed the House of Representatives in the exact form desired. That is, it provided for a stated number of medical directors, *with the rank of captain;* a stated number of chief engineers, *with the rank of commander;* etc., etc.

In the Senate the bill in the closing days of the session became attached to the naval appropriation bill and was passed as a part of that bill, but with a fatal alteration. Some influence hostile to the naval staff had so worked upon the minds of the senators in charge of the naval bill that they were persuaded to qualify the rank of the staff by the word *relative* as an adjective. With this amendment the bill went to a conference committee and the friends of the staff reluctantly accepted the change, as certain material benefits in the matter of fixing definite numbers in the different grades, an increased pay for bureau chiefs, exemption of ex-bureau chiefs of the staff from sea duty, etc., were conferred by other parts of the bill, and thus it became law, the act receiving the President's signature March 3, 1871.

The sections of this act which fixed the grades and the numbers in the grades for the engineer corps are the following:

"Sec. 7. That the officers of the engineer corps on the active list of the navy shall be as follows:

"Ten chief engineers, who shall have the relative rank of captain.

"Fifteen chief engineers, who shall have the relative rank of commander; and

"Forty-five chief engineers, who shall have the relative rank of lieutenant commander or lieutenant.

"And each and all of the above-named officers of the engineer corps shall have the pay of chief engineers of the navy as now provided.

"One hundred first assistant engineers, who shall have the relative rank of lieutenant or master; and

"One hundred second assistant engineers, who shall have the relative rank of master or ensign; and the said assistant engineers shall have the pay of first and second assistant engineers of the navy, respectively, as now provided.

"Sec. 8. That no person under nineteen or over twenty-six years of age shall be appointed a second assistant engineer in the navy; nor shall any person be appointed or promoted in the engineer corps until after he has been found qualified by a board of competent engineer and medical officers designated by the Secretary of the Navy, and has complied with existing regulations."

This, in brief, is the story of the origin of "relative rank," that apple of discord arraying line against staff in the Thirty Years' War still progressing and still distracting the naval service. That the *intention* of Congress was to confer actual rank upon the naval staff is evident from the explanations offered in both branches of that body by members who reported the bill back from conference, and it was only by attaching a peculiar significance to the word *relative* after the act became law that this intention failed to be realized. The following remarks by Senator Cragin in the Senate and by Mr. Stevens in the House, in reporting the result of the conference, show clearly enough what was the intention of those who created this law:

"Mr. Conklin—With the permission of the Senator I wish to

suggest a point to him. He says that he understands 'relative rank of' to be the same in effect with the words 'to rank with.' I wish he would tell us what would be the force of this if the word 'relative' were omitted; in other words, what 'relative' means. I understand it when you say a commodore in the navy shall have the relative rank of a major general in the army, there being two services separate and distinct. I know what that means. But when you speak of relative rank in one and the same service, what is the definition of the word 'relative' there. How does it enlarge or restrict it?

Mr. Cragin—"I will have to go back a little to answer that question. In the navy there are four or five different corps. There is the line corps, which, in the English service, is called the military branch. Then there are the medical corps, the pay corps, the engineer corps, the constructors. They have just as positive rank in their corps as the line have in theirs by law now, and the only reason why they need any relative rank at all in the line corps is to define their position with the line officers; to give them social equality, and official equality in everything except what pertains to actual command.

. . . .

"It is just the same practically as between the officers of the army and navy. A commodore by law now ranks with a brigadier general. He is not a brigadier general, but he is equal to a brigadier general socially and in public estimation. That is what this proposes to do—to place these staff officers on an equality.

There is another provision in this bill which determines what is known as precedence which does not exist now. The oldest staff officers of the navy now rank with commanders; but they rank junior to all commanders. The youngest commander outranks the highest and oldest staff officer of the line under the law as it now stands and by the construction. But by this bill they are given precedence in their own corps and with line officers in the grades where they hold this relative rank, according to the length of service in the navy, adding six years for the length of service of the staff officers, to compensate for the time spent by the line officers at the Naval Academy, and before they received their first commission. This is admitted on all hands to be eminently just, and no person can complain of it. By this provision in relation to precedence, a staff officer, a surgeon who has been in the service twenty years and one day, will outrank a line officer who has been twenty-six years in the service; that is, if a procession should be formed, that surgeon would go before the line officer, and on all other ceremonial occasions, on boards of inquiry, everywhere where they complain that injustice is now done them.

"I will say one word in relation to the executive officer. Great complaint has arisen on this subject. The Senate amendment was in about these words: executive officers of vessels of war and naval stations representing commanding officers thereof shall take precedence over all officers attached to the vessel or the station, and all orders from the executive officer shall be regarded as proceeding from the commanding officer. The provision as adopted by the committee of conference is this: after saying that commanding officers shall take precedence over all the officers under their command, we then say that the Secretary of the Navy may detail a line officer to act as the aid or executive of the commanding officer, and that as far as practicable, that officer so detailed shall be next in rank to the commanding officer, and such detailed officer, while executing the orders of the commanding officer, shall take precedence over all officers attached to the vessel or station, and all orders given by this executive officer shall be considered as proceeding from the commanding officer. Then there is a provision added that staff officers who are senior to this detailed officer may communicate directly with the commanding officer; that is to say, if a surgeon desires to leave to go ashore, he may, if he chooses, go to the captain and ask that leave. That is all there is to that.

"Now, Mr. President, I believe that this is a fair compromise. Neither side will be entirely satisfied with it. But I believe and I know that it is the best we can do under the circumstances. I want here in this public place to advise the officers, both of the line and of the staff, to accept this in good faith, and to cease this quarrel."

Mr. Washburn, of Wisconsin—" In order to save the time of the House, I will state that what the clerk has now commenced to read is the bill passed by this House regulating the staff of the navy.

"As regards the portion of the report relating to naval rank, my friend from New Hampshire (Mr. Stevens) will make some explanations, and I yield to him for that purpose."

MR. STEVENS—" I desire to say, in regard to that portion of the report regulating the official relations of the several corps in the navy, that it is in most respects the bill which passed this House some time since by a very large majority.

"Although the committee of conference were not able to embody in terms that bill in this report, yet I think I may safely say that very much has been gained to the navy, and very much to the staff corps of the navy, by the provisions of this bill as amended. Substantially there were but two points of difference between the committees of the two Houses upon this question. The first was in regard to whether the staff corps of the navy should have actual rank, in conformity to the law regulating the staff corps of the army; or whether it should be an assimilated, imperfect, inchoate rank, or a fixed, positive, actual rank; and I think that it was the opinion of the committee that had it in charge that this bill conferred upon the staff of the navy the same rank and official position that are enjoyed by the staff corps of the army. At least, the same corresponding position. There was some sensitiveness in regard to terms, and in that, particular concession became necessary. I wish to say, Mr. Speaker, that while the term 'relative' is used in conferring position and rank upon the staff corps, my belief is that a fair and liberal interpretation of the language of the bill by the Navy Department, and those charged with its execution, will place the staff corps of the navy in the same position in relation to that organization that is conferred upon the staff corps of the army. *That was the purpose of this bill as it originally passed the House, and a just interpretation will accomplish it.*

"There was another difference of opinion between the committees, and that was as to the position and precedence of the 'executive officer.' Upon that we have compromised, modified the law and regulations upon that subject, and giving authority to the Secretary of the Navy to detail an officer to act as the aid or executive of the captain or commandant, and restricting his power and functions. I have made these statements because they are matters of great interest in the navy, and *I desire this explanation to go out with the bill.*"

CHAPTER XXXII.

"Law is a spider's web, and ever was;
It takes the little flies, lets great ones pass."
—Braithwaite.

Shipbuilding Progress in the Navy, 1865–1880—The ALASKA and Class—Captured Blockade-Runners—Sale of Monitors—Rebuilding of the MIANTONOMOH Class—The PURITAN—The New SWATARA and Class—Compound Engines—Chief Engineer Wood Appointed Engineer-in-Chief—Costly Experiments with Two-Bladed Propellers—The ALERT Class of Iron Gunboats—The ENTERPRISE Class—The TRENTON—The NIPSIC—The DESPATCH—The ALARM and INTREPID.

AS WAS to be expected, the termination of the war caused almost a standstill in the work of building ships for the navy, the principal work of that nature carried on in the years immediately following 1865 being the completion of some of the larger screw vessels begun in 1863 and 1864 upon which such progress had been made that their condition justified the outlay for finishing them. In this way the large government-built commerce-destroyers whose trial trips have been described were completed; also the *Guerriere*, *Minnetonka* and *Piscataqua* of the *Java* class; the *Contoocook*, *Manitou*, *Mosholu*, and *Pushmataha* of the *Contoocook* class, and the *Algoma* of the *Serapis* class. The *Guerriere* went to the Brazil station as flagship in 1867, her performance under steam being highly satisfactory: Rear Admiral Davis reported of her that she had made on the passage down eleven knots under steam alone, adding that her bottom was so foul that this was not a fair index of what she could do. Subsequently she went to Europe and was accidently stranded, July 26, 1871, on Vado Rocks near Leghorn and so badly damaged that it was estimated the cost of repairing her would be more than she was worth. National pride however dictated that she be brought home, her name being a naval trophy in that it was the perpetuation of the name of a frigate captured by the *Constitution* in an older war, and she was accordingly repaired at great cost in the Italian government dockyard at Spezzia to fit her for the voyage home. In December, 1872, she was sold by public auction at New York for

$54,000. Her original cost, exclusive of armament, was $1,154,-325.10. The *Contoocook* (*Albany*) was sold at the same auction for $48,000.

The *Minnetonka* became the *California* by a change of name and the *Piscataqua* became the *Delaware*, under which names each performed some service on the Pacific and Asiatic stations, but the inferior materials used in their hulls deteriorated so rapidly that they soon became unserviceable. The *California* was sold in May, 1875, for $23,650, and the *Delaware* in February, 1877, for $5,175. The low price brought by the latter was on account of the fact that she was submerged when sold, having been sunk at her dock in the New York navy yard. The four vessels of the *Contoocook* class that were completed had similar brief histories, being laid aside and eventually sold for a small part of their original cost. One of them, the *Severn*, originally *Mosholu*, was traded to John Roach in 1877 at an appraised value of $25,000 in part payment for work done by him in rebuilding the iron-clad *Puritan*.

The changes in names of the vessels just referred to were general throughout the service, a great many changes being made in the summer of 1869 by circular orders issued by the Navy Department. American names were usually discarded and in many cases, especially with the monitors, names borrowed from the mythology of the ancients substituted for them; some names were changed twice within a few weeks; some were changed back to their originals, and some received for new names those that had belonged to vessels of other classes, much confusion resulting as a consequence. The report of the Secretary of the Navy for 1869 refers to the *Piscataqua* as flagship of the Asiatic station, whereas at the date of the report the *Piscataqua*, originally the *Chimo*, one of the light-draft monitors, afterward the *Orion* for a few weeks, was laid up at the Washington navy yard. The Secretary meant the *Delaware*, originally *Piscataqua*, and this is a good illustration of the mixing of names so indiscriminately that even the Department could not keep track of them.

As previously stated, the *Algoma* (*Benicia*) was the only one of the *Serapis* class of screw sloops projected in 1864 that ever reached completion, but during the five years that she was under construction the Department duplicated her in three other vessels with names different from any of the original class. These were the *Alaska*, *Omaha*, and *Plymouth*, the latter first known as *Kenosha*, and were fine ships of their kind: they were 250 feet 6 inches in length between perpendiculars; 38 feet beam; about 16 feet mean draft, and were of 2,394 tons displacement. They were powered with the 50″ x 42″ Isherwood engines built in the navy yards for the *Serapis* class.

Within five years after the close of the war all the purchased or captured vessels, with very few exceptions, had disappeared and the navy list again contained only the names of regularly built war-vessels. Three captured blockade-runners of the long graceful type so popular with the British for breaking through our blockading lines were retained in the navy for several years as despatch or special service vessels, for which employment they were well adapted. They were all side-wheel steamers. The largest of them was the *Frolic*, an iron vessel of 1,300 tons displacement, captured at sea in September, 1864, under the name of *A. D. Vance* by the *Santiago de Cuba*, condemned by the New York prize court, and turned over to the Navy Department at an assessed value of $120,-000. She performed service on two or three different stations, and in the summer of 1873 made a notable voyage from Washington to St. John's, Newfoundland, to bring home survivors of the *Polaris* arctic expedition. In 1883 she was sold to J. P. Agnew of Alexandria, Virginia, for $11,250. The *Gettysburg* was another of these captured British steamers found worth retaining in the service: she was of 1,100 tons displacement, built of iron, and had been captured off Wilmington by the *Keystone State* in November, 1863, her name when taken being *Margaret and Jessie*. She had oscillating engines of a type then a favorite with English engineers. After considerable service in the Home and Mediterranean squadrons she was sold at Genoa, Italy, in 1879, for $10,983.46. The third vessel of this kind was the *Wasp*, a wooden side-wheel steamer somewhat smaller than the others: her name when under the British flag was *Emma Henry*, and she was captured at sea (Lat. 33 N.; Long. 77 W.) in December, 1863, by the U. S. S. *Cherokee*. The ship and cargo were condemned by the New York prize court at a valuation of $294,869.01, the vessel being afterward transferred to the Navy Department at an appraised value of $83,261.

U. S. STEAMSHIP OMAHA, 1868.
(*Alaska, Benicia, Plymouth*).

For several years she did duty as a despatch vessel on the Brazil station, and was sold at Montevideo in 1876 for $2,548.47.

A joint resolution of Congress approved February 3, 1868, authorized the Secretary of the Navy to sell all the iron-clad vessels in the navy except those of the *Dictator*, *Kalamazoo*, *Miantonomoh* and *Passaic* classes if in his judgment the interests of the service did not demand their retention, the proceeds to be turned into the treasury of the United States. The resolution specified that the value of all vessels offered for sale be determined by appraisal, "to be made by a board of not less than five naval officers, two of whom shall be engineers." The first vessels sold under this authority were the monitors *Catawba* and *Oneota* of the *Canonicus* class, built in Cincinnati, Ohio, by Alexander Swift & Co. Considerable public excitement resulted from this sale, it being charged that the vessels were sold to the firm that built them for considerably less than had been bid by other parties and less than they were actually worth, they being practically new and had never been in action. The chief cause for public criticism was the fact well known and scarcely disguised that the monitors were really being sold to Peru, then at war with Spain, and the act was liable to make the United States responsible for a breach of neutrality quite as flagrant as that of England in allowing the *Alabama* and other cruisers to be built or equipped in her ports. Mr. Swift sold the two monitors immediately to Peru and they were fitted out with ammunition, provisions, etc., at New Orleans for war service, the intention being to take them directly to Havana and attack that place: fortunately the trouble between Spain and Peru was adjusted before the iron-clads were ready to proceed on their mission, and the United States was spared the disgrace of falling back upon the well-worn excuse of "not knowing that the vessels were intended for war purposes." The price paid by Swift & Co. for the two monitors was $750,000, which was covered into the treasury; their cost to the government had been considerably more than this, being about $620,000 for each.

There being no demand for vessels of the monitor type after the Peruvian war cloud had passed over, the many other monitors for sale remained laid up at the navy yards rusting away until 1874, when a number of them were sold, the purchasers being generally ship and engine builders who bought them simply as old material; the prices brought varied from about seven thousand to twenty thousand dollars each. Twenty other monitors were broken up about the same time and the proceeds used in rebuilding the large double-turreted monitors. This latter transaction became one of the suspicious items for which Mr. Robeson's administration of the Navy Department afterward underwent an investigation at the hands of Congress, but is too involved a story to be attempted in this place, except in the general way necessary to carry out the object of tracing the history of our different naval steamers.

The formidable character of the four double-turreted monitors of the *Miantonomoh* class and their fitness for ocean service so well proved by two of them gave them an especial claim for preservation. Their wooden hulls deteriorated so rapidly as to become worthless in a few years and when the subject of repairing them came up for consideration Mr. Robeson decided to make the repairs in such a radical manner that entirely new monitors with iron hulls, larger dimensions, heavier armor, and improved machinery would result. The only fund available for this building work was the annual appropriation for "care and maintenance" of vessels and "preservation and repair" of steam machinery, and at the time Mr. Robeson assumed this large undertaking those funds were being much drawn upon by the repairs of the fifteen single-turreted monitors, work made necessary by the threatened trouble with Spain in the *Virginius* affair. A specific appropriation for repairing the double-turreted monitors was not made until June, 1874, when the Secretary of the Navy was authorized to use about $900,000 for that purpose, that sum being an unexpended balance from an appropriation previously made for the construction of a floating iron dock.

Undismayed by questions of ways and means, however, Mr. Robeson went ahead and placed the work under contract; first for putting the new iron hulls in frame, then, when more money was available, another contract for putting on the inner and outer skin plating, and so on. The contractors for building these new monitors were Harlan and Hollingsworth, Wilmington, Delaware, for the *Amphitrite* (originally *Tonawanda*); William Cramp and Sons, Philadelphia, for the *Terror* (originally *Agamenticus*); John Roach,

Chester, Pa., for the *Miantonomoh*, and Phineas Burgess of Vallejo, California, for the *Monadnock*. Soon after this work was under way the Secretary of the Navy determined to "repair" the unfinished *Puritan* in the same manner, she being one of the big monitors undertaken by John Ericsson in 1862 and never completed by him. Accordingly plans were prepared for a larger and more powerful vessel and arrangements for its construction made with Mr. John Roach. The original *Puritan* was handed over to Mr. Roach at a valuation of about $43,000 and broken up for the material, some of which is said to have been used in building the new vessel. With the assistance of the *Miantonomoh* the new *Puritan* also swallowed the light-draft monitors *Cohoes*, *Casco*, *Chimo*, *Modoc*, *Napa*, *Nausett*, and *Waxsaw*, all given to Mr. Roach on account. The new *Amphitrite* in the same way consumed her original and the *Koka;* the new *Terror* absorbed her forebear and the *Shawnee*, *Wassuc* and *Tunxis*. The old *Miantonomoh* was broken up at the Boston navy yard and thus escaped being devoured by her successor. The swift cruisers *Nevada* (originally *Neshaminy*), sister-ship of the *Wampanoag*, and *Severn* (*Mosholu*) also went to Mr. Roach at a valuation of $25,000 each to help pay for the new *Puritan*. The old frigate *Roanoke* which had been razeed and converted into a three-turreted monitor was transferred to Mr. Roach for the same purpose the last day of the Robeson administration, but the new Secretary of the Navy suspended the barter and subsequently cancelled it altogether.

As the resolution of Congress authorizing the sale of old monitors directed specifically that the proceeds of such sales be turned into the treasury, these trades made with the contractors were highly irregular, not to say an evasion or violation of law, and the subject, in association with various other transactions, led to charges against the Navy Department, investigations, and the suspension of all work on the ships. After taking an immense amount of testimony, the Committee on Naval Affairs of the House of Representatives reported to the House that many of the transactions of the Robeson administration were without authority of law and in utter disregard of its authority.

"Therefore, in the opinion of your committee, that the law

may be vindicated, and respect for its mandates maintained, it is the duty of the House to mark its condemnation of the illegal practices of these former officers of the Navy Department, and to invoke the attention of the executive department of the Government, upon which rests the responsibility of further action in the premises, to these violations of law, and accordingly your committee submit for the favorable consideration of the House the following resolutions:

"*Resolved*, That the acts and conduct of the late Secretary of the Navy, George M. Robeson, and of the late Chiefs of the Bureaus of Steam Engineering, Construction and Repair, and Provisions and Clothing, and who were such since May, 1872, and as referred to in this report, as well as all others aiding and abetting therein, in the sale and disposition of public property, in their method of making contracts and in involving the government in indebtedness over and beyond the appropriations made by Congress for the support of the navy, deserve and should receive the severest censure and condemnation.

"*Resolved further*, That it shall be the duty of the Clerk of the House of Representatives to deliver certified copies of the testimony taken before the Committees on Naval Affairs and Naval Expenditures of this House, together with the reports of said committees and the views of the minority, to the President of the United States, the Attorney General, and the Secretary of the Navy."

This report was signed by Mr. Whitthorne, Chairman of the committee, and six other members. Four other members of the committee signed a minority report defending the acts of the officials of the Navy Department, and concluding with these words: "The administration of the Navy Department by George M. Robeson and his subordinates, as shown by the testimony taken, is free from fraud, corruption, and willful violation of law."

No action was taken by the House on the resolutions offered by the majority of the committee, and with the printing of the two reports and the newspaper comments thereon the matter ended. The unfinished monitors remained for a few years in the shipyards of the contractors, incurring expense for the rent of space occupied by them, and were then removed to the navy yards, where, since the

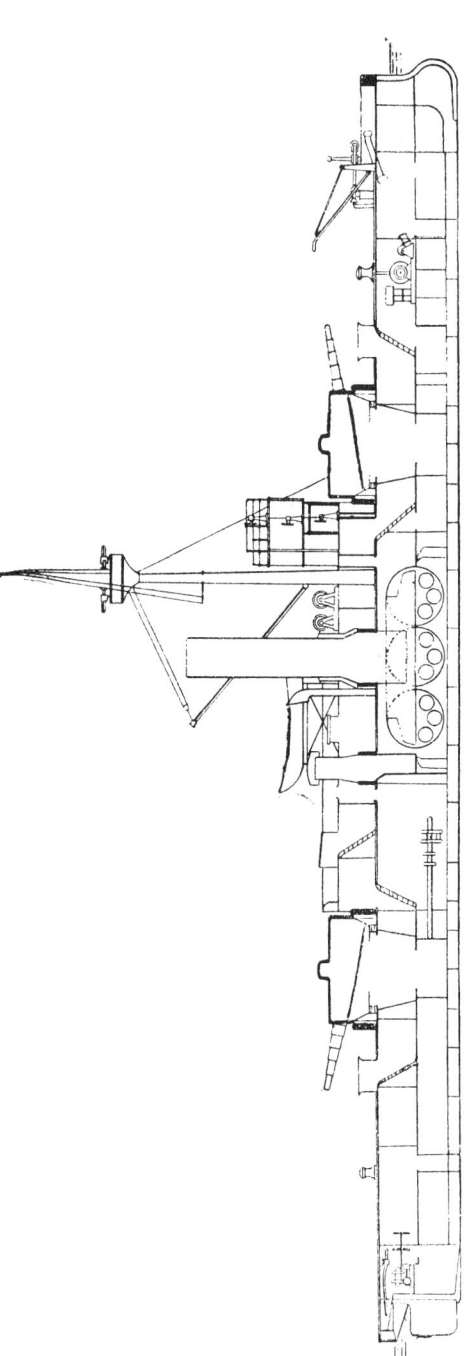

U. S. S. AMPHITRITE AS REBUILT.

Length on l. w. l., 259 feet 6 inches; beam, 55 feet 10 inches; disp., 3,990 tons; mean draft, 14 feet 6 inches.

New *Miantonomoh*, *Monadnock* and *Terror* of same dimensions; *Miantonomoh* and *Terror* are without barbettes; the *Monadnock* has triple expansion engines while the others of the class have the primitive design of 2-cylinder inclined engines crossing each other in such manner that the arrangement has caused the term "scissors engines" to be used as descriptive of them. The *Miantonomoh* is without the superstructure between the turrets.

era of the new navy dawned, work on them has been resumed and all are now completed or nearly so. As coast defense ships it is doubtful if their superiors exist in any navy; certainly not if the small crew required for their operation, low cost of maintenance, ability to enter shallow water, and other peculiar advantages are taken into consideration.

Besides repairing the iron-clads, Secretary Robeson had another difficult and more important task on his hands, and that was to keep the fleet of cruising vessels in a sea-worthy condition with the current appropriations for preservation and repair. The most serviceable ships then in the navy were the frigates and large sloops-of-war built from 1854 to 1858 and these were beginning to show the effects of years, both in hulls and machinery. Of the steamers built during the war scarcely one was in as good condition as the older vessels, the extensive use of white oak instead of live oak and the unseasoned character of much of the material hastened into their construction having resulted in rapid decay. With the fleet in the condition above stated, the Secretary of the Navy had to choose between two horns of a dilemma: he might go on expending the annual appropriations in repairing all the ships possible, putting patches and paint on over other patches and paint and in that manner keep the old hulks afloat until the disreputable appearance of the navy became such a reproach that national shame would force an appropriation for new ships from Congress; on the other hand, he might keep a few of the better ships in repair and use the remainder of the repair funds for the construction of entirely new ships under the disguise of repairs, as was done in the case of the double-turreted monitors, and this Mr. Robeson elected to do. The determination was high-handed, and, without mincing matters, was clearly an evasion of the provisions of law, but it resulted in some excellent cruisers whose appearance and service put off for some years the arrival of the day when the fleet of the United States was to become so obsolete as to be a laughing stock throughout the maritime world, even among the sea-faring people of China and Japan.

Six ships no longer considered worthy of legitimate repairs were selected to be repaired in this wholesale manner and the work of building new ships to fit the names undertaken at different navy

U. S. STEAMSHIP SWATARA, 1874.

yards in 1871–'72; the money available from year to year being limited, the work progressed slowly and from three to ten years were consumed in completing the different vessels. Two of the ships selected were the old sailing sloops *Marion* and *Vandalia*, built in 1839 and 1828 respectively, the latter having been rebuilt and lengthened thirteen feet in 1848. The experimental armored gun-vessel *Galena* was another craft to contribute a name for a new ship, as were also the newer vessels *Swatara* and *Quinnebaug* of the *Resaca* class. The last one selected was the old *Mohican*, this making one vessel for each of the principal navy yards. The new ships were built of live oak and with one exception were of the following general dimensions: Length between perpendiculars, 216 feet; beam, 37 feet; mean draft, $16\frac{1}{2}$ feet; displacement 1,900 tons. The exception was the *Vandalia*, which with the same length as the others was two feet greater beam, this increasing her displacement to 2,033 tons. They were built in navy yards as follows: The *Marion* at Kittery, Maine; the *Vandalia* at Boston; the *Swatara* at New York; the *Quinnebaug* at Philadelphia; the *Galena* at Norfolk, and the *Mohican* at Mare Island, California. The first of them to be completed was the *Swatara*, which was commissioned in 1874 and sailed from New York the eighth of June of that year with a party bound for ports in the southern hemisphere to observe a transit of Venus.

It having been determined on the strength of Engineer-in-Chief King's recommendation to supply these ships with compound machinery, a board consisting of Chief Engineers Charles H. Loring and C. H. Baker, with whom Chief Engineer David Smith was afterward associated, was ordered by the Secretary of the Navy to visit the different navy yards, examine the engines stored in them, and report as to the advisability of converting any of them into compound engines. It will be remembered that eight pairs of the 50″ x 42″ Isherwood engines had been constructed at navy yards for the *Serapis* class of sloops and that four of these sets of engines were used in the *Benicia*, *Alaska*, *Omaha*, and *Plymouth*. Mr. Loring's board recommended that the other four engines be altered for the new sloops, which recommendation was approved and the work taken in hand at the Boston and New York navy yards. The main feature in the alteration was in replacing the cylinders with new ones, a high-pressure cylinder 42' in diameter and low pressure 64", retaining the former stroke of pistons of 42" to avoid making new crank shafts and many other parts. These four converted engines were erected in the *Marion*, *Vandalia*, *Swatara* and *Quinnebaug*, the engines for the first two named having been rebuilt at Boston and the other two at New York. Entirely new compound engines with the same dimensions of cylinders as the converted engines were built for the *Galena* and *Mohican*, for the former at the Norfolk navy yard and for the latter at Mare Island. The cylinders and some other heavy castings for each of these engines were cast at the Washington navy yard. Ten cylindrical one-furnace boilers eight feet in diameter and eight feet one inch in length, constructed to withstand eighty pounds of steam pressure, were built for each vessel. The cost of these early compound engines is not known with any accuracy on account of the peculiar circumstances under which four of them came into existence, the problem being further complicated by the fact that considerable money had been spent on four other of the 50" x 42" engines partly built at navy yards and then broken up. The cost of these engines and boilers was not, however, extracted from the appropriations for repairs, as the naval appropriation act approved March 3, 1873, contained an item of $750,000 for compound engines for all these vessels except the *Mohican*.

Chief Engineer King's term of office as engineer-in-chief expired in March, 1873, and he was succeeded by Chief Engineer Wm. W. W. Wood, retiring from his office with the written thanks of the Secretary of the Navy for the efficient manner in which he had performed all his duties. Mr. Wood at the time was the senior chief engineer in the navy and possessed an enviable record for efficiency dating from his admission to the navy as a chief engineer in 1845. His name has occurred so often throughout this book as a result of his prominence in the service that it is not necessary to review his record in this place.

The board of officers that inspected and reported upon steam machinery afloat in 1869, known as the Goldsborough board, recommended among other things that all four-bladed screw propellers be removed from our vessels of war and two-bladed screws substituted for them, the idea being that the ships would sail better

CHIEF ENGINEER WM. W. W. WOOD, U. S. NAVY.
Engineer-in-Chief of the Navy from March 20, 1873, until March 3, 1877.

with the two-bladed screw fixed vertically behind the stern-post than they would with a four-bladed screw uncoupled and revolving in the water. This theory was incorrect, as was subsequently shown by experiment and observation, but the chief error existed in supposing that a two-bladed screw of sufficient propelling area could be put into the port or space between the rudder and stern posts formerly occupied by a four-bladed screw. As in the case of the strictures upon the *Wampanoag* and other cruisers built especially for high speed, the two engineer members of this board, Chief Engineers Robie and Moore, dissented from the above recommendation in their minority report. Another error was the assumption that the steaming power of a war vessel should be tampered with in the interests of the sailing quality, but the day was too early for steam to be considered as comparable with sails as a driving power. Indeed, it may be said that the navy at large still cherished a fiction to the effect that the old screw frigates and sloops were not really steamers at all, and this fond belief sometimes received official support, for as late as 1871 we find the annual report of the Navy Department referring to all these steamers in a body as "sailing-vessels with auxiliary screws."

The recommendation of the Goldsborough board was carried out and two-bladed screws made and fitted as circumstances allowed to a number of the principal screw steamers of the navy, at an aggregate cost of about $100,000. Commanding officers and chief engineers began reporting adversely concerning the change and the matter became a question of general interest in the service and one about which there was much diversity of opinion. In his annual report as admiral of the navy Admiral Porter in 1871 defended the two-bladed screw theory at considerable length, as follows:

"As you will remember, General Order 131, issued by the Department June 18, 1869, requires all officers to be careful in the expenditure of coal, and to use their sails on every occasion where great dispatch is unnecessary.

"Our steam-vessels, with a few exceptions, having hitherto been supplied with merely sufficient sail to enable them to lay to under, were converted into full-rigged ships, and the two-bladed propeller was substituted for that of four blades; the latter having been found, by the experience of officers, unfit for a ship maneuvering under sail, while the two-bladed propeller can be hoisted or placed up and down the stern-post so as to offer but slight resistance.

"The four-bladed propeller retards every movement of a ship under sail and renders maneuvering out of the question. By this change in propellers, commanding officers have been enabled to carry out the orders of the Department and effect a great saving in the expenditure of coal, restoring to the service those seamanlike qualities of our crews which seemed almost to have departed from it.

"In all the trial trips made in vessels where the propellers were changed, the two-bladed propeller invariably gave a small increase of speed with only the inconvenience of greater vibration, which latter, though desirable to avoid, is hardly to be considered where so many advantages are gained.

"According to the best authorities, the main object of a propeller is to utilize the power in such a manner that the greatest possible speed may be obtained with the least possible power. The position of the propeller should be such as not to interfere with the ordinary working of the vessel, and its effect should be produced without any disagreeable sensation to those on board. This can be done only with a two-bladed propeller, fitted to a properly constructed vessel, in which it is placed sufficiently abaft the stern-post to prevent too much reaction of water against the stern, causing vibration. . . .

"There are certain disadvantages inseparable from an increase in the number of blades. The friction of the extra blades in the water absorbs a large amount of the power of the engine, without any increase in the propulsive power.

"The assertion that with a number of blades there is less vibration is partly true, but vibration arises principally from the inequality of resistance during the successive positions of the propeller around its center, and its too close proximity to the stern-post; a fault of construction, not of propellers.

"A four-bladed propeller has one-third more weight than a propeller with two blades, and makes a ship drop heavily in an uneasy seaway. It is, in fact, a heavy drag on all occasions."

In spite of these authoritative opinions, reports kept coming in

U. S. STEAMSHIP RANGER (Alert, Huron).

Originally the *Ranger* and *Huron* were fore-and-aft rigged, but after the loss of the *Huron* the *Ranger's* rig was changed to that of a bark, the same as the *Alert*.

from the ships that had been changed showing that the substitution was producing a marked loss of speed and waste of coal due to the increased percentage of slip incident to the use of two-bladed screws of insufficient area. Engineer-in-Chief King made the subject a matter of comment in his annual reports, taking a view exactly opposite to that of Admiral Porter, and his successor, Mr. Wood, having more information on the subject by virtue of the longer time the experiment had been on trial, made it a special feature in his reports, sustaining his opinions with formidable tables of data from cruising ships, showing beyond dispute that the practice was reducing the efficiency of every ship on which the change had been made, and at the same time was largely increasing the coal bills. In 1875 the Secretary of the Navy gave Mr. Wood the asked-for authority to put the four-bladed screws back where they belonged.

Representations to Congress of the decaying condition of the navy eventually resulted in a special act, approved February 10, 1873, authorizing the Secretary of the Navy to construct eight vessels of war, the aggregate tonnage of the whole number not to exceed eight thousand tons, and the aggregate cost to be not more than $3,200,000. The act specified that four of the vessels, in whole or in part, should be built by contract with the lowest responsible bidders in public competition. Another noteworthy provision of the act was that the ships were to be "steam vessels of war, with auxiliary sail power." The cost limit was repeated in the naval appropriation bill passed the following month and placed in the appropriations for the Bureau of Construction, so it did not have to be used to pay for machinery, other appropriations providing for that.

Three of the resulting vessels were iron gun-boats of 1,020 tons displacement, named *Alert*, *Huron*, and *Ranger*. They were 175 feet between perpendiculars; 32 feet beam, and of about 13 feet mean draft. All were built by contract, the *Alert* and *Huron* at Roach's Delaware River Shipbuilding Works at Chester, Pa., and the *Ranger* by Harlan and Hollingsworth, Wilmington, Delaware. The machinery of all three was built by the Roach establishment at Chester; the engines were of the two cylinder back-acting compound type designed by the Bureau of Steam Engineering, with cylinders

$28\frac{1}{4}$ inches and $42\frac{1}{2}$ inches in diameter and 42 inches stroke, intended for a maximum horse-power of 560. Each ship had five of the single-furnace cylindrical boilers eight feet in diameter, aggregating 120 square feet of grate surface. Each had a four-bladed screw, twelve feet in diameter, that of the *Ranger* being of bureau design and the others of the Hirsch patent. The *Huron* was wrecked with terrible loss of life in 1877, after little more than two years of service, and the other two still remain on active duty. Four other gun-boats were built under the same authority, of wood, and somewhat larger than the *Alert* class. These were 185 feet long; 35 feet

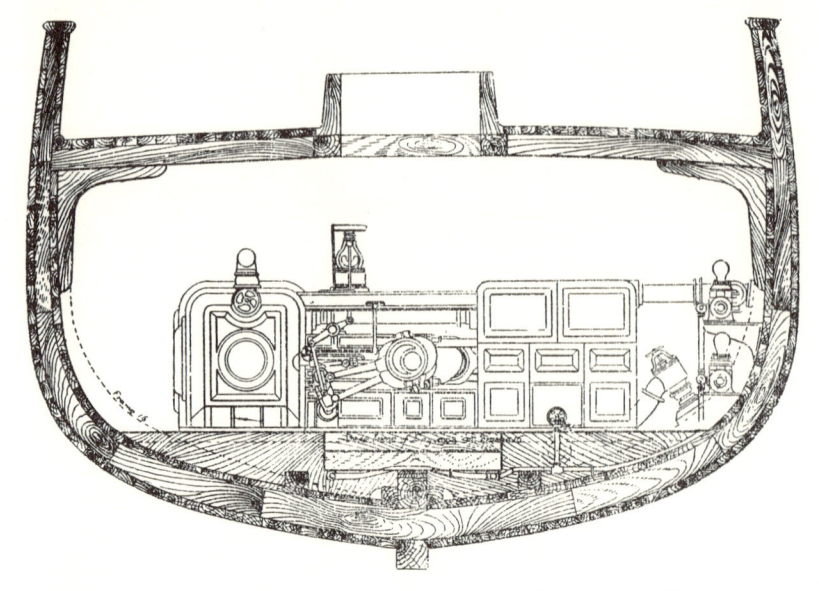

SECTION SHOWING ENGINES AS INSTALLED IN THE "ENTERPRISE" CLASS. THE SAME ARRANGEMENT OBTAINED IN THE "ALERT" CLASS OF IRON SLOOPS.

beam; about 14 feet mean draft, and of 1,375 tons displacement. The engines were compound, of bureau design, and of the same type as those of the *Alert* class, but larger, being designed for 800 horse-power. The cylinders were 34 and 51 inches in diameter and 42 inches stroke. They each had originally eight of the single furnace boilers, with 192 square feet of grate surface. The screws were all of bureau design, 14 feet in diameter and 19 feet mean pitch. Of these gun-boats, or corvettes, as they were called later,

U. S. STEAMSHIP ENTERPRISE.
(*Adams, Alliance, Essex, Nipsic, 2d*).

the *Enterprise* was built at the Kittery navy yard by a private contractor, Mr. John W. Griffiths, working in co-operation with the government officials; the *Essex* was built at the same navy yard and under the same form of dual superintendence, the contractor in this case being Mr. Donald McKay, who had a similar contract for the construction of the *Adams* at the Boston navy yard. The fourth vessel, the *Alliance*, was built at the Norfolk navy yard by the government. Machinery for the *Adams* and *Essex* was built by contract by the Atlantic Works, Boston, for $163,000 and $175,000 respectively; that for the *Enterprise* was built by the Woodruff Iron Company, Hartford, Conn., the contract price being $175,000, while that for the *Alliance* was by the Quintard Iron Works, of New York, for the same price.

For the eighth vessel authorized, the Department went beyond the idea of gun-boats and built the large frigate *Trenton*, for many years after her completion the most formidable cruising ship in our neglected navy and the only one that in type and armament at all approached the practice of other nations at the time. The hull, of live oak, was designed by Chief Constructor Isaiah Hanscom and built at the New York navy yard by Naval Constructor S. H. Pook. The *Trenton* was 253 feet long between perpendiculars; 48 feet beam; $19\frac{1}{2}$ feet mean draft, and of 3,900 tons displacement. She was full ship-rigged, and carried a ram armed with a heavy composition casting, the point nine feet below the water-line and eight feet forward of the stem. The machinery complete was built from bureau designs by contract with the Morgan Iron Works, New York, the contract price being $650,000. The engines were of the horizontal compound back-acting type, with three cylinders side by side, the high pressure cylinder, $58\frac{1}{2}$ inches in diameter, being between the two low pressures, which were 78 inches in diameter; the stroke of all pistons was 48 inches, and the engines were designed to develop 3,100 horse-power. There were eight cylindrical three-furnace boilers, 12 feet in diameter and 10 feet 3 inches in length, aggregating 464 square feet of grate surface. The propeller was a four-bladed Hirsch screw 19 feet in diameter. The *Trenton* did considerable service as flagship on different stations, and finally came to a violent end in the South Seas.

While these ships were building, the Department concluded to "repair" the gun-boat *Nipsic*, one of the *Kansas* class built in 1863, in the same way that the *Swatara* and others had been repaired. The *Enterprise* class was taken as a model and an exactly similar vessel built at the Washington navy yard, her completion being delayed until 1879 by the small appropriations for repairs available each year, this being about three years later than the completion of her sister ships. Her engines and boilers, exactly like those of the *Enterprise* class, were obtained by contract with W. Wright & Co., Newburgh, New York, the contract price being $175,000.

One steamer was added to the navy in 1874 by purchase, the Department that year buying for a despatch vessel the steam yacht *America* from Mr. Henry C. Smith of New York and changing her name to *Despatch*. This yacht is not to be confused with the more famous yacht *America*, a sailing vessel, which for a number of years belonged to the Navy Department and was stationed at the Naval Academy, she having been acquired by capture during the war. The *Despatch* was a wooden screw steamer, 174 feet long; $25\frac{1}{2}$ feet beam; about 12 feet draft, and was of 560 tons displacement. She had a two-cylinder vertical direct-acting engine, with cylinders 33 inches in diameter and 33 inches stroke, driving a single screw; the purchase price was $98,500. The *Despatch* was employed one or two summers as a practice steamer for cadet engineers; was on special service in the Mediterranean for a time; served as a surveying vessel in Samana Bay, and finally became a special service tender for the use of the President and Secretary of the Navy. In February, 1891, she ran ashore on Assateague shoal off the coast of Maryland and became a total wreck, her people losing their effects and escaping with their lives with some difficulty.

A special appropriation for extraordinary expenses of the Bureau of Ordnance enabled that bureau in 1874 to have built under its cognizance the two large torpedo vessels *Alarm* and *Intrepid*. Both were built of iron, the *Alarm* at the New York Navy Yard and the *Intrepid* at the Boston yard. The *Alarm* was 158 feet long; 28 feet beam, and of 800 tons displacement. The *Intrepid* was 170 feet long; 35 feet beam, and 1,150 tons displacement. The machinery for both was designed and built by the Morgan Iron Works, New York. That of the *Alarm* consisted of two two-cylinder compound engines with cylinders 20 and 38 inches in

U. S. STEAMSHIP TRENTON, 1876.

BOW VIEW OF TORPEDO BOAT ALARM IN DRY DOCK.

diameter and 30 inches stroke, actuating a Fowler wheel; there were four two-furnace cylindrical boilers 10 feet in diameter, aggregating 169 square feet of grate surface. The *Intrepid* had twin-screws, each driven by a two-cylinder compound engine, the high pressure cylinders being 24 inches in diameter and the low-pressures 48, the stroke of pistons being 24 inches. She had six two-furnace cylindrical boilers with 260 square feet of grate surface. The *Alarm* is still in the service, classed as a torpedo ram: the *Intrepid*, after being experimented with for several years, was hauled up on a building slip in the New York navy yard with a view to remodeling her into a light-draft gun-boat for service in Chinese waters, but that intention was abandoned and the vessel was broken up.

CHAPTER XXXIII.

"All your petty self-seekings and rivalries done,
Round the dear Alma Mater your hearts beat as one."
—J. G. WHITTIER.

The Training of Naval Engineers at the Naval Academy.

THE United States Naval Academy at Annapolis, Maryland, was established by Mr. George Bancroft when that distinguished historian was Secretary of the Navy under the administration of President James K. Polk. The first session of the school was held in 1845, Commander Franklin Buchanan being the superintendent and Lieutenant James H. Ward, in charge of the department of gunnery, the second in command. The science of marine engineering was then young, and the naval engineer corps had been established only three years; nevertheless, through the efforts of Lieutenant Ward, steam was one of the principal subjects taught during the first academic years. Lieutenant Ward was a progressive man for his day and of a decidedly mechanical turn of mind, the latter quality impelling him to become an ordnance expert and to develop into a science the rude gunnery knowledge of the time. In steam he saw a power that was destined to revolutionize naval tactics and which therefore should be mastered by naval officers as a force with which they would have to deal in the future. With this view he felt it a duty to prepare the young men of the navy placed under his charge for the change that was approaching, and he accordingly fitted himself by studying the new science and gave instruction in it by means of lectures, combining steam and gunnery as kindred subjects. When Mr. Ward left the academy in 1847 steam no longer had a champion in that institution and soon fell into neglect, being transferred first to the department of chemistry and later to a new department called natural philosophy, in each of which it was starved as a foundling child unwelcome in an already overcrowded household.

Lieutenant Ward had his lectures and notes on steam published in book form under the title of "Steam for the Million," an excellent and popular text book in its time. Ward himself rose to the rank of commander and in June, 1861, a month even before the battle of Bull Run, he was killed while gallantly attacking a Confederate battery at Mathias' Point on the Potomac River, in King George County, Virginia. In him the navy lost one of its most capable and brilliant officers and the engineer corps lost its best friend in the navy outside its own ranks. Commander Ward was the first naval officer killed in the war of the rebellion.

Before proceeding with the account of the establishment of a course of instruction for engineer students at the academy it is proper to say that the subject of educating engineers for the navy had been proposed long before the founding of the school for line officers. When making the experimental cruise with the *Fulton* in the winter of 1837–'38, Captain M. C. Perry in his contact with engines and engineers discovered that the revolution in naval education and tactics had already dawned. Reporting from Montauk Point in February, 1838, he suggested to the Department that a training school for naval engineers be established by the government; also that apprentice boys should be enlisted and trained specially for the engineer's force. The latter suggestion was carried out and firemen-apprentices were enlisted for the *Fulton*, but the proposition relative to a school for young engineers was so long in bearing fruit that Captain Perry did not live to see its perfection.

With the first actual war operations on the part of the navy in 1861 came a realization that a degree of responsibility formerly unsuspected must fall upon the engineers and their machinery. Steam at once took its place as a formidable weapon of war, and was immediately recognized as the only motive power for war purposes, however convenient, clean, and economical sails might be for peace cruising. The engineers in the navy at the beginning of the war were, as a rule, skillful and efficient, but their number, much reduced as it was by resignations and dismissals of members who were natives of the Southern States, was entirely inadequate to the work that fell upon the engineering branch when many steamers were suddenly added to the fleet and designs demanded from the naval engineers for the machinery for many others to be built. This made the influx of a great number of acting or volunteer engineers necessary, and some mishaps, delays, and disasters followed as results of the inexperience of the new men, due, in some cases, also to their incompetency, for the emergency did not permit of fine discrimination in their selection.

The great and constantly growing demand upon the engineer corps for the efficient performance of its part in war was such an important matter that it soon became a subject for consideration in the Navy Department. The need for greater scientific and technical knowledge among the engineers was one of the chief demands developed, for the many sudden emergencies and trying circumstances attending the war operations of the navy soon demonstrated that the engineers of a ship should possess considerable theoretical knowledge in addition to practical ability if the ship's machinery were to be kept in an efficient condition when far removed from the vicinity of navy-yards and consulting engineers. The conditions of service also brought forward the fact, in stronger colors than it had appeared before, that the engineer in the navy should be a naval officer as well as a marine-engineer. Mr. Isherwood fully appreciated the difficulties under which the members of his corps labored, and in the midst of the most engrossing duties he found time to address the Department on the subject, his opinions so far securing attention that in the annual report of the Secretary of the Navy for 1863 we find the following under the caption "Education of Engineers:"

"To attain and maintain our true position as a naval power, the best talent in the country must be found among the officers who are to conduct the varied operations of the service, and adequate provision to secure such ability and accomplishment should command the attention of those who have charge of our naval affairs. Our naval school is producing officers of skill, well educated for their profession, yet if our ships and steam-machinery are not at the highest attainable point of perfection, and the engineers are not skillful, the education and accomplishment of our officers will be unavailing to give us the naval superiority we should obtain.

"By the introduction of steam into naval operations a new corps is engrafted into the naval service of men combining science with mechanical skill and genius, whose professional attainments and practical power demand the fostering care of the government. Our naval engineers, like those of the army, should be thoroughly educated to their profession, for on them the motive power of our vessels and the efficiency of our steam-machinery must hereafter depend. Steam-engineering should indeed be one of the important studies of all naval officers, and should be taught at the Naval Academy. It would be well to encourage such men as exhibit aptness for mechanical studies to cultivate their peculiar talents, whether as naval constructors or engineers, in that department in which they render the highest public service. Other governments pursue this course, and we shall find our advantage in giving similar encouragement to the young men of our country.

"It is a question, indeed, as sails are subordinate to steam, whether every officer of the line ought not to be educated to and capable of performing the duties which devolve upon engineers. The means of acquiring practical as well as theoretical knowledge of the subject should be furnished by the government, and it would be well if every midshipman were to receive instruction in this now important branch of his profession. If the public is not yet prepared to combine what at present are two distinct pursuits, and make every naval officer an engineer as well as a sailor, I would recommend the formation of a class at the Naval Academy of youths, giving a preference to those who may have already evinced mechanical skill and aptitude for engineering, who might be educated with special reference to their profession as engineers. After two years' study they could be received into the corps by conferring upon them the appointment of third assistant engineers and assigning them to duty. The naval service and the country have suffered injury that can scarcely be estimated from the want of thorough, capable, and well educated engineers. Many of our most efficient vessels have been disabled and crippled in the midst of their cruise, and sometimes even at the very commencement of their service, in consequence of the incapacity of the engineers, whereby the country has been deprived not only of the use of the vessel for weeks and sometimes for months, but the officers and crew have been constrained to inactivity instead of being employed against the enemy. Some measures are necessary to correct and prevent these disasters, so injurious to the country, and I know of none so thorough and complete as that of publicly educating and training engineers to the service. The most important branch of study at the Naval Academy is, very appropriately, seamanship. A general knowledge of the application and use of steam and of practical mechanics should follow as almost equally essential. Line officers of the navy, of whatever rank, should, moreover, have the privilege of attending lectures and pursuing the studies of steam, mechanics, and, indeed, every branch that may be taught at the Naval Academy, and it is recommended that arrangements be made for carrying into effect these suggestions."

The authorship of these views, although they embody many of Mr. Isherwood's suggestions, is generally credited to the Hon. Gustavus V. Fox, the assistant secretary of the navy, upon whom fell the consideration of questions relating to the naval *personnel*. The soundness of his opinions in this matter cannot now be questioned, but at the time they appeared they were so much in advance of the theories of the day that they excited considerable opposition.

The recommendation of the Navy Department, in regard to the education of engineers, received attention from Congress without much delay, a law being enacted the following summer which gave the Secretary of the Navy authority to establish a class of cadet engineers at the Naval Academy. This was the first appearance in the United States navy of the term *cadet* as applied to a naval student or aspirant of any corps. The Act of Congress referred to was approved July 4, 1864, and became Sections 1522 and 1523 of the Revised Statutes, reading as follows:

"SECTION 1522. The Secretary of the Navy is authorized to make provision, by regulations issued by him, for educating at the

Naval Academy, as naval constructors or steam-engineers, such midshipmen and others as may show a peculiar aptitude therefor. He may, for this purpose, form a separate class at the Academy, to be styled cadet engineers, or otherwise afford to such persons all proper facilities for such a scientific mechanical education as will fit them for said professions.

"SECTION 1523. Cadet engineers shall be appointed by the Secretary of the Navy. They shall not at any time exceed fifty in number, and no persons, other than midshipmen, shall be eligible for appointment unless they shall first produce satisfactory evidence of mechanical skill and proficiency, and shall have passed an examination as to their mental and physical qualifications."

It is improbable that the provisions of this act whereby "midshipmen and others" could be educated for naval constructors and steam-engineers as specialists in these branches came up to the wishes of Mr. Fox in the premises. His desire undoubtedly was to simplify the naval service and render its official element more homogeneous by making the practical details of engineering a part of the seamanship of the time, a full mastery of which should be incumbent upon the line officers who performed the details of duty at sea. This is shown by the views which appeared in the annual report of the Secretary of the Navy for the year 1864, as follows:

"CADET ENGINEERS.

"Preliminary measures have been taken to carry into effect the law of the last session of Congress authorizing the education at the Naval Academy of cadet engineers, to be selected from youths not over eighteen years of age, who shall have been engaged at least two years in the fabrication of steam machinery. A circular has been issued and printed in the papers of the great manufacturing cities inviting applications in conformity to the law.

"Before this plan shall be put into operation, it is respectfully submitted, in view of the radical changes which have been wrought by steam as a motive power for naval vessels, whether steam engineering should not be made to constitute hereafter a necessary part of the education of all midshipmen, so that in our future navy every line officer will be a steam engineer, and qualified to have complete command and direction of his ship. Hereafter every vessel of war must be a steam vessel. Those designed for ocean service will be furnished with sails in order to economize fuel while cruising; the present and future navy will therefore combine sails and steam as motive power, and seamanship and steam-engine driving will each be necessary to make the finished professional officer. The officers to sail and navigate a ship and the officers to run the steam-engine are about equal in number.

"The Department is not aware that any line officer, whatever attention may have been given by him to the theoretical study of steam, is yet capable of taking charge of an engine, nor are steam engine drivers capable of taking charge of a man-of-war, navigating her, fighting her guns, and preserving her discipline. When vessels were propelled exclusively by sails there were but two officers, excepting in flagships, the surgeon and paymaster, who were not line officers. But under the present naval system a new and additional corps is introduced, as many steam engineers being required for a vessel as there are line officers; and, while cruising under sail, or lying in port, or performing any duty when the engine is at rest, one-half of the officers are, by existing regulations, idle and incapable of participating in duties that are often laborious and oppressive on the officers of the line, comparatively speaking. The engineers would willingly share these duties were they acquainted with them. But half the officers of a steamship cannot keep watch, cannot navigate her, cannot exercise the great guns or small arms, nor, except as volunteers under a line officer, take part in any expedition against the enemy. On the other hand, the other half of the officers are incapable of managing the steam motive power, or of taking charge of the engine-room in an emergency, nor can the commander of a vessel, though carefully taught every duty of a sailor and drill-officer, understand, of his own knowledge, whether the engineers and firemen are competent or not.

"The remedy for all this is very simple, provided the principle were once recognized and adopted of making our officers engine-drivers as well as sailors. It would not be expedient to interfere with the present status of line officers or engineers,—the change would be too radical; but we should begin by teaching each midshipman to be able to discharge the duties of line officers and engineers, to combine the two in one profession, so that officers so educated can take their watch alternately in the engine-room and on deck.

"Objection may be made that the duties are dissimilar, and that steam-engine driving is a specialty. The duties are not more dissimilar than seamanship and gunnery. When seamanship was the only education given to an officer, it was not believed he could ever learn to teach sailors to drill, and a sergeant of marines performed the duty which is now so admirably discharged by the graduates of the Naval Academy. When gunnery became a specialty, it was inconsiderately and unwisely proposed to have a corps of ordnance officers engrafted upon the naval service, a separate organization, which should draw to itself the knowledge so necessary to each, and therefore proper to be distributed among all the officers.

"Fortunately, our naval officers are taught seamanship, gunnery, and the infantry drill, and the service thereby saved from distinct organizations in these respects which would, inevitably, have impaired its efficiency. It only remains to commence, at this time, and as preparatory to the future of the navy, to teach the midshipmen steam engineering, as applied to running the engine. This would be independent of the art of designing and constructing, which is purely a specialty, and nowise necessary in the management and direction of the ship. And to this specialty, as a highly scientific body of officers, would the present corps of engineers be always required as inspectors and constructors of machinery. With the adoption of the suggestions here made, we shall, in due time, have a homogeneous corps of officers, who will be masters of the motive power of their ships in the future as they have been of seamanship in the past. By this arrangement there will be in each ship double the number of officers capable of fighting and running the vessels without additional appointments or expense. Innumerable other advantages commend the plan as worthy of trial, and it is presented for favorable consideration. The work can be commenced and carried forward at the Naval Academy without any additional appropriation, and the authority of Congress is invoked in behalf of the suggestions here submitted."

The only immediate step taken to put these recommendations

into operation was the detailing of some assistant engineers of the regular navy to duty at the Naval Academy, then at Newport, Rhode Island, as "Acting Assistant Professors of Natural and Experimental Philosophy," but they did not make engineers of any of the midshipmen then under instruction. The following year (1865) the Academy was moved back to Annapolis, where it had been before the war, and the "Department of Steam-Enginery" (afterward changed to Steam-Engineering) established as one of the regular branches of learning of the institution.

Thus far, no class of cadet engineers had been formed, but the new department at once undertook the duty of instructing the midshipmen in the principles of marine-engineering, using such appliances as were then at hand and one or two small naval steamers sent to Annapolis for that especial purpose. The present steam-building was erected in 1866, a special appropriation of $20,000 having been made for the purpose, and the greater part of its present equipment installed at that time, making a plant that for purposes of instruction in marine engineering was then unequaled in the United States. The chief item in the equipment of this building was a large marine engine set up with boilers, shafting and propeller in complete condition to be run by steam, this being the 36″ x 36″ Isherwood engine mentioned in another chapter as having been built at the Washington navy yard for the first *Quinnebaug* before foreign-built engines were ordered for that vessel. The following complimentary reference to this engine occurs in the annual report of Vice Admiral D. D. Porter, superintendent of the Naval Academy, dated September 25, 1866:

" The steam building, for which Congress appropriated twenty thousand dollars ($20,000), will be finished in November, and will, I think, be the most complete establishment of the kind in the country. We have already erected in this building, and ready for use, a beautiful propeller engine, similar to those planned by Chief Engineer Isherwood, and generally used in the vessels constructed by the Navy Department. This engine is, I think, very complete in all its parts. It is compact, strong, and simple, and well adapted for the purpose of instruction. It is a type of the engines used in our vessels-of-war, ,and to be in use for some time to come, for I

STEAM ENGINEERING BUILDING, U. S. NAVAL ACADEMY, 1878.

venture to say that no better engine can be found, although efforts have been made to bring it into discredit. I am pleased to see this monument of the skill and perseverance of the engineer-in-chief, Mr. Isherwood, erected at the Naval Academy, where it will be properly appreciated, and where it can be inspected at any time by the doubters who would delight to injure its reputation."

The picture of the steam building here presented shows that structure as it appeared during the late '70s when the cadet engineer system was at the height of its development, this being regarded as more appropriate for this work than a view of its present appearance with the alterations and changes that have occurred to it and its surroundings in later years. The two guns standing vertically at the entrance or gateway are iron 24-pounders, trophies captured on board the British frigate *Confiance*, at the battle of Lake Champlain, by Commodore McDonough. One of them is cracked and indented on the muzzle, the effect of having been struck by a shot; this same gun has been identified as the one which, by its recoil, killed Commodore Downie, the commander of the British forces.[1]

The two iron screw-propellers arranged on the lawn as ornaments are also trophies, they having been taken from the British steamer *Don*, captured in March, 1864, by the U. S. steamer *Pequot*, while trying to break the blockade off Beaufort.

The Secretary's report for 1865 again came to the defense of the new system, this time going so far as to assert that line officers would shortly find themselves in a position of secondary importance if they clung to the old seamanship as a profession. Under the head of the Naval Academy we find the following comments in the annual report for that year:

" In dispensing with vessels propelled wholly by sails from the list of regular men-of-war, it has become necessary to instruct the future naval officer in the principles and practice of steam enginery. A separate department, having this object in view, has been established at the Naval Academy, under the management and direction

---

[1] Authorities in support of this identification are cited in J. R. Soley's "Historical Sketch of the U. S. Naval Academy."

of Chief Engineer Wm. W. W. Wood, assisted by eight others, who are charged with the duty of teaching the midshipmen not only the theory of the steam-engine, but, as indicated in my last report, its actual manipulation. Sufficient experiments and progress have already been made in running the engines of the vessels attached to the Academy by the midshipmen to warrant the Department to persevere in its purpose of perfecting the education of the future line officers, by making them competent, in addition to their other acquirements, to manage and work the engine.

"The management of a man-of-war in a gale, on a lee shore, in a narrow harbor, or the splendid manœuvres of battle by sailing-vessels, have hitherto been the highest and proudest duties of a thorough naval officer. The skillful disposition of the sails, which was the result of the best training of the old school, is no longer necessary, except as auxiliary to the new motive power which modern invention and science have introduced. The naval vessel is no longer dependent on the winds, nor is she at the mercy of currents; but the motive power which propels and controls her movements is subject to the mind and will of her commander, provided he is master of his profession in the future as he has been in the past. To retain the prominence which skill and education gave him when seamanship was the most important accomplishment, the line officer must be qualified to guide and direct this new element or power. Unless he has these qualities, he will be dependent on the knowledge and skill of him who manipulates and directs the engine. To confine himself to seamanship, without the ability to manage the steam engine, will result in his taking a secondary position, as compared with that which the accomplished naval officer formerly occupied.

" For the full development and accomplishment of an object which can no longer be considered a doubtful experiment, the active co-operation of naval officers is required. When this change is effected, engineers will become the designers and constructors of engines and other marine works, and the superintendents of the mechanical employment which a navy propelled by steam has developed and may require. They will constitute in reality a highly-educated and scientific corps, and the line officers will have added to their duties the practical management of the engines."

In spite of the steps taken by the Department to carry into effect the law of 1864, authorizing the education of cadet engineers at the Naval Academy, candidates for that attention were not forthcoming. The reason probably being that the people were weary of a long war and not disposed to enter their sons in the service of the government, even to go to school. Besides this, young men who had been "engaged at least two years in the fabrication of steam machinery" were not disposed to accept conditions that would put them back into the school-room, nor likely to become very apt pupils if they did; they certainly consulted their best interests by remaining where they were, identified with the great awakening of the manufacturing industries of the North that took place at the close of the war.

In 1866, after two years of advertising of the cadet-engineer programme, the first fruits appeared in the form of two young men who were admitted to the Academy in October of that year, and two others who entered a year later. As these four cadet engineers were the first of their species in the navy, it is worth while to trace their careers.

Those who entered in 1866 were George D. McCarty, of New York City, and James P. Wilson, of Washington, D. C., and they were to some extent the victims of circumstances, being used by the Naval Academy officials as useful objects upon which to experiment in the development of a course of study for engineer students. The result of this was that when James Steel, of Wisconsin, and C. P. Howell, of New York, entered in 1867, all four were equally prepared for the same course of instruction. Toward the end of that academic year Mr. Wilson resigned, and Mr. McCarty, discovering that he had missed his vocation, got an appointment as a midshipman and entered the third class of midshipmen,—the class of 1872. About a year later he, too, tendered his resignation. Messrs. Steel and Howell proved to be bright students and were sent to sea on a probationary cruise in 1868 in the sloop-of-war *Contoocook*. Cadet Steel died at sea that same year, but Mr. Howell survived the cruise, was promoted in due time, and is now a chief engineer in the navy.

While the first cadet engineers were being experimented upon there were some engineer students of a different stamp undergoing instruction at the Academy. Not getting any results from the manufacturing cities in which the cadet-engineer system had been advertised, the Department invaded a new field for recruiting by sending circulars to the large colleges of the country in which engineering was taught. In conformity with the terms of the circular about fifty candidates, the most of whom were graduates, appeared at Annapolis in the summer of 1866 and underwent a competitive examination, the sixteen who passed highest being selected for the service. They were too well educated and too old to be made cadets of, so they were appointed acting third assistant engineers and given a special course of instruction in marine engines, and some other naval subjects not dealt with at the colleges they came from. They did not live inside the walls of the Academy, and did not form a part of the cadet organization of the time, being more on the footing of junior officers taking a post-graduate course. Five of them came from the Rensselaer Polytechnic Institute, of Troy, New York; five from Harvard; one from Yale; two from Brown University; one from Union College, and two were not college men. All sixteen graduated at the end of a two-years' course with credit and went into active service as third assistant engineers.

A melancholy accident occurred at the Naval Academy on the afternoon of October 19, 1867, resulting in the death of Chief Engineer Eben Hoyt. The steam picket-boat with which Lieutenant Cushing sank the *Albemarle* was recovered after the capture of Plymouth, repaired, and sent to the Academy as a trophy, where by direction of Vice Admiral Porter it was fitted up as a beautiful little brig-rigged steam yacht, bearing the name *Albemarle*. On the day mentioned she was taken out for a trial run, having previously developed remarkable speed for such a small craft. Admiral Porter started to go in her but not feeling well and the day being very warm, concluded not to do so, and Chief Engineer Hoyt went in charge. The run was made successfully; the boat was returning, and while nearly all the people in and about the Academy were looking at her, she blew up with a heavy explosion, killing Mr. Hoyt, Wm. Clarke, the engineer, and Samuel Driscoll, who was tending the fires, and mortally injuring the coxswain, John Shea, who died soon after. Three messenger boys who were in the boat escaped with slight injuries. The boiler had been tested to 180 pounds hydraulic pressure and the catastrophe, like most boiler explosions, has no logical explanation.

The loss of Chief Engineer Hoyt was severely felt by a wide circle of friends and official associates, among whom he was highly esteemed for his high character and professional attainments. The following from his obituary notice published in the *Army and Navy Journal* gives an outline of his important services:

"He was born in Boston, Massachusetts, May 13, 1834, educated at the public schools, and, after graduating at the high school, became a student under a prominent architect of that city. He subsequently turned his attention to civil engineering and assisted at the erection of the lighthouse on Minot's Ledge. Later, he made mechanical engineering a special study, and in May, 1857, entered the United States Navy, commencing his first cruise in October of that year on the late United States frigate *Merrimac*. The outbreak of the rebellion found him attached to the steam-sloop *Richmond*, then in the Mediterranean. The vessel was recalled and sent to join the Gulf squadron under Farragut. While in this squadron Mr. Hoyt was present at the engagement between the *Water Witch* and the rebel gun-boat *Ivy;* the fight between the ram *Manassas* and the U. S. gun-boats on the lower Mississippi; the bombardment of Fort McRae and the batteries at Pensacola; the passage of Forts Jackson and St. Philip, and the Chalmette batteries; the passage and re-passage of Vicksburg; the fight of the rebel ram *Arkansas* and the siege of Port Hudson.

"Upon his return North in 1863 he was promoted to the rank of chief engineer, and, his health having become impaired by his arduous duties in the Gulf squadron, he was assigned to duty as inspector of iron-clads and other steamers then building in Boston. In 1865, the Navy Department having determined to establish a department of steam engineering at the Naval Academy, ordered him to duty as senior assistant to Chief Engineer Wood, who was made head of that department. Subsequently, upon the detachment of Mr. Wood, Mr. Hoyt became head of the department, and occupied that position until his death.

"Mr. Hoyt was well fitted for the profession he had chosen, and both as assistant and head of department has been very largely instrumental in establishing and developing the engineering course at the Academy. Possessing no little mechanical talent, he had originated a number of useful devises, while his quick perception and generous appreciation of the labors of others lent valuable aid in bringing forward important improvements that might not otherwise have become known.

"He was a man of singular energy and industry, which, directed by a clear judgment, were always devoted to the interests of the service and the corps of which he was so prominent a member. The great desire of his later life seems to have been that the naval engineer corps should be permanently established in a prominent and acknowledged position as a body of scientific as well as thoroughly-trained practical engineers, and to that end no personal sacrifice seems to have been too great."

The examination of candidates for admission as cadet engineers in 1866 showed that the age limit of eighteen years fixed by the act of Congress providing for the system was not consistent with the other requirement that they must have had two years practical experience in the manufacture of steam machinery; this was presented to Congress by the the Secretary of the Navy in his report for the year 1866, and the law promptly modified by a section of an act to amend certain acts in relation to the navy, approved March 2, 1867, as follows:

"SEC. 2. *And be it further enacted*, That so much of the 'Act to authorize the Secretary of the Navy to provide for the education of naval constructors and steam engineers, and for other purposes,' approved July four, eighteen hundred and sixty-four, as provides that cadet engineers, when appointed, shall be under eighteen years of age, and shall have been employed at least two years in the actual fabrication of steam machinery, is hereby repealed."

The meagre results of the efforts to inaugurate the cadet-engineer system discouraged the authorities and after the graduation of the two cadets in 1868 the project was dropped for a time, and very likely would never have been revived had it not been for the efforts of Engineer-in-Chief King in 1870–'71. When Mr. King first proposed to Secretary Robeson that steps be taken to procure

CADET ENGINEERS IN UNDRESS UNIFORM.
The Every-day Dress of the Academy.

another class of cadet engineers he was met with a positive refusal: he then interested two senators in the matter and had them call on the Secretary in regard to it, their influence shaking his previous determination. When Mr. King broached the subject again, which was early in 1871, Mr. Robeson authorized him to prepare a new form of regulations for admission, which he immediately did; the proposed regulations were sent to Rear Admiral John L. Worden, the superintendent of the Naval Academy, for his opinion, and were approved by him after Mr. King had made a journey to Annapolis and urged the superintendent to aid him in re-establishing the course. The original approved copy of the paper was lost in some manner between the office of Rear Admiral Worden and that of Secretary Robeson, but Mr. King prepared another copy, obtained Worden's approving endorsement to it, and took it himself to the Secretary, when he had the satisfaction of seeing it signed and thus finally approved.

These regulations fixed the age for admission as cadet engineers at between eighteen and twenty-two, specified the manner of making application, the scope of the competitive examination, etc., and as soon as printed were sent by the Bureau of Steam Engineering to colleges and educational institutions all over the United States. Few applications were received in response to this circular, the reason for this, it is claimed, being that the officials at the colleges did not distribute the information for fear of losing students. Mr. King then appealed personally to senators and representatives in Congress to select boys and file applications for them, and in that manner about forty candidates were procured for the examination held in September of that year. From these a class of sixteen was selected by competition and admitted to the Academy as cadet engineers in October. The officers on duty at the Academy having changed in the intervening three years, the new class of cadets became experimental objects for the discovery of a course of study for them, with the result that only five passed into the senior class at the end of the academic year; two were found deficient and dropped, and nine were turned back, making, with seventeen who entered in 1872, a second class of twenty-six members. In October, 1873, sixteen more cadets were admitted, the first class then consisting of fourteen members and the second class of twenty-three, and the system of educating engineer cadets at the Naval Academy may be said to have been then well established.

By an act of Congress approved February 24, 1874, the academic course for cadet engineers was made four years instead of two, and another act, approved June 22, 1874, provided "that so much of the act entitled 'An act to authorize the Secretary of the Navy to provide for the education of naval constructors and steam-engineers, and for other purposes,' approved July 4, 1864, as provides that cadet engineers, not to exceed fifty in number, shall be appointed by the Secretary of the Navy, is hereby repealed; and cadet engineers shall hereafter be appointed annually by the Secretary of the Navy, and the number appointed each year shall not exceed twenty-five; and that all acts or parts of acts inconsistent with the provisions of this act be, and the same are hereby repealed."[1] These two laws went into effect with the class that entered the Academy in September, 1874, this being the first fourth-class of cadet engineers to become a part of the battalion of midshipmen. New regulations governing the appointment of cadet engineers, issued that same year, changed the limit of age for candidates to sixteen as the minimum and twenty as the maximum.

The cadet engineer system by this time had become well known and popular, and each succeeding year brought a greater number of candidates to the annual competitive examinations until it was not unusual for nearly two hundred alert and well-schooled youths from all sections of the country to compete for the twenty-five appointments each year. This made a system of selection that could not well be improved, although it involved disappointment to the great

---

[1] The following opinion as to this act of Congress is from the annual report of the admiral of the navy for the year 1881 and is interesting in connection with it:

"No doubt this law authorizing 25 cadets to be *annually* added to the engineer corps was passed through Congress unintentionally, for the law evidently intended that 50 should be the entire number, and the abuse has continued unchecked to the present time.

"While it was only intended that a few engineers should be annually admitted as cadets at the Academy to educate them for their profession, the Academy will become, if this system is adhered to, almost exclusively a school for steam-engineers, quite losing sight of its original purpose, viz., to educate navigators and commanders for the navy.

"I submit these remarks for your consideration, hoping that you may be able to arrive at some solution of a problem which threatens to work injury to the navy."

majority of those examined. As the number of candidates constantly increased, the Navy Department finally issued a warning to applicants in these terms: "Candidates for admission as cadet engineers are cautioned that the number of applicants is large, and the competition exceedingly close. It is, therefore, useless for candidates to present themselves unless well prepared on the subject of the examination, and unless their physical qualifications are within the prescribed standard." This warning may have deterred some who were conscious of deficient schooling from making the journey to Annapolis, but it also served to encourage the highly educated, and resulted in the admission of some each year who found little in the curriculum of the Academy, outside of the purely naval subjects, that was new to them, and who distinguished themselves in class-standing accordingly. It is a great pity that this system was eventually overturned.

The subjects for the competitive examination looked easy in the abstract to an average high-school boy, being stated in the circular as follows: "Arithmetic; algebra, through equations of the first degree; plane geometry; rudimentary natural philosophy; reading; writing; spelling; English grammar; English composition; geography; free-hand drawing; and an elementary knowledge of the principles governing the action of the steam-engine. Candidates who possess the greatest skill and experience in the practical knowledge of machinery, *other qualifications being equal*, will have precedence for admission." This last sounded well, but unfortunately had no meaning, as under the rigid system of marking examination papers it was practically impossible for two candidates to come out with the same marks, and the oral examination in steam was assigned such a low multiple in making up the aggregate marks that its weight was inappreciable.

Elementary as the examination appeared in the descriptive circular issued to candidates, it was far from being so when administered by the Academic Board. The result was that those who succeeded in getting appointments were the scholars,—often college graduates,—and any young man who had spent much time in gaining practical knowledge of machinery had no chance whatever with those who had never been diverted from their books, thus defeating one of the original provisions of the project. Of the classes that entered in 1874 and 1875 only one member of each is on record as having had any practical experience with machinery, while in the succeeding classes there was seldom even one.

A few questions taken from the examination papers of that time will show how far beyond the stated subjects the examining officers saw fit to go. In "algebra, through equations of the first degree" we find things like this,—

"Reduce $x^6 - 5x^5 + 4x^4 - 3x^3 + 2x^2 - x + 1$ to the form $Ax + B$ by means of the equation $x^2 = 2x - 3$."

"Rudimentary natural philosophy" was considered broad enough a subject to warrant this question: "Find the number of units of work expended in raising from the ground the materials for building a uniform column fifty feet in height and ten feet square, a cubic foot of the material weighing one hundred and twelve pounds. How high is the column when the work is half completed?" This was one of fifteen questions (and not the hardest one, either) given in an examination limited to three hours.

The spelling examination was an aggregation of orthographic horrors that would have struck terror to the soul of a professional philologist, and the sentences given out for grammatical analysis were simply unspeakable. In geography the uttermost parts of the earth were ransacked for strange names and unknown regions; the candidate was asked to "describe the Syr-Daria River, telling where it rises, in what direction it flows, and into what water it empties." He was asked to bound Servia and Roumania; to name the four provinces of Ireland, and to locate Cape Lopatka.

There were of course twenty-five candidates each year who weathered this ordeal better than the others and got the appointments; strange as it may seem, these twenty-five youths generally came out with very creditable marks in spite of the fact that the questions set them were far beyond what they had been notified to expect, and each class of these cadet engineers possessed one or more of those prodigies who, according to the pleasant fictions of the service, drove the esteemed heads of the various academic departments to despair, because the task of finding some new thing to teach them was a hopeless one. Be this as it may, it is a fact

Engineer Cadet-Officer, First, or Senior, class. The star on the collar was worn by a
few ranking members of each class as a mark of excellence in scholarship.
The stripes and double-diamond on the sleeve indicated cadet
rank corresponding to that of cadet captains of companies.

Cadet Engineer in "Parade Dress" Uniform.

"Service Dress" Uniform, worn by Cadet Engineers after graduation, while performing the two years' sea service prescribed.

that this system of selection, as it progressed from year to year, brought remarkably fine material into the Academy, and made it possible to build up at that institution a school of marine-engineering and kindred sciences that was admittedly not excelled in the United States at the time that the whole system was ruthlessly swept away.

In 1882, after the cadet-engineer system had been long enough established to become an important element in the academic organization, and when the course of instruction, both professionally as marine-engineers and generally as naval officers, had been developed until it was almost perfect, the whole thing was abolished by act of Congress, and the cadet-engineers then at the Academy were transformed into naval cadets of the line. The act referred to, which was approved August 5, 1882, provided that from and after that date "there shall be no appointments of cadet-midshipmen or cadet-engineers at the Naval Academy, but in lieu thereof naval cadets shall be appointed from each Congressional district and at large, as now provided by law for cadet-midshipmen, and all the undergraduates at the Naval Academy shall hereafter be designated and called 'naval cadets;' and from those who successfully complete the six years' course, appointments shall hereafter be made as it is necessary to fill vacancies in the lower grades of the line and engineer corps of the navy and of the marine corps: *And provided further*, That no greater number of appointments into these grades shall be made each year than shall equal the number of vacancies which has occurred in the same grades during the preceding year; such appointments to be made from the graduates of the year, at the conclusion of their six years' course, in the order of merit, as determined by the Academic Board of the Naval Academy; the assignment to the various corps to be made by the Secretary of the Navy upon the recommendation of the Academic Board. But nothing herein contained shall reduce the number of appointments from such graduates below ten in each year, nor deprive of such appointment any graduate who may complete the six years' course during the year eighteen hundred and eighty-two. And if there be a surplus of graduates, those who do not receive such appointment shall be given a certificate of graduation, an honorable discharge, and one year's sea pay, as now provided by law for cadet-midshipmen; and so much of section fifteen hundred and twenty-one of the Revised Statutes as is inconsistent herewith is hereby repealed.

"That any cadet whose position in his class entitles him to be retained in the service may, upon his own application, be honorably discharged at the end of the four years' course at the Naval Academy, with a proper certificate of graduation."

The standing taken by the cadet engineers transferred into the classes of midshipmen shows well the superior nature of the method by which they had been selected. A year after the exchange was made we find that seven of the first ten members of the graduating class were former cadet engineers, and four of the six "stars" of that class were engineers, although the first two members had been midshipmen: it must be remembered that the engineers of this class were seriously handicapped by going into the first class to compete in technical studies with the midshipmen who had had at least one year's study in such subjects before, and which the cadet engineers had to make up in addition to the regular work. In the next class the three leading members were former cadet engineers, the first one having a multiple fifteen units above the highest midshipman, and this same cadet engineer became the next year the "four-striper," as the cadet who commands the battalion is called in academic language. In the third class after the amalgamation took place, and in which class the cadet engineers were on an equal footing with the midshipmen, as their previous year's studies had been practically identical, we find that thirteen of the first fifteen members, nine of the first ten, and all six of the "stars" were former engineers, and one of these cadet engineers also became in turn the commander of the battalion of cadets.

For seven years following 1882 the few vacancies that occurred in the engineer corps were filled by the promotion of cadets who had been educated as line officers only; since 1889 the cadets destined for the engineer corps have had the last year of the academic course partially devoted to engineering subjects, and a little more attention is now being given to the mechanical education of the line cadets, although the older art of seamanship still retains a prominent place in the curriculum of the school. All cadets now receive during their third year (when second-classmen) theoretical and practical instruction in steam engineering about equal to that formerly given to cadet engineers of the second class, the shop-work now given being if anything an improvement upon that form of instruction under the former system. In the last, or first-class year, that portion of the class that has been selected for future admission into the engineer corps is withdrawn from the technical studies of seamanship, ordnance, and navigation, and the time thus obtained devoted to marine engines, higher mathematics, and other subjects having an affinity with the profession of engineering. It remains to be seen whether or not the present practice will inculcate that love of mechanical science produced by the cadet-engineer system, and which put forth graduates who as ship and engine designers in the recent work of rebuilding our navy have reflected great credit upon the navy, the corps to which they belong, and the system of education under which they were trained.

The law governing the present system of dividing the classes at the Academy was created by a special act of Congress, approved March 2, 1889, and entitled "An act to regulate the course at the Naval Academy." It reads in full as follows:

"That the Academic Board of the Naval Academy shall on or before the thirtieth day of September in each year separate the first class of naval cadets then commencing their fourth year into two divisions, as they may have shown special aptitude for the duties of the respective corps, in the proportion which the aggregate number of vacancies occurring in the preceding fiscal year ending on the thirtieth day of June in the lowest grades of commissioned officers of the line of the navy and marine corps of the navy shall bear to the number of vacancies to be supplied from the Academy occurring during the same period in the lowest grade of commissioned officers of the engineer corps of the navy; and the cadets so assigned to the line and marine corps division of the first class shall thereafter pursue a course of study arranged to fit them for service in the line of the navy, and the cadets so assigned to the engineer corps division of the first class shall thereafter pursue a separate course of study arranged to fit them for service in the engineer corps of the navy, and the cadets shall thereafter, and until final graduation at the end of their six years' course, take rank by merit with those in the same division, according to the merit marks; and from the final graduates of the line and marine corps division, at the end of their six years' course, appointments shall be made hereafter as it shall be neccessary to fill vacancies in the lowest grades of commissioned officers of the line of the navy and marine corps; and the vacancies in the lowest grades of the commissioned officers of the engineer corps of the navy shall be filled in like manner by appointments from the final graduates of the engineer division at the end of their six years' course: *Provided*, That no greater number of appointments into the said lowest grades of commissioned officers shall be made each year than shall equal the number of vacancies which shall have occurred in the same grades during the fiscal year then current; such appointments to be made from the final graduates of the year, in the order of merit as determined by the Academic Board of the Naval Academy, the assignment to be made by the Secretary of the Navy upon the recommendation of the Academic Board at the conclusion of the fiscal year then current; but nothing contained herein or in the naval appropriation act of August fifth, eighteen hundred and eighty-two, shall reduce the number of appointments of final graduates at the end of their six years' course below twelve in each year to the line of the navy, and not less than two shall be appointed annually to the engineer corps of the navy, nor less than one annually to the marine corps; and if the number of vacancies in the lowest grades aforesaid, occurring in any year shall be greater than the number of final graduates of that year, the surplus vacancies shall be filled from the final graduates of following years as they shall become available.

"That after the fourth day of March, eighteen hundred and eighty-nine, the minimum age of admission of cadets to the Academy shall be fifteen years and the maximum age twenty years."

CHAPTER XXXIV.

"The Arctic Ocean has been for years the nursery of heroic deeds. And had the results of enterprise been even less than they have been in that region of frost and ice, and months-long night, what has been shown there of that which is noblest and most admirable in man would have been worth all that it has cost." —*Rev.* W. L. GAGE.

Steam Vessels of the United States Navy in the Arctic Ocean—The POLARIS Expedition—Cruise of the JUNIATA and TIGRESS—The JEANNETTE Expedition—Retreat on the Ice—Heroism and Fortitude of Chief Engineer Melville—Voyage and Loss of the RODGERS—Naval and Congressional Investigations Into the Loss of the JEANNETTE—The Greely Relief Expedition—Tardy Promotion of Chief Engineer Melville for Heroism Displayed in the JEANNETTE Expidition.

AN ACT of Congress approved July 12, 1870, authorized the President of the United States "to organize and send out one or more expeditions towards the North Pole, and to appoint such person, or persons as he may deem most fitted to the command thereof; to detail any officer of the public service to take part in the same, and to use any public vessel that may be suitable for the purpose; the scientific operations of the expedition to be prescribed in in accordance with the advice of the National Academy of Sciences." Several officers of the navy volunteered to go, but as finally oganized the expedition was composed wholly of civilians and therefore cannot be regarded as a naval undertaking except to the extent that the vessel employed was taken from the navy. The commander was Mr. Charles F. Hall, a traveler of much arctic experience, and the three officers next in rank were practical seamen who as masters or mates of whaling and sealing vessels had grown familiar with the northern seas. The chief engineer was a German named Schuman, a civil engineer by profession, and the only assistant engineer was Mr. Alvin A. Odell of New London, indirectly a naval man from having been an acting third assistant engineer during the war and honorably discharged at its close.

The vessel selected for the expedition was the *Periwinkle*, a screw-steamer purchased in 1864 for $80,000, under the name of

America, and used as a gun-boat in the Civil War. She was strengthened and fitted for the voyage at the Washington navy yard, her name changed to *Polaris*, and early in July, 1871, set out on her venturesome journey. She was 135 feet long, 28 feet beam, and when loaded with stores for the exploring trip drew nearly 12 feet of water. The large screw-sloop *Congress* was detailed to carry coal and stores for the *Polaris* and proceeded as far north as Godhavn in the island of Disco, on the west coast of Greenland, she being by far the largest ship that had ever visited that port. The transfer of supplies being effected at Godhavn, the *Polaris* on the 17th of August, 1871, took her departure for the polar regions, being cheered as she got under way by the crew of the *Congress*.

From that time no tidings were received from the expedition until in May, 1873, when a telegram from the United States consul at St. John's, Newfoundland, announced that ten of the people of the *Polaris* had been brought to that port by the sealing steamer *Tigress*, which had found them adrift on the ice in Baffin's Bay. The United States steamer *Frolic* was at once despatched to St. John's and took these survivors to Washington. They knew nothing of the *Polaris* or of their shipmates, from whom they had been separated in October, 1872, by the breaking up of the ice and had been floating about on the ice since that time until rescued by the *Tigress*, a period of one hundred and eighty-seven days. Immediate preparations were made to seek for the *Polaris* and her crew: the *Tigress*, as a vessel built for ice navigation, was chartered and commissioned at New York under the command of Commander James A. Greer, proceeding to the arctic regions in July with orders to go where the *Polaris* was last seen and make every effort to find her people. The sloop-of-war *Juniata* was also sent north to carry supplies for the *Tigress* and assist in the search as far as was prudent for a vessel not built for arctic navigation.

She went as far as Upernavik on the west coast of Greenland about 250 miles north of Godhavn, whence she supplied the *Tigress*, and from which point her steam launch, named *Little Juniata*, made a most extraordinary voyage of ten days to the northward in search of signs of the *Polaris*. Two of the lieutenants of the *Juniata* who went on this boat expedition were George W. De Long and Charles W. Chipp, both fated to end their lives in the arctic regions at a later period. The chief engineer of the *Tigress* was First Assistant Engineer George W. Melville, and Lieutenant Robert M. Berry was a watch-officer in the same ship, both whom have since become distinguished for arctic deeds.

The search of the *Tigress* was not successful for the reason that the people of the *Polaris* had been rescued by other means. Their ship was crushed in the ice the day after the unfortunate portion of the crew had been carried away on the ice-floe, and the remainder of the crew had remained in camp by the wreck until the next spring when they built two boats from the ship's timbers and made their way southward until picked up by a whaling steamer off Cape York. Mr. Hall, the commander of the expedition, had died of apoplexy a short time before the disaster to the *Polaris*, but with that exception the whole ship's company survived their trying adventures. The *Tigress* got as far north as the highest point reached by Dr. Kane's expedition, her success in this particular being, according to Commander Greer's reports, largely due to the energy and skill of Mr. Melville who kept the machinery in running order under many disadvantages.

While the *Juniata* was at Godhavn Mr. Henry E. Rhoades, second assistant engineer of that vessel, was sent on an expedition with the steam launch about ninety miles to examine some coal mines on the island of Disco. He found coal in abundance and with the boat's crew aided by natives mined a quantity of it for the use of his ship, storing it at a convenient place on the beach. On the return voyage of the steam launch Mr. Rhoades made use of this coal to keep up steam, carefully observing and noting its qualities, his observations being subsequently embodied in a report which was regarded as such an addition to the subject that it was printed in full in report of the Secretary of the Navy for that year (1873).

In 1879 another arctic expedition under government auspices left the United States, it having been brought about through the liberality and public spirit of Mr. James Gordon Bennett, proprietor of the *New York Herald*. In this case the route selected was by way of Behring Straits, on the theory that less ice than elsewhere would be found in that region on account of the Kuro Siwo, or black stream of Japan, dividing and discharging some of its warm waters up through the straits. No polar expedition had ever gone by this route before, though its supposed advantages were recognized and an expedition several years before, under the command of a French lieutenant, would have gone that way but for the outbreak of the Franco-Prussian War.

Mr. Bennett employed Lieutenant De Long of the navy to examine vessels fit for arctic service in different ports in Europe and to purchase the one that in his judgment was most serviceable, the result of De Long's work being the purchase from Sir Allen Young of London of the steamer *Pandora* in which the owner had made two or three voyages to the arctic regions. She had originally been a gun-boat in the British navy and had been purchased by Sir Allen Young to enable him to gratify his taste for arctic adventure. She was 142 feet in length, 25 feet beam and drew about 13 feet when fully equipped for service. Mr. Bennett changed her name to *Jeannette*, though the name *Pandora* might very appropriately have been retained, for a veritable box of evils she proved to be for those who embarked in her. Commanded by Lieutenant De Long, the *Jeannette* proceeded from Havre to San Francisco during the summer and fall of 1888.

Congress had already passed an act in aid of the proposed expedition, reading as follows:

"Whereas James Gordon Bennett, a citizen of the United States, has purchased in Great Britain a vessel supposed to be specially adapted to arctic expeditions, and proposes, at his own cost, to fit out and man said vessel, and to devote her to efforts to solve the Polar problem; and

"Whereas it is deemed desirable that said vessel, while so engaged, shall carry the American flag and be officered by American naval officers: Therefore,

"*Be it enacted by the Senate and House of Representatives of the United States of America in Congress assembled*, That the Secretary of the Treasury be authorized to issue an American register to said vessel by the name of "Jeannette," and that the President of the United States be authorized to detail, with their own consent, commissioned, warrant, and petty officers of the navy, not to exceed ten in number, to act as officers of said vessel during her first voyage to the Arctic seas: *Provided, however,* That such detail shall be made of such officers only as the President is satisfied can be absent from their regular duties without detriment to the public service.

"Approved, March 18, 1878."

About a year later another act, approved February 27, 1879, authorized the Secretary of the Navy to accept and take charge of the *Jeannette;* to use public material in fitting her for arctic service; to ship her crew for special service and pay them from the naval pay fund, the same to be refunded by Mr. Bennett if required. The act also specified that the expedition should be carried out under the auspices and orders of the Navy Department, and that the men enlisted for it should be subject in all respects to the Articles of War and the Navy Regulations.

At the navy yard at Mare Island, California, the *Jeannette* was thoroughly fitted out for her voyage, receiving new boilers, and being strengthened by a system of heavy internal bracing to withstand the the pressure of ice. Finally with ample provisions for a long cruise and all the clothing, equipment and paraphernalia for a long sojourn in the cold, she sailed from San Francisco on the 8th of July, 1879, her officers being the following:

Lieutenant George W. De Long, U. S. N.............................Commanding.[1]
Lieutenant Charles W. Chipp,   "   ....Executive.
Master John W. Danenhower,   "   ....Navigator [2]
Passed Assistant Engineer George W. Melville, U. S. N.......Chief Engineer.[3]
Passed Assistant Surgeon James M. Ambler,   "   ....Surgeon.
Mr. Jerome J. Collins, (civilian)...Meteorologist,
Mr. Raymond L. Newcomb, (civilian)................................Naturalist.
Mr. William Dunbar, (civilian)..Ice Pilot.

The three civilians named were shipped as seamen to satisfy the terms of the act of Congress authorizing the enlistment of the crew, but were in all respects treated as officers, officially, socially, and in all ways. Besides those named, the crew consisted of twenty-four persons, all picked men as to physique, and many of

---

[1] Promoted to be Lieutenant commander, November 1, 1879.
[2] Promoted to be Lieutenant, August 2, 1879.
[3] Promoted to be Chief Engineer, March 4, 1881.

them of previous arctic service. The experience of one of these men, Wm. F. C. Nindemann, rated as Ice Quartermaster, is worthy of remark: He had been one of the crew of the *Polaris* and was one of the party drifted away from that ship and subjected to the memorable six months' hardship of the long drift on the ice-floe; when rescued and taken into St. John's he had not had enough of the polar regions and promptly volunteered to go in the search party with Commander Greer in the *Tigress*, his knowledge being found of much value on that expedition. Now we find him embarking on another attempt to penetrate the frozen zone, and it may be remarked that his services were so valuable that he was one of two enlisted men recommended by De Long for medals of honor.

On the second of August the *Jeannette* was at Ounalaska, where a quantity of deer skins, seal-skin blankets and other furs were procured. Thence she proceeded to the old Russian trading post of St. Michael's, in Norton Sound, where two Indian hunters were engaged and where the schooner *Fanny A. Hyde*, previously chartered to carry a cargo of coal, was met. With the schooner in company the *Jeannette* crossed over to a harbor just below the East Cape of Asia, transferred there the coal and some other supplies and then, on the 27th of August, turned away from the land of the living, passed through Behring Straits, and stood up into the cold and whiteness of the undiscovered northland. The wanderings of the *Jeannette* for nearly two years after the date we have reached have been fully and pathetically told in other books, for which reason the subject will be passed over quickly. Drifting ice and stormy weather were encountered from the first, and on the eighth day of September, 1879, less than two weeks after entering the Arctic Ocean, she became solidly frozen in the pack ice and never again escaped from it. For twenty-one months the luckless ship was carried hither and thither by the drifting ice, sometimes returning to positions that had been observed months before: the summer of 1880 brought no release from the grip of the ice as had been devotedly hoped for, and the wretched people ultimately had the sorrow of seeing the brief sunshine fade away and another long and silent arctic winter set in. When summer came again the ice finally opened alongside the *Jeannette*, then about five hundred miles to the northwest of where she had been first caught, and for a brief hour she was afloat; but the great masses of ice closed in on her with the power of a million gigantic vises and so crushed her sides that all possibility of ever floating in her again vanished, and the people had to abandon her with their sleds, boats, tents, provisions and some clothing, forming a camp on the ice near by. That was the eleventh day of June, 1881. About four o'clock the next morning the camp was aroused by the man on watch crying, "Turn out if you want to see the last of the *Jeannette*. There she goes! There she goes!"

"Most of us had barely time to arise and look out, when, amid the rattling and banging of her timbers and iron-work, the ship righted and stood almost upright; the floes that had come in and crushed her slowly backed off, and as she sank with slightly accelerated velocity, the yard-arms were stripped and broken upward parallel to the masts; and so, like a great, gaunt skeleton clapping its hands above its head, she plunged out of sight."[1]

After this disaster about one week was spent in allowing some of the men to recuperate from illness and in preparing for the effort to reach land, and then this devoted party set out on what is probably the most painful and remarkable march ever performed by men. With their sleds, boats, and all equipage they started toilsomely toward the Siberian coast across the broken and irregular ice floes, dragging their impediments over hummocks, through running ice and half-melted snow, piece by piece, the conditions of the march compelling them sometimes to travel back and forth as many as thirteen times over one stage of the journey in order to transport all the baggage to the advanced point. To save the men's eyes as much as possible from the glare of the sunshine on the ice and snow, the marching was done during that portion of the twenty-four hours that in another latitude would have been night, though here the men had to face the sullen blaze of the red midnight sun. The rough ice cut out moccasins and foot-gear obliging the men to toil almost barefooted, while the unevenness of the surface and the many unseen pools and streams of water under slush and snow caused so many falls and wettings that it was a usual spectacle to see half the party at a time stripped stark naked on the ice wringing out

---

[1] Chief Engineer G. W. Melville, U. S. Navy,—"In the Lena Delta," p. 32.

their clothing. It is almost past belief that men can withstand such hardship, but these men did, sleeping on the ice and in the snow for three months without serious illness or evil results.

After two weeks of this frightful toil De Long found by an observation that they had actually retrogressed twenty-four miles instead of making any distance to the southward, this being due to the fact that the whole vast ice field was afloat and had been drifting to the northward faster than the outcasts could make good their route in the other direction. He told only Chipp and Melville of this, rightly considering that the leaders of the working parties were sufficient to know it without adding the discouraging news to the troubles of the weary men. And here it will be well to speak of the invaluable qualities displayed by Chief Engineer Melville during all the discouraging events of a very discouraging voyage. A man of oaken constitution, indomitable will, and truly magnificent courage both moral and physical, he soon proved himself to be by far the most valuable helper that De Long had, and this without disparagement of the other officers, each of whom was a picked man, and resourceful to an unusual degree. De Long's journals abound in complimentary references to the skill and ability of the chief engineer and record with sketches and descriptions a great number of mechanical contrivances and make-shifts devised by Melville to meet emergencies ; there being in fact so much of this that De Long himself remarked that his journal "looked more like an engineer's notebook than a seaman's log."

Illustrative of Melville's dauntless nature and courage in adversity is the fact that during the second winter in the ice-pack, when the hearts of many of his associates were sick with deferred hope and when despair of ever again participating in the affairs of the world had reduced several of them to a condition of hebetude, he rose superior to the surrounding lethargy and employed his spare time in preparing plans and specifications for a steamship for arctic exploration, making all the drawings and describing all the structural details with as great care as though half a dozen shipyards were available to compete for a contract to build the vessel. These plans and specifications were preserved among De Long's papers and are described with reproductions of some of the drawings in

Mrs. De Long's "Voyage of the Jeannette." Perhaps the party that some day will see the North Pole will journey there in a ship whose designs were born of captivity in the midst of the frozen ocean.

A few extracts from De Long's journals are worth repeating as indicative of the qualities of Mr. Melville as an officer, engineer and man, as those qualities were impressed upon the mind of his commanding officer.

"Melville is as bright as a dollar and as cheerful as possible all the time. He sits on my left at table and helps me to carve and serve out. We broke a pump-rod two days ago. Some engineers would have wanted to stop the ship a few days for this, or perhaps turn back. Not he; he says 'all right; we will run without a pump-rod, hey brother, and when we get in I will make you a new pump-rod or fifty of them.' I believe he could make an engine out of a few barrel hoops if he tried hard. He is one of the strong points of this expedition."

"Melville is more and more a treasure every day. He is not only without a superior as an engineer, but he is bright and cheerful to an extraordinary extent. He sings well, is always contented, and brightens everybody by his presence alone. He is always self-helpful and reliant, never worries about the future, is ready for any emergency, has a cheerful word for everybody night and morning, and is, in fine, a tower of strength in himself."

"Still everything is done quietly and with precision, and aided by Chipp and Melville, whose superiors the navy cannot show, with their untiring energy, splendid judgment, and fertility of device, I am confident of being able to do all that man can do to carry on the expedition to a safe termination."

"I have decided to send a party to try to make a landing on Henrietta Island. . . . Having but one commissioned officer available, Melville, he must take charge of the party. . . . Consequently I make out orders for Mr. Melville to go in command, and to take Mr. Dunbar, Nindemann, Ericksen, Bartlett, and Sharvell with him, and to start to-morrow morning. . . .

"The party landed on the island on Thursday, June 2d (Friday, June 3d), hoisted our silk flag, took possession of the island in the name of the Great Jehovah and the United States of America, and, agreeably to my orders, named it Henrietta Island. . . . The ice between the ship and the island is something frightful. Road-digging, ferrying, and its attendant loading and unloading, arm-breaking hauls, and panic-stricken dogs made the journey a terribly severe one. Near the island the ice was all alive, and Melville left his boat and supplies, and carrying only a day's provisions and his instruments, at the risk of his life went through the terrible mass, actually dragging the dogs, which from fear refused to follow their human leaders. If this persistence in landing upon this island, in spite of the superhuman difficulties he encountered, is not reckoned a brave and meritorious action, it will not be from any failure on my part to make it known."

After nearly a month of toiling over the ice the crew of the lost *Jeannette* arrived on Bennett Island and remained there several days repairing their boats and making other preparations for a journey by water, for the ice was now sufficiently open to make this possible. The party left Bennett Island in three boats, De Long commanding the 1st cutter, Chipp the 2d, and Melville the whaleboat, Lieutenant Danenhower, Mr. Newcomb, the naturalist, and eight men being embarked in the latter. Though a staff officer and therefore not allowed by law a right to exercise command of any description, even over the men of his own department for whose conduct and performance of duty he was responsible, Mr. Melville was regularly in command of the whale-boat by De Long's orders. This came about through the physical disability of Lieutenant Danenhower, whose eyes had broken down, and there being no other line officer in the party with a right to command, Lieutenant Commander De Long selected Melville as the most competent other person and gave him this order in writing:

"U. S. Arctic Expedition.
" Cape Emma, Bennett Island,
" Lat. 76° 38′ N.,
" Long. 148° 20′ E.
" August 5th, 1881.
"*P. A. Engineer Geo. W. Melville, U. S. Navy:*
" Sir,—We shall leave this island to-morrow, steering a course

(over ice or through water, as the case may be) south magnetic. In the event of our embarking in our boats at any time after the start, you are hereby ordered to take command of the whale-boat until such time as I relieve you from that duty, or assign you to some other.

"Every person under my command at this time, who may be embarked in that boat at any time, is under your charge, and subject to your orders, and you are to exercise all care and diligence for their preservation and the safety of the boat. You will, under all circumstances, keep close to the boat in which I shall embark, but if, unfortunately, we become separated, you will make the best of your way south until you make the coast of Siberia, and follow it along to the westward as far as the Lena River. This river is the destination of our party, and without delay you will, in case of separation, ascend the Lena to a Russian settlement from which you can communicate, or be forwarded with your party to some place of security and easy access. If the boat in which I am embarked is separated from the other two boats, you will at once place yourself under the orders of Lieut. C. W. Chipp, and, so long as you remain in company, obey such orders as he may give you.

"Respectfully,
"GEORGE W. DE LONG,
"Commanding U. S. Arctic Expedition."

After perils and adventures sufficient to fill a book in the telling the three boats finally arrived at Simonoski Island only ninety miles north-east of the Asiatic mainland. On the morning of September 12th, 1881, they sailed thence with every reason for believing that their troubles were nearly over: the sea was open; the wind fair, and Cape Barkin on the Lena Delta, where they expected to find natives and food, less than one day's sail away. But the wind freshened and increased to a gale, constantly flooding the boats with icy water, and drove them far apart. Chipp's boat capsized and all in it were lost. After being hove to for a considerable time in the gale and enduring the most terrible suffering the other two boats reached the mainland, De Long on the north shore of the delta and Melville on the east coast some two hundred miles away. Leaving to the proper chroniclers the unhappy task of telling of De Long's fate, it will suffice here to say that by the time the landing was effected the winter season was so far advanced that wild game had gone from the northern part of the delta and the few natives who roam over that region had also mostly gone to the southward. After about six weeks of wandering about pitifully in quest of human beings and food this boat's crew, with the exception of two men sent ahead looking for help, perished miserably of cold and starvation.

Melville landed about a week later than De Long and so much further to the southward that he found natives, of whose assistance he was in sore need, for his party was in frightful condition with frozen hands, feet and faces, without proper clothing, and almost without food. They were sheltered in a village called Jamavaeloch inhabited by a few families of squalid Yakuts subsisting upon frozen fish, and received kindly treatment from them so far as their resources extended. Mr. Melville, despite his crippled condition, used every effort to induce these natives to assist his party to Belun, about 180 miles distant, where there was known to be a Russian outpost, but the journey was for some time impossible on account of the broken condition of the ice in the river over which a considerable part of the route lay. By the offer of a large reward Melville finally induced a Russian exile to make the journey, after the exile had refused to go with him as a guide. Fifteen days later when this man returned to Jamavaeloch he brought information that he had met on his return some natives conveying towards Belun two American sailors, as well as a promise from the Cossack commandant at Belun to extend succor to the shipwrecked people as soon as possible. The two sailors had written a note and entrusted it to the exile, saying that a search party with food and clothing was wanted to go to the assistance of Lieutenant Commander De Long, Dr. Ambler, and nine other men who were stated to be in a starving condition to the northward.

This note was delivered to Mr. Melville the evening of October 29th, and was the first intimation he had that the first cutter had reached land. That night he forced the natives to go to a neighboring village for dogs and the next morning he set out by dog sled for Belun to see the two sailors and learn from them the particulars of the landing and condition of De Long's party.

At Belun he found the men to be the faithful Nindemann and a seaman named Noros, both in a terribly exhausted and debilitated condition as the result of the hardships from which they had barely escaped with their lives. After arranging with the priest of the village to see that the two men were cared for, Melville retraced his steps as far as the station called Burulach, where, by a written agreement sent by Bartlett, a fireman belonging to his party, he met the Cossack commandant returning from Jamavaeloch with the remainder of the whale-boat's crew. Here he obtained by aid of the Cossack, dogs, sleds, and provisions for a journey to the north of the Delta, and gave Lieutenant Danenhower orders to take all the party but Bartlett as far south as Yakutsk. Bartlett he ordered to remain at Belun for thirty days, and then if he (Melville) had not returned to collect provisions, get together a team of dogs, and go in search of him. Having attended to all these matters, Melville with two natives, two dog-sleds and a small quantity of frozen fish for food for the dogs and himself set his face to the northward to search for his missing commander and shipmates. This on the 5th day of November, 1881.

On that day and in that remote and forbidding region occurred the most magnificent example of genuine heroism that this nineteenth century has seen, for the action of Chief Engineer G. W. Melville just described is entitled to that distinction. To comprehend exactly what he did it is necessary to mentally review the events of his life that had immediately preceded: the farewell to the sights and sounds of civilization more than two years before; the twenty-one months of helpless drifting in the grasp of the ice, when hope of ever seeing native land and home again must sometimes have left the stoutest hearts; the fearful march over the ice; the hardships and perils of the boat journey; the storm, and bitter disappointment when almost within touch of rescue; the separation; the loss of companions, and the final escape, frozen and half-dead from the clutches of the Polar Ocean, had all been his lot. Having passed through all this, it was his natural right, impelled by the instinct of self-preservation, to venture no more, but to save his life as something he had well earned.

To the southward toward Yakutsk whither he had ordered

Danenhower to proceed, a warmer sun was shining, and there lay the great Russian road leading to the borders of civilization; to the railway; to the blue sea; to home. Few men after passing through all the perils that Melville had survived would have thrown away that seeming last chance of personal safety, but he, being cast in a rare heroic mould, turned his back upon the means of saving himself and set his rugged face to the northward, forcing his way into the darkness and awful silence of the arctic winter like one deliberately invading the dominions of death. The cold was intense; the obstacles to progress almost insurmountable; the food supply gave out; the two natives became frightened and discouraged, refusing to go further into the dreary waste until actually clubbed by the indomitable American into awed obedience; even the dogs, inured to the climate as they were, became seized with terror and crouched down whining in the snow afraid to go further. But all this did not daunt the spirit of the leader: by entreaty; by threats, and by resorting to force at times, he kept his little band in motion, sleeping in abandoned fishing huts drifted full of snow and subsisting upon fish heads and other offal found in the scrap heaps left from the last season's fishing, until his object was attained and at the northernmost point of the delta he stood upon the waste shore of the Arctic Ocean.

There he found the spot where De Long had landed, and near by a cache from which he recovered the log-books of the *Jeannette*, some nautical and surgical instruments, and some specimens from Bennett Island, left there because De Long's people could carry them no longer. With these and with a meagre supply of fish obtained from the natives in some huts called North Belun, he returned through the delta searching for De Long until the trail was hopelessly lost because of the winter changes in the face of nature. Then, his supply of fish being again exhausted and his men and dogs in despair of their lives, he made his way back to Belun, having penetrated the bitter night nearly three hundred miles directly north, his course going and coming by the devious paths necessarily followed being more than eleven hundred miles, and returned to tell the tale; something that no white man had ever done before, and no native ever attempted at that season of the year except when spurred by dire necessity. The Skalds of old Norway would have delighted in this story as a subject for epic song.

Melville arrived at Belun November 27th, where he might well have rested from his terrible journey, but to one of his temperament there was no rest so long as work remained to be done. Feeling the need of seeing the governor of the district in person to get authority to draw upon the people of the delta for help and supplies in prosecuting the search and also being desirous of communicating with his own government, he collected reindeer teams and provisions and on the first day of December set out for Yakutsk, six hundred miles distant, over a mountain range on which he more than once slept under the white stars with the temperature seventy degrees below the freezing point. After a short sojourn at the large village of Verkeransk, where in his narrative Melville says he got the first good dinner he had eaten since leaving San Francisco, he arrived at Yakutsk December 30th, where he was royally received by General Tschernaieff, the governor, and found Danenhower and party comfortably quartered. Here a few days afterward he received telegrams in reply to others sent by him by courier soon after his landing at Jamavaeloch, the most important one reading:

"MELVILLE, *Engineer*, *U. S. Navy*, *Irkutsk:*

"Omit no effort, spare no expense, in securing safety of men in second cutter. Let the sick and the frozen of those already rescued have every attention, and, as soon as practicable, have them transferred to milder climate. Department will supply necessary funds.
"HUNT, *Secretary.*"

This and other telegrams had been brought by horse-sled more than two thousand miles over the snow from Irkutsk and arrived at Yakutsk just in time to prevent the undaunted and tireless Melville from undertaking that long journey to get at the end of a telegraph wire. He immediately arranged for the use of money in abundance and gave Danenhower orders to proceed with the men to Irkutsk and thence home, keeping with himself however the two best men, Bartlett and Nindemann, to aid in the search for De Long on the delta. With the aid and advice of General Tschernaieff, sleds, utensils, provisions, and all necessities for a stay of six months in the north were collected, not omitting many useful articles to be given to the natives who had played the Good Samaritan to the miserable boat's crew when cast up by the frozen ocean, and on the 27th of January, 1882, Melville again turned to the northward, this time with a considerable party of followers and a large provision train.

The frightful journey in snow and cold over the mountains; the winter desolation found at Belun and vicinity, and the difficulty of procuring fish for dog food are all details of delay that may be passed over. At last all obstacles were overcome and by the first week in March Melville was again in that part of the delta where he knew De Long's party should be, and with depots of supplies established was already prosecuting the search, leading one party himself and keeping others on the move under command of Nindemann and Bartlett. By that time nearly all the men, women, children and dogs on the delta had become followers of him, partly because the governor of the province had sent orders by the spravnik of the district to lend every aid in forwarding the search, and partly because Melville had collected almost all the food of the region and stored it in his depots. Facing the furious gales and drifting snow the parties tramped back and forth for about two weeks without result, until on March 23d, Melville, alone at the time except for the presence of a Yakut carrying his compass, came upon three black objects partly buried in the snow, which proved to be the bodies of De Long, Dr. Ambler, and Ah Sam, the Chinese cook. To quote from Melville's own narrative:

"I identified De Long at a glance by his coat. He lay on his right side, with his right hand under his cheek, his head pointing north, and his face turned to the west. His feet were drawn slightly up as though he were sleeping; his left arm was raised with the elbow bent, and his hand, thus horizontally lifted, was bare. About four feet back of him, or toward the east, I found his small note-book or ice-journal, where he had tossed it with his left hand, which looked as though it had never recovered from the act, but had frozen as I found it, upraised."

The bodies of the others were found in the immediate vicinity soon after, and also journals, books, and records relating to the

"FOUND."

(Published by permission from a copyrighted photograph by Mr. E. N. Hart, of Brooklyn, from the famous painting by Operti, exhibited at the World's Columbian Exposition).

voyage, now over. Here, then, was the end of the expedition of the *Jeannette* which had started forth with such lofty hopes and now found its conclusion, not unlike that of other attempts to solve the mystery of the awful North. Some of the brave company were now miserably trailing their way to the southward with the sole desire of finding home; others had been swallowed by the pitiless Arctic Ocean, and here were the remainder, buried in the snow and beaten by the elements, while dumb in a bundle of rags was the leader, the frigid marble of his face, for five months hardened by the blasts of the northern winter, proof against the keen tooth of the arctic fox or prowling wolf. An eloquent object-lesson. Yet the man who saw all this at his feet, and whose cultivated mind did not fail to perceive the moral behind it, was so endowed with that aggressive spirit that never admits defeat that as soon as he was well restored to his own country and the comforts of civilization he offered to lead another expedition, confident of being victorious over all the demoniac powers of the North.

From the timbers of an old flat boat, drifted down the Lena River, two thousand miles or more by the spring floods and left stranded in the delta years before, Melville built a huge box or coffin for his dead, and from a spar of heavy driftwood he fashioned a rude cross upon which the names of the unfortunates were deeply carved. These with infinite toil and with the assistance of all the natives and dogs on the delta, were dragged some twenty miles to the summit of a great rock, the highest point in all that weary land, and there he buried his comrades, erecting over their grave the cross and a pyramid of stones as a monument which he thought and hoped would last for all time. Afterward, by Congressional approval, the bodies were removed and brought home. The cairn tomb erected by Melville has, by means of voluntary contributions of the officers of the navy, been reproduced in granite and marble and stands on the bank of the Severn River, overlooking the beautiful grounds of the United States Naval Academy at Annapolis.

The last duty to his comrades done, Melville turned again to his stern labors. Heading one party himself and sending out others under Bartlett and Nindemann every foot of the dreary coast of the delta and the Bay of Borkhia as far eastward as Oceansk was tramped over in search for traces of Chipp and the second cutter's crew, but nothing whatever was found; nor did Melville expect to find anything, for the evidence of his own eyes made it certain that that unfortunate party had perished the night the boats were separated in the storm, Still, he felt it a duty to leave nothing undone to remove harrowing doubt and uncertainty from the minds of relatives and friends of the missing men. About the first of May Mr. Melville realized that he could do no more and determined to leave the scene of his long labors. So thoroughly had he scoured the whole delta region that he had, to use the words of his official report to the Navy Department, "exhausted all the dogs and had used so many fish that the natives in some places were almost in a starving condition; but I paid for the use of the dogs and for the fish at the regular rates in cash or trade, and had the approval of the spravnik of the district."

Mr. Melville, after a most tiresome journey of over three thousand miles, partly overland through snow and floods and partly in wretched boats on the river, arrived at Irkutsk, the capital city of Siberia, on the fifth day of July, 1882. From there he telegraphed his arrival to the Secretary of the Navy, and received a telegram in return authorizing him to return to the United States with the men of his party. At St. Petersburg he, with Lieutenant R. M. Berry of the American navy and two of the seamen, was presented to the Czar and most kindly received by him, and throughout the whole journey he was the recipient of the utmost consideration and marks of respect; for the story of his heroic exploits was then known throughout the civilized world. After short stops at Berlin and Paris, where other honors were shown him, he sailed on the steamer *Parthia* from Liverpool and set foot on his native soil and in his native city at New York the 13th of September, three years and two months from the time the unfortunate *Jeannette* had passed out of the Golden Gate with her fortunes still unknown. Of the honors tendered Mr. Melville after his return it is hardly necessary to speak. By resolutions of boards of aldermen or other city officials he was given public receptions in the cities of New York, Philadelphia, and Washington, while many similar courtesies had to be declined on account of urgent affairs in Washington connected with the history of the expedition of which he was the most responsible survivor.

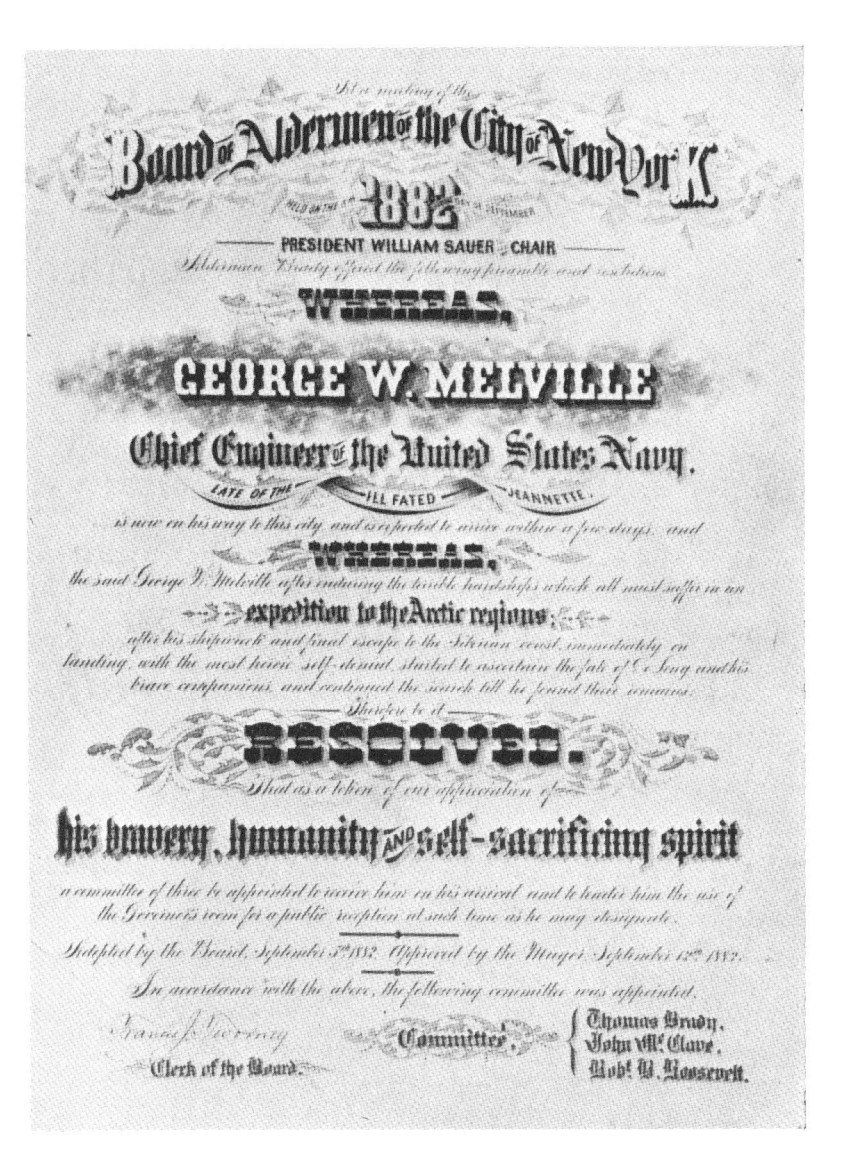

FAC-SIMILE OF RESOLUTIONS

Adopted by the Board of Aldermen of the City of New York in Honor of Chief Engineer George W. Melville, U. S. Navy.

The presence of Lieutenant Berry with Mr. Melville in St. Petersburg deserves explanation. In 1881, the *Jeannette* being then long unheard from, the government bought a Behring Sea steam whaler named *Mary and Helen* and fitted her out for a search expedition under the command of Lieutenant Berry. The name of this steamer was changed to *Rodgers* in recognition of the valuable aid rendered the Navy Department by Rear Admiral John Rodgers as president of the Jeannette Relief Board, and as a proper tribute to his eminent reputation as an officer of the navy. Berry went into the polar sea to a point beyond where the *Jeannette* had originally been caught in the ice, but of course saw nothing of her for she had then been carried far away and destroyed. He went into winter quarters in St. Lawrence Bay, near the East Cape, where, on the 30th of November, 1881, his vessel took fire and was burned in spite of all efforts to save her. The people thus rendered homeless in a northern winter season were distributed about in the villages of natives about St. Lawrence Bay and thus sustained life until the next spring when they were rescued by the whaling bark *North Star* of New Bedford. One officer of the *Rodgers*, Lieutenant Charles F. Putnam, lost his life most cruelly early in the winter by being drifted out to sea on an ice-floe and was never heard of more. Assistant Engineer A. V. Zane, U. S. Navy, shared the hardships of this unfortunate crew, he being the engineer in charge of the *Rodgers'* machinery.

Lieutenant Berry, though deprived of his ship, did not feel relieved from his duty to search for and succor the *Jeannette*, he being a man of the Melville order, not readily thwarted by disaster. Accordingly, after making all possible arrangements for the preservation of his crew, he set out with Ensign H. J. Hunt and a Kamschatka boy as interpreter to march westward along the coast of the Arctic Ocean, notifying the natives where found to watch for signs of the *Jeannette* and for some whalers that were reported missing in those waters. In this way he persistently kept up the tramp until he had journeyed nearly two thousand miles along the frozen shores and finally arrived at Oceansk only a few days after Melville had left that place on his way toward Yakutsk and home. Following on Melville's trail, Berry overtook him at Kangerack, between Verkeransk and Yakutsk, Melville having been obliged to halt his nondescript cavalcade there to allow his worn-out horses, substituted for deer at Verkeransk, to recuperate on the scant shrubbery thereabout. Berry had with his party a considerable supply of bread, sorely needed by Melville and his men, and thus in a way he actually accomplished the relief of the *Jeannette's* people, which was the duty upon which he had been ordered.

Having escaped the manifold perils briefly and imperfectly sketched in the foregoing pages, Chief Engineer Melville might have been considered deserving of rest and peace after arriving in his own country; but there was no peace. The story of the loss of the *Jeannette* and the subsequent adventures of her people had become public information through the imperfect reports of newspapers, and considerable distress had been occasioned in the minds of relatives of some who had perished, a false idea having taken root that the tragedy was due to naval discipline rather than to the rigors of the arctic region. In response to considerable public comment, Congress, a month before Melville's return to the United States, had adopted a joint resolution directing the Navy Department to investigate the conduct of the cruise, the scope of the inquiry being expressed by the wording of the resolution as follows:

"*Resolved, etc.*, That the Secretary of the Navy be requested to convene, as soon as practicable, a court of inquiry to investigate the circumstances of the loss in the Arctic seas of the exploring steamer *Jeannette*, and of the death of Lieutenant Commander De Long and others of her officers and men, including an inquiry into the condition of the vessel on her departure, her management up to the time of her destruction, the provisions made and plans adopted for the several boats' crews upon their leaving the wreck, the efforts made by the various officers to insure the safety of the parties under their immediate charge and for the relief of the other parties, and into the general conduct and merits of each and all the officers and men of the ill-fated expedition, and to submit the finding of such court of inquiry to Congress."

In compliance with this resolution Secretary Chandler ordered a court of inquiry consisting of Commodore Wm. G. Temple, president; Captain Joseph N. Miller, and Commander F. V. McNair, members, and Lieutenant Sam C. Lemly, judge advocate. This court met on the 5th day of October, 1882, and proceeded to take testimony from all competent witnesses until the 12th of February, 1883, when a detailed finding was made and subsequently approved by the Department. Certain efforts were made before the court to show that Chief Engineer Melville had dealt harshly with those placed under his authority, and to belittle his efforts when in independent command of the whale-boat and on the Lena Delta, but these charges had no foundation in fact and his conduct was praised by the court in these words in the summing up of its finding:

" Special commendation is due to Lieutenant Commander De Long for the high qualities displayed by him in the conduct of the expedition; to Chief Engineer Melville for his zeal, energy, and professional aptitude, which elicited high encomiums from his commander, and for his subsequent efforts on the Lena Delta; and to Seamen Nindemann and Sweetman, for services which induced their commander to recommend them for medals of honor.''

The finding of the court, although based upon the testimony of the survivors of the *Jeannette*, the only persons living competent to speak of their own knowledge of the matter, did not satisfy Dr. D. F. Collins, brother of the meteorologist of that name who had perished with De Long's party, he maintaining that his brother's death was due to persecution by De Long on the ship and to neglect on the part of Melville in not going in search of De Long's party as soon as he had himself landed on the Lena Delta. Dr. Collins submitted a memorial to Congress reciting at length the facts as he believed them to be, which were that his brother, Jerome J. Collins, had been " treated with every indignity and outrage, even to being deprived of all the scientific instruments and appliances of his position as meteorologist of the expedition;" that about the end of the year 1879 he was "placed under suspension or arrest by the commanding officer of the expedition, and that he remained so until he died of starvation and cold on the bank of the Lena River." "That the evidence offered to the naval court, and which the undersigned is prepared to furnish, and that has already and will be further given by the survivors, goes to show, beyond any reasonable doubt, that had Melville performed the duty devolving upon him as the commander of the party, and obeyed the directions given him by Lieutenant De Long to immediately communicate with the Russian authorities, and gone to the rescue and conducted a search for the captain's party, each and every member of that party, with the exception of Ericksen, would have been rescued and alive to-day." And finally that the naval court of inquiry "refused to admit or allow to be given valuable testimony, and that said court ruled out nearly every question that would bring out the true history of the expedition; that many of the survivors were not permitted to give their full and free testimony, and that the naval inquiry was so conducted that all possible chance or possibility of the truth coming out was destroyed."

This remarkable memorial induced the House of Representatives to direct its Committee on Naval Affairs to "investigate the facts connected with said expedition and the alleged unofficerlike and inhumane conduct therein." The investigation was conducted by a sub-committee composed of Messrs. Hugh Buchanan, William McAdoo, and Charles A. Boutelle, who patiently collected testimony until the result was a public document (Mis. Doc. 66; 48th Congress, 1st Session) of more than one thousand closely-printed pages, not including the final report of the committee. A lawyer of eminence, representing Dr. Collins, was allowed to practice before the sub-committee in the capacity of prosecutor, and Mrs. De Long in defense of her dead husband's name, and Chief Engineer Melville to defend himself, were thus forced to combine in the employment of counsel. The volume of testimony taken forbids its review within a reasonable space, but nothing not already determined by the naval court was discovered except a mass of miserable and trifling details relative to the petty personal quarrels and differences of the men of the expedition, these being extorted from the witnesses for some unknown purpose by the cross-questioning of the prosecuting attorney.

The report of the investigation made to the House of Representatives stated that so far from the indignity and outrage alleged, the treatment of officers and men by Lieutenant Commander De Long was kind and considerate, and that no fault was attached to De Long for the suspension or arrest of Collins under the circumstances. As to the charges regarding the conduct of the naval court of inquiry, the congressional committee flatly denied their truth. That part of the report relating to the accusations against Chief Engineer Melville reads as follows:

"The third boat's crew, under command of Chief Engineer Melville, did, on the 26th day of September, 1881, find a place of safety, and received supplies from the natives, some of the members of the party being in a disabled condition. The party under his command had arrived at a small Siberian village called Geeomovialocke. The country and language were entirely unknown to Melville and his party. Melville did not know that Lieutenant Commander De Long and his party had escaped destruction by the storm which overwhelmed Lieutenant Chipp and his party but it was the opinion of Melville and others of the party, that Lieutenant Chipp's boat and Lieutenant Commander De Long's were submerged by the waves and their crews drowned, and no information was received by Engineer Melville of the arrival of Lieutenant Commander De Long on the Lena Delta until his receipt of the message, by a Russian exile named Kusmah, from Nindemann and Noros. As soon after receiving this message as Melville could procure the means of making search for De Long and his party, acting on information obtained from Nindemann, he made a long and diligent search, in which he underwent great privation from cold and hunger, such as few men have ever endured and survived. In this search he came very near the place where the remains of De Long and his party were afterwards found. If Melville had known shortly after his arrival at Geeomovialocke what he afterwards knew of the arrival of De Long and party on the Lena Delta, he could and would have rescued Lieutenant Commander De Long and party, which fully appears by his immediate action on the receipt of this information.

"The committee do not believe that any blame attaches to Engineer Melville, Lieutenant Danenhower, or any of the party controlled by Melville, under the then surrounding circumstances, for the failure to rescue Lieutenant Commander De Long and his party."

Lieutenant A. W. Greely, U. S. Army, with a party numbering 25 all told, was landed in August, 1881, in Lady Franklin Bay to establish one of the two American meteorological stations in accordance with the agreement of the international meteorological congress, and left there to carry out his allotted work, it being understood that supplies and food would be sent him each year as long as his observations continued. The failure to do this and the dreadful consequences of that failure need not be entered into here, being told in detail in other books, it being sufficient for the present purpose to know that Greely had not been communicated with up to the winter of 1883–1884, and that the country then was aroused at the neglect or blundering that had left him and his gallant band to an unknown fate far within the Arctic Circle. It was then almost too late, but Congress in response to the pressure of public sentiment took up the consideration of a resolution authorizing a relief expedition, in which consideration so much time was consumed in debating about the amount of money to be used, the details of manning the vessels, etc., that Secretary Chandler, feeling that the situation required deeds rather than words, took upon himself the responsibility of buying and equipping suitable ships before Congress had completed its arguments. When finally passed, in February, 1884, the congressional resolution simply authorized the President to send the expedition and fixed no definite sum to defray the expense. In the end the actual cost was, in round numbers, $763,000.

The vessels purchased by Secretary Chandler were the steam whaler *Thetis* of Dundee, Scotland, for 140,000, and the sealing steamer *Bear* of Grenock, Scotland, for $100,000. The British government tendered the use of the steamer *Alert*, formerly the flag-ship of Captain Nares' polar expedition of 1874, and generously prepared and equipped her for service before delivering her to the American authorities. The *Thetis* and *Bear* arrived at New York during the winter and were there fitted out for their work. No expense was spared in the outfit of these ships and nothing was left undone that might in any manner contribute to the success of their mission, in which preparation the experience of Chief Engineer Melville was found invaluable. The Navy Department required from him suggestions as to the work in hand and he responded with an elaborate series of papers dealing in detail with the kind, quality, and quantity of provisions desirable; clothing; tools; boats; equipment, etc., his recommendations being generally carried out, with results that were highly satisfactory in every particular.

Mr. Melville himself joined the expedition as chief engineer of the *Thetis*, flagship of Commander W. S. Schley. Commander George W. Coffin was assigned to the command of the *Alert*, and Lieutenant W. H. Emory to the *Bear*. Chief Engineer John Lowe went in the *Bear* and Passed Assistant Engineer W. H. Nauman in the *Alert*. The ships sailed from New York at different dates from April 24 to May 10, stopped at St. John's for coal, and then proceeded northward, the *Thetis* and *Bear* joining each other at Upernavik May 29th. The *Alert* was the last to leave New York and did not reach Upernavik until June 13, being thereafter hampered by convoying the collier *Loch Garry* and so often beset with ice that she took no active part in the actual search. After ramming and jamming their way through the ice, with many narrow escapes from destruction, the *Thetis* and *Bear* on the 18th of June were off Cape York, and faced up into the North Water with the first of the venturesome Scotch whalers; with whom, indeed, they now had to compete, for Congress after providing for the expenditure of many hundreds of thousands of dollars for conducting the relief expedition had passed another act offering a reward of $25,000 to any person not in the military or naval service of the United States who would discover and rescue the Greely party, or ascertain its fate, thus pitting the whole world against the few American naval officers sent to conduct the search. In the event, the foremost of the whaling steamers were one hundred miles behind when the rescue was effected.

Without entering into details, the *Thetis* and *Bear* on the evening of June 22d found the camp of the Greely people near Cape Sabine, in Ellesmere Land, the actual discoverers being a party from the *Bear* in the steam cutter of that vessel, with which party was Mr. Norman the ice pilot of the *Thetis*. Mr. Norman was the first to enter the camp, followed closely by Mr. Ash, ice pilot of the *Bear*, and Chief Engineer John Lowe, the latter being the first person belonging to the navy to arrive. News of the discovery was quickly communicated to the ships and in a short time the officers and men of both ships were engaged in carrying the survivors on board and collecting the wreckage and records of the camp. Greely and six of his men were found alive, though so near to death's door that a delay of one day more in the arrival of succor would have sealed the fate of all: the others, soldiers of the wealthiest country in the world, had died miserably of starvation within sight of the sea that for several months each year offered a water-way to the seaports and markets of the whole world, and directly to those of their own country. The frightful sufferings which these poor men experienced may well be left to the special narratives dealing with their service in the north. The subject is one worth thinking about, however, and an idea of the utter misery to which these soldiers were reduced may be gained from the following description of their camp, written by one whose eyes, long before accustomed to scenes of human suffering, saw the place in all its hideous nakedness:

"The scene itself was indescribable, and I shall not attempt to depict our pity and horror as we viewed it. A cold, barren plateau, between a small outlying promontory and a bleak weather-riven rock of red syenite reaching to the skies, on which even the mosses and lichens would scarce grow. The raging of the wind and the pitiless sea, and the roar of the black water of the bay dashing over the ice-foot, made the lonesome picture look colder and more appalling. Drifts of ice and snow choked the ravines and hollows; but, saving ourselves and the famished, skeleton-like survivors, not a living thing appeared on the whitened landscape. The region truly seemed to be the most desolate on the face of the earth. It looked as though the curses of ten thousand witches had descended upon and blasted it, and even the birds would not dare to take their flight across the lifeless land lest they too fall victims into the death-gap below.

"Struggling up the valley of death, against the frantic wind, from the low point to the westward of the camp, where we managed with difficulty to effect a landing in our whale-boats, we first came upon the remains of the winter habitation, a parallelogram of four walls about three feet high, built of loose stone, the inside dimensions being perhaps 18 x 22 feet, with a tunnel or covered way facing the mountain to the southward. This hut had been roofed over with the whale-boats turned upside down and covered with the sails and tent-cloths; the smoke-flue, made of old tin-kettles bound with bits of canvas, was thrown to one side; and water had risen in and about the wretched dwelling-place to a height of eight inches, concealing much of the foul evidence of squalid misery in which its poor occupants had lived. Cast-off fur and cloth clothing, empty tin cans, and the sickening filth of twenty-five men for nine months lay heaped and scattered about, a veritable Augean scene."[1]

Leaving Cape Sabine the day after the rescue, the two ships proceeded southward, finding the *Alert* and *Loch Garry* on the 1st of July, near Sugar Loaf Mountain, beset in the ice-pack. One of the rescued men, Sergeant Ellison of the 10th U. S. infantry, died on board the *Bear* at Disco July 7th. The ships were at St. John's July 17th, and on the first of August landed the survivors at Portsmouth, N. H., where the North Atlantic squadron, assembled for the purpose, extended to the rescuers an imposing reception. The *Alert* was returned to the British government with suitable thanks for her use; the *Thetis* was taken into the naval service and fitted out as a gun vessel, and the *Bear* was transferred to the Revenue Cutter service, in which she has for a number of years been actively engaged in the patrol of Behring Sea and adjacent waters.

Before Chief Engineer Melville returned home from the Lena Delta in 1882 the story of his deeds had become so well known and his right to recognition for meritorious service so generally recognized that a bill providing for his advancement in the navy was introduced in Congress. The bill was favorably considered by the Committees on Naval Affairs and would have been passed had it been recommended by the Secretary of the Navy. When referred to that official for an opinion, as is always done in such cases, Mr. Chandler felt obliged to withhold his approval, and properly, for the accusations against Mr. Melville, growing out of the distress of Dr. Collins, had not been investigated, and until the court of inquiry had completed its work and found him free from blame it would have been hasty and unwise to advocate his promotion. The bill appeared in the next Congress (the 48th), this time

---

[1] Chief Engineer George W. Melville, U. S. Navy, "In the Lena Delta,," page 354.

as the result of a petition to Congress signed by a number of chief engineers of the navy over whose heads Melville would be advanced by its passage, a most generous and praiseworthy act calculated to reflect honor upon their grade had not the success of the measure been prevented by others of the same grade. A few—not more than three or four—of the chief engineers entertained such objections to losing even one number by the honorable reward of a brother officer that they addressed members of the Naval Committee in protest, and successfully.

Mr. Melville had nothing to do personally with these bills but was glad to know that they were being supported; now, however, disgusted with the action of members of his own corps, he told his friends both in and out of Congress that he did not care for the promotion proposed and hoped the matter would be dropped. In spite of his protest, members of Congress interested in him continued to introduce the bill in succeeding Congresses and it was favorably reported by the Naval Committee of the House of Representatives during the second session of the 50th Congress but did not reach a vote. In the report referred to the following complimentary reference was made to Mr. Melville:

"The qualities as officer and man displayed by Chief Engineer Melville throughout the cruise of the ill-fated *Jeannette*, and especially during the retreat of her crew over the ice and waves of the Polar Sea, to the desolate shores of Northern Siberia, and most strikingly during the search for the remains of Lieutenant Commander De Long and his party during the perils and privations of an arctic winter, have invoked the admiration of the world.

"All have united in praise of his services as well as in wonder that such services should remain without recognition from the government for which they were performed.

"There is undeniable evidence of self-sacrifice and absolute devotion to duty in serving his country."

In the Fifty-first Congress this bill found an earnest champion in Mr. Chandler, then a member of the Senate and of its Naval Committee, his knowledge of Melville and his work, gained as Secretary of the Navy during the time of the *Jeannette* investigations, convincing him of the merits and justice of the recognition asked. He reported the bill favorably to the Senate during the first session of that Congress, the report containing among many expressions of praise the following:

"In view of such a record the committee feel that the proposed promotion, so long after the deeds which it is intended to recompense, is an act of tardy justice and hardly adequate. The usual reward for distinguished bravery is an advancement of thirty numbers; this gives but fifteen. England rewarded the members of the *Nares* expedition, which was a failure after nine months on account of scurvy, by knighting the commander and promoting every officer a grade."

The bill passed the Senate soon after it was reported and a few months later came before the House of Representatives and was passed by that body, becoming a law by Presidential approval September 30th, 1890. In illustration of the tardiness of this act of simple justice, it may be remarked that three years before the passage of the bill Mr. Melville had been selected over the heads of many other chief engineers and appointed engineer-in-chief of the navy, with a special rate of pay, so that the promotion given him by Congress amounted to nothing more than changing the position of his name in the list of chief engineers and the honor of receiving from the President a special commission on which was engrossed a statement of the heroic services for which the commission was issued:

The act of Congress, besides advancing Mr. Melville, provided for the award of a medal to each member of the *Jeannette* expedition, the full text of the act here following:

"An act in recognition of the merits and services of Chief Engineer George Wallace Melville, United States Navy, and of the other officers and men of the "Jeannette" Arctic Expedition.

"*Be it enacted by the Senate and House of Representatives of the United States of America in Congress assembled*, That the President be, and hereby is, authorized, by and with the advice and consent of the Senate, to advance Chief Engineer George Wallace Melville, United States Navy, one grade, to take rank from the same date but next after the junior chief engineer having the relative rank of commander at the passage of this act, as a recognition of his meritorious services in successfully directing the party under his command after the wreck of the Arctic exploring steamer *Jeannette*, and of his persistent efforts through dangers and hardships to find and assist his commanding officer and other members of the expedition before he himself was out of peril; and that he be allowed the pay of a chief engineer as if he had been commissioned on the same date as the junior chief engineer having the relative rank of commander at the passage of this act; such increased rate of pay to begin from the date of the passage of this act.

"SEC. 2. That the said Melville shall hereafter continue to be next junior to the junior chief engineer having the relative rank of commander at the passage of this act; and whatever grade he may hereafter occupy shall be increased by one number, but the total number of chief engineers shall not be increased: *Provided*, That nothing in this act shall cause any officer to be retarded in his promotion or receive a less rate of pay than would otherwise have been the case.

"SEC. 3. That suitable medals be struck at the United States Mint in commemoration of the perils encountered by the officers and men of the said Jeannette Arctic Expedition, and as an expression of the high esteem in which Congress holds their services in the said expedition; and that one of the said medals be presented to each of the survivors of said expedition, and one to the heirs of each of the deceased members.

"SEC. 4. That a sufficient sum for the purposes of this act is hereby appropriated out of any money in the Treasury not otherwise appropriated.

"Approved, September 30, 1890. (Stat. 26, p. 552.")

CHAPTER XXXV.

"The earliest reference made to uniformity in the dress of British sailors occurs soon after the Roman invasion, when we read that fleets were supplied with speedy long-boats smeared with wax to lessen the friction of the waves, and having their sails dyed a light-blue color to resemble the sea, while, still further to lessen the chances of being seen, the crews wore clothing of the same hue."
—*Commander Charles N. Robinson, R. N.,—The British Fleet.*

UNIFORMS AND CORPS DEVICES OF THE ENGINEER CORPS.

THOUGH not perhaps entirely within the province of this historical sketch, the subject of the uniforms prescribed from time to time for the officers of the naval engineer corps is believed to possess sufficient interest to warrant its introduction. When preparing the *Fulton* for sea and arranging for the appointment of engineers for that steamer, Captain M. C. Perry foresaw the need of identifying the new class of officials with their surroundings by means of a uniform, and he made this the subject of a recommendation while addressing the Department with reference to the manner of appointing engineers. In reply the following letter was sent:

"NAVY DEPARTMENT, November 21, 1837.

"CAPT. M. C. PERRY, Com'dg Str. 'Fulton,' New York:

"SIR,—Your letter of the 16th instant, relative to the engineers of the 'Fulton' and their uniforms has been received.

"*The adoption of a uniform* such as you may approve, *if agreeable to those at whose expense it is to be provided*, meets with the sanction of the Department, and it is also desirable, as mentioned in your letter, that none be appointed engineers but those of the very best standing.

"I am, respectfully, &c.,
"M. DICKERSON, *Secretary of the Navy.*"

Captain Perry then prepared an order describing the uniform

to be worn by the engineers of the *Fulton,* which order was adopted as a general regulation and the uniform prescribed by it was worn by all naval engineers until the issue of a new uniform order in 1852. The Perry order was as follows:

COAT.

For chief engineers, dress coat of navy-blue cloth, double-breasted, black velvet rolling collar, two rows of large navy buttons on the breast, nine in each row; the cuffs to have three large navy buttons around the upper edge, with three small ones in the opening; the skirts to be lined with black silk serge, to have one large navy button behind on each hip, two at the center of each skirt in the fold, and one at the end of each; the pocket flaps to be pointed, to have three large navy buttons beneath them, showing one-half their diameter; and one embroidered five-pointed gold star, one inch and a half in diameter, to be worn on each end of the collar.

For a first assistant engineer, the same as for a chief, except that there shall be but one large navy button in the center of the fold of each skirt, and an embroidered five-pointed silver star, one inch and a half in diameter, on each end of the collar.

For a second, the same as for a first assistant engineer, except that there shall be but one embroidered silver star, of the same dimensions, to be worn on the right side of the collar.

For a third assistant, the same as for a second assistant engineer, with this exception, that the embroidered silver star shall be worn on the left side of the collar.

VEST.

For all engineers, the same as worn, according to the season.

PANTALOONS.

For all engineers, plain navy-blue or white, as the season demands.

CAPS.

For all engineers, of the usual style worn; with a gold band

COLLAR DEVICE FOR ENGINEERS, 1852-1861.

one inch and a half wide for chief engineers, and without the band for all assistants.

SWORDS AND BELTS.

For all engineers, of the usual style.

COCKED HATS.

For chief engineers only, of the usual style.

Under date of March 8, 1852, the Navy Department issued a new order making many changes in the uniforms of engineers, as follows:

UNIFORM AND DRESS—FULL DRESS.

COAT.

For a chief engineer.—Shall be of navy-blue cloth, single-breasted, with one row of nine large navy buttons in front, placed four inches and a half apart from eye to eye at top, and two and a half at bottom; stand-up collar, to hook in front at bottom and to slope thence upwards and backwards at an angle of twenty-five degrees on each side, and to rise no higher than will permit a free movement of the chin over it. It shall have on each side an embroidered device two inches high and three inches long; the anchor in silver and the wreath in gold, as per pattern. The cuffs to be two inches and a half deep, to have three large-sized navy buttons around the upper edge, with three small ones in the opening. The waist of the coat to descend to the top of the hip bone; the skirts to begin about one-fifth of the circumference from the front edge, and descend four-fifths from the hip bone towards the knee, with one button behind on each hip, and one near the bottom of the skirt in each fold. The pocket flaps to be pointed; to have three large navy buttons underneath them, showing one-half of their diameter; skirts to be lined with black silk serge; coat to be worn fully buttoned, unless otherwise permitted by the officer in command.

For a first assistant engineer.—The same in all respects as for a chief engineer, except that the cuffs shall have three medium-sized navy buttons around the upper edge.

For a second assistant engineer.—The same in all respects as for a first assistant engineer, except that the cuffs shall have no buttons on their upper edges.

For a third assistant engineer.—The same in all respects as for a second assistant engineer.

PANTALOONS.

For all engineer officers.—Shall be of navy-blue cloth or white drill, made loose to spread well over the foot, and to be worn over the boots or shoes.

Within the tropics white pantaloons will be worn at all seasons, unless otherwise permitted by the officer in command.

North of the tropics, blue cloth pantaloons will be worn from the 1st of October to the 15th of May, and the white from the 15th of May to the 1st of October. South of the tropics, blue will be worn from the 15th of May to the 1st of October, and the white from the 1st of October to the 15th of May, unless otherwise directed by written order of the commander-in-chief of a squadron or of a vessel acting singly.

VEST.

To be white, single-breasted, standing collar, with nine small navy buttons in front, and not to show below the coat.

COCKED HAT.

For chief and first assistant engineers.—When in full dress or undress, of the following description: To be not more than eight nor less than six inches and a half in height on the back (or fan) nor more than eight inches, nor less than five in front, (or cock) and not more than nineteen nor less than seventeen inches long from point to point. The curve to be one inch and one-tenth at the back; the hat to be bound with black silk lace, to show one inch and a quarter on each side; in the fold at each end of the hat a tassel, formed of five gold and five blue bullions; and on the cock,

CAP DEVICE FOR ENGINEER CORPS, 1852-1861.

a black silk cockade, five inches wide; over the cockade to be worn a loop, formed of four gold bullions three-eighths of an inch in diameter, not twisted, with a small button in the lower end of the loop.

EPAULETTES.

Chief engineers will wear two plain gold epaulettes. The strap shall be of silver lace, with the letter $\mathfrak{E}$, three-quarters of an inch long, in old English character, embroidered in gold on the frog, and the crescents to be smooth and solid.

SWORD AND SCABBARD.

Shall be cut-and-thrust blade, not less than twenty-six inches, nor more than twenty-nine inches long, half basket hilt, grip white. Scabbards of black leather, mountings of yellow gilt, and all as per pattern. Sword knot to be a strap of gold lace half an inch wide and eighteen inches long, including the tassel; gold slide; tassel of twelve gold bullions, one inch and three-quarters long, with basket-worked head, as per pattern.

SWORD BELT.

Shall be of plain black glazed leather, not less than one inch and a half, nor more than two inches wide, with slings of the same not less than one-half nor more than three-quarters of an inch wide, and a hook in the forward ring to suspend the sword. Belt plate of yellow gilt in front, two inches in diameter, as per pattern. The belt is to be worn over the coat.

CRAVAT.

Shall be of black silk, or satin, without any tie in front; for full-dress, a white shirt collar to show above it.

UNDRESS UNIFORM.

COAT.

For a chief engineer.—To be a frock coat of navy-blue cloth, faced with the same, single-breasted, with one row of nine large navy buttons on the breast, three large size buttons around the upper edge of the cuff, and three small ones in the opening.

For a first assistant engineer.—The same as for a chief engineer, except that the cuffs shall have three medium size buttons around the upper edge.

For a second and third assistant engineer.—The same as for a first assistant engineer, except the buttons around the upper edge of the cuff.

SHOULDER STRAPS.

For a chief engineer.—Shall be of blue cloth, four inches long and one inch and three-eighths wide, bordered with an embroidery of gold one-quarter of an inch in width. In the center of the strap there shall be embroidered in silver the letter 𝔈, in old English character. Shoulder-straps to be always worn as distinctive marks when the epaulettes are not worn.

CAPS.

Caps to be of blue cloth, not less than three inches and a half nor more than four inches in height, and not more than ten nor less than nine and a half in diameter on the top, with patent leather visor. An embroidered device and wreath as per pattern, the wheel embroidered in gold and the anchor in silver, similarly placed above the band of gold lace, one inch wide.

OVERCOATS.

For all officers, shall be of dark blue pilot-cloth, double-breasted, rolling collar, skirt to descend three inches below the knee. The same number of navy buttons, and similarly arranged as for undress coat; no buttons to be worn on the cuffs or pocket flaps. Officers entitled to shoulder-straps will wear the same on their overcoats, as directed for undress coats. Blue cloth cloaks may be used in boats, or when epaulettes are worn, if it be rendered necessary by cold or wet weather.

The foregoing uniform regulations were modified by an order issued September 24, 1852, directing that the bands of gold lace on the caps of all officers entitled to wear them be one and one-half inches wide instead of one inch: another uniform regulation issued January 1, 1853, directed that second and third assistant engineers should wear cocked hats, the same as for first assistants, and specified shoulder-straps as follows:

For first assistant engineers.—Of gold lace four inches long and one-half of an inch wide, to be bordered with gold bead cord one-eighth of an inch.

For second assistant engineers.—Of blue cloth four inches long and one-half of an inch wide, to be bordered with gold bead cord one eighth of an inch.

With these modifications the uniform remained as specified until February 8, 1861, when the Department issued an order relating to engineers' uniforms particularly, changing them so as to conform to uniforms worn by line and other officers of the navy, the order reading as follows:

Hereafter the coats of all engineers will be double-breasted.

Chief engineers will wear upon the cuffs of their coats the same number of stripes of gold lace as are worn by those officers with whom they have assimilated rank, and will dispense with the three large buttons.

The letter E on the epaulettes and shouler straps of chief engineers, and the embroidered wheel, anchor, and wreath on the collars of the coats of all engineers, will be dispensed with. The collar of the full-dress coat for all engineers will have an embroidered gold edging a half an inch in width, extending along the top and down the front.

The present wreath on the cap will be retained, with an embroidered centre of four oak leaves in the form of a cross, one an three-quarters of an inch in length, and the same in breadth, instead of the present wheel and anchor.

January 28, 1864, an order was issued making a number of changes in naval uniforms, chief among which was the adoption of devices indicating rank the same as were in use in the army, and increasing the number of stripes on the sleeves, the stripes for a lieutenant, for example, being changed from one three-fourths inch wide to three each one-fourth of an inch wide. The parts of this order referring specially to the engineer corps follow:

COATS.

For all engineer officers except third assistants.—Frock-coat of navy-blue cloth, faced with the same, and lined with black silk serge; double-breasted, with two rows of large navy buttons on the breast, nine in each row, placed four inches and a half apart from eye to eye at top and two inches and a half at bottom; rolling collar; skirts to be full, commencing at the hip bone and descending thence four-fifths towards the knee, with one button behind on each hip and one near the bottom of each fold; cuffs to be closed and from two and a half to three inches deep.

For third assistant engineers.—The same, except that the buttons shall be of medium size only.

OVERCOATS.

For all engineer officers except third assistants.—Shall be a caban overcoat and cape of dark blue beaver or pilot-cloth, lined throughout with dark blue flannel; skirt to extend four inches below the knee; cape to be ten inches shorter; double-breasted with pockets in side seam, and buttons arranged as for frock coat; the cape to be made so that it can be removed at pleasure, and provided with an extra cloth collar to detach so as to form a separate garment. On each end of the collar of the overcoat shall be the following devices:

Chief of Bureau of Steam Engineering.—One silver star.

Corps Device Adopted for Naval Engineers in 1861 and still worn. It is the prettiest Corps Emblem in the service when properly made, but is too often so botched in manufacture as to bear no resemblance to oak leaves.

For a fleet engineer and chief engineer with the rank of captain.—A silver eagle.

For a chief engineer with the rank of commander.—A silver leaf.

For a chief engineer with the rank of lieutenant commander.—A gold leaf.

For a first assistant engineer.—One silver bar.

For a second assistant engineer.—A small gold cord on the front edge of the collar.

For a third assistant engineer—No device, but seven buttons in a row.

CUFF AND SLEEVE ORNAMENTS.

The lace on the cuffs and sleeve is to be of navy gold lace, a quarter of an inch wide, and to be placed a quarter of an inch apart, except where a half is hereinafter designated, the first stripe being below but joining the cuff seam, and the others distributed in groups upwardly.

Chief of Bureau of Steam Engineering.—Seven stripes, with half an inch between third and fourth, fourth and fifth.

For a fleet engineer and chief engineer ranking with a captain.—Six stripes, with half an inch space between third and fourth.

For a chief engineer ranking with a commander.—Five stripes with half an inch space between first and second, fourth and fifth.

For a chief engineer ranking with a lieutenant commander.—Four stripes, with half an inch space between third and fourth.

For a first assistant engineer.—Two stripes.

For a second assistant engineer.—One stripe.

For a third assistant engineer.—Cuff plain.

SHOULDER STRAPS.

To be of navy-blue cloth, four inches and a quarter long, one inch and a half wide, including the border, which is to be a quarter of an inch wide and embroidered in gold.

The center and end ornaments or distinctions of line and staff, and indications of rank, are to be embroidered in gold or in silver, as hereinafter designated, and are to be as follows:

For the Chief of the Bureau of Steam Engineering.—A device of four oak leaves in gold in the form of a cross, one inch long, upon which is embroidered in silver a five pointed star seven-eighths diameter.

For a fleet engineer and chief engineer of over fifteen years.—A silver spread eagle resting upon a device of four oak leaves in silver in the form of a cross.

For a chief engineer after the first five years.—In the center a device of four oak leaves in the form of a cross, and at each end an oak leaf five eighths inches long, all embroidered in silver.

For a chief engineer for the first five years.—The same, except that the oak leaves at the ends shall be embroidered in gold.

For a first assistant engineer.—The same device of oak leaves in the center in silver, and at each end of the strap an embroidered gold bar half-inch long and two-tenths inch wide.

For a second assistant engineer.—The embroidered silver cross of oak leaves in the center.

Third assistant engineers are not entitled to wear straps.

CAP AND CAP ORNAMENTS.

Cap of dark blue cloth; top to be one-half inch greater diameter than the base; quarters one and a half inch wide between the seams; back of the band to be two inches wide between the points of

Undress Uniform of Chief Engineer, ranking with Lieutenant, 1861-1864. The undress or frock coat worn now (1896) is practically identical.

Undress Uniform of Chief Engineer, 1852-1861.

The "Perry" Uniform worn by Naval Engineers, 1837-1852.

the visor, with a welt half an inch from the lower edge, extending from point to point of the visor; band in front one and a half inches wide, bound; black patent leather visor, green underneath, two and a half inches wide, and rounded, as per pattern; inside of the band of heavy duck. The cap ornaments are to be worn on the band in front. During rainy weather a black cover may be worn over the cap.

Cap ornaments shall consist of a gold wreath in front, composed of oak and olive branches, three inches in width, and enclosing the following described devices:

For engineers, four oak leaves, in silver, in the form of a cross, one and one-tenth of an inch horizontally, and nine-tenths of an inch vertically.

In January, 1865, an order of the Department authorized a sack coat of navy-blue flannel or blue cloth to be worn as "service dress" by all officers on board ship and in the United States. This garment was single-breasted, with a row of five buttons in front, and was intended as an informal lounging coat for officers not on duty, the order forbidding its use on shore, or when on duty in a foreign port; as a convenient and comfortable garment it held its place in the navy for about twelve years, until at last superseded by the present tunic.

The uniforms prescribed by the order of January 28, 1864, remained unmolested for about five years, but then fell before the new broom brought to bear upon naval matters by the administration of President Grant. On March 11, 1869, a general order was issued by the Navy Department, specifying at considerable length the insignia of rank to be worn by the admiral and vice admiral, and making the following alterations in the uniforms for officers of lower grades:

Captains will wear three stripes of half-inch gold-lace, one quarter of an inch apart, on the sleeve of full-dress and undress coats.

Commanders will wear two stripes of half-inch gold lace, three quarters of an inch apart, and one stripe of quarter inch lace between them.

Lieutenant commanders will wear two stripes of half-inch gold lace, one-quarter of an inch apart.

Lieutenants will wear one stripe of half-inch gold lace, and one stripe of quarter inch lace one-quarter of an inch above.

Masters will wear one stripe of half-inch lace.

Ensigns will wear one stripe of quarter-inch lace.

Midshipmen, after graduation, will hereafter be allowed a full-dress double-breasted coat, nine buttons in each row, with a gold cord one-eighth of an inch wide around the sleeve and an anchor in gold embroidery on each side of the collar, one-inch in length (as per pattern).

No officer in the navy below the assimilated rank of lieutenant will wear shoulder-straps, cocked-hat, or epaulettes.

The cap ornament for all commissioned officers in the navy will be a silver shield with two crossed anchors in gold, arranged as per pattern. A gold cord of the same pattern as the one now worn by the midshipmen at the Naval Academy will be worn on the front of the cap by all officers.

Staff officers of assimilated rank will conform to the above regulations.

Medical officers will wear around the sleeve cobalt blue cloth, between the stripes of gold lace.

Paymasters will wear around the sleeve white cloth, between the stripes of gold lace.

Engineers will wear around the sleeve red cloth, between the stripes of gold lace.

Staff officers entitled to wear but one stripe of lace on the sleeve will wear the colored cloth so as to show one-fourth of an inch above and below the stripe.

With the above mentioned exceptions the uniform of the navy will remain as heretofore.

This order was supplemented with another issued April 27, 1869, directing that masters, ensigns, and midshipmen (and consequently engineers assimilated in rank with them) wear, in lieu of shoulder-straps or epaulettes, gold-embroidered shoulder-loops, as per pattern. Other orders at intervals restored the epaulettes and cocked hats to masters and ensigns, until since 1881 only midshipmen (naval cadets) have worn the shoulder-knots.

Another supplementary order, dated May 27, 1869, modified the order of March 11th, to the extent of directing that captains wear four stripes of one-half inch gold lace and commanders three stripes of the same, to which modification staff officers "with assimilated rank of commander" were directed to conform.

The next change in uniform of any importance was dated November 7, 1874, the order reading as follows:

On and after the first of January, 1875, all officers of the navy to whom this regulation can apply will wear on their blue-cloth trousers for full-dress, a stripe of navy gold lace down the outer seam, of the width of that on their full-dress coats.

After the above date, lieutenant commanders, and officers ranking with that grade, will wear on their sleeves two stripes of gold lace half an inch in width, with one stripe a quarter of an inch in width between them, *each* a quarter of an inch apart.

Lieutenants, and officers ranking with that grade, will wear two stripes of half-inch gold lace, one-quarter of an inch apart.

A uniform circular order issued in January, 1877, directed that after the first day of July next following the sack-coat would cease to be worn as a service coat, and its place taken by a military blouse, the same as now worn. Such a garment had been in use for several years in foreign armies and had become familiar to the navy from being worn as undress by the cadets at the Naval Academy. It is extremely neat in appearance, without metal ornamentations except rank and corps devices on the collar, and its adoption was generally satisfactory to the service, though the highly unmilitary but more comfortable sack-coat was lamented by some.

The order of March 11, 1869, establishing distinguishing colors for the different staff corps was very distasteful to staff officers in general, and especially to the engineers, who objected to the red because it was a well established corps color for the medical corps in the British and some other navies. The staff officers claimed that the colors were selected for them to wear without regard to their wishes, and that the object in adopting the colors was to make a conspicuous distinction between the appearance of line and staff officers, which allegation was based upon the claim that the devices already in use for the different corps were sufficient to show to what branch of the service the wearer belonged. At intervals for ten or twelve years after the appearance of the order referred to, staff officers prepared petitions to the Secretary of the Navy asking that the corps colors be abolished, but nothing was ever done to that end, though an order was at one time prepared, but never issued, directing that all corps marks on uniforms be abolished; that uniforms of line and staff officers be the same, and that the different corps be distinguished by the color of the field in the shoulder-straps alone, those colors to be as already established. No efforts to have the colors abolished have been made in recent years and so far as the writer's observation has extended it is probable that a majority of the younger element of the engineer corps would greatly regret the loss of their red trimmings, which they have always worn and of which they are proud, despite the occasional awkwardness of having to enter into explanations when addressed as "Doctor" by foreign naval officers.

Two or three different emblems have been used as the distinguishing mark of the Bureau of Steam Engineering according to the taste of the chief of bureau at different times: the most familiar of these is the crossed anchor and screw-propeller which was adopted about the end of 1877 by Engineer-in-Chief Shock, after a number of designs had been considered, and remained the official device of the bureau until 1893, when a general seal (spread-eagle and anchor) was adopted for the Navy Department and all its bureaus, the different bureaus being distinguished by the name printed in a circle about the emblem. Between 1881 and 1886 the bureau emblem of the anchor and propeller was worn on the sleeves of petty officers of the engineers' force, but being complicated and difficult to keep clean was superseded at the latter date by a plain emblem representing a screw-propeller of three blades.

The orders that have been quoted in this chapter now bring the uniforms down to practically what are worn at the present time, leaving out of consideration unimportant changes made from time to time regarding helmets, white clothes, cap visor, and other minor details. The uniforms for all officers now, line and staff alike, are precisely the same, with the distinctions of grade and corps devices and corps colors for the staff. Under the present regulations no officer can complain of having nothing to wear, as the following list of uniforms will show:

Service Blouse and Uniform Cap now worn.

First Assistant Engineer in Uniform prescribed by order of Feb'y 8, 1861.

Undress Uniform of Chief Engineer, ranking with Commander, 1864-1869.

Special Full Dress of Chief Engineer, ranking with Lieutenant Commander, 1895.

(1) *Special Full Dress.*—Special full-dress-coat, laced trousers, cocked hat, epaulettes, sword, and dress belt.

(2) *Full Dress.*—Same as Special Full Dress, except that the frock coat shall be worn in place of the special full-dress coat. White trousers may be prescribed.

(3) *Dress.*—Frock coat, plain blue or white trousers, cocked hat, epaulettes, sword, and plain leather belt.

(4) *Undress (A).*—Frock coat, plain blue or white trousers, blue cap (with white cover if ordered), shoulder straps, sword, and plain leather belt.

(5) *Undress (B).*—Same as Undress (A), except that the sword and sword belt will not be worn.

(6) *Service Dress.*—Blue or white service coat, plain blue or white trousers, and blue cap (with white cover if ordered).

(7) *Evening Dress (A).*—Evening dress coat, laced trousers, evening dress waistcoat, cocked hat, epaulettes, sword, and dress belt (under waistcoat).

(8) *Evening Dress (B).*—Evening dress coat and waistcoat, plain blue trousers, and blue cap.

In addition to these combinations, a blue cloth overcoat is prescribed by regulation and a boat-cloak, or mackintosh, is authorized. Five or six white service coats, or tunics, and at least ten pairs of white trousers are necessary for the wardrobe of an officer serving in the tropics. White cap-covers take the place of summer helmets since January 1, 1895. An increase in width of one-half inch in the gold lace stripe on the trousers of all officers is ordered to take effect not later than July 1, 1897.

CHAPTER XXXVI.

"The education of the people is the building up of a nation."
—R. H. THURSTON.

The Connection of the Naval Engineer Corps with Technical Education in the United States—Engineers Detailed to Colleges by Authority of Congress—Success of the Experiment—Its Discontinuance.

A BILL which had its origin in the Bureau of Steam Engineering, Navy Department, and was supported generally by the leading educators throughout the country was presented to the 45th Congress and after the usual course of consideration was passed by both Houses and became a law by approval near the end of the last session of that Congress. This was a measure of great importance to the engineer corps and to the cause of technical education, its text complete reading as follows:

"AN ACT to promote a knowledge of steam-engineering and iron-ship building among the students of scientific schools or colleges in the United States.

"*Be it enacted by the Senate and House of Representatives of the United States of America in Congress assembled*, That for the purpose of promoting a knowledge of steam-engineering and iron-ship building among the young men of the United States, the President may, upon the application of an established scientific school or college within the United States, detail an officer from the Engineer Corps of the navy as professor in such school or college: *Provided*, That the number of officers so detailed shall not at any time exceed twenty-five, and such details shall be governed by rules to be prescribed from time to time by the President: *And provided further*, That such details may be withheld or withdrawn whenever, in the judgment of the President, the interests of the public service shall so require.

"Approved, February 26, 1879."

Under the operation of this law assistant engineers, well trained themselves, were detailed gradually for duty in different colleges until there was as many as eighteen or twenty simultaneously so employed. At the time of the enactment of the law our navy was nearly at its lowest ebb in the matter of ships, which was fortunate for the colleges if not for the navy, for the scarcity of vessels in commission made it possible to find engineer officers for this special duty without robbing the fleet. Under the direction of the naval engineers, departments of mechanical engineering were established in many large institutions and new life infused into many others already established but lagging behind from lack of interest or absence of directing zeal, while the presence of the engineers themselves, with their ideas of discipline and administration gained by their own military training, was of inestimable benefit to the institutions in which they served, as is testified by great numbers of letters from college presidents on file in the Navy Department.

Details of engineer officers under the law providing for this educational work have been made as follows since the passage of the act:

1879-1881; Assistant Engineer Walter F. Worthington, to Lafayette College, Easton, Pennsylvania.

1881-1884; Assistant Engineer George S. Willits, to the Franklin Institute, Philadelphia, Pennsylvania.
Assistant Engineer Ira N. Hollis, to Union College, Schenectady, New York.
Assistant Engineer H. W. Spangler, to the University of Pennsylvania, Philadelphia, Pennsylvania.

1881-1885; Assistant Engineer M. E. Cooley, to the University of Michigan, Ann Arbor, Michigan.

1882; Assistant Engineer J. L. Gow, to South Western States Normal School, California, Pennsylvania.

1882-1883; Assistant Engineer Henry K. Ivers, to Washington University, St. Louis, Missouri.

1882-1884; Assistant Engineer Wm. B. Boggs, to Vanderbilt University, Nashville, Tennessee.

1882-1885; Assistant Engineer F. H. Eldridge, to Ohio State University, Columbus, Ohio.

Assistant Engineer C. A. Carr, to the Stevens Institute of Technology, Hoboken, New Jersey.

1882-1886; Passed Assistant Engineer Robert Crawford, to the Spring Garden Institute, Philadelphia, Pennsylvania.

1883-1885; Passed Assistant Engineer R. G. Denig, to Hamilton College, Clinton, New York.

Assistant Engineer Walter M. McFarland, to Cornell University, Ithica, New York.

Assistant Engineer W.F. Durand, to Lafayette College, Easton, Pennsylvania.

Assistant Engineer W. F. C. Hasson, to the University of Colorado, Boulder, Colorado.

Assistant Engineer Winfield S. Sample, to the Western University, Allegheny, Pennsylvania.

Assistant Engineer Jay M. Whitham, to St. John's College, Annapolis, Maryland.

1883-1886; Assistant Engineer W. H. Allderdice, to Washington University, St. Louis, Missouri.

1883-1887; Assistant Engineer A. W. Stahl, to Purdue University, Lafayette, Indiana.

Assistant Engineer Arthur T. Woods, to the University of Illinois, Champaign, Illinois.

1884-1887 Assistant Engineer Goold H. Bull, to the University of Pennsylvania, Philadelphia, Pennsylvania.

1884-1890; Passed Assistant Engineer John D. Ford, to the Baltimore Manual Training School, Baltimore, Maryland.

1885-1886; Assistant Engineer W. N. Little, to the Worcester Free Institute, Worcester, Massachusetts.

Assistant Engineer Andrew M. Hunt, to the Michigan Military Academy, Orchard Lake, Michigan.

1885-1887; Assistant Engineer F. M. Bennett, to the Chicago Manual Training School, Chicago, Illinois.

Assistant Engineer J. H. Baker, to St. John's College, Annapolis, Maryland.

1885-1888; Passed Assistant Engineer David P. Jones, to the Kansas Normal College, Fort Scott, Kansas.

Passed Assistant Engineer Frank H. Bailey, to Cornell University, Ithica, New York.

1886-1887; Assistant Engineer E. O'C. Acker, to Vanderbilt University, Nashville, Tennessee.

1886-1888; Assistant Engineer G. W. McElroy, to the University of South Carolina, Columbia, South Carolina.

Assistant Engineer T. W. Kinkaid, to the New Hampshire College, Hanover, New Hampshire.

1886-1889; Assistant Engineer F. W. Bartlett, to the Michigan Military Academy, Orchard Lake, Michigan.

1887; Assistant Engineer W. F. Durand, to the Worcester Free Institute, Worcester, Massachusetts.

1887-1890; Assistant Engineer H. W. Spangler, to the University of Pennsylvania, Philadelphia, Pennsylvania.

1887-1891; Assistant Engineer W. H. P. Creighton, to Purdue University, Lafayette, Indiana.

1888-1891; Passed Assistant Engineer G. B. Ransom, to the University of Wisconsin, Madison, Wisconsin.

Passed Assistant Engineer Wm. C. Eaton, to Madison University, Hamilton, New York.

Passed Assistant Engineer A. B. Canaga, to Cornell University, Ithica, New York.

Passed Assistant Engineer J. R. Edwards, to the University of South Carolina, Columbia, South Carolina.

Passed Assistant Engineer Wythe M. Parks, to the Chicago Manual Training School, Chicago, Illinois.

Assistant Engineer J. R. Wilmer, to St. John's College, Annapolis, Maryland.

1888-1892; Passed Assistant Engineer T. F. Burgdorff, to the University of Tennessee, Knoxville, Tennessee.

1889; Assistant Engineer Charles E. Rommell, to the Wilmington High School, Wilmington, Delaware.

1889-1890; Passed Assistant Engineer George S. Willits, to the Pratt Institute, Brooklyn, New York.

Assistant Engineer Leo D. Miner, to the University of Michigan, Ann Arbor, Michigan.

1889-1891; Assistant Engineer W. F. C. Hasson, to John Hopkins University, Baltimore, Maryland.

1890-1891; Passed Assistant Engineer John Pemberton, to the Pennsylvania State College, Centre County, Pennsylvania.

1893-1895; Passed Assistant Engineer T. W. Kinkaid, to the Pennsylvania State College, Centre County, Pennsylvania.

1894-1896; Chief Engineer John D. Ford, to the Maryland Agricultural College, College Park, Maryland.

After this method of extending governmental aid to institutions of learning had become well established and so popular as to actually embarrass the Department in meeting the requests of colleges, the work of rebuilding the navy was undertaken in earnest and the additions to the fleet of modern cruisers with complicated machinery made the services of naval engineers so necessary that few could be spared to continue the good work of technical education. At the same time that our marine engines were increasing in number and complexity the membership of the engineer corps was slowly diminished. By one of those inscrutable exhibitions of inconsistency that occasionally set the public marveling, Congress, by the very same act that appropriated money for the construction of the first steel ships of the new navy, provided for a gradual reduction of the engineer corps from two hundred and seventy members to one hundred and seventy, the reduction to take place in the grades of passed assistant and assistant engineers only. The officers of these grades being the ones upon whom the duty of standing watch at sea devolves, as well as the ones most available for college duty, the latter had to step aside for the claims of the government upon its own, and the college details were withdrawn, or allowed to expire without sending a relief.

Strenuous efforts were made by educators and naval engineers to induce Congress to reconsider its action and provide for a sufficient membership of the engineer corps to allow the continuation of the college work without interfering with the engineers' duties in building and supervising the machinery of the new navy. So much interest was taken in the matter that a committee, composed of the presidents of three of the most prominent colleges in the United

States, was appointed by the Educational Association and sent to Washington to endeavor to enlist the good will of Congress: but such things take time, and when a bill providing for the termination in the reduction of the engineer corps reached a vote and was passed, after having been before Congress for several years, it was too late. The corps had then diminished to within twenty-five of the lower number allowed, and the needs of the new ships demanded many more than there were even with this slight addition. So the educational work had to be abandoned. But two details have been made within the past five years, and these were brought about by the exercise of political influence too powerful for the Navy Department to withstand.

With no exception, so far as known, the engineer officers carried out the work assigned them in the various colleges with zeal and thoroughness, winning unqualified praise from the educators with whom they were associated, and by their abilities and bearing in the critical communities in which they lived in the college towns reflected credit upon their corps and did much to infuse abroad a better knowledge of and kindlier feeling toward the navy as an organization. The popularity of the army with the public is due in no small degree to the presence always of a considerable number of army officers as military instructors in schools and colleges throughout the country, setting such excellent examples of intelligence, self-control, and good training that the results, reflected in the minds of the growing generation, are sentiments of respect and admiration for the whole army; and the naval engineers on school duty were doing much to bring about the same for the navy. When placed in similar positions they realized that through them the naval service was on trial, often in communities where a predisposition existed to judge harshly anything and anybody connected with a military branch of the government, and to their credit it can be said that in every case the naval engineer appreciated the critical nature of his surroundings and so conducted himself in his official work and in his social life as to inspire a genuine liking and respect for the navy which he represented. In the discontinuance of these details the colleges lost much, but for the reasons just given the navy has lost more in the opportunity to set itself in a true light before the educated and scholarly elements of American society.

Space forbids a detailed account of the work done at different institutions by all the engineers trusted with the carrying out of this important work for which reason a few instances only will be briefly related as indicative of the nature of the work done by all.

In the summer of 1881 Assistant Enginneer Mortimer E. Cooley reported in obedience to naval orders to the president of the University of Michigan and was directed to establish a course of mechanical engineering parallel with the existing courses in civil and mining engineering that a complete school of engineering might exist in the university. Mr. Cooley was elected to the chair of mechanical engineering by the board of regents and proceeded to create his department from nothing to begin with by laying out a course of study, at first incomplete and difficult to execute because of the entire lack of appliances and facilities for instruction. An appropriation of $2,500 by the State Legislature soon enabled him to build and equip a small workshop or mechanical laboratory, but the trifling sum appropriated so limited the result that only six students out of about twenty applicants could be admitted to the class first to begin the new course. About a year later a larger appropriation by the Legislature enabled Mr. Cooley to enlarge his laboratories and employ an assistant professor, which allowed of the formation of a new class of eighteen students.

From this small beginning the growth of the new school was steady and rapid, until now it is one of the largest and best mechanical engineering schools in the country, its growth and success being due almost entirely to the professional and executive ability of Mr. Cooley and to his peculiar aptitude for imparting instruction. When his detail expired in 1884 such influence was used by President Angell of the university and the great value of his services to the institution so clearly set forth that the Department extended his orders one year. At the end of that time, in response to a most flattering offer made by the board of regents, he resigned his commission in the navy and accepted the professorship of mechanical engineering, which position he still holds, being one of the most prominent and popular members of the faculty as well as a leading and well-known citizen identified with the political and material development of the state in which he lives.

The work done at the Stevens Institute of Technology by

Assistant Engineer C. A. Carr, U. S. Navy, is best described by quoting from a detailed report of his duties made to the Department by him in January, 1885:

" As shown by the catalogue, I am professor of marine engineering and assistant to the professor of mathematics and mechanics. The entire senior class, numbering between forty and fifty students, are required to take the course in marine engineering. Instruction is given almost entirely by lectures and is of a practical character in which I aim to give the class the benefit of the practical knowledge that I have acquired. The class provide themselves with "Seaton's Marine Engineering," which they use as a reference book. The subjects of materials of engineering and theory of the steam engine are studied in the department of mechanical engineering, it being left for me to enable the students to become familiar with the practical design, construction, and working of the marine steam engine. The subjects treated of most in detail are,— the different methods of determining the resistance of ships; the different types of engines, their advantages and disadvantages, and a comparison of the simple and compound engine; the computation of horse-power to overcome a known resistance; the varied designs used for the different parts of the engine, boiler, and propelling instrument, and the rules for proportioning these parts; and facts regarding the practical working and care of machinery. The practical application of the Zeuner valve diagram and strain diagrams is taught by me in the draughting room. During the year the class visit the principal ocean steamers and engine-building works about New York, and make a tour of inspection of several days to the ship-yards at Philadelphia, Wilmington, and Chester, in my charge.

" In the department of mathematics and mechanics I have the freshman and sophomore classes, the instruction given them by me including the following subjects: trigonometry ; theory of equations ; coördinate geometry ; differential and integral calculus ; and elementary mechanics : also a few lectures on determinants and quaternions.

" This includes everything that has been required of me by the authorities of the institute, but I have voluntarily done a great deal of work for the mechanical laboratory, under the direction of Professor R. H. Thurston. The mechanical laboratory makes tests of engines, boilers, lubricants, etc., for outside parties, the proceeds being used in buying apparatus for the laboratory and in paying the expenses of experimental research on subjects of general interest to engineers. Much of this work is done by students under the superintendence of a competent engineer, by which means they gain a great deal of practical knowledge and experience. This work I have undertaken for my own instruction, and because it comes directly in the line of work for which I am detailed. The work which I have done, or which has been done under my superintendence, includes the following : a test to determine the efficiency of different kinds of worm and spur gearing; a test to determine the law of condensation of steam in the cylinder; tests of boilers; tests of gas engines; tests of engines running dynamos; tests to determine tensile strength and elongation of different brands of telephone wire; and a great many tests to determine the value of lubricants and of all kinds of materials for construction."

Assistant Engineers A. W. Stahl at Purdue University, Lafayette, Indiana, and A. T. Woods at the University of Illinois, Champaign, Illinois, did work very similar to that before credited to Assistant Engineer Cooley at the University of Michigan, each developing from a small beginning a thorough course in theoretical and practical mechanical engineering, systematically organized and well equipped with laboratories and modern appliances for imparting knowledge. Working in conjunction, their posts of duty not being widely separated, they combined their lectures and supplied the want of a suitable text book for students by having the lectures published in book form under the title of "Principles of Mechanism." So valuable were the services of these gentlemen that each, at the urgent solicitation of the authorities of the colleges where they were stationed, was granted an extension of one year in the length of their details, and Mr. Woods, when finally detached, was offered and accepted the chair of mechanical engineering, resigning his commission in the navy to remain with the university. Four years later he removed to St. Louis to assume the chair of dynamic engineering in Washington University, and a year afterward, having become a recognized authority on the economics of locomotive engines, was given the position of editor of the *Railway Gazette*, in Chicago. In February, 1893, he died of typhoid fever, the loss to the engineering world caused by his death being commented upon at length by all the technical journals throughout the country. He was a native of Minnesota, and a member of the class of cadet engineers that graduated from the Naval Academy in 1880.

The following letter written by the president of St. John's College, Annapolis, Maryland, commending the services to that institution of Assistant Engineer Jay M. Whitham supplies another account of this class of duty:

"Mr. Whitham was detailed by the Secretary of the Navy in July, 1883, to act as professor of mechanical engineering, &c., in St. John's College. When he reported for duty, there was not even the beginning of such a department in the institution, either in courses of study or in necessary appliances,—nothing, in short, except a demand for such instruction on the part of a goodly number of the students, and sympathy and encouragement on the part of a few members of the board and faculty.

"Under these circumstances, too much praise cannot be given to Mr. Whitham for the tact, skill and energy with which he has succeeded, with so little pecuniary assistance and in so short a time, in establishing a department which I venture to believe the friends of the college will never hereafter suffer to be withdrawn from its curriculum.

"During the first year, in consequence of the utter absence of the most essential mechanical appliances, he was compelled to limit the work of his classes chiefly to the principles and practice of mechanical drawing. In this he has achieved a distinguished success, the results being of a character, both in quality and quantity, to prove his entire fitness as instructor in this branch of his department. In connection with this, also, instruction was given in descriptive geometry, the course in which was made eminently *practical*. His success thus far, together with the interest awakened in such practical studies, naturally led to a further development and extension of the work of the department. A steam engine was purchased and a work-shop opened, in which our students may now be found laboring at anvil, bench and lathe with an interest and energy which are of themselves a sufficient proof of the wisdom displayed in the establishment of this department.

"I should, however, fail to do full justice to Professor Whitham should I omit to acknowledge our obligations to him for most timely and valuable aid in the department of mathematics. That chair having become vacant in consequence of necessary changes in the faculty, he was entrusted with the entire management of the department. His work has been as conspicuously successful as in the department of mechanical engineering. The regular course has been improved and extended, elective courses have been introduced, a new interest in mathematical studies has been awakened, and a spirit of energy and thoroughness infused into the entire department.

"Mr. Whitham is qualified by natural endowment, as well as thorough training—now also supplemented by the lessons of experience—to give satisfaction as instructor in the departments in which he has labored among us with such marked credit and success.

"I would also say that as a teacher Mr. Whitham is exceedingly painstaking and helpful, easily approached by his pupils, and animated and clear in his manner of communicating instruction; while as a disciplinarian he is firm and positive in the maintenance of order and in requiring of the student satisfactory proofs of honest and faithful application."

At the expiration of his tour of duty at St. John's, Mr. Whitham, as too many other assistant engineers have done, resigned from the navy, accepting the chair of engineering in the University of Arkansas which had been offered him. During his five years occupancy of that position he developed the department of engineering from twelve students and no assistant instructors to one hundred and five students and five assistant professors, besides building and equipping laboratories and work-shops for practical instruction. During the same time he wrote and had published two professional text books—"Steam Engine Design," and "Constructive Steam Engineering."

The few examples now cited are fairly representative and show that the duties performed by naval engineers assigned to colleges were in the main within the bounds of their profession and consistent with the wording of the act of Congress authorizing the assignments, but there are some records showing a variety of employment decidedly startling. A report of duty engaged in, made by Assistant Engineer W. F. C. Hasson from the University of Colorado at Boulder in that State, after detailing about eight hours daily class-room work in mathematics, mechanics, electricity, drawing, and astronomy, goes on to say that he is acting as secretary of the university and general assistant to the president; has command of the corps of cadets, and is a member of the lecturing force engaged in enlightening the public by means of a series of popular lectures on general subjects in the larger towns about the State. Apparently feeling that some explanation is due for all this variety, Mr. Hasson remarks at the end of his report,—"I have remained here because I am glad to be associated with a faculty composed of earnest hard-working scholars who are struggling against every obstacle to establish a scholarly institution."

Though now practically abandoned by the government, the work begun so well by many of the naval engineers is being carried on to some extent yet by former members of the corps who have resigned from the service to make educational work a profession, or by naval engineers on the retired list, the latter readily finding employment of this nature as a result of the excellent reputation for the corps established by regularly detailed active members in former years. Prominent among engineers of naval training now educators by profession may be mentioned Dr. R. H. Thurston, Director of Sibley College, Cornell University; Professor W. F. Durand, Principal of the School of Marine Construction at the same university; Professor Ira. N. Hollis, Director of the Lawrence Scientific School, Harvard University, and Professor H. W. Spangler of the University of Pennsylvania. Of retired naval engineers engaged in educational work may be mentioned as representatives Passed Assistant Engineer John W. Saville, Director of the Baltimore Manual Training School; Passed Assistant Engineer Robert Crawford, Superintendent of the Williamson School, Delaware County, Pennsylvania, and Passed Assistant Engineer W. R. King, Commandant of Cadets at the Cheltenham Military Academy.

CHAPTER XXXVII.

"Our occupation was formerly an instinct; now it is a science."
—ADMIRAL JURIEN DE LA GRAVIERE.

Brief Mention of Events of Engineering Interest Since 1872—Peril of the MANHATTAN—Titles of Assistant Engineers Changed—Chief Engineer Wm. H. Shock Appointed Engineer-in-Chief—Loss of the HURON—Cruise of the MARION to Heard Island—Reduction of Engineer Corps in 1882—Case of the Discharged Cadet Engineers—Wreck of the ASHUELOT—Longevity Pay for Passed Assistant Engineers—Chief Engineer C. H. Loring Succeeds Mr. Shock as Engineer-in-Chief—Naval Disaster at Samoa—Naval Engineers at the Columbian Exposition and Midwinter Fair—Loss of the KEARSARGE—Casualty on the MONTEREY.

TOWARD the end of the year 1873 the ships of the North Atlantic, South Atlantic, and European squadrons were assembled at Key West and all serviceable vessels at the navy yards were hurriedly fitted for service and despatched to the same point, the occasion being a possible rupture with Spain on account of that nation's action in the case of the steamer *Virginius*. One of the vessels prepared for this service was the monitor *Manhattan*, which was hastily repaired at Cramp's shipyard in Philadelphia and proceeded to sea, convoyed by the *Powhatan*, the 26th day of November. The next day when well clear of the Capes of the Delaware a gale was encountered and the evil effects of the haste with which the vessel had been prepared for sea at once showed themselves: water came in under the turret in volumes, the decks leaked badly, and the bilge pumps, constantly choking with chips and shavings left by the contractor's men, could with great difficulty be kept in operation. It was an exact repetition of the experience of the *Passaic* the night the *Monitor* went down, and one can but wonder that the lesson was so soon forgotten. After pluckily fighting against almost certain destruction for one whole day, Commander Yates of the *Manhattan* signalled the *Powhatan* that they must return to the Delaware Breakwater, where the *Manhattan* arrived eventually so disabled as to be of no immediate use for war.

While the sea was breaking at its worst over the bows of the *Manhattan* and against her turret in great masses, First Assistant Engineer John Lowe and a seaman, with great daring ventured down from the top of the turret with a hawser, which they succeeded in adjusting around the base of the turret to aid in keeping out the water. During the time that the vessel was in imminent peril Second Assistant Engineer John T. Smith remained in the bilges soaked with cold water for a period of twenty-six hours keeping the bilge pumps in operation, and with such success that his efforts prevented the *Manhattan* from foundering. When the vessel had succeeded in finding safety in the Delaware Mr. Smith was so ill from cold and exhaustion that he was sent to a hospital and never sufficiently recovered to return to active duty. The devotion to duty displayed by him was of such character as to call forth the following letter from his commanding officer:

"United States Iron-Clad MANHATTAN,
"Delaware River, November 30, 1873.

" SIR:—Your conduct during the period that this vessel was in a distressed condition on the 27th instant, while being towed by the United States Steamer *Powhatan*, was such as requires higher commendation than simply to say it met with approval. It was such as to merit the highest praise.

" Your necessary exposure, being in a wet condition during an entire day to insure the efficient working of the bilge pumps, on which the preservation of the ship depended, was an evidence of your zeal and faithfulness in the discharge of your duty. Your health, which has suffered by your exertions on the day named, will, I trust, be restored to you, and your usefulness preserved to the service.

" I am, very truly, yours,
" A. R. YATES, Commander, U. S. N., Comd'g., ' Manhattan.'
"Second Assistant Engineer J. T. SMITH,
" United States Navy (through Navy Department)."

The illness of Mr. Smith resulted in permanent disability and he was eventually condemned by a medical survey and recommended for retirement. His friends, believing that the circumstances of his disablement warranted some recognition, caused a bill to be introduced in Congress authorizing his advancement to the grade of first assistant engineer previous to being retired, which bill passed and became a law in January, 1875. The report recommending the passage of the bill, made by Senator Anthony, gave the following as a reason for Mr. Smith's advancement: "His record during the war was such as to meet the commendation of his superiors at all times; and it further appears that he lost his health by being subjected to extreme fatigue and exposure while in the line of duty. When the *Manhattan* started for Cuba in 1873, Smith was ordered on board, and it is said that by his very extraordinary exertions he saved the vessel, and at the time was highly complimented by his associates."

The act of Congress approved February 24, 1874, extending the academic course for cadet engineers from two years to four, also provided that from and after its passage the title of first assistant engineer should be changed to passed assistant engineer, and the title of second assistant engineer to assistant engineer.

In the spring of 1877, at the expiration of his term of office, Engineer-in-Chief Wood was relieved by Chief Engineer Wm. H. Shock, the latter assuming the duties of chief of the Bureau of Steam Engineering on the third of March. Mr. Wood, under whose direction the designs for new machinery for the large double-turreted monitors then being rebuilt had been prepared, was ordered to the important duty of general superintendent of that machinery. He was placed on the retired list in May, 1880, having arrived at the age limit, though in vigorous possession of all his faculties. Two years later, August 31, 1882, he was drowned by the capsizing of a canoe in a creek at his summer residence in St. Mary's county, Maryland, thus adding one more to the long list of retired sea-faring men who, after escaping the dangers of the sea for a life-time, meet death by drowning in some quiet stream or mill-pond.

Mr. Shock, the new bureau chief, had been prominent in his corps ever since his admission to it more than thirty years before and enjoyed an excellent reputation throughout the navy. Besides the many important duties performed by him, he was the inventor of a successful rotary projectile to be fired from smooth-bore guns,

CHIEF ENGINEER W. H. SHOCK, U. S. NAVY.

Engineer-in-Chief of the Navy from March 3, 1877 to June 15, 1883. From a photograph taken about ten years after Mr. Shock's retirement from active duty.

the peculiarities in the construction of the shot giving to it the advantages possessed by shot fired from rifled guns. He also had invented and patented an improved bullet for small arms, and a compensating device for setting up wire rigging in ships. The latter was very heartily approved by Admiral Porter and was used to a considerable extent in the naval service. During the International Exposition in Vienna in 1873 Mr. Shock filled the position of Vice President of the division of "Civil Enginery." He is an alumnus of Dickinson College, holding a diploma of Master of Arts from that institution. While chief of the Bureau of Steam Engineering he published an exhaustive and excellent treatise on steam boilers.

The iron screw gun-boat *Huron*, after being in commission about two years on the North Atlantic station, sailed for the West Indies from Hampton Roads November 23rd, 1877. Shortly after 1 a. m. the next morning she ran ashore on the low sandy beach in the vicinity of Nag's Head on the coast of North Carolina and became a total wreck. For some time after she struck no fears were entertained for the safety of the crew, but the ship heeled far over to the weather side, allowing the heavy incoming seas to break into and over her, washing away the men as they became exhausted, until in the end the loss of life was frightful; of sixteen officers only four were saved, or rather saved themselves, for they got ashore by their own exertions after being washed off the ship, and owed their preservation to superior endurance and to favorable accidents while struggling in the water. Only one of the marine guard of fifteen men got ashore, and only thirty of the one hundred enlisted men of the crew were equally fortunate. Two of the four officers who saved themselves were engineers—Assistant Engineer R. G. Denig, and Cadet Engineer E. T. Warburton, both young and vigorous men. Chief Engineer E. M. Olsen and Cadet Engineer E. N. Loomis were drowned.

The behavior of all on board was excellent, and especially so in the engineer's department, as brought out by the testimony before the court of inquiry that investigated the loss. The conditions below were appalling: the boilers started from their foundations and were in momentary danger of shifting bodily into the fire-room; the ship heeled so much that the amount of water in the boilers could not be known, and water from the breaking seas was rapidly filling the ship, in spite of all which, the officers and men remained faithfully at their posts, keeping up steam at full pressure to work the pumps and main engines and caring generally for the machinery the same as though the ship had been in free route. The engines were kept backing at full speed for nearly an hour after the ship struck and finally stopped only when the accumulation of sand under the stern blocked the propeller. Chief Engineer Olsen then reported the condition of the engines and obtained authority from Commander Ryan to haul fires, which was done in an orderly manner and the men permitted to go on deck and take their chances of getting ashore with others of the crew. Five of the enlisted men of the engineer's force saved themselves and seventeen were lost.

In the latter part of 1881 the screw-sloop *Marion*, then attached to the South Atlantic station, was ordered to proceed to the vicinity of Heard Island in the Southern Indian Ocean to search for a missing American whale-ship, the *Trinity*. The long and trying voyage was made and the crew of the whaler found existing miserably on the bleak and barren island where they had been wrecked fifteen months before. This humane expedition cost the life of Cadet Engineer John U. Crygier, a very popular young officer who had graduated from the Naval Academy two years before. Upon the return of the *Marion* to South America, Mr. Crygier was invalided home by order of a medical survey, he having been found suffering from a fatal disease of the kidneys brought on, as the surgeons reported, by protracted watch duty in the variable temperature of the engine and fire-rooms during the long voyage of the *Marion*. At home he was found disqualified for promotion by reason of his physical disability and was dropped from the service, not being eligible for the retired list on account of being a cadet and not a commissioned officer, although he was entitled to promotion and a commission in June, 1881, long before his disability occurred. His death occurred not long after he was dropped. He was for four years the room-mate of the author at the Naval Academy and was a genial and attractive associate, a true friend, and an accomplished young gentleman.

In adddition to the destruction of the cadet engineer system at the Naval Academy, the engineer corps suffered another severe loss by the provisions of the naval appropriation act of **August 5, 1882,** one of the sections of which fixed the number of passed assistant and assistant engineers at sixty and forty respectively in place of the one hundred previously established as the membership of each grade: the number and relative rank of the chief engineers remained as before. The actual strength of the corps at the time of the passage of the act was seventy chief engineers, ninety-nine passed assistant engineers, and sixty-two assistant engineers, in addition to which there were sixty-two cadet engineers, graduates, serving at sea, and seventy-three cadet engineers, under-graduates, in the different classes at the Naval Academy. Sixteen of the graduated cadets belonged to the class of 1880 and were therefore entitled to promotion in June, 1882, before the new law was enacted, which promotion they duly received as they became available for examination, but all other cadet engineers at sea or at the Academy were combined with cadet midshipmen to make the new corps of naval cadets. This amalgamation and an exchange of duties on board ship was directed by the following general order:

GENERAL ORDER
NO. 302.

"NAVY DEPARTMENT,

"WASHINGTON, December 12, 1882.

"The attention of commanding and other officers is called to the act of Congress, approved August 5, 1882, which provides that vacancies in the lower grades of the Line, Engineer Corps, and Marine Corps shall hereafter be filled by appointments to be made from the graduates of the Naval Academy, at the conclusion of their six years' course, and in the order of merit as shall be determined by the Academic Board of the Naval Academy.

"The above applies to all naval cadets who have not completed the prescribed six years' course of instruction.

"In order that naval cadets who have completed the four years' course of study at the Naval Academy shall have equal opportunity to prepare for their final examination, it is ordered that those who have been doing duty as cadet engineers shall in addition to those duties be assigned to deck and division duties, and shall be given every opportunity to acquire a knowledge of navigation, gunnery and seamanship, as well as of steam engineering; and that those who have been doing duty as cadet midshipmen shall, in addition to those duties, be given the duties in the fire and engine-rooms hitherto performed by cadet engineers.

"All naval cadets will, at the end of their six years' course, be finally examined at the Naval Academy by the Academic Board.

"The duty performed by each naval cadet shall be specified in the column of 'Remarks,' already provided on the Quarterly Returns called for by General Order No. 290.

"Commanding officers of naval vessels are charged with the execution of this order, which affects naval cadets who appear as cadet midshipmen on pages 25, 26, and 27, Navy Register of July 1, 1882, beginning with and junior to John L. Schock; and those who are designated cadet engineers on pages 39 and 40 of the same register beginning with and junior to Jay M. Whitham.

"Commanding officers are directed to inform the Department of the date of the receipt of this order.

"The attention of commanding officers is also called to paragraph 143, page 51, and paragraphs 3, 4, and 5, page 65, Navy Regulations, edition of 1876. These regulations will be strictly enforced.

"WILLIAM E. CHANDLER,
"*Secretary of the Navy.*"

The gradual reduction in the engineer corps directed by the act of 1882 practically stopped promotion in the lower grades of that arm, and as the line had been reduced more than one hundred numbers by the same act that branch also suffered from stagnation for a number of years. The result of this was that few vacancies existed at the end of each year for the cadets finally graduating, the most of whom in consequence were honorably discharged in accordance with the terms of the act, which is quoted in the chapter relating to the Naval Academy. The operation of this law was particularly severe upon the cadet engineers who had graduated from the Academy, for they found themselves with little time for preparation obliged to compete for the few vacancies with their midshipmen classmates who had had the benefit of three or four years instruction and practice in the technical branches upon which the examination was based. The general order No. 302 directing an exchange of duties was not received on some of the remote stations until the members of the class of 1881 were about to proceed home for final examination, and the cadet engineers of that class were therefore obliged to appear at the Naval Academy with little experience in seamanship, navigation, and gunnery, in which the midshipmen were proficient, while the examination in steam was that based upon the elementary course the cadet midshipmen had received, and in which they had an equal opportunity with the cadet engineers for excellence.

Thus handicapped, the cadet engineers of the class of 1881 had the mortification of being obliged to omit the examinations in the most important subjects, with the result that but one of them, after receiving *zero* for a mark in both seamanship and navigation, had a sufficient multiple to get one of the twenty commissions which were distributed to the combined class of ninety members. The next class of cadet engineers, that of 1882, fared much better, for with one year more time in which to prepare, its members made an excellent showing when put into competition with the cadet midshipmen, the merit roll of the combined class after the final examinations showing the first three members—Robert Gatewood, Emil Theiss and W. H. P. Creighton—to have been former cadet engineers, and eight of them took a sufficiently high standing to obtain commissions in either the navy or marine corps. The experience of the other classes of cadet engineers transformed into naval cadets has been told in the chapter devoted to the engineering course at the Naval Academy and need not be referred to again, except, perhaps, to remark that of all the injuries dealt the engineer corps by the act of 1882 the loss of these same classes of cadet engineers was not the least. From the method of their selection, sustained by their academic records, the young gentlemen of these classes were of very superior capability, and as they almost without exception went into other branches of the service than the engineer corps when finally graduated that corps lost in them an element that would have been a strong safeguard in after years.

The courses of instruction for cadet midshipmen and cadet engineers prior to the passage of the act of August 5, 1882, were the same; viz., four years at the Naval Academy and two years at sea, but a different wording of the statutes in the two cases placed the cadet engineers upon a better footing for opposing the application of that act to those of them who had already completed the academic course. The period of two years at sea for cadet midshipmen was specified as *probationary*, while for cadet engineers it was referred to as *service;* cadet engineers after leaving the Academy were also referred to in law as *graduates*, and that word was used in defining them in the very same act that specified that all *under-graduates* should thereafter be designated naval cadets. So they had ample legal grounds for claiming to be graduates not subject to the operation of the act, and for contending that the Department had committed an error in issuing the general order No. 302.

Before the final examination of the class of 1881 at the Academy in June, 1883, had taken place, a cadet engineer—Harry G. Leopold—of the class of 1882 had brought the illegality of the Department's action to public attention by bringing suit in the Court of Claims for the difference in pay between that of a cadet engineer and a naval cadet for the period that he had been regarded as a naval cadet, and his claim was sustained by the unanimous vote of that court. In its opinion in this case the Court of Claims held that the cadet engineers were graduates under the law and that the act of 1882 had been misconstrued by the Navy Department in declaring that it applied to the cadet engineers not at the Academy. This was conclusive as an opinion from a proper legal authority, but the Navy Department, instead of accepting it, demanded a rehearing of the case and in the meantime discharged all the cadet engineers of the class of 1881 with the exception of one fortunate member whose class standing entitled him to a commission. The Court of Claims sustained its previous finding in the Leopold case and also rendered an exactly similar decision in the case of De W. C. Redgrave, a member of the class of 1881 who had brought suit for his difference in pay prior to being discharged, but these decisions had no effect upon the Navy Department which adhered to its action in discharging the unfortunate cadets.

When the class of 1882 came up for final examination in 1884 and a majority of its members were mustered out, one of them, Lyman B. Perkins, obtained a more important decision by suing the government in the Court of Claims for pay as a cadet engineer *after* being mustered out. He won his case easily, having the law entirely on his side, the decision of the court being that his discharge was a violation of law and therefore void, and that he was entitled to continue to draw his pay whether the Navy Department chose to recognize him as a cadet engineer or not. This decision plainly put all the discharged cadet engineers back into the navy by virtue of being on its pay rolls, but the authorities of the Department had determined that the cadet engineers must go, and refused to recognize them. To avoid paying them in accordance with the decision of the court, the Department appealed the Perkins case to the Supreme Court and at the same time, with a view to settling the controversy finally, made a test case of the Redgrave decision and appealed that also to the Supreme Court. In January, 1886, the Supreme Court handed down an opinion in both these cases affirming in every particular the decisions of the Court of Claims and sustaining the position of the cadet engineers. The Navy Department then, acting on the advice of the Attorney General, issued a general order (No. 344, dated March 10, 1886) restoring the cadet engineers to the service and declaring them to be regarded as on waiting orders since the dates of their discharge. This order was supplemented a few months later by another restoring to the service four cadet engineers of the two classes who had been dropped for physical disability, it being admitted that the Department's action in these cases had been equally illegal with that in the cases of those who had been mustered out.

Several of these young gentlemen were prosperously established in business and declined to be restored to the service, or resigned from it soon after such restoration. The others, about twenty in all, found themselves placed junior to the assistant engineers who had been commissioned in the intervening years, and with no better prospect than of remaining cadet engineers for life, for there was no law whereby they might be advanced or promoted. In this predicament they had to lay their grievances before Congress, and bills and resolutions soon appeared before that body making provision for their restoration to their proper places in the list of assistant engineers. Without following out the fortunes of this legislative effort in all its details, it is sufficient to say that an act of Congress, approved July 9, 1888, directed that they be commissioned assistant engineers in the navy and in their original places on the list, the class of 1881 to be commissioned from July 1, 1883, and the class of 1882 from July 1, 1884.

The next lion in the path of these sorely harassed young gentlemen was the U. S. Treasury Department, which refused to pay them as assistant engineers from the dates of their commissions, although as in their original trouble the law was directly on their side. For two or three years they looked to Congress for relief, seeking to have the amount necessary to pay them what was legally due made an item in the general deficiency bill, but these efforts were slow in bearing fruit and they finally had to resort again to the employment of counsel and sue the United States through the Court of Claims for their unpaid salaries. Late in 1892, after many delays, the case reached a hearing and was decided in accordance with law in favor of the assistant engineers, who collected their pay and for the first time in ten years were out of trouble, having in the meantime acquired as much legal and legislative experience as is good for any naval officer to possess.

About four o'clock in the morning of February 18, 1883, the iron double-ender *Ashuelot* proceeding southward along the coast of China from Amoy ran upon one of the Lamock Rocks near Swatow and was so damaged that she sank forty-seven minutes later. Eleven of her people were drowned, the others escaping by the ship's boats to the island, and thence by a Chinese revenue steamer to Swatow. That greater loss of life did not result was due to the circumstance that the ship struck just at the time when both watches were up, one relieving the other. When the order to abandon ship was given, a messenger boy was sent to notify the officer in charge of the engine room, but the boy was so frightened that he jumped overboard without delivering the message and as a result the engine-room force narrowly escaped being left on the sinking ship. Assistant Engineer J. M. Pickrell, who had stood the mid-watch, was in charge of the watch, assisted by Cadet Engineer W. T. Webster, who had come below to relieve Mr. Pickrell just before the ship struck, these young officers having two watches of firemen below with them.

As the last boat was about to shove off, the executive officer, Lieutenant A. J. Iverson, whose coolness and presence of mind throughout the catastrophe won him high commendation, bethought himself of the engine-room and called down to see if anyone by chance might remain there: to his astonishment he found the two officers and all their men at their posts waiting for orders, although at that time the whole forward part of the vessel was submerged and water was pouring in a broad sheet down into the fire-room over the forward coaming of the fire-room hatch. The boats had all left the ship except the gig, which was still lying under the highly elevated stern and into which Mr. Webster and some of the men dropped from the jacob' ladder, Mr. Webster being the last person to escape from the ship and at such a late moment that a man behind him on the jacob's ladder was carried down with the ship and drowned. Mr. Pickrell, being a good swimmer and knowing that the gig could not carry them all, jumped overboard as soon as he came on deck and was picked up in the wreckage over the sunken ship a few minutes later by one of the cutters.

The conduct of these two young engineer officers on this occasion was a subject of much favorable comment on the station at the time, and was considered so meritorious that the rear admiral commanding the squadron sent each of them a complimentary letter and also addressed the following letter to the Navy Department regarding their behavior:

"U. S F. S. RICHMOND, 2nd RATE,
"Hong Kong, China, June 2nd, 1883.
"Hon. Wm. E. Chandler, Secretary of the Navy,
"Navy Department, Washington, D. C.;
"Sir:—

"I take great pleasure in mentioning to the Department the names of Assistant Engineer J. M. Pickrell, U. S. N., and Naval Cadet W. T. Webster, U. S. N., who were on duty in the fire-room at the time the U. S. S. *Ashuelot* was wrecked and in a sinking condition. Both these gentlemen remained in the fire-room keeping their men ready for any emergency, at a time when there was great danger of losing their lives. Both these young officers showed great coolness, and when they were authorized to leave the fire-room they saw that every man had left the engine department, and went on deck in order to save their lives.

"Very Respectfully, your obdt. svt.,
"Peirce Crosby,
"Rear Admiral, U. S. N.,
"Comdg. U. S. Naval Force on Asiatic Station."

As the U. S. S. *Tennessee* was proceeding to sea through the jetties of the Mississippi River the afternoon of April 2, 1883, she touched bottom sufficiently hard to heel her over for a moment, causing a surge of condensed water and then a water-hammer in a badly arranged branch of the main steam pipe, which burst. Cadet Engineer (Naval Cadet) Peter Miller on duty at the time in the fire-room, was unfortunately directly under the part of the pipe that gave way and was so horribly scalded and burned that he died the next morning. He had been appointed to the Naval Academy from Kansas and had graduated in June, 1882, number five and a "star" in a class that contained several unusually capable members. The *Tennessee* proceeded to Key West where the remains of the unfortunate young officer were interred with due military honors.

An act of Congress approved March 3, 1885, was of much importance to many members of the engineer corps, as it provided rates of longevity pay for passed assistant engineers for their third and fourth five years' periods of service in that grade. Formerly they had had but two rates of pay the same as passed assistant surgeons and passed assistant paymasters, namely $2,000 per annum sea pay for first five years, and $2,200 for second five years. Having had no special promotion as a reward for war service, and the ages of the chief engineers being so nearly their own as to constitute a barrier to their promotion, it was evident that the passed assistant engineers would remain in their grades for fifteen or twenty years and in some cases would even arrive at the retiring age in it. Lieutenants, passed assistant surgeons, and passed assistant paymasters once ranking with the passed assistant engineers had advanced to be commanders or medical and pay inspectors, but the engineer remained where he was with no hope of promotion and restricted to an inferior rate of pay until relieved by Congress. The bill was before Congress in one shape or another for about ten years before it finally became law, and it is worth mentioning that its success was eventually due to the support of the Military Order of the Loyal Legion and the Grand Army of the Republic, the sympathy of those organizations being enlisted by the circumstance that every passed assistant engineer to immediately benefit by the passage of the bill was a veteran of the Civil War.

Engineer-in-Chief Shock was reappointed at the expiration of

CHIEF ENGINEER CHARLES H. LORING, U. S. NAVY.
Engineer-in-Chief of the Navy from January 18, 1884 to July 8, 1887.

his term of office in 1881 and remained engineer-in-chief until June 15, 1883, when he arrived at the age of sixty-two and was placed on the retired list. For seven months no chief of bureau was appointed, Mr. W. H. H. Smith, the well-known and efficient chief clerk of the bureau, acting in that capacity in accordance with the provisions of law, until, in January, 1884, Chief Engineer Charles H. Loring was selected for the office and commissioned chief of the bureau. Mr. Loring at the time was the ninth in order on the list of chief engineers with relative rank of captain, and had an unblemished record of faithful and efficient service. Upon him fell some of the first knotty problems in the work then in hand of creating a new navy, a subject that will be dealt with especially in other chapters.

A disaster of unusual magnitude overtook a squadron of our naval steamers in the harbor of Apia, Samoan Islands, the 16th of March, 1889. Certain international complications had led to the assembling in that remote port, of the *Trenton*, flagship of Rear Admiral L. A. Kimberly, the *Vandalia*, and the *Nipsic*, of the U. S. Navy; the *Olga*, *Eber*, and *Adler*, of the German Navy, and the *Calliope* of the British Navy. A gale from seaward set in during the 15th of March with such threatening indications that steam was raised, topmasts housed, lower yards sent down, and all the required preparations made for meeting heavy weather. By the morning of the 16th a hurricane was raging and huge seas, gathered from the wide expanse of the Pacific Ocean, were falling into the harbor in such masses and with such force as to be almost irresistible. The American and German war vessels began dragging down upon the reefs despite the full power of their engines and the grasp of their anchors, but the *Calliope*, being a newer vessel with much greater engine power in proportion to her displacement than the others, got under way and by putting forth her utmost exertions succeeded in slowly laboring out of the harbor and into the open ocean, where she remained until the hurricane had passed, returning then to Apia to find not a single keel afloat in that harbor. The struggle of the *Calliope* against the elements furnishes probably the most eloquent illustration in the history of steam navigation of the overcoming power of steam when trusted to fight alone for the life of a ship, and the spectacle she presented when driving into the great seas and against the hurricane was such a dramatic and inspiring personification of *Power* that the men of the *Trenton* forgot for the moment their own peril and broke forth into loud cheers of admiration. For this exploit the commander and chief engineer of the *Calliope* were rewarded with promotion.

The *Nipsic*, lying nearest in shore, after vainly trying to hold on and after losing her smoke pipe and boats by collision with one of the Germans, was beached by her commander and abandoned by means of life lines, only seven of her people being drowned. Her chief engineer, Mr. George W. Hall, then considerably past fifty years of age, suffered so much from exposure and hardship that he never recovered, dying a few weeks afterward in a lonesome village in one of the neighboring islands whither he had been taken. His part in the preservation of his ship may best be told by quoting from a letter addressed the engineer-in-chief by Commander D. W. Mullan of the *Nipsic:*

"Being myself cognizant of the valuable services of the engineer officers of the navy, and especially so during the memorable hurricane at Samoa in March, 1889, I will say that had it not been for the engines of the U. S. S. *Nipsic*, which vessel I commanded at that time, (and whose chief engineer was the late George W. Hall) and also had it not been for the valuable aid rendered me by Mr. Hall throughout that terrible hurricane, the vessel and her crew would have been a total loss. During the trying hours of that storm, Mr. Hall was ever at his post and stuck to it until assistance was no longer necessary. Had poor Hall survived, his services would undoubtedly in time been recognized, but his valuable services during that time will ever be remembered by me and they shed a bright lustre on the engineer corps of the navy."

The *Vandalia* with steam on seven of her eight boilers, all the engines could use, struggled for nearly twelve hours trying to steam up to her anchors, but slowly dragged down until aground on the reef when the engines were stopped and the men sent on deck. In describing this critical period, Passed Assistant Engineer Harrie Webster, U. S. Navy, writing in the *United Service Magazine*, says this of his men: "Here the discipline and steadiness of the engineer department showed itself, for as soon as the order to stop the engines was given everything was done exactly as it would have been had the ship been coming to anchor, and when I went into the fire-room to give the order to abandon the ship the men were there, and only left in obedience to command." Of Mr. Webster himself, Lieutenant J. W. Carlin, who was in command of what was left of the *Vandalia* when the storm had passed, reported to the Navy Department: "Passed Assistant Engineer Harrie Webster remained at his post under the most trying circumstances and exhibited the greatest zeal and ability." The chief engineer of the *Vandalia*, Mr. A. S. Greene, was washed overboard and was swept sufficiently near the beach to be rescued by the Samoan warriors who by grasping hands had formed a line extending into the surf, ready to succor any who might come within reach. In this escape Mr. Greene was remarkably fortunate, for with one other exception he was the only one of many who got overboard who was not swept out to sea by the counter-current and drowned.

The *Vandalia* sank to her hammock rails after striking on the reef and her people took refuge in the rigging, over which the seas were breaking as high as the tops. Late in the evening the *Trenton* drifted down upon her and those who remained alive found safety by getting on board the larger ship. Captain Schoonmaker, Paymaster Arms, Lieutenant Sutton of the marine corps, Pay Clerk Roche, and thirty-nine enlisted men of the *Vandalia* were drowned during the day. The *Trenton* lost her steam power early in the day of the disaster, water coming through the hawse-pipes, which were located on the berth deck, in such quantity that the fires under the boilers were extinguished about 9.30 A. M. An idea of the terrific power of the incoming seas may be gained from the fact reported by the officers of the *Trenton* that in the endeavor to keep the water out, blankets and other material were wrapped upon the cables and veered into the hawse-pipes, making an obstruction that would seem immovable, but which was actually forced out time after time by the furious impact of the water driven into the pipes. The ship dragged slowly all day and soon after 8 P. M. she brought up alongside the wreck of the *Vandalia* where she sank to her gun-deck. She lost but one man, who was killed by the breaking in of a port. The *Trenton* and *Vandalia* became total losses: the *Nipsic* was temporarily repaired, floated, and taken to San Francisco to be fitted for service again. The largest of the German ships—the *Olga*—was beached and afterward saved: the two others were completely destroyed with terrible loss of life, but five people escaping from one of them. Fifteen merchant vessels in the harbor were all wrecked or stranded.

In the latter part of December 1892, the *Alliance* had a narrow escape from destruction in the same harbor, though in her case the storm was not so violent as to prevent her from steaming against it. Early in the morning of December 28 she began dragging, even after a second anchor was let go, and in a few minutes struck on the reef on her starboard quarter, which occurrence of course brought the engines into great demand. Fortunately the chief engineer had observed the possibility of this accident and on his own responsibility had got a full watch of men on duty and the fires worked up almost in condition for use, so when the order was given to get up steam it took only eight minutes to begin steaming, and the vessel worked her way off the reef and into deep water with the loss only of her two anchors and some damage to the propeller. Had it taken the usual half-hour or more to get steam from banked fires the delay would probably have been fatal to the *Alliance*. In reporting the affair to the Department, Commander Whiting of the *Alliance* referred to the rapidity with which steam was employed and said: "This was due to the energy and ability displayed by Passed Assistant Engineer H. N. Stevenson, chief engineer of this ship, whose conduct deserves the highest commendation."

The engineer corps derived much credit from the efficient manner in which Chief Engineer L. W. Robinson administered the affairs of the great department of machinery at the World's Columbian Exposition in Chicago in 1893. Mr. Robinson had had excellent experience in that class of work by being the superintendent of Machinery Hall at the Centennial Exposition in Philadelphia in 1876, he being the principal assistant of Chief Engineer John S. Albert, U. S. Navy, who held the position of chief of the bureau of machinery at that exposition. Mr. Robinson was also a civil engineer by profession before entering the navy, which specially fitted him for the work of designing foundations and supports for heavy machinery. As chief of the department of machinery Mr. Robin-

MODEL BATTLE-SHIP ILLINOIS, AT WORLD'S COLUMBIAN EXPOSITION, 1893.

An exact copy as to size, etc., of the new battle-ships of the *Indiana* class.

son had the responsible control of an exhibit covering more than thirty acres of floor space, valued at many millions of dollars, and cared for by hundreds of employes of all grades, which important trust was administered by him in such manner as to excite the highest expressions of appreciation and esteem from the directors of the exposition.

The navy as an organization gained much popularity and goodwill from the people by the unique and excellent exhibit made by the Navy Department at the Columbian Exposition. This, the conception of Rear Admiral R. W. Meade, U. S. Navy, was a full-sized and perfect imitation of a modern battle-ship of the *Indiana* class, built of brick, wood and steel on piling in the lake on the shore of the expo-ition grounds, and was so perfect in details of guns, equipment, *personnel*, and arrangement, that many who should have known better were deceived into believing it to be a genuine battle-ship, while many thousands of landsmen from the interior went home fully believing that they had seen one of the veritable giants of the new navy. The exhibits of the Navy Department were artistically arranged on the decks of this imitation battle-ship and made, with the structure itself, a display so novel and so different from all others that the "brick ship" was by all odds the most popular exhibit at the exposition. It was the good fortune of the author to be one of the officers detailed by the Secretary of the Navy to manage this naval exhibit, and in participating in the life of the wonderful White City that summer he experienced the greatest privilege and opportunity for both instruction and enjoyment that the naval service has ever afforded him, or can ever afford, for the waking splendors of all the dreams that were realized in the city built to honor the name of Christopher Columbus may not be seen again in our time.

The engineer corps of the navy was again well represented at the Midwinter Fair in San Francisco the first six months of the year 1894 by Passed Assistant Engineer A. M. Hunt, who was granted leave of absence to allow him to occupy the position of chief of the machinery exhibit, a position which he filled with great credit to himself and to the navy; unfortunately the ability which the opportunity enabled him to display led to more profitable employment in civil life, and the navy lost his services by his resignation. The following from a Pacific Coast journal, though committing the usual error of assuming that a naval staff officer has the rank and title of the grade in which he holds a commission, indicates the reputation for the navy and himself that Mr. Hunt established while associated with the Midwinter Fair:

"It should be known that the Mechanical Arts Building is under the supervision of Lieutenant A. M. Hunt, whose portrait we publish in another column of this paper. Of all the chiefs in the various departments at the Midwinter Fair, we think it will be acknowledged that Lieutenant Hunt stands almost first in popularity. With a thorough education in mechanics, which give him a clear grasp of the technical duties of his position, and with a manner at once genial and persuasive, he has made friends with all with whom he has come in contact, not alone the employes of the department who are immediately under his supervision, but also with our local manufacturers and exhibitors, who would have been fatally slow to further the plans of the Administration had they not been stimulated to interest by the enthusiastic efforts of this well-selected chief. Mr. Hunt is Passed Assistant Engineer of the United States Navy, holding the rank of Lieutenant. On account of his thorough technical knowledge and his strong executive ability, his services were requested by the promoters of the Fair at an early stage of its operations, and in accordance with that request, Lieutenant Hunt was granted leave of absence by the Navy Department to accept his present responsible position. Lieutenant Hunt was born in Iowa, thirty-four years ago, and, after receiving a good education, was appointed to the Naval Academy at Annapolis from the Seventh Congressional district of Indiana. He graduated from the Academy in 1879, and has continued in the naval service ever since. He has occupied several positions of trust, and has always acquitted himself with honor. It is a matter of pride and congratulation to our navy that it can furnish executive officers for the furtherance of such a great exhibition as the Midwinter Fair, and have them prove so eminently qualified and satisfactory as has been the case with Lieutenant Hunt."

The engineer corps was represented also at the Midwinter Fair by Mr. W. F. C. Hasson, whose resignation of his commission as an assistant engineer in the navy less than a year before was so recent that in public estimation he was still identified with the naval service, which gained the credit for his extraordinary efficiency and administrative capacity. Mr. Hasson was chief of the department of electricity, in which capacity he succeeded as admirably and won as high encomiums as did Mr. Hunt in his department.

The famous old sloop-of-war *Kearsarge*, which had outlived all her sisters by reason of the public sentiment which compelled Congress to make appropriations for her repair and preservation, ran ashore about 6 p. m., February 2, 1894, on Roncador Reef, while on her way to Bluefields, Nicaragua, and became a total loss, though but one of her crew lost his life. The people remained on the reef eight days and were taken off by the *City of Para*, leaving the bones of the historic old ship to the tender mercies of the West India wreckers. When the news became known, Congress made an immediate appropriation and despatched a steamer to the scene of the wreck to save the vessel if possible, or at least to recover property from her, but it was too late: the human buzzards, black and white, of the West Indies had stripped her clean. Her flag, bell, and numerous other relics were subsequently recovered by traveling Americans who found and purchased them in junk shops at different Caribbean ports.

A modern instance of an emergency not at all unusual in the life of a naval engineer, and of devotion to duty in meeting it, is told by the following news item from the San Francisco *Chronicle* of March 27, 1895:

"The *Monterey* reached Mare Island this evening from Sausalito. She is tied up at the quay wall. The bursting of one of the feed-pipes while the vessel was about to make an experiment with her rudder gearing resulted in the scalding of Assistant Engineer Theiss, Machinist Powell, Watertenders Arthur and Hayes, Oiler Lee, and Fireman Carlson. Every one of the men received a severe scalding.

"Theiss is in a very bad condition. It appears that his injuries were brought about by his own heroism. When the superior officer was informed of the leak it was the general belief that it was of small importance. Theiss, happening to hear the report, decided to investigate matters for himself. He found the water pouring out of the pipe into the fire-room and the men in the place in a dazed condition. His cries were : ' Boys, pull the fires, and do it quick— no telling what will happen.'

"The boiling water surged on the floor of the fire-room, but the minute Theiss gave the command every man buckled down to work. But they did not work fast enough to suit Theiss. He grasped one of the long rakes and was about to assist in the work of drawing the fires, when he fell in a pool of scalding water. The men never wavered in their work, but while their commanding officer was lying in the boiling water every man labored at the drawing of the fires.

" It turns out that the act of Theiss saved the boilers of the *Monterey*. The flesh on one side of Theiss is almost raw. All of the others had their feet scalded. Theiss was sent to the hospital, and it will be some time before he will be able to get around. While no comment is made of the work done by Theiss, it is a fact that his act saved the government thousands of dollars."

CHAPTER XXXVIII.

> "Up! Up! In nobler toil than ours
> No craftsmen bear a part;
> We make of Nature's giant powers
> The slaves of human art."
> —J. G. WHITTIER—*The Ship Builders.*

The New Navy—Naval Advisory Boards—First Acts of Congress Providing for the Rebuilding of the Navy—The ATLANTA, BOSTON, CHICAGO, and DOLPHIN—The NEWARK, YORKTOWN, and PETREL—The CHARLESTON—The TEXAS, MAINE, and BALTIMORE—The Dynamite-Gun Cruiser—The MONTEREY—The PHILADELPHIA and SAN FRANCISCO—Chief Engineer George W. Melville Appointed Engineer-in-Chief of the Navy.

THE story of the rebuilding of the American Navy is too entertaining a subject and includes too many matters of great public interest to be properly dealt with within the space remaining for this volume. Again, the New Navy is still so far from finished that any detailed account of all that has been accomplished thus far would of necessity be but the beginning of an incomplete story, for there is every reason to hope that the reconstruction work so well begun will be carried on until our navy is in every essential worthy of our race and nation. When that time comes the opportunity will be fitting for the history of the new navy to be written in detail, with minute regard for the designs and construction of all the ships; the far-reaching influences upon the manufacturing industries of the country exerted by the Navy Department in prosecuting this work; the union of political parties on the naval question; the change in public sentiment regarding the navy, and, in brief, the subject treated with the particularization it deserves.

Aside from being incomplete at present, the subject of the new navy is one so different from much that has preceded in these pages as to make it a subject by itself, only slightly connected with all that has gone before. With the first of our new ships came a great change in naval methods, amounting practically to an abandonment of all previous practices and making the new fleet a creation by itself. New ideas came into play in the designing of hulls and machinery; new forms of ships and entirely new designs and types of marine engines and boilers came into use; new types of guns were adopted; new methods of manufacture and vastly improved building material for ships, engines and guns began to be used; new and younger men began to gain attention for new ideas; in short, the change was so abrupt as to create a sharply defined line where the old and the new joined, instead of the former merging gradually into the latter, as has been the case in other navies. For this reason a general account only of our naval awakening will be here presented. An effort will be made to describe with some detail the preliminary steps that led to the establishment of a national policy of building a navy, but thereafter the ships and machinery rapidly created will be referred to briefly, and in statistical rather than descriptive manner. Some time in the future some other pen may assume the agreeable task of describing our beautiful new ships and the mighty steel embodiments of power within them.

By the year 1880 the navy of the United States had fallen to a pitifully low ebb. Its condition ten years before, when Secretary Robeson had been driven by a sentiment which the judgment of history will pronounce patriotism to stretch the law in order to build new ships, had been bad enough, but now it had reached bottom. Repairs were no longer possible, for space for more patches was lacking upon almost every ship of ours then afloat. Our ships were wooden; their machinery was, as a naval critic somewhat wittily remarked, "one cylinder behind the practice of the rest of the world;" the guns were even further behind; our cumbersome rigging and top-hamper was so antique and out of fashion as to excite curiosity in foreign ports; even the organization of our ships' companies was on an obsolete basis: the youngest of the great nations was, by its naval representation, the most ancient. A sense of humiliation dogged the American naval officer as he went about his duty in foreign lands; in the Far East; in the lesser countries along the Mediterranean Sea, and even in the seaports of South America, people smiled patronizingly upon him and from a sense of politeness avoided speaking of naval subjects in his presence. None but naval officers and a few Americans who happened to be abroad comprehend just how insignificant and cheap the Great Republic appeared in the eyes of the world at and about the time mentioned. If these classes of our citizens had to bear the contempt that had fallen upon our country as a result of naval neglect, they are likewise in a position now to appreciate and exult over the wonderful change in sentiment abroad that is the direct sequence of the regeneration of our navy.

In 1881 the Secretary of the Navy, Mr. William H. Hunt, resolved to prepare for Congress a plain and practical statement of the pressing need of appropriate vessels for the naval service, and, to reconcile as far as possible the conflicting views and theories of officers of different ages and different corps as to the types of vessels desirable, organized án Advisory Board to examine into and report upon the entire question. This board met the 11th of July of that year and remained in session almost daily until the 7th of November, on which date its report was submitted. The board was fairly representative of the naval service, containing as it did old and young officers from the different corps that deal with naval *material:* its membership was as follows:

> Rear Admiral John Rogers, President.
> Commodore William G. Temple.
> Captain P. C. Johnson.
> Commander H. L. Howison.
> Commander Robley D. Evans.
> Commander A. S. Crowninshield.
> Lieutenant M. R. S. McKenzie.
> Lieutenant Edward W. Very.
> Lieutenant Frederick Collins.
> Chief Engineer B. F. Isherwood.
> Chief Engineer C. H. Loring.
> Passed Assistant Engineer C. H. Manning.
> Naval Constructor John Lenthal.
> Naval Constructor Theo. D. Wilson.
> Naval Constructor Philip Hichborn.

The order convening this board directed it to consider and advise the Department upon the following subjects:

1st. The number of vessels that should now be built.
2d. Their class, size, and displacement.

3d. The material and form of their construction.

4th. The nature and size of the engines and machinery required for each.

5th. The ordnance and armament necessary for each.

6th. The appropriate equipments and rigging of each.

7th. The internal arrangements of each, and upon such other details as may seem to be necessary and proper, and, lastly, the probable cost of the whole of each vessel when complete and ready for service.

The Board in its report recommended that vessels of the following classes, types, material, armament, and estimated cost be built at once:

"Two first-rate steel, double-decked, unarmored cruisers, having a displacement of about 5,873 tons, an average sea speed of 15 knots, and a battery of 4 VIII-inch and 21 VI-inch guns. Cost, $3,560,000.

"Six first-rate steel, double-decked, unarmored cruisers, having a displacement of about 4,560 tons, an average sea speed of 14 knots, and a battery of 4 VIII-inch and 15 VI-inch guns. Cost, $8,532,000.

"Ten second-rate steel, single-decked, unarmored cruisers, having a displacement of about 3,043 tons, an average sea speed of 13 knots, and a battery of 12 VI-inch guns. Cost, $9,300,000.

"Twenty fourth-rate wooden cruisers, having a displacement of about 793 tons, an average sea speed of 10 knots, and a battery of 1 VI-inch and 2 60-pounders. Cost, $4,360,000.

"Five steel rams of about 2,000 tons displacement, and an average sea speed of 13 knots. Cost, $2,500,000.

"Five torpedo gun-boats of about 450 tons displacement, a maximum sea speed of not less than 13 knots, and one heavy-powered rifled gun. Cost, $725,000.

"Ten cruising torpedo boats, about 100 feet long, and having a maximum speed of not less than 21 knots per hour. Cost, $380,000.

"Ten harbor torpedo boats, about 70 feet long, and having a maximum speed of not less than 17 knots per hour. Cost, $250,000.

"Total cost of vessels recommended now to be built, $29,607,000."

The object in recommending wood as the material for the twenty small cruisers or gun-boats was to utilize the large supply of ship timber then on hand, and to afford employment to the workmen of Eastern cities in which wood ship-building was a leading industry. The board was of the opinion that all vessels of the cruiser classes be provided with full sail power, the amount of sail surface not to be less than twenty-five times the area of the immersed midship section. The 15, 14 and 13 knot classes were recommended to be ship-rigged, and the ten-knot class to be barkentine-rigged.

It was recommended that the engines of the unarmored vessels be of the horizontal, back-action, compound type, with steam-jacketed cylinders, surface condensers, and independent expansion valves on each cylinder; that the boilers should be of the ordinary cylindrical type, with return tubes above the surfaces, and of a strength capable of carrying a working pressure of ninety pounds to the square inch. That the screws should in all cases be fixed, four-bladed, and of a uniform pitch, one screw for each vessel. That the smoke-pipes of the three larger classes of vessels be telescopic, and of the smaller vessels standing with a hinged arrangement for lowering to the deck. Steam capstans and steam steering-gear were recommended for the larger classes. Nine carefully elaborated reasons were given why, in the opinion of the board, single instead of twin screws were recommended.

The report of the Advisory Board was sent to Congress with the annual report of the Secretary of the Navy that year (1881), with a full exposition of the decayed condition of the navy and an earnest recommendation that something be done in the premises. The same year President Arthur in his annual message urged upon Congress the importance of immediate action to save the American navy from total disappearance.

The next step was taken by Congress, the naval appropriation bill approved August 5, 1882, authorizing the construction of new vessels, as follows:

"Any portion of said sum (the general appropriation for the Bureau of Construction and Repair) not required for the purposes aforesaid may be applied towards the construction of two steam cruising vessels of war, which are hereby authorized, at a total cost.

when fully completed, not to exceed the amount estimated by the late Naval Advisory Board for such vessels, the same to be constructed of steel, of domestic manufacture, . . . said vessels to be provided with full sail-power and full steam-power. One of said vessels shall be of not less than five thousand nor more than six thousand tons displacement, and shall have the highest attainable speed, . . . one of said vessels shall be of not less than four thousand three hundred, nor more than four thousand seven hundred tons displacement. . . .

" The Secretary of the Navy is hereby empowered and directed to organize a board of naval officers and experts for his advice and assistance, to be called the 'Naval Advisory Board,' to serve during the period required for the construction, armament and trial of the vessels hereby authorized to be constructed, and no longer. Said board shall consist of five officers on the active list of the navy in the line and the staff, to be detailed by the Secretary of the Navy, without reference to rank and with reference only to character, experience, knowledge, and skill, and two persons of established reputation and standing, as experts in naval or marine construction, to be selected from civil life. . . .

" Before any of the vessels hereby authorized shall be contracted for or commenced the Secretary of the Navy shall, by proper public advertisement and notice, invite all engineers and mechanics of established reputation, and all reputable manufacturers of vessels, steam engines, boilers, and ordnance, having or controlling regular establishments and being engaged in the business, all officers of the navy, and especially all naval constructors, steam engineers, and ordnance officers of the navy, having plans, models, or designs of any vessels of the classes hereby authorized, or any part thereof, within any given period not less than sixty days, to submit the same to said Board. . . .

"Any part of the appropriation for said bureau (general appropriation for the Bureau of Steam Engineering) not used as above specified, may be applied toward the construction of engines and machinery of the two new cruising vessels provided for in this act."

The Naval Advisory Board thus authorized by law was organized October 9th, 1882, with the following members:

Commodore R. W. Shufeldt, U. S. Navy, President.
Chief Engineer Alexander Henderson, U. S. Navy.
Commander J. A. Howell, U. S. Navy.
Lieutenant Edward Very, U. S. Navy.
Naval Constructor F. L. Fernald, U. S. Navy.

The two civilian experts selected by the Department for employment were Messrs. Henry Steers and Miers Coryell, the former a ship architect, the latter a marine engineer, and both prominent in their professions. Assistant Naval Constructor Francis T. Bowles, U. S. Navy, was detailed as secretary of the board; Passed Assistant Engineer C. R. Roelker and Assistant Engineer H. P. Norton were also detailed to act as designers and draftsmen for the board and to perform such other duties as might be required.

After ample deliberation, this Advisory Board reported adversely to the construction of the first, or largest, cruiser authorized by the act of August 5, 1882, for the reasons that so large and expensive a vessel was not immediately required, and that in beginning a modern navy it would be better to make the start with medium-sized vessels. One steel cruiser of about 4,000 tons displacement was recommended ; also three steel cruisers of about 2,500 tons displacement, and one iron despatch boat, or "clipper," of about 1,500 tons displacement. The new Secretary of the Navy, Mr. William E. Chandler, transmitted the recommendations to Congress and asked that the previously granted authority for building the two steel cruisers be modified to suit the more recent recommendation as to what was wanted. The question came up shortly in Congress in connection with the naval appropriation bill and the debate showed that the low level to which the navy had been allowed to sink had left it few friends in public life. Those few, however, carried the day, and an act, approved March 3, 1883, made appropriations for and authorized the construction of four vessels of practically the same types proposed by the second Advisory Board. These vessels became the *Atlanta, Boston, Chicago*, and *Dolphin*. Through all these preliminary stages and in the manner thus outlined was the New Navy born.

Contracts for the building of these vessels were awarded to Mr. John Roach and the *Dolphin* was practically completed under the terms of the contract for her. No premium or penalty conditions for speed or horse-power appeared in any of these contracts. The succession of rigorous trials to which the *Dolphin* was subjected to test her horse-power, structural strength and sea-worthiness, including among others a trial-trip completely around the world, may be better detailed in a more extended work than this. So may also the unhappy story of the failure and assignment of Mr. John Roach before the other vessels were finished, and of their subsequent completion by the Navy Department, which took possession of them in accordance with a provision of the contracts. It is sufficient in this place to say that by the end of the year 1887 the three were completed and have been in active service the greater part of the time since. For their time and types they excelled in almost every element that contributes to naval efficiency, and their appearance did much to give new hope to our all but discouraged naval officers, and to inaugurate that wave of popular sentiment in favor of the navy which has now extended so generally throughout the country that the navy has become the favorite of the two military arms of the nation.

The designs for these pioneer vessels of the new navy originated with the Advisory Board of which Commodore Shufeldt was president, and the naval service is indebted to the members of that board for their work to an extent little appreciated. It is not unfashionable now to harshly criticise that board for not knowing everything that experience has taught since, but its work speaks well enough in results for the thoroughness and the earnest endeavors of its members to do the best possible for the service in the beginning of its new life. A decided influence upon the type of the ships designed was exerted by Mr. Bowles, the secretary of the board, and his classmate, Assistant Naval Constructor Richard Gatewood, then on duty in the Bureau of Construction and Repair. These two young gentlemen had graduated with great credit as cadet engineers in the class of 1879 at the Naval Academy and had subsequently undergone a course of instruction at the Royal Naval College, Greenwich, England, they being the first American cadets to be sent abroad for that purpose. Returning in 1881 to receive appointments in the construction corps, they brought with them much knowledge and information as to European methods, and this knowledge was liberally used by the Advisory Board,

U. S. STEAMSHIP CHICAGO, 1887.

Length on l. w. l., 325 feet; Beam, 48 ft. 2 in.; Mean Draft, 19 feet; Displacement, 4,500 tons.

especially in preparing the designs of the *Atlanta* and *Boston*. The hull of the *Dolphin* was designed by Naval Constructor Fernald, and the *Chicago*, as beautiful a ship as this country has produced, was also his.

Nothing especially novel entered into the machinery designs of the *Dolphin*, *Atlanta*, and *Boston*. The former was provided with a vertical compound engine so high as to be exposed to shot, though her designation as a despatch vessel put her out of the category of vessels of war. The *Atlanta* and *Boston* had horizontal back-acting engines and cylindrical return-tubular boilers, both engines and boilers being of the type described in a former chapter as having been supplied the *Trenton*. All three were fitted with single screws in deference to the prejudices of the time, though some members of the board, notably Mr. Bowles, urged the adoption of twin screws. The machinery of the *Chicago* presented a novel departure from ordinary naval practice. Two large compound engines were provided, one on each side of the ship, the cylinders standing vertically on the bottom of the ship and communicating power by means of athwartship walking-beams to the crank-shafts, the port engine driving the starboard screw and *vice versa*. As pointed out before, this installation is remarkably like the arrangement of engines put into the Stevens Battery thirty years before. The boilers of the *Chicago* were even more a radical departure from conventional forms. They were cylindrical, with return tubes, a usual arrangement, but were externally fired; that is, the furnaces were under the outer shell of the boiler, built around with brick-work, the general arrangement of the boiler being not unlike the type familiar in the American backwoods as the generator of power in saw-mills. These engines and boilers were prepared by Mr. Coryell, the civilian engineer of the board, and their adoption was, as a member of the board has told the author, "due to the popular pressure to give the outside a chance." It is proper to say that at the time similar machinery was in successful operation in an American coast-wise steamer—the *Louisiana*—and that the *Chicago* has been actively cruising for over seven years without any lengthy respite. She has recently been laid up to be fitted with modern triple-expansion machinery.

The act of August 5, 1882, directed the Advisory Board which it created to report in detail as to the wisdom and expediency of undertaking and completing the work on the double-turreted monitors whose building had languished for so many years and had been fraught with so many scandals. In a report signed by all the members the board advised the immediate completion of those vessels, which recommendation was cordially endorsed by Secretary Chandler and by him referred to Congress. Appropriations for this object followed, notably in the appropriation act of August 3, 1886, and thus after many delays these vessels have been restored to the active list of the navy. The long time occupied in their construction has

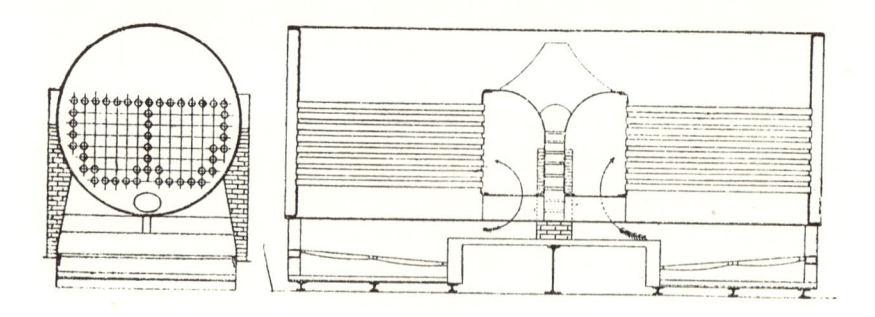

EXTERNALLY FIRED, DOUBLE-ENDED BOILER, U. S. S. "CHICAGO."
Diameter of shell, 9 feet; extreme length, 26 feet.

resulted in their appearance with obsolete machinery, with the exception of the *Monadnock*, but with their heavy guns they are efficient enough for the duty of defending harbors, which is all their original designs contemplated.

Two years elapsed after the passage of the act directing the building of the four vessels described before Congress again came to the relief of the navy; then the act of March 3, 1885, authorized the construction of "two cruisers of not less than three thousand nor more than five thousand tons displacement, costing, exclusive of armament, not more than one million one hundred thousand dollars each; one heavily-armed gun-boat of about sixteen hundred tons displacement, costing, exclusive of armament, not more than five hundred and twenty thousand dollars; and one light gun-boat of about eight hundred tons displacement, costing, exclusive of armament, not more than two hundred and seventy-five thousand dollars." The vessels thus authorized were the *Newark, Charleston, Yorktown*, and *Petrel*. In order to enlist the contractors pecuniarily in the attainment of successful results, the Navy Department began the practice with the contracts for these ships of offering premiums and exacting penalties, the requirement first selected being horse-power on the assumption that that was a true criterion of speed. The contracts fixed the horse-power of the *Newark* at 8,500; of the *Charleston*, 7,000; of the *Yorktown*, 3,000, and of the *Petrel*, 1,100. In each case a premium of $100 was specified for each horse-power in excess of that required, and a penalty of the same sum for each horse-power below that stated in the contract. Under this stipulation the *Newark* won for her builders nearly $37,000, and the *Charleston* lost over $33,000, which latter, however, was subsequently remitted by act of Congress. The *Yorktown* won nearly $40,000 and the *Petrel* lost about $500.

The designs for these vessels were various and not especially creditable, though no great results were to be expected on account of the inexperience that was one of the natural results of the long period of inaction the navy had undergone. In the proposals to bidders, choice was given between the plans of the Department and those of the bidders themselves, and the bids and contracts showed that the former were not regarded with much confidence by ship and engine builders. The *Petrel* was built by the Columbian Iron Works of Baltimore, hull and machinery complete, according to the plans furnished by the Department. The *Newark* and *Yorktown* were built by the Wm. H. Cramp and Sons Ship and Engine Building Co., of Philadelphia, which establishment accepted the plans of hulls offered by the Department but bid on designs of their own for machinery, in each case substituting horizontal triple-expansion twin-screw engines for the compound ones proposed, and the contracts were awarded on that basis.

The designs for the *Charleston* have been the subject for considerable discussion and animadversion. It is generally believed throughout the navy that she is a copy of the Japanese cruiser *Naniwa-Kan*, but such is not exactly the case. Owing to the lack of experience in war-ship building in our country, there was at that time a decided sentiment in the navy in favor of imitating the British and in the pursuit of this idea an officer attached to the

American legation in England was directed to look about the shipyards of that country and negotiate for any plans of vessels that in his judgment might be desirable to copy. This resulted in the purchase of a set of plans for a ship, believed to be the *Naniwa-Kan*, from Sir William Armstrong's establishment at Newcastle-on-Tyne. The machinery designs were not such as an engineer would have selected, and were not in accord, being a mixture of designs that had been used in different vessels built by the Armstrong Company. When received in this country and examined for the purpose of preparing specifications from them our engineers found that the general plans of machinery were those of an Italian cruiser, the *Etna*, while the details were made up from the *Giovanni Bausan*, the *Naniwa-Kan* and a fourth Armstrong ship not named on the drawings but believed to be the Chilean cruiser *Esmeralda*.

These various details did not agree with each other as to proportion and location, and as a result the contractors for the *Charleston* (the Union Iron Works of San Francisco) had to make many expensive changes in machinery as the work progressed. The Bureau of Steam Engineering had attempted to harmonize the designs before the proposals to bidders were issued, but the Secretary of the Navy, having explicit faith in the source from which the plans had been secured, directed that they should go out just as they were. Besides being out of agreement, these designs were out of date also, they being for compound instead of triple-expansion engines—"one cylinder behind," as it were. As built with this machinery the *Charleston* is the last example of this type of engine in our navy. The hull was built from the purchased plans without material alteration, but, as before stated, many changes in machinery were found desirable.[1]

With the changes in machinery the *Charleston* has been a reasonably efficient cruiser and has had much active employment. Her most important service thus far is her famous chase of the steamer *Itata* in May and June, 1891, during the civil war in Chili. The

---

[1] Many interesting details regarding the purchase and execution of the designs for the *Charleston's* machinery are given in a paper, and its discussion, entitled "Auxiliary Machinery of Naval Vessels," read by Mr. George W. Dickie, manager of the Union Iron Works, at the International Engineering Congress held in Chicago during the Columbian Exposition in the year 1893.

Itata, engaged in carrying contraband of war for the insurgents, had escaped from the custody of the United States marshal at San Diego, California, and it was considered proper that she be overhauled and captured if possible. With this object in view the *Charleston* left San Francisco May 9th and proceeded southward, with necessary stoppages for coal, as far as Iquiqui, a distance of over six thousand miles, before her mission was accomplished. This long chase was maintained under the varying conditions that would exist in war, full boiler-power and forced draft being used much of the time, and the experience gained constitutes the best lesson we have as to the behavior of a modern cruiser under war conditions. A full account of the performance of the *Charleston's* machinery, the casualties and derangements encountered, their remedies, etc., has been given the naval profession by Passed Assistant Engineer Ira N. Hollis in an admirable paper published in the "Journal of the American Society of Naval Engineers," August, 1892. A dramatic incident of the chase was a meeting in the night-time with the *Esmeralda*, the *Itata's* protector. When the identity of the *Esmeralda* was established, all outside lights were extinguished on the *Charleston*, the ship cleared for action, battery loaded, and further developments awaited with intense anxiety. Nothing happened, and the ships passed on, though the chance snapping of a primer or discharge of a small-arm on either vessel would beyond doubt have precipitated a desperate encounter, for each crew, that of the *Esmeralda* especially, longed to fight the other. The *Charleston* at the time had all boilers and her forced-draft system in use.

Besides directing the completion of the double-turreted monitors, the naval act of August 3, 1886, made extensive provision for increasing the naval establishment. One second-class battle-ship, one protected cruiser, one armored cruiser, one dynamite-gun cruiser and one torpedo boat were authorized, the names subsequently given these vessels being respectively, *Texas, Baltimore, Maine, Vesuvius* and *Cushing*. The act directed that one or more of the new vessels be constructed in government navy yards; it also specified that all armor and machinery be of domestic manufacture, but by a saving clause gave authority for the purchase of shafting abroad should it be found impossible to procure it within reasonable time from American manufacturers.

The second-class battle-ship *Texas* was selected as one of the vessels to be built at a navy yard and her construction was undertaken at the Norfolk yard; a controversy as to her stability, floating capacity, and general design so postponed her beginning that the keel was not laid until 1889, while difficulties in obtaining armor and other heavy material delayed her completion until the summer of 1895. The plans for the *Texas* were bought in England for $15,000, and were the result of a competition instituted by the United States Navy Department. The general design was by the late William John, a distinguished English naval architect at that time in the employ of the Naval Construction and Armaments Company, Barrow-in-Furness. Owing to a dispute as to whether the prize of $15,000 belonged to the designer or to his employers, Mr. John left the service of the Barrow Company, and the detailed plans for the *Texas* were worked out by his successor, Mr. A. D. Bryce-Douglas, especially distinguished as a marine engineer, though an architect of note also. Vertical triple-expansion twin-screw engines and four double-ended steel boilers were included in the plans, all the machinery being obtained by contract from the Richmond Locomotive Works of Richmond, Va. This contract required 8,600 horse-power and stipulated the usual premium and penalty of $100 for each horse-power in excess or default.

The protected cruiser *Baltimore* was built by the Cramp Company of Philadelphia, her designs, hull and machinery, being also of foreign extraction. They were bought of the Armstrong Company by the officer who had selected the designs from which the *Charleston* was evolved, but unlike that combination possessed the merit of unity. These plans had been prepared to enter a competition for a cruiser for the Spanish government and not having been successful were left on the hands of the designers. The Cramp Company made a number of changes, especially in machinery, and produced an excellent cruiser. The contract specified the development of 9,000 horse-power to be maintained for four consecutive hours and provided for the usual premium and penalty of $100 per horse-power. On her trial trip the *Baltimore* averaged 20.09 knots and exceeded the required horse-power to such an extent that she won for her builders the sum of $106,441.80. Her first important duty was during the summer of 1890 when she carried to Sweden, his native land, the remains of the great engineer John Ericsson, whose genius had done so much for the American navy in the day of its distress.

The *Maine*, known for a long time officially as Armored Cruiser No. 1, was put under construction at the New York navy yard in 1888, and a contract made with the N. F. Palmer, Jr., Company (Quintard Iron Works) of New York for the machinery, both hull and machinery being of Navy Department designs. 9,000 horse-power was specified with $100 per horse-power premium and penalty. The engines designed for the *Maine* were vertical triple-expansion, and marked the change in our navy from horizontal engines cramped into the bottom of the ship to vertical ones protected by an armored deck.

The legislation authorizing the construction of a dynamite-gun cruiser particularized as follows: "Said cruiser to be not less than two hundred and thirty feet long, twenty-six feet beam, seven and one-half feet draught, three thousand two hundred horse-power, and guaranteed to attain a speed of twenty knots an hour, and to be equipped with three pneumatic dynamite-guns of ten and one-half inch calibre, and guaranteed to throw shells containing two hundred pounds of dynamite or other high explosives at least one mile, each gun to be capable of being discharged once in two minutes, at a price not to exceed three hundred and fifty thousand dollars; said contract to be made only on condition that there shall be a favorable report made by the existing Naval Board on the system." In accordance with this authority the Navy Department made a contract for the vessel specified with the Pneumatic Dynamite-Gun Company, of New York, which company had the craft built by sub-contract with the Cramp Company. As actually built the dimensions are: Length on load water-line, 251 feet 9 inches; beam, 26 feet 5 inches; mean draft, 10 feet 7½ inches; displacement, 930 tons. The twin screw engines are of the vertical triple-expansion type with two low-pressure cylinders for each engine. The contract exacted the development of 3,200 horse-power, but offered no premium for extra power: on the official trial the *Vesuvius*, as the vessel had been named, averaged 22.5 knots and 3,795 horse-power. After a long series of experiments she has not been found a success for the purpose for which she was built, and a subsequent appropriation for another dynamite-gun cruiser has been by authority of Congress applied to other purposes.

The torpedo boat *Cushing* was built by the Herreschoff Manufacturing Company, of Bristol, Rhode Island, from the contractors' designs. She has twin-screw vertical quadruple-expansion engines, with two low-pressure cylinders for each engine, making thus five cylinders to each engine. The boilers, two in number, are of the well-known English Thornycroft type.

The act of March 3, 1887, authorized the construction of the following named vessels: *Philadelphia, San Francisco, Concord, Bennington,* and *Monterey.* The *Concord* and *Bennington* are heavily armed gun-boats, duplicates in hull and machinery of the *Yorktown*, and were built by the N. F. Palmer Co. of New York, the hulls being built at Chester, Pennsylvania, and the machinery at Mr. Palmer's establishment (Quintard Iron Works) in New York. The contracts called for 3,400 horse-power maintained for four hours and contained the usual premium and penalty clause. Each vessel won a small premium.

The *Monterey* is an improved low-freeboard monitor, and was built by the Union Iron Works, San Francisco. Horse-power (5,400) was the main requirement of the contract, with the usual premium and penalty of $100 per horse-power. On her trials she failed by more than three hundred to develop the required horse-power and a penalty of nearly $33,000 was exacted. An important departure from naval engineering precedents was made in this ship in supplying her with coil boilers for two-thirds of the generating plant. Two cylindrical, or "Scotch," boilers were supplied and four large coil boilers of the type patented and manufactured by Mr. Charles Ward of Charleston, West Virginia. On the trial trip these boilers gave great satisfaction, carrying both steam and water with fair uniformity, and passing through the ordeal without leak or mishap of any kind. The failure of the *Monterey* to realize the required horse-power was attributed to lack of skill and lack of interest on the part of the firemen hired for the occasion.

In regard to the two cruisers, the act of Congress directed that the contracts for their construction should contain provisions to the effect that a speed of 19 knots per hour should be guaranteed by the contractors and that a premium of $50,000 should be offered for

U. S. S. BENNINGTON, (CONCORD, YORKTOWN).

Length, on l. w. l. 230 feet; beam, 36 feet; mean draft, 14 feet; disp., 1,710 tons.

every quarter-knot in excess of this with a deduction of the same amount for each quarter-knot the vessels should fail to reach the guaranteed speed. These were the first ships of the new navy for which premiums were offered for speed. Both vessels had horizontal triple-expansion engines, those of the *Philadelphia* being designed by the builders, and those for the *San Francisco* by the Bureau of Steam Engineering. The *San Francisco* was built by the Union Iron Works of San Francisco. On the official trial trips the *Philadelphia* averaged for four consecutive hours 19.678 knots, and the *San Francisco* 19.51 knots, each earning $100,000 under the terms of the act of Congress.

Engineer-in-Chief Charles H. Loring resigned his position during the summer of 1887, domestic affliction of a peculiarly distressing nature impelling him to take this step, and his place was taken by Chief Engineer George W. Melville. Mr. Melville at the time was well down on the list of junior chief engineers and his elevation to the head of his corps was a surprise to himself as well as to the naval service. Having spent the greater part of his career in the navy at sea, he had not had the opportunity of making a reputation for excellence in office work or designing that is an attribute of shore-duty, and for that reason he was not supposed to be in the list of eligibles for advancement. In selecting him Secretary Whitney was influenced chiefly by the story of Melville's conduct during the cruise of the *Jeannette*. At the rate and in the direction that the navy was growing it was important that the head of the bureau most concerned should possess boldness, executive ability and sterling good judgment, and these qualities Mr. Melville's record showed him to have to an unusual degree. A quickly acquired knowledge of some of the theoretical necessities of his profession added to his great practical genius enabled Mr. Melville to produce machinery that has made our ships famous and has placed his name foremost among marine engineers throughout the world. The success that has attended our naval machinery on trial and in every-day use is phenomenal when compared with the experiences of other navies, and the mind that has directed this great work is entitled to no less qualification than that of genius. Of the many great services rendered the navy by Secretary Whitney none has been greater in resulting benefits than his selection of George W. Melville to be chief of the Bureau of Steam Engineering.

One of the first of Mr. Melville's acts after becoming engineer-in-chief was to outlaw the venerable notion that the engines of a war vessel should be horizontal that they might be stowed in the bottom of a ship, below the water-line, and in any space that might be left after other departments had made choice of all they wanted. The engines of the *Maine* were his first creation in this direction. The adoption of coil boilers for the *Monterey* was another early step of his towards freeing our navy from the tangle of conventional precedents that had grown upon it. As a measure of his professional abilities, it may be stated that after his accession to the office of engineer-in-chief bidders for new vessels ceased supplying machinery designs of their own and gladly accepted those furnished by the Bureau of Steam Engineering.

ENGINEER-IN-CHIEF GEORGE W. MELVILLE, U. S. NAVY.

CHAPTER XXXIX.

"We're creepin' on wi' each new rig—less weight an' larger power :
There'll be the loco-boiler next an' thirty miles an hour !
Thirty an' more. What I ha' seen since ocean-steam began
Leaves me no doubt for the machine : but what about the man?"
—RUDYARD KIPLING—"McAndrews' Hymn."

The New Navy, Continued—The *New York* and *Olympia*—The *Detroit* Class—The *Cincinnati* and *Raleigh*—The *Bancroft*—*Castine* and *Machias*—The Ammen Ram—Coast-Line-Battle-Ships—The *Ericsson*—The *Columbia*—Her Remarkable Voyage Across the Atlantic Ocean—The *Minneapolis*—The *Brooklyn* and *Iowa*—New Torpedo Boats and Gunboats—The New *Kearsarge*.

AN ACT of Congress approved September 7, 1888, authorized a greater addition to our new fleet than any that preceded or has followed it. The construction was authorized of one large armored cruiser of about 7,500 tons displacement; one cruiser of about 5,300 tons displacement; two cruisers of about 3,000 tons; three cruisers of about 2,000 tons, and one steel practice-vessel of about 800 tons. Premiums for speed were authorized in all cases. An important provision in this law was that—"in all their parts said vessels shall be of domestic manufacture," which shows that the steel-making industry in the United States had developed under the impetus of naval demands to the extent of disposing of the fear that shafting or other heavy forgings could not be obtained at home.

The large armored cruiser, originally designated as No. 2, and subsequently named *New York*, was built by the Cramp Company from designs furnished by the Bureaus of Construction and Steam Engineering, the contract price being $2,985,000. The contract exacted that she should develop a speed of not less than twenty knots per hour, maintained successfully for four consecutive hours, the air pressure in the fire-rooms not to exceed two and one-half inches of water. $50,000 per quarter-knot was offered as a premium for any speed in excess of the contract requirement. The engine design provided for two large vertical triple-expansion engines for driving each of the two shafts, a coupling intervening between each pair of engines. The object of this arrangement is to run at moderate speed with the after engines only, the forward ones being uncoupled. The cylinder diameters are 32″, 47″, and 72″, the piston stroke of all cylinders being 42″. Six double-ended main boilers and two single-ended auxiliary boilers provide steam, the total heating surface being 32,958 square feet, and grate surface 1,052. On her official trial trip, May 22, 1893, the *New York* developed 17,025 horse-power and averaged 21 knots for four hours, thereby earning for her builders a premium of $200,000.

Showing the extent to which steam is now used on a modern vessel of war, the following list of the steam engines on board the *New York* is inserted:

	STEAM CYLINDERS.
4 main propelling engines, vertical triple-expansion	12
4 main air-pumps	8
4 main circulating pumps	4
3 main feed pumps	6
3 auxiliary feed pumps	6
12 blowing engines for force-draft, high-speed	24
2 fire and bilge pumps	4
2 ventilating fans for engine-room	4
4 ventilating fans for ship	8
3 engines for running dynamos	6
1 steam steering engine	2
4 evaporator and distiller pumps	5
1 ice machine	1
2 auxiliary feed and fire pumps	4
4 main and auxiliary fire pumps	8
2 auxiliary boiler feed pumps	4
2 wrecking pumps	2
2 water-service pumps	4
2 auxiliary air and circulating pumps	2
1 steam capstan,	2
6 steam winches	12
2 auxiliary-boiler blowing engines	4
6 ash-hoists	12
2 turning engines	4
4 reversing engines	4
2 turrett-turning engines	4
2 steam ammunition-hoists	4
1 workshop engine	1
1 air-pump for sweeping decks	1
2 propelling engines in steam cutters	4
2 duplex feed pumps in steam cutters	4
92 engines	**170**

U. S. SECOND-CLASS BATTLESHIP TEXAS.

Length, 301 ft. 4 in.; Beam, 64 ft. 1 in.; Displacement, 6,315 tons.

It is difficult to resist the temptation to enter into a detailed description, from an engineer's point of view, of this majestic steel cruiser, and to institute comparisons between her features and performance and those of similar vessels in other navies, but the subject is one that can be properly treated only in a more detailed and extended work than this. On one occasion already, when stripped for action with hostile intent in a foreign harbor, her mere appearance was sufficient to compel a respect for the rights of American merchantmen that had previously been defiantly refused. As flagship of the squadron that represented the United States at the recent naval assemblage at Kiel, Germany, she was the most admired of all the vessels present, and the praise lavished upon her by naval experts of many countries is most gratifying to the American people as well as flattering to the naval engineers and constructors whose genius created her. The Emperor of Germany examined her critically, especially in the engine department and was so impressed with the machinery and the exquisite order in which he found it that he was profuse in complimentary expressions to Mr. Andrade, her chief engineer, and gave greater evidence of his admiration by subsequently ordering the chief engineers of the German war-ships, in the harbor, to go on board the *New York* and see how perfectly great engines can be made and how well they may be kept.

The second large cruiser—the *Olympia*—as built is of about 5,800 tons displacement and is very like the *New York* in appearance, though smaller. She was built by the Union Iron Works, San Francisco, under a contract the same in details as that for the *New York*. She exceeded her contract speed by 1.69 knots and won for the contractors the enormous premium of $300,000.

The authorizing act of Congress fixed the limit of cost of the 3,000-ton cruisers at $1,100,000 each, and when proposals for their construction were issued it was found that no ship-building firm would bid on them at that price. Under authority of the same law the Secretary of the Navy directed their construction at navy yards and they were built in that way, the *Cincinnati* at New York and the *Raleigh* at Norfolk. Triple-expansion twin-screw engines for both were built at the New York navy yard under the immediate supervision of Chief Engineers James H. Chasmar and George

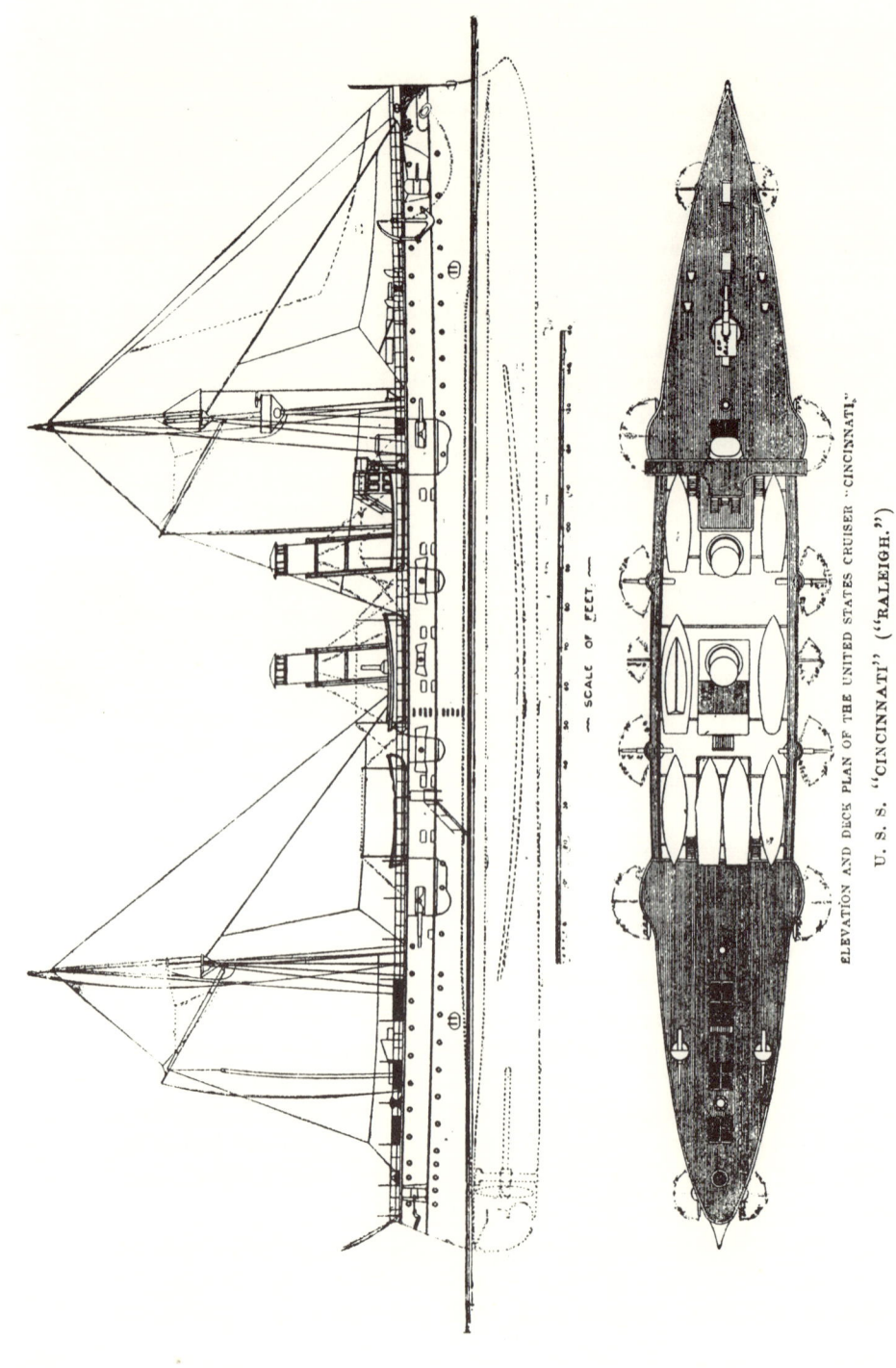

ELEVATION AND DECK PLAN OF THE UNITED STATES CRUISER "CINCINNATI,"
U. S. S. "CINCINNATI" ("RALEIGH.")
Length on l. w. l. 300 feet; beam, 42 feet; disp., 3,213 tons.

Kearney, U. S. Navy. These engines have equaled in performance any built by contract and the records of the Navy Department show that their actual cost was less per horse-power than contract-built engines. They differ from large triple-expansion engines of the usual type in having two low-pressure cylinders each, the fining in of the ship not leaving room for the location of single low-pressure cylinders of sufficient diameter.

The 2,000 ton cruisers became the *Detroit, Marblehead,* and *Montgomery.* The cost of each, exclusive of premiums, was limited by the enabling act of Congress to $700,000, and the Navy Department fixed eighteen knots as their required speed. Contractors bid in excess of the limit under these conditions and in consequence the proposals were modified by making seventeen knots the limit of required speed. Contracts for two of them were made with the Columbian Iron Works of Baltimore for $612,500 each and for the third—the *Marblehead*—with Harrison Loring, Boston, for $674,000, the premium offered in each case being $25,000 for each quarter-knot in excess of seventeen. All had vertical triple-expansion twin-screw engines of bureau design. The machinery for the *Marblehead* was built by sub-contract by the Quintard Iron Works of New York. On their trial trips all exceeded the required speed by considerably more than one knot and the *Montgomery* by more than two, earning a premium of $200,000, which is by far the greatest premium any of our new ships has won in proportion to the contract price.

The steel practice-vessel *Bancroft*, designed for the training of cadets at the Naval Academy, was built by the Samuel L. Moore and Sons Company, Elizabethport, New Jersey, the premium offered in her case being $5,000 per quarter-knot, on which basis she won $45,000. The contract price was $250,000. The name of this vessel was bestowed in memory of the distinguished American historian, Mr. George Bancroft, who was Secretary of the Navy during the first part of the administration of President James K. Polk, and through whose influence the United States Naval Academy was established.

The Fiftieth Congress, which had dealt so liberally with the navy by authorizing the ships that have been mentioned in this chapter, continued its good work at its last session by directing the construction of two steel gun-boats of the most approved type and "one ram for harbor-defence, of the general type approved by the Naval Advisory Board in their report to the Secretary of the Navy of November seventh, 1881, of the highest practicable speed." The two gun-boats, named *Castine* and *Machias*, were built by the Bath Iron Works, Bath, Maine, a speed of thirteen knots maintained for four hours with a premium and penalty clause of $5,000 per quarter-knot being the chief requirement of the contract. Each exceeded the contract speed by about two and one-half knots. When completed and put in service these two gun-boats were found so dangerously near being unstable that they were taken to the New York navy yard, cut in two, and lengthened enough to increase their displacement about one hundred and ten tons each.

The harbor-defense ram was also built by the Bath Iron Works, her general design being from plans prepared by Rear Admiral Daniel Ammen, U. S. Navy, a distinguished officer who for many years has advocated the ram as a formidable weapon in naval warfare. The name—*Katahdin*—given this craft is that of a mountain in Maine, and was formerly borne by one of the "Ninety-day" gun-boats. With the exception of a light battery of machine guns her offensive power lies wholly in her speed and ram.

During the first session of the Fifty-first Congress a new departure in our naval construction was taken by authorizing the building of three sea-going, coast-line battle-ships, "designed to carry the heaviest armor and most powerful ordnance . . . and to have the highest practicable speed for vessels of their class, to cost, exclusive of armament and of any premiums that may be paid for increased speed, not exceeding four million dollars each." These powerful ships—the *Indiana*, *Massachusetts*, and *Oregon*—are now approaching completion, the two former at the works of the Cramp Company in Philadelphia, and the *Oregon* at the Union Iron Works, San Francisco. They will be of about 10,200 tons displacement each, and their fighting factors—battery, steam power, and armor—are combined in such proportions that they will be fully the equals of any battle ships now afloat.

The same act that provided for the building of these battle ships also authorized the construction of one protected cruiser of about 7,300 tons displacement, to have a maximum speed of twenty-one

U. S. STEAMSHIP DETROIT (*Marblehead, Montgomery*).

Length on l. w. l., 257 feet; Beam, 37 feet; Displacement, 2,089 tons.

knots; one swift torpedo cruiser of about 750 tons displacement, to have not less than twenty-three knots speed, to cost not more than $350,000; and one torpedo boat. The act repeated a previous clause requiring all parts of the vessels to be of domestic manufacture. The torpedo cruiser has never been undertaken for the reason that the price fixed by Congress as the limit of cost was considered by engineers and builders insufficient to procure a vessel of the size and speed specified. The torpedo boat, named *Ericsson* in honor of the great engineer, was built by contract by the Iowa Iron Works at Dubuque, Iowa, and has not yet succeeded in running a successful steam trial. A fatality seems to have followed her from her inception; unforseen obstacles delayed her completion more than two years beyond the contract time, and repeated efforts to run a trial trip have failed from accidents to her machinery. The most distressing casualty that has befallen her was the bursting of a steam pipe while running at high speed, this killing three and severely injuring five men of the engineer's force employed by the contractors.

The large swift cruiser was given the name *Columbia*, and her remarkable speed and beautiful appearance have combined to make her the pride of the new navy and have won for her the popular appellation, "The Gem of the Ocean." The name bestowed upon her is in accordance with a law requiring vessels of her size to be to be named after states of the Union, the District of Columbia being regarded as a state for this purpose. While work was progressing on the designs for this so-called commerce-destroyer, Chief Engineer N. P. Towne, U. S. Navy, then director of the drafting room of the Bureau of Steam Engineering, facetiously dubbed her the *Pirate*, and this name, being seized upon by the newspapers as appropriate, clung to her long after the authorized name was announced, and has appeared many times in serious use both at home and abroad in descriptions of the ship. The *Columbia* was built by the Cramp Company from designs furnished by the Bureaus of Steam Engineering and Construction and Repair, the contract price being $2,725,000. A speed of twenty-one knots maintained for four consecutive hours was specified and a premium of $50,000 offered for each quarter-knot in excess of this, while a penalty was provided of $25,000 for each quarter-knot the speed might fall

Arrangement of Screws of the COLUMBIA.

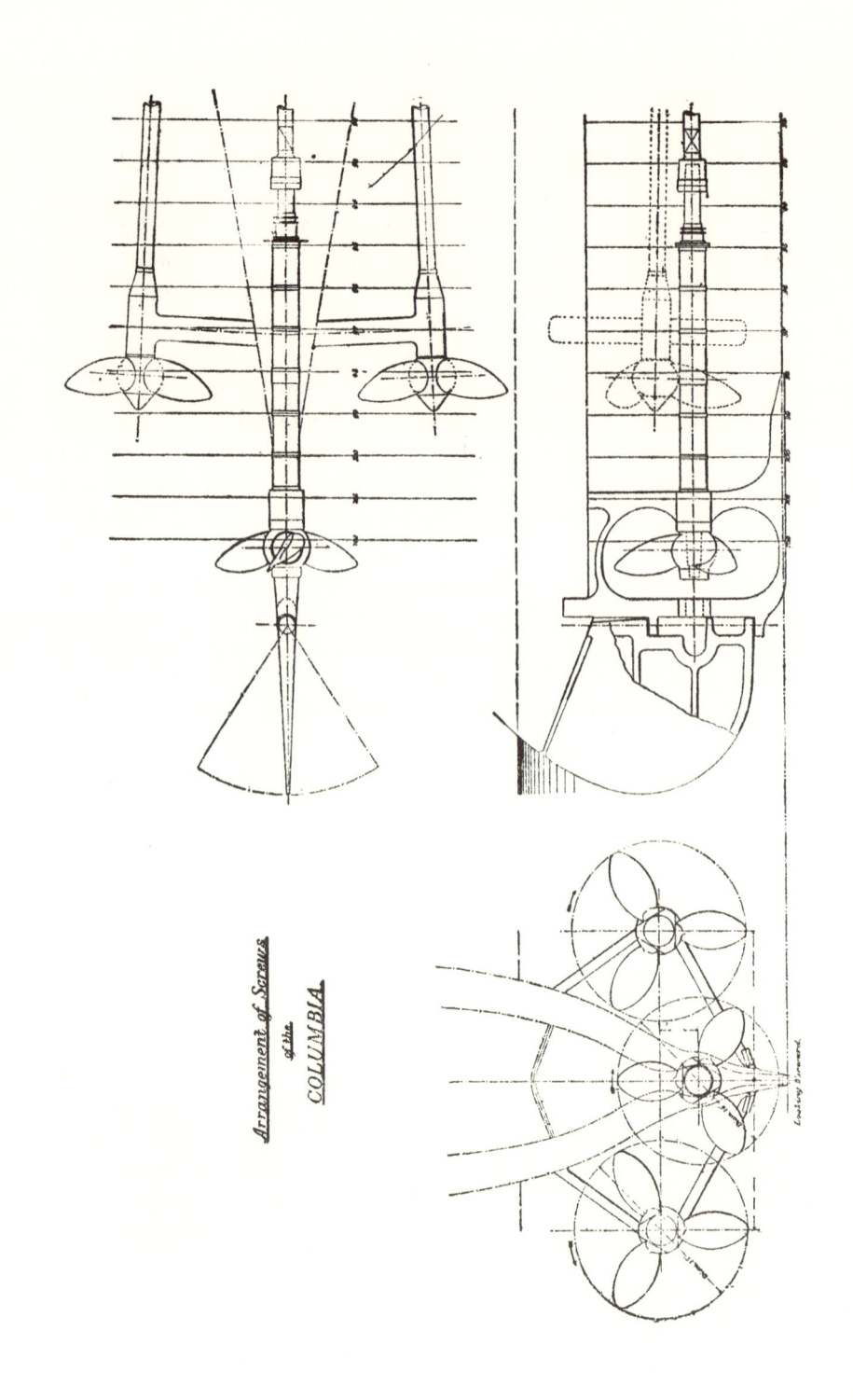

U. S. GUNBOAT, CASTINE (*Machias*).

Length on l. w. l., 204 feet; beam, 32 ft. 2 in.; displacement, 1,177 tons.

below twenty-one knots. The official steam trial took place November 18th, 1893, and the *Columbia* maintained for four consecutive hours the remarkable speed of 22.8 knots; the premium for seven quarter-knots in excess of the contract speed amounted to $350,000.

For the legislation that called this magnificent specimen of the engineer's art into existence the naval service is indebted to Honorable Charles A. Boutelle more than to any one man, while credit for her wonderful steaming qualities belongs to Engineer-in-Chief George W. Melville. Mr. Boutelle was Chairman of the Committee on Naval Affairs in the House of Representatives and he had much opposition to overcome, both in his committee room and on the floor of the House before the building of the ship was voted. This opposition was based upon doubt as to the possibility of building a ship of the size and speed proposed, and also as to the propriety of providing vessels of such a type for the navy. Mr. Boutelle knew, just as Mr. Isherwood had known years before when he had projected the *Wampanoag*, that the mere possession of such a vessel in time of war yields an invaluable advantage to the nation owning it, and his faith on the subject was not theoretical, for as a volunteer officer he had learned in the hard school of experience the most useful lessons of naval warfare.

When the question of supplying power to drive the ship at the high speed desired was being considered at the Navy Department, Engineer-in-Chief Melville proposed to secure it by installing three screws, an unusual but not novel practice, for we have seen in former chapters that some of the Mississippi River iron-clads during the Civil War had as many as four screws, and triple screws had been applied more recently to small torpedo cruisers in Europe. Secretary Tracy hesitated about undertaking such an experiment on so large and expensive a scale and gave his approval only after the most earnest arguments from Melville, who well knew that anything short of complete success would involve his own professional ruin. To all who knew the prominent part taken by Mr. Melville in establishing the characteristics of this great ship, it was a source of gratification to observe that the principal credit for the achievement was accorded him when the trial performance of the vessel became a triumph.

Though matchless in her class when compared with foreign vessels, the *Columbia* has not been free from attack by theorists within our own country. It has been asserted that she, or her type in general, is not as well adapted for war purposes as a swift armed mail steamer; that in spite of her high trial speed, no speed comparable with that of the better mail steamers can be developed by her under the usual conditions of service, and that the engineers and firemen of the navy cannot drive her at the rate obtained by the picked men used in running contractors' trial trips. The first objection to her type—that regarding her qualities as a combatant in comparison with commercial steamers—has been answered sufficiently in Chapter XXVII. To the other criticisms noted the *Columbia* herself has recently replied satisfactorily by her performance in returning to the United States from Europe after having been an object of wonder and admiration at the Kiel naval celebration.

To settle the question of her endurance at sea, the Secretary of the Navy ordered her to cross the Atlantic Ocean at full speed, without using forced draft except the last day of the voyage. The *Columbia* left Southampton, England, shortly after noon on Friday the 26th of July, 1895, and arrived at Sandy Hook at 8.59 A. M. the next Friday, having made a run of 3,090 knots in six days, twenty-three hours and forty-nine minutes, or at an average speed of 18.41 knots per hour for the whole distance. The daily performance is shown by the following summary of her log, first published in the Journal of the American Society of Naval Engineers:

"Friday, July 26.—Passed the Needles at 2 P. M., and the Lizard at 9.50 P. M.; making from 18 to 19 knots in the Channel. Light westerly wind.

"Saturday, July 27.—Moderate sea; light to fresh northerly wind. Distance run to noon, 405 miles. Coal, 196.25 tons. Average revolution of engines: starboard, 97.2; port, 97.3; center, 96.6. Leaky tubes in one boiler rendered that boiler useless for seven hours.

"Sunday, July 28.—Gentle breezes, smooth sea. Distance run, 460 miles. Coal, 201.25 tons. Average revolutions: starboard, 104.1; port, 103.9; center, 103.7.

"Monday, July 29.—Smooth sea, fresh S. S. W. wind. Dis-

HARBOR DEFENSE RAM KATAHDIN.

Length on l. w. l. 250 feet 9 inches; beam, 43 feet 5 inches; disp., 2,155 tons.

tance run, 462 miles. Coal, 225.5 tons. Average revolutions: starboard, 105.8; port, 105.8; center, 105.7.

"Tuesday, July 30.—Fresh breeze from W. by S. Distance run to noon, 450 miles. Coal, 229.75 tons. Average revolutions: starboard, 103.2; port, 103.3 ; center, 102.6. Slowed for four hours on account of fog and heavy sea.

"Wednesday, July 31.—Fresh breeze from W. S. W. Distance run to noon, 455 miles. Coal, 230 tons. Average revolutions: starboard, 105.9; port, 105.9; center, 105.1.

"Thursday, August 1.—Fresh breeze from W. S. W. Distance run to noon, 453 miles. Coal, 230 tons. Average revolutions: starboard, 105; port, 104.9; center, 104.4.

"Friday, August 2.—Passed Sandy Hook lightship at 8.59 A. M. Distance run since preceding noon, 405 miles. Coal burned to 9 A. M., 221 tons. Coal on hand at noon, 328 tons."

About eleven tons should be deducted from the daily coal consumption to account for that used in running auxiliary machinery. An inspection of the bunkers after the run showed a surplus on hand great enough to indicate that the amount charged each day exceeded that actually used by about ten per centum. The mean draft of water at the beginning and end of the voyage was 24 feet, $2\frac{1}{4}$ inches, corresponding to a displacement of about 8,150 tons, or 800 tons more than the displacement on the acceptance trial trip. Natural draft was used the whole trip, it having been found impossible with the force on board to supply coal from the remote bunkers the last day in sufficient quantity to permit of forcing the fires. The engineers' force of the *Columbia* numbered 196 men of all ratings, the working force being less than this by about a dozen men detailed as mess cooks, and by the daily sick list; sixty men from the deck force were sent to duty in the fire-rooms, but even with this help the force was inadequate and the work was most killing for all.

The few officers who directed the remarkable performance of the *Columbia's* machinery deserve mention, for upon them fell a laborious and vexing task, and a very serious responsibility: the latter not confined to the safety of machinery and boilers at high power and the lives of a large company of men, but involved also the reputation of the American navy and of American ship-builders, for the run of the *Columbia* was watched by the whole world. They were, Chief Engineer William H. Harris; Passed Assistant Engineer Martin Bevington; Assistant Engineers W. H. McGrann and George H. Sheppard, and Naval Cadets (engineer division) B. K. McMorris and Ralph H. Chappell. Only six directing officers in all. There are as many, or more, licensed engineers in each watch on board the swift trans-atlantic mail steamers with the speed of which the *Columbia* was forced to compete. Mr. Bevington was severely injured in a street-car accident shortly before the *Columbia* left Southampton, but realizing the importance of the task ahead of the ship he voluntarily undertook his duties and aided greatly in making the voyage a triumphal one. Captain Sumner speaks thus of him in his official report of the *Columbia's* run:

"I feared that I was to be deprived of the valuable services of Passed Assistant Engineer Bevington of our engineer force, as he met with a severe and painful accident just previous to our departure from Southampton, which placed him on the sick list. He left the list, however, though still suffering severely from the effects of the accident, and took his watch and duty in the engine room all the way over."

This voyage of the *Columbia* was by far the fastest trans-atlantic or long-distance passage ever made by a vessel of war, and proved that in her the United States owns a steamer that can sustain for as long a period as will ever be necessary a sea-speed greater than that of any but a very few of the Atlantic "greyhounds," while her speed under natural draft was but a little less than that of the fastest mail steamers running over the same route with adequate force in their engine departments, and habitually using forced draft. This is shown by the following table of the *best* performance of the swiftest Atlantic liners between Southampton and New York:

Fuerst Bismarck	6 days,	10	hours,	32	minutes.
Normannia	6 "	12	"	30	"
Paris	6 "	16	"	43	"
New York	6 "	17	"	14	"
Augusta Victoria	6 "	20	"	22	"
St. Louis	6 "	18	"	47	"
U. S. S. Columbia	6 "	23	"	49	"

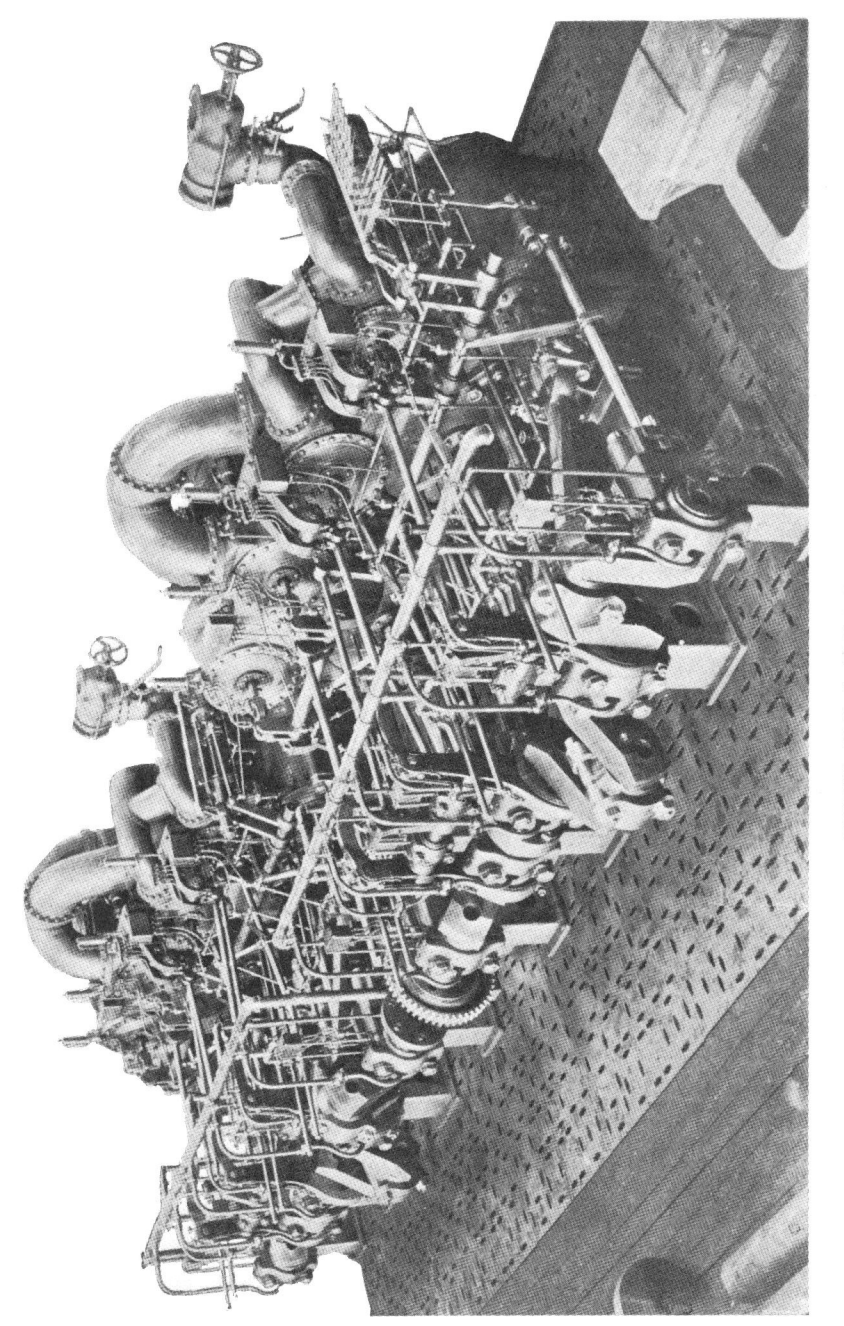

ENGINES OF U. S. RAM KATAHDIN.

Example of Modern Horizontal Triple-Expansion Engine.

When the orders for the *Columbia* to make this long sea-trial were issued, the antagonists of speed as a factor in naval warfare were happy, for they believed her incapable of maintaining a high speed for any considerable time and confidently expected her failure to furnish the final argument against the policy of building war vessels in which steam is given predominant space. Even the friends of her type, knowing the disadvantages under which she labored from lack of engineering *personnel*, were very modest in predicting the result. The two men most directly interested in her success—Engineer-in-Chief Melville, and Mr. Charles H. Cramp, her builder—did not anticipate a better record than eight days in crossing, and this estimate of time was about the average of the range established by betting men, for the sporting fraternity seized upon the event and pools were sold on it in many cities. Very few and very sanguine were those who expected to see her in New York before Saturday afternoon or Sunday morning.

Friday, August 2, was eagerly looked forward to, for it was expected that the incoming mail steamers that day would have passed the *Columbia* and would bring tidings of her progress. When, therefore, the news was flashed to New York early that morning that the *Columbia* was off Fire Island there was much surprise and doubt, but the latter was quickly dispelled by the great white cruiser herself as she rushed into New York Bay and moved majestically up the North River, being cheered as she passed by thousands of people assembled at the Battery and on the piers, and answering with hoarse blasts of her steam-whistle the congratulatory screams of innumerable river-craft. The Hamburg-American liner *Augusta Victoria* followed the *Columbia* out of the English Channel five hours behind her, with the boasted intention of beating her to New York. She did not see the *Columbia* on the voyage and her people were so confident they had passed her in the night and left her far astern that when they arrived at the New York quarantine station at noon, Friday, the bluff German captain shouted derisively, "Where is that white whirlwind now?" The answer was a bitter disappointment to him and rudely disillusioned his passengers; for it said the *Columbia* had passed up the harbor hours before.

The Fifty-first Congress completed the excellent work it had performed in strengthening the navy by authorizing at the close of its last session the construction of another commerce destroyer, a sister-ship of the *Columbia*. As in the case of the *Columbia*, Mr. Boutelle was responsible for this ship, his practical knowledge of naval affairs assuring him of the importance of possessing a few very swift cruisers as a menace to grasping powers that have a large over-sea commerce to protect. The new vessel was built by the Cramp Company and was named *Minneapolis*. The contract requirements were identical with those for the *Columbia*. On her trial trip, which took place July 14, 1894, she developed over 20,000 horse-power and maintained for four consecutive hours the unprecedented speed of 23.073 knots per hour, for which her builders received a premium of $414,600. The *Minneapolis* is probably a swifter and better ship than the *Columbia*, but as the latter has had longer and more varied sea-experience it has been thought proper to describe her performance more at length as representative of the type. The following popular comparisons of certain features of the *Minneapolis* are interesting, and are quoted from a lecture delivered at the Naval War College by Passed Assistant Engineer Ira N. Hollis, U. S. Navy, in October, 1892:

"Her low-pressure piston, which is 92 inches in diameter, has an area of 46 square feet, a very comfortable 6 feet by 8 feet stateroom on board ship, and this piston has an initial load of 100 tons, equal to the weight of three locomotives. The mean piston speed at maximum power will be 11 miles an hour, and the maximum speed 16 miles an hour. The tip of the propeller blades will move through the water at the moderate rate of 75 miles an hour. The condenser tubes, if placed end to end, would form a tube 33 miles long, and, if flattened out, would cover about $\frac{3}{8}$ of an acre. The cooling water passed through these tubes will be equal to 36,000,000 gallons per day, enough to supply a large city with water. The main boilers, if placed end to end, would form a tunnel 156 feet long, and large enough for a train of cars to pass through. If divided up into rooms, they would supply a hotel with 16 fair-sized bed-rooms. The heating surface is equal to $1\frac{1}{8}$ acres. The grate surface, if arranged on one grate, would equal one small town lot of 20 feet front and 77 feet depth. The boiler tubes, placed end to

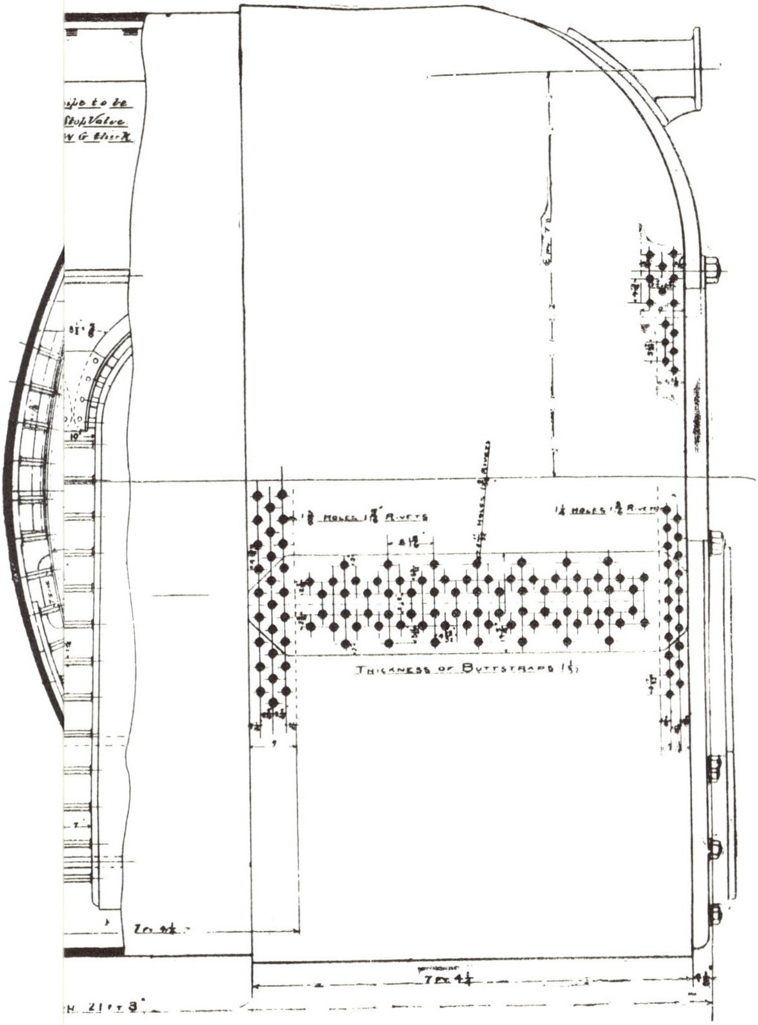

Stop Valve
THICKNESS OF BUTTSTRAPS
7 Ft 4½

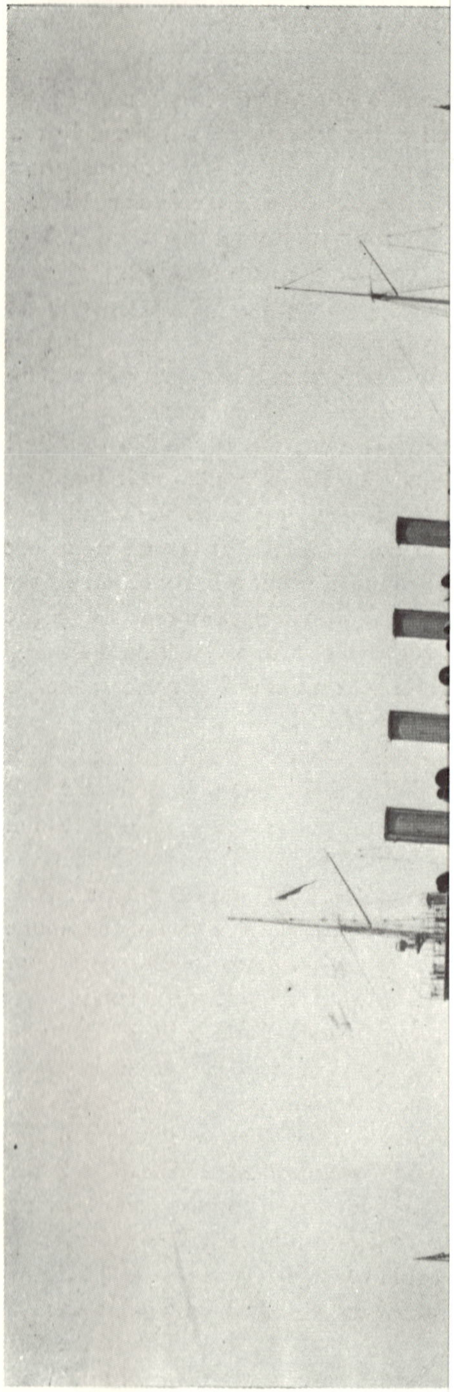

end, would be 13½ miles long. The blowers are capable of supplying 84,000,000 cubic feet of air an hour, which would supply a good-sized yacht with a ten-knot breeze.

"The coal required for a full-power run across the Atlantic would supply 150 families for one year in New York State. With 20,000 horse-power she would lift herself (7,500 tons weight) to the Brooklyn Bridge in three minutes, if hoisting ropes were coiled around drums on the shafts. If the engines were set up on shore and used as a catapult, they would throw a 300-pound weight with such velocity that it would go off into space entirely clear of the earth's influence. The fictions of Jules Verne sink into insignificance by the side of this coal-eating monster of the nineteenth century."

During the first session of the Fifty-second Congress, an act, approved July 19, 1892, authorized the construction of one armored cruiser of the general type of the *New York* and "one sea-going,

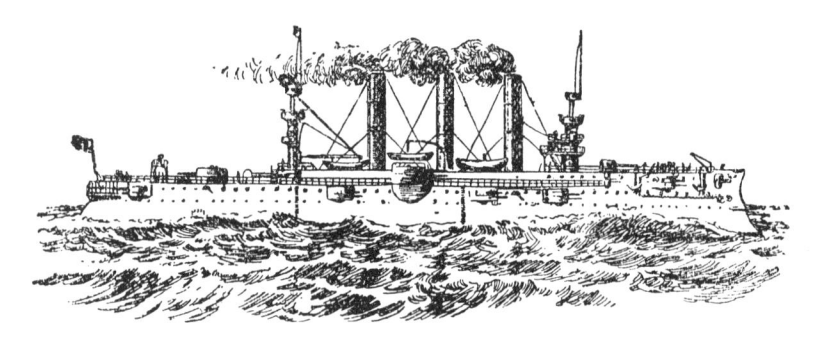

U. S. ARMORED CRUISER "BROOKLYN."

Length on l. w. l., 400 ft. 6 inches; beam, 64 ft. 8 inches; mean draft, 24 feet; displacement, 9,270 tons.

coast-line battle-ship, designed to carry the heaviest armor and most powerful ordnance, with a displacement of about 9,000 tons, to have the highest practicable speed for vessels of its class, and to cost, exclusive of armament and of any premiums that may be paid for increased speed, not exceeding four million dollars." In designing these two ships the Bureaus of Steam Engineering and Construction and Repair introduced many improvements gained by experience with the work on former vessels of the same types, and produced what are probably the best examples of ship designs now in our navy. Contracts for both vessels were awarded the Cramp Company and they are now well advanced towards completion. The armored cruiser, named *Brooklyn*, is twenty feet longer and of about seven hundred tons more displacement than the *New York*. Her engines are the same, but certain changes in the dimensions and arrangement of boilers give her about 500 square feet more heating surface. A marked departure from former practice gives her three very tall smoke-pipes (100 feet above the grates) to obtain extraordinary furnace draft without the use of blowers. The battle-ship—the *Iowa*—is over 1,000 tons displacement greater than the *Indiana* class, and is larger in all particulars. Her engines and boilers are designed for 11,000 horse-power as against 9,000 in the *Indiana* class.

Three light-draft gun-boats were authorized by the last naval appropriation bill passed by the Fifty-second Congress, and after

THE "NASHVILLE."
Length on l. w. l., 220 ft.; beam, 38 ft. 3 in.; disp., 1,371 tons.

the usual process of issuing proposals and receiving sealed bids in competition from ship-builders, contracts for all three were awarded the Newport News Shipbuilding and Dry-Dock Company, of Newport News, Virginia. First known officially as Gunboats Nos. 7, 8 and 9, these vessels have been named after the cities of Nashville, Wilmington (Delaware), and Helena, and are now nearing completion. The *Nashville*, and *Wilmington* were launched October 19th, 1895, from the same ways, they having been built "tandem" in the same slip to economize room in the ship-yard. The *Nashville*, 220 feet

U. S. BATTLESHIP "INDIANA" ("MASSACHUSETTS" AND "OREGON," 1895).

From a copyright photograph by **W. H. Rau**, Philadelphia, Pa.

long and about 1,370 tons displacement, has a peculiar arrangement of machinery. Her twin screws are actuated by two sets of vertical inverted quadruple-expansion engines, having cylinder diameters of 11, 17, 24, and 34 inches respectively, with a stroke of 18 inches. The low-pressure cylinders are placed forward of the others and so arranged that they can be disconnected when it is not desired to run the engines at full power. The remaining cylinders may be run as triple-expansion engines of the usual arrangement. This is accomplished by having two sets of boilers, four water-tube boilers of the Yarrow type carrying 250 pounds pressure, and two ordinary cylindrical boilers designed to carry 160 pounds pressure. When the engines are working at full power all the boilers will be used, the Yarrow boilers supplying steam directly to the high-pressure cylinders, while the other boilers will deliver their steam to the first intermediate cylinder—or into the first receiver—where it will meet the high-pressure exhaust at 160 pounds pressure. This novel, but purely scientific, combination was devised by Passed Assistant Engineers Frank H. Bailey and Ira N. Hollis, on duty in the Bureau of Steam Engineering. The contract requires the *Nashville*, when weighted to a mean draft of 11 feet, to average 14 knots for four consecutive hours, during which period the air-pressure in the ash-pits of the cylindrical boilers shall not exceed one inch of water, and in the ash-pits of the coil boilers two inches.

The *Wilmington*, and *Helena*, sister ships, are 250 feet, 6 inches long on the load water line, 40 feet beam, and are limited to a mean draft of about 8 feet 10 inches to adapt them for cruising in shallow rivers. They will have one military mast and no sails. A feature in their construction is the possession of two rudders, one forward of the other, to give great area for turning purposes. Twin-screw vertical triple-expansion engines of the usual type and six single-ended cylindrical boilers comprise the motive power. The contract requires a speed of thirteen knots maintained for four hours and provides a premium and penalty of $20,000 per knot, the same provision existing in the contract for the *Nashville*.

The first naval appropriation bill that came before the Fifty-third Congress received an unusual amount of attention in the form of talk, the question of further strengthening the navy being debated at length, during which debate the orators on each side did not fail to claim for their political parties all the credit for the naval construction that had gone before. The end did not justify the proceeding, for all that came of this lengthy debate was authority to build three torpedo boats. Even this did not involve any new appropriation, for the act specified that, "The Secretary of the Navy is hereby authorized to use the four hundred and fifty thousand dollars 'for the additional cruiser of the *Vesuvius* type,' appropriated by the act of March second, 1889, or so much thereof as may be necessary, for the construction, armament, and equipment of three torpedo boats, to cost, all together, not more than the said sum of four hundred and fifty thousand dollars." The three boats, designed to be large and swift, are now being built by the Columbian Iron Works, Baltimore, Maryland.

U. S. GUNBOAT "WILMINGTON" (AND "HELENA.")
Length on l. w. l., 250 ft. 6 in; beam, 40 ft. 2 in.; disp., 1,392 tons.

The next, and final, session of the Fifty-third Congress provided much more liberally for new ships, authority being granted for the construction by contract of two sea-going coast-line battle-ships of about 10,000 tons displacement, to cost, exclusive of armament, not more than $4,000,000 each; six light-draft composite gun-boats of about 1,000 tons displacement, to cost not more than $230,000 each, and three torpedo boats, to cost not more than $175,000 each. These torpedo boats have been designed to be larger than any before undertaken in our navy and the contracts for them demand a speed of 26 knots per hour.

In the plans for four of the six gun-boats, at present designated

ONE ENGINE OF U. S. STEAMSHIP MASSACHUSETTS.
Example of Modern Vertical Triple-Expansion Engine.

by the numbers 10, 11, 12, and 13, several important departures from accepted practice appear, they going back to a type similar to the *Alert* class of more than twenty years ago. The idea in this is to provide some small vessels for distant cruising that will be able to proceed under sail and not be subject to the expensive necessity of frequently seeking a dry-dock for repairs. The move is not regarded by naval engineers as a retrogression, for the excellence of the type proposed, for ordinary cruising service in time of peace,

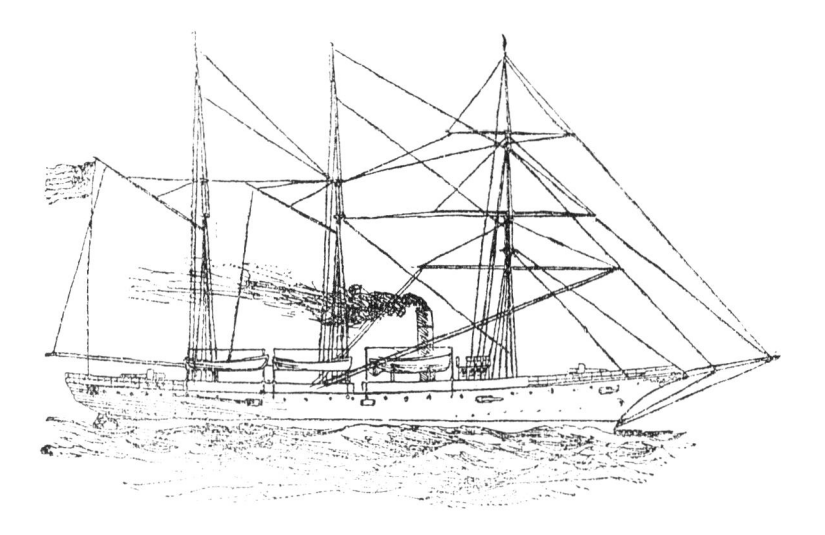

DESIGN OF SINGLE-SCREW COMPOSITE GUNBOATS NOS. 10, 11, 12, AND 13, NOW UNDER CONSTRUCTION.
Length on l. w. l., 168 feet; beam, 36 feet; disp., 1,000 tons.

is recognized by all. The under-water hull framing of the four vessels will be of steel according to the usual mode of construction, but will be planked instead of plated, and the planking will be coppered. A single screw actuated by a vertical triple-expansion engine of only 800 horse-power and two small "Scotch" boilers will be the chief items in the machinery plant. These gun-boats are to be barkentine-rigged, spreading 11,000 feet of canvas, and are designed to have the overhanging clipper-bow that looked so graceful before we became accustomed to other forms. The other two gun-boats, numbered 14, and 15, will have the same composite form of construction just described; but otherwise are of modern type, having twin-screws, and no sail power except steadying sails on two light schooner masts.

The two battle-ships have been designed for 11,500 tons displacement and will be in general very like the *Iowa* in hull and in design and arrangement of machinery. A decidedly new feature has been adopted for these big ships in locating the turrets for the VIII-inch guns on top of the XIII-inch gun turrets. The act authorizing the building of these ships concludes with the words, "and one of said battle-ships shall be named *Kearsarge*." This in deference to a general public sense of bereavement over the loss of the famous sloop-of-war *Kearsarge* on Roncador Reef a year before. The sister-ship of the new *Kearsarge* will, according to law, be given the name of one of the States of the Union. Now that the Civil War is admitted in all parts of our country to be over, and sectional feeling has so far vanished that friendly gatherings of "blue and grey" veterans on famous battle fields have become established annual features of our social life, it may be fitting time to give the battle-ship, sister of the new *Kearsarge*, the name of the State of Alabama.[1]

---

[1] Since the above left the hands of the author the ship has been named *Kentucky*

CHAPTER XL.

"Ye shall know the truth, and the truth shall make you free."—*New Testament.*

CONCLUSION.

THOSE who have read these pages to this point have obtained the means of knowing something of the introduction and development of steam as a military agent in the United States navy, and of the part in that growth taken by engineers who have been identified with the naval service. The change has been great from the *Fulton* of 1837 to the *Indiana* of 1896, but, great as it has been, one wonders after reading the story that the present form was not sooner attained. Its possibility and desirability were known long before the realization. From the day of Ericsson's *Monitor* the naval world has known perfectly well what a real war-ship should be—a steam engine and a gun, properly joined together—but it has taken a whole generation to allay the prejudices and effect the compromises necessary before the combination could be made. The result, in the form of a modern battle-ship, is a majestic monument to the skill and perseverance of man considered as an engineer.

Mr. Ruskin says that in after ages this century will be especially famous for one thing—"It will always be said of us, with unabated reverence, 'They built ships of the line.' Take it all in all, a ship of the line is the most honorable thing that man, as a gregarious animal, has ever produced." And much more in the same strain. Commenting upon this, Mr. Church in his "Life of John Ericsson" says, "It is impossible to transfer to a monitor the sentiment connected with a ship-of-the-line," and herein lies the key to the causes that have so retarded the development of the war-ship. The ship of the line was a grand object and with it great deeds were done: hence the sentiment that so exalted it and has lingered to the disadvantage of later days long after the ship of the line itself passed away. Such sentiment was as honorable as the object that inspired it and against it engineers have no right to rail, though it has done them much evil. Its effects have finally been overcome, and the engineers' battle-ship at last made possible is so far superior as a sum total of destructive energy and as an epitome of the capability of man that the past may well be allowed its own memories. Our mastodon of iron and steel, though not a ship-of-the-line, has its proper place in the line of battle and time will transfer to it, monitor though it is, the sentiment that glorified its tall predecessor.

Next to the sentiment that strove from affection to preserve old forms, engineers in their work of changing navies have been most hampered by what may be termed official precedent—a sort of slavery to past practice. The rules that hedge about a military organization foster in a peculiar degree respect for old forms and precedents because they suffice to satisfy superior authority and shield from censure those who cling to them. The bald statement, "It has always been so," is too often an all-sufficient reason against changes that may involve extra brain work or responsibility, and the progressionist finds this a stone wall in front of his endeavors. Dread of responsibility and arrogance of office are twin-brothers, and they are the discouragers of industry. The officers of our navy who have been concerned in the developments of naval architecture, steam, and the gun, know too well how iron-bound are the rules of past practice.

In illustration it is only necessary to turn back these pages and review the receptions accorded such typical vessels as the *Princeton*, *Monitor*, and *Wampanoag* when they appeared in the navy as forerunners of what was coming. After all opposition to those ships has passed into history it is noticeable that the features peculiar to them that excited the greatest opposition are now combined in a harmonious union to make the fighting ship of to-day. Is it too much to suggest that but for the insistence and persistence of engineers our *Indianas* and *Brooklyns* would not yet exist? Public opinion and to some extent naval opinion have sustained the engineer in his revolt against precedent and sentiment, but to him is due the chief praise for what has been achieved.

Steam has at last triumphed in its long warfare with sails, and navies are much better for it. Looking backward upon the history of that struggle one realizes that but for accident it would never have existed. The modern battle-ship, stripped of the refinements of science which are not essential to it, is just what Robert Fulton called his *Demologos*—a steam battery. But for the unexpected lack of opportunity of proving the superiority in battle of that structure we would have been spared the fifty years of strife, with all the engendered animosities, that have been wasted in bringing the steam fighting ship back to its original form. With the passing of sails vanishes also the dream, so long cherished, of restoring in some useful form the picturesque fabrics of other days with all their masts and spars and without engines or engineers. Few indeed to-day would seriously propose a sailing vessel for military purposes any more than we would advocate slings or spears as weapons of war or implements for the instruction of our cadets and apprentices.

The history of the steam fighting ship has now been traced from the rude beginning to the present gigantic and expensive form. In its contemplation a curious thought suggests itself. During the Middle Ages the wealth of nations and all the arts of men were lavished upon those great cathedrals that are still the admiration of the world. Now, after centuries of political and social advancement, all great nations are expending their substance and skill upon these huge battle-ships. Those of old time built for the glory of God and that righteousness might hold dominion over the spirits of men; we, with all our enlightenment, build the most powerful engines for the destruction of life and property that the earth has ever seen. This is the contrast that at first thought abruptly presents itself, but after consideration the question resolves itself into a comparison of methods for accomplishing a desirable end. Perhaps the battle-ship, as an object lesson, is better than the cathedral for compelling nations and men to practice in their dealings those fundamental precepts that lead to peace on earth and good will toward men. History seems to support this assumption.

Having reviewed the story of the steamship it is now fitting that this work should close with a few words about the man who made the steamship possible—the engineer. In all that precedes the aim has been simply to write history: to follow the growth of the war-steamer and to trace the career of the naval corps most closely identified with that growth, without speculating as to what might have been done or left undone to better advantage. Comments upon what may be termed naval politics—the strife between old and new ideas and the jealousies of corps, both incident to the introduction of steam—have been withheld. The waging of internecine naval warfare for the purpose of instituting or opposing reforms lies properly within the province of the pamphleteer, and from him the subject has always had ample attention.

By patient endeavor the corps of naval engineers has completely realized its life-long conception of the proper form of war-vessel, but it has not yet succeeded in gaining similar recognition for its own members. Indeed, a review of these pages presents a curious contrast, for we find the official status of naval engineers remaining practically unchanged during all the years that the ship whose type they have championed has been steadily advancing toward perfection. Personally, the present members of the corps may be better situated than were their predecessors, because with the same education and training as line officers there no longer exist those petty causes for friction that formerly precipitated personal and corps animosities when military and civil educations were contrasted. In official standing there has been no advance and no change of importance for fully thirty years.

In the early days when steam was merely auxiliary and seldom used there was some reason for classing the engineer with the civil or non-combatant part of the service, but the time for that ceased with the experiences of the Civil War. The steam engine is now as important a military feature as the turret-gun in the composition of a war-ship, and the director of the one is entitled by virtue of his duties to the same official standing and dignity as the other. As a matter of fact the duties of the two officers are very similar: the engineer directs the operation of machinery, which is the business he has been trained for; the gunnery officer also directs machinery and thus does the work of an engineer whether he is one or not and whether he relishes it or not. These officers with their men and machines are the main fighting force of the ship and there is no reason why one should be elevated over the other. Not only are their duties practically the same but they are performed under almost identical conditions. Each is locked in a steel-clad compartment full of men and moving machinery; each receives orders by mechanical means from a common superior and each is dependent upon himself alone for power to execute those orders. Each must, if efficient at his post, possess the quality of command and an unusual degree of self-reliance and appreciation of discipline. No other station on board ship demands the exercise of so many purely officer-like qualities.

From the very nature of steam ships of war and the objects for which a navy is maintained the identification of the engineer and the men of his division with the combatant element of the ship is complete. To refer to them as "non-combatants" is merely a foolish use of invective, the absurdity of which is self-evident, for if there were either truth or reason in the charge humanity and the established rules of war would dictate that the engineer and his men, one-half the ship's company perhaps, be removed to a place of safety when danger approaches and the remainder of the crew left to fight out its own salvation. That anything so absurd has ever been done is disproved by history; that nothing of the kind is contemplated is shown by the fact that all battle tactics for fleets and ships are based upon the use of steam power as the primary element for offense and defense.

The duties actually performed by naval engineers in war have been described to some extent in the chapters of this book relating to the Civil War. A naval lieutenant recently wrote in the *Naval Institute* that the prosecution of that war overthrew to great extent the previously existing distinctions between line and staff because "the emergencies of war caused every man to step outside his own duties and his rightful authority in order to help the general situation." That this was the case has been shown by many examples, and we have also seen that when the war ended the interrupted distinctions were restored. Unless all the rules and maxims of war that exist or ever have existed are fallacious, the duty of every person connected with a war organization is to "help the general situation," and if the peace conditions of our navy are such that any class of officers must, in the event of war, step outside their duties and exceed their "lawful authority" in order to perform the services that fall upon them, there must be something fatally wrong. The great duty of a navy in peace is universally conceded to be preparation for war, and the way to do this surely cannot be by preventing a considerable part of the official personnel from acquiring a knowledge of the duties that will devolve upon it in war. When war conditions exact the performance of duties and the exercise of authority that peace conditions deny, it would seem that inefficiency and disaster are being courted.

The varied services rendered the country by the naval engineer corps during the war were, as we have seen, well performed. And it must be remembered that much of the work was done by young men, regulars and volunteers, fresh from civil life, mostly without previous military service, and obliged, like the volunteer line officers, to learn exacting duties in the hurried school of rude and dangerous experience. That better and more varied service would have been rendered by a trained corps of engineers bred to the navy from youth, is so certain that it may be asserted without in the least disparaging the gallant engineers of the war period, or finding fault with what they did. It was an understanding of this very point that impelled the Navy Department during the war to urge successfully upon Congress the desirability of providing at the Naval Academy a system of training for the future engineers of the navy. The recommendations of the Department on this subject, quoted in Chapter XXXIII., are worth reading again in this connection.

In reading those reports one is impressed with the earnestness of the opinions regarding the necessity of line officers accepting steam engineering as an essential part of naval seamanship. If it were then important that "every naval officer should be an engineer as well as a sailor," the need is doubly important at this time, yet it does not seem to be as well appreciated now as then. There are among the writer's acquaintances some competent engineers in the line of the navy, but their mechanical talents are inherited or have been developed by circumstances external to their profession rather than by any serious effort to familiarize themselves with that naval science which constitutes so much of the real seamanship of to-day. The older seamanship was, perhaps, more agreeable as a calling and fiction has disguised it in the drapery of romance, but it cannot fight battles or carry war-ships over the seas in these days.

The prediction of Assistant Secretary Fox that the change in naval methods would result in "the sailor swallowing the engineer, or the engineer swallowing the sailor," has not yet come to pass. In fact, after thirty years of working at cross-purposes neither the sailors nor the engineers have bettered themselves or gained any advantage in the rivalry. Perhaps the admission on each side that the other has a right to live and that each is dependent for success upon the other would make mutual understanding and endeavor possible and result in benefit to the naval service, which has higher claims upon us than the interests of corps. The position of the engineer in the navy is too well established by what he has done and is doing to require defense. On shore his functions are those pertaining to the staff of a military organization, the same as those of any officer of any corps doing shore duty. At sea he directs the most needful fighting factor in the ship—*power*. Upon his ability to control that force depends the choice of position and the ability to give or refuse battle. So long as power can be maintained the ship has life; its failure involves general failure. The engineer and his division of men are so much the corner-stone upon which the fighting fabric rests that they may, to borrow an idea from their surroundings, be aptly called the Iron Brigade of the naval organization.

By custom and the requirements of service, sustained to some extent by the navy regulations, the engineer officer exercises all the functions of subordinate command over what is usually the largest division of men in the ship. Statute law, as its provisions regarding command are usually interpreted, prohibits him from exercising such command. For consistency and a logical distribution of authority more than for any reflected honor upon themselves the engineers of the navy have been for several years, and are yet, asking Congress to make their command legal, the same as that of divisional officers of the line and marine corps serving in the same ships. They also ask that real rank as a just recognition of their education and training as naval officers and commensurate with the responsibilities of their offices be conferred upon them. These are both essential steps toward harmony in the service and will make it lawfully possible for the military training that has been expended upon the engineers to be utilized in augmenting the general efficiency of the navy instead of its being wasted or suppressed.

The future of the naval engineer corps appears to be assured regardless of occasional predictions of its speedy dissolution. It is not likely that serious efforts will ever be made to operate a navy propelled wholly by steam power and composed of ships whose every function is effected by steam, without the services of steam engineers. Should a more economical source of power than steam ever be found practicable, that power and its confining machinery must still be directed by engineers. If the young men of the corps will observe the same loyalty to the service and the profession that we have seen was an admirable characteristic of that splendid body of older engineers who preceded us, we need have no fear for the future. The honor and safety of the navy must hereafter depend upon machinery and those who know how to use it. The men who will supply the intelligence for successfully directing the many operations of the fighting ship of the immediate future must be engineers. The old conception of seamanship may finally be laid to rest, and some who are now line officers may become engineers, but in any event the profession of naval engineering will remain unchanged and those who now belong to it will be all the more fortunate. Engineers, whether by that name or some other, but engineers nevertheless, will hold in their hands the fate of the coming years.

APPENDIX A.

A LIST, alphabetically arranged, of the names of all persons who have been members of the Engineer Corps of the Regular Navy since its establishment. Giving the dates of their original entry and subsequent promotions, and the manner in which they left the service, if not still in it.

	CADET ENGINEER.	NAVAL CADET.	THIRD ASSISTANT ENGINEER.	SECOND ASSISTANT ENGINEER.	FIRST ASSISTANT ENGINEER.
ABLE, AUGUSTUS H......	......	......	21 Feb. 1861	21 Apr. 1863	1 Dec. 1864
Acker, Edward O'Conner.	15 Sept, 1875	......	......	......	......
Adams, James M............	......	......	14 May, 1847	26 Feb. 1851	15 Dec. 1853
Adamson, Alfred............	......	......	13 May, 1861	17 Dec. 1862	1 Jan. 1865
Addicks, Walter R...........	1 Oct. 1878	5 Aug. 1882	......	......	......
Albert, John S...............	......	......	8 Sept. 1855	21 July, 1858	30 Aug. 1859
Albert, Sidney...............	......	......	11 Apr. 1859	17 Dec. 1861	17 Mar. 1863
Aldrich, William S..........	1 Oct. 1879	5 Aug. 1882	......	......	......
Alexander, George W.......	......	......	31 Oct. 1848	16 Feb. 1852	27 June, 1855
Alexander, John.............	......	......	......	28 July, 1845	{ 4 Mar,1842 { 26 Feb. '51
Alexander, Joseph D.........	......	......	13 Mar. 1847	......	......
Allderdice, William H......	14 Sept. 1876	......	......	......	......
Allen, David Van H.........	......	6 Sept. 1887	......	......	......
Allen, Francis B.............	......	......	1 Mar. 1862	15 Oct, 1863	......
Allen, Louis J...............	......	......	3 May, 1859	13 May, 1861	20 May 1863
Allen, Theodore.............	......	......	29 July, 1861	18 Dec. 1862	......
Allen, William A. H........	......	......	21 Apr. 1863	28 Sept. 1864	22 Nov. 1872
Allison, Oscar W............	......	......	1 Feb. 1862	15 Oct. 1863	......
Ames, John H...............	......	......	1 July, 1861	18 Dec. 1862	......
Anderson, Martin...........	13 Sept. 1877	5 Aug. 1882	......	......	......
Andrade, Cipriano..........	......	......	1 July, 1861	18 Dec. 1862	30 Jan. 1865
Annan, John W..............	15 Sept. 1875	......	......	......	......
Archbold, Samuel...........	......	......	27 July, 1843	28 July, 1845	10 July, 1847
Archer, Edward K...........	......	......	26 June, 1856	......	......
Armistead, Samuel W.......	1 Oct. 1879	5 Aug. 1882	......	......	......
Arnold, Edward R...........	......	......	1 July, 1861	......	......
Arnold, Leroy...............	......	......	16 Feb. 1852	......	......
Arnold, Solon...............	14 Sept. 1876	5 ug. 1882	......	......	......
Ashton, Francis M...........	......	......	20 May, 1863	25 July. 1866	......
Aston, Albert...............	......	......	21 Feb. 1861	8 Dec. 1862	1 Dec. 1864
Aston, Ralph................	......	......	9 Dec. 1861	8 Dec. 1863	11 Oct 1866
Atkins, James...............	......	......	26 Aug. 1859	21 Oct. 1861	1 Oct. 1863
Atkinson, James.............	......	......	......	28 July, 1845	26 May 1839
Auchinleck, Alexander......	......	......	......	22 Mar. 1848	......
Ayres, Samuel L. P..........	......	......	21 July, 1858	17 June, 1861	21 Apr. 1863
BABBITT, GEORGE H. T.	1 Oct. 1873	......	......	......	......
Badlam, William H........	......	......	3 May, 1859	8 Oct. 1861	......
Bailey, Frank H.............	1 Oct. 1873	......	......	......	......
Bailey, Horace J.............	14 Sept. 1876	......	......	......	......
Bailey, Joseph H.............	......	......	21 Nov. 1857	2 Aug. 1859	17 Mar. 1863
Bailie, William L............	......	......	16 Jan. 1863	28 May, 1864	31 Jan. 1874
Baird, George W............	......	......	8 Sept. 1863	25 July, 1866	......
Baker, Charles H............	......	......	2 Aug. 1855	21 July, 1858	2 Aug. 1859
Baker, George A.............	......	......	16 Jan. 1863	......	......
Baker, Henry T..............	......	7 Oct. 1890	......	......	......
Baker, John H...............	15 Sept. 1875	......	......	......	......
Ball, Charles H..............	......	......	......	19 July, 1861	......
Ball, Walter.................	......	6 Sept. 1888	......	......	......
Bampton, Benjamin C.......	......	......	20 May, 1857	2 Aug. 1859	17 Dec. 1862
Bankson, Lloyd.............	13 Sept. 1877	5 Aug. 1882	......	......	......
Barker, Henry S.............	......	......	26 Feb. 1851	......	......
Barlow, Frederick S.........	......	......	22 June,1860	30 July, 1862	......
Barnard, Lemuel............	......	......	16 Jan. 1863	......	......
Barnes, Charles E...........	1 Oct. 1879	......	......	......	......
Baron, Charles C............	1 Oct. 1880	5 Aug. 1882	......	......	......
Barr, William M.............	......	......	17 Mar. 1863	1 Sept. 1864	......
Barry, George J.............	......	......	26 June,1856	3 Aug. 1859	1 July, 1861
Barry, James J..............	......	......	8 Dec. 1862	8 April, 1864	1 Jan. 1868
Barry, Patrick Henry........	......	......	3 May, 1862	......	......

ASSISTANT ENGINEER.	PASSED ASSISTANT ENGINEER.	CHIEF ENGINEER.	REMARKS.
......	24 Feb. 1874	20 Nov. 1874	In service
10 June, 1881	......	......	Resigned 31 Dec. 1889
......	......	......	Res'd 2 Aug. '62; vol. Ch. Eng. war; hon. dis. '67
......	24 Feb. 1874	19 May, 1879	In service
......	......	......	
......	......	29 Oct. 1861	Died in service 3 July, 1880
......	......	21 Mar. 1870	Resigned 31 December, 1872
......	......	......	Resigned June 11, 1883
......	......	......	Resigned 5 April, 1861; went into Confed. army
......	......	......	Died in service, 26 January, 1863
......	......	......	Resigned 25 August, 1847
10 June, 1882	21 Feb. 1893	......	In service
22 Aug. 1894	......	......	In service
......	......	......	Resigned 18 February, 1868
......	......	4 Mar. 1871	In service
......	......	......	Resigned 13 June, 1865
......	24 Feb. 1874	......	Retired list 14 June, 1890
......	......	......	Resigned 8 December, 1869
......	......	......	Resigned 30 September, 1865
1 July, 1883	25 May, 1894	......	In service
......	24 Feb. 1874	11 Sept. 1881	In service
10 June, 1881	......	......	Died in service, 9 January, 1891
......	......	11 Mar. 1851	Engineer-in-Chief 16 Oct. '57; res. 25 Mar. '61
......	......	......	Resigned 3 November, 1860
......	......	......	Ensign '85; To Construction Corps '87; died '95
......	......	......	Resigned 13 April, 1864
......	......	......	Resigned 18 Feb. 1856
1 July, 1883	1 April, 1894	......	In service
......	14 Dec. 1878	......	Res'd 4 Jan.'71; reap'd. 2d. Asst. '73; died '86
......	......	12 June, 1873	Died 10 Sept. 1881
......	24 Feb. 1874	28 July, 1888	In service
......	......	......	Resigned 1 August, 1865
......	......	......	Reduced to 2d Asst. Eng. '45; dropped 18 Jan. '84
......	......	......	Dism'd 28 July,'48; Act'g. Ch. Eng. war; res. '65.
......	......	21 Mar. 1870	In service
1 July, 1877	......	......	Resigned 10 Aug. 1886
......	......	......	Resigned 10 March, 1866
1 July, 1877	7 Oct. 1884	27 June, 1896	In service
......	......	......	Resigned 28 Sept. 1877
......	......	......	Dropped 11 July, 1873
......	24 Feb. 1874	......	Retired list 30 June, 1885
......	17 June, 1874	22 June, 1892	In service; vol. 3d Asst. Eng. Sept. '62—Sept '63
......	......	29 Oct. 1861	Retired list 16 January 1893; died 6 May, 1896
......	......	......	Died in service 6 June, 1864
1 July, 1896	......	...	In service
10 June, 1881	......	......	Died in service 13 Sept. 1890 on *Monocacy*
......	......	......	Resigned 31 August, 1865
25 Feb. 1895	......	......	2d Lt. Mar. Corps, '94; exch'd. to Eng. Corps
....	......	......	Retired list 6 Sept. 1873
1 July, 1883	......	......	Appointed Asst. Naval Con. 1 July, 1889 ; In service
......	......	......	Died in service 25 July, 1855
......	......	......	Killed in action 5 August, 1864
......	......	......	Resigned 21 March, 1866
......	......	......	Resigned Nov. 15, 1881
......	......	......	Resigned Feb. 7, 1883
......	......	......	Resigned 16 April, 1866
......	......	10 Nov. 1863	Retired list 24 Mar. '74; died 10 Nov. '77
......	24 Feb. 1874	......	Retired list 2 January, 1891
......	......	......	Died in service 1 August, 1863

	CADET ENGINEER.	NAVAL CADET.	THIRD ASSISTANT ENGINEER.	SECOND ASSISTANT ENGINEER.	FIRST ASSISTANT ENGINEER.
Barstow, Havilaud			1 July, 1861	18 Dec. 1862	11 Oct. 1866
Bartholow, Frank L	15 Sept. 1875				
Bartholomew, L. S.					1 Sept. 1845
Bartleman, Richard M			24 Dec. 1853	9 May, 1857	2 Aug. 1859
Bartlett, Frank W	1 Oct. 1874				
Barton, George F			26 Feb. 1851	21 May, 1853	
Barton, James A			16 Jan. 1863		
Barton, John K	1 Oct. 1871			23 Jan. 1874	
Bates, Alexander B			16 Jan. 1863	28 May, 1864	1 Jan. 1874
Battele, Everett			27 June 1862		
Baughman, Henry C					
Baxter, William J	1 Oct. 1879	5 Aug. 1882			
Bayley, Warner B				2 Sept. 1870	
Beach, Edward L		20 May, 1884			
Beach, Robert J	13 Sept. 1877	5 Aug. 1882			
Bean, William S			15 Apr. 1847		
Beard, George W			25 Mar. 1862		
Beckwith, Henry C			27 June 1862	21 Nov. 1863	1 Jan. 1868
Belden, Charles E	14 Sept. 1876	5 Aug. 1882			
Benckert, James M			8 Oct. 1861		
Bennett, Frank M	1 Oct. 1874				
Bennett, Rudolph T			25 Mar. 1862	2 Feb. 1864	1 Jan. 1868
Bernard, Lemuel			16 Jan. 1863		
Beuret, John D		7 Sept. 1888			
Bevington, Martin	15 Sept. 1875				
Biddle, Andrew P	1 Oct. 1880	5 Aug. 1882			
Bieg, Frederick C	1 Oct. 1874				
Bilisoly, Joseph			2 Aug. 1855		
Bingham, John F			25 Aug. 1862	20 Feb. 1864	1 Jan. 1868
Birkbeck, Alexander, Jr					8 June 1844
Bispham, Harrison A	1 Oct. 1881	5 Aug. 1882			
Bissell, Frederick W			21 Apr. 1863	28 Sept. 1864	
Bisset, Henry O		6 Sept. 1892			
Bissett, John J			30 July, 1862	15 Feb. 1864	1 Jan. 1868
Blue, Victor		6 Sept. 1883			
Blye, Henry C			17 Nov. 1862	23 Mar. 1864	1 Jan. 1868
Blythe, Andrew			24 Dec. 1861	8 Sept. 1863	
Bogardus, Peter C			27 Jan. 1848		
Boggs, William Brenton	1 Oct. 1871				
Bond, William			23 June, 1863		
Bonsall, A. G.			19 Feb. 1863		
Bootes, James T	1 Oct. 1881	5 Aug. 1882			
Bordley, Thomas H			26 Aug. 1859	16 Oct. 1861	1 Oct. 1863
Borthwick, John L. D			8 Oct. 1861	3 Aug. 1863	11 Oct. 1866
Botsford, Jerard H			3 Oct. 1861	3 Aug. 1863	
Bowers, Frederick C	15 Sept. 1875				
Bowles, Francis T	15 Sept. 1875				
Boyd, Harry L	1 Oct. 1881	5 Aug. 1882			
Boynton, Edward S			26 Aug. 1859	28 Oct. 1862	
Bradford, Henry F			1 July, 1861	18 Dec. 1862	11 Oct. 1866
Brady, John R		6 Sept. 1889			
Bray, Charles D			2 July, 1868		
Breaker, Charles W			17 Dec. 1862	8 Apr. 1864	
Brecht, Theodore C			28 May, 1861	18 Dec. 1862	
Breese, E. Marshall			25 Mar. 1862	1 Nov. 1863	
Bright, George S			21 May, 1857	2 Aug. 1859	1 July, 1861
Bright, Jacob L			20 Nov. 1861	25 Aug. 1863	
Broadnix, Amos			13 Dec. 1850	26 Feb. 1851	
Brooks, Emory J			3 May, 1859	3 Oct. 1861	20 May, 1863
Brooks, Samuel R			21 Feb. 1861	21 Apr. 1863	
Brooks, William B			16 Feb. 1852	27 June, 1855	21 July, 1858

ASSISTANT ENGINEER.	PASSED ASSISTANT ENGINEER.	CHIEF ENGINEER.	REMARKS.
......	......	......	Lost in the *Oneida*, 24 January, 1870
......	......	......	Dropped 28 September, 1877
......	......	......	Resigned 20 April, 1847
......	......	28 Oct. 1861	Died 22 December, 1884
20 June, 1880	19 June, 1890	......	In service
......	......	......	Died in service 4 Sept 1853
......	......	......	Resigned 5 March, 1868
24 Feb. 1874	1 Nov. 1879	15 Jan. 1895	In service
......	24 Feb. 1874	12 Apr. 1892	In service
......	......	......	Resigned 29 June, 1865
13 Oct. 1875	......	......	Retired list, 15 July, 1886
1 July, 1885	......	......	Appointed Asst. Naval Constr. 6 June, 1888
24 Feb., 1874	21 Sept. 1877	25 May, 1894	In service; acting 3d Asst. Engr. 1864-1869
1 July, 1890	27 June, 1896	......	In service
......	......	......	Resigned 21 April, 1886
......	......	......	Resigned 23 Oct. 1847
......	......	......	Retired list 1 February, 1866
......	24 Feb. 1874	......	Retired list 2 December, 1876; died 12 July, 1885.
......	......	......	Disappeared in San Francisco, 1883; never heard of
......	......	......	Died 28 June, 1862, on board *Itaska*.
10 June, 1881	24 Apr. 1892	......	In service.
......	24 Feb. 1874	......	Retired list 21 May, 1880
......	......	......	Resigned 21 March, 1866
......	......	......	Appointed Assistant Naval Constructor July 1, 1894
10 June, 1881	22 June, 1892	......	In service.
......	......	......	Resigned 6 June, 1883
20 June, 1880	21 Oct. 1890	......	In service
......	......	......	Died 3 Sept. 1855
......	24 Feb. 1874	......	Died 3 May, 1891
......	......	2 Mar. 1847	Resigned 23 Dec. 1847
......	......	......	Ensign 1 July, 1887; in service
......	......	......	Resigned 22 October, 1867
......	......	......	In service
......	24 Feb. 1874	......	Retired list 21 Oct. 1882
1 July, 1889	......	......	Exchanged into line 12 Dec. 1892; now ensign
......	24 Feb. 1874	......	Retired list 28th Oct. 1874
......	......	......	Died 19 April, 1870
......	......	......	Resigned 6 February, 1852
1 July, 1877	18 Dec. 1885	......	Died 21 June, 1886
......	......	......	Resigned 25 May, 1867
......	......	......	Appointment revoked 12 January, 1866
......	......	......	Honorably discharged 30 June, 1887
......	......	......	Died 10 December, 1865
......	24 Feb. 1874	7 Sept. 1885	In service
......	......	......	Died in service 25, July 1864
10 June, 1881	1 July, 1892	......	In service
......	......	......	Ap. Asst. Nav. Con. 1 Nov. '81; Nav. Con. 10 Oct. '88
......	......	......	Resigned 4 February, 1884
......	......	......	Resigned 7 November, 1863
......	......	......	Died in service 16 September, 1873
1 July, 1895	......	......	In service
......	......	......	Res'd 18 March, 1869
......	......	......	Died in service, 9 Feb. 1871
......	......	......	Resigned 18 Jan. 1865; Act'g 1st Ass. Eng. 1865-68
......	......	......	Resigned 2 March, 1868
......	......	10 Nov. 1863	Retired list 5 June, 1873; died 29 May, 1875
......	......	......	Resigned 18 Oct. 1870
......	......	......	Resigned 14 Feb. 1856
......	......	......	Resigned 7 Dec. 1868
......	......	......	Resigned 13 Dec. 1865
......	......	1 Aug. 1861	Retired list 1 March. 1892

	CADET ENGINEER.	NAVAL CADET.	THIRD ASSISTANT ENGINEER.	SECOND ASSISTANT ENGINEER.	FIRST ASSISTANT ENGINEER.
Brosnahan, John G	......	......	11 June, 1862	21 Nov. 1863	1 Jan. 1868
Brower, Alfred S	......	......	16 Nov. 1861	25 Aug. 1863	......
Brown, Frederick E	......	......	21 Nov. 1857	14 June, 1861	......
Brown, Henry	......	......	17 Feb. 1860	1 Nov. 1861	1 Mar. 1864
Brown, Jefferson	......	......	17 Dec. 1862	8 April, 1864	1 Jan. 1868
Bryan, Benjamin C	15 Sept. 1875	......	......	......	......
Buckhout, Nathan W	......	......	28 Oct. 1862	15 Mar. 1864	......
Budd, Samuel P	......	......	8 Sept. 1863	......	......
Buchler, William G	......	......	21 Nov. 1857	8 Oct. 1861	6 Oct. 1862
Bulkley, Henry W	......	......	25 Aug. 1862	20 Feb. 1864	......
Bull, Frederick Jr	......	......	29 July, 1861	20 May, 1863	......
Bull, Goold H	1 Oct. 1874	......	......	......	......
Bullard, Joel A	......	......	22 July, 1862	15 Feb. 1864	......
Bunce, Benjamin	......	......	19 July, 1861	18 Dec. 1862	......
Burchard, Charles M	......	......	17 Dec. 1861	8 Sept. 1863	......
Burchard, Francis C	......	......	8 Sept. 1863	1 Aug. 1866	......
Burchard, Jabez	......	......	......	1 Sept. 1870	......
Burd, George E	1 Oct. 1874	......	......	......	......
Burgdorff, Theodore F	1 Oct. 1873	......	......	......	......
Burke, Walter S	......	17 May, 1883	......	......	......
Burnap, George J	......	......	13 May, 1861	16 Jan. 1863	1 Jan. 1865
Burritt, Harvey H	......	......	12 Aug. 1861	21 Apr. 1863	......
Burrow, Walter P	......	......	26 June, 1856	......	......
Burt, Charles P	......	6 Sept. 1892	......	......	......
Burt, Nelson	......	......	......	......	15 Nov. 1837
Bush, Arthur R	13 Sept. 1877	5 Aug. 1882	......	......	......
Bush, William W	......	5 Aug. 1882	......	......	......
Butler, Joseph L	......	......	19 Mar. 1858	1 Dec. 1860	......
Butterworth, James	......	......	23 May, 1861	29 Oct. 1862	25 July, 1866
Byles, Ten Eyck	......	......	2 Aug. 1855	21 July, 1858	......
Byrne, James E	13 Sept. 1877	5 Aug. 1882	......	......	......
CAHILL, JOSEPH N	......	......	21 July, 1858	17 Jan. 1861	17 Mar. 1863
Caldwell, Lafayette	......	......	20 Feb. 1847	......	......
Campbell, Louden	......	......	21 July, 1858	17 Jan. 1861	......
Canaga, Alfred B	1 Oct. 1872	......	......	......	......
Canfield, Francis A	......	......	21 May, 1853	......	......
Capps, Washington L	1 Oct. 1880	5 Aug. 1882	......	......	......
Carney, Robert E	......	21 May, 1885	......	......	......
Carpenter, John B	......	......	17 Feb. 1860	28 Oct. 1862	1 Mar. 1864
Carr, Clarence A	15 Sept. 1875	......	......	......	......
Carrick George W	......	......	10 June, 1862	......	......
Carroll, John	......	......	14 May, 1847	......	......
Carswell, William B	1 Oct. 1879	5 Aug. 1882	......	......	......
Carter, Thomas F	1 Oct. 1873	......	......	......	......
Castleman, Kenneth G	......	6 Sept. 1892	......	......	......
Cathcart, William L	1 Oct. 1873	......	......	......	......
Chambers, William H	1 Oct. 1878	5 Aug. 1882	......	......	......
Champion, Newton	......	......	22 Oct. 1860	17 Dec. 1862	......
Chappell, Ralph H	......	22 May, 1890	......	......	......
Chase, Thomas	......	......	4 May, 1863	......	......
Chase, Volney O	1 Oct. 1881	5 Aug. 1882	......	......	......
Chasmar, James H	......	......	7 April, 1862	2 Feb. 1864	1 Jan. 1868
Chassaing, Benjamin E	......	......	21 May, 1857	3 Aug. 1859	21 Oct. 1861
Cheney, Edward	......	......	12 Aug. 1862	15 Aug. 1864	......
Cherry, William L	......	......	16 Nov. 1861	25 Aug. 1863	......
Chipley, Charles A	......	......	......	19 July, 1861	......
Chrisman, Wilmer O	......	......	......	......	......
Christopher, Henry C	......	......	17 Mar. 1863	......	......
City, George W	......	......	12 Jan. 1864	9 May, 1857	2 Aug. 1859

ASSISTANT ENGINEER.	PASSED ASSISTANT ENGINEER.	CHIEF ENGINEER.	REMARKS.
......	24 Feb. 1874	......	Died 12 Jan. 1883
......	......	......	Died 17 Jan. 1867
......	......	......	Died 12 Dec. 1864
......	......	......	Resigned 3 March, 1869
......	24 Feb. 1874	19 Nov. 1890	Retired list 2 Aug. 1892
10 June, 1881	3 Oct. 1891	......	In service
......	......	......	Resigned 29 June, 1865
......	......	......	Resigned 10 August, 1867
......	......	10 Nov. 1863	In service
......	......	......	Resigned 14 Oct. 1865
......	......	......	Died August 9, 1863, on board *Pocahontas*
20 June, 1880	......	......	Resigned 30 June, 1889
....	......	......	Died 22 March, 1866, on board *Kearsarge* at sea
......	......	......	Resigned 17 July, 1865
......	......	......	Resigned 26 July, 1865; in volunteer service 1866-1869
24 Feb. 1874	......	......	Retired list 24 April, 1877
24 Feb. 1874	......	......	Retired list 26 Oct. 1874
20 June, 1880	4 May, 1891	......	In service
1 July, 1877	22 June, 1886	......	In service
12 Dec. 1892	5 June, 1896	......	In service; Ensign '89-'92; ex. Eng. Corps
......	24 Feb. 1874	1 Nov. 1879	In service
......	......	......	Resigned 22 Sept. 1865
......	......	......	Dismissed 17 May, 1860
......	......	......	In service
......	......	......	Resigned 20 Nov. 1839
......	......	......	Resigned 31 August, 1886
28 June, 1889	28 Mar. 1896	......	In service; entered as Cadet Midship'n, 22 Sep. '80
......	......	......	Died in service 14 Sept. 1862
......	24 Feb. 1874	10 Mar. 1881	Died in service 2 Oct. 1891
......	......	......	Resigned 25 Oct. 1858
......	......	......	Resigned 1887
......	......	......	Killed by boiler explosion, *Chenango*, 15 April, 1864
......	......	......	Resigned 12 June, 1849
......	......	......	Resigned (went south) May 6, 1861
26 Feb. 1875	10 Mar. 1881	6 Aug. 1895	In service
......	......	......	Resigned 30 April, 1856
......	......	......	Ensign '86; Asst. Naval Constr. '88; Naval Constr. '95
1 July, 1891	......	......	In service
......	......	11 June, 1774	Retired list 20 Dec. 1883; died 22 July, 1888
10 June, 1881	16 Feb. 1892	......	In service
......	......	......	Resigned 18 Nov. 1865
......	......	......	Died 21 Dec. 1852, on board *Warren*
......	......	......	Resigned 9 June, 1883
10 June, 1881	12 Apr. 1892	......	In service
......	......	......	In service
1 July, 1877	24 Dec. 1884	......	Resigned 23 Jan. 1891
1 July, 1884	28 Aug. 1894	......	In service
......	......	......	Resigned 22 Sept. 1863
1 July, 1896	......	......	In service
......	......	......	Resigned 13 Nov. 1865
......	......	......	Ensign 1 July, 1887
......	24 Feb. 1874	27 Jan. 1889	In service
......	......	10 Nov. 1863	Resigned 12 Feb. 1867
......	......	......	Resigned 31 March, 1869
......	......	......	Resigned 25 Oct. 1867
......	......	......	Resigned 9 April, 1862
18 May, 1877	......	......	Retired list 29 June, 1887
......	......	......	Retired list 16 May, 1867; died 13 Aug. 1872
......	......	......	Dropped (went south) 2 Aug. 1861

	CADET ENGINEER.	NAVAL CADET.	THIRD ASSISTANT ENGINEER.	SECOND ASSISTANT ENGINEER.	FIRST ASSISTANT ENGINEER.
Clark, Edward W...............	......	......	20 May, 1862	......	......
Clark, James M.................	......	......	3 Aug. 1863	25 July, 1866	......
Clark, Nathan Beach...........	......	......	13 May, 1861	17 Dec. 1862	1 July, 1865
Clark, Wm. J. Jr................	......	......	16 Nov. 1861	25 Aug. 1863	......
Clarke, Arthur H................	1 Oct. 1878	5 Aug. 1882	......	......	......
Claude, Gordon H...............	{ 1 Oct. '73 { 1 Oct. '74	......	......	......	......
Cleaver, Henry T................	1 Oct. 1871	......	......	23 Jan. 1874	......
Clemens, Benjamin D..........	......	......	3 Oct. 1861	3 Aug. 1863	......
Cline, Hugh. H..................	......	......	1 July, 1861	18 Dec. 1862	1 Jan. 1868
Cochran, James..................	......	......	......	......	11 June, 1840
Coggin, Frederick G.............	......	......	21 Sept. 1861	30 July, 1863	......
Coleman, Charles................	......	......	18 Jan. 1845	......	......
Coley, Frederick E...............	1 Oct. 1878	5 Aug. 1882	......	......	......
Colin, Alfred.....................	......	......	1 July, 1861	18 Dec. 1862	......
Conant, Frank H.................	1 Oct. 1878	5 Aug. 1882	......	......	......
Cone, Hutch I...................	......	5 Sept. 1890	......	......	......
Coney, Charles Tabez...........	......	......	16 Oct 1861	3 Aug. 1863	......
Cook, Allen M....................	....	22 May, 1889	......	....	......
Cook, Gilbert C...................	......	......	16 Sept, 1862	1 Mar. 1864	......
Cook, Theophilus................	......	......	22 May, 1863	6 Jan. 1866	13 Jan. 1873
Cooley, Mortimer E..............	1 Oct. 1874	......	......	......	......
Cooper, Conrad J................	......	......	9 Dec. 1861	...	......
Cooper, Francis L................	......	......	1 July, 1861	18 Dec. 1862	......
Cooper, Ignatius T...............	......	20 May, 1890	......	......	......
Cooper, James G.................	......	......	24 Dec. 1861	8 Sept. 1863	......
Cooper, John E..................	......	....	12 Aug. 1861	......	......
Cooper, Theodore................	......	......	24 Dec. 1861	8 Sept. 1863	11 Oct. 1866
Cooper, Thomas J. W...........	......	......	......	25 Apr. 1870	......
Copeland, G. M..................	......	......	21 Jan. 1842	......	......
Copeland, Robert A.............	......	......	20 Sept. 1858	28 May, 1861	......
Copeland, Thomas	......	......	......	......	19 Oct. 1842
Covell, Emerson G...............	......	......	......	......	21 May, 1847
Cowie, George Jr.................	......	......	......	9 July, 1870	......
Cowles, William..................	1 Oct. 1873	......	......	......	......
Cragg, S. Wilkins................	......	......	26 Aug. 1859	26 Oct. 1861	25 July, 1866
Crank, Robert K.................	......	6 Sept. 1888	......	......	......
Crawford, Robert................	......	......	23 June, 1863	25 July, 1866	20 Feb. 1874
Crawford, William H............	......	......	19 Feb. 1863	20 June, 1864	......
Creighton, William H. P.......	1 Oct. 1878	5 Aug. 1882	......	......	......
Crenshaw, Arthur................	......	6 Sept. 1892	......	......	......
Crisp, Richard O.................	1 Oct. 1880	5 Aug. 1882	......	......	......
Crolins, Sebastian................	......	......	1 July 1861	......	......
Cronin, Francis...................	......	......	21 July, 1858	21 Oct. 1861	20 May, 1863
Cronin, Thomas H...............	......	......	20 May, 1857	3 Aug. 1859	......
Crosby, Eli.......................	......	......	22 Sept. 1849	26 Feb. 1851	......
Cross, John C....................	......	......	8 Dec. 1862	8 Apr. 1864	......
Crummey, Thomas...............	......	......	21 Apr. 1862	......	......
Crygier, John Ulysses...........	1 Oct. 1874	......	......	......	......
Culver, William W...............	1 Oct. 1881	5 Aug. 1882	......	......	......
Cunningham, Thomas...........	......	......	3 May, 1859	13 May, 1861	20 May, 1863
Curtis, Edward...................	......	......	21 Oct. 1861	......	......
Cushman, William H............	......	......	2 Aug. 1855	21 July, 1858	3 Aug. 1859
Cuthbert, Mayland...............	......	......	24 Aug. 1861	21 Apr. 1863	......
DADE, FRANCIS C.............	......	......	20 Jan. 1849	26 Feb. 1851	21 May, 1853
Dahlgreen, Charles B....	......	......	24 Dec. 1861	......	......
Danby, Robert....................	......	......	18 Jan. 1845	10 July, 1847	26 Feb. 1851
Danforth, George W.............	......	7 Sept. 1885	......	......	......
Daniels, S. J. McK...............	......	......	19 July, 1861	18 Dec. 1862	......
Dargan, Milton...................	1 Oct. 1880	5 Aug. 1882	......	......	......

ASSISTANT ENGINEER	PASSED ASSISTANT ENGINEER.	CHIEF ENGINEER.	REMARKS.
......	......	....	Died 1 July, 1866
......	......	......	Died 24 April, 1872
......	......	......	Retired list, 16 Oct. 1868; died 18 April, 1892
......	......	......	Resigned 1 Dec. 1865
......	......	......	Second Lieut. U. S. Marine Corps, July 1 '84; dead
......	......	......	Dismissed 22 Feb. 1875
24 Feb. 1874	19 May, 1879	20 Feb. 1896	In service
......	......	......	Appointment revoked 12 January, 1866
24 Feb. 1874	......	2 Dec. 1887	Retired list 27 Aug. 1894
......	......	......	Dismissed 7 November, 1845.
......	......	......	Retired list 5 January, 1866
......	......	......	Dismissed 18 January, 1851
......	......	......	Died 19 December, 1883, on board *Onward*
......	......	......	Resigned 27 Dec. 1865
1 July, 1884	30 Sept. 1894	......	In service
1 July, 1896	......	......	In service
......	......	......	Resigned 2 Oct. 1866
1 July, 1895	......	......	In service
......	......	......	Resigned 22 July, 1865
......	24 Feb. 1874	......	Retired list 11 Oct. 1881; died 20 July, 1893
20 June, 1880	......	......	Resigned 1 Jan. 1886
......	......	......	Resigned 18 July, 1862
......	......	......	Resigned 10 Oct. 1873
1 July, 1896	......	......	In service
......	......	......	Resigned 19 Dec. 1865
......	......	......	Resigned 14 May, 1863
......	......	......	Resigned 26 July, 1872
24 Feb. 1874	6 July, 1876	......	Died 29 Jan. 1888
......	......	......	Resigned 30 Nov. 1844
......	......	......	Dismissed 19 Sept. 1861; afterward in vol. service
......	......	......	Dismissed 28 July, 1845.
......	......	......	Died 28 Dec. 1847, on board *Mississippi* in Mex. war
24 Feb. 1874	3 Dec. 1876	12 Sept. 1893	In service; was in volunteer service 1864-1865
1 July, 1877	......	......	Resigned 31 March, 1880
......	......	......	Res'd 11 Apr. '70; dism. 27 June,'64; reinstated '66
1 July, 1894	......	......	In service
......	24 Feb. 1874	......	Retired list, 30 June, 1892
......	......	......	Resigned 30 April, 1868
1 July, 1884	......	......	Retired list 26 July, 1892
......	......	......	In service
......	......	......	Resigned 18 Nov. 1884
......	......	......	Resigned 13 Aug. 1862; in volunteer service 1863
......	......	......	Resigned 10 Nov. 1865
......	......	......	Died in service 8 Dec. 1861
......	......	......	Died 24 Jan. 1854, on board *Susquehanna*
......	......	......	Resigned 21 June, 1865
......	......	......	Resigned 5 Sept. 1866
......	......	......	Dropped (physical disability) 30 Sept. 1884
......	......	......	Resigned 10 April, 1883
......	......	......	Resigned 16 Nov. 1866
......	......	......	Resigned 11 Feb. 1863
......	......	16 Oct. 1861	Died 2 Nov. 1865
......	......	......	Resigned 22 Aug. 1864
......	......	24 Oct. 1859	Retired list 26 Jan. 1889
......	......	......	Acting Ensign 15 Dec. 1862; resigned 1 Feb. 1865
......	......	26 June, 1856	Retired list 18 Aug. 1883; died 31 Dec. 1886
1 July, 1891	......	......	In service
......	......	......	Resigned 9 March, 1865
......	......	......	Dismissed 7 Nov. 1882

	CADET ENGINEER.	NAVAL CADET.	THIRD ASSISTANT ENGINEER.	SECOND ASSISTANT ENGINEER.	FIRST ASSISTANT ENGINEER.
Darrah, William F	1 Oct. 1879	5 Aug. 1882			
Dasheill, Julius M	1 Oct. 1881	5 Aug. 1882			
Davids, Henry S			26 Aug. 1859	16 Oct. 1861	1 Oct. 1863
Davids, Oscar			26 Feb. 1851	21 May, 1853	
Davis, Charles C			24 Dec. 1861		
Davis, DeWitt G			22 May, 1863		
Davis, Edward	1 Oct. 1880	5 Aug. 1882			
Davis, Nailor C				17 Jan. 1842	10 July, 1847
Davis, Willis			11 Jan. 1849		
Day, Willis B	13 Sept. 1877	5 Aug. 1882			
Deaver, James A			19 Feb. 1863	25 July, 1866	
DeGraff, Isaac			9 Dec. 1861	8 Sept. 1863	
DeHart, William H			17 Jan. 1862	1 Oct. 1863	
DeKrafft, James W			21 July, 1858	1 July, 1861	17 Mar. 1863
DeLany, Edwin H		21 May, 1890			
Delius, Herman A			26 Aug. 1859	20 May, 1863	
DeLuce, Edmund S			22 Sept. 1849	26 Feb. 1851	21 May, 1863
Deluce, George E			26 Feb. 1851		
Denby, John C			20 May, 1863		
Denig, Robert G	1 Oct. 1871			23 Jan. 1874	
DeSanno, William P			21 May, 1857	2 Aug. 1859	1 July, 1861
DeValin, Charles E			20 Sept. 1858	17 Jan. 1861	17 Mar. 1863
Diamond, Jasper H			1 July, 1863	25 July, 1866	
Dick, Thomas M		25 Sept. 1891			
Dick, Edward L			20 Sept. 1858		
Dickson, Thomas			21 May, 1843		
Diffenbach, Albert C	1 Oct. 1881	5 Aug. 1882			
Dinsmore, J			16 Jan. 1863		
Dismukes, Doctor E		21 May, 1886			
Dixon, Albert F			29 Oct. 1870		
Dobbs, Frederick A			11 Apr. 1859		
Dodge, Richard D			22 July, 1862	15 Feb. 1864	
Dove, George W. W			11 July, 1861		
Dowst, Frank B	13 Sept. 1877	5 Aug. 1882			
Drinen, George C				1 Mar. 1871	
Dripps, William A			25 Aug. 1862	20 Feb. 1864	
Driver, Reynolds			26 Aug. 1859	1 Mar. 1862	1 Oct. 1863
Dryburgh, J. R			28 July, 1845	15 Jan. 1845	
Drouillard, George L	1 Oct. 1872				
Dukehart, Thomas M			3 May, 1859	13 May, 1861	20 May, 1863
Dunbar, Asaph			19 Feb. 1863	20 June, 1864	6 June, 1868
Dungan, Horace G	1 Oct. 1874				
Dungan, William W			26 June, 1856		21 July, 1858
Dunham, William			2 Feb. 1847		
Dunn, Edward H		5 Sept. 1891			
Dunning, William B	1 Oct. 1873				
Duplaine, E. A. C			21 May, 1857	2 Aug. 1859	10 Aug. 1861
Durand, William F	14 Sept. 1876				
Duvall, Marius, Jr	1 Oct. 1879				
Dyson, Charles, W	1 Oct. 1879	5 Aug. 1882			
EASTMAN, HARRY	1 Oct. 1872				
Eastwick, Philip G			18 Nov. 1862	23 Mar. 1864	
Eaton, Charles P	1 Oct. 1879	5 Aug. 188			
Eaton, William C	1 Oct. 1872				
Eckart, William R			8 July, 1861		
Eckel, Frederick			1 July, 1861		
Eckel, Herman	14 Sept. 1876				
Eckhardt, Ernest F		5 Sept. 1891			
Edwards, John R	1 Oct. 1871				
Edwards, Richard F			1 July, 1863		

ASSISTANT ENGINEER.	PASSED ASSISTANT ENGINEER.	CHIEF ENGINEER.	REMARKS.
1 July, 1885	......	......	Died in service 25 Feb. 1889
......	......	......	Resigned 9 Feb. 1885
......	......	5 Mar. 1871	Retired list 7 June, 1884; died 8 Feb. 1888
......	......	......	Died 9 Feb. 1859
......	......	......	Appointment revoked 30 Dec. 1863
......	......	......	Lost in *Patapsco* 15 Jan. 1865
......	......	......	Honorably discharged 30 June, 1886
......	......	......	Resigned 29 Oct. 1859
......	......	......	Resigned 4 Nov. 1850
1 July, 1884	29 Jan. 1895	......	In service
......	......	......	Retired list 28 Feb. 1874; died 10 Feb. 1887
......	......	......	Resigned 23 Aug. 1866
......	......	......	Resigned 5 Nov. 1869
......	......	......	Died 19 Oct. 1870
1 July, 1896	......	......	In service.
......	......	......	Resigned 22 June, 1865
......	......	12 Oct. 1859	Retired list, 13 Dec. 1878; died 25 June, 1890
......	......	......	Resigned 28 Feb. 1853
......	......	......	Appointment revoked 1 Sept. 1864
24 Feb. 1874	25 Mar. 1880	29 Jan. 1895	In service
......	......	......	Dismissed 19 March, 1862
......	......	21 Mar. 1870	Retired list, 11 April, 1892; died 16 April, 1892
......	......	......	Dismissed 26 July, 1876
......	......	......	In service
......	......	......	Dismissed (went south) 28 May, 1861
......	......	......	Died 12 Sept. 1847
......	......	......	Appointed Ensign 1 July, 1887; in service.
......	......	......	Resigned 28 May, 1864
1 July 1891	......	......	In service.
24 Feb. 1874	4 Nov. 1877	13 July, 1894	In service
......	......	......	Died 29 Apri., 1862
......	......	......	Resigned 1 June, 1868
......	......	......	Resigned 10 August, 1863
......	......	......	Resigned 29 July, 1887
24 Feb. 1874	......	......	Retired list 19 Oct. 1875
......	......	......	Resigned 29 January, 1867
......	......	......	Died 2 Oct. 1866
......	......	......	Dropped 4 Nov. 1845
......	......	......	Resigned 10 Oct. 1874
......	......	......	Resigned 9 March, 1871
......	......	......	Retired list 31 July, 1869; died 23 Oct. 1875
......	......	......	Resigned 7 Feb. 1879
......	......	1 Feb. 1862	In service
......	......	......	Dismissed 8 April, 1847
......	......	......	In service
1 July, 1878	1 July, 1887	......	In service
......	......	......	Resigned 14 May, 1867
10 June, 1882	......	......	Resigned 15 Sept. 1887
......	......	......	Dropped 19 June, 1882
1 July, 1885	1 June, 1895	......	In service
......	......	......	Resigned 11 June, 1874
......	......	......	Resigned 5 Aug. 1865
......	......	......	Appointed Ensign 1885; Lieutenant 1894; in service
26 Feb. 1875	4 Mar. 1881	1 June, 1885	In service
......	......	......	Resigned 2 May, 1864
......	......	......	Resigned 6 Sept. 1863
......	......	......	Dismissed 3 June, 1881
......	......	......	In service
26 Feb. 1875	11 Sept. 1881	5 Nov. 1895	In service
......	......	......	Died 23 March 1866 on *Kearsarge* at sea

	CADET ENGINEER.	NAVAL CADET.	THIRD ASSISTANT ENGINEER.	SECOND ASSISTANT ENGINEER.	FIRST ASSISTANT ENGINEER.
Egbert, Daniel B.............	......	......	8 Oct. 1861	......	......
Eldridge, Frank H.............	1 Oct. 1872	......	......	......	......
Ellicott, John M.............	1 Oct. 1879	5 Aug. 1882	......	......	......
Ellinger, Julius.............	1 Oct. 1879	5 Aug. 1882	......	......	......
Ellis, Robert N.............	......	......	8 Aug. 1861	8 Dec. 1864	......
Elseffer, Harry S.............	1 Oct. 1874	......	......	......	......
Ely, Theodore R.............	......	......	26 June, 1856	2 Aug. 1859	......
Emanuel, Jonathan M.........	......	......	25 Aug. 1862	20 Feb. 1864	6 June, 1869
Emery, Charles E.............	......	......	11 July, 1861	18 Dec. 1862	......
Emmons, George D.............	......	......	3 May, 1859	21 Apr. 1862	20 May, 1863
Emrich, Charles R.............	......	19 May. 1887	......	......	......
Engard, Albert C.............	......	......	17 Mar. 1863	25 July, 1866	11 Jan. 1873
English, Morgan H.............	......	......	21 Nov. 1857	2 Aug. 1859	......
Entwistle, James.............	......	......	29 Oct. 1861	3 Aug. 1863	11 Oct. 1866
Evans, Clarence A.............	......	......	17 Mar. 1863	......	......
Evans, George R.............	1 Oct. 1881	5 Aug. 1882	......	......	......
Everding, John.............	......	......	2 Dec. 1861	25 Aug. 1863	......
Everett, William E.............	......	......	1 Sept. 1845	10 June, 1847	31 Oct. 1848
FAGAN, HENRY.............	......	......	5 Sept. 1860	......	......
Fahs, Charles M.............	1 Oct. 1880	5 Aug. 1882	......	......	......
Fallon, James E.............	......	......	17 Dec. 1862	8 Apr. 1864	......
Farmer, Edward.............	......	......	3 May, 1859	16 Oct. 1861	20 May, 1863
Faron, Edward.............	......	......	1 Sept. 1845	10 July, 1847	31 Oct. 1848
Faron, John,.............	......	......	31 Oct 1848	26 Feb. 1851	21 May, 1853
Faron, John, Jr.............	......	......	......	......	15 Nov. 1837
Fauth, Henry.............	......	......	16 Feb. 1852	27 June, 1855	......
Fennimore, Wesley.............	......	......	4 May 1863	......	......
Fenton, Theodere C.............	1 Oct. 1881	5 Aug. 1882	......	......	......
Ferguson, George R.............	1 Oct. 1878	5 Aug. 1882	......	......	......
Field, Harry A.............	1 Oct. 1879	5 Aug. 1882	......	......	......
Field, Horace A.............	1 Oct. 1880	5 Aug. 1882	......	......	......
Fisher, Arthur H.............	......	......	17 Feb. 1860	27 June, 1862	1 Mar. 1864
Fisher, Clark.............	......	......	3 May, 1859	1 July, 1861	20 May, 1863
Fiske, Samuel.............	......	......	9 Mar. 1858	......	......
Fitch, Henry W.............	......	......	3 May, 1859	3 Oct. 1861	20 May, 1863
Fitch, Reuben.............	......	......	26 Aug. 1859	29 Oct. 1861	1 Oct. 1863
Fitch, Thomas W.............	......	......	23 June, 1863	25 July, 1866	8 Oct. 1873
Fithian, Edwin.............	......	......	31 Oct. 1848	26 Feb. 1851	15 Dec. 1853
Fitts, James H.............	1 Oct. 1878	5 Aug. 1882	......	......	......
Fitzgerald, Edward T.............	......	13 Sept. 1892	......	......	......
Fletcher, Frank H.............	......	......	22 Oct. 1860	9 July, 1863	......
Fletcher, Montgomery.........	......	......	24 June, 1850	26 Feb. 1851	26 June, 1856
Follansbee, Joshua.............	......	......	17 Jan. 1842	20 July, 1845	10 July, 1847
Forbes, Cornelius A.............	......	......	18 May 1847	......	......
Ford, John D.............	......	......	30 July, 1862	15 Feb. 1864	1 Jan. 1868
Ford, John Q. A.............	......	......	2 June, 1868	2 July, 1869	......
Fornance, John.............	......	......	3 Oct. 1861	3 Aug. 1863	......
Fort, Isaac B.............	......	......	8 Sept. 1863	......	......
Fort, William F.............	......	......	27 June, 1861	18 Dec. 1862	......
Foss, Cyrus D.............	......	......	2 June, 1868	2 June, 1869	......
Franklin, John, Jr.............	......	......	10 June, 1862	21 Nov. 1863	......
Fraser, Alexander V.............	......	......	......	21 Sept. 1861	15 Oct. 1863
Freeman, Edward R.............	1 Oct. 1873	......	......	......	......
Freeman, Frederick N.........	......	9 Sept. 1891	......	......	......
Freeman, Joseph M.............	......	......	16 Feb. 1852	......	......
Freeman, Virginius.............	......	......	26 Feb. 1851	21 May, 1853	9 May, 1857
Frick, Horace E.............	......	......	......	......	......
Frick, William H.............	......	......	26 June, 1856	2 Aug. 1859	6 Jan. 1862
Frizell, Charles H.............	1 Oct. 1872	......	......	......	......
Fuller, William H.............	......	......	23 May, 1861	......	......

ASSISTANT ENGINEER.	PASSED ASSISTANT ENGINEER.	CHIEF ENGINEER.	REMARKS.
1 July, 1877	5 April, 1887	......	Resigned 21 Jan. 1865
......	......	......	In service
......	......	......	Ensign 1 July 1885; Lieut. 9 Dec. 1894; in service
......	......	......	Resigned Aug. 11, 1883
10 June, 1881	......	......	Resigned 15 Oct. 1867
......	......	......	Killed accidently in Nebraska 21 March, 1886
......	24 Feb. 1874	......	Died in service 23 Sept. 1861
......	......	......	Retired list 8 April, 1891
......	......	5 Mar. 1871	Resigned 26 Dec. 1867
1 July, 1893	......	......	Retired list 31 Oct. 1879; died 28 April, 1886
......	24 Feb. 1874	3 Oct. 1891	In service
......	......	......	In service
......	24 Feb. 1874	1 July, 1887	Died 23 Dec. 1862
......	......	......	In service
......	......	......	Resigned 4 Sept. 1865
......	......	......	Ensign 1 July, 1887; in service
......	......	30 Aug. 1852	Resigned 19 June, 1864
......	......	......	Resigned 30 Nov. 1859
......	......	......	Dropped (went South) 8 July, 1861
......	......	......	Ensign 1 July, 1886; in service
......	......	......	Resigned 21 May, 1866
......	......	4 Mar. 1871	In service
......	......	......	Resigned 1 June, 1849
......	......	23 Apr. 1859	Killed in action, 5 Aug. 1864
......	......	13 Jan. 1840	Resigned 3 April, 1848
......	......	......	Resigned 29 Aug. 1856
......	......	......	Resigned 12 Oct. 1865
......	......	......	Ensign 1 July, 1887; in service
......	......	......	Resigned 20 Oct. 1883
......	......	......	Ensign 1 July, 1885; Lieutenant 23 April, 1895
......	......	......	Honorably discharged 30 June, 1886
......	......	......	Resigned 26 Sept. 1870
......	......	23 Jan. 1871	Resigned 27 March, 1872
......	......	......	Resigned 12 June, 1858
......	......	4 Mar. 1871	Retired list 29 Sept. 1894
......	......	......	Resigned 19 April, 1869
......	24 Feb. 1874	......	Resigned 31 Dec. 1875
......	......	23 Oct. 1859	Retired list 13 Dec. 1882
1 July, 1884	......	......	Resigned 30 June, 1885
......	......	......	In service
......	......	......	Resigned 6 Feb. 1869
......	......	25 Oct. 1859	Retired list 15 Feb. 1892
......	......	31 Oct. 1848	Resigned 1 May, 1865
......	......	......	Resigned 5 Nov. 1847
......	24 Feb. 1874	27 Dec. 1890	In service
24 Feb. 1874	19 Feb. 1875	......	Died 23 Feb. 1878; Act. 3d Asst. Eng. N. Acad '66-'68
......	......	......	Lost in the *Oneida*, 24 Jan. 1870
......	......	......	Died in service 1 Dec. 1865
......	......	......	Resigned 21 April, 1865
......	......	......	Resigned 1 Nov. '73; Act. 3d Asst. Engr. N. Acad. '66 68
......	......	......	Resigned 26 June, 1865
......	24 Feb. 1874	......	Retired list 24 Mar. 1874
1 July, 1877	26 Jan. 1886	......	In service
......	......	......	In service
......	......	......	Resigned 8 Oct. 1853
......	......	......	Dropped (went South) 8 July, 1861
11 Mar. 1874	3 Mar. 1882	......	Retired list 18 June, 1890
......	......	......	Resigned 12 April, 1862
......	......	......	Resigned 16 May, 1874
......	......	......	Resigned 16 Nov. 1861

	CADET ENGINEER.	NAVAL CADET.	THIRD ASSISTANT ENGINEER.	SECOND ASSISTANT ENGINEER.	FIRST ASSISTANT ENGINEER.
Fulmer, David M...............	......	......	4 May, 1863	28 Sept. 1864	8 Dec. 1872
Fulton, Albert K...............	......	......	6 Jan. 1862	1 Oct. 1863	......
GAGE, HOWARD,........	1 Oct. 1874	......	......	......	......
Gallagher, John...............	......	......	21 Jan. 1842	22 Jan. 1846	......
Galt, Robert W...............	......	......	......	12 Oct. 1871	......
Gamble, William H...............	......	......	8 July, 1862	......	......
Gardner, John W...............	......	......	21 Apr. 1863	28 Sept. 1864	31 Dec. 1872
Garrison, Daniel M...............	......	1 June, 1891	......	......	......
Gartley, William H...............	13 Sept. 1877	5 Aug. 1882	......	......	......
Garvin, Benjamin F...............	......	......	29 Mar. 1847	31 Oct. 1848	26 Feb. 1851
Gates, George S...............	......	......	2 June, 1868	2 June, 1869	......
Gatewood, Richard...............	15 Sept. 1875	......	......	......	......
Gatewood, Robert W...............	1 Oct. 1878	5 Aug. 1882	......	......	......
Gay, Edward...............	......	......	24 Aug. 1861	21 Apr. 1863	......
Gay, Jesse...............	......	......	......	......	20 Feb. 1847
Geddes, C. Wright...............	......	......	15 Nov. 1847	11 Jan. 1849	26 Feb. 1851
Geddis, George W...............	......	......	8 July, 1862	......	......
George, F. A. R...............	......	......	11 Apr. 1859	......	......
Gideon, George, Jr...............	......	......	31 Oct. 1848	26 Feb. 1851	21 May, 1853
Gillis, Harry A...............	1 Oct. 1879	5 Aug. 1882	......	......	......
Gladding, William H...............	......	......	20 Sept. 1858	......	......
Gladstone, Daniel D...............	13 Sept. 1877	......	......	......	......
Glasscock, Eustace S...............	1 Oct. 1879	5 Aug. 1882	......	......	......
Godfrey, Jones...............	......	......	2 June, 1868	......	......
Goodwin, Francis C...............	......	......	12 July, 1861	18 Dec. 1862	......
Gorton, William F...............	......	......	16 Feb. 1852	......	......
Gow, John L...............	1 Oct. 1874	......	......	......	......
Gowing, Burdette, C...............	......	......	21 Sept. 1861	30 July, 1863	11 Oct. 1866
Grafly, Daniel W...............	......	......	21 Apr. 1862	2 Feb. 1864	1 Jan. 1868
Gragg, Samuel...............	......	......	29 Oct. 1861	3 Aug. 1863	11 Oct. 1866
Greatrake, C. L...............	......	......	......	15 Mar. 1847	......
Green, John P...............	......	......	24 Feb. 1862	......	......
Green, Joseph S...............	......	......	28 Feb. 1862	15 Oct. 1863	......
Green, Levi R...............	......	......	19 Mar. 1858	1 Dec. 1860	15 Oct. 1863
Greene, Albert S...............	......	......	17 Feb. 1860	17 Nov. 1862	1 Mar. 1864
Greene, David M...............	......	......	23 May, 1861	28 Oct. 1862	1 Jan. 1865
Greene, George M...............	......	......	25 Aug. 1862	20 Feb. 1864	1 Jan. 1868
Greenleaf, Charles H...............	......	......	3 Oct. 1861	3 Aug. 1863	11 Oct. 1866
Greer, Alexander...............	......	......	1 Dec. 1854	9 May, 1857	2 Aug. 1859
Gregory, H. P...............	......	......	21 Sept. 1861	30 July, 1863	......
Grier, John A...............	......	......	2 Aug. 1855	21 July, 1858	3 Aug. 1859
Griffin, Levi...............	......	......	......	28 July, 1845	1 Nov. 1842
Griffin, Robert S...............	1 Oct. 1874	......	......	......	......
Griffin, Thomas J...............	......	......	......	28 May, 1861	......
Griffiths, Isaac J...............	......	......	16 Jan. 1863	......	......
Gross, Charles J...............	1 Oct. 1879	5 Aug. 1882	......	......	......
Gsantner, Otto C...............	1 Oct. 1878	5 Aug. 1882	......	......	......
Guerard, Richard D...............	......	......	11 Jan. 1849	......	......
Gunnell, Robert H...............	......	......	17 Feb. 1860	27 June, 1862	1 Mar. 1864
HABIGHURST, C. J...............	......	......	23 June, 1863	2 Sept. 1865	17 Sept. 1873
Habirshaw, William M...............	......	......	29 July, 1861	......	......
Hain, Franklin K...............	......	......	{ 23 May, '61 21 Nov. '57 }	29 Oct. 1862	......
Haines, Hiram...............	......	......	16 Feb. 1852	......	......
Hall, George W...............	......	......	3 May, 1859	3 Oct. 1861	25 July, 1866
Hall, George W...............	......	......	21 Sept. 1861	3 Aug. 1863	11 Oct. 1866
Hall, Harry...............	14 Sept. 1876	......	......	......	......
Hall, Reynold T...............	......	......	......	......	......
Hall, William K...............	......	......	15 Nov. 1847	11 Jan. 1849	26 Feb. 1851

ASSISTANT ENGINEER.	PASSED ASSISTANT ENGINEER.	CHIEF ENGINEER.	REMARKS
......	24 Feb. 1874	....	Retired list 26 April, 1884
......	......	....	Resigned 25 April, 1864
20 June,1880	19 Nov. 1890	......	In service.
......	......	......	Resigned 17 Feb. 1847
24 Feb. 1874	24 Feb. 1879	26 Dec. 1894	In service
......	......	.....	Died 26 Aug. 1862
......	24 Feb. 1874	....	Retired list 18 Feb. 1889; died 16 Sept. 1891
......	......	.....	In service
.....	......	.....	Resigned 1 May, 1886
......	......	11 May, 1858	Retired list 14 Feb. 1885; died 22 Jan. 1892
24 Feb. 1874	29 Oct. 1874	......	Retired list 1884; was Act. 3d Asst. 1866-68 N. Acad
......	......	......	Asst.Naval Const'r '81; Naval Constr. '88; died '90
......	......	......	Honorably discharged at his own request, 30 June, '84
......	......	......	Died 19 Jan. 1870
......	......	31 Oct. 1848	Resigned 22 Oct. 1859
......	......	.....	Resigned 5 Sept. 1855
......	......	......	Resigned 9 March, 1864
......	......	......	Resigned 13 Aug. 1862
......	......	23 Apr. 1859	Died 16 June, 1863
......	......	......	Resigned 25 Aug. 1883
......	......	......	Dropped 4 Aug. 1863
......	......	......	Dropped 18 Oct. 1881
......	......	......	Resigned 2 July, 1885
......	......	......	Dismissed 1873; was Act. 3d Asst. Engr. N.Acad.66-68
......	......	......	Retired list 2 Mar. 1868; died 24 April, 1887
......	......	......	Died 31 Aug. 1853
20 June 1880	19 Mar. 1891	......	In service
.....	24 Feb. 1874	15 Feb. 1886	Retired list 28 Jan. 1895
......	......	......	Resigned 1 April, 1873
......	24 Feb. 1874	.....	Retired list 23 Dec. 1884; died 25 Dec. 1885
......	......	.....	Resigned 25 Oct. 1847
......	......	....	Appointment revoked 1 March, 1862
......	......	.....	Retired list 24 May, 1867
......	......	......	Resigned 2 Aug. 1869
......	......	5 Mar. 1871	Retired list 9 Aug. 1893; died 8 Mar. 1896
......	......	......	Resigned 16 Sept. 1869
......	24 Feb. 1874	......	Died 2 June, 1878
......	24 Feb. 1874	......	Retired list 18 July, 1885
....	......	21 May, 1863	Died 10 Sept. 1867
....	......	......	Resigned 27 April, 1865
......	......	31 Jan. 1862	Resigned 15 Nov. 1865
......	......	......	Resigned 2 Nov. 1847
20 June,1880	25 Aug. 1889	......	In service
......	......	......	Resigned 6 April, 1863
......	......	......	Resigned 20 Feb. 1863
......	......	......	Res gned 28 Feb. 1883
......	......	......	Resigned 17 Aug. 1886
......	......	......	Dismissed 20 July, 1850
......	......	......	Retired list 3 July 1873
......	24 Feb., 1874	2 Mar. 1892	In service
......	......	......	Appointment revoked 5 Feb. 1862
......	......	......	Resigned 24 Jan. 1863
......	......	......	Resigned 25 July, 1854
......	......	......	Resigned 16 Nov. 1866
......	24 Feb. 1874	15 Feb. 1885	Died 16 June, 1889
10 June,1882	14 Dec. 1892	......	In service
20 Apr. 1880	9 Jan. 1889	....	In service
......	......	......	Resigned 15 Feb. 1853

	CADET ENGINEER.	NAVAL CADET.	THIRD ASSISTANT ENGINEER.	SECOND ASSISTANT EEGINEER.	FIRST ASSISTANT ENGINEER.
Hallowell. Francis P............	......	......	8 Sept, 1863	......	......
Halsey, Richard E................	......	......	16 Jan. 1863	......	......
Halstead, Alexander S........	1 Oct. 1879	5 Aug. 1882	......	......	......
Hands, Robinson W............	......	......	1 Feb. 1862	......	......
Hannum, John L.................	......	......	21 Apr. 1863	28 Sept. 1864	23 Nov, 1872
Hardie, David....................	......	......	11 May 1860	28 Oct. 1862	......
Harmony, Joseph H.............	......	......	8 July, 1862	25 July, 1866	1 Jan. 1868
Harris, James M..................	......	......	16 Sept. 1853	9 May, 1857	......
Harris, Robert L.................	......	......	3 May, 1859	29 July, 1861	20 May, 1863
Harris, Thomas J................	......	......	27 Jan. 1848	......	......
Harris, William H...............	......	......	21 Sept. 1861	30 July, 1863	11 Oct. 1866
Harrison, Henry F...............	1 Oct. 1874	......	......	......	......
Harrison, William H...........	......	......	29 July, 1861	18 Dec. 1862	30 Jan. 1865
Harsen, Elisha....................	......	......	1 July, 1861	20 Apr. 1863	......
Hartrath, Armin.................	......	4 Sept. 1884	......	......	......
Harvey, Luther R................	......	......	11 Feb. 1862	15 Oct. 1863	1 Jan. 1868
Hasbrouck, Raymond D......	......	28 Sept. 1888	......	......	......
Hasson, William F. C..........	14 Sept. 1876	......	......	......	......
Haswell, Charles H.............	......	......	......	......	......
Hatcher, Jackson R.............	......	......	24 Sept. 1847	26 Feb. 1851	......
Hatfield, Robert E...............	......	......	24 Aug. 1861	......	......
Haverly, Lewis A................	......	......	19 July, 1861	......	......
Hawkins, John S.................	......	......	29 July, 1861	18 Dec. 1862	30 Jan. 1865
Hawthorne. Harry L...........	1 Oct. 1878	5 Aug. 1882	......	......	......
Hayes, Charles H................	......	5 Aug. 1882	......	......	......
Heaton, William W.............	......	......	2 Dec. 1861	8 Sept. 1863	11 Oct. 1866
Hebard, Henry...................	......	......	......	27 Jan. 1848	26 Feb. 1851
Hebard, George F...............	......	......	13 May, 1861	19 Feb. 1863	......
Hedricks, Alfred.................	......	......	24 Dec. 1861	......	......
Heiser, Henry D..................	......	......	26 Feb. 1851	21 May, 1853	9 May, 1857
Henderson, Alexander.........	......	......	8 Sept. 1863	......	......
Henderson, Andrew H........	......	......	......	......	......
Henderson, John A..............	......	......	......	......	......
Henry, James B., Jr.............	......	6 Sept. 1892	......	......	......
Herbert, William C..............	1 Oct. 1879	5 Aug. 1882	......	......	......
Herring, Benjamin..............	......	......	11 Aug. 1860	......	......
Herwig, Henry....................	......	......	......	......	......
Hewes, Charles H................	1 Oct. 1880	5 Aug. 1882	......	......	......
Hewitt, Edward L...............	......	......	24 Feb. 1862	15 Oct. 1863	......
Hibbert, Stephen D.............	......	......	11 Jan. 1849	26 Feb. 1851	26 June, 1856
Hibbs, Frank W..................	......	4 Sept. 1883	......	......	......
Higgins, Robert B...............	1 Oct. 1878	5 Aug. 1882	......	......	......
Hill, Frank K.....................	1 Oct. 1882	5 Aug. 1882	......	......	......
Hinds, Alfred W.................	......	6 Sept. 1890	......	......	......
Hine, Robert B...................	......	......	24 Aug. 1861	21 Apr. 1863	25 July. 1866
Hines, John C.....................	......	......	......	21 Nov. 1837	......
Hobby, James M..................	......	......	31 Oct. 1848	{ 26 Feb. '51 { 4 June, '61	2 May, 1863
Hodgson, Richard M...........	......	......	9 Dec. 1861	8 Sept. 1863	......
Hoffman, Frank J...............	1 Oct. 1872	......	......	......	......
Hogan, Thomas J................	1 Oct. 1874	2 Aug. 1882	......	......	......
Holland, William................	......	......	......	23 Mar. 1848	26 Feb. 1851
Hollihan, James W.............	......	......	8 Dec. 1862	8 Apr. 1864	6 June, 1868
Hollingsworth, Charles F....	......	......	29 Oct. 1861	3 Aug. 1863	......
Hollins, John.....................	......	......	25 July, 1854	9 May, 1857	......
Hollis, Ira N......................	1 Oct. 1874	......	......	......	......
Holmes, Henry...................	......	......	29 Oct. 1861	3 Aug. 1863	......
Holmes, Urban T................	......	13 Sept 1886	......	......	......
Holt, George R....................	......	......	16 Oct. 1861	3 Aug. 1863	......
Hoopes, Joseph...................	......	......	16 Sept. 1862	1 Mar. 1864	......
Hopper, William W............	......	......	11 Apr. 1859	26 Dec. 1861	17 Mar. 1863

ASSISTANT ENGINEER.	PASSED ASSISTANT ENGINEER.	CHIEF ENGINEER.	REMARKS.
......	......	......	Resigned 12 Nov. 1867
......	....	......	Resigned 30 Oct. 1863
1 July, 1885	11 Sept. 1895	......	In service
......	......	......	Lost in the *Monitor* 31 Dec. 1862
......	24 Feb. 1874	4 May, 1891	In service
......	......	......	Retired list 15 March, 1867; died 20 March, 1889
......	24 Feb. 1874	......	Died 27 Nov. 1877
......	......	......	Died 6 Oct. 1864
......	......	4 Mar. 1871	Died 9 Jan. 1889
......	......	......	Dismissed 7 July, 1849
....	24 Feb. 1874	27 Dec. 1883	In service
......	......	......	Resigned 23 May, 1877
......	......	......	Resigned 8 Oct. 1872
.....	......	......	Killed in action 5 Aug. 1864
1 July, 1890	......	......	In service
......	......	......	Died 11 June, 1886
1 July, 1894	......	......	In service
10 June, 1882	......	......	Resigned 1 Feb. 1893
......	......	12 July, 1836	Engineer-in-Chief '44-50; 1st Eng. Navy; dropped '52
......	......	......	Died 23 Dec. 1853
......	......	......	Resigned 18 Aug. 1862
......	......	......	Died 29 Aug. 1862
......	......	......	Resigned 18 Jan. 1869
......	......	......	Honorably discharged 30 June, 1884
28 June, 1889	29 Jan. 1896	......	In service; entered originally as Cadet Mid'n 22 Sept. '80
......	24 Feb. 1874	26 Jan. 1886	Died 31 May, 1895
....	......	6 Feb. 1840	Died 4 Aug. 1846
......	......	......	Dropped 17 Sept. 1856
......	......	......	Resigned 9 Aug. 1865
......	......	....	Resigned 22 April, 1865
......	......	28 June 1861	Retired list 12 July, 1894
......	......	......	Dismissed 17 April, 1866
3 July, 1876	......	......	Retired list 20 Nov. 1884
......	......	......	In service
1 July, 1885	6 Aug. 1895	......	In service
......	......	......	Dismissed (went South) 8 July, 1861
9 Sept. 1874	22 May, 1880	21 Mar. 1895	Retired 28 Jan. 1896
......	......	......	Ensign 1 July, 1886; Asst. Nav. Constr. '88, died '90
......	......	......	Resigned 2 Nov. 1866
......	......	29 June, 1861	Retired list 24 Aug. 1889
1 July, 1889	......	......	Asst. Nav. Const. 1 July, 1891; in service
1 July, 1884	15 Jan. 1895	......	In service
......	......	......	Ensign 1 July, 1886; Lieutenant 15 June, 1895
1 July, 1896	......	......	In service
......	24 Feb. 1874	14 Dec. 1882	Retired list 20 Feb. 1893; died 27 June, 1895
......	......	......	Resigned 31 Dec. 1848
......	......	......	Resigned 21 June, '55; reap'd '61; retired '70; died '82
......	......	......	Resigned 6 Jan. 1866
26 Feb. 1875	16 Sept. 1881	......	Resigned 11 June 1889
....	......	......	Resigned 12 Oct. 1886
......	......	......	Died 18 Aug. 1856
......	24 Feb. 1874	......	Retired list 31 Oct. 1879
......	......	......	Resigned 11 Sept. 1865
......	......	......	Died at sea 4 June, 1858
20 June, 1880	19 Feb. 1889	....	Resigned 30 Sept. 1893
......	......	......	Resigned 11 Sept. 1865
1 July, 1892	......	....	In service
......	......	......	Resigned 4 May, 1869
......	......	.....	Died 18 March, 1866, on board *Kearsarge*
......	......	......	Resigned 22 Nov. 1866

	CADET ENGINEER.	NAVAL CADET.	THIRD ASSISTANT ENGINEER.	SECOND ASSISTANT ENGINEER.	FIRST ASSISTANT ENGINEER.
Houston, George P............	......	......	21 May, 1857	......	......
Houston, J, Buchanan.........	......	......	21 May, 1857	3 Aug. 1859	9 Dec. 1861
Houston, Samuel H............	......	......	26 Feb. 1851	21 May, 1853	......
How, Andrew P................	......	......	......	24 Sept. 1847	......
Howell, Charles P.............	7 Oct. 1867	......	......	15 Aug. 1870	......
Howell, John..................	......	......	24 Dec. 1853	......	......
Howland, Charles H...........	1 Oct. 1878	5 Aug. 1882	......	......	......
Hoyt, Eben, Jr................	......	......	21 May, 1857	2 Aug. 1859	1 July 1861
Hudgins, John M..............	......	8 Sept. 1890	......	......	......
Huffington, Howard W........	......	18 May, 1888	......	......	......
Hughes, Arthur L..............	1 Oct. 1880	5 Aug. 1882	......	......	......
Hull, Jameson Cox............	......	......	16 Feb. 1862	{ 27 July, '55 30 Apr. '61	23 June, 1863
Hulme, Walter Q..............	1 Oct. 1880	5 Aug. 1882	......	......	......
Hunt, Andrew M..............	15 Sept. 1875	......	......	......	......
Hunt, Charles S...............	......	......	22 July, 1862	......	......
Hunt, George P...............	......	......	1 July, 1861	18 Dec. 1862	30 Jan. 1865
Hunt, Henry..................	......	......	......	......	17 Jan. 1842
Hunt, John H..................	......	......	1 July, 1861	18 Dec. 1862	30 Jan. 1865
Hunt, William H..............	......	......	24 Dec. 1853	9 May, 1857	2 Aug. 1859
Huntley, John C...............	......	......	12 Aug. 1861	......	......
Huston, Robert M.............	......	......	......	4 Oct. 1873	......
Hutchinson, Edward S.........	......	......	3 Oct. 1861	......	......
Hutchinson, James W.........	......	......	5 Nov. 1861	25 Aug. 1863	......
Huxley, John H................	......	......	19 July, 1861	28 Dec. 1862	......
INCH, PHILIP................	......	......	21 Nov. 1857	2 Aug. 1859	1 July, 1861
Inch, Richard.................	......	......	8 Sept. 1863	15 Oct. 1865	......
Ireland, George C..............	......	......	16 Sept. 1862	1 Mar. 1864	......
Isbester, Richard T............	15 Sept, 1875	......	......	......	......
Isherwood, Benjamin F.......	......	......	......	22 Jan. 1846	{ 23 May, '44 10 July, '47
Ivers, Henry K................	1 Oct. 1874	......	......	......	......
JACKSON, ALBERT........	......	......	13 May, 1861	15 Apr. 1864	......
Jackson, Thomas A.........	......	......	31 Oct. 1848	1 Oct. 1852	26 June, 1856
James, Leland F...............	......	9 Sept. 1889	......	......	......
Jeffrey, William C.............	1 Oct. 1872	......	......	......	......
Jewell, Henry C...............	......	......	16 Feb. 1852	......	......
Johnson, Charles N...........	1 Oct. 1873	......	......	......	......
Johnson, Edward C...........	......	......	18 Nov. 1862	......	......
Johnson, George R............	......	......	16 Feb. 1852	27 June, 1855	21 July, 1858
Johnson, John.................	......	......	20 May, 1857	2 Aug. 1859	1 July, 1861
Jones, David P................	......	......	25 Mar. 1862	1 Nov. 1863	1 Jan. 1868
Jones, Horace W..............	1 Oct. 1880	5 Aug. 1882	......	......	......
Jones, Owen...................	......	......	19 Feb. 1863	20 June, 1864	......
Jones, Thomas J...............	......	......	26 June, 1856	21 July, 1858	3 Aug. 1859
Jones, Truman M..............	......	......	8 Oct. 1861	3 Aug. 1863	11 Oct. 1866
Jordan, Charles W............	......	......	4 Apr. 1861	......	......
Jordan, Marshall P............	......	......	24 Dec. 1863	9 May, 1857	......
Joynes, Walker W.............	1 Oct. 1881	......	......	......	......
KAEMMERLING, G.........	13 Sept. 1877	5 Aug. 1882	......	......	......
Kafer, John C...............	......	......	16 Jan. 1863	28 May, 1864	26 June, 1872
Kaiser, Julius A...............	......	......	8 Sept. 1863	25 July, 1866	......
Karns, Franklin, D............	......	30 Sept. 1891	......	......	......
Kavanaugh, Benjamin.........	......	......	3 May, 1859	......	......
Kearny, George H.............	......	......	2 June, 1868	......	......
Keilholtz, Pierre O............	1 Oct. 1880	5 Aug. 1882	......	......	......
Keleher, James T..............	......	......	17 Feb. 1860	17 Dec. 1862	......
Kelley, Benjamin F............	1 Oct. 1873	......	......	......	......

ASSISTANT ENGINEER.	PASSED ASSISTANT ENGINEER.	CHIEF ENGINEER.	REMARKS.
......	......	......	2d Lieut. Mar. Corps, 1860; now Lieut. Colonel retired
......	......	......	Resigned 28 July, 1865
......	......	......	Died 16 June, 1854
......	......	......	Resigned 7 Aug. 1849
24 Feb. 1874	3 Dec. 1876	10 Nov. 1893	In service.
......	......	......	Resigned 3 May, 1856
......	......	......	Resigned 3 May, 1886
......	......	10 Nov. 1863	Killed explos. boiler at Naval Academy, 19 Oct. 1867
1 July, 1896	......	......	In service
......	......	......	Honorably discharged 30 June, 1894
......	......	......	Resigned 12 June, 1883
......	......	......	Resigned 1856; reappointed 1861; resigned 1866
......	......	......	Ensign 1 July 1886; in service
10 June, 1881	5 Apr. 1892	......	Resigned 31 July, 1894
......	......	......	Resigned 9 June, 1863
......	24 Feb. 1874	4 July, 1880	Died 5 April, 1887
......	......	14 May, 1847	Died 10 April, 1861
......	......	......	Died 21 Nov. 1868
......	......	19 Feb. 1863	Retired list 8 Feb. 1871; died 25 June, 1889
......	......	......	Died 20 Oct. 1863
......	......	......	Resigned 15 May, 1874
......	......	......	Appointment revoked 26 Jan. 1862
......	......	......	Resigned 6 April, 1865
......	......	......	Resigned 16 June, 1865
......	......	10 Nov. 1863	In service
24 Feb. 1874	28 Sept. 1874	3 Aug. 1892	In service
......	......	......	Resigned 10 March, 1865
10 June, 1881	......	......	Wholly retired 7 Jan. 1886
......	......	31 Oct. 1848	Engineer-in-Chief 1861 to 1869; retired list 1884
10 June, 1881	......	......	Resigned 1 July, 1885
......	......	......	Resigned 23 Sept. 1865
......	......	......	Dropped (went south) 6 May, 1861
1 July, 1896	......	......	In service
......	......	......	Resigned 2 Dec. 1872
......	......	......	Resigned 11 Jan. 1854
......	......	......	Resigned 11 June, 1874
......	......	......	Resigned 3 Sept. 1863
......	......	31 July, 1861	Retired list, 9 Nov. 1890
......	......	10 Nov. 1863	Retired list, 10 June, 1876
......	24 Feb. 1874	9 Jan. 1889	Retired list 21 June, 1892
28 June, 1889	20 Feb. 1896	......	In service.
......	......	......	Resigned 22 Dec. 1866
......	......	19 Jan. 1863	Dismissed 19 Oct. 1875
......	......	......	Died 22 Nov. 1872
......	......	......	Dropped (went south) 6 May, 1861
......	......	......	Dismissed (went south) 20 May, 1861
......	......	......	Honorably discharged 30 June, 1887
1 July, 1883	10 Aug. 1893	......	In service
......	24 Feb. 1874	......	Retired list 18 June, 1888
......	......	......	Retired list 8 July, 1873
......	......	......	In service
......	......	......	Retired list 3 April, 1866
24 Feb. 1874	1 Jan. 1876	27 June, 1893	In service; Acting 3d Asst. Engr. N. Academy '66-'68
......	......	......	Resigned 6 Aug. 1884
......	......	......	Resigned 17 March, 1868
......	......	......	Resigned 29 Oct. 1873

	CADET ENGINEER.	NAVAL CADET.	THIRD ASSISTANT ENGINEER.	SECOND ASSISTANT ENGINEER.	FIRST ASSISTANT ENGINEER.
Kellogg, Edward S..........	......	5 Sept. 1888	......	......	......
Kellogg, Mortimer.............	......	......	16 Feb. 1852	27 July, 1855	3 Aug. 1859
Kelly, John P.,................	......	......	24 Aug. 1861	21 Apr. 1863	11 Oct. 1866
Kelly, William H.............	......	......	16 Jan. 1863	28 May, 1864	......
Kenyon, Andrew J............	......	......	21 Sept. 1861	30 July, 1863	11 Oct. 1866
Kid, Charlton B..............	......	......	21 May, 1857	2 Aug. 1859	1 Feb. 1862
Kiersted, Andrew J...........	......	......	26 June, 1856	......	9 May, 1857
Kilpatrick, Thomas...........	....	......	23 Mar. 1848	13 Sept. 1849	26 Feb. 1851
Kilpatrick, William H........	......	......	11 Feb. 1862	15 Oct. 1863	......
Kimball, Henry H.............	......	......	20 May, 1863	......	......
Kimball, James B.............	......	......	8 Sept. 1853	26 June, 1856	2 Aug. 1859
King, Charles A. E...........	14 Sept. 1876	......	......	......	......
King, Glendy.................	......	......	2 Aug. 1855	21 July, 1858	......
King, James W...............	......	......	2 Sept. 1844	10 July, 1847	13 Sept. 1849
King, William Henry.........	......	......	6 Feb. 1851	26 Feb. 1861	21 May, 1853
King, William Hervey........	......	......	20 May, 1857	2 Aug. 1859	2 Dec. 1861
King, William Rufus.........	1 Oct. 1872	......	......	......	......
Kinkaid, Thomas W..........	14 Sept. 1876	......	......	......	......
Kirby, Absalom...............	......	......	3 Oct. 1861	3 Aug. 1863	11 Oct. 1866
Kleckner, Charles C..........	1 Oct. 1871	......	......	......	......
Kline, George W.............	1 Oct. 1881	5 Aug. 1882	......	......	......
Knapp, Myron H.............	......	......	5 Nov. 1861	25 Aug. 1863	......
Knepper, Chester M..........	1 Oct. 1880	5 Aug. 1882	......	......	......
Knowlton, Ingersoll F........	......	......	18 Oct. 1862	......	......
Knowlton, Minor N...........	......	......	18 Nov. 1862	23 Mar. 1864	......
Knox, Simon B...............	......	......	20 Feb. 1847	26 Feb. 1851	......
Koehl, Edward W.............	......	......	30 July, 1861	18 Dec. 1862	......
Koester, Oscar W.............	......	5 Apr. 1884	......	......	......
Kutz, George F...............	......	......	26 June, 1856	......	21 July, 1858
LA BLANC, THOMAS......	......	......	1 Feb. 1862	15 Oct. 1863	......
Lackey, Oscar H.............	......	......	21 July 1858	17 Jan. 1861	17 Mar. 1863
Laesch, Lewis C. F...........	......	......	17 Mar. 1863	......	......
Lamdin, James F.............	......	......	24 Dec. 1853	9 May, 1857	2 Aug. 1859
Lamdin, Nicholas H..........	......	......	21 Apr. 1863	17 July, 1872	......
Lamdin, William J...........	......	......	6 Feb. 1851	1 Oct. 1852	9 May, 1857
Lane, S. Cushing.............	......	......	8 Dec. 1862	......	......
Lane, Webster................	......	......	23 May, 1861	3 Aug. 1863	......
Lang, William................	14 Sept. 1876	......	......	......	......
Langer, Philip J..............	......	......	18 Nov. 1862	23 Mar. 1864	......
Latch, Edward B.............	......	......	20 Sept. 1858	8 Oct. 1861	17 Mar. 1863
Latimer, Samuel C...........	......	......	1 Dec. 1854	......	......
Latimer, William A. R.......	......	......	11 Jan. 1849	26 Feb. 1851	......
Law, William F...............	......	......	16 Nov. 1861	......	......
Lawrence, Henry R...........	......	....	{ 21 Sept.'61 { 28 Oct. 62	......	......
Lawrence, John C. E.........	......	......	28 Oct. 1850	26 Feb. 1851	......
Lawrence, J. P. Stewart......	......	......	......	......	......
Lawrence William H.........	1 Oct. 1879	5 Aug. 1882	......	......	......
Laws, Elijah.................	......	......	19 Mar. 1858	1 Dec. 1860	22 July, 1866
Laws, George W..............	......	21 May, 1887	......	......	......
Lawton, Andrew..............	......	......	24 June, 1850	26 Feb. 1851	21 May, 1853
Lawton, Elbridge.............	......	......	23 Mar. 1848	13 Sept. 1849	26 Feb. 1851
Lawton, Nelson H............	......	......	17 Mar. 1863	......	......
Lay, John L..................	......	......	......	8 July, 1861	15 Oct. 1863
Leavitt, Edward D...........	......	......	24 Aug. 1861	21 Apr. 1863	......
Lee, Caleb E..................	......	......	4 Apr. 1861	16 Jan. 1863	1 Jan. 1865
Lee, Columbus W............	......	......	26 Feb. 1851	......	......
Lee, James D.................	......	......	8 Sept. 1863	......	......
Leiper, Charles L.............	......	6 Sept. 1892	......	......	......
Leitch, Robert R..............	1 Oct. 1871	......	......	23 Jan. 1874	....

ASSISTANT ENGINEER	PASSED ASSISTANT ENGINEER.	CHIEF ENGINEER.	REMARKS.
22 Aug. 1894	......	......	In service
......	......	8 Nov. 1861	Died 16 Nov. 1870
......	24 Feb. 1874	......	Died 27 Jan. 1890
......	......	......	Cashiered 20 Nov. 1866
......	24 Feb. 1874	......	Died 27 July, 1888
......	......	......	Resigned 30 Dec. 1867
......	......	12 Nov. 1861	Retired 25 Dec. 1894
......	......	......	Resigned 22 Aug. 1853
......	......	......	Resigned 9 Feb. 1866
......	......	......	Resigned 29 June, 1869
......	......	5 Aug. 1861	Died 18 May, 1879
10 June, 1882	27 June, 1893	......	In service
......	......	......	Resigned 7 Sept. 1858
......	......	12 Nov. 1852	Engineer-in-Chief '69-'73; retired 26 Aug. '81
......	......	......	Died 25 April, 1859
......	......	10 Nov. 1863	Died 11 March, 1883
1 July, 1877	17 Mar. 1887	......	Retired 18 March, 1891
10 June, 1882	14 Dec. 1892	......	In service
......	24 Feb. 1874	2 Dec. 1886	In service
1 July, 1877	30 June, 1887	......	Resigned 5 July, 1889
......	......	......	Ensign 1 July, 1887; in service
......	......	......	Resigned 8 July, 1867
......	......	......	Ensign 1 July, 1886; Lieut. 28 April, 1895; in service
......	......	......	Resigned 17 March, 1865
......	......	......	Resigned 22 Nov. 1872
......	......	......	Died 19 Sept. 1855
......	......	......	Dropped 9 Jan. 1867
1 July, 1890	21 June, 1896	......	In service
......	......	10 Nov. 1861	Retired 26 June, 1896
......	......	......	Resigned 28 Sept. 1867
......	......	21 Mar. 1870	Retired 16 Nov. 1882; died 21 May, 1883
......	......	......	Resigned 24 May, 1864
......	......	8 Dec. 1862	Dismissed 5 March, 1867
24 Feb. 1874	3 June, 1879	......	Died 15 Nov. 1885, on board *Adams*
......	......	1 Oct. 1861	Retired list; died 12 Oct. 1888
......	......	......	Dropped 8 April, 1865
......	......	......	Resigned 22 March, 1867
......	......	......	Died 15 Nov. 1880
......	......	......	Resigned 28 April, 1870
......	......	21 Mar. 1870	Retired 22 Nov. 1878
......	......	......	Killed 24 Aug. 1855, explosion of *Hetzel's* boiler
......	......	......	Resigned 31 May, 1858; Act'g Asst. and Ch. Eng. '62-7
......	......	......	Died 24 Sept, 1863
......	......	......	Resigned 21 March, 1863
22 Mar. 1875	16 June, 1883	5 June, 1896	Resigned 2 June, 1856 In service
......	......	......	Died 1 Jan. 1885
......	......	21 Mar. 1870	Retired 20 March, 1895
1 July, 1893	......	......	In service
......	......	23 Apr. 1859	Died 17 March, 1871
......	......	26 June, 1856	Retired 3 March, 1881; died 21 July, 1889
......	......	......	Resigned 25 April, 1865
......	......	......	Resigned 22 May, 1865
......	......	......	Resigned 25 May, 1867
......	24 Feb. 1874	......	Retired 2 Dec. 1876
......	......	......	Resigned 2 June, 1855
......	......	......	Resigned 10 Nov. 1866
......	......	......	In service
24 Feb. 1874	15 Jan. 1879	30 Sept. 1894	Retired 19 Feb. 1896

	CADET ENGINEER.	NAVAL CADET.	THIRD ASSISTANT ENGINEER.	SECOND ASSISTANT ENGINEER.	FIRST ASSISTANT ENGINEER.
Leonard, Henry S...............	......	......	19 July, 1861	16 Jan. 1863	......
Leonard, John C................	1 Oct. 1878	5 Aug. 1882	......	......	......
Leonard, Samuel H., Jr.......	......	......	......	......	......
Leopold, Harry G..............	1 Oct. 1878	5 Aug. 1882	......	......	......
Levy, Charles H.................	......	......	21 Nov. 1857	2 Aug. 1859	......
Lewers, J. Henry...............	......	......	28 Oct. 1862	......	......
Lewis, Enos M...................	......	......	17 Feb. 1860	3 Aug. 1863	25 July, 1866
Lewis, Oscar C...................	......	......	1 July, 1861	18 Dec. 1862	11 Oct. 1866
Lillebridge, Frederick M......	14 Sept. 1876	......	......	......	......
Lincoln, Edmund................	......	......	6 Jan. 1862	1 Oct. 1863	......
Lincoln, Gatewood S..........	......	20 May, 1892	......	......	......
Lindsly, Cleland..................	......	......	1 Oct. 1852	3 Oct. 1861	25 July, 1866
Lining, George D................	......	......	20 Sept. 1858	17 Jan. 1861	......
Littig, James G...................	......	......	3 Aug. 1863	25 July, 1866	......
Littig, Nicholas B...............	......	......	21 May, 1857	2 Aug. 1859	1 July, 1861
Little, William N................	1 Oct. 1872	......	......	......	......
Littlefield, William L..........	......	30 Sept. 1892	......	......	......
Littlehales, George W..........	1 Oct. 1879	5 Aug. 1882	......	......	......
Livermore, Charles W.........	......	......	......	......	......
Logan, George T. W............	......	......	31 Oct. 1848	26 Feb. 1851	......
Long, James......................	......	......	16 Nov. 1861	25 Aug. 1863	......
Long, John H.....................	......	......	6 Nov. 1849	......	15 June,1861
Long, Robert H..................	......	......	11 Jan. 1849	26 Feb. 1851	21 May, 1853
Longacre, Orleans...............	......	......	1 July, 1861	18 Dec. 1862	1 Jan. 1865
Loomis, Edmund N............	1 Oct. 1872	......	......	......	......
Loomis, Frederick J...........	1 Oct. 1880	5 Aug. 1882	......	......	......
Loring, Charles H...............	......	......	26 Feb. 1851	21 May, 1853	9 May. 1857
Loveaire, Henry F...............	......	......	8 Sept. 1863	......	......
Lovering, Francis J.............	......	......	20 May, 1857	2 Aug. 1859	1 July, 1861
Lowe, John........................	......	......	21 Aug. 1861	18 Dec. 1862	25 July, 1866
Lubbe, Charles C................	15 Sept. 1875	......	......	......	......
Luce, William....................	......	......	28 July, 1845	24 May, 1843	
Lynch, Thomas...................	......	......	12 Aug. 1861	21 Apr. 1863	
Lynch, William F., Jr..........	......	......	20 Feb. 1847	......	......
Lyon, Frank.......................	......	20 May, 1890	......	......	......
MACCARTY, G. M. L......	......	......	8 July, 1861	18 Dec. 1862	30 Jan. 1865
Macomb, David B............	......	......	11 Jan. 1849	26 Feb. 1851	26 June,1856
Magee, Edward A................	......	......	27 June,1862	21 Nov. 1863	1 Jan. 1868
Magee, George W................	......	......	4 Apr. 1861	16 Jan. 1863	1 Dec. 1864
Main, Herschel...................	......	......	2 June,1868	2 June,1869	......
Mallory, Charles K.............	......	25 Sept. 1891	......	......	......
Manning, Charles E............	14 Sept. 1876	......	......	......	......
Manning, Charles H............	......	......	19 Feb. 1863	25 July, 1866	26 Oct. 1872
Manning, Edward W...........	......	......	21 May, 1853	25 June,1855	21 July, 1858
Mansfield. Newton..............	......	7 Sept. 1891	......	......	......
Manson, Charles H..............	......	......	26 Feb. 1851	......	......
Mapes, Charles A................	......	......	17 Aug. 1847	......	......
Mapes, Daniel T.................	......	......	16 Aug. 1847	26 Feb. 1851	......
Mars, Edward....................	......	......	......	......	21 Sept. 1861
Mars, Philip L....................	......	......	......	......	1 July, 1861
Marshall, Albert W.............	......	6 Sept. 1892	......	......	......
Marshall, James F...............	......	8 Sept. 1891	......	......	......
Marsland, Charles F............	......	......	8 Dec. 1862	......	......
Marsland, Edward...............	......	......	......	......	14 Aug. 1861
Martin, Daniel B.................	......	......	......	......	17 Jan. 1842
Mason, Henry....................	......	......	23 Mar. 1848	13 Sept. 1849	{ 26 Feb. '51 31 May,'61
Mather, Mason W...............	......	......	17 Dec. 1862	8 Apr. 1864	......
Mathews, Albert C..............	1 Oct. 1880	5 Aug. 1882	......	......	......
Mathews, Clarence H..........	14 Sept. 1876	5 Aug. 1882	......	......	......

ASSISTANT ENGINEER.	PASSED ASSISTANT ENGINEER.	CHIEF ENGINEER.	REMARKS.
......	......	......	Killed in action 5 Aug. 1864
1 July, 1884	14 Feb. 1895	......	In service
2 Oct. 1881	3 Aug. 1892	......	In sorvice
1 July, 1884	26 Dec. 1894	......	In service
......	......	......	Dropped.(went south) 7 July, 1861
......	......	......	Resigned 29 June, 1868
......	......	......	Died 12 Jan. 1872
......	......	......	Resigned 28 Sept, 1868
......	......	......	Resigned 20 Aug. 1879
......	......	......	Resigned 4 Feb. 1868
......	......	......	In service
......	......	......	Resigned 12 Dec. 1874
......	......	......	Resigned 18 April, 1861
......	......	......	Retired 14 July, 1874
......	......	......	Lost in the *Oneida* 24 Jan. 1870
1 July, 1877	17 Oct. 1885	......	In service
......	......	......	In service
......	......	......	Honorably discharged June 30, 1885
26 Feb. 1875	......	......	Retired list 16 Nov. 1882
......	......	......	Dropped 29 Aug. 1856
......	......	......	Resigned 17 April, 1865
......	......	10 Nov. 1863	Died 2 March, 1882
......	......	26 June, 1856	Resigned 31 Oct. 1863
......	......	......	Resigned 6 June, 1866
......	......	......	Lost in the *Huron* 24 Nov. 1877
......	......	......	Ensign 1 July, 1886; resigned 30 June, 1890
......	......	25 Mar. 1861	Engineer-in-chief 1884 to 1887; retired list, 1890
......	......	......	Resigned 26 Oct. 1868
......	......	......	Resigned 26 June, 1865
......	24 Feb. 1874	16 June, 1883	In service
......	......	......	Drowned 4 Aug. 1879
......	......	......	Resigned 29 May, 1847
......	......	......	Resigned 21 June, 1869
......	......	......	Dismissed 5 Feb. 1852
1 July, 1896	......	......	In service
......	24 Feb. 1874	16 Sept. 1881	Retired 20 June, 1896
......	......	21 Sept. 1860	Retired 27 Feb. 1889
......	24 Feb. 1874	27 Jan. 1889	Retired Nov. 4, 1895
......	24 Feb. 1874	11 June, 1876	Retired 26 June, 1893
24 Feb. 1874	20 Nov. 1874	11 Nov. 1892	Retired 10 Sept. 1895
......	......	......	In service
10 June, 1882	......	......	Resigned 30 Jan. 1891
......	24 Feb. 1874	......	Retired 14 June, 1884
......	......	......	Dismissed (went south) 6 May, 1861
......	......	......	In service
......	......	......	Resigned 25 Nov. 1853
......	......	......	Died 12 Nov. '47, on board *Mississippi* in Mexican War
......	......	......	Resigned 21 June, 1855
......	......	......	Resigned 11 Feb. 1862
......	......	......	Dismissed 2 Nov. 1861
......	......	......	In serv:ce
......	......	......	In service
......	......	......	Resigned 6 Sept. 1865
......	......	......	Resigned 4 June, 1864
......	......	14 May, 1847	Engineer-in-Chief 1853-1857; resigned 1859
......	......	21 May, 1863	Retired 16 Oct. 1868
......	......	......	Resigned 3 March, 1869
......	......	......	Honorably discharged 30 June, 1886
1 July, 1883	27 Sept. 1893	......	In service

	CADET ENGINEER.	NAVAL CADET.	THIRD ASSISTANT ENGINEER.	SECOND ASSISTANT ENGINEER.	FIRST ASSISTANT ENGINEER.
Matthews, John R................	.....	....	......	17 Jan. 1842	10 July, 1847
Matthews, Samuel................	.....	......	20 Feb. 1847	24 June, 1848	11 Jan. 1849
Mattice, Asa M..................	1 Oct. 1872	......	....	....	....
Mauglin, James..................	......	......	29 Oct. 1861	3 Aug. 1863	......
Maurice, C. Stewart.............	......	......	18 Nov. 1862	23 Mar. 1864	......
Maury, John M..................	......	......	23 Mar. 1848	26 Feb. 1851	26 Feb. 1853
Mayer, C. F., Jr.................	......	......	26 Aug. 1859	21 Apr. 1863	......
McAllister, Andrew..............	13 Sept. 1877	5 Aug. 1882	......	......	......
McAllister, Gates................	......	......	23 June, 1863	......	......
McAlpine, Kenneth..............	13 Sept. 1877	5 Aug. 1882	......	......	......
McAusland, Alexander...........	......	.....	......	......	20 Feb. 1847
McCartney, Daniel P............	......	......	1 July, 1861	18 Dec. 1862	30 Jan. 1865
McCartny, George D............	3 Oct. 1866	......	....	....	....
McCay, Henry K................	1 Oct. 1880	5 Aug. 1882	......	......	......
McCleery, Robert................	......	......	2 Aug. 1855	21 July, 1858	2 Aug. 1859
MacConnell, Charles J..........	......	......	29 Oct. 1861	3 Aug. 1863	11 Oct. 1866
McConnell, Henry...............	......	......	5 Nov. 1861	......	......
McCormick, Charles M.........	1 Oct. 1881	5 Aug. 1882	....	....	....
McCreary, Harry R.............	13 Sept. 1877	......	......	....	....
McCusker, James F.............	1 Oct. 1881	......	......	....	....
McDonough, Thomas............	......	......	27 Mar. 1843	......	......
McElmell, Edward F...........	......	......	......	7 Nov. 1871	......
McElmell, Jackson..............	......	......	2 Aug. 1855	21 July, 1858	25 Mar. 1861
McElroy, George W............	1 Oct. 1874	......	......	......	......
McElroy, Samuel................	......	......	26 Feb. 1851	......	......
McEwan, Henry D..............	......	......	1 July, 1861	21 Apr. 1863	11 Oct. 1866
McEwan, William G............	......	......	8 Mar. 1865	1 Jan. 1868	......
McFarland, Walter M..........	15 Sept. 1875	......	......	......	......
McGrann, William H...........	......	20 May, 1887	......	......	......
McGregor, James................	....	....	23 June, 1863	......	......
McGurren, J. B.................	......	......	21 Apr. 1863	......	......
McIlvaine, Henry C.............	......	......	17 Feb. 1860	6 Jan. 1862	1 Mar. 1864
McIlvaine, William D..........	......	.....	16 Nov. 1861	25 Aug. 1863	......
McIntyre, John..................	......	......	22 July, 1862	15 Feb. 1864	......
McIntyre, Sylvanus..............	......	......	24 Aug. 1861	......	......
McKay, John E.................	......	......	3 May 1859	......	......
McKay, William................	1 Oct. 1881	5 Aug. 1882	......	......	......
McKean, Frederick G..........	......	......	21 Feb. 1861	21 Apr. 1863	1 Dec. 1864
McKean, Josiah S..............	......	5 Aug. 1882	....	......	......
McLanahan, S. Calvin..........	......	......	17 Mar. 1863	25 July, 1866	......
McMorris, Boling K............	......	15 Sept. 1890	......	......	......
McMurtrie, Horace..............	......	......	3 May, 1859	29 Oct. 1861	20 May, 1863
McNamara, James B...........	......	......	8 Dec. 1862	8 Apr. 1864	......
McNary, Isaac R................	......	......	13 May, 1861	19 Feb. 1863	1 Jan. 1865
Melville, George W.............	......	......	29 July, 1861	18 Dec. 1862	30 Jan. 1865
Mercer, John D.................	......	......	16 Feb. 1852	......	......
Mercer, Joseph..................	......	......	12 Aug. 1861	......	......
Mercier, David I................	15 Sept. 1875	......	......	......	......
Mercier, William T.............	......	......	17 Jan. 1842	10 July, 1847	......
Meredith, Edward D...........	1 Oct. 1872	......	......	......	......
Merian, Henry W...............	......	......	25 Aug. 1862	......	......
Merritt, Darwin R..............	......	10 Sept. 1891	......	......	......
Messinger, William H..........	......	......	......	29 Oct. 1861	28 Sept. 1864
Michener, Abram...............	......	......	28 Oct. 1861	15 Mar. 1864	......
Mickley, Joseph P..............	......	......	......	20 Mar. 1871	......
Middleton, John M.............	......	......	28 July, 1845	{ 10 July,'47 2 May,'43 }	......
Miller, Clarence A..............	27 Oct. 1875	......	......	......	......
Miller, Frederick L.............	......	......	21 Oct. 1861	25 Aug. 1865	......
Miller, Peter....................	1 Oct. 1878	5 Aug. 1882	......	.....	......
Miller, Philip...................	......	......	20 May, 1862	15 Feb. 1864	......

ASSISTANT ENGINEER.	PASSED ASSISTANT ENGINEER.	CHIEF ENGINEER.	REMARKS.
......	......	......	Resigned 17 May, 1849
......	......	......	Resigned 18 July, 1849
26 Feb. 1875	29 Dec. 1880	......	Resigned 30 June, 1890
......	......	......	Resigned 11 Aug. 1865
......	......	......	Resigned 21 Dec. 1865
......	......	......	Resigned 17 Sept. 1856
......	......	......	Wholly retired 5 May, 1868
1 July, 1884	9 May. 1895	......	In service
......	......	......	Dropped 18 March, 1867
1 July, 1883	12 Sept. 1893	......	In service
......	......	......	Resigned 24 Nov. 1850; was Act. Ch. Eng. during war
......	24 Feb. 1874	22 Aug. 1881	Retired 10 Nov. 1892
......	......	......	Appointed Midshipman; resigned 15 Mar. 1869
......	......	......	Resigned 6 Aug. 1884
......	......	11 Aug. 1862	Died 15 Sept. 1863
......	24 Feb. 1874	2 Dec. 1885	In service
......	......	......	Resigned 6 Feb. 1868
......	......	......	Ensign 1 July, 1887; in service
......	......	......	Resigned 20 Aug. 1879
......	......	......	Resigned 15 June, 1882
......	......	......	Resigned 4 Nov. 1844
......	......	......	Retired 1 Nov. 1878
......	......	2 Feb. 1862	Retired 4 June, 1896
20 June, 1880	28 Jan. 1890	......	In service
......	......	....	Resigned 20 June, 1852
......	24 Feb. 1874	3 Mar. 1882	Retired 13 Dec. 1892; died 18 Oct. 1894
24 Feb. 1874	......	......	Appointed from vol. serv. for gallantry; retired 1875
10 June 1881	15 Sept. 1891	......	In service
1 July, 1893	......	......	In service
......	......	......	Died 22 Sept, 1863
......	......	......	Dismissed 26 Oct. 1863
......	......	......	Resigned 21 June, 1869
......	......	......	Resigned 13 Oct. 1865
......	......	......	Died 21 May, 1865
......	......	......	Resigned 19 June, 1865
......	......	......	Resigned 7 July, 1860; in Volunteer service during war
....	......	......	Honorably discharged 30 June, 1887
......	24 Feb. 1874	25 Nov. 1877	Retired 9 Nov. 1893
28 June, 1889	5 Nov. 1895	......	In service; entered as Cadet Midshipman, 29 Sept. 1879
......	......	......	Resigned 21 June, 1869
1 July, 1896	......	......	In service
......	......	......	Resigned 28 Nov. 1865
......	......	......	Died 23 June, 1864, on board *Tioga* at sea
......	24 Feb. 1874	14 Dec. 1878	Retired list 11 Sept. 1894
......	24 Feb. 1874	4 Mar. 1881	Engineer-in-Chief 9 Aug., 1887, to date; in service
......	......	......	Resigned 8 July, 1856
......	......	......	Resigned 1 May, 1862
......	......	......	Resigned 22 June, 1877
......	......	......	Dismissed 14 Aug. 1849
......	......	......	Resigned 17 June, 1873
......	......	......	Lost in the *Weehawken* 6 Dec. 1863
......	......	......	In service
......	......	......	Resigned 16 June, 1865
......	......	......	Resigned 25 Sept. 1865
24 Feb. 1874	24 Feb. 1878	28 Aug. 1894	In service
......	......	......	Dismissed 5 Oct. 1819
......	......	......	Dropped 20 Aug. 1879
......	......	......	Resigned 28 May, 1868
......	......	......	Killed 3 April, 1883, on *Tennessee*; bursting steam pipe
......	......	......	Dropped 11 Jan. 1873

	CADET ENGINEER.	NAVAL CADET.	THIRD ASSISTANT ENGINEER.	SECOND ASSISTANT EEGINEER.	FIRST ASSISTANT ENGINEER.
Miller, William G...............	1 Oct. 1881	5 Aug. 1882	......	......	......
Miller, William W...............	......	......	26 Aug. 1859	......	......
Milligan, Robert W............	......	......	3 Aug. 1863	25 July, 1866	......
Mills, Oscar B...................	......	......	16 Jan. 1863	28 May, 1864	......
Miner, Leo D.....................	14 Sept. 1876	......	......	......	......
Mintzer, William A............	......	......	16 Jan. 1863	25 July, 1866	......
Missimer, Hillary...............	......	......	19 Feb. 1861	16 Jan. 1863	......
Mitchell, Augustus.............	......	......	{ 1 July, '61 { 6 Oct. '62	......	......
Mitchell, John C................	......	......	16 Feb. 1852	......	......
Mitchell, T. Mason.............	......	......	16 Oct. 1861	......	......
Moffett, Noah W................	......	......	17 Dec. 1862	......	......
Molony, Henry H...............	......	......	19 Feb. 1861	16 Jan. 1863	1 Dec. 1864
Monroe, William C.............	......	......	21 May, 1861	29 Oct, 1862	......
Montgomery, William J......	......	......	23 May, 1861	29 Oct. 1862	25 July, 1866
Moody, Roscoe C................	......	8 Sept. 1890	......	......	......
Moore, John W...................	......	......	21 May, 1853	27 June, 1855	21 July, 1858
Moore, William S...............	......	......	2 June, 1868	2 June, 1869	......
Morgan, Cyrus R................	......	......	17 Dec. 1861	......	......
Morgan, Joseph..................	......	......	16 Nov. 1861	25 Aug. 1863	......
Morgan, Leo.....................	1 Oct. 1872	......	......	......	......
Moritz, Albert...................	13 Sept. 1877	5 Aug. 1882	......	......	......
Morley, Albert W...............	......	......	1 July, 1861	18 Dec. 1862	25 July, 1866
Morris, John R..................	......	7 Sept. 1889	......	......	......
Morrison, James H............	......	......	3 May, 1859	3 Oct. 1861	20 May 1863
Morton, James P................	......	9 Sept. 1891	......	......	......
Moses, Stanford E..............	......	6 Sept. 1888	......	......	......
Moss, Charles B.................	......	......	......	......	......
Mulford, Harry B...............	1 Oct. 1881	5 Aug. 1882	......	......	......
Mullen, Anthony T. E........	......	......	12 Aug. 1861	21 Apr. 1863	25 Jan. 1865
Murphy, Daniel..................	......	......	......	12 Nov. 1842	......
Murphy, Monroe................	......	......	18 Nov. 1862	23 Mar. 1864	......
Murray, Albert S...............	......	......	19 Feb. 1861	16 Jan. 1863	......
Murray, Jacob M...............	......	......	23 June, 1863	......	......
Musgrave, William.............	......	......	3 May, 1859	1 July, 1861	20 May, 1863
Myers, John T...................	......	27 Sept. 1887	......	......	......
NAGLE, AUGUSTUS F...	......	......	3 Aug. 1863	......	......
Nagle, Charles F...............	......	......	3 Aug. 1863	25 July, 1866	......
Nauman, William H...........	......	......	......	24 Apr. 1872	......
Neal, William S.................	......	......	25 Aug. 1862	20 Feb. 1864	1 Jan. 1868
Neill, John E....................	......	......	26 Aug. 1859	21 Oct. 1861	......
Neilson, George C..............	......	......	13 Oct. 1863	1 Jan. 1868	......
Newell, Harman.................	......	......	22 Sept. 1849	26 Feb. 1851	21 May, 1853
Newton, Isaac....................	......	......	......	......	15 June,1861
Nicholls, Arthur.................	14 Sept. 1876	......	......	......	......
Nicoll, William L..............	......	......	21 Oct. 1861	3 Aug. 1863	11 Oct. 1866
Noble, James M.................	......	......	19 Feb. 1861	20 May, 1863	......
Noell, Michael D...............	15 Sept. 1875	......	......	......	......
Nones, Henry B.................	......	......	23 Sept. 1853	28 May, 1861	1 July, 1861
Nones, Washington H........	......	......	8 Mar. 1850	26 Feb. 1851	......
Norton, Harold P...............	1 Oct. 1874	......	......	......	......
Nulton, Louis M................	......	8 Sept. 1885	......	......	......
Nutting, Daniel C., Jr........	......	21 May 1889	......	......	......
Nyman, Frank W...............	......	......	19 Feb. 1863	......	......
OAKFORD, ISAAC R......	......	......	1 July, 1861	18 Dec. 1862	......
O'Connor, Henry......	1 Oct. 1874	......	......	......	......
Ogden, Julius S..................	......	......	2 June, 1868	2 June,1869	......
Offley, Cleland N...............	......	5 Sept. 1885	......	......	......
Olmstead, L. L...................	......	......	Apr. 1861	......	......

ASSISTANT ENGINEER.	PASSED ASSISTANT ENGINEER.	CHIEF ENGINEER.	REMARKS
......	......	......	Ensign 1 July 1887; in service
......	......	......	Resigned 5 Aug. 1861
24 Feb. 1874	25 Mar. 1874	16 May, 1892	In service
......	......	......	Retired 26 Oct. 1872; died 10 Aug. 1873
10 June, 1882	11 Nov. 1892	......	In service
24 Feb. 1874	26 Sept. 1874	......	Discharged 11 Nov. 1893
......	......	......	Resigned 7 Aug. 1868
......	......	......	Lost in the *Weehawken*, 6 Dec. 1863
......	......	......	Resigned 16 Nov. 1854
......	......	......	Resigned 6 Dec. 1862
......	......	......	Appointment revoked 16 Sept. 1863
......	......	......	Lost at sea on steamer *Atlanta* Oct. 1865
......	......	......	Resigned 1 March, 1871
......	......	......	Resigned 25 Oct. 1869
1 July, 1896	......	......	In service
......	......	5 Aug. 1861	Retired 24 May, 1894
24 Feb. 1874	11 June, 1876	10 Aug. 1893	In service; was Act'g 3d Ass't eng'r N. Academy, '66-'68
......	......	......	Resigned 2 April, 1864
......	......	......	Resigned 5 Jan. 1866
......	......	......	Resigned 14 May, 1874
1 July, 1883	13 July, 1894	......	In service
......	24 Feb. 1874	17 Nov. 1882	Retired 27 March, 1896
17 Apr. 1896	......	......	In service
......	......	......	Dropped 7 Dec. 1872
......	......	......	In service
1 July, 1894	......	......	In service
......	......	29 May, 1844	Dropped 30 Jan. 1846
......	......	......	Dropped 5 Feb. 1884
......	24 Feb. 1874	......	Died 20 Sept. 1877
......	......	......	Resigned 25 Nov. 1848
......	......	......	Resigned 6 Dec. 1865
......	......	......	Killed on board *Chenango;* boiler explosion 15 Apr. 1864
......	......	......	Resigned 13 May, 1865
......	......	......	Resigned 12 Sept. 1865
22 Aug. 1894	......	......	Exchanged into Mar. Corps 25 Feb. 1895; now 2d Lieut.
......	......	......	Resigned 3 May, 1865
24 Feb. 1874	5 Apr. 1874	......	Retired 26 July, 1892
24 Feb. 1874	24 Feb. 1878	12 Sept. 1894	In service
......	......	......	Resigned 3 Sept. 1872
......	......	......	Resigned 23 Nov. 1865
24 Feb. 1874	......	......	Resigned 5 July, 1876
......	......	23 Apr. 1859	Died 24 March, 1880
......	......	......	Resigned 8 Feb. 1865
......	......	......	Resigned 20 Aug. 1879
......	24 Feb. 1874	17 Oct. 1885	Died 2 July, 1887
......	......	......	Retired 5 Jan. 1866; resigned 3 March, 1866
......	......	......	Died 1 Jan. 1878
......	......	14 Dec. 1864	Retired list 15 May, 1892
......	......	......	Died 9 Sept. 1853
10 June, 1881	12 Oct. 1891	......	In service
1 July, 1891	4 July, 1896	......	In service
......	......	......	Appointed Ass't Naval Constructor 1 July, 1895
......	......	......	Resigned 21 April, 1864
......	......	......	Resigned 13 Oct. 1865
......	......	......	Resigned 14 Jan. 1876
24 Feb. 1874	20 Oct. 1875	17 Jan. 1893	In service; was Act'g 3d Ass't eng'r, N. Acad. '66-'68
1 July, 1891	......	......	In service
......	......	......	Resigned 22 Sept. 1862

	CADET ENGINEER.	NAVAL CADET.	THIRD ASSISTANT ENGINEER.	SECOND ASSISTANT ENGINEER.	FIRST ASSISTANT ENGINEER.
Olmstead, Loring	1 Oct. 1873	......	......	......	......
Olsen, Edmund	......	......	......	12 July, 1861	15 Oct. 1863
Orr, Robert H	1 Oct. 1880	5 Aug. 1882	......	......	......
PALMER, ALBERT S	......	......	......	{ 14 Jan. '39 { 28 July, '45	......
Palmer, James E	1 Oct. 1879	5 Aug. 1882	......	......	......
Park, William D	......	......	4 Feb. 1862	......	......
Parke, Cornelius T	......	......	26 Feb. 1851	......	......
Parker, Hiram Jr	......	......	16 Nov. 1861	25 Aug. 1863	11 Oct. 1866
Parks, John W	......	......	31 July, 1847	13 Sept. 1849	......
Parks, Wythe M	......	......	......	......	......
Parmenter, Henry E	1 Oct. 1880	5 Aug. 1882	......	......	......
Parsons, Isaac B	13 Sept. 1877	5 Aug. 1882	......	......	......
Patten, Edward C	......	......	3 May, 1859	......	......
Patterson, James W	......	......	21 Apr. 1863	28 Sept. 1864	......
Patterson, Nathaniel P	......	......	15 Mar. 1847	13 Sept. 1849	26 Feb. 1851
Pattison, Thomas P	1 Oct. 1879	5 Aug. 1882	......	......	......
Patton, John B	......	21 May, 1885	......	......	......
Paul, George	......	......	16 Jan. 1863	......	......
Paxson, Isaiah	......	......	17 Mar. 1863	1 Sept. 1864	......
Peltz, Philip G	......	......	26 June, 1856	21 July, 1858	3 Aug. 1859
Pemberton, John	......	......	8 Dec. 1862	8 Apr. 1864	1 Jan. 1868
Pendleton, Joseph H	1 Oct. 1878	5 Aug. 1882	......	......	......
Pendleton, William D	......	......	......	......	29 Oct. 1861
Perkins, Con. M	......	5 Aug. 1882	......	......	......
Perkins, Lyman B	13 Sept. 1877	5 Aug. 1882	......	......	......
Perry, James H	......	......	17 Jan. 1862	{ 1 Oct. '63 { 1 Sept. '70	......
Petherick, Thomas, Jr	......	......	21 Sept. 1861	......	......
Peugnet, Maurice B	......	7 Sept. 1889	......	......	......
Pfeltz, Gustavus A	......	......	3 Aug. 1863	......	......
Phillips, Henry W	......	......	19 Feb. 1862	15 Oct. 1863	......
Phillips, William L	......	......	3 May, 1859	......	......
Phillippi, Edwin T	......	......	20 May, 1862	15 Feb. 1864	1 Jan. 1868
Pickrell, James M	1 Oct. 1874	......	......	......	......
Pierce, Granville T	......	......	8 July, 1856	......	......
Pike, Boaz E	......	......	8 Dec. 1862	......	......
Pilkington, Hugh L	......	......	27 June, 1862	21 Nov. 1863	......
Platt, William H	......	......	......	7 June, 1870	......
Plotts, Rezeau B	......	......	1 July, 1861	18 Dec. 1862	25 July, 1866
Plumley, John L	......	......	3 May, 1859	......	......
Plunkett, James	......	......	3 May, 1859	......	......
Plunkett, M. H	......	......	21 July, 1858	21 Sept. 1861	......
Plympton, G. M	......	......	14 Sept. 1853	......	......
Pollard William	......	......	17 Feb. 1860	25 Aug. 1862	......
Pollock, Emmet R	......	18 May, 1889	......	......	......
Pomroy, Joseph R	......	......	14 Aug. 1851	......	......
Porter, John S	......	25 Sept. 1888	......	......	......
Potts, Howard D	......	......	16 Nov. 1861	25 Aug. 1863	......
Potts, Richard C	......	......	15 Nov. 1847	26 Feb. 1851	9 May, 1857
Potts, Robert	......	......	17 Feb. 1860	27 June, 1862	1 Mar. 1864
Potts, Stacy	1 Oct. 1871	......	......	......	......
Powers, William A	......	......	3 May, 1862	......	......
Pratt, William F	......	......	25 Aug. 1862	20 Feb. 1864	......
Prevear, Herbert P	13 Sept. 1877	......	......	......	......
Price, Alexander H	......	......	8 Oct. 1861	3 Aug. 1863	......
Price, Arthur	......	......	10 June, 1862	21 Nov. 1863	1 Jan. 1868
Price, Claude B	......	2 June, 1886	......	......	......
Price, Henry B	......	20 May, 1889	......	......	......
Prindle, Franklin C	......	......	3 Aug. 1861	21 Apr. 1863	......

ASSISTANT ENGINEER.	PASSED ASSISTANT ENGINEER.	CHIEF ENGINEER.	REMARKS.
......	......	......	Resigned 11 June, 1874
......	......	......	Lost in the *Huron* 24 Nov. 1877
......	24 Feb. 1874	27 Oct. 1874	Honorably discharged 30 June, 1886
......	......	......	Resigned 15 July 1848
......	......	......	Honorably discharged 30 June, 1885
......	......	......	Died 11 July, 1863, on board *Richmond*
......	24 Feb. 1874	......	Resigned 31 May, 1854
......	......	......	Resigned 18 Feb. 1875
8 May, 1877	22 June, 1884	27 June, 1896	Resigned 21 May, 1853
......	......	......	In service
......	......	......	Ensign 1 July, 1886; in service
......	......	......	Resigned 24 Nov. 1887
......	......	......	Dismissed 8 January, 1861
......	......	......	Retired 21 Oct. 1869
......	......	15 Oct. 1859	Dropped (went South) 10 June, 1861
......	......	......	Resigned 4 Oct. 1882
1 July, 1891	......	......	In service
......	......	......	Resigned 9 Sept. 1865
......	......	......	Resigned 18 Nov. 1865
......	......	9 Nov. 1861	Died 21 Aug. 1868
......	24 Feb. 1874	......	Retired 14 Sept. 1891
......	......	......	Second Lieut. Marine Corps 1 July, '84; now 1st Lieu't
......	......	......	Resigned 4 Jan. 1866
1 July, 1883	......	....	Entered as Cadet Mid'n 11 Sept. '75, now 1st Lieu't
......	......	......	Resigned 12 April, 1886
24 Feb. 1874	25 Apr. 1877	1 Apr. 1894	In service
......	......	......	Appointment revoked 26 Nov 1862
1 July, 1895	......	......	Resigned 18 Sept. 1895
......	......	......	Resigned 25 June, 1866
......	......	......	Resigned 28 July, 1869
......	......	......	Resigned 6 July, 1860
......	24 Feb. 1874	......	Retired list 21 June, 1884
10 June, 1881	16 May, 1892	......	In service
......	......	......	Resigned 8 Aug. 1857; appointed Purser 3 Nov. 1858
......	......	......	Resigned 6 April, 1864
......	......	......	Resigned 27 June, 1872
24 Feb. 1874	......	......	Retired 3 Nov. 1877
......	......	......	Retired 16 Jan. 1866
......	......	......	Resigned 29 Aug. 1860
......	......	......	Resigned 6 Feb. 1861
......	......	......	Resigned 9 May, 1865
......	......	......	Resigned 19 Dec. 1854
......	......	......	Dismissed 18 Oct. 1867
1 July, 1895	......	......	In service
......	......	......	Dropped 20 Dec. 1852
1 July, 1894	......	......	In service
24 Feb. 1874	......	......	Retired 26 Oct. 1874
......	......	......	Dropped (went South) 15 June, 1861
......	......	22 Jan. 1873	In service
26 Feb. 1875	12 Oct. 1881	29 Jan. 1896	In service
......	......	......	Resigned 3 Mar. 1866
......	......	......	Resigned 29 July, 1865
......	......	......	Resigned 24 Oct. 1879
......	......	......	Retired 26 Oct. 1872
......	24 Feb. 1874	......	Resigned 1 Jan. 1890
1 July, 1892	......	......	In service
......	......	......	In service
......	......	......	Resigned 11 Sept. 1865; now Civil Engineer U. S. Navy

	CADET ENGINEER.	NAVAL CADET.	THIRD ASSISTANT ENGINEER.	SECOND ASSISTANT ENGINEER.	FIRST ASSISTANT ENGINEER.
Proctor, Andre M...............	......	6 Sept. 1889	......	......	......
Prudy, John, Jr...............	......	......	21 Nov. 1857	2 Aug. 1859	19 Feb. 1865
Purdie, Charles F............	......	......	2 June, 1868	2 June, 1869	......
Purse, Wilson K...............	......	......	12 Aug. 1858	21 Sept. 1861	11 Mar. 1863
QUIG, HENRY M...............	......	......	8 Oct. 1861	3 Aug. 1863	....
Quin, Richard B...........	......	......	21 May, 1853	27 July, 1855	......
Quinby, Isaac H...............	1 Oct. 1878	......	......	......	......
Quinn, Michael...............	......	......	......	15 Nov. 1847	6 Nov. 1849
RAE, CHARLES W.........	......	......	2 June, 1868	2 June, 1869	......
Rae, Thomas W...........	......	......	30 July, 1861	21 Apr. 1863	11 Oct, 1866
Ramsay, Henry A.............	......	......	21 May, 1853	26 June, 1856	2 Aug. 1859
Ramsden, Frederick, T. H...	......	......	25 Aug. 1862	20 Feb. 1864	......
Rank, Erastus P.............	......	......	8 Dec. 1862	......	......
Ransom, George B...........	1 Oct. 1871	......	......	......	......
Read, Frank D...............	......	6 Sept. 1889	......	......	......
Rearick, Peter A............	......	......	17 Feb. 1860	22 July, 1862	1 Mar. 1864
Redgrave, DeWitt C...........	13 Sept. 1877	5 Aug. 1882	......	......	......
Reed, Milton E.............	......	5 Sept. 1887	......	......	......
Reeves, Isaac S. K........	......	......	......	......	......
Reeves, Joseph M...........	......	8 Sept. 1890	......	......	......
Reichenback, W. C. F........	......	......	8 Sept. 1863	......	......
Reid, Robert I.............	1 Oct. 1872	......	......	......	......
Reid, William I............	......	......	2 Dec. 1861	8 Sept. 1863	......
Reiley, Peter C.............	......	......	17 Mar. 1863	......	......
Renshaw, James...............	......	......	17 Feb. 1860	8 Dec. 1862	1 Mar. 1864
Rhoades, Henry E............	......	......	......	25 Feb. 1871	......
Rice, George B.............	......	6 Sept. 1892	......	......	......
Richardson, Thornton R........	1 Oct. 1880	5 Aug. 1882	......	......	......
Rider, Frederic C...........	......	5 Aug. 1882	......	......	......
Riley, George H.............	......	......	21 July, 1858	1 July, 1861	......
Rind, S. Z. K...............	......	......	7 Sept. 1855	......	......
Roane. Alexander H...........	......	......	27 Jan. 1848	......	......
Roberts, Edward E...........	......	......	21 Sept. 1861	30 July, 1863	......
Roberts, William............	....	......	2 Aug. 1855	21 July, 1858	{ 3 Aug. '59 24 Apr. '61
Robie, Edward D.............	......	......	16 Feb. 1852	27 June, 1855	21 July, 1858
Robie, Henry W.............	......	......	3 May, 1859	9 Apr. 1862	20 May, 1863
Robinson, Lewis W...........	......	......	21 Sept. 1861	30 July, 1863	11 Oct. 1866
Robison, John K.............	......	20 May, 1887	......	......	......
Roche, George W.............	......	......	28 Oct. 1862	15 Mar. 1864	1 Jan. 1868
Roebling, Edmund............	1 Oct. 1872	......	......	......	......
Roelker, Charles R..........	......	......	8 Dec. 1862	8 Apr. 1864	1 Jan. 1868
Rogers, George W............	......	......	21 July, 1858	29 Oct, 1861	......
Rommell, Charles E..........	1 Oct. 1878	5 Aug. 1882	......	......	......
Roop, John.............	......	......	3 May, 1859	17 Dec. 1861	20 May, 1863
Ross, H. Schuyler...........	......	......	17 Nov. 1862	23 Mar. 1864	1 Jan. 1868
Ross, Nelson................	......	......	8 July, 1862	15 Feb. 1864	......
Rowbotham, William..........	......	......	......	27 Jan. 1871	....
Rowen, John H...............	......	27 Sept. 1887	......	......	......
Ruiz, Alberto de............	1 Oct. 1871	......	......	......	......
Rust, Armistead.............	1 Oct. 1881	5 Aug. 1882	......	......	......
Rutherford, Jesse F.........	......	......	......	17 Jan. 1842	26 Feb. 1851
Rutherford, William H.......	......	......	22 Sept. 1849	16 Feb. 1852	26 June, 1856
Ryan, John J...............	......	......	20 May, 1863	25 July, 1866	......
Ryan, Philip J.............	1 Oct. 1879	5 Aug. 1882	......	......	......
Ryan, John P. J.............	......	22 Mar. 1889	......	......	......
SACKETT, AUGUSTINE..	......	......	3 Oct. 1861	3 Aug. 1863	......
Safford, Levi T.............	......	......	8 Dec. 1862	8 Apr. 1864	6 June, 1868

ASSISTANT ENGINEER	PASSED ASSISTANT ENGINEER.	CHIEF ENGINEER.	REMARKS.
1 July, 1895	......	......	In service
......	......	......	Resigned 30 Jan. 1873
......	......	......	Resigned '75; was Act'g 3d Ass't Eng'r N. Acad.'66-'68
......	24 Feb. 1874	......	Retired 16 June, 1874; died 30 Dec. 1882
......	......	......	Resigned 26 Nov. 1869
......	......	......	Resigned 1 Sept. 1856
......	......	......	Dropped 16 March, 1883
......	......	15 Dec. 1853	Dropped (went south) 18 May, 1861
24 Feb. 1874	28 Dec. 1875	21 Feb. 1893	In service; was Act'g 3d Ass't eng'r N. Acad. '66-68
......	24 Feb. 1874	......	Resigned 1 Oct. 1877
......	......	......	Dropped (went south) 6 May, 1861
......	......	......	Resigned 14 April, 1869
......	......	......	Resigned 9 March, 1866
26 Feb. 1875	4 July, 1880	9 May, 1895	In service
1 July, 1895	......	......	In service
......	24 Feb. 1874	25 Mar. 1874	In service
1 July, 1883	1 Oct. 1893	......	In service
1 July, 1893	......	......	In service
30 June 1875	16 Sept. 1883	21 June, 1896	In service
1 July, 1896	......	......	In service
......	......	......	Resigned 27 Nov. 1866
1 July, 1878	19 June, 1888	......	In service
......	......	......	Resigned 29 Jan. 1867
......	......	......	Resigned 20 Oct 1863
......	......	......	Resigned 14 May, 1867
24 Feb. 1874	......	......	Retired 30 Dec. 1874; was Acting Engineer during war
......	......	......	In service
......	......	......	Honorably discharged 30 June, 1886
1 July, 1883	......	......	Entered as Cadet Midship'n '77; died on *Swatara* '85
......	......	......	Resigned 17 Oct. 1865
......	......	......	Resigned 10 Nov. 1858
......	......	......	Resigned 11 Feb. 1850
......	......	......	Resigned 19 June, 1865
......	......	21 Apr. 1863	Resigned 18 March, 1869
......	......	30 July, 1861	Retired 11 Sept. 1893
......	......	......	Resigned 25 May, 1868
......	24 Feb. 1874	19 Aug. 1883	In service
1 July, 1893	......	......	In service
......	24 Feb., 1874	25 Aug. 1889	Retired July 3, 1896
......	......	......	Dropped 27 March, 1873
......	24 Feb. 1874	10 Nov. 1890	In service
......	......	......	Resigned 23 June, 1865
1 July, 1884	12 Sept. 1894	......	In serv; 2d Lieut. U.S. Mar. C's, '84; ex'd. Eng. Corps
......	......	......	Resigned 15 Oct. 1872
......	24 Feb. 1874	28 Jan. 1890	In service
......	......	......	Retired 26 Oct. 1872; died 6 Aug. 1883
24 Feb. 1874	25 Nov. 1877	......	Retired 26 Sept. 1893; died 30 May, 1894
1 July, 1893	......	......	In service
1 July, 1878	......	......	Wholly retired 31 Dec. 1885
......	......	......	Ensign 1 July 1887; in service
......	......	......	Died 3 Jan. 1862
......	......	1 Dec. 1861	Retired 26 Oct. 1874
24 Feb. 1874	......	......	Retired 28 Oct. 1874
......	......	......	Honorably discharged 30 June, 1885
17 Apr. 1896	......	......	In service
......	......	......	Resigned 24 Aug. 1865
......	24 Feb. 1874	......	Retired 11 Oct. 1881

	CADET ENGINEER.	NAVAL CADET.	THIRD ASSISTANT ENGINEER.	SECOND ASSISTANT ENGINEER.	FIRST ASSISTANT ENGINEER.
Salisbury, George R.	1 Oct. 1874				
Sample, Winfield S.	14 Sept. 1876				
Sampson, Bias C.	13 Sept. 1877	5 Aug. 1882			
Samson, Guy			24 Dec. 1861	8 Sept. 1863	
Sanford, Hiram				21 Nov. 1837	6 Feb. 1840
Sasse, Peter A.			16 Nov. 1861		
Savage, Peter F.			21 May, 1857	3 Aug. 1859	8 Oct. 1861
Saville, John W.			28 Oct. 1862	15 Mar. 1864	
Sawyer, Daniel A.			6 Oct. 1862	15 Mar. 1864	
Sawyer, George F.			8 Sept. 1863	15 Oct. 1865	
Scattergood, Edward			26 Aug, 1859	1 Mar. 1862	1 Oct. 1863
Schell, Franklin J.	1 Oct. 1874				
Schemerhorn, William E.	1 Oct. 1872				
Schley, William R.			2 May, 1857		
Schneider, William E.	1 Oct. 1879				
Schober, Frederick			23 June,1863	25 July, 1866	
Schroeder, Charles			24 Dec. 1853	9 May, 1857	3 Aug. 1859
Scot, John A.			3 Oct. 1861	3 Aug. 1863	11 Oct. 1866
Scott, Charles P.			18 Nov. 1862		
Scott, Henry W.			1 July, 1861	29 Apr. 1863	30 Jan. 1865
Scott, William				22 Jan. 1846	20 Mar. 1840
Scribner, Edward H.	1 Oct. 1874				
Selden, William C.			26 Aug. 1859	3 Oct. 1861	1 Oct. 1863
Sellman, Henry D.			19 July, 1861	18 Dec. 1862	
Sensner, George W.			22 Oct. 1860	1 Nov. 1861	24 Aug. 1864
Senter, Charles W. C.			4 May, 1863	28 Sept. 1864	
Serra, John			{ 29 May, '43 { 14 May, '47		
Sewell, George				13 Mar. 1847	10 July, 1847
Sewell, William					
Seymour, E. H.			3 Aug. 1861		
Shallenberger, Oliver B.	13 Sept. 1877	5 Aug. 1882			
Sharey, Samuel O.			11 Feb. 1852		
Shepard, George H.		27 Sept. 1887			
Sherwood, Gilbert				21 Jan. 1842	
Shewell, Walter					
Shields, William	1 Oct. 1881	5 Aug. 1882			
Shipman, William W.			3 Aug. 1861		
Shock, George E.			16 Feb. 1852		
Shock, Thomas A.			6 Feb. 1851	21 May, 1853	26 June, 1856
Shock, Thomas A. W.	1 Oct. 1878	5 Aug. 1882			
Shock, William H.			18 Jan. 1845	10 July, 1847	31 Oct. 1848
Sibley, William E.			20 May, 1863	7 Sept. 1865	
Simpson, Henry L.	1 Oct. 1878				
Skeel, Theoron			2 June,1868		
Sloane, John D.					
Slosson, Henry L.			13 Oct. 1863	1 Aug. 1866	
Smedley, John K.			18 Nov. 1862	23 Mar. 1864	
Smith, Albert E.	14 Sept. 1876				
Smith David.			26 Aug. 1859	8 July, 1861	1 Oct. 1863
Smith, Francis G. Jr.			29 July, 1861	18 Dec. 1862	30 Jan. 1865
Smith, Henry A.			16 Sept. 1862	1 Mar. 1864	
Smith, John A. B.			21 Apr. 1863	28 Sept. 1864	22 Jan. 1873
Smith, John T.				17 June,1870	
Smith, Sidney L.			21 Oct. 1861	25 Aug. 1863	1 Jan. 1868
Smith, Thaddeus S.			12 Aug. 1861		
Smith, Walter D.			1 July, 1861	18 Dec. 1862	25 July, 1866
Smith, William S.			21 Feb. 1861	16 Jan. 1863	1 Dec. 1864
Smith, William Strother	15 Sept. 1875				
Smith, William Stuart	13 Sept. 1877	5 Aug. 1882			
Snyder, George W.					

ASSISTANT ENGINEER.	PASSED ASSISTANT ENGINEER.	CHIEF ENGINEER.	REMARKS.
10 June, 1881	27 July, 1892	......	In service
10 June, 1882	......	......	Resigned 27 June, 1887
1 July, 1883	14 Nov. 1893	......	In service
......	......	......	Resigned 2 April, 1869
......	......	......	Resigned 5 Nov. 1849
......	......	......	Died 23 July, 1862
......	......	......	Resigned 13 Jan. 1865
......	......	......	Retired 1 Feb. 1871
......	......	......	Retired 22 Jan. 1866
......	......	......	Resigned 12 Oct. 1868
......	......	......	Died 20 Sept. 1864, on board *Maratanza*
20 June, 1880	16 May, 1889	......	In service
......	......	......	Resigned 21 Oct. 1872
......	......	......	Died 25 Feb. 1858
......	......	......	Resigned 21 Oct. 1872
......	......	......	Resigned 9 June, 1873
......	......	......	Dropped (went South) 18 May, 1861
......	24 Feb. 1874	6 July, 1885	In service
......	......	......	Died 20 June, 1864 on board *Tioga*
......	......	......	Died 10 May, 1869
......	......	......	Dismissed 5 June, 1850
10 June, 1881	2 Mar. 1892	......	In service
......	......	......	Resigned 19 Oct. 1668
......	......	......	Retired 17 Nov. 1871
......	24 Feb. 1874	17 June, 1874	Retired 25 Jan. 1886
......	......	......	Lost in the *Oneida* 24 Jan. 1870
......	......	......	Dropped 27 Feb. 1851
......	......	11 Mar. 1851	Retired 17 Dec. 1885; died 13 March, 1895
......	......	15 Mar. 1845	Resigned 10 Nov. 1853
......	......	......	Died 11 Apr. 1864
......	......	......	Resigned 23 Sept. 1886
......	......	......	Resigned 3 June, 1854
1 July, 1893	......	......	In service
......	......	......	Resigned 29 Oct. 1845
27 Jan. 1876	......	......	Died 30 Nov. 1881
......	......	......	Resigned 9 April, 1883
......	......	......	Resigned 27 Feb. 1862
......	......	......	Died 11 Sept. 1853
......	......	6 Dec. 1860	Died 21 Jan. 1873
......	......	......	Honorably discharged 30 June, 1885
......	......	11 Mar. 1851	Engineer-in-Chief, '77-'83; retired 62 years old
24 Feb. 1874	......	......	Dismissed 10 Sept. 1874
......	......	......	Resigned 1 Mar. 1881
......	......	......	Retired 2 June, 1869; resigned 12 Nov. 1870
7 June, 1877	......	......	Retired 30 June, 1885
24 Feb. 1874	27 Oct. 1874	......	Resigned 15 Sept, 1883
......	......	......	Resigned 13 March, 1866
......	10 June, 1882	......	Resigned 7 Dec. 1886
......	......	5 Mar. 1871	In service
......	......	......	Resigned 28 July, 1869
......	......	......	Resigned 28 July, 1866
......	24 Feb. 1874	16 Feb. 1892	In service
......	......	......	Retired Passed Asst. Engr. 24 Feb. '75 by Act Congress
......	24 Feb. 1874	......	Resigned 29 Aug. 1884
......	......	......	Resigned 8 July, 1862
......	......	25 Mar. 1880	Died 12 Sept. 1887
......	24 Feb. 1874	20 Oct. 1875	In service
10 June, 1882	27 June, 1883	......	In service
1 July, 1883	......	......	Retired 31 Oct. 1890
9 Oct. 1876	......	......	Died 27 Dec. 1884 on board *Palos*

	CADET ENGINEER.	NAVAL CADET.	THIRD ASSISTANT ENGINEER.	SECOND ASSISTANT ENGINEER.	FIRST ASSISTANT ENGINEER.
Snyder, Henry			25 Aug. 1862	21 Feb. 1864	1 Jan. 1868
Snyder, Henry Lee			19 Mar. 1858	16 Oct. 1861	21 Apr. 1863
Sornborger, Edwin C.	1 Oct. 1872				
Spangler, Harry W.	1 Oct. 1874				
Spear, Harrison			21 Apr. 1863	25 July, 1866	
Speights, James E.			12 Aug. 1862		
Spencer, Levi T.				3 June, 1844	
Spooner, Henry W.			16 Feb. 1852	27 July, 1855	21 July, 1858
Sprague, James P.			17 Feb. 1860	1 Nov. 1861	1 Mar. 1864
Stahl, Albert W.	14 Sept. 1876				
Stamm, William S.			26 Feb. 1851	21 May, 1853	9 May, 1857
Stanworth, Charles S.	1 Oct. 1881	5 Aug. 1882			
Starr, John B.	1 Oct. 1880	5 Aug. 1882			
Starr, William C.			17 Feb. 1860		
Stebbins, Charles W.	1 Oct. 1881	5 Aug. 1882			
Stedman, Francis D.			19 Jan. 1863	20 June, 1864	
Stedman, Robert S.			17 Mar. 1863		
Steele, James	23 Sept, 1867				
Stell, John			18 Nov. 1862		
Stephens, Thomas A.			11 Jan. 1849	26 Feb. 1851	
Stevens, Benjamin R.			23 June, 1863		
Stevens, John C.			24 Feb. 1862	15 Oct. 1863	
Stevenson, Holland N.			2 June, 1868	2 June, 1869	
Stevenson, John K.			20 May, 1863		
Stewart, Henry H.			23 Mar. 1848	13 Sept. 1849	26 Feb. 1851
Stewart, Robert, Jr.	13 Sept. 1877	5 Aug. 1882			
Stickney, Herman O.		4 Sept. 1884			
Stiles, Edward A.			8 Sept. 1863	15 July, 1867	
Stimers, Alban C.			11 Jan. 1849	26 Feb. 1851	21 May, 1853
Stivers, George W.			2 Dec. 1861	8 Sept. 1863	11 Oct. 1866
Stivers, Henry H.	1 Oct. 1873				
Stone, Charles H.				24 Aug. 1861	
Strange, Clarence A.					
Strauss, Joseph	1 Oct. 1881	5 Aug. 1882			
Strickland, George D.					
Stuart, Charles B.					
Stump, T. B. C.			26 Feb. 1851	21 May, 1853	9 May, 1857
Sullivan, Lucien			12 July, 1861	18 Dec. 1862	
Sumwalt, Frederick G.			30 Aug. 1853		
Sunstrom, Mark T.			1 Feb. 1862	15 Oct. 1863	
Sutherland, Mosher A.			17 Mar. 1863	1 Sept. 1864	
Sweet, George F.			20 May, 1863		
Sydney, Joseph W.			3 Dec. 1861	8 Sept. 1863	
Symmes, Frank J.			2 June, 1868	2 June, 1869	
TAGGART, WILLIAM			5 Jan. 1843	10 July, 1847	
Talbot, Robert S.			22 Oct. 1860	26 Aug. 1862	24 Aug. 1864
Talbot, Zephaniel			3 May, 1859	13 May, 1861	20 May, 1863
Talcott, Charles G.	15 Sept. 1875				
Tapman, Henry T.			3 Aug. 1863		
Tawresey, John G.	1 Oct. 1881	5 Aug. 1882			
Taylor, David W.	1 Oct. 1881	5 Aug. 1882			
Taylor, Edward K.	1 Oct. 1878				
Taylor, P. Henry			16 Feb. 1852	21 May, 1853	
Taylor, Robert D.			21 Apr. 1863	25 July, 1866	31 Jan. 1873
Temple Arthur W.	15 Sept. 1875				
Tennent, George W.			17 Feb. 1860		
Tennent, John C.			10 July, 1847	31 Oct. 1848	
Theiss, Emil	1 Oct. 1878	5 Aug. 1882		18 Dec. 1862	
Thomas, Joseph H.			20 May, 1863	15 Sept. 1865	
Thompson, Gilbert, L.					

ASSISTANT ENGINEER.	PASSED ASSISTANT ENGINEER.	CHIEF ENGINEER.	REMARKS.
......	......	......	Resigned 21 Dec. 1873
......	......	14 Dec. 1864	Died 30 June, 1887
......	......	......	Resigned 17 June, 1873
20 June, 1880	20 Dec. 1889	......	Resigned 11 Oct. 1891
......	......	......	Retired 8 July 1873; died 18 Sept. 1874
......	......	......	Dropped 21 Mar. 1868
......	......	......	Resigned 18 Nov. 1845
......	......	......	Resigned 23 May, 1859
......	......	5 Mar. 1871	Died 15 Sept. 1881
10 June, 1882	......	......	Asst. Nav. Const. 11 Aug. 1887; Nav. Const. 9 July, '92
......	......	29 July, 1861	Retired 1 Dec. 1887
......	......	......	Ensign 1 July 1887; in service
......	......	......	Honorably discharged 30 June, 1886
......	......	......	Resigned 28 May, 1862
......	......	......	Resigned 22 Jan. 1883
......	......	......	Resigned 6 Oct. 1866
......	......	......	Resigned 5 April, 1865
......	......	......	Died 16 Aug. 1869, on board *Contoocook*
......	......	......	Resigned 18 Nov. 1863
......	......	......	Resigned 6 Sept. 1853; reappointed 1861; died 1864
......	......	......	Lost in the *Patapsco*, Jan. 15, 1865
......	......	......	Resigned 25 Oct. 1866
24 Feb. 1874	23 Dec. 1874	14 Dec. 1892	In service; Acting 3d Asst. Engr. N. Academy '66-'68
......	......	......	Dismissed 2 Aug. 1869
......	......	21 July, 1858	Retired 6 Sept. 1885; died 2 May. 1893
1 July, 1883	......	......	Retired 17 June, 1890
1 July, 1890	27 June, 1896	......	In service
......	......	......	Retired 24 Aug. 1866
......	......	21 July, 1858	Resigned 3 Aug. 1865
......	24 Feb. 1874	18 Dec. 1885	In service
1 July, 1878	......	......	Died 24 April, 1881
......	......	......	Resigned 10 June, 1865
30 Oct. 1875	......	......	Died 30 Dec. 1877
......	......	......	Ensign 1 July, 1887; in service
12 Jan. 1876	28 Apr. 1884	......	Retired 13 Feb. 1895
......	......	......	Engineer-in-Chief 1 Dec. 1850; resigned 30 June, 1853
......	......	......	Dropped (went south) 22 May, 1861
......	......	......	Resigned 5 April, 1866
......	......	......	Dismissed 29 Sept. 1864
......	......	......	Resigned 10 Nov. 1865
......	......	......	Resigned 15 Oct. 1867
......	......	......	Dismissed 30 Jan. 1869
......	......	......	Died 31 Oct. 1864, on board the *Pembina*
......	......	......	Resigned 18 July, 1871; Act. 3d Asst. Eng. under instructions at Naval Academy, '66-68
......	......	......	Resigned 12 May, 1849
......	......	......	Resigned 24 Oct. 1868
......	......	......	Resigned 16 Dec. 1865
10 June, 1881	......	......	Died 25 July, 1889, on board *Atlanta*
......	......	......	Dismissed 13 Sept. 1864
......	......	......	Ensign 1 July, 1887; Asst. Nav. Const. 1 July, 1889
......	......	......	Asst. Nav. Const. 14 Aug. 1886; Nav. Const. 5 Dec. '91
......	......	......	Died at Naval Academy 10 Dec. 1880
......	......	......	Resigned 10 Sept. 1856
......	24 Feb. 1874	......	Retired 23 April, 1892
......	......	......	Resigned 6 Feb. 1878
......	......	......	Resigned 6 Feb. 1861
......	......	......	Dismissed 5 July, 1849
1 July, 1884	1 Aug. 1894	......	In service
......	......	......	Resigned 29 Nov. 1873
......	......	......	Engineer-in-Chief 1 Sept. 1842; appt. revoked 3 Oct. '44

	CADET ENGINEER.	NAVAL CADET.	THIRD ASSISTANT ENGINEER.	SECOND ASSISTANT ENGINEER.	FIRST ASSISTANT ENGINEER.
Thompson, James................	......	......	......	......	......
Thompson, M. M.................	......	......	24 May, 1844	......	......
Thompson, Smith, Jr............	......	......	1 July, 1842	......	......
Thompson, Winfield S..........	......	......	16 Sept. 1858	......	......
Thomson, James W., Jr........	......	......	26 June, 1856	......	21 July, 1858
Thorne, George W...............	......	......	3 Aug. 1861	3 Aug. 1863	......
Thurston, Robert H.............	......	......	29 July, 1861	18 Dec. 1862	30 Jan. 1865
Tiffany, William H.............	1 Oct. 1871	......	......	......	......
Tobin, John A....................	......	......	......	4 Oct. 1870	......
Toppin, John D..................	......	......	1 July 1861	18 Dec. 1862	24 July, 1867
Tower, George E.................	......	......	17 Jan. 1862	1 Oct. 1863	1 Jan. 1868
Tower, George B. N............	......	......	21 Nov. 1857	2 Aug. 1859	16 Oct. 1861
Towne, Nathan P................	......	......	6 Jan. 1862	1 Oct. 1863	1 Jan. 1868
Townrow, Frederick W........	......	......	20 May, 1863	25 July, 1866	......
Townsend, Frank H.............	......	......	8 Sept. 1863	......	......
Trench, Martin E................	......	3 Oct. 1889	......	......	......
Trevor, Francis N...............	......	......	2 June, 1868	......	......
Trilley, Joseph...................	......	......	11 Aug. 1860	30 July, 1862	20 July, 1864
Tucker, John T...................	......	......	19 Feb. 1861	......	......
Tynan, John W...................	......	......	21 Nov. 1857	2 Aug. 1860	......
Tyson, Elijah H..................	......	......	3 Aug. 1863	......	......
UBER, CARLTON A..........	......	......	17 Mar. 1863	24 July, 1867	......
Uberroth, Preston H....	1 Oct. 1881	5 Aug. 1882	......	......	......
Upham, Joseph B................	......	......	18 Nov. 1862	23 Mar. 1864	1 Jan. 1868
VAN BUREN, JOHN D.....	......	......	13 May, 1861	21 Apr. 1863	1 Jan. 1865
Vanclain, James L.........	......	......	11 Aug. 1860	30 July, 1862	20 July, 1864
Vanderbilt, William W.........	......	......	18 Nov. 1862	23 Mar. 1864	......
Vanderslice, Thaddeus L......	......	......	8 Sept. 1863	15 Oct. 1865	......
Van Hovenberg, John.........	......	......	12 Aug. 1861	21 Apr. 1863	11 Oct. 1866
Van Tine, Charles M...........	......	......	16 Jan. 1863	28 May, 1864	......
Van Zandt, Joseph A...........	......	......	20 Feb. 1847	......	......
Victor, Henry C..................	......	......	2 Aug. 1855	20 Dec. 1860	1 July, 1861
Voorhees, Philip R..............	......	......	19 Feb. 1861	16 Jan. 1863	1 Dec. 1864
WALKER, CHARLES H.	......	8 Sept. 1891	......	......	......
Wallace, James..........	......	......	11 Nov. 1858	......	......
Walters, William L..............	......	......	21 May, 1857	......	......
Walton, Jesse F..................	......	......	25 Aug. 1862	......	......
Wamaling, Robert L............	......	......	8 July, 1862	......	......
Warburton, Edgar T............	1 Oct. 1872	......	......	......	......
Warfield, Louis E...............	1 Oct. 1881	5 Aug. 1882	......	......	......
Warner, Charles K..............	......	......	1 Feb. 1865	......	......
Warner, James H................	......	......	6 Feb. 1851	26 Feb. 1853	26 June, 1856
Warren, Benjamin H...........	1 Oct. 1871	......	......	......	......
Warrington, Joseph H.........	......	......	21 May, 1857	......	......
Washington, Pope................	......	7 Sept. 1892	......	......	......
Watters, Joseph..................	......	......	22 Oct. 1860	8 Dec. 1862	1 Dec. 1864
Watts, James E...................	......	......	17 Mar. 1863	28 Sept. 1864	......
Weaver, William D.............	14 Sept. 1876	......	......	......	......
Webb, Robert L..................	......	......	11 Feb. 1862	15 Oct. 1863	......
Webster, Charles F.............	1 Oct. 1879	5 Aug. 1882	......	......	......
Webster, Harrie..................	......	......	20 May, 1864	1 Jan. 1868	......
Webster, William T............	13 Sept. 1877	5 Aug. 1882	......	......	......
Wedderburn, Lawrence A.....	1 Oct. 1880	......	......	......	......
Weems, Edward D...............	......	......	25 Mar. 1862	1 Nov. 1863	......
Weir, Robert......................	......	......	25 Aug. 1862	20 Feb. 1864	......
Wells, Edwin......................	......	......	1 July, 1861	18 Dec. 1862	30 Jan. 1865
Wells, Chester....................	......	15 Nov. 1889	......	......	......
Wells, William S................	......	......	18 Nov. 1862	23 Mar. 1864	......

ASSISTANT ENGINEER.	PASSED ASSISTANT ENGINEER.	CHIEF ENGINEER.	REMARKS.
......	......	14 Apr. 1842	Resigned 3 July, 1845
......	......	......	Resigned 25 Aug. 1847
......	......	......	Resigned 13 Jan. 1846
......	......	......	Tendered resignation and left service (went south) '61
......	......	2 Feb. 1862	Ret red 26 June, 1896
......	......	......	Resigned 5 Nov. 1863
......	......	......	Resigned 1 April 1872
......	......	......	Dropped 24 Oct. 1872
24 Feb. 1874	2 Oct. 1877	......	Retired 20 Oct. 1890
......	......	......	Retired 11 May, 1867
......	24 Feb. 1874	30 June, 1887	In service
......	......	10 Nov. 1863	Resigned 29 Nov. 1865
......	24 Feb. 1874	3 July, 1887	Resigned 31 March, 1894
24 Feb. 1874	......	......	Dropped 11 June, 1878
......	......	......	Resigned 12 April, 1866
1 July, 1895	......	......	In service
......	......	......	Resigned '69; was Act's 3d Ass't Eng'r N. Acad..'66-'68
......	......	31 Jan. 1873	In service
......	......	......	Dropped (went south) 6 May, 1861
......	......	......	Dropped (went south) 6 May, 1861
......	......	......	Died 23 March, 1866 on board *Kearsarge* at sea
......	......	......	Retired 27 March, 1867
......	......	......	Resigned 11 June. 1885
......	24 Feb. 1874	......	Retired 27 Dec. 1875; died 13 Aug. 1889
......	......	......	Resigned 22 Sept. 1868
......	......	......	Died 27 Sept. 1874
......	......	......	Resigned 30 Oct. 1865
......	......	......	Resigned 31 Dec. 1871
......	24 Feb. 1874	23 Dec. 1884	Died 16 Oct. 1885
......	......	......	Resigned 4 Jan. 1866
......	......	......	Died 7 April, 1849
......	......	......	Resigned 16 Dec. 1863
......	......	......	Resigned 18 Feb. 1868
......	......	......	In service
......	......	......	Resigned 8 Aug. 1859
......	......	......	Died 27 May, 1858, on board *Merrimac*
......	......	......	Resigned 31 March, 1865
......	......	......	Resigned 17 Nov. 1865
1 July, 1878	1 July, 1887	......	In service
......	......	......	Resigned 10 June, 1 1884
......	......	......	Resigned 11 Oct. 1866
......	......	6 Dec. 1859	Dropped (went south) 8 July, 1861
26 Feb. 1875	......	......	Retired list 11 June, 1878
......	......	......	Resigned 1 Feb. 1860
......	......	......	In service
......	......	......	Died 13 Sept. 1866
......	......	......	Drowned 9 July, 1871
10 June, 1882	......	......	Resigned 24 Jan. 1892
......	......	......	Died 13 June, 1870
......	......	......	Honorably discharged 30 June, 1885
24 Feb. 1874	29 Oct. 1874	7 Oct. 1892	In service; was Act'g 3d Ass't Eng'r 1862-1864
......	......	......	Resigned 22 May, 1886
......	......	......	Killed at Naval Academy accidentally, 27 April, 1882
......	......	......	Resigned 6 Sept. 1867
......	......	......	Resigned 19 June, 1865
......	24 Feb. 1874	31 May 1880	Died 9 Jan. 1889 on board *Omaha*
17 Apr. 1896	......	......	In service
......	......	......	Resigned 12 Oct. 1870.

	CADET ENGINEER.	NAVAL CADET.	THIRD ASSISTANT ENGINEER.	SECOND ASSISTANT ENGINEER.	FIRST ASSISTANT ENGINEER.
Wemtz, Robert L...............	1 Oct. 1880	5 Aug. 1882	......	......	......
West, William H. G............	......	......	13 May, 1861	19 Feb. 1863	1 Jan. 1865
Wharton, Benjamin B. H....	......	......	21 Nov. 1857	2 Aug. 1859	16 Oct. 1861
Wheeler, William C............	......	......	14 Apr. 1847	26 Feb. 1851	26 June, 1856
Whipple, Edward A...........	......	......	10 July 1847	31 Oct. 1848	26 Feb. 1851
Whipple, John P................	......	......	13 Mar. 1847	13 Sept. 1849	26 Feb. 1851
Whitaker, Ezra J................	......	......	21 Feb. 1861	17 Dec. 1862	1 Dec. 1864
Whitaker, James W...........	......	......	21 Nov. 1857	2 Aug. 1859	16 Oct. 1861
White, George H................	......	......	{ 21 July,'68 { 23 May,'61	28 Oct. 1862	1 Jan. 1865
White, John M...................	1 Oct. 1873	......	......	......	......
White, Philip H.................	......	......	16 Oct. 1861	3 Aug. 1863	......
White, William W..............	13 Sept. 1877	5 Aug. 1882	......	......	......
Whitham, Jay M................	13 Sept. 1877	5 Aug. 1882	......	......	......
Whittemore, John W.........	......	......	24 Aug. 1861	......	......
Whittle, Llewellyn Fairfax..	13 Sept. 1877	......	......	......	......
Whittlesey, Humes H.........	1 Oct. 1880	5 Aug. 1882	......	......	......
Wight, Charles L...............	1 Oct. 1874	......	......	......	......
Wilkinson, George W.........	......	......	21 Sept. 1861	......	......
Willett, William. M., Jr......	......	......	24 Dec. 1853	......	......
Williams, Lloyd A..............	......	......	16 Feb. 1852	9 May, 1857	2 Aug. 1859
Williamson, Thom	......	......	21 May, 1853	27 June,1855	21 July, 1858
Williamson, William C.......	......	......	19 Feb. 1861	16 Jan. 1863	1 Dec. 1864
Williamson, William P.......	......	......	......	......	......
Willis, Clarence C..............	1 Oct. 1878	5 Aug. 1882	......	......	......
Willits, Albert B................	1 Oct. 1872	......	......	......	......
Willits, George S...............	1 Oct. 1873	......	......	......	......
Wilmer Joseph R...............	1 Oct. 1874	......	......	......	......
Wilson, Fletcher A.............	......	......	26 Aug. 1859	21 Oct. 1861	1 Oct. 1863
Wilson, James P................	5 Oct. 1866	......	......	......	......
Wilson, John.....................	......	......	19 Feb. 1861	17 Dec. 1862	......
Winchell, Ward P..............	1 Oct. 1878	5 Aug. 1882	......	......	......
Windsor, William A...........	......	......	16 Sept. 1862	1 Mar. 1864	1 Jan. 1868
Winship, Emory................	......	3 June,1890	......	......	......
Winsor, Horace E..............	......	......	21 May 1853	27 July, 1855	......
Wood, Benjamin F............	......	......	1 July, 1861	21 Apr. 1863	11 Oct. 1866
Wood, Joseph L................	14 Sept. 1876	......	......	......	......
Wood, William W. W........	......	......	......	......	......
Woodend, George R..........	......	......	21 May, 1853	......	......
Woods, Arthur T...............	14 Sept. 1876	......	......	......	......
Woodruff, Charles E.........	1 Oct. 1879	5 Aug. 1882	......	......	......
Wooster, Lucius W............	1 Oct. 1871	......	......	23 Jan. 1874	......
Worthington, John L.........	14 Sept. 1876	......	......	......	......
Worthington, Walter F......	1 Oct. 1873	......	......	......	......
Wright, Henry X...............	......	......	3 May, 1859	......	......
Wright, James D...............	......	......	21 July, 1858	17 Jan. 1861	......
Wright, Robert A..............	......	......	10 June,1862	12 Nov. 1863	......
Wylie, James.....................	......	......	19 Feb. 1863	20 June,1864	......
YARNALL, JOHN H........	15 Sept. 1875	......	......	......	......
Young, Albert O...............	14 Sept. 1876	......	......	......	......
Young, James G................	......	......	27 Jan. 1848	6 Nov. 1849	26 Feb. 1851
Young, Jefferson...............	......	......	......	......	21 Sept. 1861
ZANE, ABRAHAM, V......	1 Oct. 1871	......	......	......	......
Zeller, Theodore.........	......	......	15 June, 1843	10 July, 1847	6 Nov. 1849
Ziegler, John Q. A............	......	......	......	......	......
Zinnell, George F..............	1 Oct. 1879	......	......	......	......

ASSISTANT ENGINEER.	PASSED ASSISTANT ENGINEER.	CHIEF ENGINEER.	REMARKS.
28 June, 1889	......	......	Resigned 30 June, 1890
......	......	......	Drowned 19 July, 1872
......	......	10 Nov. 1863	Retired 14 Jan. 1895
......	......	10 Apr. 1861	Dismissed 17 January, 1863
......	......	......	Resigned 20 Feb. 1854
......	......	27 June, 1885	Died 26 Sept. 1864
......	......	6 June, 1873	Retired 8 May, 1895; died 21 Aug. 1895
......	......	10 Nov. 1863	Died 9 Mar. 1881
......	......	23 Nov. 1878	Retired 18 Nov. 1890; died 23 Feb. 1891
......	......	......	Resigned 29 Oct. 1873
......	......	......	Resigned 27 April, 1865
1 July, 1883	16 Nov. 1893	......	In service
1 July, 1883	......	......	Resigned 1 Feb. 1886
......	......	......	Killed in action 7 Nov. 1861 on board *Mohican*
......	......	......	Died on practice cruise 23 July, 1880
......	......	......	Ensign 1 July, 1886; in service
......	......	......	Resigned 1 July 1882
......	......	......	Resigned 23 Sept. 1863
......	......	......	Resigned 6 Mar. 1857
......	......	24 July, 1867	Retired 20 Dec. 1866; died 28 Dec. 1873
......	......	5 Aug. 1861	Retired 5 Aug. 1895
......	......	......	Resigned 10 Jan. 1866
......	......	20 Oct. 1842	Dropped 6 May, 1861; Eng.-in-Ch. Confederate Navy
1 July, 1884	......	......	Retired 28 June, 1890; died 11 June, 1895
26 Feb. 1875	12 Oct. 1881	28 Mar. 1896	In service
1 July, 1877	1 July, 1885	4 July, 1896	In service
20 June, 1880	10 Jan. 1891	......	Retired 4 Mar. 1892
......	......	5 Mar. 1871	In service
......	......	......	Resigned 30 Mar. 1868
......	......	......	Resigned 19 May, 1866
1 July, 1884	21 Mar. 1895	......	In service
......	24 Feb. 1874	17 June, 1889	In service
1 July, 1896	......	......	In service
......	......	......	Resigned 20 Aug. 1856
......	24 Feb. 1874	14 Dec. 1883	Retired 6 Oct. 1892
10 June, 1882	......	......	Retired 11 Nov. 1893
......	......	15 Mar. 1845	Engineer-in-Chief '73-'77; retired list '80; drowned '82
......	......	......	Resigned 20 April, 1857
10 June, 1882	......	......	Resigned 11 July, 1887
......	......	......	Dropped 28 Feb. 1883
24 Feb. 1874	1 Nov. 1879	......	Retired 29 June, 1887
......	......	......	Died 14 July, 1881
1 July, 1877	19 July, 1885	......	In service
......	......	......	Dropped (went South) 6 May, 1861
......	......	......	Resigned 16 Oct. 1861
......	......	......	Resigned 16 Oct. 1865
......	......	......	Died 26 April, 1869
......	......	......	Resigned 22 June, 1877
10 June, 1882	......	......	Resigned 30 June, 1888
......	......	......	Resigned 14 Nov. 1855
......	......	......	Retired 7 Mar. 1871; died 3 July, 1894
26 Feb. 1875	27 Aug. 1881	11 Sept. 1895	In service
......	......	27 June, 1855	Retired list 1 Dec. 1885
......	......	18 June, 1868	Act. 1st Asst. and Ch. Eng. '62-'68; died 6 July, 1885
......	......	......	Resigned 9 June, 1883

APPENDIX B.

A LIST of Steam Vessels of War that have been built for the United States Navy, from the *Fulton* of 1814 to the vessels authorized by the Fifty-third Congress. Including also the names of some of the most noted steamers that have been purchased and fitted as war vessels for the navy.

The names have been arranged in chronological order that the reader may readily identify the design of hull and machinery of any vessel with the period to which it pertains. The date given in each case is that when actual work of building the vessel was begun, that being a much closer index of the period of design and type than the date of launching usually given, the latter date in many cases having been so delayed that the type of vessel and machinery had become obsolete. All machinery data refers to original machinery of vessel.

The cost price of vessels given in these tables is the contract or actual cost of the *ship* proper—hull and machinery—and does not include the cost of guns, armor, furniture and equipment. In the case of a heavily armed and armored vessel a considerable part of the total cost is for guns and armor. The actual cost of the new battleship *Indiana*, for example, was practically twice the contract price, the chief items being distributed as follows:

Hull and machinery (including hull armor, premium and cost of trial)	$4,133,393.10
Armor for gun protection	977,134.02
Armament	966,567.58
Equipment	95,691.45
Total cost to date of being commissioned	$6,172,786.15

DATE.	NAME.	MATERIAL	PROPULSION.	DISPLACE-MENT, TONS.	TONNAGE.	LENGTH.	BEAM.
1814	Fulton............ (*Demologos.*)	Wood.....	Center wheel...		2,475	156′	56′
1822	Sea Gull	"	Side wheel.......		100		
1836	Engineer................	"	"		142	105′	17′ 2″
1836	Fulton................ (second of name.)	"	"	1,200	750	180′	34′ 10″
1839	Mississippi.............	"	"	3,220	1,692	229′	40′
1839	Missouri................	"	Hunter wheels	3,220	1,700	229′	40′
1841	Union.................	"	Side wheels......	900		185′	33′
1842	Michigan	Iron	Hunter wheels.	685	582	167′ 3″	27′ 1″
1843	Water-Witch......... (first of name)	"	Screw............		190	100′ 6″	21′ 4″
1843	Princeton............. (first of name)	Wood.....	Hunter wheels, afterw'd screw	954	672	164′	30′ 6″
1844	Alleghany	Iron.......	Side wheels......	1,020		185′	33′ 4″
1847	Susquehanna...........	Wood	"	3,824	2,450	250′	45′
1847	Powhatan.	"	"	3,765	2,415	253′ 8″	45′
1847	Saranac	"	"	2,200	1,446	215′ 6″	37′ 9″
1847	San Jacinto............	"	Screw............	2,200	1,446	215′ 6″	37′ 9″
1849	John Hancock......... (first)	"	"		208	113′	22′
1851	Princeton............. (second)	"	Screw............	1,370	900	178′	33′ 8″
1852	Water-Witch........... (second)	"	Side wheels		378	150′	23′
1852	John Hancock........ (second)	"	Screw		382	151′	22′
1853	Franklin	"	"	5,170	3,173	265′	53′ 8″
1854	Merrimack.............	"	"	4.636	3,200	256′ 9″	51′ 4″
1854	Wabash................	"	"	4,774.3	3,200	262′ 4″	51′ 4″
1854	Minnesota.............	"	"	4,833.4	3,200	264′ 8½″	51′ 4″
1854	Roanoke...............	"	"	4,772.2	3,400	263′ 8¼″	52′ 6″
1854	Colorado...............	"	"	4,772.2	3,400	263′ 8¼″	52′ 6″
1854	Niagara................	"	"	5,540	4,580	328′10½″	55′
1854	Stevens Battery........	Iron Armored	2 screws.........	6,000		420′	53′
1855	Arctic	Wood	Screw		235		
1855	Despatch	"			538		
1857	Brooklyn	"	Screw	2,686	2,070	233′	42′

BY WHOM AND WHERE BUILT.		COST.	REMARKS.
HULL.	MACHINERY.		
A. & N. Brown, New York	Robert Fulton, New York	$ 320,000.00	Destroyed by explosion, 1829.
Steam galliot, bought in New York	Steam galliot, bought in New York	16,000.00	Sold, 1840.
Bought in Baltimore	Bought in Balitimore	18,997.00	Despatch boat, Norfolk navy yard.
U.S. Govt, Navy Yard, New York	West Point Foundry Association, N Y.	299,649.81	In service 1838; burned by Confederates 1862.
U. S. Government Navy Yard, Phila	Merrick & Town, Philadelphia	569,670.70	Destroyed at Port Hudson, 1863.
U. S. Govt., Navy Yard, New York	West Point Foundry Association, N. Y.	568,806.00	Burned at Gibraltar, 1853.
U. S. Govt. Norfolk Navy Yard	U. S. Govt. Washington Navy Yard	158,128.60	Laid up at Philadelphia, 1848.
Stackhouse & Tomlinson, Pittsburg, Pa.	Stackhouse & Tomlinson, Pittsburg, Pa.	165,000.00	In commission.
U.S. Govt. Navy Yard, Washington, D. C.	U.S. Govt. Navy Yard, Washington, D. C.	53,648.00	Condemned, 1851.
U.S. Govt. Navy Yard, Phila	Merrick & Towne, Philadelphia, Pa.	212,615.00	Broken up at Boston, 1849.
Jos. Tomlinson, Pittsburg, Pa.	Jos. Tomlinson, Pittsburg, Pa.	242,595.92	Sold 1869.
U. S. Govt. Navy Yard, Phila.	Murray & Hazlehurst, Baltimore, Md.	697,215.00	Sold 1863.
U. S. Govt. Navy Yard, Norfolk	Mehaffy & Co. Gosport, Va.	795,221.00	Sold 1887.
U. S. Govt. Navy Yard, Kittery, Me.	Coney & Co. Boston, Mass	388,368.00	Wrecked, 1875.
U. S. Govt. Navy Yard, New York	Merrick & Towne, Philadelphia, Pa	408,885.00	Wrecked, 1865.
Navy Yard, Boston, Mass.	Navy Yard, Washington, D. C.	20,550.72	See John Hancock, 2d below.
Navy Yard, Boston, Mass.	Vulcan Iron Works, Baltimore, Md.	259,460.00	Sold, 1866.
Navy Yard, Washington, D. C.	Engines 1st *Waterwitch* reb'lt Wash. Navy Y'd	74,725.00	Captured by boarding June 3, 1864.
U. S. Navy Yard, Boston.	Atlantic Works, Boston, Mass.		Sold 1865.
U. S. Navy Yard, Kittery, Me.	U. S. Navy Yard, Boston.	1,331,000.00	Receiving ship, Norfolk.
U. S. Navy Yard, Boston.	R. P. Parrot, Cold Spring, N. Y.	752,279.71	Into hands of Confederates, 1861.
Navy Yard, Philadelphia, Pa.	Merrick & Sons, Philadelphia, Pa	892,373.46	Receiving ship, Boston.
Navy Yard, Washington, D. C.	Navy Yard Washington, D. C	846,336.93	In action with *Merrimac* (or *Virginia*), 1862; Mass. Naval Res.
Navy Yard, Norfolk, Va.	Tredegar Iron Works, Richmond, Va.	836,752.36	Sold, 1883.
Navy Yard, Norfolk, Va.	Tredegar Iron Works, Richmond, Va.	905,338.24	Sold 1885.
Navy Yard, New York	Pease & Murphy, New York	1,057,210.14	Sold 1885.
R. L. Stevens, Hoboken, N. J.	R. L. Stevens, Hoboken, N. J.		Never completed.
			Turned over to lighthouse board, 1859.
		139,038.17	See Pocahontas.
J. Westervelt, New York	Jas. Murphy, Fulton Eng. Wks., N. Y.	432,113.71	Sold 1891.

DATE.	NAME.	MATERIAL.	PROPULSION.	DISPLACEMENT, TONS.	TONNAGE.	LENGTH.	BEAM.
1857	Hartford	Wood	Screw	2,550	1,900	225'	44'
1857	Lancaster	"	"	3,290	2,362	235' 8"	46'
1857	Richmond	"	"	2,604	1,929	225'	42'
1857	Pensacola	"	"	3,000	2,158	230' 8"	44' 6"
1858	Saginaw	"	Side wheel		453		
1858	Mohican	"	Screw	1,461	994	198' 9"	33'
1858	Iroquois	"	"	1,488	1,016	198' 11"	33' 10"
1858	Wyoming	"	"	1,457	997	198' 6"	33' 2"
1858	Dacotah	"	"	1,369	996	198' 6"	32' 9"
1858	Narragansett	"	"	1,235	804	188'	30' 4"
1858	Seminole	"	"	1,230	801	188'	30' 6"
1858	Pawnee	"	Twin-screws	1,533	1,289	221' 6"	47'
1859	Pocahontas	"	Screw		694		28' 6"
1859	Pulaski	"	Side wheel		395		
1859	Wyandotte	"	Screw		464		
1859	Mohawk	"	"		464		
1859	Crusader	"	"		549		
1859	Sumter	"	"		464		
1859	Mystic	"	"		464		
1859	Anacostia	"	"		217		
1861	Aroostook	"	"	691	507	158' 4"	28'
1861	Cayuga	"	"		"		"
1861	Chippewa	"	"		"		"
1861	Chocura	"	"		"		"
1861	Huron	"	"		"		"
1861	Itaska	"	"		"		"
1861	Kanawha	"	"		"		"
1861	Katahdin	"	"		"		"
1861	Kennebec	"	"		"		"
1861	Kineo	"	"		"		"

BY WHOM AND WHERE BUILT.		COST.	REMARKS.
HULL.	MACHINERY.		
Navy Yard, Boston, Mass	Loring & Conry, Boston, Mass	$502,650.16	Laid up at Mare Island.
Philadelphia Navy Yard	Reanie & Neafie, Philadelphia, Pa	668,769.00	Gunnery practice ship.
Norfolk Navy Yard	Navy Yard, Washington, D. C.	566,259.46	Receiving ship League Island.
Navy Yard, Pensacola, Florida	Navy Yard, Washington, D. C.	613,252.16	Laid up Mare Island.
Navy Yard, Mare Island	Union Iron Works, San Francisco	341,493.82	Wrecked 1870.
Navy Yard, Kittery, Me	Woodruff & Beach, Hartford, Conn		Pacific station.
Navy Yard, N. Y	Fulton Iron Works, New York	323,830.81	Laid up at Mare Island.
Navy Yard, Philadelphia, Pa	Merrick & Sons. Phila. Pa	338,309.04	Sold.
Navy Yard, Norfolk, Va	Murray & Hazelhurst. Baltimore, Md	355,539.40	Sold 1873
Navy Yard, Boston, Mass	Boston Locomotive Works	297,158.54	Sold 1883.
Navy Yard, Pensacola, Florida	Morgan Iron Works, N. Y	257,418.91	Sold 1870.
Navy Yard, Philadelphia, Pa	Reanie & Neafie, Phila. Pa	457,151.12	Sold 1884.
Purchased	Purchased	139,038.17	Purchased 1855 as Despatch. Sold 1865.
Purchased	Purchased	100,000.00(?)	Sold 1863.
Purchased	Purchased	74,525.51	Sold 1865.
Purchased	Purchased	72,739.85	Sold 1864.
Purchased	Purchased	81,708.03	Sold 1865.
Purchased	Purchased	69,362.51	Sunk by collision 1863
Purchased	Purchased	70,170.76	Sold 1865.
Purchased	Purchased	38,092.45	Sold 1865.
N. W. Thompson Kennebunk, Me	Novelty Iron Works, N. Y	98,814.35	Sold.
Gildersleeve & Son, Portland, Me	Woodruff & Beach, Hartford, Conn	97,912.22	Sold 1865.
Webb & Bell, N. Y	Morgan Iron Works, New York	101,235.00	Sold 1865.
Curtis & Tilden, Boston, Mass	Harrison Loring, Boston, Mass	99,912.01	Sold 1867.
Paul Curtis, Boston, Mass	Harrison Loring, Boston, Mass	101,421.00	Sold 1869.
Hillman & Streaker, Phila. Pa	I. P. Morris & Co., Phila	98,786.57	Sold 1865.
E. G. & W. H. Goodspeed East Haddam, Conn.	Pacific Iron Works, Bridgeport, Conn	97,775.00	Sold 1866.
Larrabee & Allen, Bath, Maine	Morgan Iron Works, New York	98,868.85	Sold 1865.
G. W. Lawrence. Thomaston, Maine	Novelty Iron Works, New York	103,694.76	Sold 1865.
J. W. Dyre, Portland, Me	Morgan Iron Works, New York	101,182.30	Sold 1866.

DATE.	NAME.	MATERIAL	PROPULSION.	DISPLACE-MENT, TONS.	TONNAGE. (Old)	LENGTH.	BEAM.
1861	Marblehead	Wood	Screw	691	507	158-4	28
1861	Ottawa	"	"	"	"	"	"
1861	Owasco	"	"	"	"	"	"
1861	Pembina	"	"	"	"	"	"
1861	Penobscot	"	"	"	"	"	"
1861	Pinola	"	"	"	"	"	"
1861	Sagamore	"	"	"	"	"	"
1861	Sciota	"	"	"	"	"	"
1861	Seneca	"	"	"	"	"	"
1861	Tahoma	"	"	"	"	"	"
1861	Unadilla	"	"	"	"	"	"
1861	Winona	"	"	"	"	"	"
1861	Wissahickon	"	"	"	"	"	"
1861	Cimmerone	"	Side wheel	993	860	217.5	36
1861	Conemaugh	"	"	1,105	955	232	35
1861	Genesee	"	"	1,120	803	207	35
1861	Mahaska	"	"	1,070	832	225.33	33' 10'
1861	Maratanza	"	"		786	207	33
1861	Miami	"	"		730		
1861	Octorora	"	"	981	829	205	34.5
1861	Paul Jones	"	"	1,210	863	216' 10''	35' 4''
1861	Port Royal	"	"	1,163	805	207	35
1861	Sebago	"	"	1,070	852	225' 4''	33' 10''
1861	Sonoma	"	"	1,105	955	232	35
1861	Tioga	"	"	1,120	819	207	36' 11''
1861	Juniata	"	Screw	1,934	1,240	205	38
1861	Adirondack	"	"	1,934	1,240	205	38
1861	Housatonic	"	"	1,934	1,240	205	38
1861	Ossipee	"	"	1,934	1,240	205	38
1861	Kearsarge	"	"	1,461	1,031	198' 9''	33' 10''

BY WHOM AND WHERE BUILT.		COST.	REMARKS.
HULL.	MACHINERY.		
G. W. Jackman, Newburyport, Mass	Highland Iron Works, Newbury, N. Y.	97,736.75	Sold 1868.
J. A. Westervelt, New York	Novelty Iron Works, New York	88,240.37	Sold 1865.
Maxon, Fish & Co., Mystic River, Conn.	Novelty Iron Works, New York	99,750.00	Sold 1865.
Thomas Stack, New York, N. Y.	Novelty Iron Works, New York	88,225.00	Sold 1865.
C. P. Carter, Belfast, Me	Allain Works, New York	98,241.52	Sold 1869.
J. J. Abrahams, Baltimore, Md.	Charles Reeder, Baltimore	96,735.47	Sold 1865.
A. & G. T. Sampson, Boston, Mass.	Atlantic Works, Boston	101,681.52	Sold 1866.
Jacob Bireley, Philadelphia, Penna.	I. P. Morris & Co., Philadelphia	96,279.43	Sunk by torpedo, 1865.
Jeremiah Simonson, New York	Novelty Iron Works, New York	88,248.61	Sold 1868.
W. & A. Thatcher, Wilmington, Del.	Reany, Son & Archbold, Chester, Pa.	100,486.88	Sold 1867.
John Englis, New York	Novelty Iron Works, New York	88,000.00	Sold 1869.
C. & R. Poillon, New York	Allain Works, New York	101,240.00	Sold 1865.
John Lynn, Philadelphia	Merrick & Sons, Philadelphia, Pa.	98,771.72	Sold 1865.
D. S. Merchon, Jr., Bordentown, N. J.	D. S. Merchon, Jr., Borta, N. J.	100,000.00	Sold 1866.
Navy Yard, Kittery, Me	Novelty Iron Works, New York	193,416.70	Sold 1867.
Navy Yard, Boston	Neptune Works, New York	190,423.63	Sold 1867.
Navy Yard, Kittery, Me	Morgan Iron Works, New York	210,137.78	Sold 1868.
Navy Yard, Boston	Harrison Loring, Boston	187,128.19	Sold 1868.
Navy Yard, Philadelphia	Merrick & Sons, Philadelphia	172,341.25	Sold 1865.
Navy Yard, New York	Neptune Works, New York	173,071.81	Sold 1866.
J. J. Abrahams, Baltimore	Reany, Son and Archbold, Chester, Pa.	102,603.33	Sold 1867.
T. Stack, N. Y. (by contract in Navy Yard).	Thomas Stack, N. Y. (sub-con. Nov. W'ks.)	100,057.00	Sold 1866.
Navy Yard, Kittery, Me	Novelty Works, New York	212,771.22	Sold 1867.
Navy Yard, Kittery, Me	Novelty Works, New York	194,962.34	Sold 1867.
Navy Yard, Boston	Morgan Iron Works, New York,	199,852.14	Sold 1867.
Navy Yard, Philadelphia	Pusey, Jones & Co., Wilmington, Del.	364,820.26	Sold 1891.
Navy Yard, New York	Novelty Works, New York	411,529.38	Wrecked 1862.
Navy Yard, Boston	Jabez Coney & Co., Boston	368,817.63	Sunk by torpedo '64; raised; sold '91
Navy Yard, Kittery, Me	Reliance Machine Co., Mystic, Conn.	363,787.10	Sold 1891.
Navy Yard, Kittery, Me	Woodruff & Beach, Hartford, Conn.	286,918.05	Wrecked 1894.

DATE	NAME.	MATERIAL.	PROPULSION.	DISPLACE-MENT, TONS.	TONNAGE (OLD).	LENGTH.	BEAM.
1861	Oneida	Wood	Screw	1,488	1,032	198' 11''	33' 10''
1861	Tuscarora	"	"	1,457	997	198' 6''	33' 2''
1861	Wachusett	"	"	1,488	1,032	198' 11''	33' 10''
1861	Canandaigua	"	"	2,030	1,395	225	38' 4''
1681	Lackawanna	"	"	2,526	1,533	234' 4''	38' 2'
1861	Monongahela	"	"	2,078	1,378	225	37' 9''
1861	Sacramento	"	"	2,100	1,367	229	38
1861	Shenandoah	"		2,030	1,378	225	38' 4''
1861	Ticonderoga	"		2,526	1,533	234' 4''	38' 2''
1861	Monitor	Iron	Screw	987	776	172'	41' 6''
1861	Galena (first)	Wood (ironpl'g)	"		738		
1861	New Ironsides	Wood (iron s. a.)	"	4,120	3,486	232	57' 6''
1862	Kansas	Wood	"	836	593	179' 6''	30
1862	Maumee	"	"	"	"	"	"
1862	Nipsic (first)	"	"	"	"	"	"
1862	Nyack	"	"	"	"	"	"
1862	Pequot	"	"	"	"	"	"
1862	Saco	"	"	"	"	"	"
1862	Shawmut	"	"	"	"	"	"
1862	Yantic	"	"	"	"	"	"
1862	Agawan	"	Side wheels	1,173	974	240	35
1862	Algonquin	"	"	"	"	"	"
1862	Ascutney	"	"	"	"	"	"
1862	Chenango	"	"	"	"	"	"
1862	Chicopee	"	"	"	"	"	"
1862	Eutaw	"	"	"	"	"	"
1862	Tosco	"	"	"	"	"	"
1862	Lenapee	"	"	"	"	"	"
1862	Mackinaw	"	"	"	"	"	"
1862	Massasoit	"	"	"	"	"	"

BY WHOM AND WHERE BUILT.		COST.	REMARKS.
HULL.	MACHINERY.		
Navy Yard, New York	J. Murphy & Co, New York......................	$ 294,697.54	Run into and sunk 1870.
Navy Yard, Philadelphia......................	Merrick & Sons, Philadelphia..................	280,090.91	Sold 1883.
Navy Yard, Boston......	Morgan Iron Works, New York............	314,362.85	Sold 1887.
Navy Yard, Boston......	Atlantic Works, Boston.........................	388,541.84	Broken up 1887.
Navy Yard, New York	Allaire Works, New York......................	451,069.00	Sold 1887.
Navy Yard, Philadelphia......................	Merrick & Sons, Philadelphia..................	373,796,39	Training squadron.
Navy Yard, Kittery, Me.......................	Taunton Loco. Mfg. Co. Taunton, Mass.........	393,218.50	Wrecked 1867.
Navy Yard, Philadelphia......................	Merrick & Sons, Philadelphia......	379,717.64	Sold 1887.
Navy Yard, New York	Allaire Works, New York......................	425,426.63	Sold 1887.
Cont'l I'n W'ks, N. Y. (by sub-contract).....	Delamater Iron Works, New York.............	275,000.00	Foundered off Hatteras 1862.
C. S. Bushnell, Conn. (s.-con. Maxon-Fish,	Delamater Iron Works, (sub-contract).........	235,250.00	Broken up about 1871.
Cramp's Shipy'd, Phila. (sub-contract)..........	Merrick & Sons, Philadelphia..................	814,866.83	Burned 1866.
Navy Yard, Philadelphia......................	Captured on *Princess Royal*, English make	212,316.78	Sold 1883.
Navy Yard, New York	Stover Machine Co., New York.............	258,408.93	Sold 1869.
Navy Yard, Kittery, Me.......................	Woodruff & Beach, Hartford, Conn.......	255,943.99	Broken up about 1875.
Navy Yard, New York	S. Brooklyn Eng. Wks. Brooklyn, N. Y......	257,952.12	Sold 1883.
Navy Yard, Boston......	Woodruff & Beach, Hartford, Conn........	249,231.99	Sold 1869.
Navy Yard, Boston......	Corliss St. Eng. Co., Providence, R. I......	274,845.14	Sold 1883.
Navy Yard, Kittery, Me.......................	Corliss St. Eng. Co., Providence, R. I......	232,639.53	Sold 1883.
Navy Yard, Philadelphia......................	Merrick & Sons, Philadelphia..................	206,262.93	In commission.
George W. Lawrence, Portland, Me...........	Portland Loco. Works, Portland, Maine......	161,345.42	Sold 1867.
Navy Yard, New York	Prov. St. Eng. Co., Providence, R. I......	277,372.24	Sold 1869.
George W. Jackson, Newburyport, Mass..	Morgan Iron Works, New York	176,143.73	Sold 1868.
J, Simonson, New York......................	Morgan Iron Works, New York.............	161,273.71	Sold 1868.
Paul Curtis, Boston, Mass.........	Neptune Works, New York....................	163,239.85	Sold 1867.
J. J. Abrahams, Baltimore, Md..............	Vulcan Iron Works, Baltimore...............	160,200.00	Sold 1867.
Larrabee & Allen, Bath, Me........	Globe Works, Boston, Mass....................	164,768.68	Sold 1867.
Edward Lupton, New York......................	Washington Iron Wks. Newburgh, N. Y......	163,423.48	Sold 1868.
Navy Yard, New York	Allaire Works, New York......................	251,480.07	Sold 1867.
Curtis & Tilden, Boston, Mass...............	Globe Works, Boston.........................	160,630.41	Sold 1867.

DATE.	NAME.	MATERIAL	PROPULSION.	DISPLACEMENT, TONS.	TONNAGE. (Old).	LENGTH.	BEAM.
1862	Mattabessett	Wood	Side wheels	1,173	974	240	35
1862	Mendota	"	"	"	"	"	"
1862	Metacomet	"	"	"	"	"	"
1862	Mingoe	"	"	"	"	"	"
1862	Osceola	"	"	"	"	"	"
1862	Otsego	"	"	"	"	"	"
1862	Pawtuxet	"	"	"	"	"	"
1862	Peoria	"	"	"	"	"	"
1862	Pontiac	"	"	"	"	"	"
1862	Poutoosuc	"	"	"	"	"	"
1862	Sassacus	"	"	"	"	"	"
1862	Shamrock	"	"	"	"	"	"
1862	Tacony	"	"	"	"	"	"
1862	Tallahoma	"	"	"	"	"	"
1862	Tallapoosa	"	"	"	"	"	"
1862	Wateree	Iron	"	"	"	"	"
1862	Winooski	Wood	"	"	"	"	"
1862	Wyalusing	"	"	"	"	"	"
1862	Dunderberg	Wood— Ironarm'r	Screw	7,000	5,090	380' 4''	72' 10''
1862	Keokuk	"	"		677	159	36
1862	Chillicothe	Wood— Ir'ncasmt	2 screws and side wheels		203	155	50
1862	Indianola	"	"		442		
1862	Tuscumbia	"	"		565		
1862	Camanche	Iron	Screw	1,875	344	200	46
1862	Catskill	"	"	"	"	"	"
1862	Lehigh	"	"	"	"	"	"
1862	Montauk	"	"	"	"	"	"
1862	Nahant	"	"	"	"	"	"
1862	Nantucket	"	"	"	"	"	"
1862	Passaic	"	"	"	"	"	"

BY WHOM AND WHERE BUILT.		COST.	REMARKS.
HULL.	MACHINERY.		
A. & G. Sampson, Boston, Mass.	Allaire Works, New York.	$ 163,595.17	Sold 1867.
F. Z. Tucker, Brooklyn, New York.	S. Brooklyn, Engine Works, Brooklyn.	159,631.53	Sold 1867.
Thos. Stack, New York.	S. Brooklyn, Engine Works, Brooklyn.	159,081.27	Sold 1868.
D. S. Mershon, Bordentown, N. J.	Pusey, Jones, & Co. Wilmington, Del.	152,236.00	Sold 1867.
Curtis & Tilden, Boston.	Atlantic Works, Boston.	160,575.41	Sold 1867.
J. & D. Westervelt, New York.	Fulton Iron Works New York.	161,143.44	Sunk by torpedo 1864.
Navy Yard. Kittery, Me.	Prov. St. Eng. Co Prov R. I.	241,439.39	Sold 1867.
Navy Yard, New York.	Etna Iron Works New York.	305,199.73	Sold 1868.
Hillman & Streaker, Phila. Pa.	Neafie, Levy & Co. Philadelphia.	163,561.00	Sold 1867.
Geo. W. Lawrence, Portland, Me.	Portland Locomotive Works, Portland.	163,031.58	Sold 1866.
Navy Yard, Kittery, Me.	Atlantic Works, Boston.	249,037.97	Sold 1868.
Navy Yard, New York.	Poole & Hunt, Baltimore.	268,000.58	Sold 1868.
Navy Yard, Philadelphia.	Morris, Towne & Co. Philadelphia.	266,718.23	Sold 1868.
Navy Yard, New York.	Stover Mach. Co. New York.	256,824.52	Sold 1868.
Navy Yard, Boston.	Neptune Works, New York.	241,856.98	Sold 1892.
Reany, Son, & Archbold, Chester, Pa.	Reany, Son & Archbold Chester, Pa.	203,170.00	Wrecked 1868.
Navy Yard, Boston.	Prov. St. Eng. Co. Providence, R. I.	239,617.47	Sold 1868.
C. H. & W. H. Cramp, Philadelphia.	Pusey, Jones & Co. Wilmington, Del.	162,914.84	Sold 1867.
Wm. H. Webb, New York.	J. Roach, Etna Iron Works, New York.	1,250,000.00	Sold to French Government.
J. S. Underhill, I. W'ks for C. W. Whitney.	J. S. Underhill, I. W'ks. for C. W. Whitney.	227,507.02	Sunk, Fort Sumter 1863.
McCord&Junger, New Albany, Ind.	McCord & Junger, New Albany, Ind.	92,960.00	Sold 1865.
Jos. Brown, Cincinnati O.	Jos. Brown, Cincinnati, O.	182,372.00	Captured by Confederates 1863.
Jos. Brown, Cincinnati O.	Jos. Brown, Cincinnati, O.	229,669.73	Sold 1868.
Secor Bros, Jersey City & San Francisco.	Jos. Colwell, Jersey City.	613,164.98	Laid up.
Continental Iron Works, Greenpoint.	C. H. Delamater, New York.	427,766.78	Laid up.
Reany, Son & Archbold, Chester, Pa.	Morris, Towne & Co Philadelphia.	422,726.28	Laid up.
Continental Iron Works, Greenpoint.	C. H. Deamater, New York.	423,027.49	See text.
Harrison Loring, Boston.	City Point Works, Mass.	413,515.14	Laid up.
Atlantic Works, Boston, Mass.	Atlantic Works, Boston, Mass.	408,091.37	Laid up.
Continental Iron Works Greenpoint.	C. H. Delamater, New York.	423,171.69	Laid up.

DATE	NAME.	MATERIAL.	PROPULSION.	DISPLACE-MENT, TONS.	TONNAGE (OLD).	LENGTH.	BEAM.
1862	Patapsco.,	Iron	Screw	1,875	344	200	46
1862	Sangomon (Jason)	"	"	"	"	"	"
1862	Weehawken	"	"	"	"	"	"
1862	Canonicus	"	"	2,100	1,034	225	43' 8''
1862	Catawba	"	"	"	"	"	"
1862	Mahopac	"	"	"	"	"	"
1862	Manayunk (Ajax)	"	"	"	"	"	"
1862	Manhattan	"	"	"	"	"	"
1862	Onesta	"	"	"	"	"	"
1862	Saugus	"	"	"	"	"	"
1862	Tippecanoe (Wyandotte)	"	"	"	"	"	"
1862	Tecumseh	"	"	"	"	"	"
1862	Marietta	"	"		479		
1862	Sandusky	"	"		479		
1862	Neosho		Recessed stern wheels		523		
1862	Osage		"		523		
1862	Ozark		"		523		
1862	Dictator	"	Screw	4,438	3,033	312'	50'
1862	Puritan	"	Twin screws	4,912	3,265	340'	50'
1862	Agamenticus (Terror)	Wood--armored	"	3,295	1,564	259'	52' 4''
1862	Miantonomoh	"	"	3,401	"	257'	52' 10''
1862	Monadnock	"	"	3,295	"	259'	52' 4''
1862	Tonawanda (Amphitrite)	"	"	3,400	"	257'	52' 10''
1862	Chickasaw		Four screws		970	230'	56'
1862	Kickapoo		"		"	"	"
1862	Milwaukee		"		"	"	"
1862	Winnebago		"		"	"	"
1862	Onondaga		Screw		1,250	"	
1863	Ashuelot	Iron	Side wheels	1,370	1,030	255'	35'
1863	Mohongo	"	"	"	"	"	"

BY WHOM AND WHERE BUILT.		COST.	REMARKS.
HULL.	MACHINERY.		
Harlan & Hollingsworth, Wilmington, D.	Harlan & Hollingsworth, Wilmington, D	422,779.95	Sunk by torpedo 1865.
Reany, Son, & Archbold, Chester, Pa.....	Morris, Towne & Co. Philadelphia	422,766.73	Name changed to *Jason* 1869
Secor Bros., Jersey City............	Jos. Colwell, Jersey City.......................	436,007.29	Foundered 1863.
H. Loring, Boston, Mass.....................	Harrison Loring, Boston, Mass...........	622,963.22	Laid up.
Alex. Swift & Co., Cincinnati, O..........	Niles Tool Works, Hamilton, O........	621,424.54	Sold 1868.
Secor Bros., Jersey City.....................	Jos. Colwell, Jersey City.......	635,374.55	Laid up.
Snowden & Mason, Pittsburgh. Pa.........	Snowden & Mason, Pittsburgh, Pa.........	626,582.24	Laid up.
Secor Bros., Jersey City.....................	Jos. Caldwell, Jersey City.....................	628,879.27	Laid up.
Alex. Swift Co., Cincinnati, O...............	Niles Tool Works, Hamilton, O............	621,424.54	Sold 1868.
Harlan & Hollingsworth, Wilmington, D	Harlan & Hollingsworth, Wilmington, D	588,466.62	Sold 1891.
Miles Greenwood, Cincinnati, O................	Miles Greenwood, Cincinnati, O...........	633,327.84	Laid up.
Secor Bros., Jersey City.......	Jos. Colwell, Jersey City.....................	636,941.76	Sunk by torpedo 1864.
Tomlinson, Hartupee & Co., Pittsburgh, Pa..	Tomlinson, Hartupee & Co., Pittsburgh, Pa..	235,039.57	Sold in 1873.
Tomlinson, Hartupee & Co., Pittsburgh. Pa..	Tomlinson, Hartupee & Co., Pittsburgh, Pa..	235,039.57	Sold in 1873.
James B. Edes, St. Louis, Mo...............	James B. Edes, St. Louis, Mo...............	200,757.67	Sold as *Osceola* 1873
James B. Edes, St. Louis, Mo...............	James B. Edes, St. Louis, Mo...............	199,632.62	Sold 1867.
James B. Edes, St. Louis, Mo...............	James B. Edes, St. Louis, Mo...............	207,071.50	Sold 1865.
Delamater Iron Works New York...............	Delamater Iron Works, New York...............	1,382,991.24	Sold 1883.
Continental Iron W'ks Greenpoint, N. Y.....	Allaire Works, New York......	1,974,622.93	See Chap. XXXII.
Navy Yard, Kittery, Maine.....................	Morris, Towne & Co., Philadelphia, Pa......	1,016,071.18	Later *Terror*, 1869. Sold to Wm. Cramp, 1874.
Navy Yard, New York	Novelty Works, New York......	1,310,773.08	Broken up about 1873.
Navy Yard, Boston, Mass.....................	Morris, Towne & Co., Philadelphia, Pa.....	981,439.45	Rebuilt, (see text)
Navy Yard, Philadelphia.....................	Merrick & Sons, Philadelphia, Pa.....	1,156,323.82	See new *Amphitrite*.
Thomas G. Gaylord, St. Louis, Mo,.........	Thomas G. Gaylord, St. Louis, Mo.........	389,962.90	Sold 1874.
G. B. Allen & Co., St. Louis, Mo...	G. B. Allen & Co., St. Louis, Mo.............	391,828.24	Changed to *Harpy* and to *Kewayden*. Sold 1874.
James B. Edes, St. Louis, Mo...............	James B. Edes, St. Louis, Mo.......	387,432.88	Sunk by torpedo 1865.
James B. Edes, St. Louis, Mo...............	James B. Edes, St. Louis, Mo...............	384,969.84	Sold 1874.
Cont. I. W'ks Greenpoint, for G. Quintard	Morgan I. W'ks N. Y. for Geo. Quintard....	759,673.08	Sold by builder to French Gov't.
Donald McKay, Boston, Mass...............	Donald McKay, Boston, Mass...............	297,415.92	Wrecked 1883.
Z. Secor, Jersey City...	Fulton Foundry, Jersey City...	$ 305,928.11	Sold 1870.

DATE.	NAME.	MATERIAL.	PROPULSION.	DISPLACE-MENT, TONS.	TONNAGE, OLD.	LENGTH.	BEAM.
1863	Monocacy	Iron	Side wheels	1,370	1,030	255'	35'
1863	Muscoota	"	"	"	"	"	"
1863	Shamoken	"	"	"	"	"	"
1863	Suwanee	"	"	"	"	"	"
1863	Winnepec	"	"	"	"	"	"
1863	Ammonoosuc (Iowa)	Wood	Screw	3,850	3,213	335'	44' 4"
1863	Neshaming (Nevada)	"	"	"	"	"	"
1863	Wampanoag (Florida)	"	"	4,215	3,281	"	45' 2"
1863	Pomponoosuc (Connecticut)	"	"	4,446	3,713	"	48'
1863	Madawaska (Tennessee)	"	"	4,105	3,281	"	45' 2"
1863	Chattanooga	"	"	3,043		315'	46'
1863	Idaho	"	Twin screws	3,241	2,638	298'	44' 6"
1863	Kalamazoo (Colossus)	"	2 screws	5,600	3,200		
1863	Passaconaway (Massachusetts)	"	"	"	"		
1863	Quinsigamond (Oregon)	"	"	"	"		
1863	Shackamaxon (Nebraska)	"	"	"	"		
1863	Casco	Iron	"		614	223'	44' 3"
1863	Chimo	"	"		"	"	"
1863	Cohoes	"	"		"	"	"
1863	Etlah	"	"		"	"	"
1863	Klamath	"	"		"	"	"
1863	Koka	"	"		"	"	"
1863	Modoc	"	"		"	"	"
1863	Napa	"	"		"	"	"
1863	Naubuc	"	"		"	"	"
1863	Nausett	"	"		"	"	"
1863	Shawnee	"	"		"	"	"
1863	Shiloh	"	"		"	"	"
1863	Squando	"	"		"	"	"
1863	Suncook	"	"		"	"	"

BY WHOM AND WHERE BUILT.		COST.	REMARKS.
HULL.	MACHINERY.		
A. & W. Denmead & Son, Baltimore, Md..	A. & W. Denmead & Son, Baltimore, Md.	293,473.98	In commission.
T. S. Rowland, Con'l I. W'ks, Greenp't, N. Y.	T. F. Rowland, Con'l I. W'ks, Greenp't, N.Y.	297,678.80	Sold 1869.
Reany, Son & Archbold, Chester, Pa...............	Reany, Son & Archbold, Chester, Pa............	278,020.81	Sold 1869.
Reany, Son & Archbold, Ceester, Pa..............	Reany, Son & Archbold, Chester, Pa...........	278,662.78	Wrecked, 1868.
Harrison Loring, Boston, Mass..............	Harrison Loring, Boston, Mass...............	298,132.24	Sold 1869.
Navy Yard, Boston.....	Morgan Iron Works, New York...............	....	Sold 1883.
Navy Yard, Philadelphia, Pa.	J. Roach, Etna Iron Works, New York...	....	Sold in part payment for *Puritan*
Navy Yard, New York..................	Novelty Iron Works, York.......................	1,575,643.84	Sold 1885. (See Chap. XXIX.
Navy Yard, Boston, Mass......................	Corliss St. Eng. Co., Providence, R. I.....	....	Broken up 1883.
Navy Yard, New York	Allaire Works, New York....................	1,673,080.52	Sold 1887.
William Cramp & Sons Philadelphia............	Merrick & Son, Philadelphia, Pa............	950,159.31	Sold 1871.
George Steers, New York....................	Morgan Iron Works, New York..............	550,000.00	
Navy Yard, New York.	Delamater I'n Works, New York...............	....	Broken up on stocks.
Navy Yard, Kittery, Me.	Delamater I'n Works, New York...............	....	Broken up on stocks.
Navy Yard, Boston, Mass.....................	Atlantic Works, Boston, Mass...............	....	Broken up on stocks.
Navy Yard, Philadelphia, Pa..................	Pusey, Jones & Co., Wilmington, Del....	....	Broken up on stocks.
Atlantic Works, Boston, Mass..........	Atlantic Works, Boston, Mass...............	529,996.99	Sold for use in new vessels.
Aquilla Adams, Boston, Mass...............	Aquilla Adams, Boston, Mass...............	620,445.52	Sold for use in new vessels.
M. F. Merritt, Greenpoint, New York ...	M. F. Merritt, Greenpoint, New York......	594,012.10	Sold for use in new vessels.
Chas. W. McCord, St. Louis, Mo...........	Chas. W. McCord, St. Louis, Mo...........	589,458.82	Sold 1874.
Alex. Swift & Co., Cincinnati, Ohio	Alex. Swift & Co., Cincinnati, Ohio..........	602,985.34	Sold 1874.
Wilcox & Whitney, Camden, N. J........	Wilcox & Whitney, Camden, N. J..........	545,694.81	Sold 1874.
J. S. Underhill, New York, N. Y............	J. S. Underhill, New York, N. Y.	513,353.13	Sold 1874.
Harlan & Hollingsworth, Wilmington..	Harlan & Hollingsworth, Wilmington...	506,366.33	Sold 1874.
W. Perrine, Williamsburg, N. Y.............	William Perrine, Williamsburg, N. Y......	513,975.74	Sold 1874.
Donald McKay, East Boston, Mass.........	Donald McKay, East Boston, Mass..........	578,110.98	Sold 1874.
Curtis & Tilden, Boston, Mass	Curtis & Tilden, Boston, Mass...........	581,818.50	Sold.
George C. Bestor, St. Louis, Mo	George C. Bestor, St. Louis, Mo...........	589,428.20	Sold.
McKay & Aldus, East Boston, Mass.........	McKay & Aldus, East Boston, Mass.........	589,535.70	Sold.
Globe Works, South Boston, Mass..........	Globe Works, South Boston, Mass..........	593,674.30	Traded as old iron for new.

DATE.	NAME.	MATERIAL.	PROPULSION.	DISPLACEMENT, TONS.	TONNAGE. (OLD.)	LENGTH.	BEAM.
1863	Tunxis	Iron	2 screws		614	223''	44'' 3'
1863	Umpqua	"	"		"	"	"
1863	Wassuc	"	"		"	"	"
1863	Waxsaw	"	"		"	"	"
1863	Yazoo	"	"		"	"	"
1863	Yuma	"	"		"	"	"
1863	Antietam	Wood	Screw	3,953	3,177	312' 6''	46'
1863	Guerriere	"	"	"	"	"	"
1863	Illinois	"	"	"	"	"	"
1863	Java	"	"	"	"	"	"
1863	Kewaydin (Pennsylvania)	"	"	"	"	"	"
1863	Minnetonka (California)	"	"	"	"	316' 6''	"
1863	Ontario (New York)	"	"	"	"	312' 6''	47'
1863	Piscataqua (Delaware)	"	"	"	"	"	46'
1863	Contoocook (Albany)	"	"	3,003	2,348	290'	41'
1863	Manitou (Worcester)	"	"	"	"	"	"
1863	Mosholu (Severn)	"	"	"	"	"	"
1863	Pushmataha (Cambridge) (Congress)	"	"	"	"	"	"
1863	Arapahoe		"				
1863	Keosauqua						
1863	Mondamin						
1863	Tahgayuta						
1863	Wanalosett						
1863	Willamette						
1864	Algoma (Benicia)	Wood	Screw	2,400		250' 6''	38'
1864	Alert (first)						
1864	Epervier						
1864	Nantasket	Wood	Screw	1,129		216'	31'
1864	Quinnebaug (first)	"	2 screws	1,113		216'	30'
1864	Resaca	"	Screw	1,129		216'	31'

BY WHOM AND WHERE BUILT.		COST.	REMARKS.
HULL.	MACHINERY.		
Wm. Cramp & Sons, Philadelphia, Pa......	Reany, Son & Archbold, Chester, Pa.....	$ 648,070.99	Broken up and sold as old iron.
Snowden & Mason, Pittsburgh, Pa.........	Snowden & Mason, Pittsburgh, Pa........	595,640.36	Sold 1874.
Geo. W Lawrence, Portland, Me............	Geo. W. Lawrence, Portland, Me............	552,374.51	Sold as old iron; used in *Terror*
A. & W. Denmead, Baltimore, Md.........	A. & W. Denmead, Baltimore, Md.........	592,587.32	Sold.
Merrick & Sons, Philadelphia, Pa............	Merrick & Sons, Philadelphia, Pa............	566,364.26	Sold.
Alex. Swift & Co., Cincinnatti, Ohio.....	Alex Swift & Co., Cincinnati, Ohio......	602,985.34	Sold.
Navy Yard, Philadelphia, Pa................	Morris & Towne, Philadelphia, Pa......		Sold 1885.
Navy Yard, Boston, Mass...	Globe Works, Boston, Mass........	1,154,325.10	Sold 1872.
U. S. Navy Yard, Kittery, Me.............	Corliss Steam Eng. Co., Providence, R. I.		Broken up on stocks.
Navy Yard, New York.	J. Roach, Etna I.W'ks, New York............		Broken up on stocks.
Navy Yard, Boston, Mass............	Harrison Loring, Boston, Mass............		Broken up on stocks.
Navy Yard, Kittery, Maine....................	Woodruff & Beach, Hartford, Conn........	1,223,246.97	Sold 1875.
Navy Yard, New York	J. Roach, Etna I. W'ks New York............		Broken up on stocks
Navy Yard, Kittery Maine.......	Woodruff & Beach, Hartford, Conn........	1,177,895.04	Foundered at dock; sold 1877
Navy Yard, Kittery, Maine....................	Providence St.Eng.Co. Providence, R. I......		Sold 1872.
Navy Yard, Boston, Mass.....................	Woodrug & Beach, Hartford, Conn......	785,785.58	Sold 1883.
Navy Yard, New York.	S. Brooklyn Eng. Wks. Brooklyn, N. Y......		Sold for new *Puritan*.
Navy Yard, Philadelphia, Pa................	Morris, Towne & Co., Philadelphia, Pa......	776,380.20	Sold 1883.
Never built................	Providence St. Eng.Co. Drovidence, R. I......		Not built.
Never built................	J. Roach, New York...		Not built.
Never built................	Washington I. Works, Newbury, New York		Not built.
Never built................	Washington I. Works, Newbury, New York		Not built.
Never built................	Hazelhurst & Wiegard, Baltimore, Md........		Not built.
Never built................	Poole & Hunt, Baltimore, Md............		Not built.
Navy Yard, Kittery, Maine....................	Navy Yard, Boston, Mass................		Sold 1884.
Never built................	Navy Yard, Kittery, Maine............		Broken up.
Never built................	Navy Yard, Washington......................		Engines in store, Norfolk
Navy Yard, Boston......	Navy Yard. Kittery.....		Sold.
Navy Yard, New York.	Jackson & Watkins, London, England....		Broken up; new ship same name built.
Navy Yard, Kittery....	Navy Yard, Washington......................	360,037.64	Sold 1873.

DATE.	NAME.	MATERIAL.	PROPULSION.	DISPLACEMENT, TONS.	TONNAGE. (OLD.)	LENGTH.	BEAM.
1864	Swatara	Wood	Screw	1,113		216′	30′
1864	Fortune	Iron	"	420	350	216′	26′
1864	Leyden	"	"	"	"	"	"
1864	Mayflower	"	"	"	"	"	"
1664	Nina	"	"	"	"	"	"
1864	Palos	"	"	"	"	"	"
1864	Pinta	"	"	"	"	"	"
1864	Speedwell	"	"	"	"	"	"
1864	Standish	"	"	"	"	"	"
1864	Triana	"	"	"	"	"	"
1864	Spuyten Duyvil	Wood—Iron armr	"	207	116	84′ 2″	20′ 8″
1867	Alaska	Wood	Screw	2,394		250′-6″	38′
1867	Omaha	"	"	"		"	"
1867	Plymouth	"	"	"		"	"
1872	Galena (second)	"	"	1,900		216′	37′
1872	Mohican (second)	"	"	"		"	"
1872	Marion	"	"	"		"	"
1872	Quinnebaug ((second)	"	"	"		"	"
1872	Swatara (second)	"	"	"		"	"
1862	Vandalia	"	"	2,033		"	39′
1873	Alert (second)	Iron	"	1,020		175′	32′
1873	Huron (second)	"	"	"		"	"
1873	Ranger	"	"	"		"	"
1874	Adams	Wood	"	1,375		185′	35
1874	Alliance	"	"	"		"	"
1874	Enterprise	"	"	"		"	"
1874	Essex	"	"	"		"	"
1874	Nipsic (second)	"	"	"		"	"
1874	Trenton	"	"	3,900		253′	48′
1874	Alarm	Iron	Fowler wheel	800		158′	28′

BY WHOM AND WHERE BUILT.		COST.	REMARKS.
HULL.	MACHINERY.		
Navy Yard, Philadelphia	Navy Yard Washington, D. C.	$ 327,365.07	Broken up; new ship same name built.
James Tetlow, Boston, Mass	James Tetlow, Boston, Mass	149,600.00	In service.
James Tetlow, Boston, Mass	James Tetlow, Boston, Mass	128,000.00	In service.
James Tetlow, Boston, Mass	James Tetlow, Boston, Mass	106,240.00	Practice steamer; sold 1893.
Reany, Son, & Archbold, Chester, Pa.	Reany, Son & Archbold, Chester, Pa.	128,000.00	In service.
James Tetlow, Boston, Mass	James Tetlow, Boston, Mass	128,000.00	Sold 1893.
Reany, Son, & Archbold, Chester, Pa.	Reany, Son & Archbold, Chester, Pa.	128,000.00	In commission.
James Tetlow, Boston, Mass	James Tetlow, Boston, Mass	149,600.00	Sold 1894.
James Tetlow, Boston, Mass	James Tetlow, Boston, Mass	106,240.00	In commission.
William Perrine, New York	William Perrine, New York	128,000.00	Wrecked 1891.
S. H. Pook, Iron Works, Mystic, Conn.	S. H. Pook, Iron Works, Mystic, Conn.	45,036.29	War service James River.
Navy Yard, Boston	Navy Yard, Boston		Sold 1883.
Navy Yard, Philadelphia	Navy Yard New York		Laid up 1891.
Navy Yard, New York	Navy Yard, New York		Broken up 1884.
Navy Yard, Norfolk	Navy Yard, Norfolk		Sold.
Navy Yard, Mare Island, Cal	Navy Yard, Mare Island, Cal		Pacific squadron.
Navy Yard, Kittery, Maine	Navy Yard, Boston		Pacific squadron.
Navy Yard, Philadelphia Pa	Navy Yard, New York		Sold 1894.
Navy Yard, New York	Navy Yard, New York		Laid up 1891.
Navy Yard, Boston	Navy Yard, Boston		Wrecked 1889.
J. Roach, Chester, Pa.	J. Roach, Chester, Pa.	326,015.68	Pacific squadron.
J. Roach, Chester, Pa.	J. Roach, Chester, Pa.		Wrecked 1877.
Harlan & Hollingsworth, Wilmington.	John Roach, Chester, Pa.		Special service Pacific station.
D. McKay, Boston, Mass	Atlantic Works, Boston, Mass.		Pacific station.
Navy Yard, Norfolk.	Quintard Iron Works, New York		Training ship.
J. W. Griffiths, Kittery, Me.	Woodruff Iron Co., Hartford, Conn.		Public Marine School, Boston.
D. McKay, Kittery and Boston	Atlantic Works, Boston Mass.		Training ship.
Navy Yard, Washington, D. C.	W. Wright & Co., Newburg N. Y.		Receiving ship, Puget Sound.
Navy Yard, New York	Morgan Iron Works, New York		Wrecked 1889.
Navy Yard, New York	Morgan Iron Works, New York		In service.

DATE.	NAME.	MATERIAL.	PROPULSION.	DISPLACE-MENT, TONS.	TONNAGE.	LENGTH.	BEAM.
1874	Intrepid	Iron	2 screws	1,150		170′	35′
1874	Despatch (second)	Wood	Screw	560		174′	25′ 6″
1874	Monadnock (second)	Iron	2 screws	3,990		259′ 6″	55′ 10″
1874	Amphitrite (second)	"	"	"		"	"
1874	Miantonomoh (second)	"	"	"		"	"
1874	Terror (second)	"	"	"		"	"
1875	Puritan (second)	"	"	6,060		289′ 6″	60′ 1½″
1888	Triton	Steel	Screw	212		96′ 9″	20′ 9″
1891	Traffic	Wood	"	280		106′	29′ 4″
	Polaris	"	"			135′	28′
	Tigress	"	"				
	Jeannette	"	"			142′	25′
	Rodgers	"	"				
	Thetis	"	"	1,250		166′	30′ 3″
	Fern	"	"	840			

THE NEW NAVY.

DATE.	NAME.	TYPE.	MATERIAL.	MEAN DRAFT.	TONS DISPLACE-MENT.	LENGTH ON L. W. L.	BREADTH
1883	Dolphin	Despatch boat	Steel	14′ 3″	1,485	240′	32′
1883	Atlanta	Protected cruiser	"	17′	3,189	270′ 3″	42′
1883	Boston	" "	"	17′	3,189	270′ 3″	42′
1883	Chicago	" "	"	19′	4,500	325	48′ 2″
1887	Newark	" "	"	18′ 9″	4,098	310′	49′ 2″
1887	Charleston	" "	"	19′ 7″	4,040	312′	46′
1887	Baltimore	" "	"	20′ 6″	4,600	327′ 6″	48′ 6″
1887	Vesuvius	Dynamite-gun cruiser	"	10′ 8″	930	251′ 9″	26′ 5″

BY WHOM AND WHERE BUILT.		COST.	REMARKS.
HULL.	MACHINERY.		
Navy Yard, Boston,	Morgan Iron Works, New York............	....	Broken up 1885-'87.
Purchased of Henry C. Smith, New York	Purchased of Henry C. Smith, New York	$ 98,500.00	Wrecked 1891; wreck sold.
P. Burgess, Vallejo, Cal....................	Navy Yard, Mare Island, Cal.............	....	Not yet completed.
Harlan & Hollingsworth, Wilmington. D	Harlan & Hollingsworth, Wilmington, D	....	In commission.
John Roach, Chester, Pa......................	John Roach, Chester, Pa......................	2,102,752.22	In reserve League Island.
William Cramp & Sons. Philadelphia.	William Cramp & Sons, Philadelphia.	....	Not yet completed.
John Roach, Chester, Pa.........	John Roach, Chester, Pa.........	....	Not yet completed.
John H. Dialogue, Camden, N. J.	John H. Dialogue, Camden, N. J........	....	Tug-boat.
D. McCarty, S. Brooklyn, New York... ...	D. McCarty, South Brooklyn, N. Y......	....	Tug-boat.
...............................…	Neafie & Levy, Philadelphia, Pa............	80,000.00	Crushed in the ice, 1872.
....	...........................…	....	Chartered.—Returned to Owner.
....	....	....	See Chapter XXXIV.
....	....	100,000.00	Burned 1881.
Alex. Stevens & Sons, Dundee, Scotland...	Alex. Stevens & Sons, Dundee, Scotland...	140,000.00	In service.
...............…............	Delamater Iron Works New York, 1871......	....	Transport steamer.

THE NEW NAVY.

BY WHOM AND WHERE BUILT OR BUILDING.		COST.	PRESENT CONDITION.
HULL.	MACHINERY.		
John Roach & Sons, Chester, Pa............	John Roach & Sons Chester, Pa............	$ 360,149.28	In commission.
J. Roach & Sons, Chester, and U. S. Govt.	at New York Navy Yd	805,711.64	Repairing.
J. Roach & Sons, Chester, and U. S. Govt.	at New York Navy Yd	809,923.44	In commission.
J. Roach & Sons, Chester, and U. S, Govt.	at New York Navy Yd	1,245,776.46	Laid up to receive new machinery and boilers.
Wm. Cramp & Sons, Philadelphia, Pa.	Wm. Cramp & Sons, Philadelphia, Pa....	1,379,897.47	In commission.
Union Iron Works, San Francisco, Cal..	Union Iron Works San Francisco, Cal..	1,164,504.10	In commission.
Wm. Cramp & Sons, Philadelphia, Pa.....	Wm. Cramp & Sons, Philadelphia, Pa.	1,426,504.93	In commission.
Wm. Cramp & Sons, Philadelphia, Pa....	Wm. Cramp & Sons, Philadelphia, Pa.....	317,555.33	Laid up.

DATE.	NAME.	TYPE.	MATERIAL.	MEAN DRAFT.	TONS DISPLACEMENT.	LENGTH ON L. W. L.	BREADTH.
1887	Petrel	Gunboat	Steel	11' 7''	890	176' 3''	31'
1887	Yorktown	"		14'	1,703	230'	36'
1888	Bennington	"	Steel	14'	1,700	230	36'
1888	Concord	"	"	14'	1,740	230'	36'
1888	Cushing	Torpedo boat	"	5' 3''	116	138' 9''	14' 10''
1888	Philadelphia	Protected cruiser	"	19' 3''	4,324	327' 6''	48' 6''
1888	San Francisco	" "	"	18' 9''	4,088	310'	49' 2''
1888	Maine	Armored cruiser	"	21' 6''	6,648	318'	57'
1889	Monterey	Coast defense— barbette monitor	"	14' 6''	4,084	256'	59'
1889	Texas	Second-class battle-ship	"	22' 6''	6,300	301' 4''	64' 1''
1890	New York	Armored cruiser	"	23' 11'	8,480	380' 6''	64' 10''
1890	Olympia	Protected cruiser	"	21' 6''	5,870	340'	53'
1890	Cincinnati	" "	"	18'	3,183	300'	42'
1890	Raleigh	" "	"	18'	3,183	300'	42'
1890	Marblehead (second)	Cruiser	"	14' 6''	2,050	257'	37
1890	Detroit	"	"	14' 9''	2,068	257	37
1890	Montgomery	"	"	14' 6¼''	2,079	257	37
1890	Columbia	Protected cruiser	"	22' 6''	7,375	411' 7''	58' 5''
1891	Minneapolis	" "	"	22' 6''	7,387	411' 7''	58' 2''
1891	Bancroft	Practice vessel for naval cadets	"	11' 6''	832	187' 6''	32'
1891	Indiana	Battle-ship	"	24'	10,288	348'	69' 3''
1891	Massachusetts (second)	" "	"	24'	10,288	348'	69' 3''
1891	Oregon (second)	" "	"	24'	10,288	348'	69' 3''
1891	Katahdin (second)	Harbor defense ram	"	15'	2,183	250' 9''	43' 5''
1891	Castine	Gunboat	"	12'	1,177	204'	32'
1891	Machias	"	"	12'	1,177	204'	32'
1891	Iwana	Tug boat	"	8'	192	92' 6''	21'
1891	Narkeeta	" "	"	8'	192	92' 6''	21'
1891	Wahneta	" "	"	8'	192	92' 6''	21'
1892	Ericsson	Torpedo boat	"	4' 9''	120	150'	15' 6''

BY WHOM AND WHERE BUILT OR BUILDING.		COST.	PRESENT CONDITION.
HULL.	MACHINERY.		
Columbian Iron W'ks Baltimore, Maryland	Columbian Iron W'ks Baltimore, Maryland	$ 307,996.55	In commission.
Wm. Cramp & Sons Philadelphia, Pa.....	Wm. Cramp & Sons. Philadelphia, Pa....	498,305.45	In commission.
N. F. Palmer & Co., Chester, Pa............	Quintard Iron Works. New York.............	553,875.55	In commission.
N. F. Palmer & Co., Chester, Pa............	Quintard Iron Works, New York.............	553,117.66	In commission.
Herreschoff Mfg. Co., Bristol, Rhode Island	Herneschoff Mfg. Co., Bristol, Rhode Island	98,666.29	In commission.
Wm. Cramp & Sons, Philadelphia Pa......	Wm. Cramp & Sons, Philadelphia, Pa.....	1,424,864.85	In commission.
Union Iron Works, San Francisco, Cal...	Union Iron Works, San Francisco, Cal.	1,609,745.71	In commission.
U. S. Govt. Navy Yard, New York.....	Quintard Iron Works, New York.............	†2,500,000.00	In commission.
Union Iron Works, San Francisco, Cal..	Union Iron Works, San Francisco, Cal..	2,065,779.30	In commission.
U. S. Govt. Navy Yard, Norfolk, Va...	Richmond Loco. W'ks. Richmond, Va.........	†2,500,000.00	In commission.
Wm. Cramp & Sons, Philadelphia, Pa.....	Wm. Cramp & Sons, Philadelphia, Pa.....	3,249,224.45	In commission.
Union Iron Works, San Francisco, Cal..	Union Iron Works San Francisco, Cal..	†1,796,000.00	In commission.
U. S. Govt. at Navy Yard, New York.....	U. S. Govt. Navy Yard, New York.....	†1,100,000.00	In commission.
U. S. Govt. Navy Yard, Norfolk.........	U. S. Govt., Navy Yard, New York......	†1,100,000.00	In commission.
Harrison Loring, Boston, Mass.........	Quintard Iron Works, New York.............	†674,000.00	In commission.
Columbian Iron Wks, Baltimore, Maryland	Columbian Iron W'ks Baltimore, Maryland	†612,500.00	In commission.
Columbian Iron Wks, Baltimore, Maryland	Columbian Iron W'ks Baltimore, Maryland	†612,500.00	In commission.
Wm. Cramp & Sons, Philadelphia, Pa.....	Wm. Cramp & Sons, Philadelphia, Pa.....	†2,725.000.00	In commission.
Wm. Cramp & Sons, Philadelphia, Pa.....	Wm. Cramp & Sons, Philadelphia, Pa.....	†2,690,000.00	In commission.
S. L. Moore & Sons. Elizabethport, N. J.	S. L. Moore & Sons, Elizabethport, N. J.	297,360.17	In commission.
Wm. Cramp & Sons Philadelphia, Pa....	Wm. Cramp & Sons, Philadelphia, Pa.....	†3,020,000.00	In commission.
Wm. Cramp & Sons, Philadelphia, Pa....	Wm. Cramp & Sons, Philadelphia, Pa....	*3,020,000.00	In commission.
Union Iron Works, San Francisco, Cal..	Union Iron Works San Francisco, Cal.	*3,222,810.00	In commission.
Bath Iron Works, Bath, Maine..........	Bath Iron Works, Bath, Maine..........	*930,000.00	In commission.
Bath Iron Works, Bath, Maine..........	Bath Iron Works, Bath, Maine..........	*318,500.00	In commission.
Bath Iron Works, Bath, Maine..........	Bath Iron Works, Bath, Maine.........	*318,500.00	In commission.
Harrison Loring, Boston, Mass...............	Harrison Loring, Boston, Mass...............	33,253.57	In service.
Harrison Loring, Boston, Mass...............	Harrison Loring, Boston, Mass...............	33,648.91	In service.
Harrison Loring, Boston, Mass...............	Harrison Loring, Boston, Mass...............	33,176.52	In service.
Iowa Iron Works, Dubuque, Iowa......	Iowa Iron Works, Dubuque, Iowa........	*113,500.00	Undergoing trials.

†Limit of cost or contract price.
*Contract price, or limit fixed by appropriation.

DATE.	NAME.	TYPE.	MATERIAL	MEAN DRAFT.	TONS DISPLACE-MENT-	LENGTH ON L. W. L.	BREADTH.
1893	Brooklyn (second)	Armored cruiser.	Steel	24'	9,153	400' 6''	64'
1893	Iowa (second)	Battle-ship	"	24'	11,296	360'	72' 2½''
1894	Nashville	Gunboat	"	11'	1,371	220'	36'
1834	Wilmington	"	"	8' 8''	1,392	250' 6''	40'
1894	Helena	"	"	8' 8''	1,392	250' 6''	40'
1895	No. 3 / No. 4 / No. 5	Torpedo boats	"	5' 3''	135	160'	16
1895	Unadilla (second)	Tug boat	"	9' 6''	345	110	25'
1895	No. 5	" "	"	8' 6''	220	96' 9''	21'
1896	Kearsarge (second)	Battle-ship	"	23' 6''	11,500	368'	72' 0''
1896	Kentucky	" "	"	"	"	"	"
1896	No. 10	Gunboat	Steel and wood	12	1,000	168'	36'
1896	No. 11	"	"	"	"	"	"
1896	No. 12	"	"	"	"	"	"
1896	No. 13	"	"	"	"	"	"
1896	No. 14	"	"	"	"	174'	34'
1896	No. 15	"	"	"	"	"	"
1896	No. 6	Torpedo boat	Steel	5' 6''	180	170'	17'
1896	No. 7	" "	"	"	"	"	"
1896	No. 8	" "	"	"	"	"	"

1896 One submarine torpedo boat, detail designs not yet complete. Under contract with Maryland.

1896 { No. 7 / No. 8 / No. 9 } Battleships authorized by act of June 10, 1896; to be practically the same

1896 Not more than thirteen Torpedo boats authorized by act of June 10, 1896; details

* Contract price, or limit fixed by appropriation.

BY WHOM AND WHERE BUILT OR BUILDING.		COST.	PRESENT CONDITION.
HULL.	MACHINERY.		
Wm. Cramp & Sons, Philadelphia, Pa.....	Wm. Cramp & Sons, Philadelphia, Pa.....	*$2,986,000.00	Building.
Wm. Cramp & Sons, Philadelphia, Pa.....	Wm. Cramp & Sons, Philadelphia, Pa....	*3,010,000.00	Building.
Newport News Shipbldg. Co., Va.........	Newport News Shipbldg. Co., Va.........	*280,000.00	Building.
Newport News Shipbldg. Co., Va.........	Newport News Shipbldg. Co., Va.........	*280,000.00	Building.
Newport News Shipbldg. Co., Va.........	Newport News Shipbldg. Co., Va.........	*280,000.00	Building.
Columbian Iron Works, Baltimore, Maryland	Columbian Iron Works, Baltimore, Maryland...............	*97,500.00 (Each)	Building.
U.S. Govt. Navy Yard, Mare Island, Cal. ...	U.S. Govt. Navy Yard, Mare Island, Cal....	*80,000.00	Building.
U. S. Govt. Navy Yard, Norfolk Va.............	U.S. Govt. Navy Yard, Norfolk, Va............	*25,000.00	Building.
Newport News Shipbldg. & Drydock Co.	Newport News Shipbldg. & Drydock Co.	*2,250,000.00	Designed.
Newport News Shipbldg. & Drydock Co.	Newport News Shipbldg & Drydock Co.	*2,250,000.00	Designed.
Bath Iron Works, Bath, Maine...........	Bath Iron Works, Bath, Maine...........	*229,400.00	Contract awarded.
Bath Iron Works, Bath, Maine...........	Bath Iron Works, Bath, Maine..........	*229,400.00	Contract awarded
Lewis Nixon, Crescent Iron Works, N. J....	Lewis Nixon, Crescent Iron Works, N. J....	*238,200,00	Contract awarded.
J. H. Dialogue & Son, Camden, N. J.........	J. H. Dialogue & Son, Camden, N. J.	*230,000.00	Contract awarded.
Union Iron Works, San Francisco, Cal...	Union Iron Works, San Francisco, Cal..	*209,000.00	Contract awarded.
Union Iron Works, San Francisco, Cal...	Union Iron Works, San Francisco, Cal..	*209,000.00	Contract awarded.
Herreschoff Mfg. Co., Bristol, Rhode Isl...	Herreschoff Mfg. Co., Bristol, Rhode Isl...	*144,000.00	Contract awarded.
Herreschoff Mfg. Co., Bristol, Rhode Isl...	Herreschoff Mfg. Co., Bristol, Rhode Isl...	*144,000.00	Contract awarded.
Moran Brothers & Co. Ltd., Seattle, Wash.	Moran Brothers & Co. Ltd., Seattle, Wash.	*163,350.00	Contract awarded.

the J. P. Holland Torpedo Boat Company; being built by Columbian Iron Works, Baltimore'

as *Kearsarge* and *Kentucky.*

not yet determined.

APPENDIX C.

UNCLE SAMUEL'S WHISTLE

AND WHAT IT COSTS.

A TALE.

"He whistled as he went, for want of thought."
—Dryden

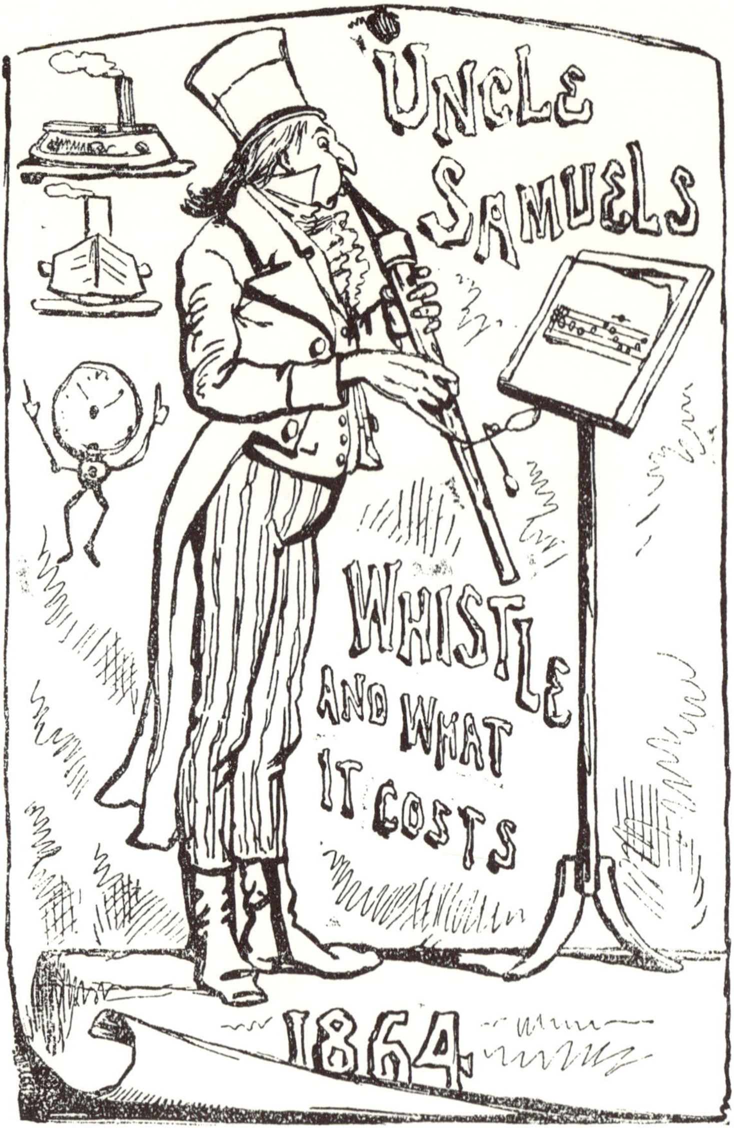
UNCLE SAMUELS
WHISTLE
AND WHAT
IT COSTS
1864

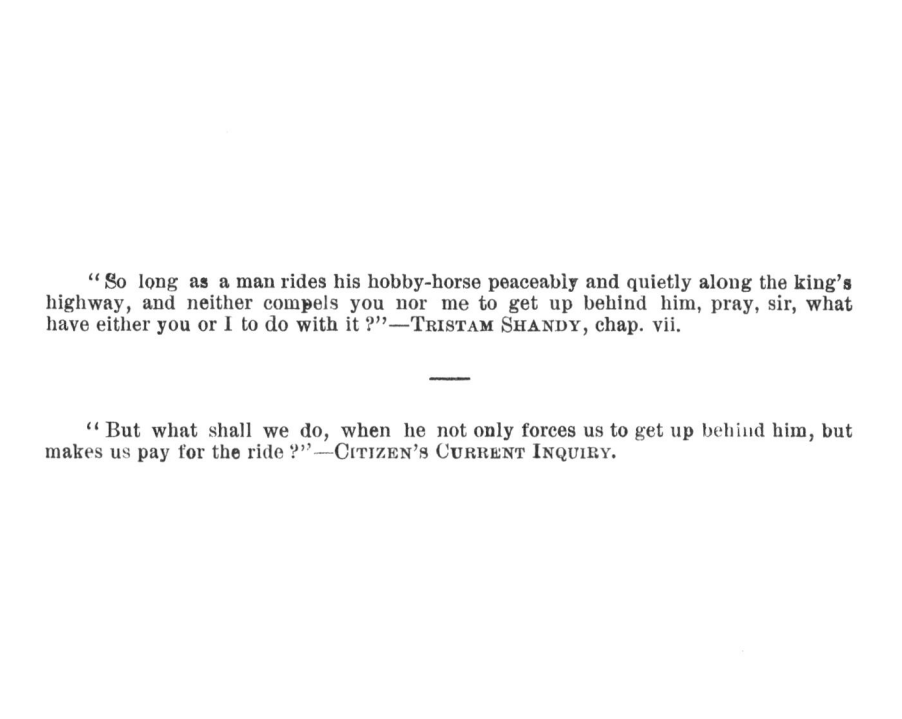

"So long as a man rides his hobby-horse peaceably and quietly along the king's highway, and neither compels you nor me to get up behind him, pray, sir, what have either you or I to do with it?"—TRISTAM SHANDY, chap. vii.

"But what shall we do, when he not only forces us to get up behind him, but makes us pay for the ride?"—CITIZEN'S CURRENT INQUIRY.

HATCHING THE EGG.

I.

It was a lovely summer morning, in the old days of peace. A cloudless blue sky bent over the glittering metropolis—a bright sun flooded its busy streets with splendor—and a gentle wind made music in the trees that grace its parks and causeways. The haunts, alike of labor and of pleasure, were already thronged. Up and down Broadway and the Avenues, surged the customary tide of human beings. Horse-cars rumbled and jingled along their various tracks, and stages, carriages, carts, and drays added volume and variety to the din of city life. All was light—activity—animation.

Especially in the City Hall Park!

There were no soldiers then in that verdurous region; nor barracks, nor recruiting tents, nor hospitals, nor artillery, nor vestiges of the "circumstance of glorious war." But the peaceful grass grew there untrampled, and birds flitted from tree to tree; and the fountain, which Mr. N. P. Willis has commemorated in song, played away in the cool and sparkling fashion peculiar to fountains; and the baked Jersey mud statute of General Washington—erected by a considerate posterity for the accommodation of the sculptor—gazed placidly at the City Hall, or seemed to smile upon the comfortable enterprise of those youthful Bohemians who thrive by polishing the boots of respectability. A scene of pastoral innocence and beauty.

Amidst that scene, and near the base of that imposing monument, there stood, on the lovely morning previously referred to, a man. He was wrapped in profound thought—and in seedy garments. His face was pale, and wore the expression of intellect tempered by timidity. His black clothes, though they had been carefully brushed, presented that glazed appearance which, except, perhaps, in the case of satinet, is the unmistakable evidence of age. His hat was greasy—his boots were soiled with dust. In his right hand he grasped a heavy walking stick : in his left, a huge roll of white paper. And so he stood—now glancing at the City Hall clock, now at the stately edifice, towards the south-east, whence issue, daily and weekly, so many organs of public opinion, in the shape of newspapers.

He had waited there already during nearly two hours—a spectacle of superfluous patience, exciting the suspicion of neighboring police officers, and stirring up the ire of contiguous apple-women. For he seemed to have no legitimate calling, and he certainly bought no apples. Nor did he incline the ear of attention to the tattered youths who repeatedly said to him, "blag yer boots." The seedy man was plainly pre-occupied, and intent on serious things.

At length, as the bell tolled the hour of ten, the stranger emerged from his reverie, walked rapidly from the Washington statue, and disappeared within the principal edifice of Printing House Square.—Let us follow in his footsteps.

We shall find him in a spacious and handsome office, adorned with a large library, and with pictures, chiefly of a marine character. A close examination of the library would disclose many books of a scientific kind, such as "Mariotte's Law" and "Isherwood's Engineering Precedents;" and mingled with these, divers volumes of poetry and *Belles Leitres*, showing that their owner, however, devoted to science, is yet addicted to occasional indulgence in "Shakspeare and the musical glasses." The other appointments of this room are correspondingly sumptuous. The carpet is rich and soft—the furniture is carved and valuable. In the centre of the apartment stands a handsome writingtable, littered with papers and drawings. Near this, in a comfortable arm chair, sits a man of singular appearance, and, as the reader will presently preceive, of still more singular talents, He is the hero of this tale.

THE HERO OF DASH-POTS AND THE SEEDY INVENTOR.

To him has entered the seedy stranger. . . . They talk.

"I am an inventor, sir,—a poor man ; but I have a fortune in these plans. You are rich—you are influential. I have come to ask your aid in presenting my invention to the notice of the United States Navy Department."

"What is your name, sir ? and what is the nature of your invention ?"

"My name, sir, is ———. My invention is a steam cut-off for application to marine engines."

"Sir," said the great man, "you have come to the right shop. My foot is on my native heath, and my name is D———n."

The seedy inventor bowed, and deposited his roll of paper upon the table.

"Sit, my friend," said the magnanimous D———n. "I will cast my eye over your drawings. The subject of economizing steam and coal has long been familiar to my thoughts. I am a devout student of Watt, and I know all about water. Mariotte is my *vade mecum*, and I abhor the very name of Isherwood. (A.) Likewise, I am a reader of the Hebrew melodies of the gifted Lord Byron. I will read them to you, if you like; but not immediately. Amuse yourself for a few moments, while I glance at these papers."

The inventor again bowed, sat down, and picking up a pamphlet, devoted his mind to the "*Tenth Annual Report of the Board of Water Commissioners to the Common Council of the City of Detroit.*" (B.)

Let us not dwell upon what he found therein; at least not yet. Suffice it to say, that he had not long to read nor long to wait for the reply of his heroic companion.

"I will take this invention, sir, under my patronage and supervision. It is not exhaustive, but it is a step in advance. So far as it goes, it harmonizes with my own views. But I warn you beforehand, that mighty obstacles must be overcome ere it can be made a practical success. Be re-assured, however ! Those obstacles are not invulnerable. It was, as remarked by the erudite Game Chicken, "within the resources of science to double up Mr. Dombey :" it is equally within the resources of science to double up Isherwood. (C.) That fellow is very destructive on coals, and it is high time that something were done about it. I behold in this cut-off the immediate means of doing something. I will let loose upon the Navy Department the entire strength of my inspiration—the whole vast power of Mariotte's Law and of Lord Byron's melodies. Nay, sir, I will even press Shakspeare into this service. So shall the cut-off carry the day. Trust yours truly for that. But, in the meanwhile, we must agree, sir, upon terms—upon terms, sir, and conditions. A cut-off is, as it were a machine, but, as noticed by the subtle Mr. Hazlitt, a man of genius is not.— Modesty forbids me to employ more definite language. I see in your intelligent countenance that you perceive the application of this remark. I shall stipulate, sir, for an interest in this invention—an interest of liberal scope and of large possible value. Upon that wall, before you, hangs a map of the United States of America, a great and glorious Republic, my friend, founded at an early period by the Father of his Country, and popularly known as an asylum for the oppressed of all nations. Those States, sir, are numerous and wealthy. These upon the northern Atlantic sea board are peculiarly so. I stipulate for the exclusive right of applying this invention in those States. I appropriate to myself New England, New York, Pennsylvania, the Middle States, and those that extend westward along the lakes. The remainder I leave to you. Accept these terms, and I lift you at once from the slough of obscurity to the heights of fame. Reject them, and I leave you to chance.

"There is a tide in the affairs of men,
Which, taken at the flood, leads on to fortune,"

That tide, sir, is now at the flood with you. Will you take it or no ? I pause for a reply."

The seedy inventor, overwhelmed by this eloquence, could only bow and point to his plans.

"I accept the terms, sir," he said, at length, "and leave my fate in your hands."

"In my hands," responded the heroic D———n, "your fate is glory. You have heard, no doubt, of the star of purest ray serene. I am that star. Henceforth it will be my vocation to shine upon you. Be happy in that reflection ! And now, sir, before we part, permit me to read a paraphrase of one of those Byronic melodies to which I have made allusion. Its application will, I think, be sufficiently evident. Here it is : (D.)

I walk in lonely beauty bright!
  The breath of steam around me flies;
And, radiant in metallic light,
  I see the brazen dash-pots rise—
A vision, glorious to my sight
  As purple peaks of Paradise!

One pot the more, one pot the less,
  Would make no difference in the view;
For all that's best of loveliness,
  And all that's best of science too,
Are garnered up, mankind to bless,
  In dash-pots of the brazen hue.

The happy thought around me coils,
  And cheers me on at every turn;
While engine-drivers pour their oils,
  And stokers make their coals to burn;
That I appropriate the spoils
  With␣ n my dash-pot's portly urn!

"There, my friend," added this bard of science and of dash-pots, "that will suffice. You are now acquainted with me, and with my sentiment. *Haec olim meminisse juvabit.* Leave me your address. I shall write to you from Washington City—from the capital—whither my steps now tend. Consider the cut-off a fixed fact. I will not say that I shall not improve upon your design. *Non tetigit, non ornavit.* But its success is all the more certain. Give me your hand, sir. Good morning!"

The dilapidated inventor withdrew, and the hero was left alone. A moment he seemed transfixed as by a mighty thought; then his tall form relaxed, and he sank back into the arm chair and closed his eyes. The recent effort of eloquence had overpowered him. The great man slept—slept and dreamed.

And this was his vision.

D———n's Dream of Triumph.

A golden cloud seemed floating in mid-air, upborne at its four corners by Watt and Mariotte, Brunel and Samuel Smiles. Upon that cloud rested an enormous throne, made of variously colored and strongly welded dash-pots. Upon that throne, in royal state, sat the angust D———n. At his feet, and serving for a footstool, appeared the scientific writings of the hated Isherwood. In his hands was upreared a a gigantic brazen dash-pot, whereinto fell a continual shower of golden eagles, poured from above by Clio, the muse of history,—a figure, however, closely resembling that of Secretary———. Around him, in every direction, floated the shapes of war-vessels, provided with the S———s cut-off. Beneath the cloud, on which rested this imposing monarchy, appeared the wretched Isherwood and the Water Commissioners of Detroit, pendant, heads downward, and grasping frantically at nothing. A gentle breeze, as of windy and ever-blowing Fame, impelled this pageant through the heavens. And thus the sleeper beheld, prefigured in light and shadow, his own immortality.

II.

Washington, D. C., —— —, 18—.

My Dear S———s:

Veni ! vidi ! vici ! So said the great Roman, after victory. So says the engineer of the period, under similar circumstances.

It was, nevertheless, an achievement of magnitude and difficulty. Prejudice, of deep root and of long continuance, opposed me at the outset. Conventionality, embodied in the form of a naval official, frowned darkly upon the champion of progress, your humble friend. Old ideas of economy—the crude notions of our antiquated forefathers—arose before me, like battle lines in Parisian streets, before the footsteps of Revolution. But, like Revolution, I nevertheless swept onward, bearing down prejudice, conventionality, and old ideas. Accordingly, these latter are dust, and I am jubilant.

Never shall I forget that memorable morning, when, with miniature dash-pot in one hand, and gilt-edged copy of "Mariotte's Law" in the other, I made my final effectual appeal to the Secretary of the Navy. Like an oracle I stood before him; and it is no exaggeration to say that I forced conviction upon his mind, with an energy and a righteous violence that literally withered him in his official arm chair. At first, I dwelt upon the simple principle of the cut-off. Then, incidentally, I gave him a detailed account of the life and services of James Watt. From this theme, by an easy and natural transition, I advanced to speak of myself; and as is not usual with mankind, I made the most of the subject. I described, with scientific prolixity and minuteness, my own novel machinery, my improvements upon the clever, though crude, idea of your active, ambitious and promising mind; and into this description I introduced, with much effect, my celebrated paraphrase of a Hebrew melody, celebrating the dash-pot. Lastly, in a peroration, worthy, though I say it, of the Ciceronian age, I called upon him to submit to the eternal laws of the Universe, as illustrated in my authentic teachings. "Respect the divine law," I exclaimed, "of which I am but the humble representative ! You may think to escape its power for a time, but you must surely submit to it at last. Yield, therefore, without fruitless resistance. Do what you will, you cannot get far ahead of the old man up above. Even Isherwood, with all his gold lace and all his money, can avail you nothing. The laws of expansion operate without regard to Isherwood. I have placed his book on a cylinder-head of one of my engines, and it never made the least difference in the operation of the piston. Will you, then, be stayed on the noble road of progress by the voice of a quack and a beast, a knave and a wretch—

> A villain,
> A cup-purse of the empire and the rule,
> Who from the shelf the precious diadem stole,
> And put it in his pocket ?

Will you butt your head against a stone wall, because, like the man in the novel, you find it "so very satisfying ?" No, you will not ! Or, if a stone wall is to be butted, you will rather choose that it be the penetrable stone wall of man's ignorance, than the indomitable barrier of eternal law. You will be mindful of sage fortitude of the pious American citizen of African descent, who said that when de Lord told him to butt a hole through a stone wall, it was his business to butt, and de Lord's business to carry him through. You will think of this, I say; and if Isherwood be powerful, you will be consoled by the reflection that all human power is weak against the power of Nature. And so, side by side with me, you will keep on butting."

"D———n," said the Secretary, when I thus concluded my harangue, "you are a great man. Take a chair, and let's liquor. I shall believe in dash-pots as long as I live; and you shall build us a new war ship."

"But Isherwood is my foe."

"Isherwood be ——."

We drank some straw-colored liquor, with our mouths, after that, and so our interview terminated.

And now the PENSACOLA is in progress of construction. The egg upon which long ago we commenced to brood, will soon break, and enable us to count our chickens—chickens of iron they will be to others, my friend—Mother Cary's chickens—but to us, chickens of gold!

"Swift fly the years, and rise th' expected morn!"

We began our work on this ship in 1858. It is now 1863. She will soon be finished, with the cut-off, and the novel machinery all complete, and 1 shall expect her to make such time as never was made before, by any craft of equal size and pretension. To-day, by way of verifying Mariotte's Law, I have applied the cut-off principle to her stern, and have had the stern cut-off. The effect was rending, and I witnessed it with emotions of awe. To-morrow we shall put the stern on again. Having satisfied the Law, we must now disappoint and effectually dispose of the prophets—these latter, collected here in great numbers by the malignant Isherwood, having stated that our ship will be good for nothing without a stern. As if the erudite D——n didn't recognize stern necessity.

The Department recognizes it, at any rate—for I have sent in my bill. All the clerks have been, for several weeks, busy in investigating the accounts: and poor creatures!—they are quite at their wits' ends. It is a comfort to think that they did'nt have far to go. As a final resort, they have procured a calculating machine. But calculating machines are vain as against dash-pots. The ship will cost $800,000 at the very least, and the Department will have to pay it.

Isherwood, I hear, suggests that such a ship ought not to cost more than $120,000, or, at furthest, more than $140,000. Strange that people will so cling to the delusions of the past. Because old-fashioned ships and engines have been built for little or nothing, is it imagined that the scientific marvels of the future are to be got without money and without price? Perish the mercenary idea—ignoble prejudice of most ignoble minds!

Indignation devours me quite.

I can no more,

D——N.

P. S.

Several Days Later.—The great work is finished. The Ship has been tried, and a competent committee reports to the Navy Department that she is considered safe to run down the Potomac with the tide. *Go Triumphe!*   D.

III.

Rumor—*ac spem fronte serenat*—had often borne to my ears the musical name of D——n, the engineer. His engines, with the celebrated —— cut-off, had been described to me—by a pious clerk in the Navy Department—as "Chief among ten thousand, and althogether lovely." As a natural consequence, I had longed to behold a specimen of the great man's art. And now the golden opportunity had come. I was at Washington. So was the Pensacola, on board which an old friend of mine held the office of Chief Engineer. She was furnished with a D——n engine. She would sail at nightfall. I did not hesitate. As the sun descended into the west, I descended into the grimy but gold-laced presence of my friend the Engineer.

On the entering the engine-room, I was filled with amazement, not wholly unmingled with consternation. On every side, as far as the eye could reach, I beheld metallic evidences of the ingenuity of D——n. With a slight effort of fancy, I might have believed myself in a museum of mechanical curiosities. The cloud of witnesses, spoken of in Holy Writ, would be as mere vapor to the dense cloud of wheels which I then beheld. In fact, the very air was black with cogs.

Cogs to the right of me,
Cogs to the left of me,
Handles and monkey-tails,
Bristled and bothered.

One wheel, in particular, presently fixed my attention. "That," said my companion, "is the reversing wheel. It adjusts the link, for going ahead, stopping, or backing. Those only can work it, however, who understand how to manipulate the cut-off implements. You will see presently. It isn't every body that's up to science, in these days."

At this moment the Captain's bell signalled to start the engine. Simultaneously twelve men joined us on the platform. The area of this latter being about two square yards, we were conscious of being crowded.

"These hands will help us," said the Engineer.

"It appears," said I, "that science still has a few representatives extant."

"A select few," he answered; "they have received instructions from D———n

FIRST GLIMPSE OF THE ENGINE-ROOM.

himself. Now, boys, start her."

The boys distributed themselves among the cogs, and resolutely commenced operations. I silently admired their resolution.

"Take it easy, boys," said a Lieutenant, looking in at this juncture. "The Captain's gone ashore, to buy a photograph of D———n; he'll be on board again in half-an-hour. If you begin now, you'll get started by the time he gets back."

They began.

Two men stationed themselves at the water-valves; two went to the injection-valves; six assumed charge of the link; one fixed his eyes on the themometer; one, in a corner, drank something out of a black bottle. The Engineer himself wound up the clock. I helped him. Six more men then came in, variously armed with handspikes, beetles, hydraulic jacks, oil cans, and wrenches. A number of small boys, all in uniform, also made their appearance, bearing buckets of water, more oil cans, and several crow-bars. They stationed themselves at the dash-pots.

"I think she will start," said I to the Engineer. "Probably," said the Engineer to me.

STARTING THE ENGINE—AND THE ENGINEERS.

So saying, he pushed with tremendous strength upon a monkey-tail. This latter, I noticed, was connected by rods and bell-crank levers with the valve spindle. Being pushed, it had, in course of time, the effect of opening a passover-valve—an auxiliary arrangement for working the engine by hand.

"The thermometer marks 153° in the shade," said a vigilant assistant.

"All right," said the Engineer. "Lend me that black bottle," he added, addressing the man in the corner. Receiving the bottle, he drank from it for five minutes.

TRIPPING-VALVES.

By this time the small boys had poured several gallons of oil into the dash-pots, and had gone out for more. The men with bars and beetles had also made a vigorous attack on the valves. Several wheels were observed to be in motion. So was the man in the corner. He reeled from side to side, as if with excessive delight at the busy scene before him. Then he suddenly fell backwards down a neighboring hatch-way.

"He has forgotten his bottle," said the Engineer.

A terrific crash was now heard. The link was down—the water valves were in operation—the engine had started.

"I think they'll cast off the lines in ten minutes," remarked a small boy near me, at the same time oversetting a bucket of water. "We shant move much at first," he added. "'Taint science to move."

I now understood the crash. The piston-rod of one cylinder had reached its dead centre, making an awful noise. The men at the water-valves redoubled their exertions. The piston-rod of the other cylinder met its centre with a yet louder bang. Boys returned, with oil for the dash-pots. The Engineer tugged at his monkey-tail. The injection-valves were knocked open with handspikes. The Lieutenant re-appeared, and announced the return of the Captain.

"He's got a capital picture of D———n," said this officer. "It's along with a sketch of the wings of Icarus."

"I'll go and see it," remarked the Engineer. "We shall have to wait some time, for a vacuum. Boys, put lots of oil in those dash-pots."

He went away, leaving the black bottle. I took charge of it. Also I wound up the clock, which, by this time, had run down. The man with the thermometer announced that instrument as marking 154°.

GOING ON WATCH.   COMING OFF.

"It's warm," he said.

In ten minutes the Engineer came back. There was, as he had predicted, a vacuum, and we were in motion. The men seemed weary, but they were certainly determined. I encouraged them by circulating the black bottle.

Thus we started, and thus we were propelled. During the entire watch, the workers in the engine-room never flagged. Regularly, as did the angels upon Jacob's ladder, the boys, with their oil cans, ascended and decended. Regularly the linkmen tugged at their wheel. Regularly the hammers rose and fell. Never were heroic exertions attended with more amazing results. On every side cogs grated and monkey-tail frisked in air. Crash! went the engine: bang! bang! zip! zip! crash! bang! zip! zip! And faintly through the din, I heard the voices of dash-pot men, crying for monkey-wrenches.

"Hurrah!" roared a small boy, from a neigboring dash-pot; "it's as good as fireworks on the Fourth of July—aint it, Mister?"

I did not hesitate to endorse the opinion of the small boy.

At this moment, the Captain rang "two bells." There was an immediate sensation in the engine-room.

"Cut off steam to the ninety-nine hundredth part of the stroke," roared the Engineer. "Stand by there, with sledge-hammers over the dash-pots! Put steam on the reversing-cylinder!"

But the link would not budge; and, in spite of closed throttle, the mill went tearing on. It is not easy to stay the march of science!

A LITTLE OIL NECESSARY.

"Heave away on that wheel!" cried the Engineer. "Send all the firemen here' and call the other division! Heave with those crow-bars, and trip the valves!"

This time success. The link arose, with unearthly shrieks and groans; and the engine was stopped, as if never to move again.

The black bottle being empty, we all drew a long breath—and wished it were full.

"Come away," said the Engineer. "Jenkins will start her; I'm tired."

The bell rang as we left the engine-room. The terrible noise recommenced, and science, under the guidance of Jenkins, once more impelled us forward at a conservative rate.

"O that D———n were here to see!" I exclaimed, taking the Engineer's arm.

"O that he were here to feel!" was his rejoinder, the thermometer being at 154°.

I looked steadfastly upon my companion. He did not appear to advantage. It would not be too much to say that science had used him up. Moreover, he was manifestly disgusted with circumstances.

"D———n is a great man," he said. "Wait till I fill this bottle, and we'll talk it over."

I waited. We nourished ourselves. Then we sat down on a gun-carriage: and this is what the Engineer said:

"D———n is a great man. I've read his Washington speech, all about the Navy, and I know by that his mighty intellect. He's acquainted with Lord Byron's verses, and with Pope and Shakspeare; and he knows all about Mariotte's Law. This is one of his engines—with the ——— cut-off. It makes 35 revolutions a minute, and it also makes a splendid noise. These are the least of its merits. It is an admirable consumer of oil. I suppose D———n learned the value of lubrication when he was a lawyer and used to oil the bench. The usual allowance to this engine is five gallons an hour—which is'nt enough, and the boys smuggle it on, at the rate of about a hundred and twenty-five gallons a-day. All the journals require it constantly (no pun intended). And then the fireman! It keeps them as busy as bees, because, you know, if the cut-off should become deranged—as I do sometimes, for instance—and steam should be used at full stroke on the engines, then the expansion application, through good fires, would rest entirely upon them. That is clear, is'nt it? When the engine is used at full stroke, and there are fifteen pounds of steam in the boilers, five revolutions will reduce the pressure to nine pounds. This again shows the wonderful utility of the cut-off, which saves the expense of large boilers for marine engines. D———n, as I said before, is a great man—a gigantic and tremendous man. I have read his tribute to Watt (E), and Watt, if he wots any thing about it, ought to be very grateful for such a first-class notice; and I have read also his remarks on expansion. And, trusting in D———n, I don't see why a donkey-boiler would'nt do for this ship, just as well as the two big ones that we carry now. But that's a point for science to determine, after we've got rid of the superfluous coal.

HE SMUGGLED THE OIL

At this point the Engineer's remarks were interrupted by a sudden commotion in the engine-room, wherefrom, presently, several men emerged, bearing the insensible body of an oiler who had just fainted among the dash-pots. They carried him away.

"It occurs frequently," resumed my companion. "Even D———n himself became a victim once—in Jerome's yacht, I think. Science must have its martyrs; you know. I've lost several fingers myself, tripping valves; and I know three engineers who, while on duty, have dropped insensible at their posts. You will notice that our stokers are very like skeletons. Thin men stand the heat better than fat ones; and the thermoneter in our engine-room rarely marks less than 140°. This is another of the beauties of the cut-off—it paves the way to promotion in the service, by cutting off so mañh numanobstacles."

THE OILER COMES ON WATCH.   HE WATCHES.

Here my companion (or was I deceived in the dim moonlight ?) deliberately winked upon me with one eye. Then, seizing the black bottle, he drank, with his mouth, for some time. Finally he resumed his remarks :

"D———n is a modest man, too. All great genius exhibits that characteristic. He never blows his own horn. He said once, that he 'was profoundly ignorant of a steam-engine, and supposed a cylinder head to be a full moon.' That was modesty ! No one, who has ever heard our cylinders work, would credit it of him. They suggest any thing but moons. Meteors, accompained by thunder, would much better typify them. But whatever may be the great man's notion as to cylinder-heads, he has certatnly got very clear ideas on the subject of DASH-POTS. Look at that engine, for instance ! It's all over dash-pots. They gleam like the brass kettle of by-gone days, in which my venerated and now defunct grandmother used to boil cabbage. Hence the tender associations with which they are fraught. I look upon them, day and night, with never-tiring admiration (F). The rings of Saturn and the splendors of Mars are really as nothing to these irridescent vehicles of science. I have, indeed, commenced a poem about them—in humble imitation of the great engineer's favorite bard. It will be comprised in four hundred cantos, commencing thus :

> The D———n dash-pots are gleaming like gold,
> And are brimming with oil as full as they'll hold;
> Neither odor nor sheen more delightful could be—
> They are pungent to smell and refulgent to see.
>   Diddle dol de ! diddle dol de !
> O the D———n dash-pot's the dash-pot for me.

"There, is, however, another feature in this engine, which illustrates to still greater advantage the grandeur of D————n's inventive genius. That is, the LINK-MOTION. The lustre of this device outshines even the lustre of the dash-pots. You

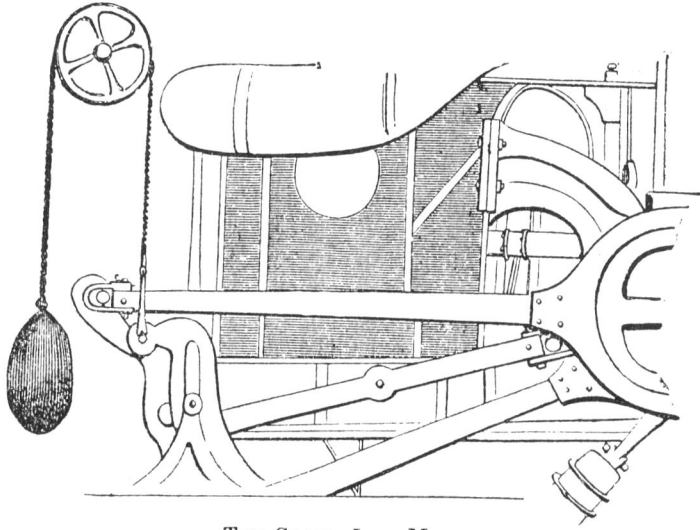

THE GRAND LINK-MOTION.

have just seen something of its achievements in starting this ship. It is not, like the common and vulgar link-motion in general use, an instantaneously adjustible apparatus, easily worked by one man. On the contrary, it requires only about fifteen men to work it, and it keeps them occupied from ten to twenty minutes in adjusting the various cogs, and cranks, and levers, in conjunction with the cut-off machinery, for going ahead or backing. Plainly enough, science marks this link-motion for its own. Only a man who, like D———n, had read 'Richard the Third,' and 'drank of the pure fountain at the source,' could have devised it. So ponderous is the mass of metal employed, that it necessitates a huge weight, acting—on a principle of sweet simplicity—over a pulley, and attached to the upper part of the arcs of both engines, thereby to lessen what otherwise would be a terrible strain on the ship. I am sure you will sympathize with my admiration for this triumph of skill. There is a great gain, too, in noise by this means—noise so salutary in its impression on the common mind. A free space is made for these weights to run up and down inside the coal bunkers; and so, at the slightest motion of the ship, they create a most exhilarating clatter, harmonizing with the delicious din of the entire engine.

"These little touches evince the philosopher. Common minds would have been content with celerity, safety, and economy, without reference to the ornamental intricacies of science. Not so the expansive D———n. His progress in the realms of thought bears no distant analogy to the wise man's progress in the realms of experience. Youth imagines that the world was made for man. Maturity discovers that man was made for the world. So in mechanism. To the budding and innocent D———n of long ago, it seemed, no doubt, the dash-pots were made for engines. To the full-blown D———n of to-day, it is manifestly clear that engines were made for dash-pots. Hence the noble machinery, with its patent cut-off and astonishing link-motion, that we have here the privilege to observe. It has been constructed under the white light of science, and without the slightest regard to expense. Its dash-pots gleam, in the yellow radiance of polished brass, and its monkey-tails are marshalled like the Assyrian cohorts of the pious Byron. Great facilities are afforded for the soothing influence of oil, and for the consequent liberal dissemination of postal currency and green-backed notes. The whistle is a dear one; but Uncle Samuel (like the old trump that he has always been) pays for it without a murmur, and wins the unqualified approbation of D———n. Could more be wished? I leave it to your judgment as a citizen.

OIL IS ACTIVE.

"You have observed—doubtless with profound amazement—the striking ceremonies with which it is necessary to approach this engine, on the respective subjects of starting and stopping. This, in itself, is evidence of almost human strength of character. In all experience it has been found that large bodies move slowly—an ancient adage, beautifully illustrated in the case of the *Clara Clarita.* (G.)

"It was D———n who selected the boiler and adapted the machinery of that 'thing of beauty,' at a cost, to the gifted Jerome, of over Twenty-One Thousand Dollars. And she sailed precisely one mile and a quarter in two hours and a half, being ultimately thwarted by a stubborn and unaccommodating tide, at Corlear's Hook. Equally valid is the venerable adage as applied to all D———n engines, with their inevitable ——— cut-off. They start slowly; they run with dignity; they stop with due deliberation. In watching this one, I am often reminded of an old gentleman, whose girls I used to flirt with, when I was a boy. A solid old gentleman he was—with the gout, and a purple noise, and staunch conservative views; and he sat by night in his drawing-room, in a marvellous arm-chair, his noble form arrayed in indescribable complications of raiment. 'Good evening, sir,' I used to say to him, on entering the room; 'it's a very cold evening.' And then I turned my attention to the girls. But the old gentleman's brain was an active one; and, after precisely fifteen minutes of preparation, his voice, emerging from many bandages, would be heard to answer, ' Yes, you're right—the evening is very cold.' There was a solidity about that old gentleman, very impressive to me in those days; and there is a similar and equally impressive solidity about this D——n engine. If it has a fault ; that fault consists in its insufficient illustration of its erudite author's idea upon the subject of bricks. With that idea he electrified a Washington Jury, in the Mattingly Case, and that idea once fully realized in practice, would electrify the entire mechanical world. Imagine a platform supporting a ton of bricks (H), placed upon the end of a one-inch piston ! Transport that image to yonder engine-room, and mark the consequence.

' How reason reels !
O what a miracle to man is man,'

especially when he happens to be such a man as D————n."

PERSUADING THE LINK TO RUN UP.

Here *conticuere omnes*, and the black bottle was circulated. But my eloquent friend, absorbed in the grand theme, soon continued his eulogium.

" The genius of D————n as been otherwise made manifest in four enormous rock-shafts, garnished with numerous parabolic cams, and designed for working the steam-exhaust and cut-off valves. It appears, too, in the valves themselves, upon which all manner of intricate instruments have been ingeniously brought to bear, in order to prevent any abrupt and decisive action that should by chance resemble that of vulgar machinery. I think it was the sublime purpose of D————n, in reference to this engine, that it should display ' neither variableness nor the shadow of turning.' His liberal ingenuity has combined the heavy metals as never heavy metals were combined before. Not only has he contrived a dash-pot, to prevent the slamming of the cut-off valve; but he has devised a lip to cushion on the steam as it is jammed against the valve-seat. I dwell upon these details with a fascinated interest. This

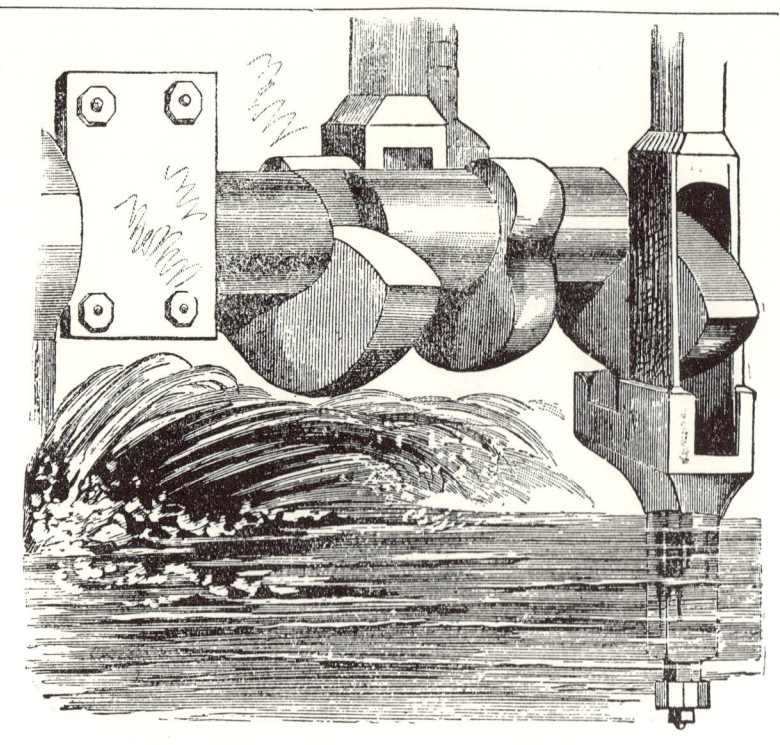

ROCK-SHAFT—ROCKING IN THE BILGE-WATER.

valve is plug-shaped. On its outside rim is a ring of metal laid upon the seat, and designed to give lead to this plug-arrangement, by expanding or contracting its circle. You can have no conception of the felicity with which it works, unless you have both seen and heard it. The principle is that of the organ-pedal, while the music—but what words can do justice to the incessant *click, click-up,* sh, *clickety-click, click-up,* so clear, so distinctly intoned, so soothing to the nervous system! What says the poet Milton?

'Can any mortal mixture of earth's sound,
Breathe such divine, enchanting ravishment!'

"I think not.

"You will marvel, perhaps, that such surpassing excellence of mechanism is not more widely appreciated in this scientific generation. I must remind you of Galileo who was incarcerated for his intelligence; and of the Scottish inventor of umbrellas, who was pelted in the streets for bearing up one of his own anti-pluvial protectors. It was not easy for even the mighty D———n to persuade Uncle Samuel to buy the whistle. The very machinery itself—coy and modest under the eye of distrustful observation—declined at first to operate. I recall the trial day of she Pensacola. The great engineer himself was on board, to superintend the engine. All was excitement. Promptly, at the word of command, the dash-pot phalanx seized their implements, and rushed into action.

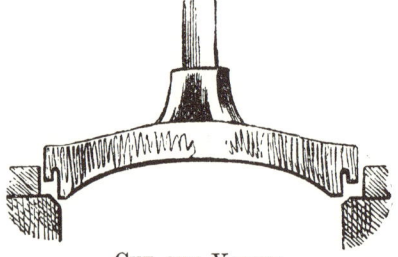

CUT OFF VALVE.

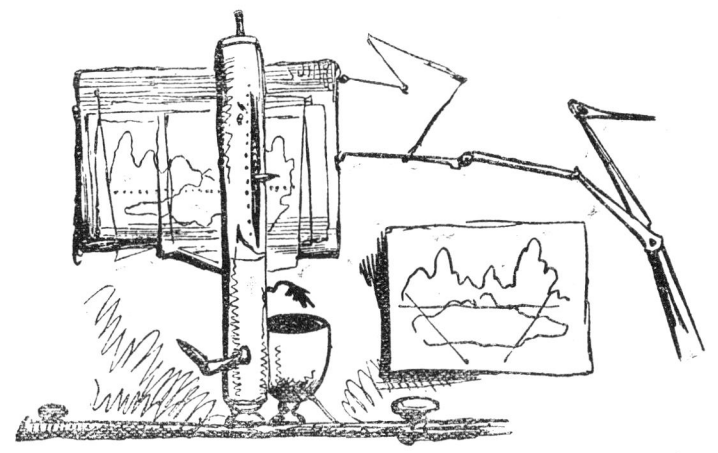

PERFECTLY CLEAR INDICATOR AND DIAGRAM.—A TRIUMPH OF GENIUS.

Gallant charge! I beheld it from my station at the valves, and thought that I had never seen a more extraordinary proceeding towards an engine. We made, I think, some ninety odd trials before the link would rise, and the desired, and I may say,

GALLANT CHARGE OF THE DASH-POT LIGHT GUARD.

indispensable vacuum, consent to form. Coyness, as I have said, is the vice of this wonderful engine; but, to cull once more from those sweet pastures of song in which its inventor loves to ramble,

"E'en its vices lean to virtue's side."

I have since noticed other manifestations of that coyness. For example, this ship has excellent lines for sailing. With a ten-knot breeze, she can out-sail her modest engines entirely. They are sensitive and sluggish under ordinary treatment. We have sometimes made nine knots an hour, with the vessel under sail, and the engines doing their utmost. That was brilliant! But coyness would seem to settle upon those cogs, and paralyze those dash-pots; and then we have disconnected the propellor, and so made eleven-and-a-half or twelve knots under the same amount of sail. At such times, the engine may have attained from forty to forty-four revolutions, cutting off, as indicated by the cut-off dial, at three and one-tenth of the stroke. Steam, as you know, soon works off; but by using the best of coal, and keep-

WORKING WATER-VALVES—A RECREATION IN HOT WEATHER.

ENGINEERS ORDERED TO REPORT FOR DUTY ON BOARD THE PENSACOLA.

APPENDIX. 941

ing the firemen in a state of incessant and wholesome activity, we have managed to keep up fourteen pounds; which implies that, under certain circumstances, a great number of revolutions may be attained by dragging the propeller through the water as you bowl merrily along.

T. M———N (LOQ.)--SHE WONT WORK, SIR. CAN'T GET HER TO GO OVER 30, NO HOW.
    D———N.--WELL--ER--GIVE HER OIL, AND SHUT OFF THREE MORE FURNACES, --AND--A--OIL THE WIPER--AND--SLACK OFF A BLADE OF THE PROPELLER,--AND--SCOUR THOSE DASH-POTS--AND SHUT THE THROTTLE--AND--YES, SET THE CLOCK BACK.

CRUISE FINISHED—THEY RETURN HOME.

"And now," said my friend, as we rose from the gun-carriage, "I think your curiosity is sufficiently gratified in reference to the D———n engine with the——— cut-off. You have seen that it is a tremendous and unparalleled affair, and you cannot doubt that its inventor is a tremendous and unparalleled man. How, then, can you censure me for my devotion to science? In such a cause, who would not gladly peril life and limb? I have lost three fingers, as you see, and one eye; and Jenkins has lost an arm. Nor have our compatriots in the great work escaped similar honors of martyrdom. Thus the cause of dash-pots is prospered; and thus, at a continued and most noble sacrifice of oil, time, and human life, Uncle Samuel enjoys and pays for the delicious D———n Whistle. And now, as remarked by Hamlet, when about to assault his respectable uncle, 'Let us go in together!'"

APPENDIX.

(A.)

ISHERWOOD DEFINED.—Ignorance and corruption--Nonsense—Snug, the Joiner--Audacity and impudence—False and not ignorant—Entirely ignorant—Utterly worthless ignoramus—The bull who took a fancy to stop a locomotive—Intriguer—Juggler—Fool--Swindler--Penny-a-liner — Bare-faced fraud — Monumental brass--Villian—Source of utter demoralization--Iago and Uriah Heep—Rascality--The son of a poor widow.—*Speech of — — D——n in the Mattingly Case*, pp. 3, 5, 12, 25, 30, 31, 32, 34, 43, 49, 60, 70, 73, 77, 79.

(B.)

"The contract was awarded to Messrs. D——n and ——. . . . . By the terms of the contract the engine was to be fully completed by the 1st day of July, 1857, but the time was subsequently extended until July 1st, 1858, and again until March 1st, 1859, in both cases by and with the consent of the sureties.

"In his report of January 1st, 1858, the engineer of the Board reported, 'that a considerable portion of the parts of the new engine have been received, and the contractors expect soon to commence the erection of the engine. The new engine house is enclosed, and every thing is prepared for the erection of the engine, and that he saw no reason to doubt that every thing on the part of the contractors would be fully carried out during the life of the contract.' But, on the 1st of Janurary, 1859, we had to report to you that the engine had not been completed, and the engineer reported to us that the work on the new engine was not as far advanced as it was anticipated it would be. The cylinders had been set. No further portions of the work had been received during the season, but a large amount of work in New York was out and nearly ready for shipment. The contractors had notified him that they had made arrangements to send the work forward by rail at once. Still, the 1st of January, 1860, came, and we were again compelled to report to you the engine uncompleted; but our engineer reported to us that the erection of the engine was nearly completed, and the boilers were placed and ready for the setting.

"During all this protracted and vexatious delay in getting this engine into service, which was deemed essential to the safety of the city, and to ensure an uninterrupted supply of water, the confidence of the engineer remained unshaken in its success, and until last summer the Board had repeated assurances from the contractors and their agent, that it would be completed and brought into use in a very short time.

"On the 1st of January, 1861, we were compelled to report to you that the engine had not yet been offered us for acceptance, although the engineer in charge of setting it up represented it as nearly completed, and that he was then at the East, with the avowed purpose of consulting his employers, the contractors, in regard to getting it into operation. On his return, in the month of February, he resumed work on it, and, after making some changes in parts of it, steam was got up, and the engine made short runs occasionally until the 14th of May. When it became necessary to throw engine No. 2 out of use, for the purpose of making important improvements on it, the engineer consented to keep up a supply of water with the new engine during the time our engine was being repaired. Engine No. 2 was out of use a longer time than it was expected it would be, and was not again brought into service until the 1st day of June last.

"Subsequently the new engine was thoroughly overhauled, rollers were removed, and slides substituted, and, after making several short runs, the engineer in charge closed the house, and left for the city of New York, taking with him the keys of the engine house, to report to his employers. Shortly after this, in the month of August last, the keys of the house were returned to the Secretary of the Board, by express, and the President of the Board recieved a communication from Mr. —— D——n, one of the contractors, apprizing him that the keys had been returned as above, and with an intimation that the contractors would probably abandon their intention of making any further efforts to complete the engine."

The above elegant extract was what the seedy inventor read from the *"Tenth Annual Report of the Board of Water Commissioners to the Common Council of the City of Detroit."*

(C.)

It will be observed that here, as in several other instances, D——n's rage (heroic and noble passion!) against Isherwood breaks out blindly, and causes him to confuse history. It was not until the D——n egg was very nearly hatched, that the offending Isherwood became Chief Engineer. D——n's first conquest—that of Mr. Secretary Toucey—was made with comparative ease. His martyrdom, so touchingly depicted by himself, did not really commence until after the advent of the new order of things, under Mr. Welles.

The poem which the great engineer has thus artfully paraphrased is the following peculiarly melodious and fanciful description which commences Lord Byron's "Hebrew Melodies:"

> She walks in beauty, like the night,
> Of cloudless climes and starry skies;
> And all that's best of dark and bright
> Meet in her aspect and her eyes,
> Thus mellowed to that tender light,
> Which heaven to gaudy day denies.
>
> One shade the more, one ray the less,
> Had half impaired the nameless grace
> Which waves in every raven tress,
> Or softly lightens o'er her face;
> Where thoughts serenely sweet express,
> How pure, how dear their dwelling place.
>
> And on that cheek and o'er that brow,
> So soft, so calm, yet eloquent,
> The smiles that win, the tints that glow,
> But tell of days in goodness spent;
> A mind at peace with all below,
> A heart whose love is innocent.

(E.)

"At this point James Watt, the Shakespeare of mechanics appeared—a man whose equal as an engineer has not stood on this earth since, nor do I see any prospect that another will come—a man on whose intellect the Almighty had impressed that intuitive knowledge of his great physical truths, as he had impressed upon the intellect of Shakspeare an intuitive knowledge of his great moral truths. He was an humble man in station, but illumined by the light of genius he rose into grandeur which will never fade. . . . . It was James Watt who fought the battles of civil liberty in the earlier part of this century. It was James

Watt—not Lord Wellington—who conquered Napoleon. He it was who, by creating that physical power, enabled England to produce out of its internal resources those means by which she sustained herself against the gigantic strength of the great Emperor, and carried on a war that resulted in his overthrow. Had James Watt never lived, the French Emperor would have wiped out from its place in the history of the world, and out of the catalogue of nations, that power and people who now domineer over land and sea. James Watt was the great pillar on which they stood, and he it was who fought the great battles that maintained them in their present position." *Speech.—Speech of D———n in the Mattingly Case*, pp. 13, 14.

(F.)

" I had read the testimony of Isherwood and appreciated its effect; and when I entered this room, there stood upon that stand one of the cubs of this lion—an engine driver from the Navy Yard—sent here to devour whatever fragments had been left from the destructive meal of the day before. He was a gorgeous creature as he stood before me; resplendent with gold lace, his delicate white hands unsullied by vile grease, and unhardened by vulgar toil; his magnificent apparel shedding an effulgence of glory around him, in which the rings of Saturn encircling his arms vied with the splendors of Mars all over his body for supremacy. There he stood as—

"The Assyrian came down like the wolf on the fold,
And his cohorts were gleaming in purple and gold;
And the sheen of their spears was like stars on the sea,
When the blue wave rolls nightly on deep Galilee.'

" I never behold one of these magnificent visions without thinking how striking is the resemblance between an engine driver of the United States Navy of this day and the lilies of the valley. Not, perhaps, from any peculiar modesty which they have in common, but because like them ' they toil not, neither do they spin ; but I say unto you, that Solomon in all his glory was not arrayed like one of these.' "
—*Speech of——— ——D———n in the Mattingly Case*, p. 11.

(G.)

MR. D———N AND THE STEAM YACHT CLARA CLARITA.

To the Editor of the———

Mr. D———n publishes in the *Times* of Tuesday last, a statement signed by Mr. Rowland, concerning the responsibility for the machinery of my steam yacht, the *Clara Clarita*, which is so erroneous and unjust that I am compelled to ask you to publish the facts of the case, so far as I know them.

That some one has very grossly blundered in the construction of that machinery, is a fact very well known. In the ship-yards along the East River it is pretty well understood who the blundering party is, but the public are not quite so well advised. Mr. D———n, by the statement alluded to, attempts to fasten the blame upon " *a gentleman* " whom he does not name, but whom he leaves every one reading the article to infer, to be me. Why, after all the trouble and expense he has put me to, he should add this extra charge, I do not know, unless it be that I am done with him, and Mr. Forbes (whom he must mean, if he means anybody,) is not. Mr. D———n knows perfectly well that I never had anything whatever to do with the construction of that machinery. I never gave an order or made a solitary suggestion respecting it. I have simply paid for the work done under his directions. Knowing nothing whatever about steam myself, I entrusted that department of my vessel entirely to the friendly supervision of Mr. Forbes. I did it chiefly to avail myself of the wonderful skill of Mr. Forbes' engineer, Mr. D———n, of whose capabilities in the way of steam I had heard glowing accounts—partly from himself and partly from other people.

Mr. Forbes knew all about my purpose of building a steam yacht from the very beginning, and took a warm and friendly interest in its construction. He knew that I wished it to be reasonably fast, and to be ready for use as soon as possible. He informed me one day that he had found an engine and boiler which might possibly answer our purpose, and that he "would have D———n examine it." A few days after this he informed me that D———n had examined it and said it *was just what he wanted; that he could adapt it to my yacht, giving her all the power she required.* The engine was thereupon purchased for the sum of $5,000, and Mr. D———n proceeded to "adapt" it. The cost of this adaptation, as may be seen by the vouchers from the Continental Iron Works, now in my possession, every dollar of which was expended under the direction of Mr. D———n, is $16,178.03. It can hardly be supposed by any man of sense, that either Mr. Forbes or myself would have purchased this engine had it not been represented as available. Nor could Mr. D———n, as an engineer, have taken in hand the job of *adapting* it, involving such an enormous cost, unless he had thought so likewise.

At last a trial trip was had. I was on board. Mr. D———n worked the engine himself, assisted by Mr. Rowland and Mr. Rowland's fireman. We started from the Continental Iron Works down the river. The day was fine, everything was in order, the model of the boat was pronounced perfection and we started off with flying colors.

Her machinery alone remained to be tried. To the best of my recollection *we made one mile and a quarter in just two hours and a half.* It was (in point of space) a brief if not a pleasant trip to all on board—including myself—especially considering that I had waited eight months for the adaptation of this machinery. I could have had fifty engines built during this time notwithstanding the "government pressure." We should have proceeded further down the river, but at Corlear's Hook we were driven back—by the tide.

For several weeks subsequent to that day the vessel was held subject to Mr. D———n's orders for the purpose of making a further trial, and he was repeatedly invited to do so, but would not. He having abandoned her, I called in the aid of two of the best engineers in New York, (next best of course to Mr. D———n,) and a second trial was had with no better results. The entire machinery of Mr. D———n was condemned as utterly worthless, and is now being sold for old iron.

Some further apology for this note—if further apology is needed—may be found in the statement of Mr. D———n yesterday in the presence of a number of gentlemen, that *he was not on board when the trial trip was made;* that "it was made by a chap by the name of Vanderbilt who was a fool." This "chap, Vanderbilt," is the superintending engineer of the Pacific Mail Steamship Company.

Yours, &c.,

LEONARD W. JEROME.

To the Editor of the Times:

As Mr. D———n has seen fit, in your paper of this date, to refer to conversation had with me at the Union Club, on the subject of the machinery of Mr. Jerome's yacht, the *Clara Clarita,* and as his reference to only a portion of the conversation must have arisen from a supposition that the remainder was immaterial to the question, I deem it but proper, both in justice to truth as well as to Mr. D———n's reputation as an engineer, to recapitulate the entire conversation.

Mr. D———n, after stating that the machinery was not such as was calculated to develop satisfactorily the fine qualities of the yacht—but that he was blameless for it, further than regarded its adaptation—answered my inquiry as to what speed could be got out of the vessel with her "adapted machinery" by the reply that she would make eleven to twelve knots an hour, (a statement, by-the-by, which, when I made it to Mr. Jerome, so surprised him as to occasion the exclamation, that "if she could not go faster than that he would scuttle her.) But, continued Mr. D————n, with such machinery as could be put in the boat, giving me the entire control of construction, I will guarantee a speed of 16 to 17 knots; and further the new machinery will require but twenty feet of the length of the vessel, in lieu of the two-thirds of her capacity occupied by the present "adaption," Now, leaving aside the fact of Mr. D————n's denial that he was present at the trial trip, and that the engine was worked by him, and therefore that its capacities were never fairly tested—the value of which denial may be ascertained by reference to the subjoined correspondence—it appears to me but fair to calculate, that as Mr. Jerome's yacht, with an estimated speed of twelve knots, went at the extraordinary rate of about half a knot, until she met the tide, when she went backward, it appears, I say, but fair to calculate that with Mr. D————n's improved machinery, she would have gone much faster than Mr. D————n's minimum of steam success, a government vessel. In conclusion, I fear that when Mr. D————n admitted, for the purpose of his discussion with the Navy Department, that he was "profoundly ignorant of a steam engine, and supposed a cylinder-head to be a full moon," he made an admission of which it will be extremely difficult to disabuse the public, if his future engineering efforts continue to be crowned with the brilliant success of his "adaptation" of the machinery of the *Clara Clarita*.

Yours, very truly,

E. RIGGS

MR. RIGGS TO CAPTAIN SMITH.

NEW YORK, Feb. 8, 1864.

Captain Alex. Smith:

DEAR SIR:—Will you please to state who were on board at the trial trip of the *Clara Clarita*, who worked the engine, who assisted, and about how long you were out?

Yours, &c.,

E. RIGGS.

CAPTAIN SMITH'S REPLY.

Feb. 8, 1864

E. Riggs, Esq:

DEAR SIR:—In reply to your favor of this date, I would state that there was on board the *Clara Clarita* on her trial trip, Mr. D————n, Mr. T. F. Rowland, and Warren E. Hill, of the Continental Iron Works; Mr. Foulkes, the builder of the yacht; Mr. Jerome, the owner; Mr. Wm. Rowland, the joiner owner; some of the mechanics of the Continental Iron Works, and the ships company for the day.

We were underway two hours and a half, the engine being run by Mr. D————n, assisted by Messrs. Hill and Rowland.

This, I believe, answers all your questions, yet I beg to add, that which seemed to me important, viz: that five weeks previously, I was instructed to get up steam, which I did, and Mr. D————n worked the engine at the dock several hours.

I also desire to inform you that on Saturday last, in a conversation with Mr. T. F. Rowland, of the Continental Works, he informed me that what Mr. Jerome had written (refering to his communication in the *Times* of Saturday last) was all true. I have been in command of the *Clara Clarita* since the 18th day of August last and I have never known any thing to have been done appertaining to her machinery, except under the direction of Mr. D————n. For so small a matter as a bilgepump, which I required, Mr. Rowland informed me that he would be obliged to consult Mr. D————n.

Yours, &c.,

ALEX. SMITH,
Commanding Yacht Clara Clarita.

(H.)

" I will suppose a little cylinder, one inch in diameter, and of indefinite length and a piston fitting in it, steam-tight, but without water friction; and I will further suppose a cubic inch of water to be passed into the bottom of that cylinder, and the piston to be then let down on the water; and I will suppose that on the top of that piston there is a platform carrying a ton weight of bricks."--*D-------n's speech in the Mattingly Case*, pp. 16.

INDEX.

ADAMS, U. S. S., 647
   Adamson, A., 426
Adirondack, 218, wrecked, 332
Advisory Board, 1st, 773; 2d, 776 et seq
Agamenticus, 347
Agawam, 357, 444
Alabama, 367; sunk, 430 et seq
Alarm, 648
Alaska, 474, 624
Albany, sloop-of-war, 92, 96
Albany, 395
Albemarle, ram, 450 et seq., sunk, 469
Albemarle, launch, explosion of, 666
Albert, John S., 567, 571, 764
Alden, James, 238, 319, 324, 388, 435, 575
Alert, 1st., 477, 2d., 643
Alert, Br. st., 706, 709
Algoma class, names of, 474
Algonquin, 357, 517 et seq
Alleghany, 53 et seq
Alliance, 647, 764
"Alvarado Hunter," 97
Ambler, J. M., surgeon, 683, 690, 694
America, yacht, 151, 648
Ammen, Daniel, 247, 452, 818
Ammonoosuc, 399, trial trip, 570
Amphitrite, 1st, 347; 2d, 628, 631
Antietam class, names of, 395
Archbold, Sam'l, engr-in-chief, 104, 154, 158, 162, 176, 202
Arctic, 153
Arctic exploration, 679 et seq
"Arms and the Man," 1
Army & Navy Journal, quoted, 606, 667
Aroostook, 221, 314
Ashuelot, 395, 590; wrecked, 756
Atlanta, 777 et seq
Atlanta, Confed. stmr., captured, 378
Atlantic cable, laid by *Niagara*, 152
Atlantic Works, 206, 340, 357, 400, 585, 647
Augusta, 247, 250, 371, 590
Aulick, J. H., 104, 127, 128

BAILEY, THEODORUS, 325, 327
   Baker, C. H., 316, 635
Balch, Geo. B., 330
Baltimore, 794
Bancroft, Geo., secy. navy, 77, 652, 817
Bancroft, 817
Baron de Kalb, sunk, 390
Barton, paym'r, 467
Batten, J. M. surgeon, 214
Bear, 706, 709
Bell, H. H., 319, 325, 367
Benicia, 474, 623
Bennett, Jas. G., 681, 682
Bennington, 802
Benton, 285, 318
Berry, R. M., 681, 698 et seq
Bevington, M. 839
Bienville, 247, 250, 437
Billings, L., paym'r, 52, 429
Blake, H. C., 367
Blockade runners, captured or destroyed, 195
"Blood is thicker than water," 43
Boiler, drop-flue, 28; ascending flue, 105; Martin's, 222; Bartol's, 223; of *Monitor*, 284; Stimer's, 349; straight-way, 515; Dickerson's, 524; of *Chicago*, 781
Bombshell, 455; captured, 457
Bonne Homme Richard, 474
Borie, A. E., secy. navy, 615

Boston, 777 et seq
Boutelle, C. A., 458, 467, 704, 825, 834
Bowles, F. T., 777, 778
Brook, John M., 290
Brooklyn, 1st, 157; 319 et seq.; 367, 435 et seq
Brooklyn, 2nd, 837
Brown, Jefferson, 386
Bryce-Douglas, A. D., 794
Buchanan, Franklin, 127, 294, 301
Buehler, Wm. G., 152, 436
Bunce, F. M., 585 et seq
Bureau of Steam Engineering, created, 361
Bushnell, C. S., 270, 272, 277, 281
Butler, Gen'l B. F., 242, 327, 444, 446
Butterworth, Jas., 599

CADET ENGINEERS, at Naval Academy, 652 et seq
Cadet Engineers, discharged, case of, 752 et seq
Cahill, Jos N., killed, 427
Cairo, 282; sunk, 390, 425
California, 623
Caliope, H. M. S., 761
Camanche, 340
Canandaigua, 218, 332, 369, 424
Canonicus, 348, 445, 484
Carondelet, 282, 318
Carr, C. A., 734, 739
Castine, 818
Casualties at Fort Jackson, 327; at Mobile, 442; at Fort Fisher, 497; in engr. corps during cival war, 509 et seq
Catawba, 348, 627
Catskill, 340, 377, 381
Cayuga, 221, 319 et seq
Ceres, 288, 451 et seq
Chain armor, by whom devised, 322, 324
Chandler, Wm. E., secy. navy, 702, 706, 709, 752, 757, 777, 782
Charleston, 789 et seq
Chattanooga, 399, 531; sunk, 532
Chenango, 357; explosion on, 427
Chicago, 777 et seq
Chickasaw, 347; 436 et seq
Chicopee, 357, 469
Chilicothe, 348
Chimo, 395, 489
Chipp, C. W., 680 et seq
Chippewa, 221, 445
Church, W. C.—"Life of John Ericsson," quoted, 71, 72, 296, 310, 313, 340, 422, 845
Cimmarone, 221, 378
Cincinnati, 1st, 282, sunk 390; 2d, 813
Clifton, 320, 329, 362, 391
Colorado, 145, 244, 319, 325, 445
Columbia, wrecked, 368
Columbia, 2d, 821 et seq
Columbian Exposition, 764
Columbian Iron Works, 789, 817, 842
Columbine, captured, 426
Commodore Hull, 375, 454, 455, 470
Commodore Jones, blown up, 425
Commodore Perry, 288, 331
Composite Gunboats, 843
Concord, 802
Conestoga, 318, 328
Congress, 395, 680
Connor, Commo., 91 et seq
Contocook, 395, 623, 665
Contocook class, names of, 395
Cooley, M. E., 733, 738
Copeland, Charles W., 21, 36, 56, 103, 104, 137

INDEX.

Cowie, George, Jr., 602
Cragg, S. W., 319, 327, 427, 428
Cramp Shipbuilding Co., 273, 399, 531, 789, 794, 801, 809, 818, 821, 838
Craven, T. A. M., 436
Crosby, Pierce, 319. 602, 757
Crygier, J. U., 750
Cumberland, sloop-of-war, 92, 231, 243, 492, et seq
Cushing, William B., 289, 330, 331, 448, 468 et seq
Cushing, 802
Cushman, W. H., 433, 434

DACOTAH, 169
Dahlgren, rear ad., 199, 380, 406, 499
Danby, Robt., 132, 133, 199, 231 et seq
Danenhower, J. W., 683, 688, 691, 693
"David," 424
Delano, B. F., 142, 176, 399, 526, 555, 589
Delaware, 623
De Long, George W., 680 et seq
Demologos, 9 et seq
Despatch, 1st, 154; 2d, 648
Detroit, 1st, 474; 2d, 817
Diana, captured, 390
Dickerson, E. N., 161 et seq.; 396, 517, 526
Dickerson, M., sec. navy, 16, 19, 713
Dictator, 340, 344, 347
Dobbin, sec. navy, 56, 138
Dolphin, 777 et seq
"Double-enders," names of, 221, 357, 395
Doughty, Th., chief engineer, 391
Drayton, Percival, 249, 333, 336, 436
Driver, Reynolds, 499
Dukehart, T. M., 319, 471
Dunderberg, 348 et seq
Dungan, W. W., 250
DuPont, S. F., 148, 245 et seq., 376 et seq., 403 et seq., 418 et seq
Durand, W, F., 734, 735, 743

EDDOWES, A. K., 370, 371
Edes, James B., 282, 347, 348
Edith, 99
Ellis, William, 54, 137
Engine, side lever, 43; half-cylinder, 65; inclined, 360; Wright's, 516; vibrating lever, 537
Engineer, 32
Engineer-in-Chief, office created, 40
Engineer Corps, U. S. Navy, established, 40; increased in 1861, 205; casualties of, in Civil War, 509 et seq.; promotes technical education, 732 et seq.; reduced in 1882, 751
Engineers, naval, first in service, how appointed, 24; how berthed and messed, 28; declared to be officers, 40; names of, 25, 76, 80; arranged in order of merit, 76 et seq.; receive commission, 75, 607, 616; titles changed, 746.
Engineers, naval, in Mexican War, 99; in Japan expedition, 132; at Port Royal battle, on *Monitor*, at Fort Jackson, 319; at Mobile, 436; at Fort Fisher, 497; lost in *Mound City*, 328; in *Weehawken*, 382; in *Tecumseh*, 438; in *Patapsco*, 498; in *Kearsarge*, 593; in *Narcissus*, 593; in *Oneida*, 598; in *Huron*, 749; volunteer, qualifications of, 205 et seq.; cadets, 652 et seq.; detailed to colleges, 733 et seq
Engineers for revenue cutters, appointed, 75
Enterprise, 644
Epervier, 477
Ericsson, John, 61 et seq.; his gun, 70, 71, 99, 262, 268; builds *Monitor*, 274 et seq.; 309, 339, 392, 396, 399, 419, 484, et seq.; 532, 801
Ericsson, 821
Esmeralda, 790, 793
Essex, 1st, 285, 318, 385; 2d., 647
Everett, William H., 151, 152

FAIRFAX, D. M., 255 et seq
Faron, John, Jr., 25, 36, 42, 76, 78, 87, 103
Faron, John, 152; killed, 438
Farragut, D. G., 318 et seq.; wounded, 329, 336, 385, 425, 435 et seq.; his statue made from screw of *Hartford*, 157
Fernald, F. L., 777, 781
Fillebrown, T. S., 109, 427
Firemen classified in 1847, 86
Florida, confed. cr., 372, et seq.; captured 442
Flusser, C W., 330, 448, 451; killed, 452
Follansbee, Joshua, 72, 152
Foote, A. H., 285, 318, 406
Fort Donelson, captured, 318
Fort Fisher, first attack, 444; captured, 496 et seq
Fort Jackson, battle at, 321 et seq
Forward affair of, 597
Fox, G. V., asst. secy. navy, 278, 310, 419, 477, 478, 484, 489, 492, 584, 589, 656, 850
Franklin, 141, 400
Frolic, 624, 680
Fulton, 1st., see *Demologos*
Fulton 2d., 19 et seq
Fulton, 3d., 29, 30, 174

GALENA, 1st., 272, 277, 315, 436
Galena, 2d., 635
Gay, Jesse, 132, 133, 157, 189
Gearing for engines discarded, 64
Genessee, 221, 387, 389, 437
Germ, 48, 50
Germantown, sloop-of-war, 231, 242, 290
Gettysburg, 497, 624
Gilmer, T. W., sec. navy, killed, 70
Gotwold, surgeon, killed, 370
Goldsborough, L. M., 286, 314, 339, 577
Grant, U S., 95, 318, 498, 615, 727
Greely Relief expedition. 706 et seq
Greene, S. Dana, 296, 302, 313
Greene, Wm. R., killed, 364
Greer, J. A., 254, 260, 680
Gregory, F. H., 408, 485, 521, 525
Grice, Francis, 103, 105
Griffis, W. E , 30, 94
Griffiths, J. W., 173, 647
Griswold, John A., 281, 310
Guerriere, 395, 622
Gunners, originally non-combatants, 2

HALL, C. F., arctic explorer, 679 et seq
Hall, Geo. W., 255, 260, 261
Hall, Geo. W., 2d. 762
Hands, R. W., 296, 333
Hanscom, Isaiah, 357, 584, 647
Harriet Lane, 174, 320, 362; captured, 363
Hartford, 157, 318, et seq., 385 et seq., 436 et seq
Hartt, Saml. 44, 103, 110
Hasseltino, D. C., 213 et seq
Hasson, W. F. C., 734, 736. 743, 769
Haswell, Chas. H., first engr. in navy, engr.-in-chief, etc., 19, 21, 36, 41, 42, 75, 86, 93, 105, 110, 120 et seq., 287, 288
Hatteras, sunk, 367
Hawkins, J. T., 456, 608
Hebard, A., 36, 47, 76, 82
Helena, 841
Henderson, Alex., 332, 500, 777
Hobby, J. M., 250, 458, 462, 464, 467
Holden, Dr. Edgar, 334, 335
Hollis, I. N., 578, 733, 743, 793, 834, 841
Housatonic, 218, 369, sunk, 424
Houston, J. B., 253 et seq., 259
Hoyt, Eben, 322, 388, killed, 666
Huber, Jos., chief engr., killed, 330
Hunt, A. M., 734, 768
Hunt, Henry, 56, 72, 118, 120
Hunt, W. H., secy. navy, 773
Hunt, Wm. H., 326, 327, 436, 439
Hunt, Lieut. W. W., his wheel, 48, et seq
Huron, 1st, 221; 2d, 643; wrecked, 749

INDEX. 951

IDAHO, 165, 396, 523 et seq., 526 et seq
Indiana, 818
Indianola, 348, 384
Inman, Wm., 47, 262
Intrepid, 648
Iowa, 1st, 571: 2d, 838
Iris, 94
Iron-clads, first, 262, river type, 282, sold, 627
Iroquois, 169, 319, et seq
Isaac Smith, 246, 247, captured, 372
Isherwood, B. F., engr.-in-chief, 55, 57, 80, 82, 99, 117, 121, 165, 176, 182, 200, 202, 217, 221, 232, et seq., 396, 399, 400, 514, 517, 535, 553, 568, 576, 589, 608, 654, 656, 663, 773, 825
Itaska, 221, 319 et seq., 436, 440
Itata, 793
Iverson, A. J., 594, 756

JAPAN, expedition to, 126 et seq
Japanese bell at Naval Academy, 135
Jeannette, arctic expedition, 682 et seq
Jeffers, Wm. N., 289, 314
John Hancock, 1st, 137: 2d, 137
Jones, Catesby, 301, et seq., 307
Jones, David P., 498, 734
Jouett, Jas. E., 436, 440
Judah, schooner, 244
Juniata, 218, 446, 680

KALAMAZOO, class, names of, 400
Kane, E. K., arctic explorer, 153
Kansas, 357, 515
Katahdin, 1st, 221, 319; 2d, 818
Kearsarge, 218, fights *Alabama*, 430 et seq., wrecked, 769
Kearsarge, 2d, 844
Kellogg, Mortimer, 131, 136, 152, 435
Kennebec, 221, 319, 436, 440, wrecked, 501
Kennon, Beverly, 53, killed, 70
Kentucky, 844
Keokuk, 348, sunk, 377
Keystone State, 370, 624
Kickapoo, 347
Kimball, J. B., 319, 328
Kineo, 221, 319, et seq., 385
King, J. W., engr.-in-chief, 147, 182, 250, 487, 544, 609, 639, 643, 668, 671
King, Wm. H., 132
Kipling, Rudyard, quoted, 371, 809
Kutz, Geo. F., 152, 385, 386, 436

LACKAWANNA, 218, 436 et seq
Lancaster, 158
Lawton, Elbridge, 138, 319
Lay, J. L., 289, 376, 468, 481
Lee, S. P., 319, 329, 332, 375, 455
Lehigh, 340, 382
Lenapee, 357, 427
Lenthal, John, 54, 56, 103, 142, 176, 525, 773
Le Roy, Wm. E., 370, 436
Lexington, 318, 328, 330
Light-draft monitors, names of, 395; failure of, 483 et seq
Lincoln, Abraham, 162, 202, 237, 278, 404, 483, 500
Lockwood, 289, 424
Long, R. H., 147, 173
Longshaw, surgeon, killed, 497
Loring, C. H., engineer-in-chief, 147, 635, 761, 773, 805
Loring, Harrison, 138, 158, 340, 348, 817
Louisiana, 287, 289, 375; used as powder magazine, 444
Louisiana, Confed., 321
Lowe, John, 707, 745

MCCAULEY, Captain Charles S., 231 et seq.
McClellan, George B., 60, 95, 297
McElmell, J., 152, 436
McEwan, William G., 440
McKay, Donald, 270, 647
Machias, 818
Mackinaw, 357, 445
Madawaska, 399, trial trip of, 532

Mahopac, 348, 445
Main, Herschel, 601
Maine, 801, 806
Mallahan, Thos., killed, 376
Manassas, Confed. ram, 321 et seq
Manhattan, 348, 436, 744
Marblehead, 1st., 221; 2d., 817
Marietta, 348
Marion, 635, 750
Marsden, Captain J., 293, 296, 299
Martin, D. B., engineer-in-chief, 56, 99, 110, 138, 148, 154, 162, 169
Massachusetts, 1st., 98; 2d., 400; 3d., 818
Mattabessett, 357, 454, 456, 466
Maumee, 357, 516
Maxey, Hon. Virgil, killed on *Princeton*, 70
Meade, R. W, 495, 767
Melville, Geo. W., engineer-in-chief, 443, 681 et seq.; 703, 705, 707, 708, 711, 805, 825, 833
Mercedita, surrender of, 370
Merchant steamers not fit for war uses, 503
Merrick & Towne, 36, 62, 110
Merrick & Sons, 147, 169, 270, 272, 399, 516, 531
Merrimac, 141, 145, 146, 230 et seq.; 290; raid of, 291 et seq.; fights *Monitor*, 301 et seq.; destroyed, 314
Messimer, H., 248, 250
Metacomet, 357. 436, 440
Mexican War, 88 et seq
Miami, 221, 320, 451 et seq
Miantonomoh, 1st., 347; 589 et. seq.; 2d., 629
Michigan, 44
Miller, P., cadet engineer, killed, 758
Milwaukee, 347; sunk, 499
Minneapolis, 834
Minnesota, 145, 148, 243, 292, 313
Mississippi, 32 et seq.; 36, 42, 91 et seq.; 128 et seq.; 189, 319 et seq.; destroyed, 386 et seq.
Missouri, 35, 36; burned, 42
Mobile Bay, battle, 435 et seq.
Mohawk, 175
Mohican, 1st., 169; 247 et seq.; 2nd., 635.
Mohongo, 395, 592
Monadnock, 1st., 347, 445; 584 et seq; 2d., 588, 629
Monitor, 274 et seq.; 295 et seq.; 301 et seq.; 314; founders, 333
Monongahela, 218, 385, 436 et seq.; 595
Montauk, 340, 376, 382
Monterey, 769, 376, 382
Montgomery, 817
Monticello, 243
Moore, J. W., 319; 322 et seq.; 388, 389, 577, 639
Morgan Iron Works, 170, 396, 427, 647, 648
Mosholu, 395, 580
Moss, Chas., case of, 76 et seq.
Mound City, 282, 328
Muldaur, A. W., 467, 598
Mullen, A. T. E., 363, 444, 445
Muscoota, 395, 594

NAHANT, 340, 377, 378, 382
Nantasket, 477
Nantucket, 340, 377, 382
Narcissus, wrecked, 593
Narragansett, 170
Nashville, 838
Nashville, Confed. Steamer 363
Naugatuck, 60, 315.
Naval Academy, 652 et seq.
Naval Constructors, 142; commissioned, 607
Neshaminy, 399, 579, 629
Newark, 789
Newell, H., 154, 445
New Ironsides, 272 et seq.; 377, 382, 445
Newton Isaac, 60, 296, 305, 307, 577
New York, 809 et seq
Niagara, 141, 151, 152
Nicholson, J. W. A., 436, 564, 593
Nindemann, W. F. C., 684. 687, 691
"Ninety-day" gunboats, names of, 221
Nipsic, 1st., 357, 515; 2d., 648; 761 et seq.
Norfolk navy yard, loss of, 230 et seq.
Norton, H P., 777

952 INDEX.

Novelty Iron Works, 221, 280, 399, 555, 589
Nyack, 357

OAK LEAVES adopted as corps emblem, 724
Octorora, 221, 435
Omlypia, 813
Omaha, 477, 624
Oneida, 218, 272, 319 et seq ; 373, 436 et seq.; sunk 597
Oneota, 348, 627
Onondaga, 347, 354
Oregon, 1st., 400; 2nd., 818
Osage, 348, 391; sunk 499
Ossipee, 218, 436 et seq
Ottawa, 221, 247, 250
Ostego, 357, sunk 443, 469 et seq
Owasco, 221, 320, 362
Ozark, 348

PALOS, 481, 599
Paraguay expedition, 174; steamers chartered for, 175
Passaic, 333 et seq,; 340, 377, 382
Patapsco, 340, 377, 382; sunk, 498
Paulding, Captain Hiram, 148, 241, 264
Pawnee, 173, 243, 247 et seq.; 426
Pay of naval engineers in 1837, 22; in 1842, 40; in 1849, 87; in 1860, 184; in 1864, 494; in 1870, 616; in 1885, 758
Pembina, 221, 247 et seq.; 437
Penobscot, 221, 368
Pensacola, 161 et seq.; 319 et seq
Pensions extended to engineer corps, 86
Pequot, 357, 516, 663
Perry, Captain M. C., 22, 26, 30, 91 et seq.; 123, 127 et seq., 653, 713
Petrel, 789
Philadelphia, 1st., 287; 2d, 802, 805
Pickrell, J. M., 756
Pinola, 221, 319 et seq.; 437
Pinta class, names of, 481
Pirsson's condenser, 55
Piscataqua, 395, 623
Pittsburgh, 282
Plymouth, N. C., battle, 471
Plymouth, sloop-of-War, 129, 131, 231; sunk, 242, 290
Plymouth, 477, 624
Pocahontas, 154, 249, 330
Poinsett, 44
Polaris expedition, 680 et seq
Polk, 94
Pomponoosuc, 399
Pook, S. H., 272, 482, 647
Port Hudson, battle, 384 et seq
Port Royal battle, 245 et seq
Port Royal, 221, 314, 436, 440
Porter, Capt. David, 11, 16
Porter, Adm'l. D. D., 213, 327, 329, 384, 390, 392, 444, 446, 472, 639, 666; his opinion of engineers, 198; of acting masters, 320; of screw propulsion, 639; of Isherwood engines, 660
Porter, J. L., 290, 314, 450
Powhatan, 105, 109, 130, 136, 445
Princess Royal, 368 et seq
Princeton, 1st., 62 et seq.; gun explosion on, 70, 72, 91, 98
Princeton, 2d, 74
Propeller, Loper's, 51; of Alleghany, 56; Ericsson's, 62; of San Jacinto, 118; experiments with two-bladed, 636
Puritan, 1st, 340; 2d, 629
Putnam, C. F., 701

QUAKER CITY, 371, 446
Quinnebaug, 1st, 477; 2d, 635
Quinsigamond, 400
Quintard Iron Works, 399, 647, 801

RALEIGH, 813
Ranger, 643
Rank, conferred upon naval engineers in 1859,
185; reaffirmed in 1861, 186; raised in 1863, 401; reduced in 1869, 610; brevet, in navy, 605; "relative," origin of, 617
Rattler, H. M. S., 63, 136
Resaca, 477
Retired list created, 357
Rhoades, H. E., 374, 375
Rhoades, H. E., 2d, 681
Richmond, 158; 319 et seq; 388; 436 et seq
Roach, John, 350, 396, 399, 544, 629, 643, 777
Roanoke, 145; 292 et seq.; 301, 354, 629
Roanoke Island, battle, 286 et seq
Robeson, Geo. M., secy. navy, 544, 602, 616, 628, 632, 668
Robie, E. D., 129, 132, 250, 344, 405, 406, 524, 526, 577, 639
Robie, H. W., 332 et seq
Robinson, L. W., 436, 764
Rodgers, C. R. P., 245 et seq
Rodgers, Geo. W., killed, 381
Rodgers, John, 138; 247 et seq.; 285, 314, 343, 378, 405, 584, 701, 773
Rodgers, voyage and loss of, 701
Roe, F. A., 319, 454, 458, 464, 467, 532

SACHEM, 295, 362, captured, 391
Saco, 357, 515
Sacramento, 218; wrecked 595
Saginaw, 166; wrecked, 599
Samoan disaster, 761 et seq
San Francisco, 802, 805
San Jacinto, 110, 114; 251 et seq.; wrecked, 495
Saranac, 109; wrecked, 110
Sassacus, 357, 445, 454, 461, 466
Saugus, 348, 445
Saville, J. W., 496, 743
Schley, W. S., 707
Sciota, 221, 319; sunk, 499
Scott, Winfield, 94, 98
Sea Gull, 16
Seminole war, 44
Seminole, 170, 247, 250, 436
Seneca, 221, 247
Sewell, Geo., 97, 109, 136, 166, 250
Sewell, Wm., 76, 105, 118
Shamrock, 357, 469
Shawmut, 357
Shawsheen, 289, 331; captured, 426
Shenandoah, 218
Shock, W. H., engr.-in-chief, 74, 80, 82, 96, 146, 730, 746, 758
Shufeldt, R. W., 777
Sloat, J. D., 89 et seq
Smith, Jos., 264, 278, 281, 486
Smith, Melancthon, 319, 326, 386, 454, 455, 575
Soley, J. R., quoted, 292, 419, 663
Sonoma, 221, 374
Southfield, 287, 451; sunk 452
Spangler, H. W., 733, 735, 743
Spitfire, 92, 96, 97
Spuyten Duyvil, 482 et seq
St. Louis, 282, 318, 328
Stahl, A. W., 734, 740
Stamm, W. S., 136, 152
Steam launch, 1st, 124
Steers, Geo., 151, 529
Stevens Battery, 57 et seq; 262
Stevens, Hon. A. F., 617, 621
Stevenson, H. N., 764
Stewart, H. H., 170, 471, 526
Stimers, A. C., 147, 262, 280, 281, 295, 296, 305 et seq., 313, 340, 349, 377, 392, 404 et seq.; 409 484 et seq
Stockton, Capt. R. F., 61 et seq.; 70, 74, 91, 97
Stodder, L. N., 296, 302, 313
Stotesbury, Wm., 469, 470, 473
Stringham, S. H., 176, 242, 262, 408
Stuart, Chas. B., engineer-in-chief, 29, 55, 74, 117, 119, 182
Susquehanna, 104, 128, 135, 152, 243, 250, 314, 373
Suwanee, 395; wrecked, 596
Swatara, 1st, 477; 2d, 635

INDEX.

TACONY, 357, 470, 471
   Talbot, Lieut. J. G., 600
Tallapoosa, 357, 495
Tatnall, Josiah, 43, 96, 246, 314
Taylor, Bayard, master's mate in navy, 131
Tecumseh, 348; sunk, 437
Tennessee, confed. stmr., 337
Tennessee, confed. ram, 437 et seq
Tennessee, U. S. S., 544, et seq., 758
Terror, 628
Texas, 794
Theiss, E. 753, 769
Thetis, 706, 709
Thompson, G. L., engr.-in-chief, 39, 41, 42
Thurston, R. H., 368 et seq.; 372, 608, 732, 743
Ticonderoga, 218, 446
Tigress, 680
Tonawanda, 347
Torpedo, unchivalrous, 425; Lay, deescribed, 481
Toucey, secy. navy, 162 185, 189
Trent, affair of, 251 et seq
Trenton, 647, wrecked, 761 et seq
Tuscarora, 218
Tuscumbia, 348
Tyler, John, President, 69, 70, 77
Tyler, 318

UNADILLIA, 221, 247, 368, 369, 445
   Underwriter, 289; captured, 423
Uniforms, 713, et seq
Union, 49 et seq
Union Iron Works, 166, 790, 802, 813, 818
United States, frigate, 231; burned, 242
Upshur, A. P., secy. navy, 53; killed, 70

VAN BRUNT, Capt., 302, 306
   Vandalia, 635; wrecked, 761 et seq
Vanderbilt, 585
Varuna, 319; destroyed, 326
Vera Cruz, bombarded, 94-95
Vesuvius, 801
Vixen, 92, 96
Voorhees, P. R., 380

WABASH, 141, 145, 147, 245, et seq.; 225, 245
   Wachusett, 218. 316, 442
Wampanoag, 399, 554, 583
Ward, J. H., 652, 653
Wasp, 624
Wateree, 357; wrecked, 596

Water Witch, 1st, 51; 2d, 52; 3d, 52, 174, 429, 667
Waxsaw, 395, 491
Webber, J. J. N., 296, 305
Webster, Harrie, 387, 389, 437, 762
Webster, W. T., 756
Weehawken, 340, 377, 378; founders, 382
Weir, Robt., 166, 389, 441
Welles, Gideon, secy. navy, 272, 274, 277, 279, 281, 339, 375, 405, 421
Wells, Wm. S., 273, 274
Westfield, 320, 362; sunk, 364
West point Foundry, 17, 20, 36
White, Geo. H., 244
Whitehall, 287, 294; destroyed, 295
Whitham, Jay M., 734, 741, 742, 752
Whitehead, 331, 451, 453, 470
Whitney, W. C., secy. navy, 805
Whittemore, J, W., killed, 249
Wilkes, Chas., 251 et seq.; 374
Williamson, Thom., 290, 436
Williamson, Wm. P., 50, 54, 76, 104, 118, 202, 290 292
Wilmington, 841
Winnebago, 347, 436 et seq
Winona, 221, 319, 373
Winooski, 357, 517 et seq
Winslow, Capt. J. H., 432
Wissahickon, 221, 319
Wood, B. F., 592
Wood, Wm. Maxwell, 90
Wood, Wm. W. W., engr.-in-chief, 76, 78, 110, 148, 158, 173, 198, 350, 468, 481, 489, 636, 643, 664, 667, 746
Woodbury, J. G., paymr., killed, 381
Woodruff & Beach, 169, 432, 516
Woods, A. T., 734, 740
Worcester, 395
Worden, J. L., 295, 296, 302 et seq.; 310, 313, 376, 526, 671
Wyalusing, 357, 454, 457, 466, 468, 470, 471
Wyoming, 169

YANTIC, 357, 446, 516
   Yates, A. R., 745
Yorktown, 789
Young, Jas. G., 379

ZANE. A. V., 701
   Zeigler, J. Q. A., 497, 585, 587, 595
Zeller, Theo., 80, 81, 100, 563, 567
Zinc first used in boilers, 124

ERRATA.

Page 64, line 17, omit "of" before the word "the."
Page 199, line 6, should be "these" instead of "their."
Page 330, line 21, "litteral" should be "littoral."
Page 465, line 24, "slooping" should be "sloping."
Folios 171-172 omitted.